Encyclopedia of
Ethnicity and Sports
in the United States

Edited by
GEORGE B. KIRSCH, OTHELLO HARRIS, AND
CLAIRE E. NOLTE

Greenwood Press
Westport, Connecticut • London

Library of Congress Cataloging-in-Publication Data

Encyclopedia of ethnicity and sports in the United States / edited by
   George B. Kirsch, Othello Harris, and Claire E. Nolte.
      p.   cm.
   Includes bibliographical references (p.   ) and index.
   ISBN 0–313–29911–0 (alk. paper)
      1. Minorities in sports—United States—History.   2. Sports—
Sociological aspects—United States—History.   I. Kirsch, George
B.   II. Harris, Othello.   III. Nolte, Claire Elaine.
GV709.5.E83   2000
796'.089'00973—dc21   99–15392

British Library Cataloguing in Publication Data is available.

Library of Congress Catalog Card Number: 99–15392
ISBN: 0–313–29911–0

First published in 2000

Greenwood Press, 88 Post Road West, Westport, CT 06881
An imprint of Greenwood Publishing Group, Inc.
www.greenwood.com

Printed in the United States of America

The paper used in this book complies with the
Permanent Paper Standard issued by the National
Information Standards Organization (Z39.48–1984).

10 9 8 7 6 5 4 3 2

Contents

Preface

The subject of this historical encyclopedia of ethnicity and sports in the United States is the sporting experience of Native Americans, African Americans, and a wide variety of immigrant groups in the United States from the age of colonization to the present. The growing interest in the history of race and ethnicity and the proliferation of sports studies suggest the need for a project of this kind. Although no one-volume reference work can cover every possible aspect of such a vast topic, the editors have striven to make this book as comprehensive as possible.

With the exception of the original inhabitants of North America—the Native American Indians—all the peoples of the United States are either immigrants or the descendants of earlier migrants to what early explorers labeled the "New World." In some sense a history of ethnic sports in the United States could be defined as synonymous with a history of sports in general in this country. But for the purposes of this project, the editors have distinguished between a "mainstream" American sporting culture that was established and developed by the earliest newcomers to the British colonies and their descendants (primarily English, but also including smaller numbers of Dutch, German, Scotch Irish, French, and other Europeans), and the sporting traditions and practices of other groups that arrived later or were treated as outsiders (especially African slaves and Native American Indians). Social historians and sociologists generally label the dominant culture as "Anglo" or "WASP" (white, Anglo-Saxon Protestant) or "American," and those terms will be used interchangeably in the entries that follow. Of course, it is also true that mainstream American culture has been dynamic and constantly changing over time, and it has frequently incorporated elements from the sporting traditions of Native American Indians, African Americans, and immigrants. The following introduction briefly refers to this process and also presents three sociological models of assimilation that are useful in understanding ethnic sports in the United States.

This encyclopedia contains five types of entries, arranged in an alphabetical A–Z format. They are racial and ethnic groups, ethnic games, mainstream sports, ethnic and racial institutions, and prominent persons. The editors believe that this system serves the needs of a wide range of readers, even though it may result in some overlap among certain articles. For example, an individual who is interested in a discussion of Irish boxers will find that topic treated in separate entries under the Irish and boxing.

Given the limitations of space and the difficulty in finding source material, it was not possible to include entries on every racial and immigrant group in the United States. The editors selected thirty groups that they believe have had the most important influence on the development of athletics in this country. African Americans receive extra emphasis because of their extraordinary degree of participation in sports, especially in the twentieth century. The English merit special attention because of their pioneering role in American sports and their continuing impact on athletics in the United States throughout the centuries. The inclusion of Canadians might surprise some readers, but we believe that although they themselves comprise a variety of ethnic groups, the Canadian national contribution to American sports is quite significant and should be recognized.

The category of ethnic sports includes games and pastimes that Native American Indians and immigrants have used (and continue to play) to help preserve ancestral traditions and cultural identity in a new setting. Some of these (such as Irish hurling, Gaelic football, bocce, or curling) were and remain favored recreations only among particular groups, while others (notably, gymnastics, golf, lacrosse, and hockey) have become more generally assimilated into American athletic culture. The term "mainstream sports" refers to popular pastimes that evolved from early English folk games or contests (such as baseball, football, and boxing) or were American inventions (basketball).

While thousands of racial and ethnic sporting clubs, leagues, institutions, and individuals have had a profound impact on American sports, we can include only a few dozen organizations and several hundred persons in this volume. We have tried to select a representative list of major teams and associations and to limit most of the biographical entries to people who achieved "Hall of Fame" status in their respective sports (although some are included who made noteworthy contributions without attaining that level of athletic immortality). Space limitations compelled us to exclude dozens of extraordinary athletes; the choices were especially difficult in the case of African Americans, because so many of them have compiled outstanding records, particularly in boxing, baseball, football, basketball, and track and field. Cross-references (indicated by an asterisk) are given only for club, association, and biographical entries.

Each entry in the encyclopedia contains a brief list of secondary sources. The volume concludes with a general selected bibliography, presenting a short list of the most useful books and articles in the fields of race and ethnicity in American sports.

The editors wish to acknowledge the assistance of the late Kevin McHugh in the preparation of the Gaelic Athletic Association entry, along with Andrew J. Shaw for the entry on Fencing; Nick Koliarakis for the entry on Greeks; Donald M. Clark for the entry on Hockey, and Forrest F. Steinlage for the entry on Turners (Turnverein).

Finally, the editors and contributors have made every effort to include all significant information and to make each entry factually correct. In those cases where it was not possible to find missing data, we have inserted a question mark. We take full responsibility for any mistakes that we may have inadvertently made.

Introduction

This volume examines the intersection of two distinct fields in American social and cultural history: ethnicity and sports. Academicians, sportswriters, journalists, and critics have written countless books, articles, and newspaper and magazine pieces on each topic, but relatively few have explored the complex relationships between them. Here ethnicity is defined broadly to include a wide range of immigrant and racial groups that have shaped the development of athletics in the United States. Long before the great migrations that began in the fifteenth century, indigenous peoples in what would later be called the New World established vibrant cultures with age-old games and pastimes. Over the next four centuries newcomers from Europe, Latin America, Asia, Africa, Australia, the Pacific Islands, and the Middle East journeyed to North American shores. While most came voluntarily, some (most notably, Africans) arrived by force in bondage. Many carried sporting traditions with them as part of their cultural baggage; they all encountered a dynamic society that included a significant and growing athletic component. Factors such as religion, social class, and gender profoundly influenced their athletic experiences in the United States, as did nativism and ethnic and racial conflicts.

Ethnic sports in the United States is a complex subject with many dimensions. One way of understanding this topic is to apply three models that sociologists and social historians have found useful in analyzing patterns of immigration and race in American society: Anglo-conformity (or Americanization), the melting pot, and structural pluralism. Each category requires a brief definition, since there has been much confusion over their precise meanings. First, Anglo-conformity refers to the assimilation of an immigrant or racial group into the dominant English or white, Anglo-Saxon Protestant culture. Some scholars prefer the term "Americanization" over "Anglo-conformity" because they believe that mainstream American culture should not be characterized as exclusively English. Second, while the term "melting pot" has taken on many different meanings, here it may be used to describe a blending of peoples or cultural elements to create a new type with hybrid cultural characteristics. In this case immigrants do not blend into the dominant culture but instead contribute to forging a new one for the United States. Finally, structural pluralism is also a tricky term, but for the sake of clarity it is defined here to mean the immigrant groups' retention of some of their respective ethnic identities, even as they experience some degree of cultural assimilation into the mainstream of American society.

In the world of sports, Anglo-conformity or Americanization refers to the degree to which newcomers participated in the mainstream sports that were either early English imports into the British American colonies, American modifications of existing English games, or new creations. As these sports evolved during the eighteenth and nineteenth centuries, they retained their popularity among the middle and upper classes. Examples from the colonial, young republic, and antebellum periods are village pastimes and games, field sports, thoroughbred horse racing, and aquatic sports such as yachting and rowing. After the Civil War wealthy sportsmen and sportswomen adopted the English games of polo, croquet, tennis, and badminton.

Prizefighting is a special case. It was associated with English sporting culture but was outlawed in the United States because it offended the sensibilities of the middle classes. Patronized by the "sporting fraternity" (composed of gentlemen from the more privileged orders and lower-class workers and immigrants) who emulated an English model, pugilism never became part of mainstream nineteenth-century American WASP culture because of its brutal nature and associations with alcohol, gambling, and related vices. Yet English and especially Irish immigrant bare-knuckle fighters gained notoriety in the United States, while boxers from later arriving groups, especially Italians, Jews, African Americans, and Hispanic Americans, fought as a means of achieving upward mobility and respect in American culture.

Team sports have provided a major avenue of assimilation for many ethnic groups in the United States. Baseball, an American adaptation of English rounders, attracted large numbers of English, Irish, and German players during its formative years. In the twentieth century, first Eastern and Southern Europeans and then Hispanics and Asians found in the national pastime their fields of dreams. American football evolved from the English games of soccer and rugby; basketball was invented by James Naismith, a Canadian trained in muscular Christianity at a WASP institution at Springfield, Massachusetts. Immigrants took up both sports with great enthusiasm prior to World War I, especially basketball, which became enormously popular in Italian, Jewish, and other ethnic neighborhoods in American cities.

The intense racism that African Americans encountered in all parts of the United States severely restricted their assimilation into both individual and team sports. Although a few black athletes competed successfully with whites after the Civil War, by the early 1890s they were encountering increasing hostility and discrimination. In the era of segregation that followed, they accommodated themselves to racist practices and institutions by developing black sporting institutions. Although the Negro baseball leagues are the best-known African American sports associations of the first half of the twentieth century, black owners and players also struggled to establish their own organizations in football, basketball, tennis, golf, and other sports. The integration of major league baseball by Jackie Robinson after World War II spurred a wave of desegregation of professional and intercollegiate athletics, which in turn stimulated and reinforced the Civil Rights movement in the United States during the 1950s and 1960s. Although black nationalists challenged black integrationists in sport during the 1960s and 1970s (in large part due to the militant leadership of Muhammad Ali), in the long run African American athletes dramatically increased their participation in mainstream American sports. By the end of the century blacks were dominant in boxing, football, and basketball both in their degree of participation and in their impact on the style and techniques of these sports.

Native American Indians have been far less successful in integrating themselves into the mainstream of American sports. While this was due in part to the racist practices of whites, in many cases it also reflected an Indian preference for their own traditional customs and games, as they resisted Anglo-conformity. During the late 1800s and early 1900s the U.S. government undertook a policy of forced assimilation of Indians into American society, suppressing native practices and promoting American activities. At government-run training schools in Carlisle, Pennsylvania, and other places, native boys were encouraged to participate in track and field, football, baseball, and basketball. A few of them, such as Jim Thorpe, Charles A. "Chief" Bender, and Joseph Guyon, later achieved stardom in track and field, baseball, and football. Such Native American prominence in mainstream American sports faded after the 1930s, partly because many residential schools closed, and reservations lacked facilities, but mostly because of the revival of interest in Indian pride and self-determination.

Before turning to a discussion of the melting pot, structural pluralism, and sports, it is important to stress the dynamic character of the interaction between racial and ethnic minorities and the most popular sports in the United States. While immigrants, African Americans, and Native Americans have frequently tried to gain greater acceptance and respect in U.S. society through mainstream sports, in certain ways they have also transformed the nature of American athletics. For example, when one considers tactics and styles of play, who could doubt the enormous impact of the Irish and African Americans in prizefighting, Jews and African Americans in basketball, or African Americans and Hispanics in baseball?

The concept of the melting pot is also useful in understanding the connections between ethnicity and sport. It is apparent in athletic forms combining elements of ethnic games and types of physical education with "Anglo" or mainstream or WASP characteristics, which became widely popular throughout most levels of American society. For example, English and especially Scottish newcomers

promoted track and field and golf, while Germans popularized gymnastics. Lacrosse, an ancestral pastime with deep religious significance for native Indian
tribes of North America, was Westernized and modernized in the mid-nineteenth
century by English residents of Montreal, Canada, who later imported it into
the United States. There it evolved into a game played mainly in high schools
and colleges. Ice hockey, another Canadian import, developed into one of the
major winter collegiate and professional sports in the United States. Soccer is a
special case. It has become a major mainstream sport for young children as well
as high school and college students, but it remains an ethnic sport for adult
participants. The Americanization of the Asian martial arts also falls under this
heading.

The meaning of the melting pot in American sports becomes clear when one
examines the process through which certain ethnic games and forms of physical
education became part of mainstream athletic culture in the United States. In
some cases, native-born sportspeople from the majority "Anglo" or "WASP"
culture adapted immigrant pastimes to suit their own recreational needs. Selec-
tively borrowing certain elements of the foreign sport, while rejecting or transforming other aspects, they created new sports that featured aspects of both the
immigrant and WASP cultures. One of the most important general questions in
sport history is why certain ethnic games and types of physical education (such
as track and field, golf, or gymnastics) take root in American soil and evolve
into mainstream sports, while others (such as cricket, curling, or Gaelic football)
fail to gain wider acceptance. In this regard, it is instructive to examine how
the rules, organization, equipment, and traditions of foreign athletic forms that
succeeded in the United States became Americanized, in order to understand the
factors that prevented the other foreign pastimes from gaining widespread
popularity.

Finally, the concept of structural pluralism is also useful in analyzing the
connections between ethnicity and sports. Here it is important to note the distinction between cultural pluralism and structural pluralism. The former refers
to the practice of groups that resist assimilation into the mainstream culture and
instead retain their distinctive language, customs, and values; the latter refers to
those newcomers who adopt major elements of the dominant host society yet
keep their personal and social relations within their own group. In the United
States many ethnic groups eventually accepted the language, political and economic values, and institutions of the dominant "Anglo" or "American" group
but were not incorporated into the structure of social or personal relationships
or institutions of American society. In other words, some ethnic groups that
became partly assimilated into American culture (especially by speaking English, finding jobs, and perhaps even becoming citizens) still tried to maintain
ties to their native lands through their traditional games and sporting associations. For this reason, certain ethnic games that attract little or no support in
mainstream American society remain quite popular among immigrants. As a
result, many ethnic groups in the United States have achieved a higher degree

of cultural assimilation than of structural assimilation, as witnessed by their allegiance to their traditional ethnic games. Examples here would be Gaelic football and hurling for the Irish (which frequently carried expressions of Irish nationalism), bocce for the Italians, and curling for the Scots. Cricket is a special case. An English game that had only limited success in gaining popularity among Americans, it was played mostly by upper-class Philadelphians and some English working-class immigrants prior to 1900. After suffering a severe decline after World War I, it has reappeared on the American sporting scene during recent decades as an ethnic pastime of West Indians and Asian Indians. Native American Indians continue to favor their own heritage over assimilation into American society by participating in lacrosse and cultivating traditional customs such as powwows and indigenous games.

Taken together, the models of Americanization, the melting pot, and structural pluralism are helpful in understanding the complex historical evolution of the interaction of ethnicity and sports in the United States. Newcomers from around the world, African Americans, and Native Americans have frequently attempted to pry open the doors of opportunity in American society through athletics, but they have also shared their own distinctive games with those who preceded them in their journeys to America. In some cases the dominant sportspeople adapted the foreign recreations to suit their own needs, while at other times they ignored the strange new pastimes. But whatever the outcome, the American sporting tradition has been enriched by the contributions of all groups, whether native-born or foreign.

A

AARON, HENRY LOUIS ("Hank") (5 February 1934, Mobile, AL–). An African American baseball player, he is best known for breaking Babe Ruth's career record for most home runs in major league baseball. He is the son of Herbert and Estella Aaron; his father was a boilermaker's assistant, and his mother was a homemaker to her eight children. Henry graduated from the Josephine Allen Institute in Mobile and received an honorary doctor of laws degree from Emory University in Atlanta, Georgia, in 1996. He played with the Indianapolis Clowns in 1951 and 1952 and signed with the Boston Braves in 1952. He was sent to Eau Claire, Wisconsin, in the Northern League, where he was named Rookie of the Year and was selected to play in the All-Star Game. In 1953 he was sent to Jacksonville, Florida, a member of the South Atlantic League, where he was selected the Most Valuable Player in the league. He started his major league career in 1954 with the Milwaukee Braves and became an Atlanta Brave in 1966, when the team relocated. In 1975 he became a member of the Milwaukee Brewers and played there in 1975 and 1976 before retiring. He was selected as the National League's Most Valuable Player in 1957; led the National League in batting in 1956 and 1959; led the National League in home runs in 1957, 1963, 1966, and 1967; and led the National League in runs batted in (RBIs) in 1959, 1960, 1963, and 1966. He won Gold Gloves in 1958, 1959, and 1960. He played in twenty-four All-Star Games over a period of twenty-one years, and he helped lead the Braves to a World Series victory over the New York Yankees in 1957. When he retired, he was baseball's all-time leader in home runs with 755; total bases (6,856); extra base hits (1,477); and runs batted in (2,297). Although he became involved in the Civil Rights movement in 1963, he stated that "it wasn't until 1966 that I crossed the line and became an agitator." As he approached and surpassed Ruth's career home run mark, he was plagued with some racist abuse and threats. He was inducted into the National Baseball Hall of Fame in 1982.

SELECTED BIBLIOGRAPHY: Hank Aaron, with Lonnie Wheeler, *I Had a Hammer* (1991); Donald Dewey and Nicholas Acocella, *The Biographical History of Baseball* (1995); Alan Minsky, *Home Run Kings* (1995); Mike Shatzkin, *The Ballplayers* (1990).

Clyde Partin

ABBOTT, SENDA BERENSON. *See* BERENSON, SENDA

ABDUL-JABBAR, KAREEM (16 April 1947, New York City–). An African American basketball player, he was born Lewis Ferdinand Alcindor, the only child of Cora and Ferdinand Alcindor. His father was a New York City Transit Authority police officer. Raised as a Roman Catholic in a middle-class family in upper Manhattan, as a youth he attended St. Jude's elementary school and Power Memorial Academy, an Irish Christian Brothers high school. At Power Memorial Alcindor was a schoolboy basketball sensation, as he led his team to seventy-one consecutive victories, three New York City Catholic high school championships, and a city career scoring record of 2,067 points. After his graduation in 1965 he journeyed to the West Coast and the University of California at Los Angeles (UCLA). Under the tutelage of legendary coach John Wooden, Alcindor had a stellar college career as a graceful and dominant center. During his three varsity seasons (1966–69) the Bruins compiled a record of 88–2 and won three National Collegiate Athletic Association (NCAA) titles, as Alcindor averaged 26.4 points per game. As a collegian he majored in history and became involved in the racial and political reform movement of the 1960s. He chose not to compete for the U.S. Olympic basketball team in 1968 as a means of protesting racial discrimination against blacks in the United States. After his graduation from UCLA he signed a contract with the Milwaukee Bucks of the National Basketball Association (NBA) after seriously considering an offer from the New York Nets of the new American Basketball Association (ABA). As he began his professional career, he underwent a major spiritual transformation, converting to the Islam religion and changing his name to Kareem Abdul-Jabbar. During his twenty seasons in the NBA with the Bucks and the Los Angeles Lakers (after he was traded in 1975), Abdul-Jabbar became the premier center of all time and arguably (with Michael Jordan*) the best basketball player ever. His record included one NBA title with the Bucks (1971) and five with the Lakers (1980, 1982, 1985, 1987–88). A six-time winner of the league's Most Valuable Player award, when he retired, he held nine NBA career marks, including most points scored (38,387). He was inducted into the Naismith Memorial Basketball Hall of Fame in 1995.

SELECTED BIBLIOGRAPHY: Kareem Abdul-Jabbar, with Peter Knobler, *Giant Steps* (1983); Kareem Abdul-Jabbar, with Mignon McCarthy, *Kareem* (1990); Arthur R. Ashe, Jr., *A Hard Road to Glory: A History of the African American Athlete since 1946* (1988); Bill Becker, "Alcindor Is Eager to Start Varsity Career," *New York Times*, 15 October 1966; Sam Goldpaper, "Alcindor Clarifies TV Remark, Criticizes Racial Bias in U.S.,"

New York Times, 23 July 1968; James Haskins, *From Lew Alcindor to Kareem Abdul-Jabbar* (1978).

George B. Kirsch

ADAMS, JOHN JAMES ("Jack") (14 June 1895, Fort William, Ontario, Canada–1 May 1968, Detroit). A hockey player, coach, and general manager, he was the son of John Adams, a locomotive engineer, and Sarah Ann Adams. He built the Detroit Red Wings into a National Hockey League (NHL) powerhouse, while in the process establishing hockey as a major sport in the Motor City. Adams won two Stanley Cups as a player with the Toronto Arenas (1918) and Ottawa Senators (1927) and three more as the Red Wings' coach and general manager (1936, 1937, 1943). Tommy Ivan* took over as coach in 1947 while Adams focused on building the team through the use of an extensive farm system—a method he pioneered. A fierce competitor with a propensity for verbal tirades, Adams was disliked by opposing coaches and players, referees, and some of his own players for his abrasive behavior. All, however, were forced to respect his ability to judge talent and build a hockey club. The powerful Red Wing squad led by Gordie Howe* won an NHL record seven consecutive regular season championships, along with four Stanley Cups between 1947 and 1955, distinguishing Adams as the only man ever to win the Stanley Cup as a player, coach, and general manager. In 1959 Adams was elected to the Hockey Hall of Fame. Adams' contribution to hockey in Detroit was immeasurable. When he came to the city in 1927, hockey was a foreign game that was paid little attention. In order to establish a following for the sport Adams became a zealous promoter; his ability to publicize the hockey club through the media, combined with the team's strong showing on the ice, led the sporting public to embrace the Red Wings. Adams proudly became an American citizen, adopting his new country as enthusiastically as the fans of Detroit had adopted the once-alien game of hockey. In recognition of his dedication and perseverance in promoting the sport, he was selected in 1966 as the inaugural recipient of the NHL's Lester Patrick Award for outstanding service to hockey in the United States.

SELECTED BIBLIOGRAPHY: Richard Bak, *Detroit Red Wings: The Illustrated History* (1997); Jack Berry, "Jack Adams Left Indelible Mark on Detroit, CPHL Ice Scenes," *The Hockey News* 21, No. 32 (June 1968): 13; David Cruise and Alison Griffiths, *Net Worth: Exploding the Myths of Pro Hockey* (1991); Phil Loranger, *If They Played Hockey in Heaven: The Jack Adams Story* (1976); Roy MacSkimming, *Gordie: A Hockey Legend* (1994).

Dennis Ryan

AFRICAN AMERICANS. Today African American athletes generate an enormous amount of publicity from the mass media. The public views elite black superstars as celebrities, valued citizens, heroes, and sometimes pariahs. Their sport performances and other activities reflect and influence the ways in which the American people view them as individuals and perceive African Americans as a group. The prestigious positions that many black sport stars hold are due in large part to the accomplishments of their predecessors—the pioneers of African American participation in American sports. For the past two centuries, black athletes have struggled through eras of accommodation to segregation and discrimination, racial integration, and forceful expressions of black nationalism and pride. Today they are demanding full equality and respect throughout the sport communities of the nation.

Much of African Americans' participation in sports in America began on plantations. Slavery in the United States was a harsh, cruel institution. Plantation slaves were worked from sunup to sundown. Yet, despite the truculent character of slavery and the long hours of labor, slaves were not without a social life. After sundown and away from work and masters, slaves hunted, fished, gathered wild crops, sang, danced, and engaged in storytelling and other forms of entertainment.

American southerners participated in a number of recreational activities; among them were horse racing, cockfighting, gambling, wrestling, and boxing. Slaves were involved in most of these activities, primarily for the entertainment, but sometimes for the profit, of planters. Perhaps the most profitable of plantation sports, for planters and a few slaves, was boxing.

Boxing matches provided entertainment for whites and a diversion from the hard life of a slave. A slave who showed exceptional boxing ability was rewarded, because his talent could render a fortune for a master who bet heavily on him and won. Therefore, extraordinary boxing slaves were given special privileges to inspire them to victory. In a few cases, slaves were manumitted as a result of their boxing ability. Even more rare was the black man who was able to earn a living at boxing. One of these rare boxers was Tom Molineaux.*

Molineaux, a slave on a Richmond, Virginia, plantation, was from a family of boxing slaves. In one fight against another slave his master wagered $100,000 and offered to manumit him if he won. Molineaux defeated his opponent, and his master profited handsomely. Molineaux then bolted America for England, where boxing was more popular. Under the guidance of Bill Richmond, the first African American to make a living at boxing, Molineaux positioned himself for a fight against the British (and then world) heavyweight bare-knuckle champion, Tom Cribb. Molineaux and Cribb met in December 1810 before a crowd of more than 20,000 people. They fought for more than twenty rounds before Molineaux knocked Cribb unconscious. Molineaux's corner began to rejoice, but Cribb's corner accused Molineaux of having lead weights in his glove. The referee suspended the count, which allowed Cribb to regain consciousness. The bout was continued, and Molineaux lost in the fortieth round. The next year in a return engagement, Molineaux was knocked out in the eleventh round. The losses were obviously hard on him; his boxing career and health declined, and he died a few years later, broke and dispirited.

Molineaux is a startling example of the "rags to riches to rags" cycle, which still plagues black athletes nearly 200 years after his boxing career ended. His boxing ability took him from plantation slave to freeman to a match against an esteemed white pugilist. He was involved in the first interracial heavyweight title bout. Molineaux was a contender for the most coveted athletic prize during his lifetime—the heavyweight championship of the world. He most certainly knew fame and fortune, but in the end the acclaim and possessions escaped him. While it may be an overstatement to suggest that he was the prototype of the African American athlete, it would not be hyperbolic to state that many black sportsmen have followed suit in their quest for, grasp of, and loss of privilege and prosperity.

In the nineteenth century African Americans played a prominent role as jockeys in thoroughbred horse racing. In the South most jockeys were slaves, while in the North they were usually English, Irish, or native-born whites. In the early 1800s, before the advent of thoroughbred racing meets in America, black jockeys won a number of prestigious match races.

At the first Kentucky Derby (1875) the winner—Oliver Lewis—was black, as were thirteen of the other fourteen jockeys. Another black rider, Jimmy Winkfield, recorded two victories in four starts, a second and a third place finish to give him the best winning average in Kentucky Derby history. He later went to Europe and continued racing and winning. Isaac Murphy* won the Kentucky Derby in 1884, 1890, and 1891—the first to win the Derby three times. Murphy won a number of other important races as well. Willie Simms* won the Kentucky Derby twice (1896 and 1898), won at Sheepshead Bay (New York) five times, and went to England, where he attained international fame.

During the late 1800s black jockeys faced increasing resentment from white riders, who sometimes worked in concert to force blacks to the rails. Eventually, they were excluded from the sport of horse racing, especially after the Jockey Club (a licensing agency for jockeys formed in 1894) banned blacks from membership.

As black jockeys were being forced out of horse racing in the 1800s, black boxers were struggling to gain acceptance as pugilists. For nearly 100 years after Molineaux's fight against Cribb, no African American was allowed an opportunity to compete for the heavyweight title. However, this was not due to a lack of talent or interest among black boxers. George Godfrey and Charles Hadley are but two of the black boxers who sought a match with the popular champion John L. Sullivan*; their offers, like others, were refused. Sullivan fought blacks on his way to fame and the title, but when he reached prominence as a fighter, he drew the color line. One he became world heavyweight champion, Sullivan never again faced a black boxer.

Peter Jackson perhaps came closer than any other African American in the nineteenth century to fighting for the heavyweight title. He was born in the Virgin Islands and emigrated to Australia when he was very young. After becoming the Australian heavyweight champion in 1886, Jackson emigrated to San Francisco in search of prestige and financial gain.

Jackson attempted to arrange for his first fight in America against a white boxer, Joe McAuliffe, but when he refused, Jackson instead defeated George Godfrey for the colored heavyweight championship of the world. As colored champion, Jackson found white boxers were more eager to fight him, because a victory over the best black boxer could garner for whites an important and perhaps even a title fight. Jackson hoped that his defeats of white opponents (e.g., McAuliffe, Patsy Cardiff, Frank Slavin, and Jem Smith) would do the same for him—set him up for a title bout.

Jackson was not alone in seeking a fight against Sullivan. In 1890 several athletic clubs made impressive offers to host a fight between the two boxers. Sullivan turned down all offers; he would not meet a black fighter in the ring and certainly not one as talented as Jackson. Discouraged, Jackson continued to fight. In 1891 he fought James Corbett* to a sixty-one-round draw. While the Jackson-Corbett fight failed to enhance Jackson's position with Sullivan, it propelled Corbett to a title fight with Sullivan, which Corbett won. This turn of events caused Jackson to cut short his stay in England to seek a rematch with Corbett.

Jackson and Corbett agreed to a fight, but they disagreed on the location of the bout. Corbett wanted to fight in Jacksonville, Florida, but Jackson refused. Interracial contests were not a welcome spectacle in America, and an interracial heavyweight championship fight in the American South could be particularly dangerous to a black man who emerged victorious over a white fighter. Jackson thought it wise to avoid fighting Corbett in the Deep South. Thus, he surrendered his chance to compete for the title. It is possible that Corbett's tactics were designed to avoid risking his title against Jackson. Jackson turned to heavy drinking. He died at the age of forty from tuberculosis or, perhaps, from a broken heart. His misfortune was being black in a society that valued the ability and accomplishments of whites only.

While Jackson and others sought heavyweight title bouts against white challengers, African Americans in the lower weight classes were making their mark on boxing. Because they were smaller in size, their fights did not carry the same implications for racial and national superiority that accompanied heavyweight fights. On 27 June 1890 George "Little Chocolate" Dixon* defeated Nunc Wallace, the British featherweight champion, with an eighteenth-round knockout, to become the first African American to hold a title in any sport. The next year he won the American bantamweight title with a knockout of Cal McCarthy in Boston.

A decade later—in 1901—a second African American became a boxing titleholder when Joe Walcott won the welterweight title from Rube Ferns. The following year another African American, Joe Gans, won the lightweight title with a first-round knockout of Frank Erne. In 1904, two top black boxers fought for the welterweight title—Walcott and Aaron "Dixie Kid" Brown—which Brown won on a foul in the twentieth round.

Like their heavyweight counterparts, most of the previously mentioned boxers retained little of their fortune during their later years. Dixon, who won an enormous amount of money, succumbed to alcohol and died broke at the age of thirty-seven. Walcott lived to be sixty-three, but he, too, died broke (the victim of a hit-and-run accident). The "Dixie Kid" died penniless after attempting suicide at the age of fifty-two. Of the early black boxing champions, only Joe Gans was financially secure when he died.

The decade of the 1890s has been referred to as the "darkest period in race relations in U.S. history" because of a record number of lynchings (1,217) and the 1896 "separate but equal" Supreme Court ruling (*Plessy v. Ferguson*). But ironically, this decade also witnessed the crowning of the second African American champion in any sport (after Dixon in boxing), when Major Taylor* became the world and American sprint cycling champion in 1899.

Major Taylor was a champion cyclist during the period preceding the advent of the automobile and auto racing, when cycling was one of the most popular spectator sports in America. In 1898 Taylor held seven world records in his specialty—the sprints. In 1899 he won the one-mile world championship in Montreal, followed by the American championship in 1899 and 1900 (on total points from qualifying events). During the early 1900s he successfully toured Europe, where cycling was the most popular sport at the time. He was heartily welcomed by the French, and he dominated the sport, but his refusal to race on Sundays—for religious reasons—did not allow him to compete for the world championships in Europe in 1902 or 1903. Still, he was able to add to his victories, earnings, and popularity in Europe without enduring the prejudice he faced in America. When Taylor retired from the sport of cycling, he was thirty-two years old, an international star, and very wealthy. However, bad business investments cost him his savings, his house, and other valuables. When he died of heart and kidney problems, his body lay unclaimed in Chicago for more than a week. He was buried in a common "pauper's grave" in a Jim Crow section of a cemetery, where he remained until he was reburied sixteen years later by a Chicago bicycle association. In 1982, Indianapolis, his hometown and the city that banned him from one of its racetracks in 1896, named its velodrome after him.

Racism, highlighted by segregation laws and practices, governed nearly every aspect of life in the United States during the early twentieth century. The institution of sport also operated in ways that maintained white supremacy; many of the contests were for whites only. As in the late 1800s, African Americans contended for the "colored heavyweight" title, but whites refused to meet African Americans for heavyweight title fights. It was a common practice for white fighters to meet black boxers on their way to prominence but to draw the color line—avoid black boxers—once they distinguished themselves as pugilists.

John Arthur "Jack" Johnson,* who had been the "colored heavyweight champion," wanted to fight for the "world" heavyweight title, but he, like other African Americans, was initially ignored. However, Johnson was relentless in his pursuit of the title; he followed Tommy Burns from New York to England, France, and Australia in search of the bout. Despite the disapproval of many boxers, including former champion Sullivan, Burns parted company with the white athletes' custom of drawing the color line. In Australia in December 1908, Jack Johnson taunted, laughed at, and defeated Tommy Burns to become the first black heavyweight titleholder. The American press trivialized Johnson's accomplishment, claiming that he wasn't in the same category as Sullivan, Corbett, and Jeffries, former white champions. Jim Jeffries, the former heavyweight champion, was summoned out of retirement to remove the ever-present "golden" smile from Jack Johnson's face and to restore white superiority to boxing.

Johnson's fight with Jeffries in Reno, Nevada, was a colossal affair. More than 20,000 fans—including over 100 correspondents and writers from the United States, Europe, and Australia—came to witness what many viewed as the fight for racial superiority. Jeffries was America's "great white hope." Most expected Jeffries to win because he was white but also because he was believed to possess physical ability, discipline, courage, restraint, and intellectual ability, which Johnson (and by extension, "the race") was said to lack. Johnson became the first fighter to ever knock Jeffries down (which he did several times) and out. Johnson's win over Jeffries also signaled an end to unchallenged notions of white supremacy in the ring. African Americans rejoiced after Johnson's victory. Many felt that he had "uplifted" a downtrodden race. Others likened Jeffries' defeat to a second Emancipation Proclamation. African Americans had, once again, thrown off whites' shackles, freeing themselves, this time, from another kind of slavery—ideological racism.

Not surprisingly, whites were angered by Johnson's triumph. Some whites sought to suppress black jubilation by preventing parades and other festivities honoring Johnson's accomplishment. Rioting broke out in many cities and towns in America. Major cities forbade the showing of the film, claiming that the sight of a black man thrashing a white man heightened racial tension (although the sight of whites whipping blacks was not considered to be similarly disquieting). Johnson's lifestyle, especially his penchant for ignoring important social taboos, was an affront to many Americans. He was extravagant; he drove expensive cars; he was an impeccable dresser who often changed clothes three or four times daily; he adorned himself with expensive diamonds; he carried a roll of thousand-dollar bills, which he loved to spend having a good time; and he showed disdain for, rather than deference to, whites.

But what most incensed whites was Johnson's liaisons with white women, which got him in trouble with the federal government under the Mann Act. The Mann Act, or "White Slave Traffic Act," enacted in 1910, forbade the interstate transportation of women for immoral purposes. It was intended to prohibit commercial vice—cases where foreign women were smuggled into the United States to engage in prostitution. Johnson was charged with violating the Mann Act for sending money to Belle Schreiber, a prostitute and Johnson's former mistress, enabling her to travel from Pittsburgh to Chicago. Johnson was fined $1,000 *and* sentenced to one year in prison. He then fled the United States for Europe.

Although he was still the heavyweight champion, he had difficulty finding fights and making a living in Europe. He turned to wrestling, bullfighting and vaudeville performances for income. In 1915, two years after his escape from America, Johnson put his title on the line in a fight against the gargantuan—6' 6", 260-pound—Jess Willard. By knocking Johnson out in the twenty-sixth round, Willard became the great white hope that Jeffries had sought to be. Whites rejoiced. Boxers and promoters vowed to keep the title from black inter-lopers. For twenty-two years, no other African American would be allowed to fight for the heavyweight title. Prospective black contenders would have to first prove that they were not a threat to the established order. Johnson returned to Europe for another five years before coming back to the United States in 1920 to serve his one-year prison sentence. While Johnson was held in high esteem by many African Americans for his convincing display of black prowess, the black middle class disavowed and denounced him, believing that he had brought hardship to African Americans (some had lost their jobs in the wake of his defeats of white fighters) and that he had embarrassed the black community through his liaisons with white women. Still, Johnson was among the first in a long line of African Americans to demonstrate blacks' abilities to participate in heretofore white sports. He paved the athletic road for African American athletes to follow. However, they would have to follow a different path to social accep-tance.

Jack Johnson was the torchbearer for the first generation of twentieth-century African American athletes. The next generation witnessed the formation of the Negro Leagues* in professional baseball; barnstorming teams such as the all-black New York (Harlem) Renaissance Big Five* in basketball; and the inclu-sion of a few African Americans on white professional football teams before the color line was drawn in 1933. In college a few black athletes, including Fritz Pollard and Paul Robeson,* played on northern and western teams. In 1916 Pollard, All-American from Brown University, became the first of many African Americans to compete in the Rose Bowl. In the 1920s he also became the first African American to coach and play quarterback in the National Football League (NFL). Robeson, All-American at Rutgers, was a teammate of Pollard on the Akron Pros. Robeson, a Phi Beta Kappa, attended law school at Columbia Uni-versity and later became a renowned actor, singer, and activist. Most black college athletes, however, were in track-and-field programs. By the time of the 1936 Olympics there were 100–200 African American athletes scattered throughout programs in the United States. Black athletes were more prominent than before, but they were still not revered as heroes to white America. Jesse Owens* and Joe Louis* would change that.

Jesse Owens and Joe Louis were both born to black sharecroppers in Ala-bama. Their families left the South seeking better jobs and opportunities in the urban northern cities of Cleveland and Detroit, respectively. Owens attended college at Ohio State University, where he became one of the most outstanding athletes in history. To illustrate, at the Big Ten Championship meet at the Uni-versity of Michigan, 25 May 1935, an injured Jesse Owens tied the world record for the 100-yard dash (9.4 seconds) and broke the world mark for the 220-yard low hurdles (22.6 seconds), the 220-yard sprint (20.3 seconds), and the long jump (26 feet, 8-1/4 inches). In one hour he broke three long-held world records and tied another. The next month Owens scored 40 of Ohio State University's 40-1/5 points in a meet that his team lost against the University of Southern California.

Owens is best known for his performance at the 1936 Berlin "Nazi" Olympics. The Eleventh Olympic Games were important to Germany, as they indicated the European nations' willingness to reconcile with Germany. But given Hitler's views about the inferiority of non-Aryans and the fact that Germany was becoming a totalitarian police state, there was bound to be controversy. American Jews, appalled by Hitler's open discrimination against Jews, called for a boycott of the "Nazi Games" by the United States. Meanwhile, the German government asked that black athletes be barred from the games, claiming that it was degrading and disgraceful for whites to compete with "Negroes" for trophies. The American black press, although divided, also had strong opinions about the German Olympics. Some newspapers advocated boycotting the games, as participation might be taken as a sign of approval of Nazi beliefs and practices. Others felt that the Olympic Games would be the perfect setting to challenge Hitler's notions about the inferiority of non-Aryans. Every defeat of a German would be a blow to Aryan supremacy.

It was the decision of the American Athletic Union to participate in the Olympics. Although the Germans won the unofficial medal count, Jesse Owens' performance was magnificent. He tied the world record of 10.3 seconds in the 100-meter dash; set an Olympic record of 26' 5-1/4" in the long jump; set an Olympic record of 20.7 seconds in the 200-meter sprint; and ran the opening leg in the finals of the record-setting 400-meter relay (which was run in 39.8 seconds). Owens alone scored forty points; the German male track team scored sixty points. Owens, the brightest of the Olympic stars, had become a hero to black and white Americans (although whites referred to him, condescendingly, as "a credit to his race"). In winning four gold medals, he had led a team of Americans, which included eighteen other African Americans, that demolished notions of Aryan preeminence in physical contests.

Joe Louis would later pick up where Owens had left off. Before the opening of the Olympic Games, Joe Louis met German boxer Max Schmeling in a bout that was expected to position the winner for a match against James Braddock, the heavyweight titleholder. While there were a few references to a fight between a representative of the "master race" and a son of Africa, there was little animosity toward Schmeling. In fact, many Americans viewed this as a fight between a black man and a white man, not a German and an American. Therefore, because he was white, Schmeling had many fans in America. Surprisingly, Schmeling, a 10–1 underdog, scored a twelfth-round knockout over Louis. Upon his return to Germany he was praised by Hitler, with whom he lunched, for a

"German victory." A despondent Louis worked to get himself back into contention for the title. He felt he had let himself and African Americans down.

Louis, more than Owens, was viewed as an emissary for the black community. Few other African Americans were in the public eye as was Louis, and he was careful not to "bring shame to the race" by antagonizing whites as Johnson had. Louis' public persona was humble, nonthreatening, and modest. He was counseled to never show pleasure in beating whites and to never have his picture taken with white women. In short, Louis was coached to be acceptable to whites. Because he was talented and observed the prescribed roles that whites had for African Americans, he was, indeed, accepted by whites. In 1935 he was named "Boxer of the Year" by *Ring Magazine* and "Athlete of the Year" by the Associated Press—honors that Jack Johnson would never have received no matter how many opponents he had defeated.

In the year after losing to Max Schmeling Louis defeated seven fighters in eight months. In June 1937 he became the first African American in twenty-two years to fight for the heavyweight championship. He defeated James Braddock with an eighth-round knockout in front of 45,000 spectators—20,000 of them black fans—to become the second black heavyweight champion. But his most important fight was yet to come.

During the two years since Louis and Schmeling had met in the ring Hitler had sought to expand his influence over Germany. This, along with Germany's persecution of Jews, disturbed Americans. In addition, Schmeling's reception by Hitler following his first fight with Louis and the German's use of the victory as a sign of Aryan superiority troubled Americans. This led to increased American hostility toward Germans and Schmeling as a representative of Nazism.

Whereas the first fight between Louis and Schmeling was viewed as a bout between a black and a white opponent, the second was viewed by many Americans as a contest between nations, the United States versus Germany, and ideology, democracy versus fascism. America was now represented by an African American, a decided change in Americans' position toward nonwhites. Even President Franklin D. Roosevelt got involved; he sent his private car to bring Louis to the White House, where he felt Louis' muscles and proclaimed, "Joe, we're depending on those muscles for America." Louis, like Owens, had become a key functionary for America—he was performing a crucial role for the entire system. For once, his performance had the support of America, not just the black community. He was expected to send Germany a message about America's ability to do combat.

In one round Louis completely destroyed Schmeling and concerns about Aryan supremacy; democracy had triumphed over fascism. Later, Louis solidified his position as a beloved (black) American when he enlisted, as a private, in the U.S. Army, preferring to forgo a deferment that he might have been granted. His presence and recruitment activities for the military encouraged others to participate in the World War II effort. He also fought numerous exhibitions, contributing his share of purses—a considerable amount of money—to the Navy Relief and Army Relief Funds. Yet, all the while, Louis was one of the "colored troops," as the U.S. military was segregated by race.

Although they were American champions, Owens and Louis were not immune from the prevalent racial stereotypes of their era (e.g., blacks are better athletes because they are closer to the primitive than whites), nor were they excused from loathsome racial customs such as being confined to the "colored section" of restaurants, buses, theaters, and so on. During the early part of Louis' career he was often depicted as a "Sambo" by newspapers—he was presented as an apelike figure with a small head, apelike arms, large lips, dark skin, and bulging eyes.

Owens and Louis were both nationally celebrated figures and black men—holding two contradictory standings in the public mind during the 1930s. Nevertheless, they became the first two black heroes to America for much the same reason: they had performed phenomenally in international events where, as representatives for America, they defeated "foreign enemies." They were, later, credited with improving race relations in America, in large part because of their deferential behavior. Louis' nonthreatening bearing caused many influential whites—from former heavyweight champions to politicians—to declare that interracial bouts were no longer disruptive of racial harmony, a reversal of views from those of Johnson's reign as heavyweight champion. Moreover, Louis and Owens are credited with opening the door for Jackie Robinson* and other African Americans to play integrated professional ball. They were the first to go from race heroes to national idols.

Jackie Robinson is widely credited with breaking the color line in professional team sports in America when he signed a contract with the Brooklyn Dodgers in 1945. This is a misrepresentation of his accomplishment. Professional football had a few, although not more than five, African Americans on team rosters in the 1920s. While it appears there was no organized boycott, some teams objected to playing against African Americans. By 1933 professional football had drawn the color line.

Even professional "white" baseball had included black players on its rosters before Robinson's signing, but that was before the turn of the century. In 1872 John W. "Bud" Fowler joined a minor league team in New Castle, Pennsylvania, to become the first black professional baseball player. By the next decade as many as thirty African Americans participated on white professional teams. This number included Moses Fleetwood Walker,* who, as a catcher for the Toledo Blue Stockings in 1884, became the first black major leaguer; his brother, Welday Walker; and other standouts, such as Frank Grant and George Stovey. But increasing resistance by white ballplayers led the International League to ban the signing of African Americans in 1887. Shortly thereafter there was a general blackout in professional baseball.

The Negro Leagues showcased black talent for black and white audiences;

they were known for great play and improvisation. For example, night baseball and East-West All-Star Games both originated in the Negro Leagues; white baseball adopted these innovations years later. The Negro Leagues were also known for barnstorming-playing exhibitions, which constituted most of their games, against all kinds of opponents ranging from black to white teams as well as from local teams to intact major league "white teams" (which they often defeated). Negro Leaguers also endured all kinds of conditions—playing in major league parks; playing on open fields without backdrops; sleeping in buses, dugouts, and on the side of the road (due to hotels' policy of racial discrimination); sleeping two or three to a bed; and playing several games in a day. Roy Campanella,* who played a decade in both the Negro Leagues and the white majors, claimed to have played catcher in four games in one day on several occasions while with the Baltimore Elite Giants of the Negro Leagues. Although life was hard in the Negro Leagues, they gave black players a chance to make a living playing a sport players loved, and they were a training ground for a number of the most outstanding African Americans to play baseball. That group included Josh Gibson* and Smokey Joe Williams, who never played white baseball, as well as many who later played in the white major leagues, such as Satchel Paige,* Willie Mays,* Hank Aaron,* Larry Doby,* and Jackie Robinson—the first player to go from the Negro Leagues to white baseball.

In the mid-1950s, as black baseball was declining due to the integration of the major leagues, the Indianapolis Clowns hired a few African American women, primarily as gate attractions to boost attendance. In 1953 Toni Stone,* a second-base player, signed with the team as the first woman to play Negro League ball. The following year the Clowns replaced her with another African American female, Connie Morgan. That year the team also recruited Mamie "Peanut" Johnson as the first black woman to pitch in the Negro Leagues.

Robinson, it was widely felt, was not the best ballplayer in the Negro Leagues; that honor would arguably go to Satchel Paige, the extraordinary pitcher who was, at one time, the highest paid ballplayer, black or white, in America. However, Branch Rickey, general manager of the Brooklyn Dodgers, felt that Robinson had the perfect "combination" of characteristics to become the pioneer black player in the white majors. Having thoroughly investigated Robinson's college, military, and sports background, he decided that Robinson had the skills to play for the Dodgers, but his other "assets" were just as important: Robinson was a veteran of predominantly white teams. He had earned a varsity letter in four sports at the University of California at Los Angeles (UCLA), where he was a star in football, baseball, basketball, and track. In addition, Robinson was college-educated and had served as a second lieutenant in the army during World War II. While in the army Robinson demonstrated his willingness to fight for his rights on numerous occasions, including attempting to integrate facilities at military bases. Rickey saw in Robinson a courageous and talented man who would suppress his feelings and emotions, in the face of whites' insults, for the good of Rickey's "experiment." Or, as Buck Leonard, one of the Negro League stars, saw it, "we had a whole lot better ballplayers than Jackie, but Jackie was chosen 'cause he had played with the white boys."

The collaboration of Rickey and Robinson was important, but other factors, outside of baseball, facilitated desegregation in the white leagues. Black patriotism and participation in World War II caused some people to rethink discriminatory policies; black reporters demanded tryouts for black athletes and often identified candidates for white teams; and New York state passed the Quinn-Ives antidiscrimination law in 1945, which forbade racial discrimination in hiring. This was an opportune time for Rickey to pursue his interest in securing black talent for his team.

Robinson was encouraged to emulate the behavior of Joe Louis—appease rather than offend whites. But Robinson was not like Louis. He was not accustomed to suffering indignities; he took pride in retaliation. Yet, he was convinced, by Rickey, that any retaliation would have tragic consequences for himself and other African Americans who hoped to play professional white baseball. For two years Robinson endured racist taunts by baseball fans and opponents, hate-mail, segregated accommodations and restaurants, and an attempt by his prospective teammates—and later by the St. Louis Cardinals—to boycott games if he was included in the lineup, all without retribution. He continually made sacrifices to avoid jeopardizing the chances of other African American ballplayers. However, when black players were firmly established in the league, Robinson was free to express himself like other ballplayers; he was free to respond, as he deemed appropriate, to attempts to humiliate him. Thereafter, many who had admired him for submissive and nonretaliatory public behavior began to view him as an ungrateful insurgent. Robinson felt he had done his job—he had nullified all of whites' reasons for excluding African Americans from baseball. An onslaught followed.

Robinson became an outstanding major leaguer. During his first year with the Brooklyn Dodgers he was named the National League Rookie of the Year. Two years later, in 1949, Robinson led the league in batting and stolen bases and was named the National League Most Valuable Player. A six-time All-Star who helped his team to six league pennants, Robinson ushered in an era of black dominance in professional team sports. Shortly after Robinson signed with the Dodgers, they added four other black players to the roster. Although some teams lagged behind, by 1959 every major league baseball team had at least one black player.

Robinson's signing and later performance reverberated throughout team sports. Professional football reintegrated in 1946, when Robinson's former UCLA backfield mate, Kenny Washington,* signed with the Los Angeles Rams. Woody Strode,* another former UCLA teammate of Robinson, was also signed by the Rams that same year. Nearly four years later, Chuck Cooper* and Earl Lloyd became the first black players in the National Basketball Association. An important obstacle had been conquered in sport during the 1940s and 1950s.

Black athletes would soon come to dominate the same sports that had, for years, ignored their performances. They were thrilled to be included in the white leagues. However, the next decade would bring restlessness and rebellion as they witnessed white America's ambivalence toward them: they were accepted on the field only.

During the 1950s and 1960s a number of racial barriers fell in sport. Althea Gibson* won the French Tennis Open in 1956, followed by back-to-back titles both at Wimbledon and Forest Hills, New York, in 1957 and 1958. There were also black firsts in the National Hockey League (Willie O'Ree in 1957); in golf on the Professional Golfers' Association (PGA) (Charlie Sifford* in 1961) and Ladies Professional Golf Association (LPGA) (Renee Powell in 1967) tours; in professional basketball as head coaches (John McLendon in the American Basketball Association [ABA] and Bill Russell* in the National Basketball Association [NBA]); in baseball (Emmett Ashford as first black umpire in 1965); and in various other areas of professional sport.

In college sports, African Americans began to show up on more team rosters in the major sports. By 1948 black athletes appeared on one out of every ten predominantly white college teams, although they constituted only 1% of all basketball players at these colleges. From this it is easy to see that few teams had more than one black player representing them. Furthermore, black athletes were not allowed to be second or third teamers; a disproportionate number of them were Rookies of the Year, conference Most Valuable Players, and All-Americans. Moreover, southern colleges refused to compete against teams with black players.

Most southern college conferences did not relax their ban on integration until the latter part of the 1960s. Some northern colleges with integrated sports refused to play against southern schools; others simply left black players on the sidelines when they visited or hosted southern teams. In a sure sign that white southern schools were not prepared to welcome black athletes, African American students (nonathletes) were met by angry white mobs when they attempted to integrate the University of Mississippi in 1962 and the University of Alabama in 1963. Furthermore, Mississippi colleges sat out National Collegiate Athletic Association (NCAA) basketball tournaments in 1959 and 1961 and a bowl game in 1961—both prestigious events—rather than compete against black athletes.

In 1966, Texas Western (now the University of Texas, El Paso), recruited an all-black starting five—a first for a basketball team at a predominantly white university—and upset the all-white University of Kentucky team to win the national championship. Shortly thereafter Kentucky accepted black players on its teams. Most other white colleges desegregated, if they had not already done so.

After World War II African American women asserted themselves in collegiate and Olympic sports, first in track and field and later in basketball. Tuskegee Institute and Tennessee State University led the way, and by the 1950s black women constituted more than two-thirds of U.S. females chosen to compete at the major international meets and the Olympic Games. Alice Coachman* was the first black woman to win an Olympic gold medal when she won the high jump in 1948 at London. Wilma Rudolph* was a sensation in 1960 in Rome, capturing three gold medals. Following her in the limelight as track celebrities from the 1960s through the 1990s were Wyomia Tyus-Tillman,* Evelyn Ashford Washington,* Florence Griffith-Joyner,* Jackie Joyner-Kersee, Gail Devers, Valerie Briscoe, Gwen Torrence, and others.

African American female participation in basketball was slower to progress, but the feminist revolution of the 1960s and 1970s and especially the passage of Title IX of the Education Amendments Act of 1972 opened the gates of opportunity for all women of all races in the United States. First the Association of Intercollegiate Athletics for Women and later the National Collegiate Athletic Association promoted and regulated varsity athletics for women, with basketball as the premier sport. Pioneering black women who starred on the court during the 1970s and 1980s include Lusia Harris of Delta State, Lynette Woodard* of Kansas, and Pam and Paula McGee and Cheryl Miller* of UCLA, among others. Many also helped U.S. teams win medals at the Olympic Games; Woodard, Pam McGee, and Miller led the American women to a gold medal victory at the 1984 games at Los Angeles.

Desegregation in American sports did not mean full acceptance for African American athletes. Black players in college and the professional ranks were roomed in undesirable hotels while their white teammates often reposed in luxury; many restaurants, even in hotels that would admit them, were off-limits to black players; and black players who were permitted to stay at white hotels were not allowed to be roomed with whites. Moreover, interracial interaction was frowned upon, if not banned.

During the 1960s a number of black athletes began to complain about their treatment by the predominantly white sports establishment. Professional athletes protested about being underpaid and barred from occupying certain sports leadership positions. Collegiate athletes felt that they were exploited by schools that welcomed their athletic ability yet ignored their academic and social needs. After their academic eligibility was completed, they were treated like pariahs by their alma mater.

Many whites—fans, coaches, administrators, students, and alumni—failed to understand what black athletes had to lament. Sport, they felt, had lifted scores of black men and women from the "ghettos" and improved their lot in life. According to the athletic director at the University of Texas, El Paso, "In general, the nigger athlete is a little hungrier, and we have been blessed with having some real outstanding ones. We think they've done a lot for us, and we think we've done a lot for them." Many black athletes disagreed; they challenged white demands that they be humble and grateful. Collegiate athletes presented universities with their own demands: an end to restrictions on their social activities, including interracial dating; the discontinuation of demeaning, racist language directed at black athletes; the curtailment of segregated accommodations; and an end to stacking—the practice of assigning players to positions by race.

Some college programs responded by suspending black athletes for insubordination; others simply removed them from the team, effectively curtailing their athletic careers. But many black athletes of the 1960s were not inclined to be like Louis and Owens—obsequious and nonthreatening. Instead, many chose to be like Muhammad Ali.*

Ali was, as Cassius Clay, a blessing for boxing. He was brash, loquacious, attractive, talented, and, for sports reporters, quotable. He danced around opponents, daring them to hit him. He spouted self-penned poetry about his upcoming matches, giving his antagonists often humorous, but not altogether innocuous, nicknames. He brought attention and flair to boxing and helped to rescue it from the doldrums. Cassius Clay was tolerated by many Americans and well liked by some until he announced, two days after becoming the heavyweight champion, that he had joined the Nation of Islam, a religious group headed by Elijah Muhammad. He further incensed many Americans by declaring that he was dropping his "slave name," Cassius Clay, to be known as Cassius X. Later he took the "divine" name, Muhammad Ali.

Many whites and some African Americans were upset by Ali's affiliation to the Nation of Islam (or "Black Muslims," as the Nation of Islam was commonly called). The Nation of Islam, through its most prominent spokesperson, Malcolm X, was outspoken about America's history of oppression of African Americans and very critical of whites. But, more importantly to Ali and a host of other people of color, the Nation of Islam preached black pride to African Americans, countering feelings of black inferiority.

Former black heavyweight champions Floyd Patterson* and Joe Louis denounced Ali for joining the Nation of Islam. Patterson declared the Black Muslims "a menace to the United States and to the 'Negro race,' " adding: "The image of a Black Muslim as the world heavyweight champion disgraces the sport and the nation." He promised to defeat Ali and return the title to (Christian) America, which he was unable to do. Other African Americans were similarly upset by Ali's religious conversion.

Two years after declaring himself a member of the Nation of Islam, Ali saw his draft status changed from 1-Y (not qualified for military service) to 1-A. He announced that he would not serve in the armed forces, requesting that he be awarded conscientious objector status on religious grounds. In 1967, his request denied, Ali refused to be inducted into the service. One hour later—before he was charged or convicted of a crime—New York state's Athletic Commission suspended his boxing license. Every other jurisdiction soon followed, thus barring him from further fights.

Initially, after his association with the Nation of Islam was disclosed, many black athletes were probably ambivalent toward Ali; he was anti-Christianity, anti-vice, anti–race-mixing. All told, he was too chaste for their tastes. However, black athletes came to revere Ali as he refused to waver on his principles: he would not serve in the armed forces (or as he said, support the domination of people of color by a white government) even if it meant being stripped of his title. Ali was in the forefront of the black athletic revolution of the 1960s. He made it easier for black athletes who followed to challenge the system. Ali influenced generations of black athletes and ushered in the era of a new black athlete—a more assertive athlete, who was prepared to challenge racial injustice.

In 1968, at the Olympic Games in Mexico City, African Americans Tommie Smith* and John Carlos* finished first and third in the 200-meter dash. When they raised their black-gloved fists in a "black power" salute on the victory stand, they engendered feelings of pride in many African Americans. Smith, Carlos, and many other African American athletes had used the Olympic international stage as a forum to protest against racial inequities in America. The proposed boycott of the Olympics and the resultant protests by black athletes contributed significantly to the awakening of black America during the late 1960s.

Black athletes of the 1960s and early 1970s demanded better treatment from a white public and Establishment that often felt African American athletes were lucky to receive the rewards and adulation they bestowed on them. Some prominent former athletes demanded the same.

In October 1972, before the second game of the World Series between the Cincinnati Reds and the Pittsburgh Pirates, Jackie Robinson was honored for his contributions to baseball. A fighter to the end, Robinson said to the thousands gathered, "When I look down the third base line, I want to see a black man coaching. Then I'll be able to say we've made progress." Robinson never lived to see that day in baseball history. He died a week later.

Nearly fifteen years after his death Al Campanis, Robinson's white former teammate with the Montreal Royals and one of the few white players to join Robinson's all-star barnstorming team, appeared on a television program that paid tribute to Robinson and his legacy. Campanis, then the vice president of the Los Angeles Dodgers—the franchise that made Robinson a pioneer— claimed that African Americans lack the "necessities"—his reference to intellectual and other abilities—to manage baseball teams. He added, however, "They are outstanding athletes, very God-gifted, and they're wonderful people. . . . They're gifted with great musculature and various other things." These, according to Campanis, are the assets that make African Americans great athletes but do not qualify them for front office positions. With this Campanis reignited a heated debate about black ability—whether sports ability is determined by race and whether African Americans and black people around the world are genetically superior as athletes (and, according to some people, inferior intellectually).

Over the past few decades numerous commentators—including "scientists"— have condescendingly complimented African Americans for their sports accomplishments, especially since the breaking of the color barriers in team sports, concluding that they had physiological (e.g., better suited for sports), psychological (e.g., relaxation under pressure), and historical (i.e., slavery) advantages over whites that led to their outstanding sports performances. Thus, whites had, in a brief period of time, gone from claiming that African Americans lacked the ability to participate in sports with whites (which was used as a justification for segregated sports), to declaring that African Americans are better at sports through no "fault" of their own (certainly not through hard work) but, rather, because of innate advantages. Thus, it was possible to admire black athletes' performances as one would other creatures' magnificence, while simultaneously maintaining strongly held beliefs about racial superiority (i.e., blacks are not as intelligent, disciplined, or industrious as whites).

The belief in black athletic superiority may at once serve to mollify white concerns about their athletic ability (i.e., "It's not that you're inept; it's that they were born better") and keep African Americans out of the sports positions many whites covet when their playing days are over. Still, some African Americans have managed to obtain some positions directing and administering sport franchises.

In the 1980s few professional teams had black head coaches, general managers, or other front-office personnel. Excluding basketball, the number of black coaches was truly abysmal. By 1994 the NBA still led the leagues with five black coaches (19%), followed by major league baseball with four (14%) and the NFL with two (7%). In addition, a small percentage of African Americans were in top management positions (e.g., president or vice president of the organization), and a few were part owners of franchises, although, when this entry was written, there were no African American majority owners of any major professional sports franchise. African Americans have won a number of "coach of the year" awards and a few championships in sport. Sport, perhaps more than other institutions in America, has allowed African Americans to become managers and executives. But they continue to be underrepresented relative to the number of athletes in these sports. During the 1992–93 seasons African Americans made up 16% of the professional baseball, 68% of the football, and 77% of the basketball players; their percentages as coaches and front-office personnel pale by comparison.

In college sport, African Americans constituted only 6% of the students at predominantly white colleges and universities in 1994 but 42% of the football players, 37% of the women basketball players, and 60% of the men basketball players at the most competitive (Division I-A) level. Yet only 4% of college head coaches were African American, with a higher percentage in basketball (fewer than 20%) than in football (where there were only a handful) or baseball (where there were no collegiate managers). It is apparent that black athletes are readily accepted on college and professional teams as athletes but only in non-supervisory positions. Basketball and football especially are sports where, typically, whites control and direct black talent. It is unlikely that Jackie Robinson would see progress in this.

During the 1980s and 1990s there was a resurgence of discussion about black intellect and athletic ability and the exploitation of African American youth in college sports. In college, new regulations heightened the public conversation about black intellect and sport. The National Collegiate Athletic Association (NCAA) implemented a series of guidelines (Proposition 48, Proposition 42, and Proposition 16) that raised the minimum grade point average and standardized test scores that athletes would have to obtain to accept an athletic scholarship. While some argued that the standardized tests were culturally or racially biased and a way to diminish the number of African Americans at predominantly white universities, others argued that new, higher standards were necessary to avoid the continued exploitation of black athletes (e.g., by bringing academically unprepared student athletes into colleges and universities where they could not make the grade). The public discussions led many to question the academic competence of black athletes. This occurred at a time when sport was simultaneously making stars, superstars, and megastars or celebrities out of a few African American athletes.

As spectator sports have become more popular in America, black athletes have been at or near the top of the escalating salaries in sports. African Americans constituted all the top-paid players in basketball for the 1996–97 season and the top four in major league baseball (MLB) for the 1996 season. (They were not among the five top-paid football players—only white quarterbacks were represented—nor among the top hockey players.) All of the players on the preceding list made in excess of $5 million per year in salary alone, headed by Michael Jordan's* estimated $30 million for one season. The top professional boxers often exceed Jordan's expected salary, and nearly all of them are black. During the late 1990s several black professional basketball players signed seven-year contracts worth more than $100 million each.

In addition, some athletes have commercial endorsements that exceed their salary (e.g., Michael Jordan's commercial endorsements were estimated at $40 million). While the salaries of most professional athletes pale in comparison to the preceding group, the average salary in the NBA and MLB exceeds $1 million, and football is nearing that mark. The minimum season wage in the NBA is now more than $250,000. If one adds the money from business interests (e.g., Magic Johnson* was a part owner of the Los Angeles Lakers and has a chain of "Magic Theaters"), money and fame from movies, videos, and so on in which athletes star or appear, it is easy to see how some black athletes have gone from stars to celebrities. In fact, in an interesting twist on celebrity, in cities like New York, Chicago, Dallas, and Los Angeles, it is unusual *not* to see movie stars, television show hosts, politicians, and other celebrities starstruck by black athletes. African American athletes are now among the brightest of the stars. They have gone from the shadow to the summit.

SELECTED BIBLIOGRAPHY: Arthur R. Ashe, Jr., *A Hard Road to Glory: A History of the African-American Athlete* (1988); Susan K. Cahn, *Coming on Strong: Gender and Sexuality in Twentieth-Century Women's Sport* (1994); Ocania Chalk, *Pioneers of Black Sport* (1975); Othello Harris, "African American Predominance in Sport," in D. Brooks and Ron Althouse, eds., *Racism in College Athletics: The African American Athlete's Experience* (1993); Jack Orr, *The Black Athlete: His Story in American History* (1969);

Robert Peterson, *Only the Ball Was White* (1970); Donn Rogosin, *Invisible Men: Life in Baseball's Negro Leagues* (1983); Edna Rust and Art Rust, Jr., *Art Rust's Illustrated History of the Black Athlete* (1985).

Othello Harris

AGASSI, ANDRE (29 April 1970, Las Vegas, NV–   ). A tennis player, he is the son of Armenian immigrants, Emmanuel Michael and Elizabeth Agassi. His father was a boxer in the 1952 Olympics. He attended a Christian school until the age of sixteen, and he completed his high school education through correspondence courses. Agassi was exposed to tennis at age four. As a child, he had the opportunity to hit with tennis greats such as Bjorn Borg, Ilie Nastase, and Harold Solomon. He left school to attend the world-renowned Nick Bollettieri Tennis Academy near Bradenton, Florida. With his trademark forehand, Agassi exploded onto the Association of Tennis Professionals (ATP) tour in 1986, ranking ninety-first in the world by the end of the year. He won his first professional title in 1987 at Itaparica, finishing the year ranked twenty-fifth. In 1988 Agassi became a full-fledged talent, winning six titles and making semifinal appearances at both the French Open and U.S. Open, finishing the year at third in the world. In 1990, Agassi took home three titles, made final appearances in the French Open and U.S. Open, and also won the inaugural ATP Tour World Championships. In 1992, he became Wimbledon champion, his first grand-slam title, by defeating Goran Ivanisevic in the final. After battling with a wrist injury, Agassi returned to the tour with a new coach, former player Brad Gilbert, and claimed U.S. Open titles in 1994 and 1999 and the Australian Open in 1995. In April 1995, Agassi reached the number one ranking in men's tennis. At the 1996 Olympics in Atlanta, Agassi won gold for the United States in the men's singles. Known for his showmanship, rock-and-roll appearance, and rebel image, he injected a youthful energy and trendy style to the sport not only in America but around the globe as well. His Andre Agassi Foundation has raised thousands of dollars to help at-risk youth in his hometown of Las Vegas. When he won the French Open in June 1999, he became the fifth man to capture all four Grand Slam titles. He has also been a consistent member of the U.S. Davis Cup Team.

SELECTED BIBLIOGRAPHY: Andre Agassi, "Diary of a Rookie on Tour," *World Tennis* 35 (December 1987): 32–36, 50; Peter Bodo, "Image Isn't Everything," *Tennis* 28 (February 1993): 34–39; Robin Finn, "On Wimbledon's Grass, Agassi Hits Pay Dirt," *New York Times*, 5 July 1992; Curry Fitzpatrick, "Born to Serve," *Sports Illustrated* 70 (13 March 1989): 63–74.

Thomas Cesa

ALI, MUHAMMAD (17 January 1942, Louisville, KY–   ). An African American prizefighter, he was born Cassius Marcellus Clay, Jr. His father was a billboard and sign painter and his mother, Odessa (Grady) Clay, was a household domestic. He attended public schools in Louisville and first gained national notoriety in 1960 by winning the light-heavyweight gold medal at the Olympic Games in Rome. After turning professional, he was outspoken about his boxing ability. He claimed to be "the Greatest," although others called him "the Louisville Lip" and "the Mouth That Roared." He also sometimes created disparaging names for his opponents, announced the round of their defeat prior to the match, and taunted them before and during the fight. He reinvented the ritual of the weigh-in as well as pre- and postfight interviews. He would become the first man to win the heavyweight title three times, defeating such outstanding champion fighters as Sonny Liston,* Floyd Patterson,* Joe Frazier,* and George Foreman.* After his stunning victory over Liston in 1964 Clay announced his new name—Muhammad Ali—and his membership in the Nation of Islam. Many boxing officials, fans, and former boxers, including former heavyweight champion Joe Louis,* denounced Ali for joining that Muslim sect, whose main spokesperson was Malcolm X. Former heavyweight champion Patterson sought a match with Ali, promising to return the title to "Christian America." Ali was disappointed with the preoccupation with his religious conversion, but he was not disheartened. After his easy win over Patterson he became more vocal about America's racial practices, denounced integrationist movements, which he found to be too ingratiating, and declared, like Malcolm X and other members of the Nation of Islam, that segregation was preferable to fawning. In 1967 Ali refused induction into the military. He sought conscientious objector status, claiming his religious teachings forbade his involvement in any war except a holy one. Later that year he was found guilty of draft evasion and received the maximum penalty: five years in prison and a $10,000 fine. (This decision was reversed by the Supreme Court in 1971.) One hour after he refused induction Ali was stripped of his title by the New York State Athletic Commission; other states refused to allow him to fight. For three years he was banned from boxing, but he was not without supporters, especially among African Americans (and black athletes in particular) and students who were protesting the United States' involvement in Vietnam. When the ban on boxing was lifted in 1970, Ali, who was undefeated before his forced layoff, fought and lost to Frazier in a title fight. In 1974 he regained his crown by stopping Foreman in a fight in Kinshasha, Zaire. In 1978 Leon Spinks would take the heavyweight title from Ali, only to lose it in a rematch that same year. Ali lost his last two fights—one to Larry Holmes, the other to Trevor Berbick, perhaps because of the onset of Parkinson's Syndrome. Yet after his retirement Ali's popularity increased; he received rewards and recognition from many of the same establishments that once shunned him. President Carter sent Ali as an official emissary to Africa when he wanted to drum up support for the United States' boycott of the 1980 Olympics. In 1990 Ali went to Iraq to meet with Saddam Hussein. He returned with fifteen Americans who had been held hostage by the government of Iraq. During the 1990s the public viewed Ali as an icon of the 1960s—rebellious and determined to change the system. He was also admired as an example of the changes the United States experienced over the last third of the twentieth century. He was one of the most reviled and one of the most admired men of his time. During his career he espoused both accommodationism and separatism in response to America's treatment of African Americans. He became an inspiration for African Americans by proposing a boycott of the 1968 Olympics, but three decades later he inspired and even moved many fans to tears as he struggled to light the Olympic torch to open the 1996 games at the stadium in Atlanta. In short, Muhammad Ali was an enigma to much of America.

SELECTED BIBLIOGRAPHY: Muhammad Ali, with Richard Durham, *The Greatest: My Own Story* (1975); Othello Harris, "Muhammad Ali and the Revolt of the Black Athlete," in Elliott Gorn, ed., *The People's Champ* (1995), 54–69; Thomas Hauser, *Muhammad Ali: His Life and Times* (1991); Frederic C. Jaher, "White America Views Jack Johnson, Joe Louis, and Muhammad Ali," in Donald Spivey, ed., *Sport in America: New Historical Perspectives* (1985), 239–262; Robert Lipsyte, *Free to Be Muhammad Ali* (1978); David Remnick, *King of the World* (1998); Jose Torres, *Sting Like a Bee: The Muhammad Ali Story* (1971).

Othello Harris

ALLEN, DUDLEY (? 1846, Lexington, KY–22 October 1911, Lexington, KY). An African American thoroughbred owner and trainer, he was born a slave in Fayette County, Kentucky. He enlisted in the Fifth U.S. Colored Cavalry Regiment in 1864, rising to the rank of quartermaster sergeant before leaving the army in 1866. After the war he returned to Lexington, where he operated his own stock farm, successfully buying, then training and reselling young horses to wealthy eastern sportsmen. By 1891 Allen was a thoroughbred trainer of note, as well as the first African American to own a Kentucky Derby winner, the second Derby winner he trained. His burial site in Lexington is unknown.

SELECTED BIBLIOGRAPHY: Nancy O'Malley, "Kinkeadtown: Archaeological Investigation of an African-American Neighborhood in Lexington, Kentucky" (Program for Cultural Resource Assessment, University of Kentucky, Lexington, 1996); Lynn S. Renau, *Racing around Kentucky* (1995).

Lynn S. Renau

ALLEN, MEL (14 February 1913, Johns, AL–16 June 1996, Greenwich, CT). A sportscaster primarily employed by the New York Yankees, he was born Melvin Allen Israel to Julius and Anna (Leib) Israel, Jewish immigrants from Russia. His father owned a clothing store, then became a traveling salesman during the depression. In high school, Allen won letters in basketball, football, and baseball. At the age of fifteen he enrolled at the University of Alabama, where he earned a B.A. in political science in 1932 and a law degree in 1936. He started his career as a broadcaster on the public address system for the University of Alabama football home games. Allen's first professional assignment came in 1936, when he was hired by CBS as a radio announcer for news and sports. He dropped his last name, "Israel," because, he claimed, CBS considered it "too Jewish." Allen was the distinctive "Voice of the Yankees" from

1939 to 1964, excepting a few years in the U.S. Army during World War II. First on radio, then on television, he reached the height of his fame as the broadcaster for the great Yankee teams that dominated baseball from 1949 to 1964. He broadcast the exploits of all the Yankee greats of that era, dubbed DiMaggio* "Joltin' Joe," and exclaimed "How about That!" in response to heroics by the likes of Joe DiMaggio, Yogi Berra,* Mickey Mantle, and Roger Maris. Allen was abruptly fired by the Yankees in 1964. Subsequently, he was the narrator for *This Week in Baseball* for nineteen years and called forty Yankee games a year for SportsChannel from 1978 to 1985. Bright, descriptive, and exuberant, in 1978 he was among the first group of inductees into the broadcaster's wing of the National Baseball Hall of Fame.

SELECTED BIBLIOGRAPHY: Mark Bechtel, "The 1996 Regular Season: A Yankee Legend Signs Off," *Sports Illustrated*, 13 November 1996, 41; David Halberstam, *Summer of '49* (1989); *New York Times*, 17 June 1996, B9; *New York Times*, 18 June 1996, B15.

Richard FitzPatrick

ALOU, FELIPE ROJAS (12 May 1935, Haina, Dominican Republic–   ). A baseball player and manager, he was one of the first Latin Americans to succeed in the major leagues. His father was a carpenter and blacksmith; his mother looked after six children in the coastal town of Haina, a few miles west of Santo Domingo. Alou played for seventeen seasons in the major leagues with six different ball clubs. In 1958 Alou became the second Dominican player to reach the big leagues. On 10 September 1963 he and his brothers Mateo and Jesus constituted the outfield for the San Francisco Giants, marking the only time three brothers played together on the same team in the major leagues. After his playing career ended in 1974, Alou managed for twelve years in the minor league system of the Montreal Expos. In 1992 Alou was named manager of the Expos, becoming the first Dominican to guide a major league team. In 1994 he led the Expos to first place and was chosen as the manager for the National League team at the 1995 All-Star Game, becoming the first Latino to manage in the midyear event. He also managed for twelve winter seasons in the Dominican Republic, winning the championship of the Caribbean Series in 1990. Alou was an early and outspoken critic of discrimination in the United States. In his first season he was assigned to play on a team in Lake Charles, Louisiana, but was forced to leave after only five games due to racial segregation. In 1963 he wrote an article in *Sport* magazine detailing the prejudice Latin players faced in the United States.

SELECTED BIBLIOGRAPHY: Felipe Alou, with Arnold Hano, "Latin Ballpayers Need a Bill of Rights," *Sport* (November 1963): 21; Felipe Alou, with Herm Wesikopf, *My Life and Baseball* (1967); John Devaney, "Felipe Alou: The Gentle Howitzer," *Sport* (June 1967): 63–67; Charles Einstein, "Alou, Alou," *Sport* (September 1962): 25.

Milton Jamail

AMERICAN SOCCER LEAGUE. This organization was formed at a meeting of delegates representing eight of the soccer organizations in the country at the Hotel Astor in New York City on the evening of 7 May 1921. The clubs represented were the New York Football Club (FC), Robins Dry Dock of Brooklyn, Bethlehem Steel FC of Bethlehem, Pennsylvania, Erie Athletic Association of Newark, Jersey City FC, Fall River Rovers of Fall River, Massachusetts, J. & P. Coats FC of Pawtucket, Rhode Island, and the Philadelphia FC. The meeting was addressed by Thomas W. Cahill, secretary of the U.S. Football Association (USFA), who outlined the scope of the new league. Luther Lewis of the Bethlehem Football Club was elected temporary chairman, and J. Scholefield was appointed secretary pro tem.

The league began play in September of that year with eight clubs, all located along the eastern seaboard. Those teams were Philadelphia Field Club, New York Football Club, Jersey City Celtics, Todd Shipyards of Brooklyn, Harrison FC, J. & P. Coats of Pawtucket, Holyoke Falcos of Holyoke, Massachusetts, and Fall River United.

From these small beginnings the American Soccer League (ASL) grew into a league of international renown. The heyday of the league began in 1924 with the expansion from eight teams to twelve. At the start of the 1924–25 season the ASL included the following clubs: Fall River Marksmen, Bethlehem Steel, Brooklyn Wanderers, Boston Wonder Workers, New Bedford Whalers, Providence Clamdiggers, J. & P. Coats of Pawtucket, New York Giants, Indiana Flooring of New York, Fleischer Yarn of Philadelphia, Newark Skeeters, and Philadelphia Field Club. Over the years the most successful ASL team was the Fall River Marksmen, named for their owner, Sam Mark. The Marksmen won the ASL championship six times and the cup competition once. The league imported many star players from Europe and developed many star players of its own, including Billy Gonsalves* and Archie Stark,* while its players formed the nucleus of the highly successful U.S. World Cup team of 1930. Unfortunately, as with so many ambitious attempts to establish a professional soccer league in the United States, its existence was relatively short-lived. This was due in part to squabbling within the U.S. soccer community and also because of the devastating effects of the Wall Street crash of 1929 and the subsequent depression. If it were not for the combined effect of these two events, then the ASL might well have succeeded. When the ASL finally collapsed in 1932, it was replaced with a reformed and less ambitious version in 1933. This "second," scaled-down ASL survived the depression and World War II and following the war was made up largely of teams with ethnic connections such as the Philadelphia Ukrainian Nationals. It remained an East Coast league until 1972, when it expanded to the Midwest and then the far West, with greater accent being placed on American players. However, the second ASL folded in 1983 through lack of support. A "third" ASL was formed in 1988, which then merged with the Western Soccer League in 1990 to form the American Professional Soccer League.

SELECTED BIBLIOGRAPHY: Sam Foulds and Paul Harris, *America's Soccer Heritage* (1979); Tony Cirino, *U.S. Soccer vs. the World* (1983); Zander Hollander, ed., *The American Encyclopedia of Soccer* (1980); Colin Jose, *NASL—A Complete Record of the North American Soccer League* (1989); Colin Jose, *The United States and World Cup Soccer* (1994); Colin Jose, *The American Soccer League, 1921–1931* (1997).

Colin Jose

AMERICAN SOKOL ORGANIZATION. The Sokol organization is more than a gymnastic club; rather, it aspires to improve moral values through a variety of educational and social activities. Its program is a combination of historical, educational, and physical activities promoting the ideal of a sound mind in a healthy body. The American organization is a copy of the Czech Sokol, which was founded by Miroslav Tyrš and Jindřich Fügner in Prague in 1862.

A professor of aesthetics at the university in Prague, Miroslav Tyrš believed in the Hellenic ideal of a healthy body and an enlightened mind. Both he and Fügner saw the building of physical and moral strength as a way to revive the Czech nation. In his capacity as director of gymnastic training, Tyrš developed the Sokol ideology and also the first complete gymnastic terminology in the Czech language. Within five years of its founding, there were sixty-eight Sokol clubs, several of them founded by Czech immigrants in the United States.

The first Sokol club in the United States was founded in St. Louis in 1865, and others followed in Chicago, New York, and other areas of Czech immigration. In 1878, thirteen clubs joined to form the National Sokol Union, which was renamed American Sokol Organization in 1917. The first women's club was founded in Cleveland in 1880. Additional immigration broadened the Sokol base and allowed the organization to expand its program. By 1937, there were almost 20,000 adults and an equal number of younger people enrolled in eighty-six clubs in the American Sokol. The organization is currently headquartered in the Chicago suburb of Berwyn, a center of Czech life in America.

An eleven-member Board of Governors oversees the Executive Committee, which administers the daily business of the organization. The 1995 convention elected Fred Kala as president, David Harlan as director of the Men's Program, and Jan Kalat as director of the Women's Program. The most important role is played by the Board of Gymnastic Instructors, which oversees all gymnastic and sports activities, conducts gymnastic courses, and prepares the national gymnastic festivals called *slets*. The *slets* are five-day festivities held every four years that include gymnastic and sports competitions and conclude with a mass calisthenic display that can include thousands of participants. The club paper, *American Sokol*, has been published since 1879 and features articles on gymnastics and other Sokol activities. The organization depends on volunteers to run the educational and gymnastic programs in the sixty remaining clubs, of which thirty-four are active, composed of 6,000 adult members and an equal number of younger people.

Tyrš' program has been developed over the years into a training system for children. It begins with warm-up exercises, followed by work on three apparatuses, then resistive exercising and games to instill the values of teamwork and fair play, and concludes by cooling off with mass calisthenics and, sometimes, marching or singing. Sokol instructors are trained in special courses that provide instruction in demonstrating routines, spotting, judging, and understanding calisthenics, as well as lectures on the meaning of the Sokol and related topics.

Although the American Sokol Organization is primarily concerned with training American youth and accepts any child or adult of good character as a member, it has also produced a number of champions. A pillar of the Gymnastic Section of the American Athletic Union (AAU), the Sokol organization has hosted many national meets in its halls. Three Sokol members, Frank Kriz,* Jim Hartung,* and Laddie Bakanic,* were Olympic medal winners, while Rudolf Novak was a member of the U.S. gymnastic team at the 1924 Olympics in Paris, where Sokol member Edward Knorek competed in the pole vault. In addition, Paul Fina was a member of the U.S. gymnastic team at the 1940 Olympics and Phil Cahoy and Jim Hartung at the 1980 Olympics, and Tim Hintnaus made the pole vault team for the 1980 Olympics.

In addition, several Sokol members were AAU National Gymnastic Champions in various competitions, and the Sokol team won first place in the 1941 national championship. Several members of the Czech Olympic team came to the United States as Sokol instructors, many of whom, such as Jarka Jelínek, Josef Kos, and Frank Příhoda, stayed permanently. As part of the Czech immigration following the communist takeover in 1948, Marie Provaznik* (1890–1991), chair of the International Gymnastic Federation and women's gymnastic director of the Czech Sokol, arrived in this country. Her tireless efforts on behalf of gymnastics made her a key figure in the organization.

American Sokol women were early pioneers in the field of women's gymnastics. Mildred Prchal (1895–1983), the first director of women in any Sokol organization, introduced the concept of rhythmic gymnastics into women's training. After studying this new technique in Prague and Paris in the 1920s, she went on to become the president of modern rhythmics, and she also served on the U.S. Olympic Committee. One of her students, Norma Zabka, judges international gymnastic competitions and has been vice chairperson for rhythmics in USA Gymnastics. Male Sokol members have filled similar roles, such as Jerry Hardy, who has judged international gymnastic meets and has been an AAU administrator as well as a member of the U.S. Olympic Committee.

Several Sokol members have had their names placed on the Honor Roll of USA Gymnastics, a testimony to the importance of the Sokol to gymnastic life in the United States. Even if ethnicity has faded, the Sokol idea still lives and was recognized when the U.S. government issued a commemorative Sokol centennial stamp in 1965.

SELECTED BIBLIOGRAPHY: Stanley Barcal, "American Sokol Organization" (unpublished manuscript, American Sokol Organization, 1991); *Centennial of the Sokols in America, 1865–1965* (1965); Claire E. Nolte, "Our Brothers Across the Ocean: The Czech Sokol in America to 1914," *Czechoslovak and Central European Journal* 11 (Winter 1993): 15–37; Sokol Archives, Berwyn, IL.

Vladislav Slavik

AMERICAN TENNIS ASSOCIATION. Tennis was an elite sport played primarily at country clubs and on private courts. Blacks were barred from participation in U.S. Lawn Tennis Association (USLTA)-sanctioned events and were not welcome at private, all-white country clubs. However, records indicate that wealthy blacks built private courts in the 1890s. In 1899, black tennis clubs organized matches between New York, Philadelphia, and Washington, D.C., clubs. Tennis was also popular at black colleges. The American Tennis Association (ATA) was founded in 1916 by African Americans. The first national championship was held in 1917 at Druid Park in Baltimore. The first national men's champion was Tally Holmes, who repeated the feat in 1918, 1921, and 1924. Lucy Slowe was the first women's champion. The most dominating national champion was Reginald Weir, captain of the City College of New York men's tennis team. He was ATA national champion in 1931, 1932, 1933, 1937, and 1942. The most dominating female player was Ora Washington,* who won eight titles in nine years.

The original goals of the American Tennis Association were (1) to develop tennis among black people in the United States, (2) to encourage the building of courts and the formation of clubs, (3) to form local associations, and (4) to encourage the development of junior players.

In the early years, the ATA and the USLTA were involved in a confrontation over the entries of Reginald Weir and Gerald Norman, Jr., in USLTA events. The National Association for the Advancement of Colored People (NAACP) was involved in the confrontation. It wasn't until the 1940s that blacks were allowed to participate in USLTA-sanctioned tournaments. The ATA is the oldest black sports organization in the United States. It continues to host its national championships in different locations throughout the United States the second week in August and boasts a membership of over 6,000.

SELECTED BIBLIOGRAPHY: Arthur R. Ashe, Jr., *A Hard Road to Glory: A History of the African-American Athlete 1919–1945*, vol. 2 (1993); Edna Rust and Art Rust, Jr., *Art Rust's Illustrated History of the Black Athlete* (1985).

Gary A. Sailes

ANDRETTI, MARIO (28 February 1940, Montana, Italy–   ). The son of Italian immigrants, he became one of the world's most celebrated race car drivers.

His parents, Louis and Rina Andretti, moved Mario and his twin brother to Lucca, Italy, in 1948. There Mario's father took a job in a toy factory; his boys worked in a garage owned by Seggiolina & Biagini and drove a Stanguellini Formula Junior Car. The family moved again, arriving in America in June 1955 and joining relatives in Nazareth, Pennsylvania. Mario's cousin, Louis Messenlehner, owned a garage in Nazareth, which provided employment and an ideal hangout for young racing enthusiasts. Hoping to attend high school, the teenagers were placed in seventh grade instead, so eventually Mario left school, paid for correspondence courses, and hired a tutor, Dee Ann Hoch. He received his diploma and married Dee Ann. Andretti's American racing career started in a Hudson. By 1960 he had twelve wins, and on Labor Day in 1963 he won three races. He raced U.S. Auto Club (USAC) sprint cars in 1964 and in both 1965 and 1966 placed first in the national standings of race car drivers. In 1967 he won the Daytona 500 Stock Car and the Twelve Hours of Sebring. In 1969 Andretti captured one of the major prizes in racing, the Indy 500 in a Turbocharged Hawk under Andy Granatelli STP sponsorship. Andretti raced the Grand Prix circuit and continued driving the Indy 500 in the years that followed. He won the coveted World Championship in 1978. In the 1980s he placed second twice in the Indy 500 (1981 and 1985). In 1992, he won the Driver of the Quarter Century award. His fifty-second victory came with a win at the Indy Car Grand Prix at Phoenix, Arizona, on 4 April 1993. Andretti raced the Indy 500 and the Bank of America 300 at Monterey's Laguna Seca Raceway in May and in October 1994, respectively; he won neither. That same year he retired, leaving racing to his sons, Michael and Jeff.

SELECTED BIBLIOGRAPHY: Mario Andretti, *What's It Like Out There?* (1970) and *Andretti* (1994); Clint Brawner and Joe Scalzo, *Indy 500 Mechanic* (1975); Ian Morrison, *The Guinness Guide to Formula One* (1989); Nigel Roebuck, *Grand Prix Greats: A Personal Appreciation of 25 Famous Formula I Drivers* (1986); Joseph Siano, "Last Ride: Andretti 500 Miles from the Finish Line," *New York Times*, 29 May 1994, Sec. 8, 1–2.

Philip M. Montesano

ANITONI, VAEA (20 September 1970, 'Utulau, Tongatapu, Tonga–   ). Born the only child of mother Patiola Naufahu Mataipule and father Finau Salt, Vaea Anitoni came to Ontario, California, as a twenty-one-year-old student in 1991 and has gone on to become the U.S. national rugby team's most prolific try scorer. Anitoni learned the game in his native country, reaching the elite level as a teenager and once representing Tonga in seven-a-side rugby, an abbreviated game that is rugby union's equivalent of full-court, three-on-three basketball. But his greatness unfolded in the very different realm of American rugby, where the sport is much less developed, and ethnic Polynesians have been outsiders. After joining the Pomona rugby club, Anitoni debuted for the United States only one year after his arrival, coming on as a replacement player to score the first of his seventeen international tries against Canada. Anitoni then stayed away from international rugby for two years, moving north to the San Francisco Bay Area. But when he returned in 1994, he played in sixteen consecutive games for the U.S. national team before finally missing a game in 1997. In the midst of that streak, during the 1996 Pacific Rim season, Anitoni scored a phenomenal ten tries in six games, including four in one match against Japan. Both are American records. Anitoni entered 1998 with twenty-three test appearances ("caps") and seventeen tries for the United States, an outstanding scoring ratio. Meanwhile, Anitoni made frequent appearances for the United States in sevens as well, helping the Eagles to a consolation bracket championship at the 1997 sevens World Cup. Domestically, Anitoni was a key figure with San Francisco's Olympic Club before a group of fellow Polynesian immigrants persuaded him to join the rival San Mateo club in 1995. The move proved a real shot in the arm both for San Mateo, which went on to become a national power and in 1997 claimed the national sevens championship, and for Polynesian clubs in general, long present on the margins but now proliferating throughout the western United States. A quiet man of 5'8" and 170 pounds and an airline employee, Anitoni is a wing in fifteen-a-side rugby but a flyhalf in sevens, an unusually versatile combination that has sometimes led his fellow national teamers to call him the best player in the United States.

SELECTED BIBLIOGRAPHY: Manchester (England) *Guardian*, 13 January 1997, 1–21.

Kurt Oeler

ARCARO, GEORGE EDWARD ("Eddie") (19 February 1916, Cincinnati, OH–14 November 1997, Miami, FL). Son of Pasquale, an Italian fruit peddler, and Josephine Giancola Arcaro, Eddie was too small to compete in team sports, but at 5'2" and 114 pounds he combined his small size with intelligence and determination to become one of the world's greatest jockeys. After his family moved to Kentucky, Eddie quit school as a young teenager, much to the disappointment of his father, and learned the horse racing trade by working in stables. He showed his potential at age sixteen when he won fourteen races in one week. He learned to control his fiery temper after he was suspended in 1942 over a violent clash with another jockey in the Cowdin Stakes. In 1938, Arcaro won the first of his five Kentucky Derby victories. He won five Belmont Stakes and six Preakness Stakes races. He became a Triple Crown winner twice: on Whirlaway in 1941 and on Citation in 1948. He was the leading money winner in 1940, 1942, 1948, 1950, 1952, and 1958. His 4,779 victories helped to earn a gross purse of $3,039,543. He is a member of the National Horse Racing Hall of Fame. After riding in his last race on 16 November 1961, he worked as a television commentator during racing events.

SELECTED BIBLIOGRAPHY: Eddie Arcaro, *I Ride to Win* (1951); Jim Murray, "Fast Eddie," in Lawrence DiStasi, *Dream Streets, the Big Book of Italian Culture* (1989);

Nancy Stout, *Great American Thoroughbred Racetracks*, Foreword by Eddie Arcaro (1991); *New York Times*, 15 November 1997, A15.

Frank J. Cavaioli

ARMENIANS. Athletics have always been an effective way to bring young adults together. Many Armenian organizations recognize this and have included both individual and team sports in their agendas. Organizations often plan socials, dances, and similar activities in conjunction with athletics to encourage Armenian youth to meet and make new friends. Athletics have thus become a contributing factor in galvanizing the Armenian community and helping instill pride in Armenian heritage and culture.

The American-based Armenian General Athletic Union (AGAU Homenetmen), the oldest Armenian athletic organization in the United States, was founded in 1921 by ten individuals in New York City. The initial organizer was Jack Karabekian. The other charter members of the original Board of Directors were Bayenderian, Fred Dagavarian, Zeron Deundian, Archie Howsenian, Onnig Kamanjian, Dick Khoian, Mamas Khoubesserian, Mgrdich Maroukian, and Melkon Yemanjian.

The AGAU held its first Olympic athletic games at Elmer's Park, Brooklyn, New York, in 1923. The AGAU continues to be active in the New York-New Jersey area, organizing athletic events and awarding annual athletic scholarships to many deserving athletes of Armenian descent. The *AGAU Bulletin*, its quarterly publication, is mailed to thousands of longtime members and supporters.

The Armenian Youth Federation (AYF) was founded in 1933 by Karekin Nejdeh, a general who served under the legendary General Antranig. The AYF initiated one of the most popular Armenian athletic events, the AYF Olympics, which have been held every year. The First Annual AYF Tzeghagron Sports Festival was held in 1934 at Walker Playground, Brockton, Massachusetts. AYF members and previous competitors provide solid leadership and enthusiasm that make the AYF athletic games one of the most popular and strongest events of the year. The annual competition brings together chapter teams from all over the United States and Canada in a family atmosphere. AYF participants meet and compete while their parents renew old friendships.

A number of other athletic programs organized after World War II are still active today. The Armenian Church Youth Organization of America (ACYOA), under the guidance of the Eastern Diocese of the Armenian Church of America, is a prime example. The ACYOA started its basketball competition to bring together members as well as World War II servicemen for athletic and social purposes. Since then, the ACYOA has added many other athletic events to its sports weekend. These annual competitions take place in the eastern United States.

The Armenian Church Youth Organization of California (ACYOC) initiated its first sports weekend in 1964, beginning with basketball competitions between San Joaquin Valley and Los Angeles ACYOC teams. These events are organized with the support of the Western Diocese of the Armenian Church of America and have expanded to other sports and are held in the Fresno area each year. In 1967 the Beirut (Lebanon)-based Homenetmen established its first chapter in Los Angeles. Its enthusiastic leader, Kerop Arakelian of Beverly Hills, is known as the "Father of the Homenetmen." The Homenetmen have several chapters in California, as well as in many other areas throughout the United States and Canada.

The first Homenetmen Athletic Games were held in 1975 in Los Angeles. Today, the Homenetmen is one of the largest active sports organizations in the United States. It has active sports programs all over the United States. In California, it is organized in many cities and regions with active regional competitions from the very young all the way up through people in their late thirties. These regional competitions take place every two or three months on a statewide basis with hundreds of youths taking part. They are backed by an active group of adults who raise funds through dances, raffles, banquets, and especially bingo, which has realized thousands of dollars each month for funding this highly successful program. The Western Armenian Athletic Association (WAAA), now known as the "Armenian Summer Games," was formed in 1969 by Richard Demirjian and Ben Morjig, who was then vice president of the Pacific Association of the Amateur Athletic Union (AAU). In its first year, the Armenian Olympics were sponsored by St. Vartan's Armenian Church Youth Organization (ACYO) of Oakland, California. In 1970 the organization expanded to include the general public, organized and incorporated as the WAAA. The primary purpose of the WAAA is to organize athletic competition in various sports for athletes of Armenian descent. The only eligibility requirement to compete is that one parent must be of Armenian descent.

The latest athletic organization formed in recent years is the Armenian General Benevolent Union (AGBU). Its North American Olympic Games was originated by the Central Youth Committee in 1981. In 1982, Eugene Karadjian of Toronto was appointed first director of these games, and Toronto was selected as the site of the first AGBU North American Olympian Games. From 1982 to 1989 the games were held in Toronto, Detroit, Boston, Montreal, Los Angeles, Toronto, Miami, and Kingston (Ontario). The AGBU also organizes international games every two years with the participation of all of its worldwide youth chapters. The 1987 games were held in Geneva; 1989, Buenos Aires; 1991, Los Angeles; 1995, Paris. In addition, the AGBU holds Middle Eastern and Mediterranean Regional Games every two years.

SELECTED BIBLIOGRAPHY: Arra S. Avakian, *The Armenians in America* (1977); Richard N. Demirjian, *Armenian-American/Canadian WHO's WHO of Outstanding Athletes, Coaches and Sports Personalities 1906–1912* (1989); Richard N. Demirjian, *Triumph and Glory: Armenian World War II Heroes* (1996).

Richard N. Demirjian

ARMSTRONG, HENRY (12 December 1912, Columbus, MS–24 October 1988, Los Angeles). An African American prizefighter with a multiracial black,

Irish, and Cherokee ancestry, he was born with the name Henry Jackson, Jr. His father, the son of a white plantation owner and a black slave, was a farmer and butcher. His mother, America Armstrong, was half Cherokee. Armstrong moved with his family to St. Louis at the age of four and graduated from Toussaint L'Overture School and Vashon High School in that city. He began his boxing career as Melody Jackson and then changed his name when he relocated to Los Angeles. There he fought as an amateur, ran a shoeshine business, and turned professional after he failed to qualify for the 1932 Olympic boxing team. He won the world featherweight title with a knockout of Petey Sarron on 29 October 1937. The following year proved to be the greatest in his career, as he defeated Barney Ross* to take the world welterweight championship on 31 May and then outlasted Lou Ambers to gain the world lightweight crown on 17 August. With that triumph he became the first man to hold three world boxing titles at the same time. He relinquished his featherweight championship in 1938 because of that division's weight restriction, and he lost his lightweight title to Ambers in a rematch in 1939. In 1940 he yielded his welterweight belt to Fritzie Zivic, and he continued to box until 1945. Known as "homicide Hank" or "little perpetual motion" because of his incessant, windmill style of offense, he was one of the best pound-for-pound pugilists of all time. He was poorly paid or cheated out of much of his earnings, and he squandered most of the remainder of his money. After his retirement from the ring he suffered from a serious alcohol problem, but a religious conversion changed his life. Ordained as a Baptist minister, he became a preacher and humanitarian, and in 1950 he established the Henry Armstrong Youth Foundation for the prevention of juvenile delinquency. He was inducted into the International Boxing Hall of Fame in 1990.

SELECTED BIBLIOGRAPHY: Henry Armstrong, *Gloves, Glory, and God* (1956); Bud Greenspan, "Henry Armstrong," *Parade Magazine* (24 October 1982): 19–20; Peter Heller, *In This Corner: Former World Champions Tell Their Stories* (1973).

George B. Kirsch

ASHE, ARTHUR, JR. (10 July 1943, Richmond, VA–6 February 1993, New York City). An African American tennis player, he was raised by his father, Arthur Ashe, Sr., a city parks employee. His mother, Mattie Cordell (Cunningham) Ashe, died in March 1950 at age twenty-seven. Ashe started playing the sport at age seven. He joined the all-black Richmond Racquet Club at ten years old. He was discovered by Dr. Walter Johnson of Lynchburg, who also sponsored Althea Gibson.* He was placed in a group of aspiring black junior tennis players. Ashe won the U.S. Lawn Tennis Association (USLTA) Junior Indoors titles in 1960 and 1961. He was ranked number eighteen by the USLTA in boys eighteens in 1961. Ashe attended the University of California at Los Angeles (UCLA) on a tennis scholarship. He moved up in the USLTA ranking to number two while attending UCLA. He won the U.S. Amateur Championship in 1963, and while still a UCLA student he became the first black to play on the U.S. Davis Cup Team. He won the U.S. Open in 1968, defeating Tom Okker of the

Netherlands. He was the first black national champion since 1957, when Althea Gibson won, and the first black male to win the title. Ashe won the Australian Championship in 1970 and defeated Jimmy Connors in 1975 to become the first black male to win the Wimbledon title. He retired from competition in 1979 after suffering a mild heart attack and later had quadruple bypass heart surgery. He was named Davis Cup captain for the United States in 1980. Ashe spent the remainder of his life as a political activist fighting against apartheid in South Africa and for AIDS awareness. He was one of the original founders of Artists and Athletes against Apartheid. It is likely that he contracted AIDS as a result of a blood transfusion he received during bypass heart surgery in 1983. During his career Ashe also served as president of the Association of Tennis Professionals (the players' union) and as chairman of the board of the Black Tennis and Sports Foundation. He was inducted into the International Tennis Hall of Fame in 1985.

SELECTED BIBLIOGRAPHY: Arthur R. Ashe, Jr., with Neil Amdur, *Off the Court* (1981); Arthur R. Ashe, Jr., *A Hard Road to Glory: A History of the African-American Athlete* (1988); Arthur R. Ashe, Jr., with Arnold Rampersad, *Days of Grace* (1993); *New York Times*, 25 October 1992, Sec. 8, 1 and 8 February 1993, Sec. C; Edna Rust and Art Rust Jr., *Art Rust's Illustrated History of the Black Athlete* (1985).

Gary A. Sailes

ASHFORD, EVELYN. *See* WASHINGTON, EVELYN ASHFORD

ASIAN INDIANS. Sports activities among Asian Indians in America have largely followed the patterns of other Asian American groups. They have been guided by the belief that education is the main vehicle for success in life and that all other pursuits have a secondary role, if any. Thus, much of their energy has been directed toward education-based pursuits and careers and very little toward sports endeavors.

Still, Asian Indians appear to be more underrepresented in sports in the United States than their Asian American counterparts. One hardly finds an equivalent of Michael Chang* or Kristi Yamaguchi* in the Asian Indian community. There are two main reasons for this phenomenon: first, Asian Indians are relative newcomers to America compared to most Chinese and Japanese Americans, many of whose families have been in this country for generations. The influx of Asian Indians into America began only in the mid-1960s with the liberalization of U.S. immigration laws. The majority of Asian Indians in America are first-generation immigrants. Second, Indian immigrants in America grew up in a culture that emphasized sports that were popular throughout the old British empire—especially cricket, field hockey, and soccer. They had little or no familiarity with American football, basketball, or baseball. In consequence, Asian Indian households have been somewhat reluctant to embrace the major team sports of the United States, and thus the parents do not pass on a love of, and appreciation for, these pastimes to their American-born children. For young

Asian Indians, exposure to these American sports is due mainly to their partic- ipation in school and community recreation programs.

Against this background, one finds two distinct trends in sports activities among Asian Indians in America. The first generation, most of whom arrived in this country as adults, has been naturally drawn into activities with which they have an affinity. In addition, as members of the professional class of doc- tors, engineers, scientists, computer scientists, and professors, their involvement in sports has been more of a leisure activity and pastime than a conscious, competitive athletic pursuit. Conversely, second-generation Asian Indians, who were born and raised in this country, have been more receptive to mainstream American sports and on occasion have chosen professional sports as career pur- suits.

It is not surprising that cricket is the favorite sport among first-generation Asian Indians. The recent revival of cricket in America following nearly a cen- tury of neglect can be largely attributed to Asian Indians and other expatriates from British Commonwealth countries, most notably, Pakistanis and West In- dians. The fascination with cricket among first-generation Asian Indians is at- tributable to a desire to derive some measure of security and belonging in an alien and individualistic society. This desire, in turn, has produced a sense of communal solidarity among diverse groups, transcending traditional nationalistic rivalries.

Asian Indians play in various capacities for an estimated 600 cricket teams and an equal number of unregistered teams in the United States. The majority of these cricket clubs are concentrated in metropolitan areas with large immi- grant populations from the British Commonwealth countries. A large number of the most active cricket clubs are in the New York metropolitan area, which, together with New Jersey, Connecticut, and Pennsylvania, reportedly accounts for half of all cricket teams in America. Asian Indians participate in individual tournaments, exhibition matches, and league competitions. These are played in city, county, state, and national parks as well as on college and university grounds. In New York City, more than a dozen cricket teams play regularly on the eleven grounds in Van Cortlandt Park in the Bronx and also in Corona Park and Baisley and Edgemere Parks in Queens, Walker Park and Miller Field in Staten Island, and Sunken Meadow in Randall's Island. Outside the New York area, Asian Indians also play cricket on such historic sites as the Parade Ground at Fort Ethan Allen, Colchester, Vermont, and the Princeton University campus.

In general, cricket teams in large metropolitan areas have a multiracial com- position consisting of expatriates from India, Pakistan, England, Australia, New Zealand, South Africa, West Indies, Sri Lanka, and other countries. But it is not rare to find cricket teams formed along specific national lines, especially in small and medium-sized cities where there might be a preponderance of one com- munity versus the others. Thus, in the Midwest and South (excluding Florida), where West Indian communities are rare, cricket clubs often consist exclusively of Indians or Pakistanis or both.

Asian Indians have also played for U.S. cricket teams in international matches.

Florida-based Sarasota International Cricket Club (SICC), which includes Indians, South Africans, Canadians, Zambians, West Indians, British, and Americans, toured England in 1992 to play matches against a number of English teams. In return, SICC hosted teams from England in addition to teams from Los Angeles, Houston, and Toronto. Asian Indians and Pakistanis have been instrumental in organizing a number of international cricket matches in America. They promoted the India-Pakistan Match in 1989, which featured Imran Khan and Sunil Gavaskar, two internationally known cricket stars from India and Pakistan, respectively.

Cricket activities in America are governed by the U.S. Cricket Association (USACA), a member of the International Cricket Council (ICC), the parent association supervising cricket worldwide. In the past, Nazir Khan, a Pakistani, and Jimmy Colabavala, an Indian, respectively served as president and vice president of USACA. Lately, USACA has come under increasing challenge from a rival organization named U.S. Cricket Federation (USCF) of Philadelphia, a city generally regarded as the home of American cricket.

Much of the revival of cricket in America also owes to the contribution of Asian Indian students on university campuses. Indian students in almost every major American college or university have formed cricket clubs either by themselves or along with fellow international students. Some of these well-known university cricket clubs include those of Columbia, Rutgers, St. John's, the University of Kentucky, and others. These university clubs play mostly against each other in regional competitions. For example, the Columbia cricket team plays in the Commonwealth Cricket League in New York, with matches against other university clubs in the Northeast, including the Ivy League teams.

If interest in sports among first- and second-generation Asian Indians in America has mostly diverged in opposite directions, in at least one premier sport, tennis, the two generations have shared a mutual interest. Many first-generation Asian Indian immigrants play recreational tennis on both public and private courts, but occasionally a few of the more talented players compete in U.S. Tennis Association (USTA)-sponsored local or regional tournaments. Some have served as tennis coaches in clubs and summer camps. Vijay Amritraj, the best-known Indian-born tennis player, has made Los Angeles his residence and has been active in promoting tennis among young people in America in addition to playing a role as an "ambassador" for world cultures.

Second-generation Asian Indians also have been drawn to tennis. Laxmi Poruri achieved the number one ranking in the U.S. girls eighteen-and-under group when she was fifteen years old. She won the national title in 1988 and twice made the list of the U.S. national team. A Stanford graduate, Poruri subsequently went on to obtain World Tennis Association (WTA) rankings in women's tennis for several years and played against seeded players in all major international tournaments, including the grand slams. Poruri's diary of daily recollections of her experiences during the International Tennis Federation (ITF) Women's Circuit tours was covered by ABC's *Nightline with Ted Koppel* a few years ago.

Perhaps the best-known athlete among second-generation Asian Indians in America is Alexi Grewal. Grewal made a sensation in the 1984 Los Angeles Olympics by winning the gold medal in men's individual road race cycling—an event normally dominated by Europeans.

American-born Asian Indians have begun to make their mark in sports administration as well. One of the main architects for making Major League Soccer (MLS) a reality in America is Sunil Gulati, the league's thirty-eight-year-old deputy commissioner. Gulati was also instrumental in putting together a World Cup soccer team for the United States in 1990. Until then America had not participated in the event for forty years. Gulati's efforts paid off in 1994, when the American team reached the second round at the World Cup before being beaten by Brazil, which won the championship that year.

The achievements of Poruri, Grewal, and Gulati demonstrate that Asian Indians are capable of distinguishing themselves in mainstream American sports in spite of a cultural heritage that generally de-emphasizes athletics in favor of academics. It is likely that as second-generation Asian Indians increasingly participate in basketball, baseball, tennis, soccer, squash, and other sports in middle and high schools and colleges, more of them will earn greater recognition in American sports.

SELECTED BIBLIOGRAPHY: Mihir Bose, "ICC Embrace American Revolution," *Electronic Telegraph*, 14 September 1996 [Online] URL: http://www.cricket. org/link_to_database/A . . . 6/Sep96/CRICKET_IN_AMERICA_14SEP1996.html [4 April 1998]; "Corel WTA Tour Notes & Netcards," 26 February 1996 [Online] URL: http://www.tenniscountry.com/wta226.html [11 May 1998]; "ESPNET SportsZone: Cycling Past Results" [Online] http://espn.sportszone.com/editors/atlanta96/almanac/ cycmirr.html [10 April 1996]; "MLS Deputy Commissioner Likes Behind-the-Scenes Role," 31 March 1996 [Online] URL: http://www.nando.net/newsroom/ap/oth/1996/oth/ soc/feat/archive/033196/soc8242.html [24 April 1998]; Lavina Melwani, "Cricket in Little India: How's That?" *Little India*, 31 May 1995, 10–23; Laxmi Poruri, "It's Lonely, Even If You're Not at the Top," *New York Times*, 17 November 1996, S9; John Riha, "Tennis Lessons," *World Traveler* (May 1998): 42–44, 46–48, 71.

Shankar Chaudhuri

ATTELL, ABE (22 February 1884, San Francisco–6 February 1970, Libertyville, NY). A prizefighter, he was born Albert Knoehr, the son of Russian Jewish immigrants. Attell, nicknamed "the Little Hebrew" to drum up support among Jewish fight fans, held the featherweight title from 1901 to 1912. Claiming to have fought in 360 contests, he won 91 of his documented 168 prizefights, 47 by knockout, while losing 10. The rest, having gone the distance, were counted as draws or no decisions, according to the rules of the day. Shortly after turning pro, Attell relocated from San Francisco to Denver in 1901, at that time one of the centers of boxing in the United States. That year, at age seventeen, he won the featherweight title by defeating George Dixon,* becoming the youngest champion in any weight class until Wilfred Benitez* in the 1970s. Attell's record undoubtedly would have been better had he not been an inveterate gambler. He was regularly accused of carrying other boxers to make them look good in order to guarantee a more lucrative rematch, in which he would bet heavily on himself. He finally lost the title to Johnny Kilbane in California in 1912 while suspended by the New York State Athletic Commission for gambling and cocaine use during a bout. Attell retired from the ring in 1917. He became involved with Arnold Rothstein, the notorious gambler and gangster, and was implicated in the 1919 Black Sox scandal, allegedly providing $100,000 in bribes to Chicago White Sox players to throw the World Series. Charges against him were dropped for insufficient evidence.

SELECTED BIBLIOGRAPHY: Ken Blady, *The Jewish Boxers' Hall of Fame* (1988); Peter Levine, *Ellis Island to Ebbets Field: Sport and the American Jewish Experience* (1992); Steven A. Riess, "A Fighting Chance: The Jewish-American Boxing Experience, 1890–1940," *American Jewish History* 74 (1985): 223–254; *New York Times*, 7 February 1970, 29.

Marc Singer

AUERBACH, ARNOLD JACOB ("Red") (20 September 1917, New York City–). The son of Hyman, a Russian Jewish immigrant and owner of a dry cleaning shop, and Marie (Thompson), an office worker prior to marriage, he became a prominent basketball coach for the Boston Celtics. As a boy he resided in Brooklyn and graduated from Eastern District High School. Auerbach, a good schoolboy and collegiate basketball player, attended Seth Low Junior College prior to earning bachelor's and master's degrees from George Washington University. He married Dorothy Lewis in 1941 and subsequently served in the navy (1943–46). Auerbach was a professional basketball coach and executive. He coached the Washington Caps (Basketball Association of America [BAA], 1946–49), Tri-Cities Blackhawks (National Basketball Association [NBA], 1949–50), and the Boston Celtics (NBA, 1950–66). A shrewd judge of talent and a master psychologist, the fiercely competitive and autocratic Auerbach emphasized the fundamentals, defense, and the team over the individual. The greatest coach in professional basketball history, he led the Celtics to nine NBA championships during his final ten seasons of coaching. Auerbach retired from NBA coaching with a then-record 938 regular season wins against only 479 losses. After retiring from coaching, Auerbach remained the Celtics' general manager until 1984 and then served as the franchise's president from 1984 to 1997. Despite the vicissitudes of numerous changes in ownership, the Celtics won seven additional championships with Auerbach running the front office. A Basketball Hall of Fame inductee (1968) and a charter member (1979) of the Jewish Sports Hall of Fame, Auerbach frequently expressed pride in his Jewish heritage. His brashness, manifested by fiery clashes with referees and lighting a victory cigar prior to game's end, epitomized chutzpah. His support of black athletes, including Chuck Cooper* and Bill Russell,* reflected Judaism's commitment to social justice.

SELECTED BIBLIOGRAPHY: Arnold "Red" Auerbach and Joe Fitzgerald, *Red Auerbach: An Autobiography* (1997); Red Auerbach, with Joe Fitzgerald, *On and Off the Court* (1985); Peter Levine, *Ellis Island to Ebbets Field: Sport and the American Jewish Experience* (1992); Robert Slater, *Great Jews in Sport* (1983); Arnold "Red" Auerbach File, Naismith Memorial Basketball Hall of Fame.

William M. Simons

B

BAER, MAX (11 February 1909, Omaha, NE–21 November 1959, Hollywood, CA). Raised in Livermore, California, by a German Irish Catholic mother and a nonreligious Jewish father and married to a Catholic woman, Baer was nonetheless seen as a "Jewish" heavyweight fighter and promoted himself as such, wearing a Jewish star on his boxing trunks to attract fans. His identity as a Jewish fighter was reinforced in the wake of his 1933 victory over Max Schmeling, the boxer closely associated with Hitler and Aryan supremacy. As a result, by virtue of his knockout of champion Primo Carnera in 1934, "the Livermore Larruper" is considered by some to have been the only Jewish heavyweight champion. Baer's Jewish identity was more symbolic than actual, serving as a powerful counter to stereotypes of Jewish physical weakness and ungainliness, as well as a rallying point in fights against rivals symbolically linked to Nazism and fascism. Despite this, he apparently did not take boxing seriously and had a reputation for sloppy training and clowning, although this may have been due to a "clown" stereotype applied to Jewish boxers by the press. True or not, Baer lost the heavyweight title to James Braddock in 1935 in his first and only defense. Baer was also notable for appearing in the first-ever televised bout, losing to Lou Nova in 1939. He retired from the ring in 1941; in keeping with his reputation as a showman, he appeared in several Hollywood films.

SELECTED BIBLIOGRAPHY: Sam Andre and Nat Fleischer, *A Pictorial History of Boxing* (1959, rev. 1993); Peter Levine, *Ellis Island to Ebbets Field: Sport and the American Jewish Experience* (1992); Jeffrey T. Sammons, *Beyond the Ring: The Role of Boxing in American Society* (1988).

Marc Singer

BAEZA, BRAULIO (26 March 1940, Panama City, Panama–   ). A jockey, his grandfather and father were both jockeys and trainers in his native Panama, where he became a sensation in 1959 at the age of nineteen. The next year he moved his tack to the United States, where he led all riders in purses won five times (1965–68, 1975). A consummate horseman, he sat tall and erect in the post parade but bent to his task when the gate opened, riding with a fluid grace and keen sense of pace that characterized his handling of twenty-four different champions. He won the Champagne with two-year-old champions Bold Lad, Buckpasser, Successor, Vitriolic, and Honest Pleasure; the Travers with three-year-old champions Buckpasser, Arts and Letters, Key to the Mint, and Majima; the Jockey Club Gold Cup with Horses of the Year Roman Brother, Buckpasser, and Arts and Letters. He set the mile record with Buckpasser in 1966, lowered it to 1:32-2/5 with Dr. Fager in 1968. In 1972 Baeza stunned British observers with his front-running ride on Roberto in the Benson and Hedges Gold Cup to hand Brigadier Gerard his only career defeat. He also rode such champions as Damascus, Susan's Girl, Ack Ack, Chateaugay, Foolish Pleasure, and Affectionately. Over his seventeen-year career in the United States, which ended in 1976, he compiled a record of 3,140 victories out of 17,239 mounts (18.2%). He was inducted into the National Thoroughbred Racing Hall of Fame in 1976.

SELECTED BIBLIOGRAPHY: Bill Christine, "Proud Baeza Is Still among Jockeys," *Los Angeles Times*, 9 June 1995, C9; New York Racing Association Press Releases; *Thoroughbred Record*, 29 May 1976; *Schenectady Gazette*, 30 July 1995.

Courtesy of the National Thoroughbred Racing Hall of Fame

BAKANIC, LADDIE (3 May 1924, New York City–   ). She was a member of the U.S. gymnastic team that won the bronze medal at the 1948 Olympics. Laddie was the only child of Charles and Sophia Hniz, immigrants from Czechoslovakia who owned a tailor shop in New York City. Both parents were active in the Bohemian Gymnastic Association Sokol of New York. Her father was a gymnastic instructor and also served three terms as president, while her mother trained at gymnastics and was a member of the Sokol drama and singing societies. Laddie began her gymnastic training in the New York Sokol at the age of five and soon had mastered the intricate routines, winning most of the Sokol gymnastic meets. At age thirteen she won first place in the Sokol Junior Girls Championship held in Madison Square Garden, and in 1946 she won the Sokol Senior Women's Championship. The following year, she placed second in the Championship Division at the all-Sokol *slet*. She also successfully competed in Amateur Athletic Union (AAU) gymnastic meets, winning first place in the Junior Championship in 1941 and second in the Senior Championship in 1944. She won a place on the U.S. Olympic team by placing sixth in the National AAU Championship in 1948 and helped the U.S. Olympic team win the bronze medal later that year by garnering 50.10 points, fifth place among Americans at the London games. Unlike today's gymnasts, Laddie had neither coach nor choreographer. Her father and other Sokol gymnastic instructors helped, mostly by instilling in her the will to succeed. Laddie also served as a gymnastic instructor of young girls in the New York Sokol Hall.

SELECTED BIBLIOGRAPHY: *Centennial of the Sokols in America, 1865–1965* (1965); A. B. Frederick, *Roots of American Gymnastics* (1995); Richard Edd Laptad, *A History of the Development of the United States Gymnastics Federation* (1972); Minot Simons, *Women's Gymnastics: A History* (1995).

Vladislav Slavik

BANKS, ERNEST ("Ernie") (31 January 1931, Dallas, TX–   ). An African American baseball player, he is the son of Eddie (a laborer) and Essie Banks. Raised in a poor household, as a child he did housework and picked cotton to help support his family. He attended Booker T. Washington High School in Dallas, and during two summers as a schoolboy he played baseball for a black barnstorming team, the Detroit Colts. After graduating in 1950, he joined the Kansas City Monarchs of the Negro American League. After serving two years in the U.S. Army, Banks made the transition from Negro League* ball to the major leagues when he signed a contract with the Chicago Cubs in September 1953. The second black member of the Cubs (second baseman Gene Baker preceded him), he became one of baseball's star performers as a power-hitting shortstop in 1955, when he batted .295, with forty-four home runs and 117 runs batted in (RBIs). A wiry and slender athlete with powerful wrists, his greatest year came in 1958, when he led the National League in home runs with forty-seven and in RBIs with 129. He added another home run crown in 1960 (forty-one) and another RBI title in 1959 (143). In 1962 he switched to first base and continued his slick fielding and offensive production until his retirement after the 1971 season. Although Banks had the misfortune of playing on losing Cub teams (he set a record for most major league games played without an appearance in a postseason contest), he maintained his enthusiasm for his sport during his decades with his team. Immensely popular with fans, "Mr. Cub" conveyed his love of baseball through his famous saying "Let's play two." After his retirement Banks worked as a coach and as a goodwill ambassador for baseball, and he also served charitable organizations that helped children. Banks was inducted in the National Baseball Hall of Fame in 1977, the third black player to be elected.

SELECTED BIBLIOGRAPHY: Arthur R. Ashe, Jr., *A Hard Road to Glory: A History of the African-American Athlete since 1946*, vol. 3 (1988); Ernie Banks, with Jim Enright, *Mr. Cub* (1971); *Chicago Cubs Vineline* 2 (April 1987): 8–10, and 6 (December 1991): 9, 12 and 7 (January 1992): 21; Eddie Gold and Art Ahrens, *The New Era Cubs, 1941–1985* (1985); James R. Riley, *The Biographical Encyclopedia of the Negro Baseball Leagues* (1994).

George B. Kirsch

BARBUTI, RAYMOND J. (6 June 1905, Brooklyn, NY–8 July 1988, Pittsfield, MA). A track athlete, he was the son of Thomas and Elizabeth (McClain) Barbuti. His family moved to Long Island, where he excelled in all sports at Lawrence High School. His Italian father was a Nassau County Court reporter.

He received a football scholarship to Syracuse in 1924, where he became an All-American and starred in track, graduating with honors in 1928. Barbuti was the only American male to win an individual gold medal in a running event, the 400-meter race, at the Ninth Olympic Games of 1928, held in Amsterdam. He also won a second gold medal by running anchor on the victorious American team that set a world record in the 1,600-meter relay race. General Douglas MacArthur, then president of the U.S. Olympic Committee, persuaded him to compete in the relay race. Although he was a star halfback, he received more attention for his track performances. His victories included the Penn Relay Championship one-mile relay, National Intercollegiate Champion, 220- and 440-yard dashes, National Champion 400-meter dash, and IC4A one-mile relay. From 1928 to 1963, he officiated at track meets and in more than 500 college football games. Among his honors is his election to the National Track and Field Hall of Fame in 1967 and to the Long Island Sports Hall of Fame in 1986. During World War II he enlisted as a private in the Army Air Corps, served in Europe, China, Burma, and India, and was discharged in 1945 with the rank of major. Barbuti worked for New York state for thirty years, retiring as director of the state's Civil Defense Commission.

SELECTED BIBLIOGRAPHY: Frank J. Cavaioli, "The Italian American Chariot of Fire," in Francis X. Femminella, ed., *Italians and Irish in America* (1985), 35–42; John Kieran and Arthur Daly, *The Story of the Olympic Games* (1973); David Wallechinsky, *The Complete Book of the Olympics* (1992).

Frank J. Cavaioli

BARRERA, LAZARO S. (8 May 1924, Marianao, Cuba–25 April 1991, Downey, CA). A thoroughbred horse trainer, his father (Crispin) was a Cuban quarterhorse jockey. His mother (Blanca Fouquest Sosa) was French, and his paternal grandfather was a dairy and sugarcane farmer. Prior to migrating to the United States he was a leading trainer in Cuba and Mexico. His first major success in the United States came in 1971, when he sent out Tinajero to win the Jerome Handicap. Thereafter came a plethora of good horses, as well as a pair of open heart operations. In addition to sprinter-turned-classics winner Bold Forbes and two-time Horse of the Year Affirmed, he won major stakes on both coasts with Adored (Santa Margarita and Delaware), Island Whirl (Hollywood Gold Cup and Whitney), and It's the One (Strub and New Orleans Handicap). Voted Eclipse Awards as the outstanding trainer in the United States a record four times (1976–79), Laz Barrera also led North American trainers in earnings four times. He conditioned five champions, including Triple Crown winner Affirmed (which broke Kelso's long-standing earnings record in 1979) and Kentucky Derby-Belmont winner Bold Forbes. His other champions included juvenile filly It's in the Air, sprinter J. O. Tobin, and older male Lemhi Gold. Over his thirty-nine-year career (1945–84) he saddled 104 stakes winners; he was inducted into the National Thoroughbred Racing Hall of Fame in 1979.

SELECTED BIBLIOGRAPHY: Deirdre B. Biles, "Laz Barrera, 1924–91: A Life with Horses," *The Blood Horse* 117 (4 May 1991): 2365; Rick Bozich, "Laz Barrera Had Winning Touch with People, Too," *Louisville (KY) Courier-Journal*, 26 April 1991, E1, E6; *Daily Racing Form*, 27 April 1991; Jay Hovdey, "A True Conquistador," *Thoroughbred Record* 224 (April 1990): 100–105; *New York Times*, 30 April 1991, B12 (N); *Thoroughbred Times* 7 (3 May 1991): 1, 10.

Courtesy of the National Thoroughbred Racing Hall of Fame

BASEBALL. Ethnicity and race have been major elements in baseball since the mid-1800s, when the modern version of the game first gained widespread popularity across the United States. As wave after wave of immigrants reached American shores, a few of the newcomers and many more of their offspring tried the national pastime on sandlot and school yard diamonds. Those who became proficient enough to play professional ball became heroes in their respective ethnic communities, as their fellow countrymen flocked to ballparks to cheer them on to greater glory. Eventually, club owners realized the commercial value of ethnic players who could enhance ticket sales. Meanwhile, journalists and social commentators engaged in ethnic stereotyping and sociological theory as they pondered the meaning of foreign participation in what they viewed as the American national pastime. Even as they perpetuated derogatory views of the immigrants, these writers celebrated the game as a democratic institution that would assimilate aliens into the mainstream of American society. In December 1923 *The Sporting News* reaffirmed the value of ethnic diversity in baseball even as it acknowledged the exclusion of blacks: "In a democratic, catholic, real American game like baseball . . . there has been no distinction raised except tacit understanding that a player of Ethiopian descent is ineligible. . . . No player of any other 'race' has been barred. . . . the Mick, the Sheeny, the Wop, the Dutch and the Chink, the Cuban, the Indian, the Jap or the so-called Anglo-Saxon—his 'nationality' is never a matter of moment if he can pitch, hit, or field." Daily and weekly newspapers and magazines of the early twentieth century frequently applauded efforts to "Americanize" foreigners through athletics, especially baseball.

The ethnic experience in baseball has reflected the changing nature of American immigration from the 1840s to the present. The "old" pre–Civil War migrations of persons from Great Britain and Northern and Western Europe gave way to new hordes of foreigners from Southern and Eastern Europe from the 1880s to World War I. During recent decades Latin America and Asia have provided the largest share of newcomers. Although it is certainly true that ethnic baseball players from all of these continents have shared similar experiences, an important distinction must be made between those who emigrated from the British Isles and Europe as opposed to those who came from Latin America and Asia. In the former case, those from Irish, Scottish, English, German, Dutch, Scandinavian, or other European stock did not draw upon any baseball heritage from their country of origin, since the sport was either unknown or of minor status in their ancestral lands. But in Latin America and Asia baseball had taken root in several countries prior to 1900. As a result, during the late 1800s and early 1900s the prominent Irish, German, and European players (most of whom were born in the United States) had little impact on the status of the game across the Atlantic. But in the twentieth century Cuba, Mexico, Puerto Rico, Venezuela, Santo Domingo, and other Caribbean and Central American nations exported talented players to the United States, as did Korea and Japan in the Far East. In recent years the success of Latin American and Asian ethnic stars in American baseball has bolstered the sport's popularity in their native regions.

When one shifts the perspective from national origin to race, further distinctions and comparisons must be made concerning the treatment of Native Americans and African Americans. In the case of Indians there is more common ground with the experience of immigrants than with blacks. Indians endured much racial stereotyping and prejudice from the press and the major and minor leagues, but they were not barred from playing with whites. A few achieved stardom and even selection in the Hall of Fame in Cooperstown, New York. For African Americans the story has been very different. From the late 1800s down to the present black players and club owners have pursued two strategies: accommodation to white racism and the pursuit of equal opportunity and integration into the baseball fraternity. Only recently have black players, clubs, and leagues received recognition, but the struggle for respect and fair treatment continues.

Space limitations prohibit a detailed narrative of ethnic and racial participation in baseball, but it is possible to present an outline of the different stages in the experience of European, Native American, Latin American, Asian, and African American ballplayers. Since the modern version of the sport was an adaptation of the old English game of rounders, it is not surprising that most of the men of New York City's Knickerbocker Base Ball Club who invented it were of British or Northern European, white, Anglo-Saxon, Protestant ancestry. But although most of the members of the Knickerbocker and other upper-middle-class amateur organizations of the 1840s and 1850s were from English, Dutch, or French Huguenot families, a few Irish-born boys and young men were playing the game in Brooklyn and New Jersey prior to the Civil War.

The Irish became the first ethnic group to distinguish themselves on the baseball diamond. A few were premier players for the first celebrated amateur and professional nines of the 1860s and early 1870s. Forty-one percent of those who entered the National League from 1876 to 1884 were of Irish ancestry, as were 36% during the period 1885–1890. The fraction of Irish among major league players declined to about one-fifth for the years 1890 to 1915, but it appears that the percentage seemed higher to the public because of the number of Irish veteran and star players, captains, and managers, including Michael "King" Kelly* and John McGraw.* In 1915 eleven of the sixteen managers were descendants of Erin. Many fans of the late 1800s associated Kelly and other Irish ballplayers with an assertive, flamboyant style of play that featured aggressive base running and the stolen base. The public also tended to link Irish players with excessive alcohol consumption, and the owners acted on these beliefs by tightening their restrictions on the players' conduct off the field.

Germans also made their mark on the early history of baseball, and their influence was felt long into the twentieth century. Players of Teutonic ancestry (including a few Dutch, Swiss, and Austrians) constituted about one-fifth of all those who joined the National League between 1876 and 1884. The proportion rose to about 30% in the 1890s (including a few with German Jewish backgrounds) and then held at about that level down to 1915. Thus, between 1890 and World War I the Germans outnumbered every other ethnic group among professional baseball players except "non-Irish" British Isles descendants (English, Scottish, Welsh). Among the most celebrated German Americans in baseball history were John Peter "Honus" Wagner,* George Herman "Babe" Ruth,* Lou Gehrig,* and George Edward "Rube" Wadell. Prominent club executives and owners include George Weiss of the Baltimore Orioles and New York Yankees, August Adolphus "Gussie" Busch, son of the cofounder of Anheuser-Busch of St. Louis, and the German Jew Barney Dreyfuss* of the Pittsburgh Pirates.

After World War I Southern and Eastern Europeans increasingly challenged the Irish and German contingents on the nation's diamonds. Among them were two of the fastest growing ethnic communities in American cities—Italians and Jews. Their youngsters played the game on city streets and in more formally organized programs sponsored by immigrant social clubs, business and private organizations, public schools, and other institutions. Owners of major league franchises took notice of the burgeoning fan base as these children and their parents rooted for their favorite hometown teams and heroes. Other factors that shaped the experience of Italians and Jews in baseball were ethnic stereotypes and ominous political developments in Europe. As Italy emerged as a fascist state and potential threat to American security, and as anti-Semitism intensified in Nazi Germany, the performance of Italian and Jewish ballplayers in the United States took on heightened symbolic meaning. With the outbreak of World War II, ethnic baseball heroes such as Joe DiMaggio* and Hank Greenberg* displayed both their prowess on the field and also their patriotism and their loyalty to the American creed of democracy.

A few Italian Americans earned spots on major league rosters prior to World War I, but they did not assert themselves in the baseball world until the 1920s and especially the 1930s. Louis Pisano (playing under the name of Buttercup Dickerson) was a left fielder in 1878 for the Cincinnati Red Stockings, and Ed Abbaticchio joined the Phillies in 1897. The first Italians in professional baseball often changed their names to conceal their ethnic identity; a notable example was Ping Bodie (born Francesco Stefano Pezzolo), who played for the Philadelphia Athletics and the New York Yankees from 1917 to the late 1920s. During the interwar period and after World War II dozens of Italians in addition to DiMaggio (and his brothers Vince and Dom) had distinguished careers as players, coaches, and managers. They included Tony Lazzeri* of the Yankees (known as "Push 'em Up Wop" because he bounced up so often after being hit by a pitch), Ernie Lombardi,* Frank Crosetti, Dolph Camilli, Phil Rizzuto,* Billy Martin, Yogi Berra,* Tom Lasorda, and many others. But "Joltin' Joe" DiMaggio stands alone among Italian players because of his brilliance on the field, his military service during World War II, and even his ill-fated marriage to Marilyn Monroe. He began his career as an ethnic star, but he ended it in the 1950s as an American idol, symbolizing the fully assimilated immigrant.

As was the case with the Italians, there were a few Jewish professional ball-players prior to World War I, but many more earned a modest place for themselves in the game after 1920. According to one account, between 1871 and 1980 there were 115 Hebrew major leaguers. All of these men faced enormous hurdles because of their religion's traditional hostility toward athletics and the pervasive anti-Semitism they encountered in society. America's national pastime posed a problem for Orthodox immigrant Jews in the early twentieth century because parents feared that it would distract their youth from their religious training. But as Jewish boys took up the sport, the older generation grudgingly gave permission for them to play. As Abraham Cahan advised in his column in the Yiddish-language *Jewish Daily Forward*: "[L]et your boys play baseball and play it well, as long as it does not interfere with their education or get them into bad company. . . . Bring them up to be educated, ethical, and decent, but also to be physically strong so they should not feel inferior. . . . Let us not so raise the children that they should grow up foreigners in their own birthplace." But anti-Semitism was a powerful force in American society, and it shaped the experience of Jews in baseball in a number of ways. After the shock of the "Black Sox" scandal with the fixing of the 1919 World Series, Henry Ford wrote two long articles entitled "Jewish Gamblers Corrupt American Baseball" and "The Jewish Degradation of American Baseball," in which he accused the Jewish underworld figures Arnold Rothstein and Abe Attell* of masterminding the sordid affair. Although Rothstein and Attell were involved in this incident, Ford exaggerated their roles and played up the incident as an example of an international Jewish conspiracy to corrupt Anglo-Saxon institutions. Jewish players who made it to the big leagues during the 1920s and 1930s endured a great deal of anti-Semitic heckling.

Club owners of this era realized the box office appeal of Jewish players in cities where there were large numbers of Hebrew immigrants. The best example is the case of the New York Giants' hopes for Moses Solomon in 1923 and especially Andy Cohen in the late 1920s. Neither one became a star, but the Jewish community of Detroit soon gained a genuine hero with the rise of Hank Greenberg, raised in the Bronx in New York City. Although he was never an observant Jew, Greenberg did gain respect in his community when he refused to play on Yom Kippur. His early entrance into military service and his many years of duty as an officer in the Air Corps elevated his reputation as a Jew who was willing to sacrifice his career for his country. Like DiMaggio, he began as an ethnic star and ended as an assimilated American hero. Nearly twenty

years later Jewish fans enjoyed the exploits of another Hebrew, Sandy Koufax,*
whose brief, but spectacular, career as a pitcher for the Dodgers earned him a
place (with Greenberg) in the Hall of Fame.

In some ways the experience of Native Americans in baseball resembles that
of white immigrants, but with an important qualification. Indians were subject
to a difficult kind of prejudice that was more intense than the ethnic stereotyping
and abuse directed at the Irish, Germans, Italians, Jews, or other European players. Native Americans got the opportunity to play baseball primarily through
the federal government's Indian schools and several private educational organizations. These boarding institutions were established to eradicate Indian culture
in the youth and teach them American cultural values. Public officials and administrators believed that sports in general and baseball in particular were ideal
means to use to assimilate Native Americans into the mainstream culture. The
best-known school of this type was founded at Carlisle, Pennsylvania, in 1879.
Its most famous product was Jim Thorpe,* who was destined to lose his gold
medals won at the 1912 Olympic Games because of his participation in a semiprofessional baseball summer league several years earlier. Several dozen Indian
or part-Indian players rose to the major league level prior to World War II,
beginning with Louis Sockalexis,* who joined the Cleveland club in the National League in 1897. Besides Thorpe, others included such standouts as
Charles Albert "Chief" Bender* and John "Chief" Meyers.* The common nickname of "chief" given to Indian ballplayers reflects the stereotypical views of
the white media, as do the team names and mascots of the Cleveland Indians
and the Atlanta Braves. Meyers has stated that he felt that he had been treated
as a foreigner during his career; recently, several Native American organizations
have protested the use of Indian nicknames, mascots, and symbols by baseball
teams as racist and demeaning.

African Americans were among the first to play the modern form of baseball
in the United States, but they had the most difficulty of any group in achieving
equal opportunity to compete on the nation's diamonds. Baseball fever swept
through the black communities of many American cities and towns during the
1860s, as all-black nines appeared in Newark, Camden, and New Brunswick,
New Jersey; Chicago; Philadelphia; Pittsburgh; Brooklyn; New York City; Baltimore; and New Orleans, among other places. Some of these clubs, such as the
Philadelphia Pythians,* recruited from the upper ranks of African American
society, while others enlisted men of lower status—for example, the Chicago
Blue Stockings were hotel and restaurant waiters. Although the Pythians and
other black clubs occasionally competed against white teams during the late
1860s, they were barred from joining state and national baseball associations.
During the 1880s the Cuban Giants and several other black professional nines
played in white leagues and also against clubs of their own race. Between 1883
and 1898 fifty-five black ballplayers gained admission to white professional
baseball leagues. In 1884 two of them, Moses Fleetwood Walker* and his

brother Weldy, made it to the American Association, which then held major league status.

As racism intensified during the late 1880s the Walker brothers and other blacks were barred from the major leagues, and African American players accommodated themselves to the segregation and discrimination in baseball that would last until the 1940s. Black youth continued to play the game in segregated schools, colleges, and recreational programs and on sandlots in the North and South. Adults also formed sandlot and semiprofessional clubs, a few of which became renowned in black communities as they barnstormed across the country. During the early decades of the twentieth century perhaps the most famous of these were the Homestead Grays* and the Pittsburgh Crawfords,* both of Pittsburgh. The formation of the Negro National League* in 1920 by Andrew "Rube" Foster* and the creation of the Negro American League* in 1937 gave some structure to black baseball, but barnstorming tours, exhibitions against white stars, and postseason trips to the Caribbean were still important sources of income for the black clubs. The games against the celebrated white players were featured attractions, with black clubs defeating their counterparts in many of these contests. The junkets to Latin America were especially prized by the players because of the extra revenue and the relief from the racial prejudice that plagued them in the States.

The Negro Leagues struggled during the 1930s but thrived during and immediately after World War II, despite numerous operating difficulties. Most of the clubs were controlled by black politicians or gamblers who invested profits earned in the numbers rackets in their nines. Owners were dependent on white professional clubs and cities that rented them ballparks for both All-Star and regularly scheduled games. Furthermore, players frequently broke their contracts and switched teams, even in midseason, and weaker teams often folded, even before completing their schedules. Yet fans turned out by the thousands to see the great stars of this era—Josh Gibson,* "Cool Papa" Bell,* Satchel Paige,* Buck Leonard,* Ray Dandridge, Willie Wells, Leon Day, and many others—especially at the annual All-Star Games held in Chicago.

The age of integration in baseball began with Branch Rickey's signing of Jackie Robinson* to a contract with the Brooklyn Dodgers in 1945. Although the National Association for the Advancement of Colored People and the black press had urged major league baseball to end the ban on black players during World War II, the owners had resisted for a number of reasons. They believed that southern ballplayers would not compete against blacks, that southern cities and towns that hosted spring training camps would not permit racially mixed teams in their communities, and that no black ballplayers could compete at a major league level. Some were concerned about the possible effects of integration on attendance by white fans, while others predicted that admitting blacks would lead to the demise of the Negro Leagues and a loss of income for white clubs that rented their ballparks to black nines. Rickey selected Robinson for his great experiment because Robinson had attended the University of California at Los Angeles (UCLA), had served in the army as an officer, and had the temperament and character to take the abuse he was certain to experience without fighting back on the field. Robinson's debut with the Dodgers in 1947 proved that the most talented players from the Negro Leagues could more than hold their own at the major league level.

Robinson's success led directly to the demise of the Negro Leagues, but the full integration of baseball proceeded slowly during the late 1940s and early 1950s. Don Newcombe, Roy Campanella,* and Joe Black joined the Dodgers, while Larry Doby,* Paige, and Luke Easter signed with the Cleveland Indians. Although the 1950s brought the arrival of such superstars as Willie Mays* and Hank Aaron,* teams such as the New York Yankees and the Boston Red Sox were slow to sign talented black stars. During recent decades many African Americans have distinguished themselves on major league diamonds, but only a few have played the central positions of pitcher, catcher, and middle infielders. Off the playing field there has been relatively little opportunity for blacks, as is evident from the small number who have gained employment as managers, coaches, and front-office executives.

The experience of Hispanics in baseball is far more complicated than that of European immigrants, Native Americans, or blacks because of two factors. The first is the interaction of players and clubs from North, Central, and South America and the Caribbean; the second is the issue of race. The introduction of American baseball during the late 1800s into Mexico, Nicaragua, Panama, Cuba, Santo Domingo, Venezuela, Colombia, and other Latin American lands created a craze for the sport that intensified in the twentieth century as white major leaguers and blacks from the Negro Leagues toured through the region. Cuba in particular was a hotbed for the sport in the early 1900s, but its best players could aspire to play in the United States only if their skins were light enough to pass the color test in a racist American society. The most celebrated Cuban to star in the major leagues during this period was Adolfo "Dolf" Luque, who won 193 games over a twenty-year career. Beginning in the 1930s Joe Cambria scouted for Clark Griffith's Washington Senators and signed over 400 players over a twenty-five-year career.

Dark-skinned Cubans, Dominicans, and other Latin Americans could only dream about competing in the Negro Leagues until Jackie Robinson broke the color barrier in the National League in 1947. Martin Dihigo* of Cuba excelled as both a pitcher and batter and became the only Latin ballplayer from the Negro League era to earn a place in the Hall of Fame. After Robinson integrated baseball, he opened the door for blacks in both the United States and Latin America. The first to capitalize on this opportunity was another Cuban, Saturnino Orestes Arrieta Armas, renamed Minnie Minoso in the United States. Since then more than 500 Latin-born players have reached the "Big Show," including Roberto Clemente* of Puerto Rico, Felipe Alou* and Juan Marichal* of the Dominican Republic, Luis Aparicio of Venezuela, and Rod Carew* of Panama.

During recent decades the city of San Pedro de Macoris in the Dominican Republic has earned the distinction of having the most major leaguers per capita in the entire world. In the 1990s economic, political, and social problems in communist Cuba under Fidel Castro contributed to the decline of that nation's sports programs. As a result, its athletes became far more willing to seek asylum in the United States to continue their careers. Joe Cubas, a Cuban American sports agent based in Miami, helped seven baseball players defect from Cuba in 1996 alone. One year earlier he lured away Livian Hernández, who signed a $4.5 million contract with the Florida Marlins and starred in the 1997 major league baseball playoffs and World Series. In December of that year Hernández's half brother, Orlando Hernández, escaped to the United States. Within a few months he signed a contract with the New York Yankees, and he duplicated his relative's achievement with stellar performances in the World Series for the champion Yankees in 1998 and 1999.

Like the European ethnic ballplayers who preceded them, the Hispanics have been subject to abuse, ridicule, stereotyping, and prejudice. Many of them struggled to learn the English language and encountered racism that was much more virulent than anything they had experienced in their native lands. But also like their predecessors, they became gate attractions in those cities that numbered large Latino populations, especially New York, Los Angeles, and Miami. Fernando Valenzuela, a native of Mexico, made a sensational debut with the Los Angeles Dodgers in the early 1980s. In 1993 Wayne Huizenga of the Florida Marlins launched his expansion team in the National League with a marketing strategy aimed at Miami's sizable Hispanic community.

Asians have also entered the baseball scene in recent decades, partly through the success of Little League boys' teams from Taiwan and Japan but mostly through the importation of Japanese and Korean pitchers in the 1990s. As was the case in Latin America, American professionals helped promote the sport in Japan via postseason tours, and some joined Japanese clubs. A new era began in the mid-1990s with the arrival of Hideo Nomo from Japan and Chang Ho Park from Korea. Both pitched for the Dodgers in a city with a rapidly growing Asian population. The signing of Hideki Irabu by the Yankees in 1997 raised the further possibility that Japanese clubs were willing to relax their restrictions on free agency and allow more of their stars to seek fame and fortune in the United States. The coming of the Asians in major league baseball also highlighted the marketing possibilities of the American national pastime in the Far East.

SELECTED BIBLIOGRAPHY: Robert F. Burk, *Never Just a Game: Players, Owners, and American Baseball to 1920* (1994); Jack E. Davis, "Baseball's Reluctant Challenge: Desegregating Major League Spring Training Sites, 1961–64," *Journal of Sport History* 19 (Summer 1992): 144–162; Walter L. Harrison, "Six-Pointed Diamond: Baseball and American Jews," *Journal of Popular Culture* 15, No. 3 (Winter 1981): 112–118; Robert Heuer, "Latin Ballplayers Load the Bases," *Americas* 42 (March 1990): 18–23; Robert Heuer, "Look What They've Done to My Game," *Americas* 47 (May 1995): 36–41; John

B. Holway, *Voices from the Great Black Baseball Leagues* (1975); John B. Holway, *Blackball Stars: Negro League Pioneers* (1988); John B. Holway, *Black Diamonds: Life in the Negro Leagues from the Men Who Lived It* (1989); Milton Jamail, *Full Count: An Inside View of Cuban Baseball and the United States* (2000); Peter Levine, *Ellis Island to Ebbets Field: Sport and the American Jewish Experience* (1992), chs. 5–7; Effa Manley and Leon H. Hardwick, *Negro Baseball before Integration* (1976); Michael M. Oleksak and Mary Adams Oleksak, *Beisball: Latin Americans and the Grand Old Game* (1991); Robert Peterson, *Only the Ball Was White* (1970); John C. Phillips, "Race and Career Opportunities in Major League Baseball, 1960–1980," *Journal of Sport and Social Issues* 7, No. 2 (Summer-Autumn 1983): 1–17; Samuel O. Regalado, *Viva Baseball! Latin Major Leaguers and Their Special Hunger* (1998); Steven A. Riess, *Touching Base: Professional Baseball and American Culture in the Progressive Era* (1980); Steven A. Riess, "Race and Ethnicity in American Baseball: 1900–1919," *Journal of Ethnic Studies*, 4 (Winter 1977): 39–55; Donn Rogosin, *Invisible Men: Life in Baseball's Negro Leagues* (1983); Rob Ruck, *Sandlot Seasons: Sport in Black Pittsburgh* (1987); Harold Seymour, *Baseball: The People's Game* (1990), chs. 6, 24, 33–37; William Simons, "Jackie Robinson and the American Mind: Journalistic Perceptions of the Reintegration of Baseball," *Journal of Sport History* 12 (Spring 1985): 39–64; Jules Tygiel, *Baseball's Great Experiment: Jackie Robinson and His Legacy* (1983); G. Edward White, *Creating the National Pastime: Baseball Transforms Itself, 1903–1953* (1996), ch. 8; Sol White, *Sol White's Official Baseball Guide* (1907; reprint, 1984); Joel Zoss and John Bowman, *Diamonds in the Rough: The Untold Story of Baseball* (1996), chs. 4–6.

George B. Kirsch

BASILIO, CARMEN (2 April 1927, Canastota, NY–   ). A prizefighter, he is the son of Italian immigrants and one of ten children. His father was an onion farmer. Basilio was twice welterweight boxing champion and once middleweight champion. He quit high school before he was eighteen years old to join the marines in 1945, where he began boxing. He turned professional in 1948. Basilio defeated Billy Graham in 1953 to win the New York state welterweight championship. In 1955, in the Syracuse War Memorial, he defeated Tony DeMarco to win the world welterweight title. On 14 March 1956, he lost the title to Johnny Saxton but regained it on 12 September of that year, defeating Saxton. Basilio advanced to the middleweight class and defeated the legendary Sugar Ray Robinson* to win the world middleweight title, 23 September 1957. In a rematch on 2 March 1958, he lost the title to Robinson. In his last fight, his seventy-ninth, he was defeated by Paul Pender in a world middleweight title fight at Boston, 22 April 1961. After retiring from boxing, Basilio became an instructor in physical education at LeMoyne College in Syracuse and a public relations representative for the Genesee Brewing Company.

SELECTED BIBLIOGRAPHY: Carmen Basilio, *The Boxing Register* (1997), 184–187; Peter Heller, *In This Corner: Former World Champions Tell Their Stories* (1973); Gilbert E. Odd, *Encyclopedia of Boxing* (1983); *Syracuse Herald-American*, 28 October 1979, 4–6, 8, 10, 12, 16–17, 37, 39.

Frank J. Cavaioli

BASKETBALL. The claims of boxing, baseball, and soccer notwithstanding, basketball is America's most ethnic game. It was created in 1891 by an immigrant, James Naismith,* a Canadian of Scottish descent, in an institution of English origins, the Young Men's Christian Association (YMCA). The unique ideology, sporting enthusiasm, and amateur principles of the YMCA were largely imported from Britain, for young, muscular, Christian males. Yet basketball was scarcely a year old before a female Jewish immigrant from Lithuania, Senda Berenson (Abbott),* introduced it to women at Smith College.

Beyond its English and Scottish origins, basketball appealed to another older immigrant community: German Americans whose forebears had created the gymnasium as a place where ropes and pulleys, vaulting apparatus, and parallel bars provided vigorous, disciplined exercise for urban folk. Under pressure to enliven their gymnastics programs with competitive athletics, German turners in Louisville, Cincinnati, and Newark reluctantly introduced basketball to their gyms. In 1895, just four years after Naismith invented the game, a German YMCA in Buffalo founded a team under the guidance of Fred Burkhardt, a former student with Naismith at Springfield.

Competing against other YMCAs, college teams, and semiprofessional clubs, the Buffalo Germans* quickly became the premier basketball squad in the United States. In 1901 they won the Amateur Athletic Union championship at the Pan-American Exposition in Buffalo; in 1904 they dominated a tournament held in conjunction with the St. Louis Olympics. Turning professional, they barnstormed to 111 consecutive victories in 1908–11. Over twenty-nine years, including nine as amateurs, the Buffalo Germans won 762 games and lost only 85.

Around the turn of the century, public schools and churches promoted basketball as a winter sport safer and more respectable than boxing, cheaper as well as safer than football. Neighborhood schools gave the game an official stamp of public approval as a wholesome sporting activity linked to the flag, the English language, and law-abiding precepts (playing by the rules) for the patriotic socialization of sons and daughters of newcomers from afar. Unfortunately, many children of immigrants did not stay in school beyond the primary level. Instead, they received their tutelage in citizenship from a more traditional, familiar source, the local Catholic church. Likely as not, second-generation immigrants from Central and Eastern Europe learned to play basketball in their parish church hall or in a gym built adjacent to the sanctuary, under the watchful eye of a Catholic priest.

This pattern especially held true for booming cities like Chicago where ethnic communities, heavily Catholic and working-class, soon outnumbered the native-born. Second-generation Czechs, Poles, and Slavs eagerly took to hoops. In 1921 a Czech team won the citywide public parks basketball championship; two years later, Catholic organizations representing Chicago's ethnic communities founded the National Catholic Interscholastic Basketball Tournament at Loyola University. At the onset of the depression, the Polish National Alliance (PNA) sponsored twenty three teams in three PNA basketball leagues spread around the city of Chicago. Mike Krzyzewski,* the highly successful coach at Duke University, first learned his basketball in a Chicago ethnic enclave.

The Catholic Youth Organization* (CYO) provided a kind of umbrella organization for these disparate, ethnic-based teams and leagues. Founded in 1930 by Chicago's auxiliary bishop Bernard J. Sheil, the CYO emphasized boxing and basketball as means to prevent juvenile delinquency. In 1931 a Chicago CYO tournament featured 415 teams. The winner, St. Joseph, went off to play the CYO champion of New York City.

If some ethnics—like the Irish—turned more to pugilism than to basketball, others found other ball games more attractive, especially in those areas of the country where a mild climate encouraged year-round outdoor activity. The Italian neighborhood on "Dago Hill" in southwest St. Louis is a good example. Baseball and soccer teams flourished on the Hill, in the shadow of St. Ambrose church. Basketball was not a popular pastime there or in other notable Italian American communities such as Boston's South End or New York City's Little Italy. Californian Angelo Joseph "Hank" Luisetti,* a three-time All-American at Stanford University in the late 1930s, is the only Italian name that readily comes to mind as a well-known basketball player of the sport's formative years.

By way of contrast, the early history of basketball would be much the poorer without the participation of numerous second-generation immigrant Jews from Eastern Europe. Basketball not only provided Jews the usual means of cultural assimilation but also helped to destroy the stereotype of the Jew as bookish, quaintly religious, and physically weak. On school yards, at settlement houses, and in Young Men's Hebrew Associations,* Jewish youths eagerly played and promoted the game. Early community teams such as the Atlas in New Haven, Connecticut, the Dux in Brooklyn, and the Talmud Torah Athletic Club ("the Fighting Rabbis") in Minneapolis attracted fervent partisan support from friends who proudly cheered their exploits and enjoyed family outings at dances following the games.

Two institutions of higher learning in New York City, New York University (NYU) and the City College of New York (CCNY), exercised unique attractions for the sons and daughters of Jewish immigrants. Not surprisingly, NYU and CCNY dominated intercollegiate basketball in the first half of the twentieth century. Joseph "Gid" Girsdansky, a son of one of the founders of the Socialist Party in the United States, played on NYU's very first team in 1907; two years later he was elected captain of a squad that went undefeated. In 1934 all five NYU starters were Jewish, leading the Violets to an 18–1 record and a national championship.

CCNY, a public institution that charged no tuition, became an even greater magnet for second-generation Jews. By the mid-1920s more than 85% of its student body claimed Jewish ancestry. Their first big basketball name was a little man, Bernard "Barney" Sedran,* whose 115 pounds on a frame of 5'4" made him exceedingly small even for that era. Appropriately born on the Lower East Side of New York in the same year that James Naismith invented basketball, "Mighty Mite" Sedran won All-Star honors for three years at CCNY. Over the next thirteen years he played for fifteen different professional teams, subsequently coached six professional and semiprofessional squads, and in 1962 was inducted into the Naismith Memorial Basketball Hall of Fame.

Another traveler on the road from New York's Lower East Side to Springfield, Massachusetts' Hall of Fame by way of CCNY was Nathan "Nat" Holman,* whose long, successful coaching tenure at City College made him one of the most visible coaches in the entire history of the game. For several years in the 1920s he starred most of the time as the only Jew on the team—amid a galaxy of stars, the original Celtics. His coaching career overlapped his playing days. Beginning in 1919, over a span of thirty eight years he directed CCNY teams to 422 victories and only 188 losses. In 1950 they captured both the National Collegiate Athletic Association (NCAA) and National Invitational Tournament (NIT) titles, the only team ever to win both tournaments. Of the 518 players Holman coached, some 83% were Jewish.

In the 1950s, however, second- and third-generation Jews joined the American exodus from urban ethnic communities to the suburbs, and Jewish youths aimed for something more than basketball goals. The Jewish presence in college and professional basketball waned dramatically. Larry Brown and Lennie Rosenbluth at the University of North Carolina in the late 1950s, Art Heyman at Duke University in the early 1960s, and Danny Schayes at Syracuse University in the 1970s were exceptions, not the rule, of postwar Jewish participation in basketball at its highest levels of play.

In recent years the most visible Jewish basketballer is Nancy Lieberman* (Lieberman-Cline after marriage in 1988), who played on the silver medal-winning American women's team at the Montreal Olympics in 1976 before leading Old Dominion University to two national championships in the late 1970s. A three-time All-American, Lieberman then played professionally for several years and has kept herself in the limelight by coaching and promoting and providing television commentary for women's basketball.

No longer on the floor, Jews can now be found in coaching and managerial roles. Harold "Red" Auerbach* of the Boston Celtics, William "Red" Holzman* of the New York Knicks, and Larry Brown of several clubs have excelled as coaches since World War II. On the owners' trail blazed by a Jewish businessman who sponsored the interwar Cleveland Rosenblums are men such as Eddie Gottlieb* of the Philadelphia Warriors and William Davidson of the Detroit Pistons. David Stern, the innovative, forceful commissioner of the National Basketball Association (NBA), caps an impressive, century-long history of Jews in basketball.

When Jewish athletes dropped the ball in the 1950s, African Americans picked it up. In truth, blacks had long played the game, but largely in segregated schools and universities whose activities remained invisible to white America. John McLendon, for example, learned the game from the old master himself, James Naismith, at the University of Kansas and for some twenty-five years coached at all-black institutions such as North Carolina Central College, Hampton Institute, and Tennessee A&I. His teams won 523 of their 685 games, a sensational 76%. Yet not until the 1960s did McLendon, at the end of his coaching career, break out of the racially segregated orbit.

Prior to the 1950s two professional barnstorming teams, the New York (Harlem) Renaissance Big Five* and the Harlem Globetrotters,* were the only African Americans who regularly and prominently competed against whites. Both teams derived from racial barriers against black participation on white teams and also from an absence of black professional basketball leagues on the order of the Negro League* in baseball. Yet the Rens and Globetrotters thrived because white professional teams welcomed the skill and showmanship that attracted big crowds for one-night exhibitions.

Both teams were created by immigrants other than African Americans. The founder of the Rens, Robert J. Douglas,* was only four years of age when he came with his parents from the British West Indies. In 1922 he founded the Rens at the Renaissance Casino ballroom in Harlem, with jazz, dancing, and big band music in the background. For twenty-six years the team stayed mostly on the road, winning more than 100 games a year throughout the East and South. Each year they played several games against the all-white original Celtics and often as not beat them. In 1931 the Rens defeated their barnstorming counterparts, the Harlem Globetrotters, for the mythical professional world championship.

The Globetrotters trace their roots to Abraham Michael "Abe" Saperstein,* an immigrant whose Jewish parents left Poland for England, then moved to Chicago in 1905. A four-sport star in high school, Saperstein coached several black basketball squads in adjacent inner-city neighborhoods and in 1927 tagged his newly formed barnstorming team with the Harlem reference for publicity purposes. At first the Globetrotters toured mostly in the Midwest. In 1940 they won the unofficial World's Basketball Championship but were already finding that spectators were most attracted to athleticism when it was combined with comedic showmanship. In 1950 they launched an annual summer tour of Europe.

Saperstein and his Globetrotters momentarily hindered the admission of black players onto the rosters of the new National Basketball Association (NBA), which was founded in 1949. As exhibition games between struggling NBA teams and the Globetrotters invariably filled the stands, owners were reluctant to tamper with Saperstein's easy access to the best black talent. In 1950, however, that cozy arrangement collapsed with a vengeance when New York Knicks' owner, Ned Irish, announced his intentions to hire Nat "Sweetwater" Clifton from the Trotters. In the 1950 NBA draft of college players, the Boston

Celtics selected Charles "Chuck" Cooper from Duquesne University, and the Washington Capitols took Earl Lloyd from West Virginia State.

Black talent did not immediately flood into the NBA. By 1960 African Americans made up only 20% of NBA rosters, a far cry from the 75% that would be the case by 1995. Of the many factors that have gone into this racial turn-around, two invite explanations: the centrality of black athletes in the emergence of college basketball as a televised spectacle and the transformation of the game as a result of the black aesthetic.

Win-loss columns spoke volumes in favor of several college and university coaches who recruited their first black players in the 1950s. Bill Russell* and K. C. Jones at the University of San Francisco, Elgin Baylor* at the University of Seattle, Wilt Chamberlain* at the University of Kansas, and Oscar Robertson* of the University of Cincinnati all made winners of their teams. So did the five black starters on the previously unknown Texas Western University squad, who won the NCAA crown in 1966.

Yet the black centerpiece in televised college basketball glowed most vividly in a single game in 1968, when African American centers Lew Alcindor (later Kareem Abdul-Jabbar*) of the UCLA Bruins and Elvin Hayes* of the Houston Cougars faced each other in a packed house at the Houston Astrodome. As millions watched on television, the action surged up and down the court with the lead repeatedly changing hands before Houston—led by Hayes' thirty-nine points—squeaked out a 71–69 victory. The hype surrounding this event can best be viewed as a kind of prelude to the recent "March madness" created by the television moguls.

A distinctive black style of play adds to the appeal. Whereas white players had for decades run, passed, and shot in predictably set patterns, blacks jazzed up the game with the faster, louder, more explosive improvisations that came right off the urban ghetto courts. In order to compete, whites have had to adapt to a more imaginative, innovative style of play that features the cross-over, between-the-legs dribble, the look-off pass, the double-pump move to the basket, and the demonstrative slam dunk. Some combination of Earvin "Magic" Johnson* and Michael Jordan* constitutes the black style at its best: an artistry that borders on wizardry, a hard-won, practiced accuracy that is nevertheless full of surprises.

From its narrow Scottish and English beginnings, basketball came into the American mainstream through the avid participation of European immigrants. Now, with the dominant presence and athleticism of African Americans, the game soars in popularity.

SELECTED BIBLIOGRAPHY: Stephen Fox, *Big Leagues: Professional Baseball, Football, and Basketball in National Memory* (1994); Gerald Gems, *The Windy City Wars: Labor, Leisure, and Sport in the Making of Chicago* (1997); Nelson George, *Elevating the Game: Black Men and Basketball* (1992); Peter Levine, *Ellis Island to Ebbets Field: Sport and the American Jewish Experience* (1992); Gary Ross Mormino, *Immigrants on the Hill: Italian-Americans in St. Louis, 1882–1982* (1986); Robert W. Peterson, *Cages to Jump Shots: Pro Basketball's Early Years* (1990); Thomas M. Tarapacki, *Chasing the American Dream: Polish Americans in Sports* (1995).

William J. Baker

BAYLOR, ELGIN (16 September 1934, Washington, DC–   ). An African American collegiate and professional basketball player, he is the son of John Baylor and Uzzel Baylor. He began playing the sport at the relatively advanced age of fourteen, in part because racial segregation limited his access to public playgrounds. He progressed rapidly, making the All-City Washington, D.C., team while competing for Phelps Vocational High School. In his senior year he attended Spingarn High School. After graduation he was recruited to play football at the College of Idaho in faraway Caldwell, Idaho, but he transferred after his freshman year to Seattle University. After sitting out one season of college ball (during which he played for an American Athletic Union (AAU) squad in Seattle), he became a national star from 1956 to 1958. A graceful player with great leaping ability and superb body control, he pioneered a new athletic style of basketball that profoundly changed the nature of the sport. In 1958 he led his Seattle team to the National Collegiate Athletic Association (NCAA) finals, which lost to the University of Kentucky. That year he was an All-American and was selected as the NCAA University Division Most Valuable Player (MVP). He skipped his final year of college eligibility to join the Minneapolis Lakers in the National Basketball Association (NBA). There he helped to revive a struggling franchise, which relocated to Los Angeles in 1960. As team captain he sparked the Lakers to greater glory during the 1960s. Highlights of his fourteen-year career include the Rookie of the Year award in 1959 and selection to the All-NBA first team every year from 1959 to 1969. Despite his brilliant playmaking and shooting performance, his Laker teams lost the NBA finals to the Boston Celtics six times. A knee injury forced him to retire early in the 1971–72 season, so he missed out on much of the satisfaction when the Lakers won the championship that season after years of frustration. After his retirement he coached the New Orleans Jazz for four years, and he later became vice president and general manager of the Los Angeles Clippers. He was elected to the Naismith Memorial Basketball Hall of Fame in 1976.

SELECTED BIBLIOGRAPHY: Arthur R. Ashe, Jr., *A Hard Road to Glory: A History of the African-American Athlete since 1946*, vol. 3 (1988); Frank Deford, "A Tiger Who Can Beat Anything," *Sports Illustrated* 25 (24 October 1966): 40–48; Buddy Martin, "The Final Four and the National Media," in *Rocky Mountain Basketball—Naismith to Nineteen-Ninety* (1989); Elgin Baylor file, Naismith Memorial Basketball Hall of Fame.

George B. Kirsch

BEAMON, BOB (29 August 1946, Jamaica, NY–   ). An African American track-and-field athlete, he was orphaned before his first birthday. He was raised by his stepfather, James Beamon, a construction worker, and his grandmother,

Minnie Beamon. After attending a reform school for juvenile delinquents, he graduated from Jamaica High School in 1965. After attending North Carolina Agricultural and Technical University, he transferred to Texas Western University at El Paso. As a student there Beamon was the national collegiate and triple-jump champion, and he also won the National Amateur Athletic Union (AAU) outdoor title. Beamon arrived at the 1968 Mexico City Olympics under a cloud of controversy, having recently been suspended from his college track-and-field team for refusing to compete in a meet against Brigham Young University as a protest against that institution's racial policies. During the qualifying round, Beamon fouled on his first two attempts, but with the encouragement of his friend and fellow competitor Ralph Boston,* who had won a gold medal in 1960 and a silver in 1964, Beamon hit his third takeoff perfectly and soared 29 feet 2-1/2 inches. With this spectacular long jump at the Olympics, Beamon became the first person to clear not only 28 feet but also 29 feet. The word "Beamonesque" was coined by sport historians in honor of one of the greatest athletic performances in history. His long-jump record stood for twenty-three years until Mike Powell broke the mark by two inches at the Track and Field World Championships held in Tokyo during the summer of 1991. Beamon became the AAU Champion again in 1969 following his phenomenal Olympic accomplishment and competed intermittently until 1972, when he made an unsuccessful attempt at an Olympic comeback. He became a professional athlete in 1973 and was elected to the U.S. Olympic Hall of Fame in 1983. He earned his undergraduate degree at Adelphi University in 1972 and later received a master's degree in psychology and counseling at San Diego State University.

SELECTED BIBLIOGRAPHY: Ira Berkow, "Beamon's Moment Suspended in Time," *New York Times Biographical Service* 15 (March 1984): 289–290; Mark Heisler, "Captured by One Moment in Time," *Los Angeles Times*, 25 July 1984, pt. 8, 24, 30; Bill Mallon and Ian Buchanan, *Quest for Gold: The Encyclopedia of American Olympians* (1984); Coles Phinizy, "The Unbelievable Moment," *Sports Illustrated* 29 (23 December 1968): 53–56; Dick Schaap, *The Perfect Jump* (1976).

                                                                    Debra A. Henderson

BEDNARIK, CHARLES ("Chuck") (1 May 1925, Bethlehem, PA–   ). A collegiate and professional football player, he is the son of Slovak immigrants. His father, Charles A. Bednarik, was an open-hearth steelworker, and his mother, Mary Pivovarnicek Bednarik, was a factory worker. He attended a Slovak ethnic parish, Saints Cyril and Methodius, but went to a public secondary school (Liberty High School) in order to participate in interscholastic sports. He then served in the air force and flew thirty combat missions. After World War II, he attended the University of Pennsylvania, playing center and middle linebacker and achieving All-American recognition in 1947 and 1948. He also received the prestigious Maxwell Award in 1948, an honor reserved for the most outstanding college athlete. Bednarik then moved to the professional ranks and played with the Philadelphia Eagles from 1949 until 1962. He became the team's center and occasionally played linebacker, especially when injuries plagued the team. Over his career he established a reputation for durability, missing only three games. He made the National Football League's (NFL) All-Pro team at offensive center in 1949 and 1950 and at defensive linebacker from 1951 to 1956 and in 1960. In the 1960 season, Philadelphia defeated the Green Bay Packers, 17–13, for the NFL title. During the championship match, on the last play of the game, Bednarik made the game-saving tackle that kept Green Bay fullback Jimmy Taylor out of the end zone. He is remembered as one of the last players to play both offense and defense for the length of the game. Bednarik has been inducted into both the Pro Football Hall of Fame and the College Football Hall of Fame.

SELECTED BIBLIOGRAPHY: Chuck Bednarik and Dick Schaap, "Who Says Pros Can't Play 60 Minutes?" *Saturday Evening Post* 234 (25 November 1961): 54–56ff; Ralph Hickock, *A Who's Who of Sports Champions* (1995); Joseph Krajsa, ed., *Slovaks in America: A Bicentennial Study* (1978); John D. McCallum and Chuck Bednarik, *Bednarik: Last of the Sixty-Minute Men* (1977); "*The Slovaks,*" *The Columbus Legacy*, videotape (1992); M. Mark Stolarik, *The Slovak-Americans* (1988).

Michael J. Kopanic, Jr.

BELL, JAMES THOMAS ("Cool Papa") (17 May 1903, Starkville, MS–7 March 1991, St. Louis). An African American baseball player, he was the grandson of an Oklahoma Indian. His father was a farmer. In 1920 he moved to St. Louis to finish high school and to find work. Two years later he began his career in the Negro Leagues* with the St. Louis Stars as a pitcher; he earned his nickname by maintaining his poise while performing under pressure in close contests. An arm injury forced him to the outfield in 1924, and for the rest of his career he became legendary for his hitting prowess and his blinding speed on the base paths and in the field. A switch-hitter, he was renowned for his bunts, infield hits, and stolen bases. In regular Negro League games he compiled a lifetime batting average of .337. He played twenty-five seasons for many teams in the United States, Latin America, and Mexico, including the St. Louis Stars (1922–31), the Pittsburgh Crawfords* (1933–36), and the Homestead Grays* (1943–46). Like most of the black ballplayers in the era of segregated baseball, he competed in countless barnstorming games. He also excelled in exhibition matches against white major leaguers. During his later years he was a player-manager for several clubs, a scout for the St. Louis Browns of the American League, and a custodian and security officer at the St. Louis City Hall. He was inducted into the National Baseball Hall of Fame in 1974.

SELECTED BIBLIOGRAPHY: James Bankes, "Flying Feet: The Life and Times of Cool Papa Bell, the Fastest Base Runner Baseball Has Ever Known," *Baseball History* 1 (Fall 1986): 39–50; James Bankes, *The Pittsburgh Crawfords* (1991); John Holway, *Voices from the Great Black Baseball Leagues* (1975); Robert W. Peterson, *Only the Ball Was White* (1970); James A. Riley, *The All-Time All-Stars of Black Baseball* (1983).

George B. Kirsch

BELMONT, AUGUST (8 December 1816, Alzei, Germany–24 November 1890, New York City). A banker and patron of horse racing, he was of Jewish ancestry. The son of Simon and Frederika (Elsaas) Belmont, his father was a wealthy landowner. As an agent for the Rothschilds he traveled to Naples and Cuba before founding his own company in New York City during the financial panic of 1837. A successful banker, during the 1840s he became a prominent Democrat and also served as consul general for Austria in the United States. He rose in the ranks of New York society through his diplomatic post, his great wealth, and his marriage to the daughter of Commodore Matthew C. Perry. In 1853 President Franklin Pierce appointed him minister to the Netherlands. Although he opposed Lincoln's election as president in 1860, during the Civil War he was an ardent supporter of the Union cause. As a turfman he enjoyed great success as a breeder at his farms at Babylon, New York, and Lexington, Kentucky. His horses won many stakes races and purses, and in the season just prior to his death his twenty-two entries headed the earnings list. For twenty years he served as president of the prestigious American Jockey Club, and in 1866 he joined Leonard W. Jerome to build Jerome Park, a magnificent new racetrack in the Fordham section of Westchester County (now in the Bronx, New York City). Belmont soon became the dominant personality among the horsemen at Jerome Park, and the first Belmont Stakes, named in his honor, was run there in 1867. At the time of his death he was a governor of the Coney Island Jockey Club and a steward of the New York Jockey Club. He was also a founder of the Monmouth Park (New Jersey) Racing Association.

SELECTED BIBLIOGRAPHY: August Belmont, *A Few Letters and Speeches of the Late Civil War* (1870); Dan M. Bowmar III, *Giants of the Turf: The Alexanders, the Belmonts, James R. Keene, the Whitneys* (1860); R.J.H. Gottheil, *The Belmont-Belmonte Family* (1917); *New York Times*, 15 November 1890, 1–2; William H. P. Robertson, *The History of Thoroughbred Racing in America* (1864); W.S. Vosburgh, *Racing in America, 1866–1921* (1922).

George B. Kirsch

BENDER, CHARLES ALBERT ("Chief") (5 May 1884, Crow Wing County, MN–22 May 1954, Philadelphia). A professional baseball player, he was the son of a White Earth Indian Reservation Chippewa mother (Mary Razor) and a German father (Albertus Bliss Bender, a farmer). "Charley," as he called himself, first shone as a pitcher under coach Glen "Pop" Warner at the Carlisle Indian Industrial School. In 1903 Bender catapulted from Dickinson College as a nineteen-year-old to the Philadelphia Athletics. He played an integral role on five Athletics pennant-winning teams that claimed World Series crowns in 1910, 1911, and 1913. While overshadowed by the accomplishments of teammates Eddie Plank and Rube Waddell, Bender through workman consistency fashioned a lifetime 212–127 record in 3,017 innings, with a career 2.46 earned run average (ERA). This two-time twenty-game winner, whose repertoire included the spitter, had his career season in 1910, when he went 23–5 with a 1.58 ERA. He threw a no-hitter against Cleveland in 1912. A versatile team player, Bender also frequently relieved and sometimes played the outfield. He led the American League (AL) in saves during the 1921 season with thirteen. Bender was comfortable with his Indian identity in spite of the militaristic, anti-Indian cultural environment he experienced at Carlisle. The much admired Chippewa was an affable, pragmatic gentleman who became a golf professional, billiards player, Pennsylvania clay pigeon champ, and baseball expert. He coached for almost thirty years, most of it in the minors. He was elected to the National Baseball Hall of Fame in 1953.

SELECTED BIBLIOGRAPHY: Mike Shatzkin, ed., "Chief Bender," *The Ballplayers: Baseball's Ultimate Biographical Reference* (1990), 68; *The Sporting News*, 24 December 1942, 30 December 1953, 2 June 1954; Robert Tholkes, "Chief Bender—The Early Years," *Baseball Research Journal* 12 (1983): 8–13.

Joseph M. Giovannetti

BENITEZ, WILFRIDO ("Wilfred") (12 September 1958, Bronx, NY–   ). Son of Puerto Ricans Gregorio and Clara Rosa Benitez, he was the youngest prizefighter ever to win a professional title when he defeated Antonio Cervantes on 6 March 1976 for the Junior Welterweight crown. Benitez's father had boxed as a boy and taught his sons the sport in the Bronx. He directed Wilfred's training during much of his professional career. When Benitez was seven, he moved with his family to Puerto Rico and participated in Golden Gloves competition. He turned professional in 1973 and finished his boxing career in 1990 with an overall 53–8–1 professional record. In addition to his junior welterweight title he won championships as welterweight (1979) and superwelterweight (1981). He lost the welterweight championship to Sugar Ray Leonard* in 1979 and the superwelterweight to Thomas Hearns in 1982. Although he was still a young man in the mid-1980s, Torres' skills were declining, and he lost all major bouts that he fought against quality opponents. Financial difficulties forced him to continue to box long after his prime. He entered the Boxing Hall of Fame in 1996. Boxing injuries led to posttraumatic encephalitis, which left him seriously incapacitated.

SELECTED BIBLIOGRAPHY: Richard Baker, "Clinging to Yesterday: The Sad Saga of Wilfred Benitez," *The Ring* 70 (April 1991): 32–33; Gregorio Benitez, "Why Benitez Won't Win," *The Ring* 58 (November 1979): 22; Mario Rivera Martino, "Benitez Takes Jr. Welter Title from Cervantes," *The Ring* 55 (June 1976): 13–17; William Nack, "On Top of the World," *Sports Illustrated* 51 (22 January 1979): 16–17; Bert Randolph Sugar, *The 100 Greatest Boxers of All Time* (1984); Bert Randolph Sugar, "Ringside Reports," *The Ring* 62 (February 1983): 46–47.

Richard V. McGehee

BENOIT, JOAN. *See* SAMUELSON, JOAN BENOIT

BERENSON, SENDA (19 March 1868, Vilna, Lithuania–16 February 1954, Santa Barbara, CA). The daughter of Russian Jewish immigrants (Albert Valvrojenski and Julia Mieliszanski), she was a physical educator and the inventor of a set of rules for women's basketball, modifying the men's game. Born in a shetl as Senda Valvrojenski, she came to Boston at age seven. Emigrating in 1874, her father, a peddler, changed the family name to Berenson. Berenson attended the Boston Latin School and the Boston Normal School for Gymnastics, where her health improved, and she became interested in gymnastics. In 1892 Berenson became the director of physical training at Smith College, Northampton, Massachusetts, at the new Alumnae Gymnasium. She observed Dr. James Naismith's* new game of basketball at Springfield College and then organized a women's basketball game in 1892 at Smith College. Known as the "Mother of Women's Basketball," Berenson supervised the first "official" women's game, which pitted the Smith sophomores against the freshmen at Alumnae Gymnasium on 22 March 1893. To avoid the roughness of the men's game, Berenson adapted the rules for women: dividing the court into zones, prohibiting snatching the ball from another player, allowing five to ten players on a team, and emphasizing teamwork. In June 1899 at the Physical Training Conference to draw up modified rules for women's basketball, participants selected Berenson to author the official rules. Berenson edited *Spalding's Athletic Library Basket Ball for Women* in 1901, explaining that the women's game avoided "undue physical exertion." Berenson chaired the U.S. Women's Basketball Committee from 1905 to 1917, popularizing women's basketball throughout the country at colleges, schools, Young Women's Christian Associations (YMCAs), and Young Women's Hebrew Associations* (YWHAs). Retiring from Smith in 1911, she then chaired the Physical Education Department at Burnham School in Northampton until 1921. As the pioneer of women's basketball, in 1985 Senda Berenson Abbott became one of the first three women (and the first Jewish female) to be enshrined in the Naismith Basketball Hall of Fame.

SELECTED BIBLIOGRAPHY: Senda Berenson, ed., *Spalding's Athletic Library Basket Ball for Women* (1901); "Senda Berenson," in Geoffrey Wigoder, ed., *Encyclopaedia Judaica Year Book, 1983–1985* (1985); Betty Spears, "Senda Berenson Abbott: New Woman, New Sport," in Joan S. Hult and Marianna Trekel, eds., *A Century of Women's Basketball: From Frailty to Final Four* (1991); Athletics, Nearprint File—Special Topics: Senda Berenson Material, American Jewish Archives, Cincinnati, OH; Senda Berenson, "Basket Ball for Women," n.d., Speeches, Senda Berenson Collection, College Archives, Smith College, Northampton, MA.

Linda J. Borish

BERG, MORRIS ("Moe") (2 March 1902, New York City–29 May 1972, Belleville, NJ). A baseball player, his parents were Ukrainian Jewish immigrants. Berg's father (Bernard) was a pharmacist, and his mother (Rose) was a housewife. A graduate of Newark's Barringer High School, Berg received a bachelor's degree from Princeton, studied linguistics at the Sorbonne, and earned an LL.B. from Columbia. Linguist, attorney, and spy, he was also a major league baseball player. During Berg's fifteen seasons in the major leagues (1923, 1926–1939), he played for Brooklyn of the National League and Chicago, Cleveland, Washington, and Boston of the American League. Primarily a reserve catcher, Berg possessed good defensive skills. Nonetheless, as his career statistics—.243 batting average, six home runs, and 206 runs batted in—indicate, Berg had limited offensive abilities. An enigmatic and reclusive bachelor, Berg was known as baseball's preeminent intellectual. After his death, declassified documents revealed that Berg conducted important atomic counterintelligence for the Office of Strategic services during World War II.

SELECTED BIBLIOGRAPHY: Ethel Berg, *My Brother Morris Berg: The Real Moe* (1976); Nicholas Dawidoff, *The Catcher Was a Spy: The Mysterious Life of Moe Berg* (1994); Louis Kaufman, Barbara Fitzgerald, and Tom Sewell, *Moe Berg: Athlete, Scholar, Spy* (1974); Peter Levine, *Ellis Island to Ebbets Field: Sport and the American Jewish Experience* (1992); Robert Slater, *Great Jews in Sport* (1983).

William M. Simons

BERRA, LAWRENCE PETER ("Yogi") (12 May 1925, St. Louis–   ). A baseball player, manager, and coach, he is the son of Pietro and Pauline (Longsani) Berra, both Italian immigrants. Yogi grew up in the Italian "Hill" section of St. Louis. He quit school at age fourteen, took odd jobs, excelled at baseball, and signed with the New York Yankees for $500. In 1943, at age eighteen, Berra played for the Yankee farm team in Norfolk, Virginia, joined the navy, and after his discharge in 1946 played for the Newark Bears. From there he played for the Yankees until 1964. Berra was an American League All-Star catcher from 1948 through 1962. He played in fourteen World Series, ten on the winning side. After retiring, he managed the Yankees to a pennant but was fired when he lost the World Series. He coached for the New York Mets (1965–72); in 1973 he managed the Mets to the National League pennant, only to lose again in the World Series. From midseason 1975 through 1983, he coached the Yankees and the following year managed the Yankees to an 87–75 record. After a slow start in 1985, the Yankees fired him, and the Houston Astros later hired him as a coach. In 1972 Berra was elected to the Baseball Hall of Fame. The Yankees retired his uniform, number 8. A longtime resident of Montclair, New Jersey, in 1998 Montclair State University named its new baseball facility and a museum in his honor. During and after his playing career Berra was well known for his humorous malapropisms, such as "It's like *Déjà Vu* all over again."

SELECTED BIBLIOGRAPHY: Yogi Berra, with Tim Horton, *Yogi: It Ain't Over* (1989); Bob Burnes, "My Favorite Yankee," *The Sporting News Baseball Register 1958* (1958); Joe Garagiola and Dave Anderson, "Yogi of the Yankees," *Reader's Digest* 85

(July 1964): 110–113; David Halberstram, *Summer of '49* (1989); Phil Pepe, *The Wit and Wisdom of Yogi Berra* (1974).

Frank J. Cavaioli

BLACK COACHES ASSOCIATION. The Black Coaches Association (BCA) was founded in 1988 by a group of African American assistant coaches, primarily from the sport of basketball at the Division I level, who were concerned about the lack of head coaching positions available to them and other minorities. The formation of the BCA came on the heels of a national debate concerning the qualifications and dearth of African Americans in coaching and administrative positions at all levels of sport. The genesis of the debate was the now well-known comments by Al Campanis, then vice president of the Los Angeles Dodgers, who told a national television audience on the ABC Television program *Nightline* in April 1987 that blacks lacked "some of the necessities" to serve as field managers. Campanis was forced to resign his position from the Dodgers, but his comments brought forth heated exchanges among members of both races, numerous publications and media attention, and the formation of such organizations as the BCA and Harry Edwards' proposed National Organization on the Status of Minorities in Sports. The BCA, under the continuing leadership of executive director Rudy Washington, head basketball coach at Drake University, initially focused on the hiring practices of intercollegiate athletic programs at predominantly white institutions. Although this is still a topic high on its priority list, the BCA has expanded its agenda to include all policies and decisions in intercollegiate athletics that discriminate against African Americans. More than anything else, the BCA is an activist organization dedicated to assuring equal opportunity in college sport while at the same time raising the consciousness of athletic administrators, society at large, and the media. The BCA, with a membership of approximately 3,000, disseminates information through its *BCA Journal*. Each issue of the journal provides information about coaching positions, changes in rules established by the National Collegiate Athletic Association (NCAA), and a host of other topics. The BCA also holds an annual conference at various sites around the country. The highlights of each conference are the featured speakers and panel discussions that address subjects of particular interest to association members. The BCA has also recently organized an annual basketball game titled the Martin Luther King, Jr./BCA Classic, and it has also made plans to establish local chapters. The most visible incident in the life of the BCA was its confrontation with the NCAA during the early 1990s. In October 1993, thirty basketball coaches from the BCA boycotted the meeting of the National Association of Basketball Coaches and met with the Congressional Black Caucus in Washington, D.C. to protest the NCAA's new guidelines that toughened academic requirements for freshmen athletes, limited coaches' contacts with athletes, and cut the number of basketball scholarships for men. The coaches also threatened to boycott the first day of basketball practice, the upcoming NCAA convention, and the Final Four basketball tournament the following spring. In February 1994, leaders of the BCA and NCAA held a conference call mediated by the community relations service of the U.S. Department of Justice in an attempt to forge a resolution to their differences. The following month representatives of the two groups finally came face-to-face in a nine-hour meeting in Chicago. The outcome of that meeting was a signed agreement between the BCA and NCAA that guaranteed a closer working relationship between the two groups and a promise to ensure equal opportunities for African Americans and other minorities in intercollegiate sport.

SELECTED BIBLIOGRAPHY: Debra E. Blum, "Black Coaches versus the NCAA," *The Chronicle of Higher Education* (26 January 1994): A39–A40; Dana Brooks and Ronald Althouse, "Racial Imbalance in Coaching and Managerial Positions," in Dana Brooks and Ronald Althouse, eds., *Racism in College Athletics: The African-American Athlete's Experience* (1993); Timothy Davis, "The Myth of the Superspade: The Persistence of Racism in College Athletics," *Fordham Urban Law Journal* 22 (1995): 615–698; Charles Farrell, "Scarcity of Blacks in Top Jobs in College Sports Prompts Founding of Group to Monitor Hiring," *The Chronicle of Higher Education* (6 May 1987): 40, 42; Charles S. Farrell, "NCAA Effort to Spur Black-Coach Hirings Gets Mixed Reviews," *The Chronicle of Higher Education* (23 September 1987): A39–A40.

David K. Wiggins

BLACKBURN, CHARLES HENRY ("Jack") (3 May 1883, Versailles, KY– 25 April 1942, Chicago). An African American prizefighter, he became best known as a trainer of Joe Louis.* The son of a minister, as a youth he moved with his family to Terre Haute, Indiana, where he began to box, and later to Pittsburgh and Philadelphia, where he gained notoriety in local clubs as "the Philadelphia Comet." Standing 5'10" tall but weighing only between 132 and 140 pounds, he frequently fought heavier opponents to earn a living. His career was interrupted in 1909, when Blackburn shot his wife and two other persons in a family quarrel. He was convicted of manslaughter and sentenced to serve fifteen years in prison, but he was paroled after four years and eight months because of good behavior and the pleas of friends and supporters (including Booker T. Washington). He then took a position as physical culture director at a Philadelphia health school before becoming a full-time boxing instructor for amateur and professional pugilists. His greatest opportunity came when John Roxborough and Julian Black selected him to train Louis during the early 1930s. For nine years Blackburn schooled the Brown Bomber on boxing techniques, especially balance and punching with accuracy. When Blackburn died, Louis remembered him as a "teacher, father, brother, nurse, best pal to me." He was inducted into the International Boxing Hall of Fame in 1992.

SELECTED BIBLIOGRAPHY: Nat Fleischer, "The Philadelphia Comet," *The Ring* (July 1942): 34–35; "Louis' Ringmaster," *Newsweek* 19 (4 May 1942): 52.

George B. Kirsch

BLANDA, GEORGE (17 September 1927, Youngwood, PA–   ). A football player, he is the son of Slovak American parents. His father, Michael Blanda, was a coal miner. A graduate of Youngwood High School, he played twenty six years of professional football, the longest career of any player in the history of the game. He began his career as an All-American quarterback at the University of Kentucky, then joined the Chicago Bears in 1953. Frustrated after several disappointing seasons and an injury, he prematurely retired from pro football in 1959 but came back to play starting quarterback for the expansion Houston Oilers in 1960. Blanda then led his team to two American Football League (AFL) championships and headed the AFL in passing yardage (3,330) and touchdowns (thirty six) in 1961. He was also named the AFL's player of the year. He continued to lead the league in 1963, 1964, and 1965, with 224, 262, and 186 completed passes. The 1963 total also included a conference-high 3,330 yards. In 1966, Blanda was moved to field goal kicker and led the league in scoring with his 116 points. Blanda was traded to the Oakland Raiders and made one of the most startling comebacks in NFL history. In 1970, when he was forty three years old, he acquired a reputation for miracle comebacks and became the most talked about "old man" in football. The American Football Conference (AFC) and Associated Press both named Blanda the player and male athlete of the year. He finally retired after the 1975 season at the age of forty-eight. By the end of his career, the "old man" had completed 1,911 of 4,007 passes for nearly 27,000 yards and 236 touchdowns. He kicked 943 extra points after touchdowns and made an incredible 335 field goals. When he retired, he held the record for the most points scored (2,002) in the NFL. He was elected to the Pro Football Hall of Fame in 1981.

SELECTED BIBLIOGRAPHY: Ralph Hickock, *A Who's Who of Sports Champions* (1995); Joseph Krajsa, ed., *Slovaks in America: A Bicentennial Study* (1978); *Los Angeles Times*, 8 August 1983, pt. III, 2; Wells Twombly, *Blanda Alive and Kicking* (1972).

Michael J. Kopanic, Jr.

BLAZEJOWSKI, CAROL (29 September 1956, Elizabeth, NJ–   ). A basketball player and executive, she is of Polish descent. She grew up in Cranston, New Jersey, with her father, Leon, a laborer, and her mother, Grace, a bank employee. Her high school did not have a varsity girl's team until her senior year. Upon graduation she chose to stay near home and attend Montclair State College and major in physical education. Montclair State was the only non-scholarship school to make the championship women's final four in 1978. While at Montclair State, Blazejowski was a three-time All-American and was awarded the Wade Trophy (best collegiate female basketball player) the first time this award was presented. She also scored a career total of 3,199 points and averaged 31.7 points per game without the benefit of the three-point shot. She was a silver medalist at the 1979 Pan-American Games and a gold medalist in the World Championship Games. In 1980, Blazejowski was on the U.S. Olympic women's basketball team, but the Moscow Games were boycotted. During the 1980–81 basketball season, she played for the New Jersey Gems of the Women's Professional Basketball League and was the league's leading scorer. During her playing days, Blazejowski was known for her great scoring ability. She once tallied 52 points against Queens College in Madison Square Garden, setting a record for the college ranks at that arena. In 1994 Carol was inducted into the Naismith Basketball Hall of Fame. During the late 1990s she was vice president and general manager of the New York Liberty of the Women's National Basketball Association (WNBA).

SELECTED BIBLIOGRAPHY: *At the Rim: A Celebration of Women's Collegiate Basketball* (1991); Joan S. Hult and Marianna Trekell, *A Century of Women's Basketball: From Frailty to Final Four* (1991); Janet Woolum, *Outstanding Women Athletes* (1992).
Shawn Ladda

BOCCE. Bocce has served as a cherished pastime among Italian Americans for more than a century. The Italian immigrants brought a love of bocce to their adopted country, and the sport appealed to them even more once they were here. Finding themselves in overcrowded cities and with little money, the immigrants found in bocce a sport that did not require an extensive playing area or expensive equipment. As the immigrants assimilated, bocce's popularity spread. America soon discovered what its newest citizens had known all along: although bocce requires a lifetime of practice to play well, anyone can learn the rules and then begin having fun within minutes. Even more importantly, success at bocce does not depend on one's physical attributes; in other words, young people can play against individuals twice their age. Indeed, the true joy of bocce lies in the fact that families as a whole can play together—children with parents and with grandparents. With the Italian heritage placing such importance on the family (and with other Americans wanting familial "quality time"), it can be no wonder that bocce's appeal flourished.

Bocce, often referred to as "Italian lawn bowling," is one of the oldest known sports in human history. An Egyptian hieroglyph dating back to 5200 B.C. clearly depicts two boys playing bocce. The sport would find much popularity among ancient civilizations, especially with the Romans. The ancients used rounded rocks instead of today's composite balls, and the rules of play have changed over the years; but the object in winning has remained unchanged since those Egyptian boys first matched their talents: two sides compete against each other, with one competitor beginning the round by rolling out a small ball (today called the pallino). Each side then tries to get its boccia ball as close to the pallino as possible, either by rolling or throwing the boccia ball. The side whose boccia ball lies closest to the pallino wins.

One of the most prominent bocce players and administrators today is Philip Ferrari of Bensenville, Illinois. Ferrari was the first American to win the 1993 national singles championship, a competition traditionally dominated by Italian-born players. Like countless others, Ferrari learned the game as a youngster, first by watching, then by playing under his father's tutelage. Pointing to the fact that 2 million Americans now play bocce at least once a week, Ferrari refers to bocce as "the best kept secret in sports." Determined to "spread the word" about bocce, Ferrari organized the World Bocce Association (WBA) in August 1993. The WBA serves as a governing body of the sport, providing (for the first time) bocce players with a voice on the national level. The WBA was also created to encourage and improve the sport, by overseeing the rules of play, by promoting bocce through various educational programs, and by sponsoring competitions that benefit the Special Olympics. For more information, contact the World Bocce Association at 1098 West Irving Park Road, Bensenville, IL 60106 or via telephone no. 800\OK-BOCCE (800\652–6223).

SELECTED BIBLIOGRAPHY: Rico C. Daniele, *Bocce: A Sport for Everyone* (1994); Mario Pagnoni, *The Joys of Bocce* (1995).

Philip Ferrari and Ciro C. Poppiti

BOSTON, RALPH (9 May 1939, Laurel, MS–). An African American track-and-field athlete, his mother, Eulalia, was a housemaid. He attended Laurel High School and Tennessee State University, where in 1960 he came from out of nowhere to win the national collegiate long-jump title. Just two months later Boston broke Jesse Owens'* long-standing world record of 26' 11-1/4", becoming the first long jumper to leap over the 27' mark. As one of the most dynamic and spectacular field performers in U.S. Olympic history, Boston won a gold medal in the long jump at the 1960 Olympics in Rome. At the next two Olympic Games Boston was a silver medalist at Tokyo in 1964 and earned a bronze in 1968 at Mexico City. Although not a participant in the controversial black glove salute carried out during the Mexico City Olympics in protest against racism in the United States, Boston supported his teammates Tommie Smith* and John Carlos* by taking the victory stand shoeless and wearing long black socks. During his career, Boston set and tied the world long-jump record five times. His final mark of 27' 4-3/4" was broken by Bob Beamon* during the Mexico City Olympics. He also won six straight National Amateur Athletic Union long-jump championships and an indoor title as well. Boston was also an exceptional high jumper and high hurdler. After his retirement in 1968 he entered the field of college administration and television commentary. In 1974 he was selected a charter member of the National Track Foundation Hall of Fame, and in 1985 he was inducted into the U.S. Olympic Hall of Fame.

SELECTED BIBLIOGRAPHY: Fred Katz, "Record Breaker," *Sport* 33 (February 1962): 38–39; *The Lincoln Library of Sports Champions*, vol. 2 (1975), 108–112; Bill Mallon and Ian Buchanan, *Quest for Gold: The Encyclopedia of American Olympians* (1983); James A. Page, *Black Olympian Medalists* (1991).

Debra A. Henderson

BOUDREAU, LOUIS, JR. (17 July 1917, Harvey, IL–). A baseball player, manager, and broadcaster, his father (Louis, Sr.) was a machinist of French ancestry and minor league baseball player, and his mother (Birdie) was a home-maker of German descent. A graduate of Thornton High School in Harvey, he attended the University of Illinois, where he played baseball and basketball. Boudreau was an outstanding college athlete who lost his senior year of eligibility when he agreed to sign a contract with the Cleveland Indians after graduation. He played two seasons in the minor leagues and became the Indians' regular shortstop in 1940. He excelled defensively, leading the American League in fielding eight times, and hit better than .300 four times. In 1942, at age twenty-four, he was named player-manager, handling these responsibilities well despite his youth. Known as the "Boy Manager," he devised the "Williams shift," a special defensive alignment to counteract Ted Williams. He led the Indians to a World Series championship in 1948 and was voted American League Most Valuable Player. Released by the Indians after the 1950 season, he finished his career with the Boston Red Sox. Boudreau managed Boston and the Kansas City Athletics before beginning a second career as a broadcaster for the Chicago Cubs in 1958. He managed the Cubs briefly in 1960 and then returned to broadcasting until 1988. He was elected to the Baseball Hall of Fame in 1970.

SELECTED BIBLIOGRAPHY: Lou Boudreau, with Ed Fitzgerald, *Player-Manager* (1949); Lou Boudreau, with Russell Schneider, *Lou Boudreau: Covering All the Bases* (1993); "Lou Boudreau," in Martin Appel and Burt Goldblatt, *Baseball's Best: The Hall of Fame Gallery* (1977).

Steven P. Gietschier

BOWMAN, WILLIAM SCOTT ("Scotty") (18 September 1933, Montreal, Quebec, Canada–   ). The National Hockey League's (NHL) winningest coach, he is the only man to direct three different teams to the Stanley Cup. He coached in St. Louis (1967–71), Montreal (1971–79), Buffalo (1979–87), Pittsburgh (1991–93), and Detroit (1993–   ), earning League Coach of the Year honors on two occasions (1977, 1996). A brilliant tactician and intense competitor, Bowman often clashed with his players. After many years of apprenticeship in the Montreal organization Bowman earned his first NHL head coaching job with the expansion St. Louis Blues, leading the team to the Stanley Cup Finals in their first three seasons. Back in his hometown Bowman directed the Canadiens to five Stanley Cup triumphs in eight seasons. His Montreal squads of the late 1970s are recognized as among the best ever seen in the NHL. Bowman led Pittsburgh to the Stanley Cup in 1992 and in 1997 guided Detroit to its first championship in forty-two years. In 1991 the sport's ultimate honor was bestowed upon Bowman as he was elected to the Hockey Hall of Fame in the Builders category. His contribution to hockey in the United States has been noteworthy. The success of the Blues in the early years of their existence helped solidify the game in the city and region, as well as increase the stability of the league in an uncertain time. In addition, Bowman built quality teams in Buffalo,

Pittsburgh, and Detroit, increasing the profile and popularity of the sport in these areas of the country.

SELECTED BIBLIOGRAPHY: Ken Dryden, *The Game* (1983); Stan Fischler, *Coaches* (1994); Dick Irvin, *Behind the Bench* (1993); Dick Irvin, *The Habs: An Oral History of the Montreal Canadiens 1940–80* (1991); Claude Mouton, *The Montreal Canadiens: A Hockey Dynasty* (1980).

Dennis Ryan

BOXING. At first glance, the subject of boxing and ethnicity seems simple enough. The ring is a meritocracy. Men (almost never women, so the ring is a meritocracy that excludes half the population, hardly meritocratic) compete under conditions of total equality to determine who is the most powerful, the quickest, the most skillful—to determine who is the best fighter. Keep winnowing the best from the rest, and a champion emerges. Boxing, then, seems a classic Darwinian struggle that respects only quality, never extraneous factors like ethnic background.

Of course, it's not that simple. True, the ring itself is no respecter of anything but finesse and speed, power and skill. True again, ethnic groups and minorities have indeed found in boxing an expression of their desire to excel, and they have pointed with pride to championships as evidence of group mobility. Benny Leonard,* Primo Carnera, and Jack Johnson* were ethnic heroes who won with their fists what society too often denied in life's larger arenas.

But there is a contradiction here. If American society's claims of equal opportunity for all truly worked, there would be little need for symbolic expressions like boxing. Equality would not require constant reenactment, constant proofs of its reality; it would simply be taken for granted. So while there is much truth in the idea that there has been an ethnic succession to boxing championships—English and Anglo Americans predominating as title-holders, followed in rough order by the Irish, Jews, African Americans, Italians, Latinos, and Asians—we need to ask why this occurs and whether or not it is a sign of social mobility or of a lack of it.

Certainly, boxing, like other sports, has been a marker of Americanization. Generally speaking, immigrants themselves are less likely to become participants or spectators than their descendants (though the Irish were involved in the sport from its American inception because they had been familiar with it back in the old country). John L. Sullivan,* the great heavyweight champion of the late nineteenth century, was a perfect example. When he fought, he wore symbols of both Irish and American nationalism, the Stars and Stripes as well as the green. This Americanization process can be seen even in the names boxers took, especially after the turn of the century. Welterweight champion Ted "Kid" Lewis was born Gershon Mendlehoff in London; middleweight champion Stanley Ketchel* began his life in Grand Rapids as Stanislaus Kiecal; Johnny Dundee, known as "the Scotch Wop" while he reigned as featherweight champion, was christened Giuseppi Carrora in his native Sicily; and lightweight champion Benny Leonard, "the Ghetto Wizard," was born Benjamin Leiner in New York City. Of course, taking an American name expanded a man's potential base of fan support, for his countrymen almost invariably knew his real identity anyway. Equally important, to partake of a sport like boxing—as a fighter or a fan—was to engage in something that seemed quintessentially American and therefore was part of the process of assimilation. But generally, that assimilation was hedged by strong, ongoing ties to the ethnic community, so that John L. Sullivan and his fans did not have to choose—he was an Irish *and* an American champion.

Even if professional boxing were a true meritocracy, we know empirically that generally only the truly disadvantaged choose to enter the ring. Sociological studies have consistently shown that professional prizefighters come from low socioeconomic backgrounds and have limited education. For them, boxing is a job and a very poorly paying one at that. Of course, this is related to the ring's attractiveness to ethnic groups; rarely have those from privileged backgrounds chosen to become professional fighters. Certainly, it would be an exaggeration to say that the ring appeals only to those who have no alternatives, but it is true that boxing draws its practitioners from those whose options in life are limited, and such people tend to come from oppressed ethnic groups. So if boxing seems like a form of social mobility, the perception is shaped by the relative hopelessness of those it attracts. Simply put, few boxers ever made it past local fights, poverty-level wages, and permanent physical disability. Historically, those with limited life chances accepted the dangers and paltry wages associated with the ring.

It is impossible in this small space to give a comprehensive picture of the many subtle ways ethnicity has entwined itself with the ring. But relating several historical examples will at least give some sense of the problem.

Even before men boxed in America, bare-knuckle prizefighting had been hailed as the national sport of England. Great heroes of the ring like James Fig and Jack Broughton helped develop the sport and its rules during the eighteenth century. During these early days, fighters of Irish descent were a presence in the English ring. Moreover, during the late eighteenth century one of the greatest champions of the English ring was Daniel Mendoza, also known as "Mendoza the Jew." The rise of this Sephardic Jew, a relatively small man but extremely quick and scientific, did not signal a general acceptance of Jews in English society. On the contrary, Mendoza became a model in Jewish ghettos of the importance of physical toughness, and many other Jews, following his example, learned the fundamentals of boxing, then used their skills to defend themselves against London's deep-rooted anti-Semitism.

As the eighteenth century became the nineteenth, Americans, too, began to enter the English ring. The two most notable men of this era were African Americans, Bill Richmond and Tom Molineaux.* Both were thoroughly obscure in their home country; boxing simply did not exist in American consciousness. But in England, they became quite prominent. Richmond was born on Staten

Island in 1763, then at the beginning of the American Revolution he came to the attention of General Percy, the duke of Northumberland. Percy made a servant of Richmond, brought him back to England, then secured his apprenticeship to a cabinetmaker. While working as a journeyman in his trade, Richmond became interested in the ring, learned to box (probably with the duke's patronage, as was the custom), and soon engaged in regular ring battles. Never a champion, he nonetheless was known for his quickness at planting a few good blows, then retreating. Richmond relied on his pugilistic fame to help secure customers when he opened a London tavern, the Horse and Dolphin, where he trained hundreds of the English "fancy" (as fight fans were known).

After Richmond had retired from the prize ring, an obscure newcomer walked into the Horse and Dolphin, Tom Molineaux, whom the English journalist Pierce Egan called "the Tremendous Man of Colour." We know very little about Molineaux. Legend has it that he had been a slave in Virginia but that he won an enormous sum of money for his master by defeating another slave in the ring and that Tom was freed as a reward. The story seems unlikely, since there is no evidence that boxing was known in the South. Perhaps he was born a free black. Molineaux picked up the rudiments of fistfighting working among English seamen on the docks of New York City. He learned quickly, and by 1810, having been well prepared by Bill Richmond, he was ready to challenge for the championship of England. What is perhaps most interesting in the English coverage of Molineaux's assault on the title is that it was interpreted less through the lens of race—black versus white—than nationality. The thought that champion Tom Crib might lose to Molineaux in either of their two great fights in 1810 and 1811—Crib won them both—rankled because a foreigner would then hold the title. After these heroic battles, Molineaux slipped into the life of dissipation so common to aging fighters, and he died penniless in Dublin twenty years later.

Not until the middle of the nineteenth century did prizefighting under the bare-knuckle rules become a major sport in America, mostly with working-class men in large cities. But from the very beginning, ethnicity was important, and fights that featured ethnic rivalry attracted considerable attention. Native-born Americans, Englishmen, and Irish immigrants all competed against each other, but there was greatest intensity in American versus Irish rivalries, especially as the potato famine beginning in 1845 brought hundreds of thousands of impoverished Irish to these shores. Sometimes, when two Irishmen fought, one would try to claim the mantle as the real representative of America, so the ethnic rivalry could be perpetuated, a practice that continued in the twentieth century with boxers assuming false ethnic identities—say, a Jew fighting under an Irish name—and even black "white hopes" to stir up excitement.

Boxing rivalries spilled over into street violence, as seen in the 1855 murder of nativist leader and pugilist William Poole at the hands of a gang whose leader was the champion John Morrissey,* an Irish immigrant. But nowhere was the importance of ethnic rivalry more clear than in the first great championship battle ever fought on American soil, the 1849 fight between Tom "Young America" Hyer and James "Yankee" Sullivan of County Cork. The rivalry of these two men for boxing supremacy (Hyer won) went way beyond the ring. Each fighter represented whole factions of men, and those factions were rivals within New York City politics for power. Boxing was crucial to urban street life, which included gangs, saloons, brothels, ward offices—a whole host of plebeian institutions. Boxers and their friends provided muscle in the competition for control of turf, businesses, and political power, all of which divided along ethnic lines.

Anti-Irish sentiment abated considerably by the late nineteenth century, and the rise of a consumer culture made leisure activities like sports more acceptable to Americans. Even boxing was reformed with the new marquis of Queensberry rules, which made prizefighting seem less violent and anarchic. Equally important, the great charisma of champion John L. Sullivan brought new fans to the ring. But even as the native-born versus Irish rivalry waned, the antipathy toward African Americans—made even stronger by the end of Reconstruction in 1877 and a spate of new apartheid laws in the 1880s and 1890s—found expression in the ring. Partly out of fear of losing his championship, partly out of simple racism, Sullivan refused to fight one of the most able contenders of his generation, Peter Jackson, an Australian black of enormous talent. By refusing to mix with blacks, the Irish in effect became white. Moreover, on the same card with Sullivan during his last fight in 1892, George "Little Chocolate" Dixon* won the featherweight crown by thrashing Jack Skelly, and many people, especially in the South, swore it would be the last time a black man raised a hand against a white with impunity.

So once again we see the inherent tension of boxing's mythology of inclusiveness and equal opportunity for all and the desire to limit entry into the ring. Perhaps the most interesting and shameful episode was the story of Jack Johnson. Based on the available films, some boxing experts argue that Johnson was the greatest heavyweight who ever fought. Yet he failed to get a chance to fight for the title until he was thirty years old, simply because others would not fight him. Finally, in 1908, after holding the black heavyweight crown for several years, he badgered champion Tommy Burns into a match. They fought in Burns' homeland, Australia, and Johnson won handily. A larger-than-life figure, the son of a slave who grew up in rigidly segregated Galveston, Texas, Johnson now flaunted his newfound wealth and his serial marriages to white wives. For the next six years, the search for "the great white hope" was on. Johnson defeated a string of white opponents, including former champion James J. Jeffries; after his victories, whites rioted in the black section of towns. While some African Americans were dubious about Johnson's flamboyant life, he was an authentic black hero because he broke so many racial barriers, and he did it publicly. Those who sought revenge against "Papa Jack" got it when the federal government arrested him for violation of the Mann Act. Johnson was accused of transporting a white woman across state lines for immoral purposes. Johnson fled the country on the trumped-up charge and was allowed to return, so the story goes, only when he agreed to deliberately lose his title, which he did to Jess Willard in 1915 in Havana, Cuba.

While Johnson was one of the most egregious examples, the tension between inclusion and exclusion remained intense in the years before World War II. For example, in virtually every year during the 1920s and 1930s, a Jew held at least one major divisional title, certainly a sign of the ring's openness. Yet champion Jack Dempsey* reverted to John L. Sullivan's pattern when he refused to fight black contenders. Moreover, where there was ethnic inclusion, it often came at the cost of demeaning rivalries between groups for the sake of improving the gate. Thus, a local fight between a Jew and a Pole, for example, might be freighted with religious or nationalist antagonisms having nothing to do with the contenders but useful to promoters selling the fight. In recent decades, the manipulation of ethnic rivalries has continued, though most often now with black, Asian, and Latino fighters.

Exclusion of the sort that victimized Jack Johnson grew less common, but the politics of boxing and race remained intense. Joe Louis* became the first black champion since Johnson when he defeated James J. Braddock in 1937. Louis was a quiet and dignified man by nature, but he was also coached by his handlers to maintain a low profile and, above all, never to show emotion when he defeated his white opponents. By not flaunting racial taboos, Louis managed to avoid the troubles that plagued Johnson. Moreover, when he fought German champion Max Schmeling, he did so as a representative of a free nation opposed to Nazi tyranny. As a patriot who served his country during the war and a black man who would not make an issue of race, Louis gained a following among whites; but among African Americans his exploits in the ring made him one of their great culture heroes. Nonetheless, critics have argued that it was only by playing the docile and grateful black that Louis avoided running afoul of American racial mores.

Certainly by the age of Cassius Clay in the 1960s, America had traveled a long way from Jack Johnson's time. Immediately after winning the title in 1964, Clay declared that he had converted to the Nation of Islam, that his old name was a slave name, and that from then on he would be called Muhammad Ali.* His deep faith in his new religion meant supporting the rhetoric of militant black nationalism. Even during this era of the Civil Rights movement, the Nation of Islam was seen as a radical group, and Ali did little to modify that image. The champion was not helped among most white Americans when he refused to be drafted and declared his opposition to the Vietnam War. Every state boxing commission stripped him of his license to fight (an outrageously illegal act). The white vilification of Ali was predictable. But what was less expected was a small, but growing, number of people, white and black, who embraced him as a hero, as a man of courage and conviction standing up for principles. After the Supreme Court overturned Ali's conviction for violating the Selective Service Act, and after he rewon his championship, lost it, then won it again, after countless magnificent fights in the 1970s and after his struggle with Parkinson's disease became public knowledge, Ali's image was rehabilitated. As the twentieth century ended, he was universally acclaimed one of the great American heroes.

So boxing has reflected many of America's complex attitudes toward race and ethnicity. At times, we come close to the ideal of inclusion and equal opportunity that the ring promises; certainly, few people are seriously looking for white hopes anymore. But more disturbingly, boxing remains a place where we see most clearly how ethnicity and poverty come together in America. The presence in the ring of so many men who are at once poor and members of minority groups forces us to realize how the structure of American society remains disturbingly unequal.

SELECTED BIBLIOGRAPHY: Ken Blady, *The Jewish Boxers' Hall of Fame* (1988); Allen Bodner, *When Boxing Was a Jewish Sport* (1997); Elliott J. Gorn, *The Manly Art: Bare-Knuckle Prize Fighting in America* (1986); Thomas Hauser, *The Black Lights: Inside the World of Professional Boxing* (1986); Peter Levine, *Ellis Island to Ebbets Field: Sport and the American Jewish Experience*, chs. 8, 9 (1992); Steven Riess, "A Fighting Chance: The Jewish-American Boxing Experience, 1890–1940," *American-Jewish History* 74 (March 1985): 223–254; Jeffrey Sammons, *Beyond the Ring: The Role of Boxing in American Society* (1990).

Elliott J. Gorn

BRESNAHAN, ROGER PHILIP ("the Duke of Tralee") (11 June 1879, Toledo, OH–4 December 1944, Toledo, OH). A baseball player and the son of Irish immigrants, Bresnahan always maintained that he was born in Tralee, Ireland—hence his nickname. His professional baseball career spanned five decades, ending in 1931 as a coach with the Detroit Tigers. Although Bresnahan was the first catcher in major league baseball history to be inducted into the National Baseball Hall of Fame, he got his start in 1897 as a pitcher with the Washington Senators (National League [NL]), posting a winning record of 4–0. After contract negotiations failed, Bresnahan was sent packing and resurfaced in the majors in 1900, playing in two games with the Chicago (NL) club. The following season he signed with John McGraw's* Baltimore Orioles (American Legue [AL]) and eventually followed McGraw to the National League. Still a player without a set position, Roger served wherever he was needed, playing all nine positions, plus acting as player-manager for five seasons, by the end of his seventeen-year career. In 1905, with the New York Giants, Bresnahan finally became their full-time catcher, bringing to the position his innovative catching techniques, a game strategy, and his leadership abilities. He was constantly showing his inventive side. After he retracted an idea for protective headgear, he inevitably came up with what all catchers might agree to be his best contribution to the game—shinguards. When Bresnahan ended his coaching career with the Detroit Tigers in 1931, his list of accomplishments was impressive; he had been an owner, manager, coach, and player. As a player, he appeared in

1,430 major league games and compiled a lifetime batting average of .279. He was named to the Baseball Hall of Fame in 1945.

SELECTED BIBLIOGRAPHY: Irving A. Leitner, *Baseball: Diamond in the Rough* (1972); Lowell Reidenbaugh, "Roger Bresnahan," *Baseball's Hall of Fame: Cooperstown: Where the Legends Live Forever* (1993); James K. Skipper, Jr., *Baseball Nicknames* (1992), 30; John Thorn and Pete Palmer, eds., *Total Baseball IV: The Official Encyclopedia of Major League Baseball* (1995), 739, 1458, 2332, 2355.

Scot E. Mondore

BROCK, LOUIS CLARK (16 June 1939, El Dorado, AR–   ). An African American baseball player, he is the son of Maud and Paralee Brock. After his parents separated, his mother moved her family to Colliston, Louisiana, and did farmwork and cleaning. Brock attended a segregated grade school in Mer Rouge, Louisiana. As a youth he was inspired while listening to a radio broadcast of a game that featured Jackie Robinson.* While a student at Union High School in Mer Rouge, he excelled in basketball and baseball. After graduation he matriculated at Southern University on a work-study program and earned a scholarship beginning with his sophomore year. During his junior year he helped Southern win the National Association of Intercollegiate Athletics baseball championship. After college he signed with the Chicago Cubs, reaching the major leagues late in the 1961 campaign. Although Brock's performance was only average during his first two and half years, his productivity improved dramatically after the Cubs traded him to the St. Louis Cardinals in mid-June 1964. He starred with the Cardinals for the remainder of his nineteen-year career as a steady hitter and run scorer and especially as a feared base stealer. In 1977 he surpassed Ty Cobb's long-standing career record of 892 steals, and his total of 938 at his retirement has been exceeded by only Rickey Henderson. As a major leaguer he played in 2,616 games and registered 3,023 hits. He also batted .391 in three World Series with the Redbirds (1964, 1967–68). Active in charitable causes while a player, he helped raise funds for scholarships for needy youth, and he has received several community service awards. He was inducted into the National Baseball Hall of Fame in 1985.

SELECTED BIBLIOGRAPHY: Arthur R. Ashe, Jr., *A Hard Road to Glory: A History of the African-American Athlete since 1946*, vol. 3 (1988); Lou Brock and Franz Schulze, *Stealing Is My Game* (1976); Bob Broeg, *Redbirds: A Century of Cardinal Baseball* (1981); Bob Fortus, "Success Story: Lou Brock's Climb to the Hall of Fame," *Baseball Digest* 44 (November 1985): 39–44.

George B. Kirsch

BROWN, EDWARD DUDLEY ("Brown Dick") (1850, Lexington, KY–24 March 1906, Lexington, KY). He was an African American thoroughbred trainer. Thoroughbred breeder R. A. Alexander purchased Brown at the Lexington slave market when the boy was eight years old. A protégé of Ansel Williamson,* Brown, by the time he was sixteen, was one of the two best jockeys in the country. By age twenty-two, he had outgrown the saddle. In 1874 he began training the first of many champion runners, including the 1877 Kentucky Derby winner Baden Baden for Daniel Swigert, for whom he had ridden the 1870 Belmont Stakes winner Kingfisher. He was leading trainer at Churchill Downs' Spring Meets in 1877, 1881, and 1882 and leading Fall Meet trainer in 1875, 1878, 1881, 1884, and 1885. Before his death he trained, raced, then sold the 1896 and 1898 Kentucky Derby winners. In 1895, *The Thoroughbred Record* stated: " 'Brown Dick' is one of the richest colored men in Kentucky, being worth $75,000 surely and $100,000 probably, with nearly all his assets in cash." At his death Brown, a generous man, was nearly broke. When Brown was inducted into the Racing Hall of Fame in 1984—only one of three African Americans ever accorded that honor—*The Blood-Horse* called him "one of the most celebrated trainers of any era."

SELECTED BIBLIOGRAPHY: Alexander Mackay-Smith, *The Race Horses of America 1832–1872: Portraits and Other Paintings by Edward Troye* (1981); Lynn S. Renau, *Racing around Kentucky* (1995).

Lynn S. Renau

BROWN, JAMES NATHANIEL (17 February 1936, St. Simons Island, GA–   ). A star African American running back in football, he was the son of Swinton Brown and Theresa Brown. His father, an inveterate gambler, left home when Brown was two years old. His mother went north to find a job, leaving Brown to be raised by his grandmother and aunt. He went to school in a seg-regated two-room shack. When he was eight, his mother sent for him from Manhasset, New York, where she had found a permanent position as a domestic servant. As a high school athlete he won thirteen varsity letters and received forty-five scholarship offers, plus an invitation to play minor league baseball for the New York Yankees. He accomplished all of this despite the fact that in his youth gang activities became a dominant force in his life. Although Syracuse University did not offer Brown a scholarship, a group of Syracuse alumni raised funds to support him during his freshman year at Syracuse. As a result of his sterling play Brown received a "full ride" for the rest of his time at Syracuse. At Syracuse in 1953 he was the only black freshman on the football team. Brown described the time and place as a "crossroads of segregation." While at Syracuse Brown was a dominant ball carrier. In 1956 as a senior he scored forty-three points against Colgate, and at the end of that season in the Cotton Bowl he ran for 132 yards and scored twenty-one points against Texas Christian University. As an Orangeman he also participated in basketball, track and field, and lacrosse. He later was elected to the National Lacrosse Hall of Fame. At 6' 2" and 232 pounds Brown had the ideal running back physique. In nine seasons (1957–65) with the Cleveland Browns he won rushing titles on eight occasions. Brown was inducted into the Pro Football Hall of Fame in 1971. When he left the game to try his hand at a Hollywood film career, he held the following records: career rushing yards (12,312), single-season rushing yards (1,863), single-game rushing yards (237), average yards per game (104.4), average yards per carry (5.22), 100-yard rushing games (58), 1,000-yard rushing seasons (7), and touchdowns (126). Many football pundits speak of Brown as very possibly the game's greatest running back. After his retirement Brown became an actor in a series of "B" films. He succeeded because of his unique charisma, his astounding physique, and the demand for a black power sex figure. Between 1965 and 1984 Brown was involved in a series of nasty criminal cases. In three of these incidents women accused him of assault and battery. But it is also true that Brown's positive social impact was considerable. In 1987 he started the Amer-I-Can program specifically designed to turn recidivist gang members into contributing members of society.

SELECTED BIBLIOGRAPHY: Donald Bogle, *Toms, Coons, Mulattoes, Mammies and Bucks: An Interpretive History of Blacks in American Films* (1989), 220–223; Brad Herzog, *The 100 Most Important People in American Sports History* (1995), 232–235; Peter King, "Rushing toward a Record Book," *Sports Illustrated* 81 (10) (5 September 1994): 134; Peter King, "Jim Brown," *Sports Illustrated* 81 (12) (19 September 1994): 57–58; Joan Mellen, *Big Bad Wolves: Masculinity in the American Cinema* (1977), 331; Materials received from Saleem Choudhry, Pro Football Hall of Fame Library-Research Center, Canton, OH.

Scott A.G.M. Crawford

BUFFALO GERMANS. The first basketball team to achieve national prominence, the Buffalo Germans originated in 1895 as a club for boys under fourteen years of age at the German Young Men's Christian Association (YMCA) on Genesee Street in Buffalo. The founder of this fabled five and its coach was the Y's physical education director, Fred Burkhardt, who had learned the sport under the tutelage of James Naismith* at the YMCA training school at Springfield, Massachusetts. By 1900 the squad had compiled a record of eighty-seven wins and only six losses and claimed the championship of western New York state. By 1901 the boys had matured into young men, and they earned their first major amateur title by winning the Amateur Athletic Union championship at the Pan-American Exposition, held in their hometown. Their roster included captain Al Heerdt, George Redlein, William Rohde, Henry Faust, John Maier, and Ed Miller. Their next significant victory came at the third modern Olympic Games, held in 1904 at St. Louis as part of the celebration of the centennial of the Louisiana Purchase. Although basketball was only a demonstration and not an official medal sport at those Olympics, the basketball tournament did attract clubs from around the nation. The Germans swept all five of their games, including a hotly contested finale against the reigning YMCA national champions, the Central Y of Chicago.

During the following winter of 1904–5 the club turned professional and undertook an extensive tour, billing themselves as "world's champions." For the next two decades the Germans barnstormed across western New York and north-western Pennsylvania, with occasional forays into Ohio and northeastern New York. Their itinerary was limited because all of the players had regular jobs in Buffalo. For the first ten years of the club's professional era its roster was remarkably stable, with Heerdt, Faust, and Miller still active in 1915. Partly because the club never joined one of the fledgling pioneer professional leagues (probably because of transportation costs), the Germans ran up an incredible record. Playing most of their games against YMCA, college, semipro, and small-town teams, the Germans racked up victory after victory. Between 1908 and 1911 the Buffalo five won 111 consecutive games, finally losing to a strong professional squad representing the Thirty-First Separate National Guard of Herkimer, New York.

The Buffalo Germans continued to barnstorm until the mid-1920s, and it finally joined a professional league when it entered the new American Basketball League for the 1925–26 season. Renamed the Buffalo Bisons, the club had a new generation of players but was still managed by Al Heerdt. The team struggled through a losing campaign and dropped out of the circuit after only one year. The legendary five eventually expired in 1929. Over the course of its long history the Buffalo Germans won 792 games, lost 86, and set a very high standard for team unity, discipline, and excellence. The club was inducted into the Basketball Hall of Fame as a team in 1961.

SELECTED BIBLIOGRAPHY: John Devaney, *The Story of Basketball* (1976); Joe Jares, *Basketball: The American Game* (1971); James Naismith, *Basketball: Its Origin and Development* (1941); Robert W. Peterson, *Cages to Jump Shots: Pro Basketball's Early Years* (1990).

George B. Kirsch

BULGARIANS. The Bulgarian community in the United States is one of the smallest and most disunited ethnic groups in the country, with minimal participation in the political, cultural, and sporting life of the nation. After the breakdown of the political system in Bulgaria during the early 1990s, approximately 35,000 Bulgarians emigrated to the United States. Most of those people were young and ambitious, with a high degree of education and professional training. Their arrival changed the outlook of the Bulgarian community in the United States. After 1991 two Bulgarian newspapers and a Bulgarian radio station were established in the United States. Consequently, the arrival of so many young Bulgarians led to the first Bulgarian sporting club in the United States—the Bulgarian Lions. Organized on 5 November 1993 in Chicago, it joined the Illinois indoor soccer championship during the same year. The founders of the team were Piter Petrov, George Todorov, Piter Toptchev, and Traitcho Spasov, with the financial support of George Matchev. The Lions' first official game was played at the indoor soccer stadium in Palatine, a suburb of Chicago, against Northwest Union. The Bulgarian team won by a score of 6–1. The Lions players in this historical game were Piter Toptchev, Angel Pepeliankov, Lazar Spasov, Sam Todorov, Marko Ratchev, Marin Purlev, Symon Vladimirov, and Steve Fihpov. In the mid-1990s, Piter Toptchev, a former goalkeeper for the Bulgarian national soccer team, became coach of the Bulgarian Lions. Their team uniform consists of white socks, green shorts, and green shirts. In 1994 the Lions achieved a rank of third in the general classification of soccer clubs in the United States. The Bulgarian American soccer community received a major boost in 1994, when the Bulgarian national team reached the semifinals of the World Cup tournament, winding up fourth in the world.

SELECTED BIBLIOGRAPHY: Nikolay Altanov, *The Bulgarian-Americans* (1979); Claudia Carlson and David Allen, *The Bulgarian Americans* (1990).

Orlin Krumov

BUTKUS, RICHARD (9 December 1942, Chicago–). A football player, his parents, John Butkus and Emma Goodoff, were Lithuanian. He attended Chicago Vocational High School, where he played fullback and linebacker on defense. Graduating in 1961, Butkus accepted a football scholarship at the University of Illinois under coach Pete Elliott. There he played at both offensive center and defensive linebacker positions. Named twice to the All-American team, he was chosen as the American Football Coaches' Association Player of the Year in 1964, and he cocaptained the 1965 College All-Star Team, which played the Cleveland Browns. He was the number one draft choice of the Chicago Bears in 1965 and played middle linebacker in his rookie year, leading the Bears in fumble recoveries and pass interceptions and being named to the middle linebacker position on the All-Pro team and the Pro-Bowl team. During his nine years with the Chicago Bears, Chicago never had a championship season, but Butkus was named to the All-NFL (National Football League) team seven of those nine years and played in eight Pro Bowl games. He was a good student in college and has been described as one of the smartest, fastest, and fiercest persons ever to have played his position. Injuring his knee during the 1970 season, he continued to play hurt until 1973, when, in midseason, he retired. Butkus has been called the premier linebacker of his era and was inducted in the Pro Football Hall of Fame in 1973 and the College Football Hall of Fame in 1983.

SELECTED BIBLIOGRAPHY: Robert W. Billings and Richard Butkus, *Stop Action* (1972); George Vass, *George Halas and the Chicago Bears* (1971); *Great Athletes of the Twentieth Century—Football* (1992); *TSN Football Register* (1974).

Lawrence Huggins

C

CAMPANELLA, ROY ("Campy") (19 November 1921, Philadelphia–26 June 1993, Woodland Hills, CA). An African American baseball player, he was the son of fruit and vegetable market owner John and Ida Campanella. He began his career in the Negro Leagues* in 1937, where he competed until 1945. He was one of five black players signed by Brooklyn Dodgers executive Branch Rickey before the 1946 season. He reached the major leagues with the Brooklyn Dodgers in 1948 and remained with that team until 1957. Campanella was the first black catcher to break baseball's color line. He was named the Most Valuable Player in the National League in 1951, 1953, and 1955. He led the league in runs batted in (RBIs) in 1953 and was selected as an All-Star catcher 1947 through 1954 and again in 1956. He was elected to the Hall of Fame in 1969. He was severely injured in an automobile accident in January 1958 and became a quadriplegic as a result. An exhibition game on 7 May 1959 to benefit him drew 93,103 fans, the largest crowd in major league history. Although hampered by injuries to his hands and legs throughout his career, he was considered the standard by which catchers were measured, not only for his era but for all time. Despite being confined to a wheelchair for thirty-five years he coached Dodger catchers for two decades. He also served on the Dodgers Community Services Staff, making innumerable appearances before the public.

SELECTED BIBLIOGRAPHY: Roy Campanella, *It's Good to Be Alive* (1959); Donald Dewey and Nicholas Acocella, *The Biographical History of Baseball* (1995); Gene Schoor, *Roy Campanella: Man of Courage* (1959); Mike Shatzkin, *The Ballplayers* (1990); Dick Young, *Roy Campanella* (1952).

Clyde Partin

CANADIANS. The Canadian American contribution to the sporting culture of the United States is a subject fraught with ambiguity. Many persons would challenge the notion that Canadians are a distinct ethnic group. Canada as a nation has struggled to support the sovereignty of different cultures, ethnicities, and even nationalities within a unified sociopolitical framework. For this reason, the concept of a uniquely Canadian ethnic contribution to American sporting culture through the immigration or prolonged residency of Canadians to the United States verges on being a political anachronism. Apart from this, however, Canada is recognized around the world for some of its unique sporting traditions. For example, the popular characterizations of boyhood in Canada are steeped with references to hockey. Regardless of the country's inconsistent record at the Winter Olympic Games, a perception exists that Canada is a haven for winter sports. Indeed, most Canadians do not shy away from the out-of-doors during their long, cold winters. Also, Canadians hold their own perceptions about the link between national sporting traditions and national identity. For example, whether imagined or real, the ties between their modern athletic traditions and those of the North American Indians linger in the imaginations of many Canadian sportspersons, regardless of their ethnic heritage. The ongoing debate about the status of lacrosse as the national sport of Canada is a perfect example of this phenomenon. Similar ethnic/cultural myths prevail and embellish present-day experiences in activities such as canoeing, kayaking, and snowshoeing.

Lacrosse provides an interesting case study of the importation of a Canadian game into the United States. During the middle decades of the nineteenth century William George Beers and other upper-class Montreal residents of British ancestry adapted the Native American game of stickball to create the modern version of lacrosse. That pastime soon made inroads into the United States, where a few amateur and collegiate clubs fielded teams during the late 1870s. During the twentieth century lacrosse established itself on the high school and college levels, while a modified form of indoor play achieved a modest following as a professional arena sport. Lacrosse was also taken up by American women in many of the prominent women's colleges in the northeastern states. There, English, Canadian, and American headmistresses who were trained physical educators introduced the sport to their students.

It is impossible to discuss all of the individual Canadians who deserve recognition for their enduring contributions to American sports. This entry focuses on a select number of persons in several general categories: physical educators and sport scientists of the late nineteenth and early twentieth centuries; amateur athletes; university and college students; professional athletes; and business people who have become involved with professional sport in the United States.

Perhaps the best-known Canadian who moved to the United States and contributed significantly to American sporting culture is the man credited with the invention of the game of basketball. James Naismith* was born in 1861 in Almonte, Ontario, a Scottish community in the historic Ottawa Valley. He received postsecondary education at McGill University in Montreal and trained to be a Presbyterian minister. His theological studies led to an association with the Young Men's Christian Association (YMCA), which resulted in a teaching po-

sition at Springfield College in Massachusetts. There, in 1891, he drafted the
first rules and orchestrated the first game of basketball. The fact that Naismith
began his physical education career at Springfield College reflected the strong
Scottish and Presbyterian ethic that was part of his small-town Ontario upbringing. A self-proclaimed, muscular Christian, he was greatly influenced by the
doctrine of Amos Alonzo Stagg. After Naismith married, he completed a degree
in medicine, but he was not especially interested in becoming a practicing physician. Ultimately, Naismith and his family moved to the University of Kansas,
where he was hired as director of the chapel, physician, head of athletics and
physical education, and, naturally, basketball coach. He died in 1939.

Naismith's impact on American sporting culture is closely linked with another
prominent Canadian physical educator who literally followed in the footsteps of
the father of basketball. Robert Tait McKenzie was a lifelong friend and col-
league of Naismith's. Both men came from the same tiny Ontario town of Almonte; born in 1867, McKenzie was six years younger than Naismith. He also
attended the prestigious McGill University in Montreal, where he earned a B.A.
and a graduate degree in medicine. Much of McKenzie's early career mirrored
that of Naismith. His intellectual horizons expanded beyond medicine as he
taught anatomy and designed physical education programs for students at Mc-
Gill. He also became interested in the arts, especially sculpture, that illustrated
the anatomy of the human body. Almost immediately, his sculptures gained
international recognition. In 1904, he found the ideal outlet for his interests in
medicine, physical education, and art at the University of Pennsylvania, where
he became a professor in the faculty of medicine and director of the department
of physical education. His pioneering enthusiasm for physical education, medicine, and the aesthetics of the human body made a lasting impression on American as well as Canadian culture. In Philadelphia he was instrumental in
establishing the city's playground system. Internationally, he was recognized by
such illustrious organizations as the International Olympic Committee when he
submitted a sculpture in the first art competitions associated with the modern
Olympic Games in Stockholm, 1912. There he won a bronze medal. R. Tait
McKenzie died in 1938.

The late nineteenth and early twentieth centuries witnessed the rise of international amateur sport. Between 1894 and 1908 the quadrennial Olympic Games
festival did not have an established participation format that would enable athletes to compete freely as individual amateurs and still represent their native
countries. Eventually, these growing pains brought about the formation of National Olympic Committees. Before this occurred, however, several Olympic
athletes simply competed for the teams or institutions that were the most con-
venient. For example, a Canadian named George Washington Orton won the
steeplechase in the Olympic Games of Paris, 1900. At the time, he was a graduate student at the University of Pennsylvania and was selected and competed
for the American team in Paris. As a Canadian, Orton's sporting contributions
to the United States are not completely unique. Certainly, many Canadians were

traveling south for postsecondary education and participated in the athletic programs of their colleges and universities. Orton's role is exceptional because of
his athletic talent and his winning performance at the Olympic Games. His gold
medal was added to the American tally. This occurred because Canada did not
have an Olympic team competing at the Paris Olympic Games of 1900. Orton
was no traitor to Canada's international athletic reputation; he simply took advantage of a situation south of the border that was not available to him in
Canada. Canada's first official Olympic Games delegation was not assembled
until 1908 for the games in London, England.

For generations, sportspersons of Canadian origin have made significant contributions to American college and university sports. The American varsity
system, which openly permits institutions to recruit and provide athletic scholarships, is very different from the system in Canada, where, traditionally, athletic
scholarships have not been condoned. One very prominent Canadian who traveled south to pursue academics and athletics is Duncan McNaughton, who won
the high-jump gold medal at the Olympic Games in Los Angeles, 1932. Mc-
Naughton moved to the United States to study geology at the University of
Southern California and Cal Tech. He won the U.S. high-jump championship
and set a state record during his university years. After completing a Ph.D. in
geology, he remained a resident of the United States. Thousands of Canadians
have followed a path similar to that of McNaughton. A more recent example,
from the 1980s, are the Gait twins, Gary and Paul, from British Columbia.
Following distinguished junior lacrosse careers in Canada, the twins went to
Syracuse University and led that school's field lacrosse team to a number of
National Collegiate Athletic Association (NCAA) championships. Today, the
Gait twins are credited with the revived interest in American intercollegiate field
lacrosse. Many Canadians who have accepted American athletic scholarships
have returned to Canada, while many others have remained in the United States
and have pursued careers in and out of sport. For Canadian varsity athletes, the
boundary between the United States and Canada has been relatively fluid.

Another group of Canadian sportspersons for whom the border between Canada and the United States has also been rather permeable is professional athletes.
Of those who have moved across the border (and at times back again) with
relative ease, hockey players have made the greatest and most sustained contribution to American sporting culture. Like lacrosse, hockey emerged in the latter
decades of the 1800s and quickly gained enthusiastic followers in the United
States. But unlike lacrosse, hockey evolved into a popular professional sport
during the early 1900s. Many Canadian hockey players and enthusiasts became
disillusioned with, or were simply expelled from, the rigid amateur system that
dominated the governance of Canadian hockey well into the second decade of
the twentieth century. These players found that they could make a living for
themselves playing hockey in several of the northern states, especially in Michigan and Pennsylvania. One example of such a player was John Liddell Macdonald Gibson, who organized a semipro team in Houghton, Michigan. Gibson

was a Canadian-trained dentist who moved to Detroit to set up his practice. With the help of a local entrepreneur, he established the Portage Lakers and helped give American hockey a much needed boost.

Lester Patrick, who was born in Quebec but moved to Vancouver early in his adult life, eventually relocated to New York City as coach, sometime player, and general manager of the New York Rangers. His tenure with this club lasted twenty years and helped New York City become recognized as a true "hockey town." Prior to his New York years, Lester Patrick made another very important contribution to the sport of hockey in the United States. While living in Vancouver between 1919 and 1926, Patrick helped form professional hockey teams in Spokane and Seattle, Washington. Today, the National Hockey League (NHL) honors Lester Patrick, a Canadian who resided in the United States for most of his professional career, with the Lester Patrick Memorial Trophy for outstanding contributions to hockey in the United States.

Several generations after Lester Patrick's playing career ended, another Canadian was awarded this prestigious trophy for his contribution to hockey in the United States. Bobby Hull, the patriarch of a Canadian hockey dynasty, was born in 1939 and spent a considerable period of his professional career in the United States. Like many of the prominent players of his generation, Hull had a long and dedicated career with one of the classic NHL teams, the Chicago Black Hawks (1957–72). Hull's involvement with the formation of the rival World Hockey Association in 1972 resulted in his exclusion from Team Canada in the famous Canada/Soviet Union Hockey Series. That same year, Hull was also passed over by the Canadian Olympic hockey program. In the end, Hull donned an American jersey and played for the United States' Olympic hockey team in the Winter Olympic Games in Sapporo, Japan.

Throughout this century the migration of Canadian hockey players to the United States has never ceased. In most cases, their professional NHL careers have taken them initially to the United States, where, when their playing days were over, they stayed. Ted Lindsay and a number of other prominent players of his generation are responsible for the formation of the NHL Players' Association. Lindsay played thirteen seasons with the Detroit Red Wings and was traded to the Chicago Black Hawks for the 1958–59 season. His tenacious character resulted in many nicknames, including "Terrible Ted," "Tempestuous Ted," and "Forever Furious." This tenacity was perhaps one of the attributes that enabled Lindsay to spearhead the controversial formation of the NHL Players' Association. For a number of years after his playing days were over, he coached the Detroit Red Wings. He later remained a resident of Detroit. Of the same era as Lindsay, Gordie Howe* was equally dedicated to the formation of the NHL Players' Association. Like Lindsay, his professional career resulted in his becoming a long-term resident of Detroit. Howe was distinguished as recipient of the Lester Patrick Memorial Trophy. The list of Canadian hockey players who have moved to the United States is long, indeed. In recent decades, the most influential player is, unquestionably, Wayne Gretzky, nicknamed the

"Great One." Some attribute the rebirth of fan interest in hockey in the south-western United States to the historic trade that sent Gretzky from the Edmonton Oilers to the Los Angeles Kings.

As either intercollegiate or professional athletes, Canadian women have had many fewer opportunities to move to the United States for the express purpose of pursuing sports careers. This does not mean, of course, that Canadian women have not moved to the United States and left their mark on American sporting culture. One simply needs to look in different places to find evidence of these contributions. Canada's post–World War II pride and joy, Barbara Ann Scott, moved to the United States almost immediately after she won the gold medal in the women's figure skating competition at the Winter Olympic Games in St. Moritz, 1948. There, she pursued a professional show business career as a figure skater, married an American, and settled in Chicago. She has continued to live an active, sporting lifestyle and is especially involved in equestrian sports. With the recent phenomenon of televised professional figure skating competitions, Barbara Ann Scott returned to the limelight as a judge and a referee for these new media spectacles. She brought a unique personality to professional figure skating that reflected the values of what seems to have been a more innocent and certainly less complex sporting world for American and Canadian women. While Barbara Ann Scott seems to have lingered in the collective memories of Americans and Canadians, other Canadian women figure skaters have relocated to the United States and made equally valuable contributions to American sport. One prominent Canadian is Barbara Wagner, who, with her partner, Bob Paul, won the world pairs figure skating championship four times between 1957 and 1960. Wagner and Paul also won a gold medal at the Winter Olympic Games in Squaw Valley, 1960. Following this success, the pair skated professionally for a number of years. After splitting up as athletes, both Wagner and Paul pursued separate careers as figure skating instructors, coaches, and choreographers. Coincidentally, both Wagner and Paul worked in California, where each of them has coached a number of American skaters who have gone on to win world and Olympic championships.

In the ranks of professional athletes, Canada's women golfers have certainly made an impact on sporting life in the United States. The advantageous climate of the southern United States and indeed the very nature of the Ladies Professional Golf Association (LPGA) tour have encouraged a number of Canada's best golfers to establish residences south of the Canadian border. Possibly the most influential athlete of this group is Sandra Post, who resides in Boynton, Florida. Among her many golfing honors, Post was voted Rookie of the Year for the LPGA in 1968. In total, Post won eight LPGA tournaments.

Many Canadians have also migrated to the United States to pursue the mythically favored American pastime, baseball. Most of the notable Canadian baseball players distinguished themselves in the late nineteenth and early twentieth centuries. That era produced such players as George "Mooney" Gibson and "Chewing Gum" John O'Brien. Gibson played for the Pittsburgh Pirates between

1904 and approximately 1920, and O'Brien played on a number of teams in the National League between 1891 and 1899. During this century, Dick Fowler was one of the most successful professional Canadian ballplayers in the United States, playing nine seasons in the American League, beginning in 1941. More recently, Ferguson Jenkins* earned admission to the Baseball Hall of Fame in 1991 for nineteen seasons of brilliant pitching, mostly with the Chicago Cubs.

Guy Lombardo, of Guy Lombardo and his Royal Canadians fame, seems an unlikely candidate for this entry. While his career as a big band leader is, perhaps, his greatest source of notoriety, he was also an inductee into the U.S. Speedboat Hall of Fame. Lombardo, who was born in London, Ontario, in 1902, was an accomplished and winning speedboat racer between 1946 and 1956. He won international competitions and the U.S. National Championships and set various speed records in the propeller-driven category of boats. He also served as secretary for the American Power Boat Association. For the greater part of his life, Lombardo was a resident of Freeport, New York.

It is important to note that several Canadian businessmen have moved to the United States and with their entrepreneurial savvy contributed to American sporting culture. For example, Jack Kent Cooke brought professional hockey to Los Angeles in 1967. Cooke, who hailed from Toronto, spent most of his life as a sports entrepreneur in the United States. His business ventures extended into the National Basketball Association (NBA), NHL, and major league baseball. Another Canadian who joined the ranks of professional sport franchise owners in the United States is Pat Bowlen. Bowlen, once a lawyer from Edmonton, moved to the United States and bought the Denver Broncos football team.

Finally, the extent to which Canadian athletes, coaches, physical educators, and sport entrepreneurs have contributed unique ethnic qualities to American sport is debatable. In fact, the multiethnic makeup of the two countries is very similar. Perhaps Canadian sportpersons who move to the United States to pursue sporting careers do so because they share more things in common with American sporting culture than differences.

SELECTED BIBLIOGRAPHY: Frank Cosentino, *Almonte's Brothers of the Wind: R. Tait McKenzie and James Naismith* (1996); Cleve Dheensaw, *Lacrosse 100: One Hundred Years of Lacrosse in B.C.* (1990); Bob Ferguson, *Who's Who in Canadian Sport* (1977); David McDonald and Lauren Drewery, *For the Record, Canada's Greatest Women Athletes* (1981); Alan Metcalfe, *Canada Learns to Play: The Emergence of Organized Sport, 1807–1914* (1987); Don Morrow, Mary Keyes, Wayne Simpson, Frank Cosentino, and Ron Lappage, *A Concise History of Sport in Canada* (1989).

Douglas A. Brown

CAPONI, DONNA (29 January 1945, Detroit–   ). A golfer of Italian descent, as a girl she learned to play the sport from her golf pro dad, Harry, and, under his tutelage, won the Los Angeles Junior title in 1956 at age eleven. She turned professional immediately after graduating from high school. By 1965, she had joined the Ladies Professional Golf Association (LPGA). During her career she won twenty-four major tournaments, including the U.S. Women's Open in 1969 and the LPGA Championship in 1979. She also scored two LPGA holes in one. Her LPGA victories brought her fame and over $1.3 million. She is a member of the Italian American Sports Hall of Fame. In the 1990s Caponi was also employed as a women's and men's golf tournament analyst for the Golf Channel, and she served on the Advisory Panel of the Family Golf Association (Hopewell, New Jersey).

SELECTED BIBLIOGRAPHY: Ira Berkow, "Changes Are for the Better," *New York Times Biographical Service* 12 (August 1981): 1039–1041; "1997 Record Book," *Golf Digest* 48 (January 1997): 161–179; Barry McDermott, "Prima Donna by a Nose," *Sports Illustrated* 54 (22 June 1981): 66–69; Sarah Pileggi, "Donna Was Prima in the Dinah," *Sports Illustrated* 52 (14 April 1980): 54–57.

Philip M. Montesano

CAREW, RODNEY ("Rod") (1 October 1945, Gatfin, Canal Zone–). A baseball player, he is the son of Olga and Eric Carew. His father was a maintenance worker on the Panama Canal. His mother brought her children to New York City when Rod was a teenager, and he had little contact with his father after that. Rod honed his baseball skills playing sandlot ball while working and attending George Washington High School. He signed with the Minnesota Twins organization in 1964, and after minor league seasons in Florida (as the first black player on the Orlando team) and North Carolina, he joined the Twins in 1967. In nineteen major league seasons, twelve with Minnesota (1967–78) and seven with the California Angels (1979–85), Carew won seven American League batting titles and had four 200-hit seasons and fifteen straight seasons of over .300 batting averages. His career records included a .328 batting average and 3,053 base hits. He played in eleven All-Star Games during his Minnesota years and four more with California. Carew was known for his hitting consistency rather than power, although he hit fourteen homers in the 1975 and 1977 seasons. A second baseman during his early career, injuries forced him to shift to first base after the mid-1970s, and he also served as designated hitter in this later period. In 1969 he stole home seven times, tying a record set in 1946. For six years after retiring at the end of the 1985 season Carew operated a batting school for children through major leaguers. In 1992 he became batting instructor for the California Angels. Carew grew up speaking Spanish and belonged to the Episcopalian Church. However, his wife is Jewish, and after his marriage, Rod observed Jewish holidays, including not playing on Yom Kippur. In 1995–96 his oldest daughter's unsuccessful battle with leukemia received national attention, and Carew's public appeals yielded a doubling of the bone marrow registry. Carew was American League Rookie of the Year in 1967 and league Most Valuable Player (MVP) in 1977, and he was inducted into the National Baseball Hall of Fame in January 1991, his first eligible year.

SELECTED BIBLIOGRAPHY: Larry Batson, *Rod Carew* (1977); Rod Carew, with Frank Pace and Armen Keteyian, *Rod Carew's Art and Science of Hitting* (1986); Ron Fimrite, "Portrait of the Artist as a Hitter," *Sports Illustrated* 56 (1983): 74–88; Ralph Hickock, *A Who's Who of Sports Champions: Their Stories and Records* (1995).

Richard V. McGehee

CARLOS, JOHN (5 June 1945, New York City–   ). An African American track athlete, he withdrew from East Texas State University because of racial discrimination and enrolled at San Jose State College. His athletic career is one hidden in the shadows of his 1968 Olympic teammate Tommie Smith.* For the most part Carlos is known (and will always be known) as the other 200-meter sprinter in the defiant medal stand pose at the 1968 Mexico City Olympics, as he received his bronze medal for third place. After this demonstration to protest racial injustice in the United States, Carlos and Smith were ejected from the Olympic Village by the International Olympic Committee. Carlos was not nearly as outspoken as Smith, and he gained notice mostly as an afterthought to him. Although Carlos is often seen as merely a sidekick to Smith, he did have an impressive career before and after the famous episode. His best performance was a time of 19.7 seconds, using illegal, spiked shoes for the 200-meter event at the 1968 Olympic trials. In 1969 he was Amateur Athletic Union (AAU) and National Collegiate Athletic Association (NCAA) champion at 200 meters and 220 yards, and he also tied world records in the 60-yard and 100-yard dashes. In 1970 he tried unsuccessfully to pursue a career in professional football. In 1977 he founded the John Carlos Youth Development Program in Los Angeles, a program aimed at stressing the importance of a solid education over big-time athletic competition. He also served on the 1984 Los Angeles Olympic Organizing Committee.

SELECTED BIBLIOGRAPHY: Arthur R. Ashe, Jr., *A Hard Road to Glory: A History of the African-American Athlete since 1946*, vol. 3 (1988), 190, 193–195, 198; Harry Edwards, *The Revolt of the Black Athlete* (1969); Reid M. Hanley, *Who's Who in Track and Field* (1973).

Earl Smith and George B. Kirsch

CARNESECCA, LUIGI ("Lou") (5 January 1925, New York City–   ). An Italian American college and pro basketball coach, he guided St. John's University to a 526–200 record in twenty-four seasons. The son of Alfredo Carnesecca, a delicatessen proprietor, and his wife, Adele, he was raised on Manhattan's East Side and graduated from St. Ann's Academy in 1943. After serving in the U.S. Coast Guard during World War II, he received a B.A. from St. John's in 1950. He then returned to St. Ann's as head basketball coach, building a powerful program that captured three national Catholic championships in his seven years there (during which time the school moved to Queens and was renamed Archbishop Molloy). St. John's coach Joe Lapchick took notice and hired Carnesecca as an assistant coach in 1957, a role that Lou filled for eight seasons before taking over as head coach of the Redmen. Carnesecca led the team for twenty-four of the next twenty-seven seasons, taking a three-year hiatus from 1970 to 1973 to coach and manage the New York Nets of the American Basketball Association. Carnesecca's tenure at St. John's produced consistently strong teams; his squad went to a postseason tournament every year. In 1985 the Redmen went to the Final Four of the National Collegiate Athletic Association (NCAA) Tournament, and in 1989 they won the postseason National Invitational Tournament. Within the ultracompetitive Big East, St. John's shared the regular season title four times (1980, 1983, 1986, 1992), won it once outright (1985), and triumphed in the postseason tournament twice (1983, 1986). Throughout his career Carnesecca was a tremendous ambassador for the game of basketball around the world, touring with teams and conducting clinics on four continents. He was honored by Governor Mario Cuomo for his contributions to youth and athletics in New York state. Carnesecca was awarded the prestigious title of Cavaliere by the Italian president, an honor that recognizes prominent Italian Americans who have distinguished themselves in their field. Carnesecca's coaching prowess was recognized with national Coach of the Year Awards in 1983 and 1985. In 1992, Carnesecca received the sport's ultimate honor with induction into the Naismith Memorial Basketball Hall of Fame.

SELECTED BIBLIOGRAPHY: Lou Carnesecca, with Phil Pepe, *Louie: In Season* (1988); Mike Douchant, *Encyclopedia of College Basketball* (1995); *Redmen Basketball Media Guide* 1991–92; *Redmen Basketball Magazine* (1991–1992); William C. Rhoden, "Hometown Talent Creates a Charisma," *New York Times*, 13 January 1985, S-9; George Vecsey, "Louie Makes the Four," *New York Times*, 25 March 1985, C1, C6; Vic Ziegel, "The Gospel according to Lou," *New York Magazine* 16 (7 February 1983), 78–79.

Dennis Ryan

CARPATHO-RUSYNS. Carpatho-Rusyns are a numerically small eastern Slavic people whose homeland lies near the Carpathian Mountains in north-eastern Slovakia, southern Poland, and western Ukraine. Their language, religion, and other cultural traits, including sports, have been influenced by neighboring groups such as Czechs, Hungarians, Poles, and Slovaks. At the time of their mass migration to America, which commenced around 1880, the great majority were members of the Greek Catholic Church, united with Rome. The Greek Catholic Union, a church-related society with clerical and lay membership, initially promoted their athletic activities.

The Sokols (Falcons), the gymnastic division of the union, was organized in 1910 and by 1932 reported about 20,000 members in its brotherhoods and sisterhoods. Modeled on the Czech Sokols, which began in 1862 in Bohemia, individual and team calisthenics and other individual sports were favored. Intellectual growth, religious faith, and American citizenship were promoted. Carpatho-Rusyn Sokols were glorious in June 1920, when six American men competed in a Pan-Slavic international gymnastics exhibition in Prague. They met with President Thomas G. Masaryk, since most of the ancestral homeland was then within the borders of Czechoslovakia.

By the 1920s and 1930s a few Carpatho-Rusyn professional athletes were well known outside the ethnic community. Most famous were world welterweight boxing champion Pete Latzo* (1902–68; reigned 1926–28), perennial heavyweight boxing contender Johnny Risko (1902–53), and baseball Hall of Famer Joe "Ducky" Medwick (1911–75). Boxing is an individual sport, but it is noteworthy that the immigrants' children took readily to American team sports such as baseball, basketball, and football, and, for its part, the Sokol quickly organized leagues in men's and women's basketball, men's baseball, and men's and women's softball. Carpatho-Rusyns and other Slavs identified with Latzo, and the association's newspaper publicized his title bouts. Surprisingly, a caption in its 1922 yearbook encouraged female participation in boxing!

World War II's end brought opportunities for veterans to attend college and opportunities in college sports, the expanding professional basketball and football leagues, and the hundreds of professional baseball teams. Successful in this era were major league baseball players Steve Ridzik (b. 1929) and Andy Seminick (b. 1920), baseball umpire Al Honichick (b. 1918), football college and professional player, coach, and executive Mike Holovak (b. 1919), and, more recently, ice hockey's Ed Hospodar (b. 1959).

Among Carpatho-Rusyn Americans, the popularity of the individual participant sports, bowling and golf, accelerated during the 1960s. From then until the 1990s, the biweekly *Greek Catholic-Union Messenger* reported on local leagues and national tournaments sponsored by the society. Meanwhile, pro football quarterback Bernie Kozar (b. 1963) and hockey high scorer Peter Bondra (b. 1968) were standouts. However, the ethnicity of Carpatho-Rusyn sports figures was not usually noticed by other Americans. Nonetheless, parental and in-group support for athletic competition was still aiding their success.

SELECTED BIBLIOGRAPHY: Paul Robert Magocsi, *The Carpatho-Rusyn Americans* (1989); *Opportunity Realized: The Greek Catholic Union's First One Hundred Years, 1892–1992* (1994); Michael Roman, ed., *Diamond Jubilee Almanac of the Greek Catholic Union* (1967).

Richard Renoff

CASALS, ROSEMARY (16 September 1948, San Francisco–   ). A tennis player, she was born to poor immigrant parents from El Salvador. She was raised by her great-uncle (Manuel Casals Bordas), a former member of the El Salvador National soccer team, and her great-aunt (Maria). A graduate of George Washington High School in San Francisco in 1966, "Rosie" Casals became an accomplished tennis player without ever taking a professional lesson. Coaching and encouragement from her uncle led her to a U.S. singles ranking of eleven by the time she was seventeen years old. Casals' victories include eleven singles and 112 doubles professional titles. She spent a total of eleven years in the U.S.

top ten and held a ranking of number two in 1970, 1971, and 1976 and number three in 1973, 1974, and 1976. She is best known for having teamed with Billie Jean King to win several grand-slam titles. Together with King, Casals won the U.S. Championship and the South African Championship and was a five-time winner at Wimbledon (1967, 1968, 1970, 1971, 1973). More recently, she won the U.S. Open Senior Women's Doubles Championship in 1990. In 1996 Casals was inducted into the International Tennis Hall of Fame. She also made major contributions to the development of the Virginia Slims Invitational and World Team Tennis, both of which increased the popularity of professional tennis in the 1970s. Due in great part to her activism, professional tennis events became open to both amateur and professional players, and women's events began to approach equity with men's in terms of prize money.

SELECTED BIBLIOGRAPHY: Bud Collins, "Casals Is in the Big Time," *Boston Globe*, 13 July 1996, 28:3; Bud Collins, *My Life with the Pros* (1989); Linda Jacobs, *Rosemary Casals: The Rebel Rosebud* (1975); Angela Lumpkin, *Women's Tennis: A Historical Documentary of the Players and Their Game* (1981); A. J. Johnson, *Great Women in Sports* (1996), 72–75; Alida M. Thacher, *Raising a Racket: Rosie Casals* (1976).

Katherine M. Jamieson

CATHOLIC YOUTH ORGANIZATION. The Catholic Youth Organization (CYO) embarked on an Americanization program that transcended race, ethnicity, and class in the delivery of its sports programs and social services. The Catholic assimilation program in Chicago, initiated during World War I, met with limited success and stiff resistance, particularly in ethnically controlled parishes. As in Europe, Catholics' leisure activities centered around the church, where immigrant and largely working-class parishioners looked to the clergy for guidance. In such enclaves ethnic concerns and nationalistic issues thwarted Catholic cohesion, isolated congregations from the mainstream society, and inhibited full participation in American culture. Nearly a century of such insularity dissolved rapidly during the depression of the 1930s, when the CYO merged religion with sport.

The widespread Progressive reform movement introduced immigrant youth to American sport forms in the schools, parks, and playgrounds of America's cities. The Catholic Knights of Columbus fraternal association began organizing formal tournaments by the turn of the century. By 1910 Chicago's Catholics boasted the largest religious baseball league in the United States. Priests often organized and administered parish sports teams as a means to retain a religious influence and offer more wholesome forms of leisure than the urban vices that tempted their flock. Catholics participated in both parish-centered leagues and a broader athletic network against Protestant, Jewish, and independent foes. Victories bolstered both ethnic and religious pride as World War I brought nativist attacks.

In Chicago, Archbishop, later Cardinal, George Mundelein attempted to spur greater Americanization by centralizing the bureaucracy, limiting parish autonomy, and placing American-born, English-speaking priests in the ethnic parishes. Mundelein ordered Holy Name fraternal societies to be established in each parish, but interest languished until such groups assumed athletic functions. One of the cardinal's young lieutenants, Bernard J. Sheil, proved adept at adapting such infrastructure and nurturing youthful sporting interests. Sheil had forsaken a professional baseball career for the priesthood, where duties as a parish priest and jail chaplain influenced his social activism.

As bishop, Sheil officially incorporated the existing parish athletic programs into the centrally administered CYO in 1930. Assuming personal leadership shortly thereafter, he initiated a widespread boxing program and the world's largest basketball league, numbering 120 teams by 1931. The annual boxing tournaments appealed to thousands of working-class youths representing all ethnic groups and eventually produced an international traveling team and a number of Olympians. Others became professional fighters. All participants received free instruction, equipment, and medical care, with winners awarded college scholarships.

The phenomenal success of the boxing program fostered a more comprehensive athletic program and social agencies. The bishop founded Sheil House, a social settlement in the African American community, as well as similar neighborhood centers for the nissei, Italians, Puerto Ricans, and Navajo Indians. Sheil's social activism, his stance against anti-Semitism, and his involvement in labor issues brought him national attention and membership on presidential commissions. A disgruntled assassin failed in an attempt on Sheil's life at a 1939 rally for the Congress of Industrial Organizations.

CYO athletes competed internationally, and Sheil expanded activities to include media services, a radio station, and publications in Polish, French, and German. He financed and directed the National League of Decency and provided social services for war veterans, parolees, the poor, the sick, the blind, and the uneducated. His concern for the last prompted summer vacation schools held in Chicago's public parks and the founding of two institutions of higher learning.

Upon the death of Mundelein in 1939, Sheil failed to receive the expected cardinal's hat, as his flamboyance and profligacy did not endear him to his superiors. Sheil resigned his post and retired an embittered man in 1954. The Catholic archdiocese discontinued funding for his many projects, but parish sports programs held on for decades. Sheil remained a legendary hero to working-class people, who eagerly participated in the CYO programs that nurtured not only religion but patriotism, as they sustained dreams of socioeconomic mobility and greater inclusion in American culture.

SELECTED BIBLIOGRAPHY: Mary Elizabeth Carroll, "Bishop Sheil: Prophet without Honor," *Harper's Magazine* 211 (1954): 45–51; Gerald R. Gems, "Sport, Religion, and Americanization: Bishop Sheil and the Catholic Youth Organization," *International Journal of the History of Sport* 10 (August 1993): 233–234; Roger L. Treat, *Bishop Sheil and the CYO* (1951).

Gerald R. Gems

CENTRAL INTERCOLLEGIATE ATHLETIC ASSOCIATION. The Central Intercollegiate Athletic Association (CIAA) is an athletic conference consisting of historically African American institutions of higher education. Originally titled the Colored Intercollegiate Athletic Association, the CIAA was established in 1912, largely through the efforts of Ernest J. Marshall, a teacher of chemistry and football coach at Howard University who convened the first meeting of the association. The founding members of the CIAA were Hampton Institute, Shaw University, Howard University, Lincoln University, and Virginia Union University. The CIAA was organized to add legitimacy and provide structure to black college sport, which was marred by a host of evils during the early twentieth century. Almost immediately after its formation, the CIAA established academic standards for its athletes, implemented procedures for the selection of officials, and arranged schedules and championship play in a variety of sports. One of the CIAA's most famous events was its annual track-and-field championships. Organized for the first time in 1922, the championships, which were usually held at Hampton Institute's Armstrong Field, involved hundreds of athletes, attracted even more spectators, and garnered much attention from the *Chicago Defender, Pittsburgh Courier Journal*, and other well-known black weeklies. The CIAA, which for a number of years disseminated information on athletics through its annual *Bulletin*, served as the model for similar organizations established to regulate college sport among historically African American institutions of higher learning. Such organizations as the Southern Intercollegiate Athletic Association (1913), Southwestern Athletic Conference (1920), and South-Central Athletic Association (1932) took the lead from the CIAA and set standards for college sport among historically African American institutions in different sections of the country. Like the CIAA, these organizations sponsored championships in a number of sports and dealt with such issues as eligibility requirements for athletes, scheduling conflicts, poor sportsmanship among athletes and spectators alike, and the repudiation of financial obligations. The CIAA has become a decidedly different organization since its founding. By 1932 its membership had expanded from five to twelve institutions. It still includes twelve institutions but competes at the Division II level of the National Collegiate Athletic Association (NCAA). Divided into Eastern and Western Divisions in all sports, excluding football and baseball, the CIAA sponsors thirteen championships for both men and women athletes. The men compete for championships in tennis, golf, baseball, basketball, cross-country, indoor track, and track and field. The men's title in football is determined by the best regular season record. In contrast to the men, women in the CIAA compete for championships in volleyball, basketball, softball, cross-country, indoor track, and track and field. The CIAA is also frequently represented by member institutions in NCAA postseason championships in a variety of sports.

SELECTED BIBLIOGRAPHY: Central Intercollegiate Athletic Association, Web site http://www.theciaa.com/about/excellence.htm.; Edwin Bancroft Henderson, *The Negro in*

Sports (1939); Patrick B. Miller, "To Bring the Race Along Rapidly: Sport, Student Culture, and Educational Mission at Historically Black Colleges during the Interwar Years," *History of Education Quarterly* 35 (1995): 111–133; Charles H. Williams, "Twenty Years Work of the C.I.A.A.," *Southern Workman* 61 (1932): 65–76.

David K. Wiggins

CHADWICK, HENRY (5 October 1824, Exeter, Devon, England–20 April 1908, Brooklyn, NY). Known as the "Father of Baseball," British-born Chadwick was one of the game's greatest advocates. Son of English journalist James Chadwick, he emigrated in 1837 at age thirteen with his parents to the United States, settling in Brooklyn, New York. He was a journalist who used his columns in almost twenty newspapers to promote fan interest in the game and ensure that baseball remained an honest and fair endeavor. At age nineteen he followed his father into journalism when he took a position with Brooklyn's *Long Island Star* newspaper. In 1856 he accepted a position with the *Brooklyn Eagle*. Writing primarily about baseball, he remained at the *Eagle* until 1894. In 1858 he also began writing for the *New York Clipper*, the nation's leading sport and entertainment newspaper. He remained at the *Clipper* until 1888. At these papers, Chadwick improved the box score and established systems of scoring that are essentially similar to those in use today. Primarily through these positions at the *Eagle* and the *Clipper*, Chadwick saw the potential of baseball as America's national pastime and took an active role in supporting the game in its infancy. He was one of the game's earliest reformers, lashing out against gambling and drinking by players. Chadwick created the first baseball annual, *Beadle's Dime Base Ball Player* (1860). From 1869 to 1908 he edited leading baseball handbooks: *DeWitt's Guide* (1869–80) and *Spalding's Base Ball Guide* (1881–1908). Chadwick's friendly dispute with Albert G. Spalding about the origins of baseball led to the Mills Commission, which investigated the beginnings of the sport in the United States. Chadwick correctly viewed baseball as an adaptation of the English game of rounders, whereas Spalding sought an American origin for the national pastime and supported the tale that Abner Doubleday had created the game in Cooperstown, New York, in 1839.

SELECTED BIBLIOGRAPHY: John B. Foster, "Henry Chadwick: 'The Father of Base Ball,' " in *Spalding's Official Base Ball Guide* (1909), 7–20; David L. Porter, ed., "Chadwick, Henry," *Biographical Dictionary of American Sports: Baseball* (1987); various items from Chadwick, Henry, Officials File at the National Baseball Hall of Fame Library.

Corey Seeman

CHAMBERLAIN, WILTON ("Wilt") (21 August 1936, Philadelphia–12 October 1999, Los Angeles). An African American basketball player, he is the son of William Chamberlain, a custodian and neighborhood handyman, and Olivia

Chamberlain, a laundress and cleaning woman. A scholastic star at Overbrook High School, he led his team to two Philadelphia city championships. An all-around superlative athlete, he was also a standout in track and field in the sprints, the shot put, and the high jump. After graduating in 1955, he accepted a scholarship to the University of Kansas, where he earned All-American honors in basketball during his sophomore and junior years; he also lettered and won championships in track and field. His prolific scoring and superlative defensive and rebounding skills revolutionized college basketball and forced rule makers to institute several changes, including widening the free-throw lane from eight to twelve feet and banning offensive goaltending. Annoyed by collapsing defenses and stalling tactics used against his team and eager to begin competing for pay, Chamberlain left Kansas after his junior year to tour with the heralded Harlem Globetrotters.* In 1959 he signed with the Philadelphia Warriors and began a fourteen-year career in the National Basketball Association (NBA) that included six seasons with the Warriors, three with the Philadelphia 76ers, and five with the Los Angeles Lakers. Although he set numerous single-season and career records, he was often criticized for not being a team player because his clubs won only two NBA titles (the 76ers in 1967 and the Lakers in 1972). He is also remembered for his many competitive battles with Bill Russell* of the Boston Celtics. Although he usually defeated Russell in these confrontations, the Celtics won most of the NBA championship series played against Chamberlain's clubs. Nicknamed "the Big Dipper" and "Wilt the Stilt," Chamberlain became the first NBA player to score over 30,000 points, and when he retired, he held the NBA record for career game scoring average. A durable competitor, he was also a standout in assists, shot blocking, and rebounding. He became the first person to lead the NBA in assists, field goal percentage, and rebounding in a single season (1960–61). After leaving the NBA, he coached the San Diego Conquistadors in the American Basketball Association for one year but then turned his attention to founding the International Volleyball Association, sponsoring several volleyball and track teams in California, and appearing in commercials and feature films. He was elected to the Naismith Memorial Basketball Hall of Fame in 1978. Chamberlain was known for his outspoken, boastful nature and his frequent feuds with his coaches. On racial matters he was critical of black militants. In 1968 he attended the Republican National Convention and supported Richard Nixon in the presidential election campaign. His practice of dating white women was especially unpopular among black feminists.

SELECTED BIBLIOGRAPHY: Arthur R. Ashe, Jr., *A Hard Road to Glory: A History of the African-American Athlete since 1946*, vol. 3 (1988); Wilt Chamberlain, "Why I Am Quitting College," *Look* 22 (10 June 1958): 91–94ff; Wilt Chamberlain, as told to Tim Cohane, "Pro Basketball Has Ganged Up on Me," *Look* 24 (1 March 1960): 51–55ff; Wilt Chamberlain, *A View from Above* (1991); Wilt Chamberlain and David Shaw, *Just Like Any Other 7-Foot Black Millionaire Who Lives Next Door* (1973); John Garrity, "Wilt Chamberlain," *Sports Illustrated* 75 (9 December 1991): 22–25; Bill Libby, *Go-*

liath: The Wilt Chamberlain Story (1977); *New York Times*, 13 October 1999, A1, B10;
A. S. Young, "The Track Team That Wilt Built," *Ebony* 37 (October 1982): 68–72.

George B. Kirsch

CHANEY, JOHN (21 January 1932, Jacksonville, FL–). A prominent African American basketball player and successful college coach, he was abandoned by his father when he was still a baby. His mother, Earley Chaney, had to work all day and into the night as a maid and seamstress in a sweatshop to support her family. At age fourteen he moved from Florida to Philadelphia with his mother and abusive stepfather, where he turned to basketball as an escape from poverty. Playing for Ben Franklin High School, Chaney was awarded Philadelphia's Public League Most Valuable Player award in 1951. Graduating from high school about five years before African Americans were given a chance to play for Philadelphia's Big Five (La Salle, Villanova, St. Joseph's, Penn, and Temple), he had to return to the segregated South to attend a small school in Daytona Beach, Florida, Bethune-Cookman College, to earn a scholarship. After graduating in 1955, he accepted an offer to play for the Harlem Globetrotters* for $350 a month because the National Basketball Association at the time still had little interest in African American players. Stunned to discover the Globetrotters' games were fixed, he quit after only two months. Chaney moved back to Philadelphia to work three jobs: junior high physical education teacher, waiter, and semiprofessional player for the Eastern Basketball League. After compiling an impressive 59–9 record as coach at the junior high level, he moved on to Simon Gratz High School in Philadelphia. In 1972 he accepted the coaching job at Cheyney State University, thirty five miles outside Philadelphia, where in 1978 he won a National Collegiate Athletic Association (NCAA) Division II national championship and was awarded Pennsylvania's Distinguished Faculty Award for his work in the community, classroom, and gym. In 1982 Temple University offered him the head basketball coaching job, making him the first African American coach at one of the Big Five schools. While at Temple he has become an outspoken defender for society's disfranchised. A member of the executive committee of the Black Coaches Association,* he has passionately argued for the repeal of new NCAA rules that set new minimum standards for freshmen eligibility, on the grounds that the new regulations discriminate against minority youth. At Temple he regularly recruited underprivileged student athletes and then demanded that they attend classes and earn degrees.

SELECTED BIBLIOGRAPHY: Charles S. Farrell, " 'Big Four' Spread Influence of Black Coaches," *Black Issues in Higher Education* 11 (29 December 1994): 24–25; William F. Reed, "A New Proposition," *Sports Illustrated* 70 (23 January 1989): 16–19; Gary Smith, "The Whittler," *Sports Illustrated* 80 (28 February 1994): 72–80; Steve Wartenberg, *Winning Is an Attitude: A Season in the Life of John Chaney and the Temple Owls* (1991).

Troy D. Paino

CHANG, MICHAEL (22 February 1972, Hoboken, NJ–). A tennis player and the son of Chinese immigrants, his father (Joe) and his mother (Betty) are research chemists. After winning many United States Tennis Association (USTA) junior titles, Chang began his professional career in 1987 and became the youngest player (fifteen years, six months) to win a main draw match at the U.S. Open. In 1988, he won his first tournament in San Francisco and finished the year ranked number thirty in the world. In 1989 Chang defeated Stefan Edberg to win his first and only grand-slam title at the French Open. Chang not only became the youngest grand-slam champion in history (seventeen years, three months) but was also the first American male to win at Roland Garros since Tony Trabert in 1955. After an injury in 1990 and an off-year in 1991, Chang rebounded in 1992, winning three titles, allowing him to reach the number four ranking in the world and qualify for his first Association of Tennis Professionals (ATP) Tour Championships. He continued his winning ways in 1993, reaching seven finals and winning five of them. Chang found much success in Asia, where he won four of his five titles and earned over $1 million in prize money. 1994 was a banner year for Chang, winning a career-best six titles and qualifying for his third straight ATP Tour Championship. In 1995, Chang was runner-up in the French Open, his first grand-slam final since he won the title there in 1989. He also won four titles, compiled an 18–1 record in Asia, and was runner-up at the ATP Tour Championships. Chang reached the number two ranking in the world in 1996, taking second place at the Australian and U.S. Open and winning at least three titles for the fifth consecutive year. Chang has been one of the most consistent tennis players on the men's professional tour, as he developed an all-court game that allowed him to utilize his steady ground strokes and his unparalleled speed and quickness. He has also taken an active role in spreading tennis in Hong Kong through his "Stars of the Future" program.

SELECTED BIBLIOGRAPHY: Rachel Alexander, "Chang's Grand Slam Fund; With Just One Title in Major Tournament, Hard Work Continues," *Washington Post*, 19 September 1997, D8; John Blake, "Media with a Message ONLINE; Chang Takes His Faith to Cyberspace," *Atlanta Journal/Atlanta Constitution*, 5 April 1997, F2; Brian Cleary, "Little Big Man," *Tennis* 31 (August 1995): 64; Joel Drucker, "Michael Chang's Unfinished Journey," *Tennis* 34 (May 1998): 38–42; Dale Robertson, "Chang Reflects Country's Rise and Fall," *Houston Chronicle*, 3 June 1997, B1; Dale Robertson, "Chang's Actions Not Always Lauded," *Houston Chronicle*, 11 June 1995, B1; David Zinczenco, "Michael Chang Never Lets Up," *Men's Health* 10 (June 1995): 110.

Thomas Cesa

CHARLES, EZZARD MACK (7 July 1921, Lawrenceville, GA–28 May 1975, Chicago). An African American prizefighter known as "the Cincinnati Cobra," he was the son of William and Alberta Charles. His father was a janitor. Born into a life of rural poverty, he moved with his family to Cincinnati when he was a young boy. At the age of fourteen he began his amateur career as a skinny

140-pound fighter. He won a Golden Gloves championship and the 1939 National Amateur Athletic Union middleweight title. After turning professional as a middleweight, he eventually moved up to the light-heavyweight division. He sacrificed three years of his boxing career to military service during World War II. After the war he suffered only one defeat between 1946 and 1950. His punishing victory over Sam Baroudi in 1948 left Charles profoundly shaken; Baroudi died a few days after that bout, and for the rest of his career Charles lacked the "killer instinct" to knock out a beaten opponent. In 1949, after Joe Louis* retired as heavyweight champion, Charles won a decision over Jersey Joe Walcott to win the National Boxing Association's crown. He defended his championship eight times before losing to Walcott in 1952. His fifteen-round decision over Joe Louis in 1950 was memorable in part because of Louis' attempt to regain his title as an aging boxer, but more because of Charles' apparent unwillingness to knock out his former idol in the later rounds. Two losses to Rocky Marciano* in 1954 ended Charles' dream of regaining the heavyweight crown. He fought for five more years, long past his prime. After his retirement in 1959 he suffered from bad investments and briefly tried professional wrestling. He was inducted into the International Boxing Hall of Fame in 1990.

SELECTED BIBLIOGRAPHY: W. C. Heinz, "The Strange Career of Ezzard Charles," *Saturday Evening Post* 227 (7 June 1952): 34; Abbott J. Liebling, "Reporter at Large: Doc Picks the Rock," *The New Yorker* 30 (2 October 1954): 75–82; *New York Times*, 29 May 1975, 38.

George B. Kirsch

CHINESE. Through American sports, Chinese Americans creatively expressed themselves and their ties to Chinese American communities. A very few found fame and, in the case of modern-day tennis star Michael Chang,* wealth. Yet Chinese Americans often also found that as they ran down the court or around the base paths, "racism's traveling eye," to quote Elaine H. Kim, followed them.

Chinese people began to immigrate to America in significant numbers during the mid-nineteenth century. By the 1870s, the work of Chinese immigrants was vital to development of West Coast railroads and industries. Nevertheless, Chinese immigrants and their offspring encountered racism and nativism on the U.S. mainland. Beginning in the late 1880s, the U.S. Congress enacted laws that severely restricted Chinese migration to the United States and declared Chinese immigrants ineligible for citizenship. Those Chinese already here were expelled from the most dynamic sectors of the mainland U.S. economy and further barred from the industrial working-class opportunities offered European immigrants.

In Hawaii, Chinese Americans were less likely to face the politics of racial exclusion than the politics of class. Hawaiian Chinese formed an important part of a multicultural workforce. Their labor was too vital to the Hawaiian economy to be marginalized in ethnic enclaves. At the same time, they and other Asian

Hawaiian workers, as well as native Hawaiian workers, crossed ethnic boundaries to develop a formidable nonwhite working class that plagued the generally European American elite for decades.

It has not always been easy for Chinese Americans to achieve even the minimum of their athletic dreams. In part this was because racial discrimination denied them equal access to recreational facilities during the early decades of the twentieth century. This was especially the case in California communities such as Oakland, where, between the world wars, Chinese and Japanese Americans were discouraged from joining certain recreational clubs. To offset this arrangement, the city's superintendent of recreation organized special clubs for Oakland's Asian American residents. Moreover, the overcrowded conditions and poverty found in many urban Chinatowns tended to discourage all but the more affluent from engaging in sporting competition.

During the late nineteenth and early twentieth centuries prizefighters of Chinese ancestry showed that Chinese Americans were more than just victims of exploitation and exclusion. They defied racial stereotypes, won bouts, and gained the respect of the European American sporting world. Chinese males were often racialized as too "unmanly" to compete effectively against European Americans in sports such as boxing. Still, in the early 1900s, Ah Wing, a porter living in Sacramento, gained notice and victories. According to the *San Francisco Chronicle*, he "possessed . . . rare gameness, a quality which his race is not generally supposed to exhibit." On the eve of World War II bantamweight Hawaiian Chinese David Kui Kong Young was described by veteran ring reporter Eddie Muller as "pound for pound . . . the greatest puncher we've had in the past 25 years."

As a second generation matured during the early decades of the twentieth century, Chinese American communities throughout the United States were represented by baseball nines. Meanwhile, Hawaiian Chinese made news in the baseball world of the 1910s and 1920s. Hawaii University's Chinese team undertook rigorous and generally successful tours of the mainland from 1910 through 1916. In the process, they played college, semipro, and black professional nines.

Hawaiian players of Chinese ancestry sought unsuccessfully to gain entrance into organized professional baseball at a high minor and even major league level. In December 1914, the Portland Beavers of the Pacific Coast League signed Lang Akena, who was half native Hawaiian and half Chinese. However, Portland's manager, Walter McCreadie, bowed to the threat of a European American player boycott and released Akena. Another Chinese Hawaiian, "Buck" Lai Tin, was given a tryout by the New York Giants after playing with the famed Bushwicks of Brooklyn semipro club. While an adept fielder, Tin's hitting failed to impress the Giants' legendary manager John McGraw, and he was cut.

In 1932, a Chinese American got a brief opportunity to play in the Pacific Coast League (PCL). At that time, the Great Depression subdued PCL financial operations, and PCL magnates, like minor league owners and operators throughout the country, considered fresh notions to bolster attendance. Early in August the Sacramento Solons hired Kenso Nushida, a Japanese American pitcher, as a way of perking interest in a club mired in mediocrity. Nushida, as it turned out, performed and drew well. The next month, the Oakland club signed a local semipro pitching standout, Lee Gum Hong, who was recruited just in time to pitch against Nushida in Oakland. This pitching duel of Asian Americans occurred as the Sino-Japanese War inflamed the passions of people of Chinese and Japanese descent in the United States. The game pitting Hong and Nushida was marketed as more than just one more game in the long PCL schedule, but a game that symbolized a war of nations, even though both pitchers were American-born.

Community football teams were formed as the second generation of Chinese came of age in the United States. In 1919 the Kai Kee football team played out of the San Francisco Bay Area and challenged opponents averaging 145 pounds or less. In the mid- and late 1930s, Chinese Americans in Los Angeles and the San Francisco Bay Area organized several community teams.

Individuals of Chinese descent not only performed on integrated elevens but, in some cases, impressed contemporaries. Son Kai Kee was no star, but he played major college football for the University of California in the late 1910s. In the late 1940s the University of California had another Chinese American on its squad. George Fong was a fine all-around back on the powerful Pappy Waldorf elevens. On the Hawaiian Islands, football players of Chinese descent often stood out. During the 1920s the Dayton Triangles of the youthful National Football League signed Walter Achiu, a Hawaiian drop kicker of Chinese ancestry.

Basketball attracted tremendous support in Chinese American communities between the world wars. For example, early in 1939 one could wander into San Francisco's Kezar Pavilion Sunday evenings and find Bay Area quintets of Chinese Americans playing each other from 6:30 P.M. to 11 P.M. However, one would have to pay a fifteen-cent admission price to catch the excitement. Since the sport's inception, basketball's appeal has cut across gender lines. One of the most powerful things about Chinese American basketball was its attraction to young women. In Portland during the 1930s the Chung Wah five was a champion team led by a former high school star, La Lun Chin, who defied racial and gender stereotypes of Chinese women as passive and exotic. At the same time, young women associated with the Lowa Athletic Club organized a basketball team in Los Angeles that lasted through much of World War II. After World War II the St. Mary's Catholic Church in San Francisco's Chinatown sponsored one of the best female teams in the Bay Area. Helen Wong, one of the finest female athletes in San Francisco's history, was the star of the St. Mary's five.

Chinese American men, too, played basketball enthusiastically. The Lowa Athletic Club's male squad toured California and Mexico in the 1930s. After World War II some of the best of San Francisco's Chinese American basketball players barnstormed throughout the United States. One of the finest of these players was Helen Wong's brother Willie, who earned the reputation as a scintillating ball handler and shooter. Moreover, basketball historian Robert Peterson claims that a Chinese American professional squad called the Hong Wah Q'ues played Midwestern fives before World War II.

Tennis became a relatively popular sport among some second-generation Chinese Americans before World War II. In 1935 eleven-year-old Henrietta Yung gained attention as a tennis prodigy in San Francisco and remained one of the finest female amateurs in California for years. The aforementioned Helen Wong became even more famous as an amateur tennis player. Another San Franciscan, "Peanuts" Louie, developed into a leading female amateur player during the 1960s. Of course, Michael Chang has emerged as one of the best tennis players in the world. In golf, a Chinese Hawaiian, Charley Chung, performed professionally in the 1920s. Chung was just one of many very fine golfers of Chinese descent playing in Hawaii during the 1920s. Before and after World War II Chinese Americans on the mainland and Hawaii organized golf clubs and tournaments.

In recent years Chinese American athletes have attracted international attention and have won national and international championships. In the 1980s Tracy Wong was a top-flight female long-distance runner for the University of Texas, while Wei Wang ranked as one of the best female table tennis players in the United States. In the mid-1990s Michelle Kwan* and Amy Chow were considered among the greatest female ice skaters and gymnasts in the world, respectively.

SELECTED BIBLIOGRAPHY: Sucheng Chan, *This Bittersweet Soil: The Chinese in California Agriculture, 1860–1910* (1986); Joel S. Franks, "Chinese Americans and American Sport, 1880–1940," in *Chinese America: History and Perspectives* (1996); Elaine Kim, "Preface," in Jessica Hagedorn, ed., *Charlie Chan Is Dead: An Anthology of Contemporary Asian American Fiction* (1993); Ronald Takaki, *Strangers from a Different Shore: A History of Asian Americans* (1989).

Joel S. Franks

CHYZOWYCH, WALTER (20 April 1937, Ukraine–2 September 1994, Winston-Salem, NC). A soccer player, Chyzowych emigrated from the Ukraine to Germany with his family at the age of six, coming to Philadelphia when he was twelve. A high-scoring forward at Temple University, he was selected to the National Collegiate Athletic Association (NCAA) All-American Soccer Team in 1959 and 1960. He coached soccer with great success at the Philadelphia College of Textiles and Science from 1961 to 1963 and 1966 to 1975. Chyzowych played professionally with the Philadelphia Urkainian Nationals (U.S. Open Cup Winners, 1963), the Newark Ukrainians, the Newark Sitch (American Soccer League Most Valuable Player, 1966), and in the National Professional Soccer League and the Canadian Pro-League. One of the most talented goal scorers of the 1960s, he made his debut with the U.S. National Soccer Team in 1964 and then later coached the National Team from 1976 to

1981. He also coached the U.S. Olympic and U.S. Youth Team during this period. Chyzowych perhaps is best known and acclaimed for his work as director of coaching for the U.S. Soccer Federation (USSF), 1975–81 and 1984–86. In this role in the early 1970s he was instrumental in creating the USSF's highly successful National Coaching Schools. His book, *The Official Soccer Book*, the sport's bible, has been widely used in coaching ranks, both in the United States and abroad. At the time of his untimely death in 1994, Chyzowych had coached soccer at Wake Forest University since 1986. In 1997 he was elected to the USSF's National Soccer Hall of Fame.

SELECTED BIBLIOGRAPHY: Walter Chyzowych, *The Official Soccer Book* (1978); Zander Hollander, ed., *The American Encyclopedia of Soccer* (1980); Len Oliver, "The Ethnic Legacy in U.S. Soccer," *SASH Historical Quarterly* 9 (Winter 1996): 1–4, 10, and (Spring 1996): 1–4.

Leonard P. Oliver

CLEMENTE, ROBERTO WALKER (18 August 1934, Carolina, PR–31 December 1972, San Juan, PR). A baseball player, he was the son of Puerto Rican sugar-mill workers. His father (Melchor) was a mill foreman, and his mother (Luisa) a mill laundress. Clemente was a star right fielder for the Pittsburgh Pirates, batting .317 with 240 home runs and 3,000 base hits from 1955 to 1972. In 1952 and 1953 the teenaged Clemente played for the Santurce Crabbers, a Puerto Rican team that featured a mix of Latin, Negro League, and major league players, including Willie Mays.* In 1954 Clemente signed a minor league contract with the Brooklyn Dodgers organization. When the Dodgers failed to place Clemente on their forty-man roster, the Pirates selected him in a special draft. During the 1960s, Clemente developed into one of the game's greatest all-around right fielders. Clemente's whipping bat speed helped him capture National League batting crowns in 1961, 1964, 1965, and 1967, and his powerful throwing arm and quickness afoot aided him in winning twelve consecutive Gold Glove awards. In 1966 Clemente earned the National League (NL) Most Valuable Player honors. Labeled "the Great One" by broadcaster Bob Prince, Clemente played exceptionally well in the postseason. A lifetime .362 hitter in fourteen World Series games, Clemente helped the Pirates to surprising World Championships over the Yankees in 1960 and the Orioles in 1971. In 1972, in his final regular season at bat, Clemente collected his milestone 3,000th base hit. In December 1972, after a devastating earthquake struck Nicaragua, Clemente responded to reports that relief supplies were being intercepted by Nicaraguan authorities. Clemente organized a collection of food, clothing, and medicine and accompanied the airlifting of supplies from San Juan Airport. Shortly after takeoff, the DC-7 encountered engine trouble and plunged into the Atlantic Ocean. Clemente, whose body was never found, was presumed dead at the age of thirty-eight. After the Hall of Fame announced that it had waived its standard five-year waiting period, the baseball writers made Clemente the first Latin American member of the Cooperstown shrine. As a Puerto Rican and black man, Clemente considered himself a double minority, often speaking out against racism. Clemente, who involved himself in charitable community efforts, laid the groundwork for the building of the "Roberto Clemente Sports City," an athletic complex for Puerto Rican youngsters. On 17 August 1984, the U.S. Postal Service issued a commemorative stamp honoring him as a "humanitarian and athlete."

SELECTED BIBLIOGRAPHY: Jay Feldman, "Roberto Clemente Went to Bat for All Latino Ballplayers," *Smithsonian* 24 (September 1993): 6; Phil Musick, *Who Was Roberto?* (1974); Rob Ruck, "Remembering Roberto Clemente," *Pittsburgh Magazine* (December 1992): 36–41; Claire Smith, "Clemente's Widow Keeps His Dreams Alive," *New York Times*, 23 November 1994, B15; Deron Snyder, "Clemente Inspires Even after Death," *USA Today Baseball Weekly* (29 December 1992): 35; Kal Wagenheim, *Clemente!* (1973); Paul R. Walker, *The Pride of Puerto Rico: The Life of Roberto Clemente* (1988); Steve Wulf, "Forty for the Ages," *Sports Illustrated* 81 (23 November 1994): 110–111.

Bruce Markusen

COACHMAN, ALICE B. (DAVIS) (9 November 1923, Albany, GA–   ). An African American track-and-field athlete, specializing in the high jump and sprints, she was the only daughter of Evelyn, a widow. Coachman attended Madison High School, Tuskegee Institute, and Albany State College in Georgia. Her success in track and field began in elementary school, and she went on to compete for Tuskegee Institute High School and earned her first medal at a meet in Connecticut. Coachman won a total of twenty-five National Amateur Athletic Union (AAU) titles. From 1939 through 1948 she won the outdoor high-jump championship. A superb sprinter, she also captured several national titles in the outdoor 50-meter and 100-meter dashes and the indoor 50-meter dash and high jump. In addition to her involvement in track, Coachman studied dressmaking and played on the basketball team at Tuskegee. She transferred to Albany State College in 1947 and completed requirements for a home economics degree. At the 1948 Olympics in London, Coachman set a new record in winning the high jump at 1.68 meters or 5' 6-1/8", making her the first woman of African heritage to win a gold medal in the Olympic Games. She retired from competition after the Olympics and became a physical education teacher and coach in Atlanta. Coachman is a member of several Halls of Fame, including National Track and Field, International Women's Sports, Black Athletes, Tuskegee, Georgia State, and Bob Douglas. Each spring Albany State hosts the Alice Coachman Relays.

SELECTED BIBLIOGRAPHY: Michael A. Davis, *Black American Women in Olympic Track and Field* (1992); Ralph Hickok, *A Who's Who of Sports Champions: Their Stories and Records* (1995); James A. Page, *Black Olympic Medalists* (1991); Victoria Sherrow, *Encyclopedia of Women and Sports* (1996).

Susan Rayl

COMISKEY, CHARLES ALBERT (15 August 1858, Chicago–26 October 1931, Eagle River, WI). A first-generation Irish American, baseball player, and eventual "baseball magnate," Comiskey was the son of immigrants John and Annie Kearns Comiskey. His father was a Chicago alderman. After attending St. Mary's College, Kansas, Charles was to become a plumber's apprentice, but Ted Sullivan, whom he had met at St. Mary's, signed him to the Northwestern League Dubuque Rabbits in 1878. At first Comiskey was a substitute player and earned his living selling candy and newspapers on trains running out of Dubuque. Comiskey rose steadily through the baseball ranks, however. While with Dubuque he revolutionized the static first-base position, playing it wide and relying on the pitcher to cover the bag. In 1882 Comiskey joined the St. Louis Browns, becoming manager the following year and leading the team to four consecutive American Association pennants (1885–88). He managed the Chicago team for the ill-fated Players' League in 1890 but returned to the fold and the Browns the next year. In 1900 he was able to realize his ambition to return to Chicago. He built the powerful White Sox team and, with Ban Johnson, was instrumental in forming the American League. In 1920, two of his star players confessed to fixing the 1919 World Series with other members of the team. Comiskey's parsimonious salaries have been suggested as one reason the players consented to the scheme. The "Black Sox" scandal caused the breakup of one of the strongest teams in baseball history, exposed the pervasive influence of gambling within the sport, and is widely believed to have precipitated a personal and professional decline for Comiskey from which he never recovered. However, at the time of his death the onetime plumber's apprentice was the sole owner of a significant major league franchise and a millionaire, and he was elected to the National Baseball Hall of Fame in 1939.

SELECTED BIBLIOGRAPHY: Eliot Asinof, *Eight Men Out: The Black Sox and the 1919 World Series* (1987); Gustav Axelson, *"Commy": The Life Story of Charles A. Comiskey* (1919); Daniel M. Pearson, *Baseball in 1889: Players vs. Owners* (1993); Comiskey file, National Baseball Hall of Fame Library, Cooperstown, NY.

Lesley L. Humphreys

CONN, WILLIAM DAVID, JR. (8 October 1917, East Liberty, PA–29 May 1993, Pittsburgh). A champion Irish American prizefighter, he was the son of William David Conn, Sr., a Westinghouse steamfitter, and Margaret McFarland Conn of Cork, Ireland. He was a disinterested student in parochial school in Pittsburgh. He found his calling after a nun advised him to stop wasting time and learn a trade. Recognized for his boxing skills, Billy grew into a light-heavyweight. He turned professional at the age of seventeen. Managed by Johnny Ray, his career spanned seventy-six bouts. Ranked among the ten best fighters in his class by *Ring Magazine*, he won a fifteen-round decision over Melio Bettina in July 1939 for the vacant light-heavyweight title. Billy, the

"Pittsburgh Kid," was world light-heavyweight boxing champion until 1941, successfully defending his title twelve times against the toughest opponents. He vacated that title to fight Joe Louis* for the heavyweight championship on 18 June 1941. Conn, often remembered as the last in a long line of the Irish American world champions, reportedly lost because he could not resist his Irish impulses. The Louis-Conn match was a stunner. Thirty pounds lighter, Conn gave the Brown Bomber a dazzling boxing lesson and was far ahead in scoring up to the thirteenth round. Rejecting advice from handlers, Billy decided to try to win by knocking out Joe Louis. Slugging it out with the champion, he was knocked out with two seconds left in the round. Soon after, Louis and Conn joined the army and did not to fight again until after World War II. The rematch was held in Yankee Stadium on 19 June 1946, ending in an eighth-round knockout by Louis. Conn was inducted into the International Boxing Hall of Fame in 1990.

SELECTED BIBLIOGRAPHY: Peter Heller, *In This Corner: Former World Champions Tell Their Stories* (1973); Ralph Hickock, *Who's Who of Sport Champions* (1995); "Life of Billy Conn," *Boxing and Wrestling* 7 (August 1957); John McCallum, *Encyclopedia of World Boxing Champions since 1882* (1975); *New York Times*, 30 May 1993, 38; J. B. Roberts and Alexander G. Skutt, *The Boxing Register, International Boxing Hall of Fame Official Record Book* (1997).

Lawrence Huggins

CONNOLLY, HAROLD (1 August 1931, Somerville, MA–   ). Harold Connolly distinguished himself as an exceptional hammer thrower among the athletes to emerge from the athletic renaissance of the 1950s and 1960s. Overcoming a birth defect, from 1956 to 1964 he dominated the hammer throw with seven world records and nine Amateur Athletic Union (AAU) championship titles. He was also a four-time Olympian (1956, 1960, 1964, and 1968). His contribution to the hammer throw would reach far beyond his impressive feats in the hammer circle. He was an innovator in hammer training and technique as well as a worthy ambassador for this ancient Celtic sport. On 2 November 1956 at the age of twenty-five, he set his first world record with a throw of 224' 10-1/2", but the dramatic events leading up to and following the 1956 Melbourne Olympic Games would transform his story into a legend. At the height of the Cold War the battles that were fought on the athletic field between American and Russian rivals symbolized the competition between capitalism and communism. At Melbourne Connolly defeated the Soviet hammer thrower Mikhail Krivonosov for the gold medal with an Olympic record distance of 207' 3-1/2". Connolly later served as director of U.S. Programs for Special Olympics International in Washington, D.C. He also volunteered his services as a coach for Georgetown University; among his athletes was 1996 Olympian Kevin McMahon. In July 1973 a Senate Hearing Committee was formed to review the dangers of anabolic steroids in international athletics. Connolly prophetically voiced his concern for the increasing use of steroids among college and high school athletes.

SELECTED BIBLIOGRAPHY: Bill Mallon and Ian Buchanan, *Quest for Gold: The Encyclopedia of American Olympians* (1984); Cordner Nelson, *Track's Greatest Champions* (1986); Roberto L. Quercetani, *A World History of Track and Field Athletics, 1864–1964* (1964); David Wallechinsky, *The Complete Book of the Olympics*, rev. ed. (1988).

Margaret Mary Hennessey

CONNOLLY, JAMES BRENDAN (28 October 1868, South Boston, MA–20 January 1957, Boston). An Olympic athlete and a writer, chiefly of sea stories, his parents (John, a fisherman, and Ann) were immigrants from the Aran Islands in the west of Ireland. He attended Harvard University in 1895–96. Connolly had only recently enrolled at Harvard when he learned of the inclusion of the hop, step, and jump—the contemporary form of the triple jump and his specialty as an amateur track-and-field athlete—on the schedule of the first modern Olympic Games at Athens. Though denied leave of absence from Harvard, Connolly felt compelled to participate and left for Athens with twelve other American athletes as the sole representative of Boston's Suffolk Athletic Club. The final in the hop, step, and jump was held on the games' inaugural day (6 April 1896); Connolly won easily, thus becoming the first Olympic champion of the modern era. Later that week he tied for second in the high jump and placed third in the long jump, as the Americans dominated the program in athletics. Connolly would participate in two more Olympics, but after 1900 his reputation as a writer of sea fiction—especially his evocations of the Gloucester fishing fleet—eclipsed his early achievements as an athlete. In his journalism and fiction he did find occasion to espouse the Olympic ideal, most notably in a 1908 novel based on the most resonant event of the 1896 games, the victory of the Greek Spiridon Loues in the marathon.

SELECTED BIBLIOGRAPHY: James Brendan Connolly, *An Olympic Victor: A Story of the Modern Games* (1908); James Brendan Connolly, "The Spirit of the Olympian Games," *Outing Magazine* 48 (1906): 101–104; John J. MacAloon, *This Great Symbol: Pierre de Coubertin and the Origins of the Modern Olympic Games* (1981); Ernest Cummings Marriner, *Jim Connolly and the Fishermen of Gloucester* (1949); Albert J. Miles, "James B. Connolly," in Bobby Ellen Kimbel, ed., *Dictionary of Literary Biography*, Vol. 78, *American Short-Story Writers, 1880–1910* (1989), 111–116.

George Rugg

CONNOLLY, THOMAS HENRY, SR. (31 December 1870, Manchester, England–28 April 1961, Natick, MA). An umpire, he was born in England. He played cricket as a child, and at age thirteen his family immigrated to the United States, settling in Natick, Massachusetts. Connolly first learned of baseball when he served as a local team's bat boy. Fascinated by the rules, he became more interested in officiating than competing in the game. He was discovered by National League umpire Tim Hurst umpiring games at the local Young Men's Christian Association (YMCA) in Natick. Through this connection, Connolly became an umpire in the New England League from 1894 to 1897. For the next three seasons, Connolly officiated in the National League. He quit his position with the National League when league president Nicholas E. Young repeatedly failed to support his decisions. In 1901 Connolly signed with the American League and single-handedly officiated its first game. As with all umpires, he worked games alone until 1907, when the American League began using multiple umpires. He served with distinction as a full-time American League umpire for thirty years. In 1931, American League president William Harridge appointed Connolly the league's first umpire in chief, responsible for improving the quality of officiating. In this position, Connolly instituted the four-person umpire crew. He held that position through January 1954, when he retired at age eighty-three. In 1953 Connolly and fellow umpire Bill Klem were the first two umpires elected to the National Baseball Hall of Fame.

SELECTED BIBLIOGRAPHY: David L. Porter, ed., "Thomas Henry Connolly, Sr.," *Biographical Dictionary of American Sports: Baseball* (1987); "Thomas H. Connolly," in the *American League Red Book* (1954); various items from Thomas H. Connolly, official file at the National Baseball Hall of Fame Library.

Corey Seeman

COOPER, CHARLES T. ("Tarzan")

COOPER, CHARLES T. ("Tarzan") (30 August 1907, Newark, DE–19 December 1980, Philadelphia). A professional basketball player, he was one of the first African Americans to excel at that sport. The son of Theodore and Evelyn Cooper, he was a standout performer at Philadelphia Central High School, graduating in 1925. At 6'4" and 215 pounds he was one of the biggest men in the game during its formative years. After high school he joined several local Philadelphia teams for four years before signing with the soon-to-be legendary Harlem Renaissance club. From 1929 to 1939 he was the center on the team that was one of the best clubs of that depression decade, compiling a record of 1,303 wins against only 203 losses. He and his teammates barnstormed across the country, playing most games far from their home base in New York and often encountering discrimination in traveling and lodging. Although the "Rens" were an all-black squad, they often played against white teams. Some of Cooper's most memorable encounters were against the Original Celtics and their star center, Joe Lapchick.* The highlights of Cooper's career were his club's eighty eight straight wins in 1932–33 and his selection as the Most Valuable Player as the "Rens" defeated the Harlem Globetrotters to win the World Champions tournament in 1939. During World War II Cooper joined the Washington Bears, leading them to a "World's Pro Title" in 1943. He was elected to the Naismith Memorial Basketball Hall of Fame in 1976.

SELECTED BIBLIOGRAPHY: *New York Times*, 24 December 1980, A-14; Robert W. Peterson, *Cages to Jumpshots: Pro Basketball's Early Years* (1990); Charles Cooper file, Naismith Memorial Basketball Hall of Fame.

George B. Kirsch

COPELAND, LILLIAN (25 November 1904, New York City–7 July 1964, Los Angeles). Although she was a native of New York City, Lillian Copeland attended the University of Southern California (USC) and gained prominence as an outstanding track-and-field athlete and Olympic champion. Copeland was an all-around athlete at USC, playing basketball and tennis. She excelled in track and field, winning nine national titles beginning in 1925 with her win in the shot put. Copeland resumed her studies at the University of Southern California Law School after the 1932 Olympics and worked for the Los Angeles County Sheriff's Department; she served as a juvenile officer for twenty-four years. In 1926, winning three national titles in the discus, shot put, and javelin, Copeland broke the world record in the javelin throw with a mark of 112' 5-1/2" inches and the discus toss with 101' 1". In the 1928 Olympics Copeland earned a silver medal in the discus event and set a world record. At the Brussels international track meet in August 1928, Copeland led the American women's Olympic team against the European stars, breaking the world's record for the shot put, and she also won first place in the javelin and discus throw. In the 1932 Olympic Games Copeland won the gold medal in the discus setting a world record with a distance of 133' 1-5/8". She achieved recognition as one of the world's great woman athletes with her records and national titles. As a participant in the 1935 Maccabiah Games in Tel Aviv, Copeland won all three of her events—discus, shot put, and javelin. Lillian Copeland was inducted into the Jewish Sports Hall of Fame in Israel and into the B'nai B'rith/Klutznick National Jewish Museum, Jewish Sports Hall of Fame, Washington, D.C.

SELECTED BIBLIOGRAPHY: "Miss Copeland Sets Mark in Shot-Put," *New York Times*, 13 August 1928, 12; *New York Times*, 8 July 1964, 35; Bernard Postal, Jesse Silver, and Roy Silver, *Encyclopedia of Jews in Sports* (1965); Robert Slater, ed., *Great Jews in Sport*, rev. ed. (1992).

Linda J. Borish

CORBETT, JAMES JOHN (1 September 1866, San Francisco–18 February 1933, Bayside, NY). A prizefighter, Corbett's parents (Patrick, a livery stable owner, and Catherine) were Irish immigrants. As a boy he left school around 1883 to work in a bank. James J. "Gentleman Jim" Corbett was heavyweight boxing champion of the world from 1892 to 1897. He learned to box not on the street but at San Francisco's Olympic Club, where he took lessons while rising to the position of assistant teller at the Nevada Bank. In 1889 he left the bank to fight professionally and over the next two years met, without defeat, such outstanding fighters as Joe Choynski, Jake Kilrain, and Peter Jackson. On 7 September 1892 Corbett challenged longtime champion John L. Sullivan* for the heavyweight title at New Orleans' Olympic Club. In a bout popularly portrayed as a triumph of speed and "science" over brute force, Corbett won easily by knockout in twenty-one rounds. Many additional circumstances of the fight suggested boxing was entering a new era: this was the first heavyweight title bout fought with gloves, the first promoted by an athletic club, and the first held in an urban arena. As champion Corbett refined the public persona of the dapper "Gentleman Jim" in a stage play conceived by manager William A. Brady. Brady sought to exploit Corbett's matinee good looks and his image of middle-class respectability, but while the play was a financial success, the new champion never approached the popularity of Sullivan. Corbett lost his title by knockout to Bob Fitzsimmons at Carson City, Nevada, 17 March 1897 and retired after his second reclamation attempt against James J. Jeffries in 1903.

SELECTED BIBLIOGRAPHY: James J. Corbett, *The Roar of the Crowd: The True Tale of the Rise and Fall of a Champion* (1925); Nat Fleischer, *"Gentleman Jim": The Story of James J. Corbett* (1942); Michael T. Isenberg, *John L. Sullivan and His America* (1988); Alan Woods, "James J. Corbett: Theatrical Star," *Journal of Sport History* 3 (1976): 162–175.

George Rugg

CORDERO, ANGEL (8 November 1942, Santurce, PR–   ). His father (Angel T. Cordero, Sr.) was a jockey, trainer, and owner; his mother (Mercedes Hernandez) was the daughter of a jockey and trainer. He studied at the Institute of Puerto Rico. Cordero rode his first winner in 1960 at El Commandante Race Track in his native Puerto Rico. He emmigrated to the United States in 1962 and quickly developed into a leading rider, winning numerous titles at tracks in New York and Florida. A fierce competitor and a popular athlete with the racing public, Cordero won the Kentucky Derby with Cannonade (1974), Bold Forbes (1976), and Spend a Buck (1985); the Preakness with Codex (1980) and Gate Dancer (1984); and the Belmont Stakes with Bold Forbes (1976). The 5' 3" 113-pound Cordero was voted consecutive Eclipse Awards as the nation's leading jockey in 1982–83. Over the first twenty-five years of his career (1962–87) he recorded 6,110 victories out of 33,612 mounts (18.1%), earning more than $121 million in prize money. He was inducted into the National Thoroughbred Racing Hall of Fame in 1988 while still an active jockey.

SELECTED BIBLIOGRAPHY: *Current Biography* (1975), 91–93; *New York Post*, 15 March 1975, 22; Clayton Riley, "Angel on Horseback," *New York Times Magazine*, 27 April 1975, 16, 64–68; Ron Smith, *The Sporting News Chronicle of Twentieth Century Sport* (1992); *Sport* 47 (April 1969); 52.

Courtesy of the National Thoroughbred Racing Hall of Fame

CORNBLIT, JOSEPH ("Joey") (15 November 1955, Montreal, Canada–   ). Educated at Carol City High School in Miami, Florida, he was the first graduate of the North Miami Amateur Jai-Alai School under the tutelage of Epifanio

Saenz. A professional jai alai player, he began competing in the game at the age of twelve. When he was fifteen, he led the United States to its first bronze medal in the World Amateur Jai-Alai Championships, held in France in 1970. Prior to 1970 no American team had ever won a game in international competition. At sixteen Cornblit broke into the professional ranks while still attending high school. He made his professional debut at World Jai-Alai's* Miami fronton in 1972. During a brief stint at World Jai-Alai's Ocala fronton that year he captured the Championship Singles, Frontcourt Doubles, and Most Wins titles. He quickly established himself as a dominant player. Playing under the name of "Joey," Cornblit had a profound impact upon jai alai with his aggressive style of play. His *remate* (a type of kill shot) became a lethal shot to win points. Previously, jai alai was traditionally a catch-and-throw game. However, Cornblit rarely volleyed, as he attempted to kill the point immediately. His style was emulated by players of the time, especially those aspiring young stars at his alma mater, the North Miami Amateur Jai-Alai School. Cornblit's tenure with World Jai-Alai lasted from 1972 to 1986 at the Miami, Fort Pierce, Hartford, and Ocala frontons. While at Miami Jai-Alai he won three Singles Championships, seven Frontcourt Doubles Championships, and four Most Wins titles. He was also a five-time Tournament of Championships winner and captured the National Championship in 1982. He continued his playing career at Dania Jai Alai in Dania, Florida, collecting ten more titles. Back and shoulder problems forced him to retire from the sport in September 1995. Cornblit was the first American superstar in a sport dominated by the Basques.

SELECTED BIBLIOGRAPHY: J. Garcia Lourdes, "*Jai-alai* Flourished in Florida," in *International Prosperity, Florida in Shape for the Future* (1984); Clark Spencer, "Ailing Joey, 40, Retires from *Jai-alai*," *Miami Herald*, 10 November 1995, 12D; Miami Jai-Alai Public Relations File, "Joey," Miami, Florida.

                                                                           James R. Varella

COSELL, HOWARD (b. COHEN) (25 March 1918, Winston-Salem, NC–23 April 1995, New York City). A sportscaster, his parents, Isadore Cohen, an accountant, and Nellie Cohen, a housewife, were of Polish Jewish descent. They moved to Brooklyn in 1920. A graduate of Brooklyn's Alexander Hamilton High School, Cosell earned undergraduate and law degrees from New York University. During World War II he served in the army and married Mary Edith Abrams, with whom he had two daughters. Cosell's successful creation of a Little League radio show in 1953 led him to abandon his law practice for sportscasting. From 1953 to 1992, Cosell was a sportscaster for ABC-TV and radio, and from the late 1960s through the mid-1980s, he was the preeminent figure in the profession. Candid, socially conscious, erudite, and arrogant, he simultaneously attracted a multitude of devotees and detractors. At the peak of his notoriety, Cosell was ubiquitous, featured in virtually every important ABC sportscast from *Monday Night Baseball* to horse racing. On television's *Wide*

World of Sports, his interviews with heavyweight boxing champion Muhammad Ali* elicited memorable verbal sparring. As an irreverent television commentator on *Monday Night Football* (1970–83), Cosell, synthesizing sports, entertainment, and journalism, acquired his greatest celebrity. As a lonely widower battling cancer and heart disease, Cosell, in his final years, issued self-righteous condemnations of sports and acerbic assessments of former colleagues. At his best, however, defending Muhammad Ali's right of expression and providing moving commentary when terrorists murdered eleven Israeli athletes at the 1972 Olympics, Cosell articulated Judaism's traditional concern with justice. Through his penetrating questions and courage, Cosell contributed significantly to sportscasting's acquiring journalistic legitimacy.

SELECTED BIBLIOGRAPHY: Norman Chad, "Point After: Howard Cosell, Signing Off," *Sports Illustrated* 4 (1992); 68; Howard Cosell, with Mickey Herskowitz, *Cosell* (1973); Howard Cosell, with Peter Bonventre, *I Never Played the Game* (1985); *New York Times*, 24 April 1995, B-11; Benjamin G. Rader, *In Its Own Image: How Television Transformed Sports* (1984).

William M. Simons

COVELESKI, STANLEY A. (13 July 1889, Shamokin, PA–20 March 1984, South Bend, IN). A baseball player, he came from a Polish immigrant family whose original name was Kowalewski, though it was spelled Coveleski for most of his career. Stan dropped out of St. Stanislaus Elementary School after the fourth grade and went to work in the Pennsylvania coal mines at age twelve, working twelve-hour days. At night he would throw stones at tins and developed such a reputation that a semipro team offered him a tryout as a pitcher. He signed a minor league contract and developed a spitball, which was a legal pitch at the time. He moved up to the majors with Cleveland in 1916 and became a consistent winner. His best season was probably 1920. That year he had a 24–14 record with a league-leading 133 strikeouts for the pennant-winning Indians. In the World Series against Brooklyn he threw complete-game shutouts in three games and posted a 0.67 earned run average (ERA). He was called "the Silent Pole" because of his quiet demeanor. On the mound he was a fast worker with outstanding control. In one game he pitched for seven innings without throwing a ball. The spitball was outlawed in 1920, but Coveleski and sixteen other pitchers were "grandfathered" and allowed to continue throwing the pitch. Coveleski later pitched for the Washington Senators and New York Yankees before retiring in 1928 with 215 career wins and a 2.88 ERA. He settled in South Bend, Indiana, where he operated a service station, which was a gathering place for admiring youngsters.

SELECTED BIBLIOGRAPHY: *Cleveland Plain Dealer*, 21 and 23 March 1984; Mike Shatzkin, ed., *The Ballplayers: Baseball's Ultimate Biographical Reference* (1990); Stanley Coveleski file, National Baseball Hall of Fame Library, Cooperstown, NY.

Thomas M. Tarapacki

CRICKET. The English game of cricket was the first team sport in the United States. Introduced in the British colonies in North America during the 1700s, its modern era dates from the 1830s. Although baseball surpassed cricket as the national pastime during the 1850s and 1860s, the English sport remained popular after the Civil War among British working-class immigrants and some upper-class, native-born sportsmen, especially in Philadelphia. During the early twentieth century and especially after World War I cricket suffered a severe decline in the United States, but during the late 1900s a new wave of immigrants from British Commonwealth countries revived the sport's fortunes in America.

Affluent and working-class English immigrants founded cricket clubs in New York City and Philadelphia during the 1830s and 1840s. The St. George Cricket Club* of Manhattan, launched in 1838, was the first regular outfit governed by rules and regulations. In the spring of 1844 the St. George Club gained a new rival, the New York Cricket Club, created by John Richards, the English-born publisher of *The Spirit of the Times*. Although New York and its neighboring cities dominated American cricket during the sport's formative years, Philadelphia was destined to become the cricket capital of America. That city's Union Cricket Club appeared in 1843, when Robert Waller of the St. George Club moved to Philadelphia and brought together several English importers, a few Kensington men, and a sprinkling of American-born townball players. The Union Club followed many of the English customs connected with cricket, such as sending out invitations for interclub contests and providing tent accommodations for ladies and collations for players on match days. These Philadelphia sportsmen did break with one important English tradition in that they did not as a club sanction betting, although they knew that their matches stimulated considerable private wagering.

Many of the Englishmen who started the first American cricket clubs were merchants, professionals, or representatives of their government, but some were craftsmen of more modest means. These sportsmen joined together to enjoy themselves but also to preserve their ethnic heritage as British residents in a foreign land. In addition to Waller's efforts in Philadelphia, two other Dragon Slayers from the St. George association, Robert Bage and George Wheatcroft, organized a group of skilled craftsmen into the Newark Cricket Club in 1845. George Aitken, the British consul in San Francisco, founded that city's first modern sporting organization in March 1852, when he launched the San Francisco Cricket Club. Several British players helped in the formation of the Lowell, Massachusetts, club, whose secretary wrote in 1857 that "we Americans never saw a game of cricket played, and knew nothing of it, until we formed a club and got some Englishmen to learn [*sic*] us."

After the Civil War the continuing migration of British officials, businessmen, and skilled craftsmen to the United States prevented cricket from dying out in areas where clubs had existed prior to 1861. Fresh blood from England reinvigorated both white- and blue-collar organizations. In San Francisco the California

Cricket Club, founded in 1867, met in the same rooms as the British Benevolent Society, and its president was the British consul, William Lane Booker. In Trenton, New Jersey, potters from Staffordshire, England, were prominent in that city's industrial and recreational life. They formed lodges affiliated with the Sons of St. George and organized cricket clubs to secure and strengthen their ethnic identity, even as they also stimulated interest in cricket among the natives in New Jersey's capital throughout the 1860s and 1870s. Their promotion of the sport in Trenton repeated the earlier contribution of English craftsmen in Newark before the war.

American cricket during the mid-1800s provides interesting and complex ethnic patterns of participation, for England's national game did attract significant numbers of Americans in certain localities, especially in Newark and Philadelphia. This is apparent from the increasing frequency of special contests that matched Englishmen against Americans. In Newark, natives and "old countrymen" each contributed 45% of the total club members before 1861. Philadelphia (including its environs) was far and away the capital of American cricket both before the Civil War and for the rest of the nineteenth century, with the vast majority of its cricketers born in the United States. The sport became much more popular among Americans in Philadelphia than in other cities because of the willingness of that city's British residents to promote their pastime and because of the greater receptiveness of middle- and upper-class residents. Englishmen controlled New York City cricket, although Albany, Yonkers, and Long Island (including Brooklyn) fielded an impressive number of players.

Ethnic issues played a role in the triumph of baseball over cricket in the United States during the Civil War era, although other factors (especially the lack of good playing fields, the length and slow pace of matches, and problems with adaptability) were more important in determining the outcome of the competition between the two sports. Nineteenth-century Americans associated cricket with Great Britain and baseball with the United States, but they did not reject the former pastime simply because it was British. Anglo Americans had imported British customs and recreations in colonial days, and after 1776 the new nation still shared much of the culture of the former ruling country, enjoying such English amusements as hunting, fishing, horse racing, and boating. The special problem cricket faced in the United States was not simply one of origin but rather that the sport was controlled by an immigrant community that used it in part to preserve its own ethnic identity. The intense nativism of the 1850s did generate some anti-British sentiment in American cities, and there was certainly some hostility toward cricket because of it. But this liability could have been overcome through proper sponsorship and promotion. In 1861 the *New York Clipper* stated that "we must endeavor to remove the prejudices that exist against a game that emanates from a foreign country, and . . . we must overcome the same prejudice that exists among cricketers against the American game of ball." To eliminate or reduce American antagonism toward cricket, Englishmen had to be willing to reach out to American youth and adult ballplayers. In New York City it appears that the St. George Cricket Club was not especially active in such missionary work. In 1868 the *New York Times* maintained that "had our resident English cricketers observed a less exclusive and more liberal policy of action in the government of their clubs . . . we have not the least doubt that cricket would have gained much of the popularity its innate attraction is deserving of. But instead of this being done, an English exclusiveness has marked the government of the leading organizations, while no encouragement has been afforded young players." One important factor that inhibited American acceptance of cricket was the Englishmen's tendency to monopolize play in both practice sessions and formal matches. This was frequently a problem in batting, for novices were usually retired quickly, while experts retained their turn for long periods. The British customs of multiple club memberships and permitting professionals to participate in challenge matches also deprived the native sportsmen of sufficient opportunity to learn cricket. Except in Philadelphia, older natives of Great Britain tended to dominate the action at all levels of competition.

The golden age of American cricket began in the late 1880s, when upper-class Philadelphia clubs earned a string of victories against British elevens. Although it ended with World War I, that catastrophe was not the major cause of the sport's decline in the United States. More important were changing recreational trends, especially for the youth in Philadelphia. Country clubs adopted new British sports such as tennis and golf, and the growing popularity of the automobile and the advent of scouting and summer camps also drew boys away from the cricket fields. As the elite abandoned the game, the English working-class immigrants were unable by themselves to sustain the sport's previous standing.

During the twentieth century a few American college and private clubs kept the sport alive, but ultimately cricket's status in the United States depended on English and Australian residents and especially Asian, West Indian, and other immigrants whose countries had once been colonies in the British empire. During the late 1900s English and Australian diplomats, professionals, and businessmen founded clubs and leagues in Virginia, California, and Colorado, while along the East Coast most cricketers were natives of such South American or Caribbean nations as Guyana, Trinidad, Barbados, and Jamaica. Indians, Pakistanis, and Sri Lankans constituted strong contingents on West Coast and midwest elevens. In the mid-1990s there were about twenty cricket leagues in the United States, with these ethnic communities particularly active in metropolitan New York City, Boston, northern and central New Jersey, Washington, D.C., Atlanta, and northern and southern California. Thus, at the end of the twentieth century cricket in the United States was multicultural and multiracial, as white, black, and Asian players from a variety of nations around the globe pitched their wickets on American grounds. According to a Guyanese cricketer, the sport brought diverse peoples together, including Englishmen and Caribbean peoples.

He explained that "the Guyanese and Jamaicans don't always get along back in our separate countries, but we come here and cricket brings us together. We'll have South Africans, Australians, and West Indians socializing like it really is a big melting pot in this country."

SELECTED BIBLIOGRAPHY: Melvin A. Adelman, *A Sporting Time: New York City and the Rise of Modern Athletics, 1820–1870* (1986), ch. 5; J. Thomas Jable, "Latter-Day Cultural Imperialists: The British Influence on the Establishment of Cricket in Philadelphia, 1842–1872," in J. A. Mangan, ed., *Pleasure, Profit, Proselytism: British Culture and Sport at Home and Abroad* (1988), 175–192; J. Thomas Jable, "Social Class and the Sport of Cricket in Philadelphia, 1850–1880," *Journal of Sport History* 18 (Summer 1991): 205–223; George B. Kirsch, *The Creation of American Team Sports: Baseball and Cricket, 1838–1872* (1989); John A. Lester, ed., *A Century of Philadelphia Cricket* (1951); Tom Melville, *The Tented Field: A History of Cricket in America* (1998); Peter Monaghan, "Students and Professors from the British Commonwealth Help Preserve a Grand Old American Game: Cricket," *The Chronicle of Higher Education*, 21 October 1987, A41–42; Britt Robson, "Star-Spangled Cricket," *Utne Reader*, September–October 1995, 32–34.

George B. Kirsch

CRONIN, JOSEPH EDWARD ("Joe") (12 October 1906, San Francisco–7 September 1984, Osterville, MA). A baseball player, manager, and executive, he was born to parents of Irish descent only a few months after the great earthquake of 1906. His father (Jeremiah) was a teamster from County Cork, and his mother (Mary Carolin Kelly) was born in the United States to parents from County Athlone. He graduated from Christian Brothers School of the Sacred Heart. Cronin began his major league career in 1926 with the Pittsburgh Pirates but did not see much playing time until he was dealt to the Washington Senators in 1928. He was a very talented shortstop with a lifetime fielding average of .951, and he was also known as a smooth hitter, compiling a lifetime batting average of .301. The Senators dealt him to the Boston Red Sox for the 1935 season, and he completed his major league playing career in 1945 after twenty years. Cronin also served as player-manager for both the Senators and the Red Sox, during which time he developed a reputation as an intelligent field manager. This reputation helped him to gain a position in the Red Sox front office from 1948 until 1959, when he was chosen as the American League president by the team owners. During his tenure as president he led the league through two separate expansions and introduced the designated hitter. He was elected to the Baseball Hall of Fame in 1956.

SELECTED BIBLIOGRAPHY: Al Hirshberg, *From Sandlots to League President: The Story of Joe Cronin* (1962); Stewart Wolpin, "Joe Cronin," in Mike Shatzkin, ed., *The Ballplayers* (1990), 236–237; Joseph Edward Cronin file, National Baseball Hall of Fame Library.

James L. Gates, Jr.

CSONKA, LAWRENCE RICHARD (25 December 1946, Stow, OH–   ). A premier college and professional football player, he is of Hungarian descent. He was raised on a farm by his parents, Joseph Csonka and Mildred (Heath) Csonka. His father worked as an engineer at Goodyear Tire and Rubber Company and as a radio and television repairman. Larry played on the Stow High School football team before enrolling at Syracuse University, where he starred as a powerful running back, breaking all the rushing records of such Syracuse immortals as Jim Brown,* Ernie Davis, Floyd Little, and Jim Nance. At Syracuse, Csonka was elected to the College All-American Team in his junior year, 1967, and again as a senior in 1968. Not unexpectedly, he was the first running back picked in the American Football League (AFL) draft in 1968 and joined the Miami Dolphins. Don Shula became the head coach of the Miami Dolphins in 1969 and began to build what would prove to be a dynasty around Csonka, whose running prowess provided the likes of Bob Griese, Paul Warfield, Mercury Morris, and Jim Kiick more room to operate. Csonka has often been compared to Bronko Nagurski,* and many consider him to be one of the finest, if not the finest, fullback ever to play the game. During the 1972 season the Dolphins went undefeated and won the Super Bowl, only to come back again in the 1973 season to win all but two of their games and the Super Bowl once more. During 1973 Csonka set a new record for the most touchdowns scored in a postseason game and was named the Most Valuable Player in the 1974 Super Bowl game. At the formation of the newly conceived World Football League (WFL) in 1974, Larry was signed away from the Miami Dolphins and played for Memphis for one season, after which the league folded. He returned to the NFL with the New York Giants, where he played very little because of a severe knee injury. Back with the Miami Dolphins in what was to be his final season, 1979, Csonka rushed for 837 yards and scored twelve touchdowns, leading the Dolphins to another Divisional title.

SELECTED BIBLIOGRAPHY: Howard Balzer, "Csonka Trying to Form New Union for Players," *Sporting News*, 28 May 1990, 36; Aaron Bernstein, "Hey, Larry, What Are You Doing Here?" *Business Week* (25 June 1990): 56–57; Marshall Burchard and Sue Burchard, *Larry Csonka* (1975); Larry Csonka and Jim Kiick, with Dave Anderson, *Always on the Run* (1973); Kavanah, *Great Athletes of the Twentieth Century—Football* (1992); George Sullivan, *Larry Csonka: Power and Pride* (1975).

Lawrence Huggins

CUBANS. Cuban athletes have attained their greatest success and recognition in American baseball, although they have also distinguished themselves in boxing and a few other sports. As legend has it, Cuban-born Nemesia Guillot brought baseball to the island after attending Fordham University in New York. Whether or not this tale is true, it is likely that Guillot's influence, coupled with increased economic and social ties between the United States and Cuba, encouraged the spread of baseball throughout Cuba during the late nineteenth century. Esteban Bellan was the first Cuban to play professional baseball in the

United States when he competed in the National Association of Professional Base Ball Players in 1871. Racial views in the United States at the time greatly hampered the recruitment of Cubans. Bellan was allowed to play only because he was light-skinned. In 1910, American major league teams played exhibition games in Cuba and saw many extraordinary Cuban players. In addition, during the first decade and a half of the twentieth century the desire to hire cheaper labor also encouraged American teams to tap into the growing Cuban market. As a result, a few more light-skinned Cubans were invited to play in America. In 1911 the Cincinnati Reds signed infielder Rafael Almeida and outfielder Armonda Marsan, and a year later Mike Gonzalez started with the Boston Braves. In 1918 the Cincinnati Reds signed Dolf Luque. Luque was an exceptional player. Despite his talent, blue eyes, and light-skinned complexion, fans often greeted him with racial slurs. This kind of prejudice kept dark-skinned Martin Dihigo* out of the major leagues. Instead, he played in the Negro Leagues* in the United States, where he excelled as a pitcher and batter and at all defensive positions except catcher. Helping to break down the color barrier was perhaps one of the greatest contributions Cubans made to the sport. Although black Cubans were not allowed to play, light-skinned Cubans were. Black Americans were hopeful that the presence of Cubans in the major leagues indicated a liberalized attitude toward race. In 1911 Lester Walton, sports editor for the *New York Age*, wrote, "With the admissions of Cubans of a darker hue in the two Big Leagues it would then be easy for colored players who are citizens." Baseball's color barrier did not officially end until the late 1940s with the admission of Jackie Robinson,* but the entrance of Cubans throughout the early twentieth century set the ball rolling. Between 1871 and 1994, 129 Cuban-born athletes played in the major leagues. The most prominent among them are Esteban Bellan, Rafael Almeida, Armonda Marsan, Mike Gonzalez, Dolf Luque, Minnie Minosa, Sandy Amoros, Pedro Ramos, Mike Cuellar, Tony Perez, Luis Tiant, Tony Oliva, Jose Canseco, Rafael Palmeiro, Orestes Destrade, Tony Fossas, Rene Arocha, and Tony Menendez.

Cubans have also impacted the American boxing scene. Kid Chocolate, "the Cuban Bon Bon," was one of the most popular fighters in New York in the 1920s and 1930s. Kid Gavilan, "the Cuban Hawk," introduced America to the bolo punch, a powerful uppercut that resembled the motion he had used with a machete in Cuban sugar fields. More recently, Ultimino Sugar Ramos, Jose Naples, Alfredo Duvergel, and Lorenzo Aragon have challenged American boxers in both professional and Olympic bouts. Joel Casamayor and Ramon Garby, two of Cuba's star boxers, defected to the United States in 1996.

Athletes of Cuban descent have excelled at various other sports and impacted the American sport scene to a lesser extent. Pedro Bascallao won the U.S. National Squash Tennis Championship nine years in a row and served as president of the U.S. Squash Tennis Association from 1969 to 1982; Marie Colon Ruenes, Ana Quirot, Yoelbi Quesada, Alberto Juantorena, and Javier Sotomayor challenged and impressed American athletes at track-and-field events during Olympic Games; Miraide Garcia-Soto, Ortiz Puente, and Ivan Travejo Perez made names for themselves in fencing competitions; Diaderis Luna is a top woman's judo contender, and Pablo Lara and Ariel Hernandez won medals in various weight-lifting categories in the 1996 Olympic Games.

Compared to other nationalities, the number of Cuban athletes who have influenced the American sport scene seems quite small. After 1959, when Fidel Castro's communist regime took power, Cuban athletes were restricted from traveling to the United States. Throughout the late 1980s and early 1990s, the world witnessed the demise of communism. As a result, Cuba suffered from economic and political hardships, causing security to become somewhat lax. Cuba's sports programs have eroded, and athletes are now far more willing to defect to the United States to continue their careers. Joe Cubas, a Cuban American sports agent based in Miami, helped seven baseball players defect from Cuba in 1996 alone. One year earlier he lured away Livian Hernández, who signed a $4.5 million contract with the Florida Marlins and starred in the 1997 major league baseball playoffs and World Series. In December of that year Hernández's half brother, Orlando Hernández, escaped to the United States. Within a few months he signed a contract with the New York Yankees, and in 1998 and 1999 he duplicated his relative's achievement with stellar performances in the World Series for the champion Yankees. Track-and-field athletes, gymnasts, and other Cuban athletes have defected to the United States in large numbers in recent years as well. Therefore, it is safe to assume that athletes of Cuban descent will have an even greater impact on the American sport scene in the near future.

SELECTED BIBLIOGRAPHY: Peter C. Bjarkman, *Baseball with a Latin Beat—A History of the Latin American Game* (1994); Thomas D. Boswell and James R. Curtis, *The Cuban American Experience—Culture, Images and Perspectives* (1983); Milton Jamail, *Full Count: An Inside View of Cuban Baseball and the United States* (2000); Michael M. Oleksak and Mary Adams Oleksak, *Beisbol: Latin Americans and the Grand Old Game* (1991); Paula J. Pettavino, *Sport in Cuba: The Diamond in the Rough* (1994); Steven A. Riess, *Touching Base: Professional Baseball and American Culture in the Progressive Era* (1980).

Diane D'Angelo

CURLING. The oldest artifacts from the ice sport of curling are stones that prehistoric peoples slid toward a target along frozen rivers or lakes. These peoples may also have used primitive brooms to clear snow from the path of their sliding stones. In 1565 Holland's Peter Breugel painted *Hunters in the Snow* and another work depicting scenes resembling modern curling. Breugel's paintings support the premise held by some that curling originated in continental Europe. The Scots, however, are the undisputed developers and formalizers of the modern game. By 1638 curling was considered, with golf and archery, one of their recreational pastimes. After a huge growth spurt in the nineteenth century, curling was played by thousands in nearly every Scottish parish. Between the sixteenth and twentieth centuries, Scotland's climate warmed, and today the lochs rarely freeze. The climate change hindered curlers, who played outdoors on natural ice until the twentieth century. Nonetheless, the Scots had, by the mid-1800s, formalized curling's rules of play and equipment and had established the "mother club" of curlers worldwide, the Royal Caledonian Curling Club (RCCC). The RCCC is today the national governing body of curling in Scotland, with 20,000 active members now playing indoors on refrigerated ice.

The game of curling spread throughout the world through the efforts of thousands of Scottish soldiers and émigrés. In North America curling's origins likely date to the late 1700s. The first documented record is the founding of the Montreal Curling Club in 1807. In 1832 the Orchard Lake Curling Club near Detroit became the first curling club in the United States, organized at the home of one Dr. Robert Burns! The Orchard Lake group curled on Lake St. Clair. The oldest continuously operating curling club in the United States is the Milwaukee, Wisconsin, club, founded in 1845. The Scottish founders' roster included such names as Murray, Ferguson, Dunlop, Gunyon, Findlay, Kinney, McFarland, and McFadyen. Since the mid-1800s curling has spread and thrived in northern states, including Wisconsin, Minnesota, and North Dakota, and in the Great Lakes, New England, and mid-Atlantic states. There are pockets of curling activity in other states, including Alaska, Washington, California, Texas, Colorado, Nebraska, Kansas, Missouri, and North Carolina. In the United States in the late 1990s there were over 15,000 curlers in over 135 clubs, most of which owned their ice facility. While many U.S. curlers have Scottish roots, modern curling club membership rosters tend to reflect an ethnic cross-section of their communities, which are preponderantly small-town and rural. The U.S. Curling Association (USCA—founded 1958) governs curling in the United States. Like that other Scottish sport, golf, curling is both a recreational and an athletic pastime, marked by a strong code of fair play and courtesy, "the Spirit of Curling." The USCA is a member of the U.S. Olympic Committee and the World Curling Federation and has 131 member clubs in eleven regions. Curling debuted as a medal sport in the 1998 Winter Olympic Games in Japan. About 1.5 million people from ages eight to eighty in over thirty-three countries curl.

The best-known American curler is Raymond "Bud" Somerville, the first inductee in the USCA's Hall of Fame. Somerville, of Superior, Wisconsin, skipped his team to its first world championship in 1965 at age twenty-eight. In 1992, at age fifty-five, he skipped his team to a bronze medal at the Albertville Olympics (curling was a demonstration sport). The largest curling club in the United States is the St. Paul, Minnesota, club, with over 700 members. The ice sport of curling, although never well known in the United States, has developed steadily throughout American history. The sport is often passed down through families and has provided enjoyable winter recreation to thousands of Americans.

SELECTED BIBLIOGRAPHY: John Kerr, *A History of Curling* (1890); W. H. Murray, *The Curling Companion* (1981); David B. Smith, *Curling: An Illustrated History* (1981); Tim Wright, *United States Men's Curling Championships, the First Thirty Years* (1986).

David J. Garber

CZECHS. As is true of many other ethnic groups, the Czechs came to the United States primarily because of religious or political persecution or economic want. The first sizable migration to North America from the Czech lands, then the kingdom of Bohemia, took place in the first half of the eighteenth century. These immigrants, known under the name Moravian Brethren, were the spiritual heirs of the Bohemian Unitas Fratrum, followers of the Czech martyr John Hus and Jan Amos Komensky (Comenius). They settled first in Georgia, then Pennsylvania, Ohio, North Carolina, and the nearby states. They went to exile because of their religious persecution in their homeland and eventually migrated to North America. The largest migration of Czechs to America occurred around the revolutionary year 1848 and lasted until the second decade of the twentieth century. This mass migration was precipitated partly by political reasons and partly, and more importantly, because of unsatisfactory economic conditions and large unemployment in the Habsburg empire, of which the kingdom of Bohemia was then a part. Some of the emigrants settled in large cities, such as St. Louis, Chicago, Cleveland, and New York. The bulk of the emigrants settled, however, in the rural areas of the Midwest, including Nebraska, Kansas, Ohio, Iowa, Minnesota, and Wisconsin. Later on, groups of Czech emigrants went as far as the Dakotas, Oklahoma, and Oregon. There were three more waves of Czech migrations: the first, prior to World War II, the second, after the communist coup d'état in 1948, and the third in 1968, after the suppression of the experiment with liberalization in communist Czechoslovakia called the Prague Spring and the occupation of the country by Soviet troops.

Sports, athletics, and gymnastics have been an integral part in the life of Czechs for at least the last 150 years. The idea has its foundation in the Sokol (Falcon) movement, inspired by its founders Miroslav Tyrš (1832–84) and Jindřich Fügner (1822–65). It became an important factor in Czech national life, not only in the old country but in the United States as well. It was officially founded in 1862 in Prague, at the time when the Czech nation was awakening from lethargy produced by over 200 years of repression of the national language and national feeling by the ruling Habsburgs. The cities and towns became completely Germanized, and it was a miracle the Czech language survived among the peasantry. With the birth of the Sokol movement a new national program was born. "Equality, harmony, fraternity" and "A healthy mind in a healthy body"—these were their aims and mottos. The Sokols stressed physical training for the body and national and patriotic training for the mind. The movement grew and prospered and has always played an important part in the affairs of the young Czech nation. Being composed largely of younger men and later also of younger women, it stood for virility, energy, and enthusiasm, as well as for democracy and patriotism. The movement was so powerful that it spread through Central and Eastern Europe.

Most of the immigrants from the Czech lands were raised on these ideas, and it was only natural to bring them along to the United States. From their first Gymnastic Society in St. Louis, in a short time its members spread to nearly every Czech settlement in the United States, many of which soon boasted of their own Sokol Halls. The Sokol movement in America has survived to this day. The members of Sokol clubs meet regularly for practice, give public exhibitions, and compete in tournaments. With German turners, they have been the true pioneers in gymnastics and light athletics in this country. The Sokols do not confine themselves to physical activities alone but also participate in various cultural and other ethnic activities.

Considering the emphasis of Sokol organizations on health and general body exercises, it is not surprising that Czech Americans excelled, above all, in gymnastic sports. Among the earliest contenders was Charles Edward Dvorak of Chicago (b. 1878), who was a holder of Olympic and intercollegiate pole vault records. Then came the legendary Frank Kriz* (b. 1894), who won Amateur Athletic Union (AAU) All-Around Championships in 1922 and 1924 and who represented the United States in three Olympiads, winning several medals. Laddie (Hniz) Bakanic* (b. 1924) of New York City won first place in the AAU Junior Championship in 1944. She was a member of the 1948 U.S. Olympic team, which won a bronze medal. James Hartung* (b. 1960) from Omaha, Nebraska, won the 1975 and 1976 All Around Championship, as well as the United States Gymnastics Federation Junior Olympics. He was a National Collegiate Athletic Association (NCAA) All-Around Champion in 1980 and 1981. He holds a total of twenty-two All-Around American Awards. Kim Zmeskal (b. 1976) of Houston, Texas, was the first U.S. gymnast to win the all-around in the world championship. She emerged as one of the country's top women gymnasts in 1989, when she won the all-around balance beam and floor exercise in the American classic. She also scored her first perfect 10.00 in the floor exercise, while winning the all-around in the Arthur Gardner Memorial meet in Switzerland. In 1990 Zmeskal won the first of three consecutive U.S. All-Around Championships and had two perfect scores in the vault and floor exercise in winning the All-Around Championship and the U.S. Challenge meet. She was the 1991 World All-Around Champion, and during the 1992 world championship she was the only athlete to win two gold medals.

In track and field Hugo Morris Friend (b. 1882) emigrated from Prague, Czechoslovakia, to the United States when he was two years old. A standout in the long jump and high hurdles, he won AAU championships in both events in 1905 while a student at the University of Chicago. As a member of the Chicago Athletic Association, he placed fourth in the hurdles and captured a bronze medal at the 1906 Olympics. Olga Fikotova Connolly (b. 1932) from Prague took the Czech discus title in 1955 and 1956 and then went on to win the Olympic gold medal with a new record of 176' 1". At the Olympics she met Hal Connolly,* the U.S. hammer thrower champion, whom she subsequently married. As an American citizen, she represented the United States at the next four Olympiads. She won five AAU titles between 1957 and 1968, and, at the Olympics, she finished seventh in 1960, twelfth in 1964, and sixth in 1966. In May 1972 she beat Earlene Brown's twelve-year-old record with a throw of

179' 2" and later that month improved the record to 185' 3". At the 1972 Olympics she was selected to carry the U.S. flag at the opening ceremonies. There was another discus thrower of Czech origin—Richard Aldrich Babka (b. 1936) of Cheyenne, Wyoming. He won the AAU "Rink" Throw in 1958. In August 1960 he set a world record of 196' 6.5" before going to Rome, where he placed second behind Al Oerter at the Olympics, winning the silver medal. Babka enjoyed a remarkably long career at the top, and his best mark ever came in 1968, when, at the age of thirty-two, he threw 209' 9".

One of the most popular sports that Czechs brought with them to America is soccer. They soon established their own team—Sparta ABA (Athletic and Benevolent Association), Chicago, the oldest Czech sport club in America, which marked its eightieth anniversary during the 1995–96 season. Even though the actual Sparta club was established in 1917, its direct predecessor, Slavia, had fielded an excellent team in 1915. During that year several other new Czech soccer teams appeared, including S. K. Union, Cechie, West Side, Bohemians, Olympia, and Sokol Slavsky. The first league game between two Czech clubs in the United States took place on 21 November in Chicago, when Cechie tied S. K Olympia 1–1. The beginning of 1916 brought two more Czech teams into the league: AC Rangers and S. K. Atlas. Because of the number of interested teams the league had to form a new division where more Czech teams competed. New members of the league became American-Bohemians, S. K. Union, and S. K. Slavoj. All these clubs but Sparta would later dissolve or merge with other clubs. Initially, Sparta played a minor role in the Chicago soccer scene, which was dominated by the Irish and Scottish teams. However, in 1923 Sparta was able to sign several good players from Czechoslovakia and became one of the elite clubs of Chicago. Sparta was also one of the first clubs to field women's teams. It achieved its biggest triumph in 1938, when the team became Champion of the USA with an impressive record, winning thirty-six out of thirty-nine matches. By the time of its eightieth anniversary, Sparta teams could boast of two U.S. and eleven league championships.

One of the earliest Americans of Czech descent to make a name for himself in football was Joseph K. Taussig (b. 1873), who started as a quarterback for Navy in 1897 and 1898. Hugo F. Bezdek (b. 1884), a native of Prague, Czechoslovakia, nicknamed "Thirteen-Inch Shell" by his classmates, was the only man to coach major college football and manage big-league baseball. He played for the University of Chicago and coached Arkansas (1908–12), Oregon (1906, 1913–17), Penn State (1918–29), and Delaware Valley (1949). He also managed the Pittsburgh Pirates (1917–19). Attaining national fame also was George S. Halas* (1895–1983) of Chicago, the last of eight children of first-generation Bohemian immigrants, nicknamed "Papa Bear." The player-coach for the Staley football team, which later became the Chicago Bears, he was associated with the team until his death in 1983. He was a pioneer in many aspects of the game. He introduced the T formation, man-in-motion attack in 1940 that set the style for modern football. He was the first coach to hold daily practices, to utilize films of opponents, to barnstorm teams, to have games broadcast on the radio, and to use a tarpaulin on the field for weather protection. One of the most successful football players was George F. Blanda* (b. 1927) of Youngwood, Pennsylvania, whose mother was a native of Prague and whose father was of Slovak ancestry. All of George's brothers—Peter, Paul, and Tom—were outstanding athletes in basketball or football. George was drafted by the Chicago Bears in 1949 and played with them through 1958. In 1960, after a year's absence, he was signed as a free agent by the Houston Oilers, and in 1967 he was dealt to the Oakland Raiders. He played more seasons than any other pro player and holds many records. More recently Jay McKinley Novacek (b. 1962) of Gothenberg, Nebraska, has gained fame as the Dallas Cowboys' tight end.

The earliest Czech American baseball player was Edward Joseph Konetchy (b. 1883) of La Crosse, Wisconsin. He began playing first base for the Cardinals in 1907, had a twenty-game hitting streak in 1910, and in 1911 led the National League (NL) with thirty-nine doubles. Batting over .300 four times, Konetchy compiled 100 or more hits in fourteen consecutive seasons and broke up four no-hitters. Another old-timer was Joseph Franklin Vosmik (b. 1910) of Cleveland, Ohio. He was considered by baseball experts the best hitter to come from the Cleveland sandlots, averaging .300 in his major league career. Another baseball player of note was Robert H. Cerv (b. 1926) of Weston, Nebraska. He spent most of his major league career with the New York Yankees and the Kansas City Athletics. The much celebrated star Stanley Frank Musial* (b. 1920) of Donora, Pennsylvania, was half Czech (after his mother) and half Pole. Reportedly, his mother encouraged him to enter baseball. Among the recent players, a person deserving notice is Kent Alan Hrbek (b. 1960) from Minneapolis. He was an instant favorite when he joined the Twins in 1981. With the Twins until he retired in 1994, the left-handed-hitting, right-handed-throwing first baseman ranked among the best all-around American League (AL) players.

Tennis is one of the most popular summer sports in the Czech lands, and its players have ranked among the best in Europe, starting with the sensational win of Jaroslav Drobny at Wimbledon in 1954. At the height of the communist oppression a number of top players defected from Czechoslovakia to the West, some of whom emigrated to the United States and Canada. Of these, two players in particular, Ivan Lendl* and Martina Navratilova,* achieved international fame.

One of the most popular winter sports in the Czech lands is hockey, and it is therefore not surprising to find its players among the best in Europe. Following the overthrow of communism in Czechoslovakia, a number of their players have been offered lucrative franchises by various American professional hockey teams. The National Hockey League clearly benefited from the arrival of these players. Jaromir Jagr (b. 1972) from Kladno, the right wing of the Pittsburgh

Penguins, and Dominik Hasek (b. 1965) from Pardubice, the goaltender of the Buffalo Sabres, have almost become household names in the United States. During the 1998 Winter Olympiad these two players were briefly released to the Czech National Hockey Team and were largely responsible for the Czechs' success in winning the Olympic gold medal.

In figure skating early stars of the Ice Capades were Aja Zanova (née Alena Vrzanova) (b. 1931) and Otto and Maria Jelinek, all Czech-born and Olympic and world champions, the former for Czechoslovakia (1949 and 1950), the latter two for Canada (1962). Among the younger generation, Nicole Bobek (b. 1977) of Chicago, daughter of Czech refugee Jana Bobkova, shows real promise. She won her first title in 1991—a gold medal at the Olympic Festival and another at the 1991 Vienna Cup in Austria. In 1995 she won the U.S. Women's Figure Skating championship by beating the favored Michelle Kwan.* She then went on to win a bronze medal at the world championship.

Finally, Czech Americans have excelled in a variety of other sports in the United States. The best-known basketball player of Czech ancestry is John Havlicek* of Lansing, Ohio. He was an All-American at Ohio State University who later played football for the Cleveland Browns. He earned his greatest fame as a star for the Boston Celtics in a career that stretched from 1962 to 1978. In ski jumping the 1967 U.S. champion was Gene Kotlarek of Duluth, Minnesota. In boxing Jack Root (née Korinek) (1876–1963), a native of Prague, Bohemia, knocked out Charles Upton and Pat Brastand in his first and second pro middleweight bouts in 1897. He remained undefeated in thirteen fights in 1898. He had a standoff with Australian Jimmy Ryan in 1899 but won his next six fights that year by knockout in only fifteen composite rounds. Root had been the top-ranking middleweight until 1903, during which time he developed into an intelligent, "scientific" boxer. When the 175–pound class was created, Root easily won the first contest against Kid McCoy at Detroit in April 1903. He held the championship until his next bout against George Gardner, which he lost. In weight lifting Anthony A. Matysek (b. 1893), originally from Moravia, was a champion wrestler and bodybuilder, billed as "America's Strongest Man." In 1915 he established a world weight-lifting record of 241 and 3/5 pounds. He followed this in 1917 by a world shoulder lifting record of 278 pounds.

For some unexplained reasons most of the Czech American wrestlers have come from Nebraska. They include Joe Zikmund, who immigrated to the United States from Czechoslovakia and settled in Barnard, Nebraska. He became one of the greatest wrestlers, competing with the best in the game for the Lightweight Championship of the world. Then there were three Stecher brothers, Anton, Lewis, and Joe, sons of Czech Nebraska pioneer Frank Stecher, from Dodge County, Nebraska. The greatest glory came to the youngest son, Joe Stecher (b. 1893), who was acknowledged by his contemporaries as the greatest wrestler who ever lived. Joe's strong legs earned him the nicknames "Python-like Legger" or "Scissors-King." He won the world's title first in Omaha in 1915 against Charlie Cutter, the second time from Earl Caddock in 1920, and the third time from Stanislaus Zbyszko, the "Polish Giant," in 1925. Another wrestler among the Czech Nebraskans was John Pesek, who became the wrestling Heavyweight Champion of the World in 1932. In 1957, he was named to the Nebraska Sports Hall of Fame as the greatest wrestler of his time. He was called the Nebraska "Tiger-Man" because of the ferocity of his attack in matches. Pesek's victory over Charlie Hanson in 1920 was described as the fiercest and most terrifically fought battle in mat history. His son, Jack Pesek, followed in his famed father's footsteps, winning the Nebraska state heavyweight championship. Jerry (Jaroslav) Adam of Omaha, whose parents immigrated there from Bohemia, became known as Nebraska's professor of wrestling. Upon enrolling at the University of Nebraska, he lettered in both football and wrestling. After graduation, Jerry was named the University of Nebraska mat coach. He also became an assistant football coach and a professional wrestler.

SELECTED BIBLIOGRAPHY: George Halas, with Gwen Morgan and Arthur Veysey, *Halas by Halas: The Autobiography of George Halas* (1979); Ralph Hickok, *A Who's Who of Sports Champions* (1995); Vladimir Kucera and Alfred Novacek, *Czechs and Nebraska* (1967); Bill Mallon and Ian Buchanan, *Quest for Gold: The Encyclopedia of American Olympians* (1984); Zdenek Nerada, ed., *Sparta Chicago 80* (1996); Claire E. Nolte, "Our Brothers across the Ocean: The Czech Sokol in America to 1914," *Czechoslovak and Central European Journal* 11 (1993): 15–37; Rose Rosicky, *History of Czechs (Bohemians) in Nebraska* (1929); Denise Willi, *Martina Navratilova: Tennis Star* (1994).

Miloslav Rechcigl, Jr.

D

DEHNERT, HENRY ("Dutch") (5 April 1898, New York City–20 April 1979, Far Rockaway, NY). A professional basketball player and coach, he was of German descent. Dehnert did not play high school or college basketball but gained experience in local leagues. At 6'1" and 220 pounds he played a strong all-around game, exhibiting speed, ball-handling skill, clever passing, and solid defense. Original Celtics owner Jim Furey signed "Dutch" and many other top players to exclusive contracts, a novel practice. To capitalize on his investment, Furey withdrew the team from league play to barnstorm. Due to their innovative play and outstanding skill the Celtics were immensely popular and financially successful. Since they played together exclusively, they developed exceptional teamwork and pioneered many new concepts that became staples of the game from that point forward. Among these were the give-and-go play and switching man-to-man defense. Dehnert personally authored one of the Celtics' most important innovations, the "pivot play." It was conceived in Chattanooga, Tennessee, against a local team. In order to prevent a "standing guard" from breaking up his team's passing game, Dehnert stood in front of him and received a pass. He found that he then was able to pass to a cutting teammate whose man he would screen. If Dehnert's man committed to try to stop the pass, Dutch could then turn the opposite way with a clear path to the basket. Dehnert became one of the highest paid and best-known players in pro basketball. Following years of barnstorming success the Celtics joined the American Basketball League (ABL), playing home games at the new Madison Square Garden, and took two consecutive championships (1926–28) with so little difficulty that the league forced the team to disband in order to enhance competitive balance. Dehnert joined the Cleveland Rosenblums, continued his outstanding play, and led them to two consecutive league titles (1928–30). With the ABL's collapse in 1931, Dehnert joined a reconstituted Original Celtics squad, which continued barnstorming. He retired having played in over 1,900 Celtics victories. During the

1940s he coached for several professional teams, and in his later years he worked as a mutuel clerk for the New York State racetracks. He was elected to the Naismith Basketball Hall of Fame in 1968.

SELECTED BIBLIOGRAPHY: Stanley Cohen, *The Game They Played* (1977); G. Dickey, *The History of Pro Basketball since 1896* (1982); Larry Fox, *The Illustrated History of Basketball* (1974); Zander Hollander and A. Sachare, *The Official NBA Basketball Encyclopedia* (1989); Joe Lapchick, *My Life in Basketball* (1965); David Neft and Richard Cohen, *The Sports Encyclopedia: Pro Basketball 1891–1989* (1989); Robert W. Peterson, *Cages to Jump Shots: Pro Basketball's Early Years* (1990).

Dennis Ryan

DELAHANTY, EDWARD JAMES ("Big Ed") (30 October 1867, Cleveland, OH–2 July 1903, Niagara Falls, NY). A baseball player, his father (James) was of Irish-French-Norman lineage, and the family name was originally spelled "de la Hante." He graduated from Cleveland's Central High School and also attended St. Joseph's College nearby. Delahanty's baseball career began in 1887, when he signed with Mansfield in the Ohio State League, whereupon he embarked upon a career that would extend through a variety of teams and professional leagues. His major league career began in 1888 with Philadelphia in the National League and included seasons with Cleveland (1890) of the Players League, a reprise in Philadelphia (1891 to 1901), and two years in the newly founded American League with Washington (1902–3). During his sixteen seasons as a major league ballplayer he compiled a collection of impressive offensive statistics. These included a lifetime batting average of .346, with three years with averages over .400 (1894: .407, 1895: .404, and 1899: .410). His premodern era .505 slugging percentage is indicative of his hitting power. Delahanty had a noted disdain for team training rules, and in June 1903 he was suspended from the Washington club for code violations during a trip to Detroit. On the train to New York he was ordered off by a conductor for being drunk and disorderly. He was last seen walking toward the International Bridge near Niagara Falls. While there is controversy as to whether it was an accident, suicide, or homicide, Delahanty's body was discovered several days later on the Canadian shore. His death was directly attributed to having gone over the falls. He was elected to the Baseball Hall of Fame in 1945.

SELECTED BIBLIOGRAPHY: Allen Lewis, "Ed Delahanty," in Mike Shatzkin, ed., *The Ballplayers* (1990), 265; Mike Sowell, *The Mysterious Death of Hall-of-Famer Big Ed Delahanty: July 2, 1903* (1992); Edward James Delahanty, research file, National Baseball Hall of Fame Library.

James L. Gates, Jr.

DEMPSEY, WILLIAM HARRISON ("Jack," "the Manassa Mauler") (24 June 1895, Manassa, CO–31 May 1983, New York City). A heavyweight champion boxer, he was the son of Hyrum Dempsey, a teacher, sharecropper, and rancher of Irish descent, and Mary Celia (Smoot) Dempsey. His father had worked in West Virginia before moving his growing family to western states to seek a better life. Dempsey completed the eighth grade in Lakeview, Utah, and became a miner and saloon fighter in Utah and Colorado. After a series of victories in 1915 and 1916 and a dispute with his first manager, John Reisler, he came to public attention through his affiliation with Jack "Doc" Kearns, who took control of Dempsey's career. During World War I Dempsey worked in a shipyard; he received a draft deferment as the sole support of his wife, mother, and younger siblings. Dempsey captured the heavyweight crown on 4 July 1919, when he severely punished and knocked out the gigantic Jess Willard. The result was stunning because at 6' and 180 pounds, Dempsey was six inches shorter and nearly seventy pounds lighter than Willard. His lack of military service in World War I became a major issue in 1921 in Dempsey's fight with French war hero Georges Carpentier. The press labeled Dempsey a "slacker" and draft dodger but he easily defeated Carpentier in the first boxing match ever to bring in $1 million in gate receipts.

Victories in 1923 over Tommy Gibbons and Luis Angel Firpo of Argentina boosted his popularity but his two fights against Gene Tunney elevated him to one of the great sport heroes of the 1920s. He lost a decision to Tunney on 23 September 1926 in Philadelphia, but it was the rematch the following year that became legendary in boxing history. On 22 September 1927, in Chicago, Dempsey knocked Tunney down in the seventh round but failed to go promptly to a neutral corner. His delay caused the famous "long count" which gave Tunney time to recover and eventually win the bout. The two defeats to Tunney ended Dempsey's boxing career, but after his retirement he enjoyed much success and great popularity through exhibition bouts, employment as a referee, and especially his restaurant business in New York City. During World War II he earned the rank of commander in the Coast Guard, directed the Coast Guard's physical fitness program, and served as a morale officer. He was inducted into the International Boxing Hall of Fame in 1990.

SELECTED BIBLIOGRAPHY: Jack Dempsey, *Dempsey* (1977); Jack Dempsey, *Round by Round: An Autobiography* (1940); Nat Fleischer, *Jack Dempsey* (1972); Roger Kahn, *A Flame of Pure Fire: Jack Dempsey and the Roaring '20s* (1999); Randy Roberts, *Jack Dempsey: The Manassa Mauler* (1979); Bert R. Sugar, "Jack Dempsey: A Legend for All Times," *Ring* (July 1983): 24–33.

George B. Kirsch

DIHIGO, MARTIN (25 May 1906, Matanzas, Cuba–22 May 1971, Cienfuegos, Cuba). A baseball player known as "El Maestro," Dihigo grew up in a small town east of Havana. As a teenager his talent on the ball field was recognized. Dihigo played every position on the diamond except catcher. His skills took him to the United States, where he played in the Negro Leagues* from 1923 to 1935 and in 1945. Dihigo began his professional career in the United States in 1923 with Alex Pompez's Eastern Cuban Stars. In 1928 he moved to the Homestead Grays* of Pittsburgh for a year before joining the Philadelphia Hilldales in 1929 and 1931. In 1930 he returned for a short stint with the Cuban Stars. Most of his remaining years in the United States were spent with the New York Cubans and Baltimore Black Sox. In 1937 he returned to Latin America to play in Santo Domingo, Venezuela, and Mexico. There he performed mainly as a pitcher, compiling a lifetime 115–60 record in Cuba and a 119–57 record in Mexico. Dihigo had a lot of power and speed, which helped him hit .421 in 1926, followed by .370 season the next year. He led the league with home runs in 1926 and tied for the lead in 1927 with Oscar Charleston. Each man hit eighteen home runs, though Dihigo accomplished his feat in fewer times at bat than Charleston. He was selected to play in two East-West classics and was inducted into the National Baseball Hall of Fame in Cooperstown, New York, in 1977. Dihigo is also enshrined in the Cuban and Mexican Halls of Fame. Other players described Dihigo as one of the top five players they ever saw at each position he played. After his playing career Dihigo retired in Cuba as a national hero, where even Fidel Castro admired him. He owned a wide array of real estate holdings and acted as Cuba's minister of sports until his death.

SELECTED BIBLIOGRAPHY: Dick Clark and Larry Lester, *The Negro Leagues Book* (1994); John Coates II and Merl Kleinknecht, "Historically Speaking: Martin Dihigo," *Black Sports* (November 1973): 13–14; James A. Riley, *The Biographical Encyclopedia: The Negro Baseball Leagues* (1994), 233–235.

Leslie Heaphy

DIMAGGIO, JOSEPH PAUL ("Joltin' Joe," "the Yankee Clipper") (25 November 1914, Martinez, CA–8 March 1999, Hollywood, FL). A baseball player, he was the son of Italian immigrants Giuseppe DiMaggio, a fisherman, and his wife, Rosalie, both of whom were from Isola Della Fammine, a small island northwest of Palermo in Sicily. Joe was raised in the San Francisco Italian American fishing community of North Beach. He followed his older brother Vince into professional baseball by joining the San Francisco Seals of the Pacific Coast League at the end of the 1932 season. In 1936 he was sold to the New York Yankees and remained with them for his entire professional career until his retirement in 1951. In thirteen seasons as a Yankee DiMaggio set numerous team and league records and had very strong career statistics despite missing the 1943–45 seasons due to military service. The apex of his baseball career was a remarkable fifty-six-game hitting streak in the summer of 1941. The "Yankee Clipper" is thought by many to be the greatest all-around ballplayer ever. DiMaggio's classic smooth swing made the difficult task of hitting a baseball look easy. A superb fielder with a strong arm, he always seemed to be in the right place at the right time. These skills, combined with a style and grace on and off the playing field, made him a leader in the clubhouse and an idol to baseball fans worldwide.

SELECTED BIBLIOGRAPHY: George DeGregorio, *Joe DiMaggio: An Informal Biography* (1981); Joe DiMaggio, *Lucky to Be a Yankee* (1946); Joseph Durso, *DiMaggio:*

The Last American Knight (1995); Jack Moore, *Joe DiMaggio: A Bio-Bibliography* (1986); *New York Times*, 9 March 1999, A-1, D-4, 5.

Gregory S. Harris

DITKA, MICHAEL KELLER (18 October 1939, Carnegie, PA–   ). A football player and coach, he is the son of Mike Ditka, Sr., a railroad worker whose parents were immigrants from the Ukraine. Ditka's mother, Charlotte Keller, was of Irish and German ancestry. Mike, Jr. was active in baseball, basketball, football, and wrestling at Aliquippa High School before entering the University of Pittsburgh in the fall of 1957. There, in addition to his football career, he briefly participated in baseball and basketball. During his senior year at Pittsburgh he was a consensus All-American while captaining the team and winning the university's Hartwig Award for the most outstanding contribution to that school's varsity athletics. During his senior year he played in the Hula Bowl, the College All-Star Game, and the East-West Shrine All-Star Game. As the first-round choice of the Chicago Bears in 1961, "Iron Mike" played at tight end. He won the National Football League (NFL) Rookie of the Year award, scoring twelve touchdowns while catching fifty-six passes for 1,076 yards and was named to the All-NFL team, a feat he was to duplicate for each of the ensuing three years. He also participated in five straight Pro Bowls. In 1964 he achieved his career high by catching seventy-five passes, including a single-game performance of thirteen receptions for 168 yards against the Washington Redskins. Ditka played for the Philadelphia Eagles during the 1967–68 season and for the Dallas Cowboys from 1969 through 1972. Appointed as a special teams coach for Dallas in 1973, he was subsequently chosen by George Halas* to coach the Chicago Bears in 1982. Building the program there, in 1985 Ditka was named Coach of the Year by both the Associated Press and United Press International after leading his team to a 15–1 season record, the NFC crown, and a victory in Super Bowl XX over the New England Patriots, 46–10. Ditka's personal playing career record of 427 receptions for 5,812 yards and forty-three touchdowns was cited in his 1988 enshrinement in the Football Hall of Fame. In recent years Ditka has worked as a sportscaster as well as a head coach.

SELECTED BIBLIOGRAPHY: Armen Keteyian, *Ditka, Monster of the Midway* (1992); David L. Porter, ed., *Biographical Dictionary of American Sports: Football* (1987).

Lawrence Huggins

DIXON, GEORGE ("Little Chocolate") (29 July 1870, Halifax, Nova Scotia, Canada–6 January 1909, New York City). An African American prizefighter, he was descended from blacks who had migrated to Canada from the American colonies during the Revolutionary War. After moving to Boston with his parents, he took up boxing after working as an apprentice to a photographer who specialized in pugilistic pictures. Standing only 5'3" tall and weighing only about 100 pounds, he became one of boxing's greatest fighters in the lower weight classes. Managed by Tom O'Rourke, he turned professional at the age of sixteen. On 27 June 1890 he became the first black to win an international title when he knocked out the British featherweight champion, Nunc Wallace. He claimed the American bantamweight crown in 1891 with a victory over Johnny Murphy. The following year he captured the world featherweight championship with a fourteen-round knockout of Fred Johnson. He lost and regained that title three times before yielding it for the final time to Terry McGovern in 1900. Perhaps his most celebrated and controversial match occurred on 6 September 1892, when he fought white amateur Jack Skelly in a bout that was part of a three-day Carnival of Champions at the Olympia Club in New Orleans. (The feature attraction was the heavyweight title fight between John L. Sullivan* and "Gentleman" Jim Corbett.*) Although racially mixed public bouts were illegal in New Orleans, the Dixon-Skelly contest was permitted because it was held in a private club. Dixon gave Skelly a punishing, brutal, and bloody beating that shocked the spectators and generated a wave of revulsion among sportswriters, especially in New Orleans. The unexpected outcome of a black man's beating up a white opponent resulted in a racial backlash against mixed fights. Afterward black fighters had only limited opportunities to challenge whites in the ring, especially in heavyweight bouts. After losing his title for good in 1900, Dixon fought for six more years, but his chronic alcoholism and his spendthrift ways contributed to his premature demise.

SELECTED BIBLIOGRAPHY: Arthur R. Ashe, Jr., *A Hard Road to Glory: A History of the African-American Athlete, 1619–1918*, vol. 1 (1988), 22–24; Nat Fleischer, *Black Dynamite: The Story of the Negro in the Prize Ring from 1782 to 1938* (1947).

George B. Kirsch

DOBY, LAWRENCE EUGENE

DOBY, LAWRENCE EUGENE (13 December 1923, Camden, SC–   ). An African American baseball player, he is the son of David Doby, a horse groomer, and Etta Brooks, a domestic worker. Doby was raised by his maternal grandmother in a small, racially segregated southern town. In 1938 he joined his mother, who had earlier migrated to Paterson, New Jersey, and attended East Side High School, earning eleven varsity letters in four sports. Prior to graduation, Doby made an impressive professional debut with the Newark Eagles of the Negro National League* under an alias in order to preserve his amateur status. After brief stints at two colleges, he was drafted into the navy and served as a physical education instructor. In 1946 he rejoined the Eagles as an infielder. He played in two Negro League All-Star Games and, with Monte Irvin and Leon Day, led the Eagles over the Kansas City Monarchs in the Negro World Series. In 1947, Bill Veeck, president of the Cleveland Indians, purchased his contract at midseason. Doby became the first African American baseball player in the American League, just eleven weeks after Robinson had joined the Dodgers in the National League, and the first player to go from the Negro Leagues directly to the major leagues. In 1948 he moved to the outfield and emerged as an offensive force and helped lead his club to a World Series victory. From 1949 to 1956, Doby established himself as one of the best power hitters in the game and one of its best center fielders, leading the American League with thirty-two home runs in 1952 and 1954. Although he played in the shadow of Mickey Mantle, Willie Mays,* and Duke Snider, Doby set an American League record of 164 consecutive games without an error in 1955. During his thirteen years in the majors, mostly with Cleveland, he made six consecutive All-Star appearances and became only one of four men in the history of baseball to play in the World Series of both the Negro and major leagues. After the major leagues, Doby played in Japan for one year and became a minor and major league coach for the Montreal Expos and Cleveland Indians. In 1978 Bill Veeck, president of the Chicago White Sox, promoted him to manager in midseason, making Doby the second African American manager in major league history. Despite the team's improvement during the last six weeks of the season, Veeck fired Doby as manager that October. In the 1980s Doby served as director of community relations for the New Jersey Nets basketball team.

SELECTED BIBLIOGRAPHY: Larry Moffi and Jonathan Kronstadt, *Crossing the Line: Black Major Leaguers, 1947–1959* (1994); Joseph Thomas Moore, *Pride against Prejudice: The Biography of Larry Doby* (1988); Mark Ribowsky, *A Complete History of the Negro Leagues, 1884 to 1955* (1995).

Larry K. Menna

DONOGHUE, JOSEPH F. (11 February 1871, Newburgh, NY–1 April 1921, New York City). This son of an 1843 Irish immigrant family from County Kerry was speed skating's first "official" World Champion. His father (Tim, Sr.) was a renowned oar maker for the world's best amateur and professional rowers and also U.S. national speed skating champion of the 1860s. His mother (Margaret Kennedy) was a homemaker who had eleven other children, including the "straight mile" world record holder Tim, Jr. (1887). Although the United States did not have a strong speed skating tradition in 1888, Tim, Sr., helped develop Joseph into a legitimate international star through many years of stern parental training on the frozen uppers of the Hudson River. Tim, Sr., monitored Joe's training methods from his oar shop on the Hudson. The rigorous training allowed Joe to sweep the European circuit from 1888 to 1891. Donoghue's presence on the world scene would, in effect, cause the formation of the International Skating Union in 1892. Eventually, Donoghue would suffer from the effects of stardom and media scrutiny that haunt modern-day celebrities. During his amateur days Donoghue was treated royally as an eighteen-year-old international "gentleman." When he turned professional at twenty-three in 1893, no one dared to race him for fear of losing their money, and his star began to dim. Donoghue was primarily a "straight" open river skater specialist who never did master tight turns, which the artificial oval rink required. Although Donoghue set the world record for a 100-mile race, beating the long-distance skating champ John Ennis (a well-known Irish pedestrian), his long-distance training would eventually cause injury to his ankles and force him into an early retirement. Initially, his celebrity was "Barnumized" by promoters; later he grew tired of training, lost interest, suffered from painful ankle joints, fell on hard times, hocked his trophies, including diamond medals and a fur coat, developed a reputation as a ladies' man, never married, and died nearly alone at age fifty. After Donoghue's professional prime and after his father's death in 1897, he continued for a few years to run his father's crew oar business from their oar shop located on the Hudson River. In his final years he settled accident claims as a lawyer for the Metropolitan Street Railway Company in New York City.

SELECTED BIBLIOGRAPHY: John M. Heathcote and Charles G. Tebbutt, *Skating, Figure Skating, Curling, etc.* (1892); John J. Nutt, *Newburgh: Her Institutions, Industries and Leading Citizens* (1891); J. Van Buttingha Wichers, *Schaatsenrijden* (1888).

Paul J. DeLoca

DOUGLAS, ROBERT L. (4 November 1882, St. Kitts, British West Indies– 16 July 1979, New York City). An African American professional basketball owner and manager, he was the son of Robert Gould Douglas, a commercial ship purser. Douglas immigrated with his family to New York City in 1902. In 1908 Douglas, George Abbott, and J. Foster Phillips organized the Spartan Field Club. This club provided amateur sport competition in cricket, track, soccer, and basketball for the black youth of Harlem. Douglas participated on the track and basketball teams until 1918, when he became the general manager of the club. In the fall of 1923 Douglas organized the New York (Harlem) Renaissance Five* professional black basketball team. The "Rens" practiced and played home games at the newly constructed Renaissance Ballroom in Harlem and quickly became one of the top teams in the country. With the onset of the depression the "Rens" barnstormed in the Midwest and the South, playing club, college, and All-Star teams. In the 1932–33 season the Rens had an eighty-eight-game winning streak, and in 1939 they won the first world professional basketball championship, which was held in Chicago. During World War II, Douglas curtailed the schedule of the "Rens" and allowed his players to move to various teams to make a living. The "Rens" served as the first all-black team to enter a league, the National Basketball League, when they replaced the Detroit Vagabond Kings in 1948. Known as "the father of black basketball," in 1971 Douglas became the first African American elected as a contributor to the Naismith Memorial Basketball Hall of Fame.

SELECTED BIBLIOGRAPHY: Arthur R. Ashe, Jr., *A Hard Road to Glory: A History of the African-American Athlete, 1919–1945*, vol. 2 (1988); Ocania Chalk, *Pioneers of Black Sport* (1975); Glenn Dickey, *The History of Professional Basketball since 1896* (1982); Susan J. Rayl, "The New York Renaissance Professional Black Basketball Team, 1923–1950" (Ph.D. diss., Pennsylvania State University, 1996); Robert L. Douglas file, Naismith Memorial Basketball Hall of Fame.

Susan Rayl

DREYFUSS, BARNEY (23 February 1865, Freiburg, Germany–5 February 1932, New York City). The owner of the National League Pittsburgh Pirates and one of the leading figures in major league baseball during the first third of the twentieth century, he was the son of German Jews Samuel Dreyfuss and Fanny (Goldsmith) Dreyfuss. He was educated at the Karlsruhe Gymnasium in Germany and immigrated to the United States when he was sixteen years old. He moved to Paducah, Kentucky, where he worked at the Bernheim Brothers distillery. Initially a laborer, Dreyfuss moved up in the company and served as an accountant. He took over the semipro baseball team at the distillery and, after moving to Louisville with the company, purchased an interest with the Louisville National League Club. In 1899 Dreyfuss bought out his partners and merged Louisville, a team that featured future Hall of Famers Fred Clarke and Honus Wagner,* with the Pittsburgh Pirates. In 1901, Dreyfuss bought out his partners and became the sole owner of the Pirates. He embraced baseball and became one of its most knowledgeable owners, keeping meticulous records of players across the country in his famous "dope books." Under Dreyfuss the Pirates won six National League pennants and two World Series. He was noted for his ability to create a balanced schedule, evenly distributing holiday games to all teams. An ardent peacemaker, Dreyfuss was central to the conclusion of the National and American League war in 1903 and the creation of both the World Series (1903), and the office of the commissioner (1921).

SELECTED BIBLIOGRAPHY: Ralph S. Davis, "Barney Dreyfuss—The Man," *Baseball Magazine* (July 1908); David L. Porter, ed., "Dreyfuss, Barney," *Biographical Dictionary of American Sports: Baseball* (1987); Barney Dreyfuss file, National Baseball Hall of Fame Library.

Corey Seeman

DUFFY, HUGH (26 November 1866, Cranston, RI–19 October 1954, Boston). A baseball player, manager, scout, and coach, he was of American Irish descent. He spent sixty-six years in professional baseball. In 1888 Duffy signed his first major league contract with Cap Anson's Chicago White Stockings, despite being offered more money to play with the Boston club. He idolized Anson, but Anson was not impressed with the 5' 7" Duffy. In 1890 Duffy jumped to the Players League and then the American Association before he settled in 1892 with the Boston Braves of the National League (NL), where he spent the next nine years. In 1894 Duffy enjoyed his best year in the major leagues. He led the league in home runs (eighteen) and runs batted in (RBIs, 145) and set a record in batting average (.440) that still stands today. Duffy ended his playing career in 1906 with the Philadelphia Phillies (NL) with a lifetime batting average of .324. Duffy was a better player than manager, finishing with a record of over .500 only twice. He ended his managerial career with 535 wins and 671 losses, never taking any team above fourth place. Working as a hitting instructor with the

Boston Red Sox, Duffy gave some pointers to some of their great hitters, including Ted Williams. In 1945 he was elected by the Veterans Committee to the National Baseball Hall of Fame.

SELECTED BIBLIOGRAPHY: Peter Filichia, *Professional Baseball Franchises: From the Abbeville Athletics to the Zanesville Indians* (1993), 15, 25; *New York Times*, 20 October 1954, 29; Lowell Reidenbaugh, "Hugh Duffy," in his *Baseball's Hall of Fame: Cooperstown, Where the Legends Live Forever* (1993); John Thorn, ed., *Total Baseball V: The Official Encyclopedia of Major League Baseball* (1997), 754, 2336, 2358.

Scot E. Mondore

DUTCH. The Hollanders of New Amsterdam and Fort Orange (Albany, New York) were very unlike their stern contemporaries in Puritan New England. They were rather fun-loving and uninhibited in their pursuit of sports and *volksvermaken* (popular folk pleasures). So it is informative to read the comprehensive ordinance issued by the director general and the Council of New Amsterdam in 1656, describing the "lower or unlawful exercises or games" that were forbidden to the denizens of that town. We can glean a clear idea of the recreational interests of the time from reading this document. Among the leisure-time pursuits of New Amsterdamers forbidden by ordinance were the firing of guns, riding the goose, planting of Maypoles, carousing, drunkenness, beating of drums, retailing of spirits, and "other insolence." The following activities were banned on the Sabbath: cardplaying and "dicing"; playing ball; trick-track, tennis, cricket, or ninepins; pleasure parties in a boat, cart, or wagon; fishing, hunting, and gathering strawberries or nuts. Director Pieter Stuyvesant condemned "pulling the goose" or "riding the goose" as "unprofitable, heathenish, and pernicious" and issued ordinances against this cruel sport. In this event a goose, whose head was well greased, was fastened to a rope that was stretched across a road. Riding on horseback, a man tried to catch the bird by the neck in order to pull the head off at a gallop.

During the colonial era the Dutch settlers in North America enjoyed many pastimes. They introduced the German sport of bowling (ninepins, kingpin) to the New World and arranged the pins in the shape of a diamond. The Dutch version, *kegelspel*, was played with large wooden balls and ninepins on a bowling green. The name "Bowling Green" in lower Manhattan reflects the universal popularity of this sport among the early residents of New Amsterdam. Washington Irving immortalized this game in his story of Rip Van Winkle. An outdoor version of cricket called *stoelbal* (or "stool-ball") was popular with New Amsterdam women. A variant, when played in winter on the ice, was called *kalviten* (or "curling"), a team game with a modification that involved sliding two "stones" or balls at a tee. Early histories devote much space to describing in great detail archery matches and shooting with the crossbow. Battledore or shuttlecock, an early form of badminton, was a favorite game. *Trock* was a seventeenth-century modification of croquet, played on the grass. *Klos* or *kloot-haan* involved an iron ring at the end of an alley so as to form a gate. The point was for the contestant to play his bowl through this ring by means of a spadelike bat. In *kaetsen* a player struck the ball with his hand or racket against a wall. His opponent drove it back after its rebound. It was also played person to person with a cord or net in between. Both in the homeland and in the New World, Dutch youngsters enjoyed playing *kooten* or *cockalls* or *knucklebones*, primitive forms of dice games. Stoopball was made possible by Dutch settlers of New Amsterdam. A ball was thrown against the *stoep* or front veranda of the house, and the player then ran to a base. "Double Dutch rope" employs two jump ropes moving in opposite directions, touching the ground alternately. It was invented in the Netherlands and came to America with some of the earliest New World settlers.

Card, board, and parlor games were also popular. "Devil cards," "Pedro cards," and "high, low, jack" were frequently denounced from the pulpit by Holland American *dominies*. It is ironic that what earlier generations of Hollanders decried was improved upon and, in fact, given its official rules by a member of a later generation, Harold S. Vanderbilt.* Trick-track was a Dutch version of backgammon, an ancient game of warfare between black and red forces, played with both men and pegs, whose outcome was determined by the fall of the dice. A trock-table was similar to a pool table, on which an ivory ball was struck under a wire wicket by a cue.

With memories of the ponds and canals of the Netherlands, skating was not so much a sport as a way of life. Frozen waterways were filled with crowds of people of all ages, wearing skates made of iron and wood, some screwed to boots, others fastened with leather straps. *Kolf*, an ancient Dutch game, was played on ice with sticks and a hard leather ball that was knocked toward a stave or another target.

Racing with wagons, carts, and sleighs was popular. Sleighs were often built in shapes resembling animals or ships and were gilded or painted in bright colors. The lure of ice was always present, and racing sleighs on ice is often described. Although prohibited by law, horse racing was very widespread and very popular.

The Dutch contributions to the world of games and sports have continued in the popularity of bowling, ice skating, horse racing, and contract bridge. But with the loss of sovereignty over New Netherland to the English in 1664, emigration from the Netherlands fell off severely. Accommodation and assimilation into the mainstream culture—Americanization—were the inevitable outcome. Quotas in the nineteenth century and the nativism generated by World War I further reduced immigration, discouraged preaching in any language other than English, and brought the publishing of many non-English-language periodicals to an end. Postwar intermarriage put an end to the homogeneity of the Netherland American community. So it is not surprising that there is little awareness today that the pastimes that so characterized the seventeenth century were brought from the Netherlands to a Dutch colony established at the tip of Manhattan island in 1624.

In the twentieth century several Dutch Americans have distinguished themselves in the world of American sports. In football Norman Van Brocklin* (known as "the Dutchman") was a collegiate and professional star quarterback at the University of Oregon and the Los Angeles Rams and Philadelphia Eagles. Harold S. Vanderbilt* was a legendary yachstman and the inventor of contract bridge. Jim Kaat was a pitcher in major league baseball whose career stretched over twenty-four seasons and four decades (1958–83). Johnny Vander Meer, nicknamed the "Dutch Master," earned baseball fame in 1938, when he hurled two consecutive no-hit games for the Cincinnati Reds.

SELECTED BIBLIOGRAPHY: Donna R. Bames, "Dutch Games: Seventeenth-Century Dutch Depictions of Children's Games, Toys, and Pastimes," in Rhonda L. Clements, ed., *Games and Great Ideas* (1995); Ellis Lawrence Raesly, *Portrait of New Netherland* (1945); William R. Shepherd, *The Story of New Amsterdam* (1926, 1970); "Sports, Festivals, and Pastimes," in Esther Singleton, *Dutch New York* (1968); "Holidays and Celebrations," in Charlotte Wilcoxen, *Seventeenth Century Albany: A Dutch Profile* (1981, 1984).

Thomas E. Bird

E

EDWARDS, HARRY (22 November 1942, East St. Louis, MO–   ). Raised by his mother (Adelaide) and father (Harry, a laborer) in East St. Louis, Missouri, Edwards was a basketball and track athlete at San Jose State. A graduate of San Jose State (B.A.) and Cornell University (M.A., Ph.D.), Edwards is a professor of sociology at the University of California, Berkeley, who has written extensively on the role of African Americans in sport and has led boycotts to ensure equality in both sport and the larger American society. Edwards first came to national attention in the fall of 1967, when he led a highly publicized protest movement of black students at San Jose State, which culminated in the cancellation of the season-opening football game between that institution and the University of Texas at El Paso. Shortly after the racial confrontation at San Jose State, Edwards organized a proposed boycott of the 1968 Olympic Games in Mexico City. Calling the venture the Olympic Project for Human Rights (OPHR), Edwards assembled a group of outstanding black athletes who threatened to boycott the Mexico City games unless certain demands were met, including the restoration of Muhammad Ali's* heavyweight boxing title, exclusion of South Africa from participation, and the ouster of Avery Brundage as president of the International Olympic Committee (IOC). The black athletes ultimately decided to compete in the games, choosing instead to show forms of protest to illuminate the racial discrimination in America and around the world. Since the Mexico City games, Edwards has assumed positions in the sports establishment himself. In addition to working with the San Francisco Forty-Niners, Edwards was hired in 1987 by baseball commissioner Peter Ueberroth to seek out minority candidates for upper-level administrative positions. Edwards has continued, however, to be highly critical of organized sport, the racism still prevalent in American society, and the overemphasis on sport among many African Americans. He has expressed his views on these topics in a plethora of articles in popular periodicals and academic journals. He has also made his views known in a number of books, including *The Revolt of the Black Athlete* (1969), *Black Students* (1970), *The Sociology of Sport* (1973), and *The Struggle That Must Be: An Autobiography* (1980). In addition to his publications, Edwards is frequently asked to speak on issues relating to African American athletes at professional conferences and on radio and such popular television newscasts as *Nightline*.

SELECTED BIBLIOGRAPHY: Vincent Matthews, with Neil Amdur, *My Race Be Won* (1974); Donald Spivey, "Black Consciousness and Olympic Protest Movement, 1964–1980," in Donald Spivey, ed., *Sport in America: New Historical Perspectives* (1985), 239–259; William VanDeburg, *A New Day in Babylon: The Black Power Movement and American Culture, 1965–1975* (1992); David K. Wiggins, "The Year of Awakening: Black Athletes, Racial Unrest, and the Civil Rights Movement of 1968," in David K. Wiggins, *Glory Bound: Black Athletes in a White World* (1997), 104–122.

David K. Wiggins

ELDER, ROBERT LEE (14 July 1934, Dallas, TX–   ). An African American professional golfer, he began caddying in Dallas, Texas, where he grew up. When he was eleven, his father (a coal truck driver) was killed in the army during World War II, and he then moved with his family to Los Angeles. He dropped out of Manual Arts High School in Los Angeles after attending two years. After he finished second to Joe Louis in an amateur competition sponsored by the United Golfers Association (UGA),* he became a protégé of noted African American golfer Ted Rhodes.* Elder was drafted into the army in 1958, where he captained the army golf team at Ft. Lewis, Washington. He competed in all-service tournaments against some white professionals who were also temporarily in military service. When he was discharged from the service, he went to Washington, D.C., where he began teaching golf at Langston Golf Course. In 1959 he turned professional and began competing regularly on the UGA tour, where he dominated play over a nine-year period, winning the National Professional UGA Championship in 1963, 1964, 1966, and 1967. In 1963 he met and married Rose Harper, herself an accomplished golfer, who was to play a significant role in his golf career on the Professional Golfers' Association (PGA) tour, as well as in his efforts to end discrimination in golf. Because of complicated requirements that favored white golfers, it wasn't until 1967 that Elder was able to secure his PGA card, which entitled him to compete on the PGA tour. In 1968 he went five sudden-death holes against Jack Nicklaus on national television, eventually losing the American Golf Classic at the Firestone Golf Club in Akron, Ohio. Elder played a key early role helping to break down apartheid policies in South Africa, which prohibited interracial sports competitions. He and Gary Player competed in a series of exhibition matches in South Africa in 1970. Despite his success on the PGA tour, an invitation to the Masters eluded him because of the convoluted point system devised by Masters organizers. However, beginning in 1971, invitations to the Masters were issued to all winners of PGA tournaments in the previous year. In 1974, Lee Elder won the Monsanto Open, and the following year he became the first African American golfer to play in the Masters. In 1979 he would achieve the same distinction on the American Ryder Cup team. He was one of the charter members of the PGA Senior Tour, where he continued to compete during the late 1990s.

SELECTED BIBLIOGRAPHY: Arthur R. Ashe, Jr., *Hard Road to Glory*, vol. 3 (1988); Al Barkow, *The History of the PGA Tour* (1989); F. Finley McCrae, "Hidden Traps between the Placid Greens: A History of Blacks in Golf," *American Visions* 6 (April 1991): 26–29; Louis Robinson, "Lee Elder, Hottest Sophomore in Pro Golf," *Ebony* (September 1969): 61; *Sports Illustrated* 42 (10 March 1975): 24.

Larry Londino

ENGLISH. The English influence on American sports, as on so many other aspects of American life, has been profound. Americans imported English sports, athletic equipment, and regulations. Americans applied English gambling rules, read English sports magazines and newspapers, and wore English sporting clothes. English immigrants created communities centered around sport that fostered the development of sporting clubs and associations in the United States. The English wove into the cultural fabric of America a love of sport and the human connections it can provide. English colonists introduced into the New World such sports as ninepins, skittles, bowls, ball games, horse racing, fox hunting, rugby, soccer, and wrestling. After the American Revolution, English immigrants were influential in bringing into the new country such sports as rowing, boxing, cricket, archery, croquet, track and field, tennis, badminton, polo, and yachting.

Social class and nationalism were important elements in the English contribution to American sports. The upper and middle classes of the United States emulated their English counterparts and patronized horse racing, fox hunting, cricket, rowing, archery, croquet, tennis, badminton, polo, and yachting, while bowling, rugby, soccer, baseball, wrestling, boxing, and track and field tended to be favorite pastimes of the hoi polloi. Nationalism was also an important factor in the dynamic relations between English and American sportsmen, as the rivalry between the two great nations played itself out on fields, courts, and waterways. International competition between Americans and Englishmen was particularly keen in yachting, horse racing, rowing, cricket, boxing, and tennis.

Bowling. Bowls, also called tenpins, was played in England in the Middle Ages. Along with other similar games like ninepins and skittles, it developed into modern bowling. These sports were brought to America by the earliest English colonists. Dutch explorers also brought a form of bowling to the New World. In the colonies, skittles was usually played by the lower classes in alleyways or outside taverns. Bowls was played by the earliest settlers in Jamestown, Virginia. The survival of the Jamestown colony was endangered by the colonists' unwillingness to do the work necessary to provide for themselves. When the new governor, Sir Thomas Dale, arrived in 1611, appalled by what he saw, he instituted the "Laws Divine, Morall and Martial." Consistent with the Puritan vision of a community in covenant with God, these laws were meant to govern all aspects of the settlers' lives. Dale had found the colonists playing bowls, which he promptly forbade.

This Puritan vision, common in the young colonies, hampered the development of sports in America. The Records of the Court of Assistants of the Colony of the Massachusetts Bay, 1630–1644, reveal that in 1633 a court ordered "that noe person howsehoulder or other, shall spend his time idely or unprofitable under paine of such punishment as the Court shall think meete to inflicte." Football, sledding, horse racing, gambling, theater, and all Sunday pastimes were banned.

Despite the pronouncements against sports in Jamestown and New England, most American colonists played English sports. In Williamsburg, Virginia, they took part in bowling-type games, handball, wrestling, and battledore shuttlecock. In New York they bowled and played battledore shuttlecock, tennis, and cricket.

Horse Racing. The English brought thoroughbred racing to the colonies, and it was America's first organized sport. Horse racing began in England over 300 years ago, when owners raced their horses against each other for a wager. As early as 1715, Boston newspapers published racing advertisements and notices. However, in the seventeenth and eighteenth centuries, because of the Puritan New Englanders' opposition to gambling, orders were passed banning horse racing. The sport was never as popular in New England as it was farther south. In 1665 New York's first English governor, Richard Nicolls, established the first organized horse races, offering a silver cup for the winner. They were held at the Newmarket Course on Hempstead Plains, Long Island, which was named after the famous racing center in England. For the rest of the colonial period races were held twice a year at Newmarket, while other races were run near Jamaica. Racing's popularity grew at such a rate that a race in Manhattan in 1736 attracted over 1,000 people.

In the 1730s the horse Bulle Rock was brought from England to Virginia to breed. Soon thereafter the colonial South developed into the center of horse breeding and horse racing in America. The southern landowners imitated the English gentry's lifestyle, with horse racing their most important sport. Americans adopted the English rules from Newmarket. By the late eighteenth century tracks and racing centers were operating in Virginia, Maryland, Kentucky, South Carolina, and Tennessee. The National Race Course at Washington, D.C., opened in 1802, and the first permanent racecourse opened in Maryland in 1820.

During most of this developmental period, horse racing was illegal. The Continental Congress banned horse racing in 1774, but because the British occupied New York, racing continued there. After American independence, horse racing was forbidden, although races continued to be held in New York. In 1821 the restriction was finally lifted, and subsequent races in Queens County were attended by thousands of people.

Foxhunting. Modern foxhunting became popular in England in the 1600s and 1700s as a national upper-class sport. The English brought the sport of foxhunting to the colonies when, on 30 June 1650, Robert Brooke, Esq. brought a pack of hounds from England to Queen Anne's County, Maryland. The first foxhunt in America took place shortly thereafter. The earliest record of an organized group foxhunt tells of one given by the Sixth Lord Fairfax in Virginia in 1747. By the 1760s James de Lancey had brought foxhounds from England, and the gentry and farmers of the English settlements of Oyster Bay, Long Island, and Westchester County engaged in their version of formal English foxhunting. Americans trained their dogs according to the English techniques, conducted their foxhunts according to English rules, and dressed in the English fashion. They favored dogs imported from England or those whose pedigree could be traced to England.

The oldest recognized hunt club in the United States is the Rose Tree Foxhunting Club in York County, Pennsylvania, founded in 1859. The Masters of Foxhounds Association was established in 1907 to regulate foxhunting. Men and women continue to enjoy the sport of foxhunting in America with 176 organized hunt clubs in existence in the United States today.

Rugby and Soccer. The early forms of rugby and soccer stemmed from a game played in England as early as the fourteenth century. The first colonists brought soccer to America. Colonial men played soccer casually in the streets in New England. There is one reference, in 1685, to an organized soccer match. It was not until the nineteenth century that soccer became truly popular in America. Soccer was the most popular sport among late nineteenth-century English immigrants. English immigrant workingmen in the textile mills organized games among themselves and started soccer clubs in Paterson, Newark, Philadelphia, Fall River, Massachusetts, and New York. By 1890, Philadelphia had seven soccer clubs, and Fall River had approximately twenty-five.

Rugby's auspicious birth occurred at a soccer game at the Rugby School in England in the mid-nineteenth century. According to one popular account of the origins of the game, in clear violation of soccer rules a Rugby School student picked up the ball and ran with it. In the late nineteenth century English businessmen and travelers introduced rugby to distant parts of their empire, including Canada. In 1874 McGill University challenged Harvard University to two matches. Rugby play in America during this time was largely intercollegiate, and the games were often a combination of soccer, rugby, and football, with each team favoring one of the three sports. These matches contributed to the development of American football, which soon replaced both rugby and soccer in popularity in the United States.

Cricket. Cricket originated in England from a children's game and was played as a sport as early as the thirteenth century. The first rules and regulations were established in England in the early eighteenth century. The English colonists brought cricket to America, and by the 1790s they had organized cricket clubs in Boston, New York, and Philadelphia. Throughout the 1830s, 1840s, and 1850s, clubs were established by upper-class merchants, diplomats, and professional men as well as by English immigrant knitters, weavers, and woolen workers in Philadelphia, Newark, Brooklyn, Boston, Lawrence, and Lowell, Massachusetts.

Organized cricket began in the United States with the formation of the famous St. George Cricket Club in New York in 1839–40. The club's trainer was an English professional cricketer. Members of this club included English-born, upper-class businessmen, professionals, diplomats, and military officers, as well as English immigrant craftsmen and artisans. When the Union Cricket Club was founded in Philadelphia in 1843, mechanics, including a saw maker, a frame smith, and a wood turner, were listed among its members. In 1848 more than 20% of the members of the St. George Cricket Club were artisans. By 1865, however, that number had dropped to 5.7%. In the first half of the nineteenth century, cricket was more popular than baseball in the United States. In 1860 approximately 10,000 cricketers played as members of about 400 clubs. Many factors contributed to its loss of favor, including the decline of English immigration and the assimilation of the English into American society. Also, the working-class Americans who were playing cricket felt alienated from the English elite who governed the game and the clubs. As the percentage of American-born players declined, English immigrants kept the sport alive, along with upper-class Philadelphians who identified with elite English cricketers.

Baseball. Rounders, an English schoolchildren's game dating from as late as the 1740s, is probably the most direct ancestor of baseball. The English colonists in America played fives or handball, trap ball, stool ball, and rounders. These were simple games all featuring bats, balls, and bases. In 1869 English-born Harry Wright, a professional bowler and cricket player at the St. George Cricket Club of New York, led in the formation of the first professional baseball team, the Cincinnati Red Stockings. Many early baseball players had previously been English cricketers.

Wrestling. Modern wrestling began in England in the eighteenth century. Wrestlers like Thomas Topham of London would challenge one and all at fairs and circuses in England. English settlers brought the sport to America, and wrestling became popular, particularly on the frontier.

Rowing. The sport of rowing in England began to develop in the thirteenth century from what had been a means of transportation. Watermen transported people around London on the River Thames. Later, in the sixteenth century, passengers bet on races between the boats. These early races led to the organized sport of rowing. Rowing developed similarly in the United States, with races initially between ferrymen. The first documented race occurred in New York on 23 June 1802 between two famous boats, one built by Chambers of London and the other by John Baptiste of New York. The competition between the English and American boat builders generated a great deal of interest, and there was a subsequent series of races in 1811. In that year New York longshoremen and English and American seamen were rowing competitively on the Hudson River. By the 1820s young men joined boat clubs such as the Knickerbocker Club and the Whitehall Aquatic Club, both of New York. These clubs held frequent races with purses from $20 to $10,000 accompanied by a great amount of spectator betting. The first international race was held on 9 December 1824 between an English boat, *Certain Death*, rowed by English sailors, and an American boat, *American Star*, rowed by members of the Whitehall crew. This four-mile race was watched by 50,000 spectators. The American boat won the $1,000 prize.

Boxing. In the late eighteenth and early nineteenth centuries English sailors introduced boxing to the United States. Around the same time, young American men who had become familiar with boxing while at college in England began engaging in the sport at home. In 1823 an American newspaper reported on a boxing match in New York. The match used English rules with a specific number of rounds. Also in the 1820s the famous English boxers William Fuller and George Kensett arrived from England and staged boxing matches considered brutal and disgusting by most American newspapers. However, William Fuller's gentlemanly conduct and first-class prizefighting gymnasium gave respectability to the sport of sparring for gentlemen, and it gained in popularity. However, bare-knuckle prizefighting was banned in the United States, but despite this prohibition the featured fights attracted large crowds and considerable coverage in the press. In the first half of the nineteenth century one-fifth of the boxers in New York were English immigrants, and the Americans used the English prize ring rules. One of the most celebrated sporting events in the nineteenth century was the great international match in England in 1860 between the English champion pugilist Tom Sayers and the American challenger John C. Heenan. This controversial bout ended in a riot as the crowd disrupted the match with Sayers badly injured.

Archery. Archery societies existed in England as far back as the sixteenth century. In America the sport of archery has both English and Native American roots. The first archery club in the United States, the United Bowmen, was formed in Philadelphia in 1828. The National Archery Association was organized in 1879 and held its first tournament in Chicago, which was opened to both men and women.

Croquet. The French game of pallemaille (pall-mall) was played in England in the sixteenth century, and a more complicated form became croquet. In the 1860s Americans, imitating the middle and upper classes in England, began playing croquet in the United States. It was one of the few sports in which men and women played together.

Tennis. Tennis came to England from France in the early fifteenth century. In 1873, a British cavalry officer adapted indoor court tennis to outdoor lawn tennis and called it sphairistike. Tennis was introduced into the United States from England in three different places in the 1870s. In February 1874 Mary E. Outerbridge of Staten Island, New York, watched British officers play sphairistike in Bermuda and brought racquets and a net back to the Staten Island Cricket and Baseball Club. A few years later, she and some friends formed the Ladies Club, and tennis became popular among the wives and daughters of the club members. In 1874, James Wright, having watched tennis in England, set up a court in Massachusetts. Around the same time, English people living in New Orleans started playing tennis, and in 1876 they formed the first tennis association in the United States, the New Orleans Tennis Club.

Badminton. An English children's game called battledore shuttlecock developed into the sport of badminton, which was played by early English colonists in Williamsburg, Virginia. In 1878 some upper-class American men who had seen badminton played in England and India founded the Badminton Club of New York. Battledores and shuttlecocks were brought from England. The club had nine courts, which could accommodate up to 150 men and women, who played in tuxedos, long dresses, and dancing shoes. Badminton, like croquet, tennis, and archery, was among the few sports in which both men and women participated.

Track and Field. The development of the modern sport of track and field, also called athletics, began in England in the second half of the nineteenth century. The Scots and English brought their athletics to the United States, and the private athletic clubs in American cities were modeled after English ones. In the middle of the 1800s there were track-and-field races at Hoboken's Beacon Race Course, but the founding of the New York Athletic Club in 1868 firmly established the sport in the United States. Two of the three founders of the New York Athletic Club were Americans of English descent.

Polo. James Gordon Bennett, the publisher of the *New York Herald*, watched a polo match in Hurlingham, England, in 1876 and subsequently brought polo to the United States. He and his friends founded the Westchester Polo Club in 1877. Demonstrations of polo in Newport, Rhode Island, by the Westchester Polo Club spurred the interest of America's elite in this new sport. In 1886 the United States played its first international polo match against England's Hurlingham Club, but it was not until 1909 that the Americans succeeded in defeating the English at the sport.

Yachting. King Charles II was responsible for the birth of English yachting in the mid-seventeenth century. Since then, yachting has been the pastime of the wealthy and fashionable. It was brought to America by the Dutch in New York in the seventeenth century, but the English popularized it. In 1851 the Royal Yacht Squadron of Great Britain offered the Hundred Guinea Cup to the winner of a race around the Isle of Wight. The now famous American schooner *America* won the race, and its owner, John C. Stevens, donated the cup to the New York Yacht Club in 1857, thus christening the race the America's Cup. At the end of the nineteenth century, Joshua Slocum, an English immigrant and naturalized American, demonstrated the seaworthiness of smaller boats when he sailed the 11.3-meter *Spray* around the world. This trip popularized smaller and lighter craft, making the sport affordable for a greater number of people.

SELECTED BIBLIOGRAPHY: Melvin L. Adelman, *A Sporting Time: New York City and the Rise of Modern Athletics 1820–70* (1986); John Richards Betts, *America's Sporting Heritage: 1850–1950* (1974); Jennie Holliman, *American Sports (1785–1835)* (1975);

George B. Kirsch, *The Creation of American Team Sports: Baseball and Cricket, 1838–72* (1989); Tony Mason, ed., *Sport in Britain* (1989); Betty Spears and Richard A. Swanson, *History of Sport and Physical Activity in the United States*, 2d ed. (1983).

Juliana F. Gilheany

EPSTEIN, CHARLOTTE (? September 1884, New York City–26 August 1938, New York City). The daughter of Mortiz H. and Sara Epstein and of Jewish ancestry, she played a major role in the development of U.S. women's Olympic swimming. Educated at the Ethical Culture School, New York City, she worked as a court stenographer in New York City. Known as the "Mother of Women's Swimming in America," Epstein founded the renowned Women's Swimming Association (WSA) of New York in 1917 to teach the health benefits of swimming. In 1914, before founding the WSA, "Eppie" (as she was known) started the National Women's Life Saving League and competed in its swimming meets. Epstein served as the chair of the Athletic Committee of the National Women's Life Saving League in 1915. At that time she appealed to the Amateur Athletic Union to allow women to register as athletes in swimming events. With Epstein's outstanding administrative ability as the swimming club team manager in 1917 and president in 1929, WSA members gained great success in diving and swimming competitions, producing such prominent Olympic champions as Aileen Riggin and Gertrude Ederle. "Eppie" was the team manager-chaperon on the 1920 Women's Olympic swimming team, the first time females were allowed to compete in the Olympic Games. She had a crucial role in giving Riggin and other WSA members the chance to compete in the Olympics. During Epstein's term of leadership, 1920–36, WSA members dominated swimming, earning world records in competitions. Epstein achieved the official position of Olympic team manager of the U.S. women's swimming team in the 1920, 1924, and 1932 games. She was appointed chair of the U.S. Olympic Women's Swimming Committee and chair of the Amateur Athletic Union, National Women's Swimming Committee. Epstein chaired the swimming committee for the 1935 Maccabiah Games in Tel Aviv. In 1936 she refused to attend the Berlin Olympic Games. As a Jewish American she withdrew from the American Olympic Committee in protest of Nazi policies. To recognize Epstein's distinguished services to the American Olympic Committee, in 1939 the committee issued a special resolution. The International Swimming Hall of Fame, Florida, inducted Epstein as a contributor, and she is a member of the Jewish Sports Hall of Fame in Israel. In 1994 Epstein became one of the first women inducted into the B'nai B'rith/Klutznick National Jewish Museum, Jewish Sports Hall of Fame, Washington, D.C.

SELECTED BIBLIOGRAPHY: Linda J. Borish, "Charlotte Epstein," in Paula Hyman and Deborah Dash Moore, eds., *Jewish Women in America: An Historical Encyclopedia* (1997); Charlotte Epstein Collection and Women's Swimming Association Archives, Henning Library, International Swimming Hall of Fame, Ft. Lauderdale, FL; *New York Times*, 27 August 1938, 13; John Simons, ed., *A Biographical Dictionary of Living Jews of the United States and Canada*, vol. 3: *1938–1939* (1939); Robert Slater, *Great Jews in Sport*, rev. ed. (1992); Paula D. Welch and Harold A. Lerch, "The Women's Swimming Association Launches America into Swimming Supremacy," *The Olympian* (March 1979): 14–16.

Linda J. Borish

ERVING, JULIUS WINFIELD, II ("Dr. J") (22 February 1950, Hempstead, Long Island, NY–   ). An African American basketball player, his father left home when Julius was three years old. He was raised by his mother, Callie (Erving) Lindsey, a domestic worker. After graduating from Roosevelt High School, Long Island, he enrolled at the University of Massachusetts, where he developed his breathtaking and athletic style of play. Prompted by his family's financial problems, he left college following his junior year in 1971 and signed with the Virginia Squires of the fledgling American Basketball Association (ABA). In his first season Erving was selected the ABA's Rookie of Year, and in his second season he led the league in scoring with a 31.9 points per game average. In 1973 Erving was traded to the New York Nets, where he led them to two ABA championships while winning three league Most Valuable Player (MVP) awards and two playoff MVP awards. Following the ABA-National Basketball Association (NBA) merger and a lengthy contract dispute with the Nets, Erving joined the Philadelphia 76ers in 1976. He led the 76ers to the NBA playoffs in each of his eleven seasons with the team, which won the NBA championship in 1983. He was an NBA All-Star in every one of his eleven seasons, winning the NBA All-Star Game MVP in 1977 and 1983 and the NBA MVP in 1981. He retired in 1987, having scored over 30,000 points for an average of 24.2 points per game. In retirement Erving became a highly successful businessman and a popular basketball analyst on television. Famous for his acrobatic moves and spectacular slam dunks, he was elected to the Naismith Memorial Basketball Hall of Fame in 1993.

SELECTED BIBLIOGRAPHY: Marty Bell, *The Legend of Dr. J.* (1975); *Ebony* 30 (March 1975): 44 and (May 1975): 35; Nelson George, *Elevating the Game: Black Men and Basketball* (1992); Tony Kornheiser, "Exit Dunking," *Sport* 78 (June 1987): 56–57; Jim O'Brien, "Dr. J's Magic Puts Nets Fans on Their Feet," *The Sporting News* (12 January 1974).

David Andrews

ESPOSITO, PHILIP ANTHONY (20 February 1942, Sault Ste. Marie, Ontario, Canada–   ). The son of Pat Esposito, a second-generation Italian Canadian steel factory foreman, and Frances, he was one of the National Hockey League's (NHL) most prolific scorers. "Espo" played center for the Chicago Blackhawks (1963–67), Boston Bruins (1967–75), and New York Rangers (1975–81). His passionate leadership and deft scoring touch helped the Bruins to Stanley Cup victories in 1970 and 1972. During a remarkable eight-year span as a member of the Bruins, Esposito won five Art Ross Trophies (scoring champion) and two

Hart Trophies (Most Valuable Player) and set NHL records for most goals and points in a season. Esposito became a national hero in Canada as a result of his outstanding performance in leading a team of Canadians to victory over the Soviet National Team in the 1972 Summit Series. In 1975 Esposito reached 500 goals faster than anyone before him—achieving the feat in just 803 games. Upon retirement in 1980 Esposito stood second to Gordie Howe* in career goals (717) and points (1,590). In 1984 he was enshrined in the Hockey Hall of Fame. He also made an impact off the ice, serving as president of the NHL Players Association from 1979 to 1981. After his retirement Esposito established a foundation offering career counseling and job training to former players, in order to facilitate their smooth transition into new careers. Esposito has always been a willing ambassador for hockey in the United States. In 1978 he received the Lester Patrick Award from the NHL for his outstanding contribution to hockey in the United States. During the 1990s he served as the general manager of the NHL's Tampa Bay Lightning, striving to increase the popularity of the sport in Florida.

SELECTED BIBLIOGRAPHY: Phil Esposito and Tony Esposito, with Tim Moriarty, *The Brothers Esposito* (1971); Phil Esposito, with Gerald Eskenazi, *Hockey Is My Life* (1972); Morgan Hughes and Joseph Romain, *Hockey Legends of All Time* (1996); Tom Murray, "Esposito Foundation to Aid Retired Players," *The Hockey News* (24 December 1982): 27; Harry Sinden and Dick Grace, *The Picture History of the Boston Bruins* (1976).

Dennis Ryan

F

FENCING. Social class, ethnic, and racial issues constitute an important part of the history of fencing in the United States. Men and women of the upper classes patronized the first fencing clubs in colonial America, and by the mid-1800s several gentlemen and ladies of the urban elite enrolled in private clubs. During the nineteenth century immigrants from Germany who founded gymnastic clubs (turnverein) included fencing as one of the athletic exercises, while instructors and itinerant theatrical performers from Europe (especially from Germany, Austria, France, and Italy) demonstrated the sport for the American public. In the twentieth century Jews and other Eastern Europeans, African Americans, Latin Americans, and Asians earned recognition and an impressive number of championships in foil, epeé, and sabre competitions.

Beginning in the 1880s aristocratic sportsmen promoted fencing in elite eastern colleges and private clubs. At that time the sport also became fashionable among ladies of the privileged classes. The Amateur Athletic Union sponsored the first U.S. national championships in 1888, but a dispute over the format of competition led in 1891 to the creation of the Amateur Fencers' League of America (AFLA), which was renamed the U.S. Fencing Association (USFA) in 1981. The AFLA and the prominent New York City fencing clubs restricted membership to persons from families prominent in aristocratic society and excluded professionals, Jews, African Americans, and others.

Jewish participation in American fencing dates from the early twentieth century, as Camille Waldbott won the national championship in foil in 1907. Waldbott was an immigrant from the Alsace Lorraine region of Germany who learned to fence at the Chicago Turn Gemeinde and also represented the Chicago Fencing Club. He became both the first Jewish national champion and the first foil titlist who did not reside on the East Coast. It took three more decades for Jewish fencers to gain entry into the more exclusive New York City clubs. By the 1930s more Jews were entering major competitions, with national foil titles won by Norman Lewis (1939), Bennet Nathaniel Lubell (1948), and Dr. Daniel Bukantz (1949, 1952, 1953, 1957). Later in the century numerous Jewish fencers competed on collegiate teams, especially at the City College of New York, New York University, Columbia, and Harvard.

From the 1920s to the 1950s Southern and Eastern Europeans made their mark on the American fencing establishment. Among the Italians, Dean Victor Cetrulo and Silvio Louis Giolito each won two national foil titles. Giorgio Santelli, of Italian descent, came to the United States from Budapest and was an influential coach during the 1920s. The Hungarians first became a significant factor in American fencing as early as the 1920s, but the end of World War II and the failed revolt against Soviet domination in 1956 sent streams of refugees and defectors to America. Many became prominent competitors and teachers. Among the earliest native Hungarians who achieved fame in fencing in the United States was Nickolas Muray, national sabre champion in 1927–28 and a member of the U.S. Olympic team in 1928 and 1932. Helena Mroczkowska was U.S. Olympic foil champion four times between 1940 and 1948. Hungarian Olympic champion George Jekelfalussy Piller worked as a fencing coach in California. Lajos (Louis) Csiszar was head fencing coach at the University of Pennsylvania, the U.S. Olympic team in 1956, and the U.S. team at the Pan-American games. Tibor Nyilas, a seven-time American sabre titlist, was a member of the U.S. Olympic fencing team in 1948, 1952, 1956, and 1960 and of the Pan-American team in 1951, 1955, and 1959. Csaba Elthes, a professional fencing master, trained the U.S. fencing teams for a number of Olympic and Pan-American Games in the 1960s and 1970s. Five-time national fencing champion Alex Orban was a member of the U.S. Olympic fencing team in Mexico in 1968 and in Munich in 1972 (sabre). Paul Pesthy was a four-time member of the U.S. Olympic pentathlon and épée fencing teams and a four-time winner of the U.S. épée championship. Csaba Miklos Pallaghhy was American Sabre Team champion from 1958 to 1962, and Pan-American Sabre Team champion in 1963. Other prominent Hungarian American fencers over the years have been Joseph Vince, George V. Worth, Thomas Orley, Laszlo Pongo, John Thomas Balla, and Dr. Ervin Acel.

African Americans were active in fencing during the 1930s, when Young Men's Christian Associations (YMCAs) and Young Women's Christian Associations (YWCAs) provided basic instruction in the sport. But racial discrimination practiced by the AFLA severely curtailed their opportunities to compete at the local and national levels. A case in point is the experience of Violet Barker, who learned to fence at the Harlem YMCA under the tutelage of Alex Hern, a Jew who was teaching fencing in settlement and neighborhood houses throughout New York City. Barker won a recreational league championship sponsored by the Works Progress Administration, which earned her a membership card in the AFLA. But when she arrived at the New York Fencers Club for an AFLA open foil meet, she was barred from the competition because of her race; when she produced her AFLA membership card, an official tore it into little pieces. Hern and the National Association for the Advancement of Colored People initiated a lawsuit against the AFLA but dropped the action when Barker refused to pursue the case. Hern welcomed blacks at his Foils Club on Fourteenth Street, which his enemies at the AFLA dubbed the "Abyssinian School of Fencing." Another racial incident occurred in 1949, when Columbia University's varsity fencing team withdrew from all meets sponsored by the AFLA because of pressure applied by that organization to withdraw its two black members from a competition at the New York Athletic Club. In the aftermath of the Columbia boycott the Board of Directors of the AFLA split over the issue of excluding blacks from its meets. Its president, Miguel Angel deCapriles, supported desegragation, stating: "It is time to recognize that fencing has changed from the aristocratic sport that it was to the democratic sport that it is."

By the 1950s African Americans were gaining acceptance by the AFLA and were winning fencing titles in intercollegiate meets. In the following decades several blacks captured prestigious national honors. Sophronia Pierce Stent was captain of the New York University team; in 1951 she became the first black woman to gain admission into the AFLA. Collegiate champions include Bruce Davis of Wayne State University (Detroit); Tyrone Simmons of the University of Detroit; Peter Lewison of the City University of New York; and Peter Westbrook, Michael Lofton, and Ruth White of New York University. In 1969 White became the first black athlete to win a national fencing title, when she won the under-nineteen crown in foil. She was trained by several Hungarian coaches, including Bela de Csajaghy. Subsequent African Americans who have won national championships include Lewison, Westbook, Lofton, Uriah Jones, Burt Freeman, Ed Ballinger, Terrence Lasker, Mark Smith, Erin Smart, Bob Cottingham, Nikki Tomlinson Franke, and Sharon Monplaisir, among others. Westbrook, who is half Japanese and half black, also took home a bronze medal in the sabre at the 1984 Olympic Games in Los Angeles. To a great extent these honors are the result of increased participation by African Americans at black fencing clubs in several cities.

Finally, since the 1930s American fencing has exhibited an increasing multiethnic and multiracial character, as Hispanic and Asian athletes have become prominent as administrators and champions. The deCapriles brothers were men of great education, status, and wealth from Mexico who represented the older aristocratic tradition. Julia Castello, Hugo Martinez Castello, Natalia Clovis, Marcel Pasche, Maria Cerra Tishman, and Henrique Santos were all of Spanish or Latin American heritage. Among Asians, Heizaburo Okawa of Japan won two titles in the 1960s and then settled in California, while Jennifer Yu of California won the women's foil title in 1990.

SELECTED BIBLIOGRAPHY: Arthur R. Ashe, Jr., *A Hard Road to Glory: A History of the African-American Athlete since 1946*, vol. 3 (1988), 216–218; Luigi Barbasetti, *The Art of the Foil, with a Short History of Fencing* (1932); Gay Kirstine Jacobsen D'Asaro, "A History of the Amateur Fencers League of America," M.A. thesis, San Jose State University, 1983; William M. Gaugler, *The History of Fencing: Foundations of*

Modern European Swordplay (1988); John Kardoss, *Sabre Fencing: History, Theory, Practice* (1955); *New York Times*, 1 December 1949, 47, 9 December 1949, 40, 14 December 1949, 46.

                                              Andrew J. Shaw and George B. Kirsch

FERNANDEZ, BEATRIZ ("Gigi") (22 February 1964, San Juan, PR–). A Puerto Rican tennis player, she is the daughter of a doctor of medicine, Tuto Fernández Plá, and Beatriz Ferrer Calderón. Gigi went to high school at the Academia San José in San Juan and later attended Clemson University. She represented Puerto Rico in the Los Angeles (1984) Olympics, where tennis was an exhibition sport. She played for the United States and won two Olympic gold medals in women's doubles in Barcelona (1992) and Atlanta (1996) with Mary Joe Fernández. For Puerto Rico, Gigi also won a gold medal in women's doubles with Marilda Juliá and bronze in mixed doubles with Miguel Nido in the Central American and Caribbean Sports Games in La Habana (1982). As a professional athlete, Gigi won two singles titles (1991 in Albuquerque and 1986 in Singapore) and sixty-eight doubles titles. Fernández also won seventeen women's grand-slam doubles crowns: two Australian Open, six French Open, four Wimbledon, and five U.S. Open. She has played with a variety of partners, including Robin White, Martina Navratilova,* Jana Novotna, and Natasha Zvereva. Even while representing the United States, Gigi has always expressed that she feels and is Puerto Rican. Gigi announced her retirement from professional tennis after losing in the finals of the U.S. Open in 1997, playing with Zvereva as her partner. Zvereva and Fernández ended their partnership in the grand slams ranked as one of the all-time great doubles teams.

SELECTED BIBLIOGRAPHY: Frances Concepción and Aurea Echevarría, "Gigi Fernández," *Tres Mujeres Deportistas, un Discurso Patriarcal* (1997) 57–76; Jaime Vega Curry, "La mejor en la historia," *El Nuevo Día, Domingo Deportivo*, 21 September 1997, 4–9.

                                                      Raúl Mayo-Santana

FERNANDEZ, LISA (22 February 1971, Long Beach, CA–). A softball player, she is the daughter of Cuban-heritage father (Antonio) who played semipro baseball in Cuba, and Puerto Rican-heritage mother (Emilia). She graduated from St. Joseph High School in Lakewood, California, and earned a bachelor's degree in psychology from the University of California, Los Angeles (UCLA). Despite one coach's suggestion that she was "not built to pitch," Fernandez persevered and amassed statistics that made her the best all-around softball player of her era. Once a batgirl for her mother's slow-pitch softball team, by age eleven Fernandez had won her first Amateur Softball Association (ASA) championship and was on her way to a high school career that included sixty-nine shutouts, thirty-seven no-hitters, twelve perfect games, and an earned run average of 0.07. While at UCLA, Fernandez compiled a 93–7 record, leading her team to two national championships. As a senior she had an earned run average of 0.25, pitched 348 strikeouts, and batted .510. Fernandez was named the National Collegiate Athletic Association (NCAA) women's collegiate athlete of the year (1993), ASA woman of the year (1991, 1992), and Olympic athlete of the year (1992, 1993). Fernandez has also led three teams to gold medals in the Olympic festival, earned gold in the Pan-American Games, and pitched the first-ever U.S. women's Olympic softball team to a gold medal in 1996. During the late 1990s Fernandez worked as a consultant for Louisville Slugger and was one of very few visible Latina spokeswomen for sport in general and softball in particular.

SELECTED BIBLIOGRAPHY: Lisa Fernandez, "Fast Pitch: How I Do It," *Scholastic Coach and Athletic Director* 64, No. 8 (March 1995): 26–30; A. J. Johnson, *Great Women in Sports* (1996), 163–166; J. Ludden, "Fernandez Knows Gold Waits on Deck: Pitcher Always Well-Equipped for Success," *Washington Post*, 25 July 1995, D-6: 5; S. Smith, "Sports People: Lisa Fernandez," *Sports Illustrated* 78, No. 20 (24 May 1993): 52.

Katherine M. Jamieson

FINNS. While the Finns were among the first immigrant groups to journey to America, joining the English, Dutch, and Swedes in the early 1600s, Finnish Americans compose one of the smallest ethnic groups in the United States. However, they built over 300 social halls, which included athletic clubs where they engaged in gymnastics, track and field, boxing, and wrestling. Many of these halls (e.g., those in New York; Fitchburg, Massachusetts; Ashtabula and Fairport Harbor, Ohio; and Covington, Michigan) produced fine athletes. Suomi College, Hancock, Michigan, the only college the Finns founded in America, also promoted a sports program.

The sometimes stocky, muscular, sometimes wiry, not-too-tall, fierce Finn made a good distance runner, ski jumper, and ice hockey player. Those sports produced the most outstanding athletes. Strength, fearlessness, and endurance were the Finns' strong suit as opposed to wit, quickness, and trickery. They preferred slower, but sustained, movement, combined with rhythm.

Distance Running. Ville Ritola ran most of the distance runs in the 1924 and 1928 Olympics, winning five gold and three silver medals. Ritola's achievements are relatively unknown, being overshadowed by those of Finland's Paavo Nurmi. In the 1924 Olympics in Paris he won gold medals in the 10,000 meters (setting a world record), the 3,000-meter hurdles, the 10,000-meter cross country team race, and the 3,000-meter team race. He captured silver medals with second place finishes to Paavo Nurmi in the 5,000- and 10,000-meter events. In 1928 in Amsterdam, Holland, he was victorious in the 5,000 meters and finished second to Nurmi at 10,000 meters. In each Olympics he ran for Finland, but the Finnish American community paid a large part of his expenses. Ritola resided in the United States for fifty-eight years (forty-eight of them in New York City). Ironically, he did not receive his citizenship papers until the last decade of his life, when he was living in Finland. Prior to Ritola, Hannes Kolehmainen ran the Finns to world recognition in the 1912 Olympics while he lived in New York for two years. In later times Bob Kempainen is the all-time greatest Finnish or Finnish American marathon runner, with a time of 2:08:45 at Boston in 1996. Other fine marathon runners have been Carl Linder, David Komonen, Otto Laakso, and William Wick, all from the 1920s.

Ice Hockey and Skating. In mainline sports, the first professional hockey league in the United States centered in Michigan's Keweenaw Peninsula (Houghton) in 1903, with the farthest team being Pittsburgh. A number of Finns played on the world championship team of 1904 for the McNaughton Cup, including Sam Kokko and another Kolehmainen. The Olson family of nine boys and two girls is the classic symbol of second-generation Finnish American skaters. Ruth Olson-Matt was a speed skater; Virginia Olson-Carlson became a figure skater and teacher, while all the brothers (Wesley, Allan, Paul, Gordon, Edward, Roy, Theodore, Marcus, and Weldon; born 1911 to 1932) played amateur, semipro, college, professional, and Olympic hockey. Six of them (Allan, Ed, Roy, Ted, Mark, and Weldon) played college hockey for Michigan Technological and Michigan State Universities. Their family originated in Hancock, Michigan, where most Finns stopped upon arrival, and resided primarily in Marquette. They produced their own family hockey team. Eddie Olson reached the highest laurels of the nine, enshrined in the U.S. Hockey Hall of Fame (1960). Parents Frank and Ida (née Anttila) were Finnish immigrants. No other Finnish American family so exemplified the Finnish spirit on ice as did the Olsons. Other fine hockey players among Finnish Americans were Willard Ikola of Eveleth, Minnesota (Hall of Fame, 1970), Gus Hendrickson of Duluth, Minnesota, Eddie Maki and Rod Paavola of Hancock, Michigan, and the Joupperi brothers and Charles Uskila of Calumet, Michigan. Ikola was a prominent player for the University of Michigan and a member of the 1956 U.S. Olympic hockey team; he later became a coach. Uskila was the first American-born player to participate in the Stanley Cup playoffs. In addition to his career in professional hockey, he teamed up with his sister Leena (an internationally famous skater) for figure skating tours in the United States and Australia. Later he officiated in the National Hockey League and became a producer and choreographer for the Ice Capades. Respected as one of the foremost skating authorities on the North American continent, he was inducted into Michigan's Upper Peninsula Sports Hall of Fame in 1978.

The Finnish affinity to ice and snow is borne out further in the final decade of the 1900s by the representation of dozens of hockey players from Finland in the National Hockey League, led by stars such as Jari Kurri, Esa Tikkanen, Teemu Salanne, Pentti Lund, Pay Timgren, Henry Akervall, and others. It is not uncommon for Finnish names to appear on modern college hockey rosters, but they usually retain Finnish citizenship.

Ski Jumping. The oldest ski jumping tourney in America of continuous existence began in 1887 at Suicide Hill in Ishpeming, Michigan, which is why the Hall of Fame is located there. It was begun and perpetuated by Norwegian and Finnish jumpers, particularly the Bietila brothers. The legendary Bietila family of six brothers of Ishpeming, Michigan, is without parallel in the early history of ski jumping. The sons of Jacob and Mary (née Snell) Bietila became known as the "Flying Finns" and dominated the American jumping scene from the 1930s to the 1960s. The brothers, sons of an immigrant iron miner, were Anselm, Leonard, Walter, Paul, Roy, and Ralph Bietila. Walter competed in the 1936, 1940, and 1948 Olympics and served in 1960 as the coach for the U.S. Olympic team. He was inducted into the National Ski Hall of Fame in 1965. Ralph, the best ski jumper of the family, won six national titles and was a member of the U.S. Olympic teams in 1948 and 1952. He was inducted into the National Ski Hall of Fame in 1975. Some other flying Finns over the years were Leo Anderson of Ironwood, Michigan, Rudy Maki and Coy Hill of Ishpeming Michigan, and Willie Erickson of Iron Mountain, Michigan. Walter and Ralph Bietila, Maki, Hill, and Erickson are U.S. Ski Hall of Fame members. Other skiing accomplishments include a Finnish immigrant, Asario Autio, who was the American national cross-country ski champion in 1907, claiming the title in Ashland, Wisconsin. Mary Seaton-Brush of Hancock, Michigan, represented the United States in downhill skiing in the winter Olympics in 1976.

Other notable American sports personalities with Finnish ancestry include Richard "Dick" Enberg and Greg Norman. Enberg, one of the nation's premier television sportscasters, is the son of Finnish immigrants who migrated to the United States in the early 1900s. A graduate of Central Michigan University in 1957, he also earned a Ph.D. in health science from Indiana University in 1961. Norman's mother, Toini Hovi, was a Finnish immigrant to Australia who introduced her son to golf in his early teens. Norman, known as the "Great White Shark" because of his light blond hair, joined the Professional Golfers' Association (PGA) tour in 1983 and then relocated from Australia to Hobe Sound, Florida. A two-time British Open winner, in 1995 he set a tour season record for highest earnings and received the PGA Tour Player of the Year honor. He has won the Arnold Palmer Award for being leading money winner three times, having earned over $1 million a year worldwide seven times up to 1996.

At least seven Finnish Americans are in national Halls of Fame of skiing and hockey, and over two dozen Finnish Americans have participated in the modern Olympics. For an immigrant folk numbering only one-third of 1% of the American population, Finnish Americans can hold their heads high that sports is one of their favorite pastimes, along with the sauna, Sibelius (music), Saarinen (design), and Suomi College (education). "S" seems to be their favorite consonant. On one hand, Finns in America are like the football team whose coach, when asked to comment on his players, said: "They're small but they're slow." More like the tortoise than the hare in the old story, Finnish Americans may not be as slow as once thought. Small, maybe, but still winners. The 1996 Olympics serve as a case in point. Thanks to Annette Salmeen and Dan O'Brien, their two gold medals were one more than the total earned by Finland.

SELECTED BIBLIOGRAPHY: John E. Ketonen, *Finnish American Horizons* (1976); Werner Nikander, *Amerikan Suomalaisia* (American Finns) (1927); Harri Siitonen, "Sports," *The Finnish American Reporter*; Kaarlo P. Silberg, *The Athletic Finn* (1927);

Finnish American Historical Archives, Finnish-American Heritage Center, 601 Quincy St., Suomi College, Hancock, MI; National Ski Hall of Fame, Ishpeming, MI 49849.

Les E. Niemi

FLEISCHER, NATHANIEL S. ("Nat") (3 November 1887, New York City– 25 June 1972, New York City). A boxing writer, referee, and publisher, he was born into a Jewish family and grew up on Manhattan's Lower East Side. He attended P.S. #15 and was a graduate of Townshend Harris High School. As a schoolboy track athlete he was Public Schools Athletic League champion in the 220-yard sprint. As a student at the City College of New York he competed in track and was cofounder of that institution's intercollegiate basketball team. After earning a B.S. degree in botany and chemistry in 1908, he taught in the New York City public schools and took courses in commercial chemistry and forestry. In 1912 he found his true vocation in journalism, beginning as a reporter for the *New York Press* and becoming its sports editor four years later. He later worked as sports editor for the *New York Sun* and *New York Telegram*, but his most significant contribution to the sport of boxing and sports journalism began in 1922, when he and three partners founded the magazine *The Ring*. Fleischer capitalized on the growing respectability and popularity of boxing during the 1920s, and his publication became the most influential periodical in the world of pugilism. Fleischer was also a prolific author and editor who wrote dozens of biographies and boxing histories, the best-selling *Training for Boxers*, and *The Ring Record Book and Boxing Encyclopedia*. For more than a half century he worked tirelessly to promote and reform prizefighting. Among his many contributions to the sport were his monthly ratings of fighters and his awarding of championship belts to world titlists. He also supported physical examinations for contestants, lobbied for better medical care for injured fighters, and helped to establish boxing commissions to regulate the sport. A popular referee of title bouts around the world, a writer and publisher, a collector of prizefighting historical materials and memorabilia, and a passionate defender of pugilism, he became well known as "Mr. Boxing." He was elected to the International Boxing Hall of Fame in 1990.

SELECTED BIBLIOGRAPHY: Howard Cohn, "Boxing's Boswell," *Sportfolio Magazine* (August 1948); K. Carichton, "Mister Boxing," *Colliers* 120 (6 December 1947): 58; Nat Fleischer, *50 Years at Ringside* (1958); Nat Fleischer, *The Ring Record Book and Boxing Encyclopedia* (1964); *New York Times*, 26 June 1972, 36.

George B. Kirsch

FLEMISH. The Flemish, the immigrants from the Dutch-speaking northern part of Belgium, have not excelled in American sporting life. Their two most prominent figures in America's history were not sportsmen but Catholic missionaries: Father Pieter Jan De Smet (1801–73) and Father Damian, alias Jozef De Veuster (1840–89). The former was called the apostle of the Indians of the Rocky Moun tain West. The latter became the hero of Molokai (Hawaii), where he lived and died among the lepers.

The creation of an independent Belgium in 1830, after having been (re)united briefly with the Netherlands from 1815 till 1830, incited some Flemish to emigrate for political reasons. Detroit would become the main location where Flemish immigrants would settle. Further major settlements occurred in Chicago and Moline, Illinois. The vast majority of these Flemish newcomers came from the provinces of West and East Flanders. They immigrated from the 1880s onward until World War I. Most of them were members of farm families driven by poverty, hoping to find a better fate in the New World. A second wave of immigration took place after World War I and before the 1929 stock market crash. A total of about 200,000 Flemish emigrated to North America, 60,000 of whom settled in Canada. They were attracted by the growth of the automobile industry in Detroit and the availability of cheap land in the Midwest.

In crucial situations of ethnic identity crisis—as, for instance, in the case of immigration—traditional games from the homeland can become salient emblems of the ethnic self. This probably explains why these Flemish Americans have preserved and fostered some of the typical Flemish folk games as a vehicle for ethnic expression in North America. Compared to some other ethnic groups such as the Scottish, the Irish, or the Italians, the Flemish immigrants were in a more unfavorable position. Not only did they arrive later and in much smaller numbers, but they were also non-English-speaking Catholics from the poorest layers of society. So, as they were not highly literate (what they still call today "Belgian" is actually dialects of West and East Flanders), they clung to their local folk games as a means to express their cultural roots.

Archery, undoubtedly the most popular folk sport in Flanders at the time the emigrants left Europe, is still popular among today's Flemish Americans. Moreover, these archery contests consist of the typical Flemish versions of "popinjay shooting" either at "jays" fixed on top of a tall mast or at horizontal targets. Detroit, for instance, still has its Willem Tell Archery Club, which was founded in 1894.

Rolle Bolle, played in the Detroit area and especially popular in and around Moline, Illinois, is a typical Flemish bowling game (somewhat similar to bocce), played with heavy flat bowls on an elliptical track. The United Bolders Club of Western Illinois celebrated its 75th anniversary in 1997 and organized a *Rolle Bolle* tour and tournament for American players and for visitors from the old homeland. Another haven for *Rolle Bolle* is the municipality of Ghent (Minnesota), which celebrated its 100th anniversary in 1980. So-called world championships of *Rolle Bolle* take place almost yearly and are alternatively organized in Flanders and in North America (American Midwest or Ontario, Canada).

The Flemish passion for pigeon racing and cycling has not completely vanished; neither has a typical Flemish version of darts nor some old-style card games. All these activities are still practiced in the Cadieux Café in Detroit, enjoyed with excellent mussels "à la flamande." The calendar of these cultural and sporting encounters is printed in the bilingual weekly (English and Dutch) *Gazette van Detroit*, which was first published in 1914.

SELECTED BIBLIOGRAPHY: Danielle De Kegel, "Sport and Ethnicity: Folk Games among the Flemish Immigrants in North America" (unpublished licentiate thesis in physical education, Leuven: K.U. Leuven (1981), 163 pp.; Hentenryk Ginette Kurgan-Van, "Belgian Immigration to the United States and Other Overseas Countries at the Beginning of the Twentieth Century," in G. Kurgan and E. Spelkens, eds., *Two Studies on Emigration through Antwerp to the New World* (1976), 9–49; Roland Renson, "The Flemish Archery Gilds, from Defense Mechanisms to Sports Institutions," in Roland Renson, P. P. De Nayer, and M. Ostyn, eds., *The History, the Evolution and Diffusion of Sports and Games in Different Cultures* (1976), 135–159; Roland Renson, Danielle De Kegel, and H. Smulders, "The Folk Roots of Games: Games and Ethnic Identity among Flemish-Canadian Immigrants," *Canadian Journal of History of Sport* 14, No. 2 (1983): 69–79; P. D. Sabbe, L. Buyse, and R. Roose, *Belgians in America* (1960).

Roland Renson

FLOOD, CURTIS CHARLES (18 January 1938, Houston, TX–   ). An African American baseball player, he is the son of hospital employees Herman and Laura Flood. His parents moved their six children to Oakland, California, in 1940. Curt starred at McClymonds and Oakland Technical High Schools, signing with the Cincinnati Reds in 1956. He played with minor league clubs in 1956 and 1957 and then was traded to the St. Louis Cardinals, where he played from 1958 through 1969. He sat out the 1970 season and then spent his final season in 1971 with the Washington Senators. However, he appeared in only thirteen games that year and retired in April 1971. He was selected to the All-Star Team in 1964, 1966, and 1968 and was a Gold Glove winner as an outfielder, 1963 through 1969. He held the record for consecutive errorless chances (568) as an outfielder. The streak ended in 1967. In 1969, at age thirty-one, he chose to quit baseball rather than be traded against his will, when the St. Louis Cardinals wanted to trade him to the Philadelphia Phillies. He fought the reserve clause and asked baseball commissioner Bowie Kuhn to declare him a free agent. He filed suit against Commissioner Kuhn in 1970, stating that baseball had violated the U.S. antitrust laws. The case went before the Supreme Court, but that Court upheld the district court and court of appeals, rulings that favored organized baseball. Although Flood lost on a 5–3 vote, the language upholding baseball's exemption from antitrust status was so riddled with contradictions that it invited a closer look at the sport's status. Thus, the door was opened for the 1975 Messersmith-McNally rulings and the advent of free agency.

SELECTED BIBLIOGRAPHY: "Baseball's Forgotten Man," Newsweek 93 (2 April 1979): 18; Donald Dewey and Nicholas Acocella, *The Biographical History of Baseball* (1995); Curt Flood, with Richard Carter, *The Way It Is* (1970); William Leggett, "Not Just a Flood, but a Deluge," *Sports Illustrated* 29 (19 August 1968): 18–21; Richard Reeves, "The Last Angry Man," *Esquire* 89 (1 March 1978): 41–48; "What Ever Happened to Curt Flood?" *Ebony* 36 (March 1981): 55–56.

Clyde Partin

FOOTBALL. Upper-class college students at elite eastern colleges and universities invented American football during the last third of the nineteenth century. Although the game began as a pastime of privileged white, Anglo-Saxon Protestants, it soon gained popularity among African Americans, Native Americans, and a variety of European immigrant groups. An 1869 soccer game between Princeton and Rutgers Universities eventually evolved into the present form of football by World War I. The transition in the sport both reflected and promoted changes in American society as diverse racial and ethnic groups found greater inclusion in the mainstream culture.

Race proved an early factor. While fledgling football programs in southern schools excluded African Americans, some northern institutions displayed a more tolerant position. The Amherst teams of 1891–93 included William Henry Lewis and William Tecumseh Sherman Jackson. Lewis, the team captain in 1891, is generally considered to be the first African American collegiate player. He continued to play as a law student at Harvard, earning All-America designation in 1892 and 1893. Lewis later wrote a book on football and served as an assistant coach at Harvard.

Biddle (now Johnson C. Smith University) defeated Livingstone College in the first game between black schools in 1892. Throughout the remainder of the decade several African American players appeared on northern teams: George Flippen at Nebraska; Joseph Lee at Harvard; George Chadwell at Williams; and William Washington at Oberlin. Matthew Bullock played at Dartmouth from 1901 to 1903; he then became the first African American head coach, beginning at Massachusetts Agricultural College in 1904. William Craighead, another black, captained the team in 1905.

From the mid-1890s and thereafter African Americans began to earn recognition for their prowess at both the high school and collegiate levels. The Pollard brothers (Luther, Leslie, Hughes, and Fritz) and Sam Ransom starred on Chicago interscholastic teams, and both Robert Marshall (Minnesota, 1905–6) and Edward Gray (Amherst, 1908) became All-Americans. Another All-American, Fritz Pollard, became the first African American in the Rose Bowl game when his Brown team faced Washington State in 1916. Paul Robeson* earned All-America honors as a Rutgers end in 1917 and 1918. Such achievements led to greater opportunities for African American players throughout the succeeding decades, but only at northern schools. Black football players remained banned from southern college teams until the 1960s.

Before that time northern schools with black players had to agree not to play them when they scheduled games in the South, which sometimes affected the results significantly. On one such occasion in 1937, Wilmeth Sidat-Singh, the black adopted son of a Hindu, was benched for a game at Maryland. His team, Syracuse, lost, 13–0. Syracuse won the return match, with Sidat-Singh, 52–0. Slowly, black players brought integration to the South. In 1947 Charles Pierce played for Harvard at Virginia. A year later, Penn State brought two African Americans to the Cotton Bowl. Integrated games followed irregularly. Prentiss

Gault entered the University of Oklahoma in 1958, but schools in the Deep South remained committed to segregation until the 1970s.

Professional football, a northern phenomenon for most of its history, integrated more quickly. Western Pennsylvania athletic clubs began paying the best college players to appear in single games against their rivals, when community pride and significant wagers were at stake. By 1903 the practice had spread to northeastern Ohio, and Charles Follis became the first African American pro when the Shelby team hired him for the entire 1904 season. Akron paid another black, Charles "Doc" Baker, from 1906 to 1908. In 1911 Henry McDonald became the first black player in the New York pro league. Canton of the Ohio league hired Gideon Smith in 1915.

Black players found greater opportunity as independent pro teams organized into a national league. Robert Marshall, the Minnesota All-American, returned to play with four different teams until he retired at age forty-seven. The Akron team hired Fritz Pollard as player-coach, the first African American to fulfill that role on the professional level. His team won the first National Football League championship in 1920, when he was joined by Paul Robeson. Several pro teams featured black stars throughout the 1920s. Fred "Duke" Slater, an All-American lineman at Iowa, enjoyed a long career and All-Pro honors before retiring to his law practice after the 1931 season. The Hammond, Indiana, team employed four African Americans between 1923 and 1925, but opportunities dwindled in the 1930s as white owners opted for the segregation policy already in effect in professional baseball. Despite his stellar play, Joe Lillard's contract was not renewed by the Chicago Cardinals after the 1933 season. Ray Kemp had been released by the Pittsburgh Pirates earlier in the season. From 1934 to 1946 African Americans had no recourse but to play in football's minor leagues.

Segregation ended abruptly in 1946, when the Cleveland Rams moved to Los Angeles and signed former University of California at Los Angeles (UCLA) greats Kenny Washington* and Woody Strode,* who had been stars in the Pacific Coast League. The Cleveland Browns of the rival pro league, the All-America Football Conference, also signed Bill Willis and Marion Motley* that year. As the latter two earned Hall of Fame credentials, other teams began employing black players, with the Washington Redskins being the last to sign an African American, Bobby Mitchell, in 1962. By the 1960s such stars as Jim Brown* and Gale Sayers made it impossible to deny the accomplishments of African Americans. By the late 1990s about two-thirds of professional football players were black; and black players, like Walter Payton* and Jerry Rice, own most of the records in professional football. On the college level, Eddie Robinson of Grambling has won more games than any other coach.

African Americans were not the only group to earn fame on the football fields. Like blacks, Native Americans enjoyed early success in the sport, particularly through the Carlisle Indian School. From 1879 to 1918 the institution operated as a means to assimilate Native Americans into white culture, and Anglo sports played a prominent role. By 1895 the Carlisle football team embarked on a national schedule against the best teams.

Bemus Pierce from the Seneca tribe in New York became Carlisle's first All-American as a lineman. After his graduation in 1899 Pierce played professionally, then became an assistant coach at Carlisle under Glenn "Pop" Warner. He later served as head coach at Buffalo, Kenyon, Carlisle, and Haskell. Under Warner, Carlisle and its players gained a national reputation as they engaged in the most rigorous schedule in the nation and always played on the opponents' field. Despite such handicaps numerous Carlisle players won acclaim as All-Americans, including Isaac Seneca, Martin Wheelock, Frank Hudson, Jimmie Johnson, Elmer Busch, Albert Exendine, Jim Thorpe,* and Joe Guyon.* The last three earned distinction after college. Exendine became Warner's assistant before securing head coaching positions at six different institutions. Thorpe, a 1912 Olympic champion, was acknowledged as America's greatest athlete of the first half of the twentieth century. In 1912 Carlisle led the nation in scoring, with Thorpe leading the way. A professional baseball and football player, he nominally headed the National Football League (NFL) as its first president. Guyon made All-America at both Carlisle and Georgia Tech, where he played on the 1917 national championship team. He enjoyed a long career in the professional ranks.

In 1922 and 1923 a white promoter, Walter Lingo, sponsored an all-Indian team in the NFL, featuring Thorpe, Guyon, and Pete Calac among the ten tribes represented on the roster. William "Lone Star" Dietz, another Carlisle player, later coached the professional Boston Braves (now Washington Redskins) after a successful career as a college coach.

Carlisle was only one of three Indian schools. Haskell Institute served the Midwest in Lawrence, Kansas. Though overshadowed by Carlisle, Haskell produced its own stars, most notably, John Levi and Mayes McLain. In 1926 McLain set the single season scoring record with 253 points.

While African and Native American players received early recognition, foreigners, particularly Southern and Eastern Europeans, earned acclaim by the 1930s. Pat O'Dea, an Australian, won renown as a kicker for Wisconsin in the 1890s. Irish-born James Hogan was a three-time All-American at Yale. A Czech, Hugo Bezdek, an All-American at the University of Chicago in 1905, went on to a distinguished coaching career. Other immigrants also reached stardom as coaches, such as German-born Bob Zuppke at the University of Illinois and Scotsman Jock Sutherland at Pittsburgh. The legendary Knute Rockne,* who led Notre Dame to fame and fortune, was born in Norway.

Although known as the "Fighting Irish," Notre Dame featured many ethnic stars over its fabled history, thus earning a pluralistic support that crossed class and ethnic boundaries. Ironically, not all were Catholics. Jewish Marty Brill and Marchy Schwartz led the team as All-Americans from 1929 to 1931.

Other Jewish stars rose to prominence during the interwar years. Arnold Horween captained, then coached the Harvard team. Bennie Friedman* quarterbacked Michigan from 1924 to 1926, and Marshall Goldberg* became an All-American at Pitt, 1936–38. Sid Luckman* starred at Columbia and for the Chicago Bears, and Sid Gillman had a long career as a coach on the professional level. Over 150 Jewish Americans have played in the NFL, most before 1950. Such demonstrations of Jewish prowess during the Holocaust carried great symbolic value for American Jews.

Polish immigrants fielded their own football team in Chicago by the turn of the century, and many second-generation Poles appeared on college teams by the depression. The most famous, Bronko Nagurski,* was born in Canada of Polish and Ukrainian parents. He starred at the University of Minnesota before engaging in a stellar career as a professional with the Chicago Bears. Other Polish Americans, such as Alex Wojciechowicz* and Dick and Ed Modzelewski, earned fame on football fields, and Vic Janowicz won the Heisman Trophy in 1950.

Players of Eastern European stock have made a major impression on the game. George Halas,* the son of Czech immigrants and longtime owner of the Chicago Bears, was one of the pioneers of pro football. Chuck Bednarik,* of Slovakian parentage, and Johnny Unitas,* of Lithuanian descent, became two of its biggest stars.

Italian Americans, too, have had an impact on the sport. Frank Carideo quarterbacked Notre Dame from 1928 to 1930, and teammate Joe Savoldi starred at fullback. Angelo Bertelli won the 1943 Heisman Trophy for Notre Dame, as did Joe Bellino at Navy in 1960. A Fordham lineman, Vince Lombardi* became a celebrated professional coach. Gino Marchetti and Italian-born Leo Nomellini dominated other pro linemen during the 1950s. Italian American quarterbacks, such as Dan Marino* and Joe Montana, hold numerous professional passing records.

Scandinavian athletes often appeared on University of Minnesota teams, and more recently Jan Stenerud and Morton Andersen became prominent kickers on pro teams. The advent of soccer-style kicking brought other ethnics into the sport by the 1960s. Pete Gogolak, a Hungarian, developed the innovation at Cornell and brought it to the professional ranks as a kicker for the Buffalo Bills in 1964. (His brother Charles starred at Princeton using the same technique.) The success of the Gogolak brothers led to the wholesale adoption of the new style and the importation of Europeans. Garo Ypremian, an Armenian, enjoyed a pro career with the Miami Dolphins, as did Jan Stenerud, Kansas City's Scandinavian kicker in the 1970s. Ali Haji-Sheikh and Fuad Reveiz appeared as kickers in the 1980s.

Hispanic players, such as Efren Herrera and Luis and Max Zendejas, also rose to prominence as kickers. Lyle Alzado and Anthony Munoz earned All-Pro status as linemen; while Jim Plunkett, of Mexican Indian descent, earned honors as a quarterback.

For many ethnic groups football has provided a measure of inclusion in mainstream American culture. Sport, in general, provided a vehicle for hope and aspirations, but when baseball excluded African Americans as early as the 1870s, football still provided opportunities. The rough, physical nature of the game appealed to the immigrant working class and allowed both blacks and Jews to overturn myths of physical inferiority. By virtue of their abilities, members of diverse ethnic groups won inclusion in American society, and ethnic football heroes allowed other immigrants to share in that process of identification and assimilation.

SELECTED BIBLIOGRAPHY: Arthur R. Ashe, Jr., *A Hard Road to Glory: Football* (1993); John M. Carroll, *Fritz Pollard: Pioneer in Racial Advancement* (1992); Peter Levine, *Ellis Island to Ebbets Field: Sport and the American Jewish Experience* (1992); Charles H. Martin, "Integrating New Year's Day: The Racial Politics of College Bowl Games in the American South," *Journal of Sport History* 24 (Fall 1997): 358–377; David L. Porter, ed., *Biographical Dictionary of American Sports: Football* (1987); Myron J. Smith, Jr., ed., *The College Football Bibliography* (1994).

Gerald R. Gems

FOREMAN, GEORGE (22 January 1948 or 10 January 1949, Marshall, TX–). A champion African American heavyweight boxer, his parents were J. D. Foreman, a railroad worker, and Nancy (Nelson) Foreman. A chronic truant at school, he did not earn a junior high school diploma. At the 1968 Mexico City Summer Olympics Foreman won a gold medal in the heavyweight division. His win brought him considerable popular appeal. At a time of political saber rattling between the Soviet Union and the United States, Foreman's knockout of USSR representative Iones Chepulis was doubly symbolic as a political and athletic triumph. Moreover, Foreman was photographed as a happy winner brandishing a miniature Stars and Stripes flag. This was most significant as other African American athletes, notably, Tommie Smith* and John Carlos,* had used their victory podium to lash out at what they perceived to be a racist and exploitative America. Their resentful stares contrasted markedly with Foreman's geniality and patriotic fervor. Foreman's first professional fight took place in New York City on 23 June 1969. He steadily worked his way up the ranking list with twelve wins in 1971 and 1972. Then on 22 January 1973 in Kingston, Jamaica, Foreman captured the heavyweight championship of the world with a stunning victory over Joe Frazier.* On 30 October 1974 Muhammad Ali* knocked out Foreman in eight rounds in an extraordinarily staged fight in Kinshasa, Zaire—the "rumble in the jungle." The 1997 Oscar Award-winning documentary *When We Were Kings* is a superb contextual examination of the Foreman-Ali contest. In March 1977 Foreman gave up pugilism for preaching. However, he started on the comeback trail in March 1987. On 19 April 1991 Foreman fought Evander Holyfield for the world championship. Despite losing, Foreman garnered much support for his gritty and tenacious performance. His box appeal was such that he was matched with Michael Moorer for the World Boxing Association and International Boxing Federation (IBF) championships.

In an amazing upset Foreman won and at the age of forty-five years and nine months became the oldest boxer ever to win a heavyweight crown. Foreman has also participated in contests where he looked ancient, vulnerable, and suspect. On 24 April 1995 in Las Vegas three Nevada judges awarded Foreman a points victory over Eastern Germany's Axel Schulz for the IBF heavyweight title. English journalist David Miller labeled the judges as "overcome by sentiment, myopia or bald-faced bias," labeling their ruling for Foreman as a "sickening decision." By the late 1990s Foreman had successfully capitalized on a number of food-marketing strategies and was still considered a possible opponent for champion Evander Holyfield. Foreman will be remembered because of his famous fight with Ali and his metamorphosis as an aged boxer into a figure of national and international appeal. The onetime "distant angry thug" was reborn as a man who was full of love for everyone, and the public loved him back.

SELECTED BIBLIOGRAPHY: Muhammad Ali and Richard Durham, *The Greatest: My Own Story* (1975); David Ansen, "The Return of the Rope-a-Dope," *Newsweek* 129, No. 7 (17 February 1997), 66; C. L. Browne, "Crowning Glory," in *Ring Power* (January–February 1996), 15–22; George Foreman and Joel Engel, *By George* (1995); David Miller, *Our Sporting Times* (1996); Joyce Carol Oates, "Interview," *Playboy* 40, No. 11 (November 1993): 63–76; John Roberston, "George Foreman," in David L. Porter, ed., *African-American Sports Greats—A Biographical Dictionary* (1995); Jeffrey T. Sammons, *Beyond the Ring: The Role of Boxing in American Society* (1988); J. Tuite, ed., *The Arthur Daley Years* (1975); *When We Were Kings* (film, 1997); Materials received from the International Boxing Hall of Fame, Canastota, NY.

Scott A.G.M. Crawford

FOSTER, ANDREW ("Rube") (17 April 1879, Calvert, TX–9 December 1930, Kankakee, IL). An African American baseball player and executive, he grew up in a small Texas town. His mother's name was Sarah, and his father, Andrew, was a minister in the Methodist Episcopal Church. He began his baseball career after completing the eighth grade in the Negro school in Calvert. He debuted with the Fort Worth Yellow Jackets in 1897 at the age of seventeen. Foster's career took him to Chicago in 1901 to join the Leland Giants. He moved on to pitch for the Philadelphia Giants in 1904 before returning to Chicago in 1907. Foster slowly took over more and more responsibilities with the Chicago team, becoming the manager in 1907 and later owner of the Chicago American Giants, an original entry in the Negro National League* (NNL) in 1920. In 1910 as manager Foster led the team to a record of 123–6. Foster is best known as the "Father of the Negro Leagues." He brought together eight clubs in Kansas City in 1920 to found the first Negro League. Foster served as president until 1926, when he became ill and was hospitalized until his death in 1930. Foster was the guiding force of the NNL, and after he retired the league struggled through the 1931 season and then folded. Foster's career achievements as a player, manager, owner, and league president led to his election to the National

Baseball Hall of Fame in 1981. Foster's half brother William pitched in the Negro Leagues and entered the Hall of Fame in 1996.

SELECTED BIBLIOGRAPHY: "Historically Speaking: Andrew "Rube" Foster," *Black Sports*, (November 1977): 59–60; James A. Riley, *The Biographical Encyclopedia of the Negro Baseball Leagues* (1994), 290–292; Russell Streur, "Rube Foster, Father of Negro League Baseball," *Sports Collectors Digest* (8 February 1991): 186–187; Charles E. Whitehead, *A Man and His Diamonds: A Story of the Great Andrew Rube Foster* (1982); Frank Young, "Rube Foster—The Master Mind of Baseball," *Abbott's Monthly* (November 1930): 42–49, 93; Andrew "Rube" Foster Papers, National Baseball Hall of Fame, Cooperstown, NY.

Leslie Heaphy

FOX, RICHARD KYLE (12 August 1846, Belfast, Ireland–14 November 1922, Red Bank, NJ). Fox's father (James) was a carpenter and mason, and his mother (Mary) was the daughter of a Presbyterian minister. He was editor and publisher of the weekly *National Police Gazette* from 1877 to 1922 and an important early sports promoter. He was employed by Belfast newspapers from age twelve until his emigration to New York in 1874. Taking over the moribund *Gazette* in lieu of back wages, he sought to revitalize it as America's leading journal of the lurid and sensational, focusing on crime, sex, the theater, and sports. By the early 1880s he was selling 150,000 copies per week and had made his paper a fixture wherever working-class men gathered—in barbershops, saloons, hotels, and livery stables. Fox came to realize the potential of sport for increasing circulation through his coverage of the Paddy Ryan–Joe Goss fight of 30 May 1880. Not content to wait for spectacles to occur, he soon became the ring's foremost promoter, defining weight classifications, offering championship belts, and contributing greatly to boxing's new legitimacy. Numerous other sports were featured in the *Gazette*'s pink pages, especially the blood sports of the old urban underworld and contrived events like pie-eating contests. Fox had no reservations about appealing to the ethnic prejudices of his working-class readership, targeting Americans of African, Asian, and Jewish descent with equal virulence. The *Gazette*'s sales declined after 1900 as its journalistic techniques and subject matter were appropriated, in diluted form, by the New York dailies.

SELECTED BIBLIOGRAPHY: Elliott J. Gorn, "The Wicked World: The *National Police Gazette* and Gilded-Age America," *Media Studies Journal* 6 (1992): 1–15; Sam G. Riley, "Richard Kyle Fox," in Sam G. Riley, ed., *Dictionary of Literary Biography*, vol. 79, *American Magazine Journalists, 1850–1900* (1989), 143–48; Gene Smith and Jane Barry Smith, eds., *The Police Gazette* (1972).

George Rugg

FRAZIER, JOSEPH W. ("Smokin' Joe") (12 January 1944, Beaufort, SC–   ). An African American heavyweight champion prizefighter, he was the twelfth child of Rubin and Dolly Frazier, who raised him in rural poverty on their farm. His parents also labored on neighboring white people's land to earn enough money to pay for the necessities of life. As a boy he attended a segregated local public school until he dropped out in the tenth grade at the age of fourteen. After marrying at the age of fifteen, he moved north, settled in Philadelphia, and worked in a kosher slaughterhouse. After some early training in boxing in a local gym he became a successful amateur fighter, but he lost to Buster Mathis in the 1964 Olympic trials. After Mathis sustained an injury, Frazier replaced him on the Olympic boxing team and won the gold medal as a heavyweight. Managed by Yancy "Yank" Durham, he turned professional the following year, and by 1967 he was the leading contender for the heavyweight title. On 4 March 1968, after the New York State Athletic Commission stripped Muhammad Ali* of his title for refusing induction into the U.S. Army, Frazier defeated Mathis for New York state's version of the heavyweight crown. On 16 February 1970 he won the World Boxing Association world heavyweight title by a technical knockout of Jimmy Ellis. After court rulings cleared Ali to resume his boxing career, he challenged Frazier for the world title. Ali enraged Frazier when he portrayed him as a surrogate "white hope," a "stand-in" champion, and the pawn of white people. On 8 March 1971 in a bout that was promoted as "the Fight of the Century," Frazier retained his championship by defeating Ali in a fifteen-round decision. Frazier lost his world title to George Foreman* in 1973, and later he was defeated in two memorable battles with Ali in 1974 and 1975. Boxing historians view the latter match, "the Thrilla in Manila," as one of the greatest fights of all time. Frazier retired after another loss to Foreman in 1976; his abortive comeback attempt five years later ended after only one unimpressive win. Although during his prime he was overshadowed by the more flamboyant Ali, he earned a reputation as a tough slugger who was willing to take an enormous amount of punishment as he wore his opponents down. After retiring from the ring, he trained boxers and had limited success in a career as a singer. He was inducted into the International Boxing Hall of Fame in 1990.

SELECTED BIBLIOGRAPHY: Gerald Astor, "Joe Frazier: The Six-State Champ," *Look* 33 (24 June 1969): 89, 91; Robert H. Boyle, " 'Smokin Joe' Burns Out," *Sports Illustrated* 44 (28 June 1976): 68–71; Joe Frazier, with Phil Berger, *Smokin' Joe* (1996); Bruce Jay Friedman, "Will Joe Frazier Be the Next Champ?" *Saturday Evening Post* 240 (23 September 1967): 97–101; "Heavyweight Joe Frazier: A Stockholder's Dream," *Ebony* 23 (November 1967): 136; Jeffrey Sammons, *Beyond the Ring: The Role of Boxing in American Society* (1988).

                                                                    George B. Kirsch

FRAZIER, WALTER, II (29 March 1945, Atlanta, GA–   ). An African American basketball player, he was raised in a modest duplex in Atlanta's inner-city ghetto. The son of Walter and Eula (Wynn) Frazier, he was a football, baseball, and basketball standout at Howard High School. He turned down football scholarship offers to Indiana and Kansas Universities to play basketball at the University of Southern Illinois at Carbondale. He lost his scholarship after his sophomore year (1964–65 season) due to poor grades, but he returned to school the following year to concentrate on school and regain his scholarship. Returning to the team for the 1966–67 season, Frazier averaged eighteen points per game and earned the Most Valuable Player award at the National Invitational Tournament. He then left school with one year of college eligibility remaining and was picked in the first round of the 1967 National Basketball Association (NBA) draft by the New York Knickerbockers. After a mediocre rookie season he averaged over seventeen points, six rebounds, and nearly eight assists per game during his second year. In 1970 he helped the Knicks win their first NBA championship by averaging nearly twenty-one points per game. Known as an aggressive defensive player with all-around offensive skills, Frazier led the Knicks to another title in 1973. He was named six times to the All NBA team, seven times to the NBA All-Star team, and seven times to the NBA All Defensive team. Considered one of the greatest guards to ever play the game, he retired after thirteen seasons playing for the Knicks and the Cleveland Cavaliers with an 18.1 points, 6.1 assists, and 5.9 rebounds per game career average. During his prime in the early to mid-1970s, Frazier developed a reputation as a partygoing bachelor and stylish dresser. His teammates nicknamed him "Clyde" (after the lead character in the film *Bonnie and Clyde*) for his modish, 1930-ish attire. Ironically, Frazier was a quiet man who preferred solitude and sleep to crowds and parties. During his playing days he proved to be a savvy businessman by developing several outside financial interests, such as ownership in a hairstyling salon, president of a sports management company, and part-time radio broadcaster. After his career he became a full-time television and radio commentator for New York Knicks games.

SELECTED BIBLIOGRAPHY: "Walt Frazier," *Current Biography* (1973); 141–143; Walt Frazier and Joe James, *Clyde* (1970); Walt Frazier, with Neil Offen, *Walt Frazier: One Magic Season* (1988); Martin Taragano, *Pro Basketball Statistics: Top Players and Teams by Game, Season and Career* (1993).

Troy D. Paino

FREEDMAN, ANDREW (1 September 1860, New York City–4 December 1915, New York City). A baseball owner, he was of German Jewish ancestry, the son of Elizabeth (Davies) and Joseph. He attended St. Aloysius Academy and graduated from the College of the City of New York with a law degree. Freedman purchased a controlling interest in the New York Giants baseball club after the 1894 season. The Giants were champions by virtue of their Temple Cup victory. Under Freedman's ownership the quality of the Giants' play steadily deteriorated. Freedman was reputed to be overbearing, ill tempered, and capricious. His ownership was characterized by frequent managerial changes and squabbles with players, umpires, other owners, and the press. Freedman and three other owners devised a plan to reorganize the National League into a syndicate trust. Stock ownership would be held in the league, and gate receipts pooled. The plan was not adopted, as the foursome could not find a fifth vote to break the deadlock. Freedman sold his interest in the Giants after the 1902 season to John Brush, who had been owner of the Cincinnati franchise. The deal was part of a larger plan that included new ownership for Cincinnati and John McGraw's leaving Baltimore to manage the Giants. Freedman worked as a real estate lawyer and bondsman. He gained additional wealth through real estate speculation. He had close personal ties to Tammany Hall, which he used to further his business interests. Freedman wielded tremendous power in the political and financial spheres of New York. As an owner he used his power to prevent the American League from establishing a competing franchise in New York by holding leases on possible park sites and threatening to cut streets through sites that he did not control. After selling the Giants, Freedman devoted himself to the financing and building of the New York City subway system. He died a bachelor and left his entire fortune to charity.

SELECTED BIBLIOGRAPHY: "Andrew Freedman," *Dictionary of American Biography*, Vol. 7 (1931), 8; Mrs. John J. McGraw, *The Real McGraw* (1953); Steven A. Riess, *City Games: The Evolution of American Urban Society and the Rise of Sports* (1989); Ray Robinson, *Matty: An American Hero* (1993).

Randy B. Klipstein

FRICKER, WERNER (24 January 1936, Karlsdorf, Yugoslavia–   ). A soccer player, he emigrated from a German-speaking area of Yugoslavia to Austria at the age of eight and came to Horsham, Pennsylvania, in 1952 at the age of sixteen as an apprentice carpenter. He founded Fricker Corporation, a prosperous home-building and land-developing firm in Horsham, while continuing to play soccer. He captained the United German-Hungarians for eleven years, winning the U.S. National Amateur Championship in 1965. In 1964 he played for the U.S. Olympic team in qualifying rounds. Fricker served as president of the Eastern Pennsylvania Soccer Association, and then, in 1984, he was elected president of the U.S. Soccer Federation (USSF), taking over an organization in disarray and $1.4 million in debt. He set about strengthening the American national teams so that by the late 1980s, the United States was competitive with some of the world's best soccer nations at both the senior and youth levels. In 1990, for the first time in forty years, the United States qualified for the World Cup. Another goal was bringing the World Cup tournament, soccer's most prestigious event, to the United States. In 1983, under Fricker, the USSF unsuccessfully tried to lure the 1986 World Cup to the United States. In 1988, the USSF was $1.5 million in the black and again, under Fricker's guidance, sought to bring the 1994 World Cup to the United States. The bid was successful, resulting in the United States' hosting the world's biggest sporting event. An elder statesman of American soccer, his greatest achievements were giving opportunities for young American players to compete successfully on the international level, providing the base for commercial sponsors and television interests in soccer, and helping to bring the 1994 World Cup to the United

States. Fricker was inducted into the USSF's National Soccer Hall of Fame in June 1992.

SELECTED BIBLIOGRAPHY: Walter Chyzowych, *The Official Soccer Book* (1978); Zander Hollander, ed., *The American Encyclopedia of Soccer* (1980); Len Oliver, "The Ethnic Legacy in U.S. Soccer," *SASH Historical Quarterly* 9 (Winter 1996): 1–4, 10 and (Spring 1996): 1–4.

Leonard P. Oliver

FRIEDMAN, BENJAMIN ("Benny") (18 March 1905, Cleveland, OH–23 November 1982, New York City). A collegiate and professional football player and coach, his parents, Lewis, a tailor, and Mimi, a housewife, were Russian Jewish immigrants. An outstanding schoolboy athlete at Glenville High School in Cleveland, the 5'10", 172-pound Friedman played football for the University of Michigan from 1923 to 1926, earning his undergraduate degree the following year. An offensive quarterback and defensive safety, he guided Michigan to Big Ten championships in 1925 and 1926. An All-American selection as a junior and senior, Friedman was a brilliant passer, elusive runner, and deft place kicker. His celebrity as a quarterback and defensive back continued during seven seasons (1927–33) in the National Football League. An All-Pro selection from 1927 to 1931, Friedman played for the Cleveland Bulldogs (1927), Detroit Wolverines (1928), New York Giants (1929–31), and Brooklyn Dodgers (1932–33). His gridiron exploits and Jewish following generated significant support for the struggling National Football League. Following his retirement from active play, Friedman coached football at City College of New York (CCNY) from 1934 to 1941. Given the meager resources at his disposal, his CCNY coaching record of twenty-seven wins and thirty-two losses was more than respectable. After naval service during World War II, Friedman was the first athletic director (1949–63) and football coach (1950–59) at Brandeis University. Possessed of an analytical mind and charismatic presence, he built a successful football program at Brandeis, posting a record of thirty-four wins, thirty-three losses, and four ties. A Jewish standard-bearer during his playing days, Friedman's coaching successes at Brandeis gave the first Jewish-sponsored, liberal arts university important recognition during its initial decade. After academic critics of Brandeis' athletic program forced the abolition of football prior to the 1960 season, disappointment shadowed Friedman's later years.

SELECTED BIBLIOGRAPHY: Peter Levine, *Ellis Island to Ebbets Field: Sport and the American Jewish Experience* (1992); *New York Times*, 24 November 1982, D21; Abram Sachar, *Brandeis University: A Host at Last* (1976); William Simons, "Brandeis: Athletics at a Jewish-Sponsored University," *American Jewish History* 83 (1995): 65–81; Robert Slater, *Great Jews in Sports* (1983).

William M. Simons

FRIEDMAN, MAX ("Marty") (12 July 1889, New York City–1 January 1986, ?). A pioneer of college and professional basketball, he was raised in the heavily Jewish blocks of Manhattan's Lower East Side. Beginning in 1903, he played for the "midget" team of the University Settlement House, which was coached by a Jewish immigrant from Austria. There he first joined with his longtime teammate Barney Sedran,* as the two youngsters led their squad (the "busy Izzies)" to settlement house and metropolitan Amateur Athletic Union championships. Unlike Sedran, he skipped college and began competing for money at the age of sixteen. Although at twenty-one he was only 5' 7.5" tall, on the court he was not much shorter than his teammates and opponents, most of whom were under 6' in height. Frequently paired with Sedran, the two were top gate attractions, celebrated as the sport's "Heavenly Twins." Between 1910 and 1927 Friedman played in most leagues in the East and led his teams to numerous championships. He frequently played on several squads during the same season, competing on most nights and often twice on Sundays. In 1914 his Utica, New York, squad claimed a world title, while the following year his team in Carbondale, Pennsylvania, won thirty-five straight games. During World War I he participated in U.S. Army basketball and helped to organize a tournament for soldiers that evolved into the Inter-Allied Games, the first international basketball tournament. After the war Friedman starred in 1921 on the New York Whirlwinds; from 1923 to 1927 he was captain and coach of the Cleveland Rosenblums. Renowned for his defensive skills as a guard, during his pro career Friedman scored over 1,300 points. In 1971 he was elected to the Naismith Memorial Basketball Hall of Fame.

SELECTED BIBLIOGRAPHY: Peter Levine, *Ellis Island to Ebbets Field* (1992), 27–29, 53–56; Max Friedman file, Naismith Memorial Basketball Hall of Fame, Springfield, MA.

George B. Kirsch

FRISCH, FRANK FRANCIS ("the Fordham Flash") (9 September 1898, Queens, NY–12 March 1973, Wilmington, DE). A baseball player, manager, and broadcaster, he was the son of German immigrant and wealthy linen manufacturer Franz Frisch. His mother was Katherine (Stahl) Frisch. Raised in the Bronx, he attended Fordham Prep and Fordham University, where he was a sprinter on the track team, captain of the basketball squad, a second-team All-American halfback and captain of the football team, and a catcher and captain of the baseball nine. Choosing a baseball career, he signed with the New York Giants in June 1919 and never played in the minors. During his seven seasons with the Giants he played second and third base, reaching stardom as a switch-hitting, aggressive, base-stealing, and slick fielding second baseman. He contributed mightily to the Giants' winning four consecutive pennants between 1921 and 1924, with World Series victories in 1921–22. His stormy relationship with manager John McGraw ended in a sensational trade after the 1926 season, which sent him to the St. Louis Cardinals in exchange for their six-time batting champion and player-manager Rogers Hornsby. He attained even greater notoriety as leader and eventually manager of the Cardinals, dubbed the "Gashouse Gang" in the 1930s. The National League's Most Valuable Player in 1931, he helped the Cardinals capture league pennants in 1928, 1930–31, and 1934, with World Series championships in 1931 and 1934. Named manager on 24 July 1933, he retired as a player in 1937 and was released as Cardinals pilot in 1938. He later managed the Pittsburgh Pirates from 1940 to 1946 and the Chicago Cubs from 10 June 1949 to 21 July 1951. A fiery competitor who enjoyed baiting umpires, who frequently tossed him out of games, in his private life he loved horticulture and classical music. After his retirement he was celebrated as a colorful raconteur and host of a postgame television show for the New York Giants. Over his long career of nineteen seasons he batted .316 with 2,880 hits and 1,244 runs batted in, led the league in stolen bases three times, and set numerous fielding records for second basemen in regular season and fifty World Series games. He was inducted into the Baseball Hall of Fame in 1947.

SELECTED BIBLIOGRAPHY: Bob Broeg, *The Pilot Light and the Gas House Gang* (1980); Frank Frisch, as told to J. Roy Stockton, *Frankie Frisch: The Fordham Flash* (1962); *New York Times*, 13 March 1973, 42; *The Sporting News*, 24 March 1973.

George B. Kirsch

G

GAELIC ATHLETIC ASSOCIATION. Founded in 1884 by Michael Cusack and Maurice Davin in Thurles County, Tipperary, Ireland, the Gaelic Athletic Association (GAA) aimed to preserve and foster such traditional Irish games as hurling* and Gaelic football.* A sporting expression of Irish cultural nationalism, it was designed to counter the growth of English football, rugby, and other games and Anglicizing influences in Ireland and to support independence among Irish Catholics. From its inception the GAA had links with Irish political nationalism, especially the Fenians. The formation of the GAA led to the founding of the Gaelic League, which was created in 1893 to preserve the Irish language, once banned by the British government.

Meanwhile, in the United States during the late 1800s the Irish American communities of New York City, Boston, Chicago, and other cities were already supporting several Gaelic football, hurling, and track-and-field clubs. New York City alone had about a dozen particularly well known teams in that era, notably, the Irish Americans, the Barrys, the Wolfe Tones, the Stars of Erin, the Mitchels, the Thomas Francis Meaghers, the Emmets, and the Kickhams. In 1888 an "American Invasion" of more than fifty Irish athletes toured the United States, competing in hurling contests and track-and-field meets in several cities. All of this activity spurred the creation of the first Gaelic Athletic Association in the United States, organized in Chicago in 1890. In New York City the Irish-American Athletic Association yielded control of Gaelic football and hurling to the Irish Counties Athletic Union in 1904. This organization later became known as the United Irish Counties (UIC), which stills exists today. Ten years later a New York City branch of the GAA was founded, and it took over the administration of that city's Irish sports. Unlike in Ireland in the late 1800s, the teams in New York and later in Philadelphia, Boston, Chicago, and San Francisco were named not after counties but rather Irish nationalist leaders and patriots such as Wolfe Tone and Robert Emmet. However, the teams soon became incorporated into the various Irish county organizations that had existed in the city since 1849. For example, in 1904 the Kickhams changed their name to the Tipperary football team, to be affiliated with the Tipperary Society. In New York City, Boston, Chicago, and other cities the grounds of clubs sponsored by the GAA were often named Celtic or Gaelic Park.

At the end of the twentieth century games were played in most prominent U.S. cities. Outside New York, which has its own separate managing board, all GAA teams fall under the auspices of the North American County Board. Each year, usually on Memorial Day weekend, teams from across the United States gather in one city to pick the best teams in Gaelic football and hurling. Comprising twelve Divisional Boards in twenty major U.S. cities, the GAA of North America currently has a total of eighty-five adult clubs from across the country. Most clubs feature a roster of approximately fifty players with an additional 100 nonplaying members. Competitions are held locally to select clubs to qualify to play in the national championships.

SELECTED BIBLIOGRAPHY: Ronald H. Baylor and Timothy J. Meagher, eds., *The New York Irish* (1996); Brian deBreffney, *Ireland: A Cultural Encyclopedia* (1983); Marcus de Burca, *The G.A.A.: A History of the Gaelic Athletic Association* (1980); W. F. Mandle, *The Gaelic Athletic Association* (1987).

George B. Kirsch

GAELIC FOOTBALL. This fifteen-a-side field game is played exclusively in Ireland and in Irish immigrant communities, including those in the United States. Players seek to score by kicking or fisting a round ball between two uprights, either under an eight-foot crossbar (a goal, worth three points) or over it (a point, worth one). The ball may be kicked, punted, caught, handled, or fisted but not thrown or picked directly from the ground. Players may also run with the ball, provided it is periodically "hopped" off the ground or relayed between foot and hand.

The determining event in the history of Gaelic football was the founding of the Gaelic Athletic Association* (GAA) in Ireland (1884). As part of its overtly nationalist agenda, the GAA sought to counter the growth of English football codes (i.e., soccer and rugby) by promoting its own uniquely Irish game, ostensibly a revival of local village traditions. Certainly, forms of field and cross-country football were played in Ireland until the time of the famine (1845–47). But researchers have found little to suggest that football enjoyed any particular prominence in Irish culture or that it was played in any singular way. Maurice Davin's initial code of ten rules (1885) was ambiguous in the extreme, and the modern game evolved by trial and error only over the ensuing thirty years. But if Gaelic football's pedigree is open to doubt, the GAA was nonetheless successful in developing a code that could be (and continues to be) defined in opposition to nonindigenous traditions and that subsequently established itself as an Irish sporting institution.

The earliest known references to "Irish foot-ball" in the United States date from 1857 (New York) and 1859 (New Orleans). After the Civil War forms of the game—which must have been rough and unstructured—were played at the weekend gatherings of Irish American political, cultural, and benevolent organizations, and teams bearing nationalistic nicknames were established. But the emergence of something akin to the modern game can only have resulted from the dissemination of the GAA code. Here Irish Americans were culturally receptive, for sport figured strongly in the Gaelic revival already under way by 1880. The GAA's "American Invasion" tour of 1888, while not expressly showcasing football, nonetheless spurred its growth by promoting the code with Irish American athletic organizations and sowing the seed for local GAA affiliates. The first of these was organized in Chicago in 1890; by 1893 it was sponsoring ten Gaelic football teams.

In New York the GAA arrived for good in 1914 and soon established itself as the dominant force in Gaelic football in the United States. Indeed, it has on occasion fielded teams as powerful as any in Ireland, winning the championship of the Irish National League for 1948–49 and repeating the feat twice in the 1960s. But few of the New York teams' players learned the sport in America. Historically, the GAA has maintained local fan interest by recruiting recognized Irish players, using the prospect of wages and secondary jobs to appeal to athletes who, in Ireland, perform as amateurs. The transatlantic traffic in Gaelic footballers reached a peak in the 1950s but slowed as circumstances in Ireland improved, and urban enclaves of Irish Americans around venues like New York's Gaelic Park disappeared into the suburbs.

SELECTED BIBLIOGRAPHY: Eoghan Corry, *Catch and Kick—Great Moments of Gaelic Football 1880–1990* (1989); Tom Humphries, *Green Fields: Gaelic Sport in Ireland* (1996); W. F. Mandle, "The Gaelic Athletic Association and Popular Culture, 1884–1924," in Oliver MacDonough, W. F. Mandle, and Pauric Travers, eds., *Irish Culture and Nationalism, 1750–1850* (1983), 104–121; Ralph C. Wilcox, "The Shamrock and the Eagle: Irish Americans and Sport in the Nineteenth Century," in George Eisen and David K. Wiggins, eds., *Ethnicity and Sport in North American History and Culture* (1994).

George Rugg

GAINES, CLARENCE ("Big House") (21 May, 1923, Paducah, KY–   ). An African American college basketball coach, he graduated from Paducah High School in 1941, where he starred in football. At Morgan State University in Maryland he was an All-American tackle for two years and played basketball to keep in shape during the off-season. After earning his bachelor's degree in 1946, he added a master's degree in physical education from Columbia University in 1947. While an undergraduate Gaines majored in chemistry, hoped to become a dentist, and never seriously considered a coaching career. But his life plans changed when he was offered a position at Winston-Salem Teachers College, teaching math and physical education. During his first years there he coached football, basketball, boxing, and tennis and even served as interim athletic director. But after 1950 he concentrated on basketball, mostly because it was easier to recruit the seven or eight players needed for that sport than the forty or fifty required for football. Over a forty-seven-year career that ended in 1993 his teams compiled a record of 828 wins against 447 losses, including eighteen twenty-win seasons. At the time of his retirement his total career victories ranked second only to Kentucky's Adolph Rupp. His Winston-Salem squads achieved their greatest success during the 1960s, with Earl "the Pearl" Monroe leading the team to a 31–1 record and a National Collegiate Athletic Association (NCAA) College Division championship in 1966–67—the first NCAA title won by a predominantly African American college. That year Gaines was honored as the NCAA College Division Coach of the Year. During the late 1960s and 1970s he encountered more difficulty in recruiting talented black players, primarily because the major private and public universities in the nation were integrating their campuses and enrolling African American athletes. Gaines was inducted into the Naismith Memorial Basketball Hall of Fame in 1981.

SELECTED BIBLIOGRAPHY: *Charlotte Observer*, 24 February 1993; *New York Times*, 6 December 1983, II–13.

George B. Kirsch

GATES, WILLIAM ("Pop") (30 August 1917, Decatur, AL–1 December 1999, New York City). Son of Lulu and Dan Gates, he and his family migrated from Alabama to Cleveland and then to New York City in 1920. He graduated from Benjamin Franklin High School in 1937. Gates was a professional basketball player and coach. He played on three Young Men's Christian Association (YMCA) basketball teams that won All-City Titles. In high school he earned All-Conference honors in 1937 and 1938 and made the All-City First Team in 1938. During his senior year Benjamin Franklin won the New York City Public School Athletic League title. Within months of graduating from high school in 1938, Gates joined the New York Renaissance* professional team. The Rens won the first world professional basketball championship, held in Chicago in 1939. During World War II Gates played for several professional teams, including the Rens, Grumman Flyers, and Washington Bears, earning All-Pro Tournament team status while playing for each of these clubs. In 1946 he served as one of the first African Americans to play in a league when he signed with the Tri-City Blackhawks of the National Basketball League (NBL). The following season he rejoined the Rens, and the team represented Dayton in 1948–49, the first all-black team in the NBL. When the Rens were leased to Abe Saperstein in 1949, Gates signed with the Scranton Miners of the American Basketball League. The Miners won the 1950 league championship, and Gates made the All-League first team. Between 1950 and 1955, Gates served as a player-coach with the Harlem Globetrotters.* In 1989 "Pop" Gates was elected to the Naismith Memorial Basketball Hall of Fame.

SELECTED BIBLIOGRAPHY: Arthur R. Ashe, Jr., *A Hard Road to Glory: A History of the African-American Athlete, 1919–1945*, vol. 2 (1988); *New York Times*, 5 December 1999, A63; Susan J. Rayl, "The New York Renaissance Professional Black Basketball Team, 1923–1950" (Ph.D. diss., Pennsylvania State University, 1996); William "Pop" Gates file, Naismith Memorial Basketball Hall of Fame.

Susan Rayl

GEHRIG, HENRY LOUIS (19 June 1903, New York City–2 June 1941, New York City). A baseball player, he was the son of German-speaking parents. His father, Heinrich, a skilled mechanic and native of Baden, and his mother, Christina (Flack, born in Denmark), settled in New York City. Always shy, Gehrig suffered frequent humiliation as a youngster due to the anti-German hysteria that pervaded the nation during World War I. He attended Public School #132 and the High School of Commerce. In 1921 he was invited by the New York Giants to play baseball in the major leagues but declined so that he could study at Columbia University. As an undergraduate sports enthusiast Gehrig was on the football, swimming, and baseball varsity teams, for which he still holds a record as the Columbia pitcher with the most strikeouts in a game, fanning seventeen Williams batters even though in the end he lost the game. Then in 1923, reportedly because his coach at Columbia received a $500 recruiter's bonus, Gehrig signed with the New York Yankees, where he became known as the "Iron Horse." Outstanding as a first baseman and in many instances superior in batting to Babe Ruth,* Gehrig had a lifetime slugging average of .341, played 2,130 consecutive major league games, and participated in seven World Series. Coached and abetted by Babe Ruth, whom Lou idolized, Gehrig in 1927 was voted Most Valuable Player in the American League, an honor he also earned in 1931, 1934, and 1936. On 3 June 1932 Gehrig performed a feat never matched by Babe Ruth—four home runs in a single game against the Philadelphia Athletics. Due to mysterious problems of ailing health, Gehrig in 1939 began consultations at the Mayo Clinic in Rochester. On 4 July of the same year, some 62,000 fans and a grateful nation, among them millions of German Americans, gathered to honor their soft-spoken hero. The same year, at the age of thirty-five, Gehrig retired from baseball, following which at the behest of Mayor Fiorello La Guardia, he became parole commissioner of New York City, only to die two years later in 1941 of amyotropic lateral sclerosis, known today as Lou Gehrig's disease.

SELECTED BIBLIOGRAPHY: Bob Broeg, *Superstars of Baseball* (1971); Raymond J. Gonzalez, "The Gehrig Streak Reviewed," *Baseball Research Journal* 4 (1975): 34–37; Raymond J. Gonzalez, " 'Larrupin' Lou and 23 Skidoo," *Baseball Research Journal* 12 (1983): 22–26; Raymond J. Gonzalez, "Lou Who? Stole Home 15 Times," *Baseball Research Journal* 7 (1978): 109–111; Raymond J. Gonzalez, "Still the Greatest One-Two Punch," *Baseball Research Journal* 6 (1977): 98–101; Frank Graham, *Lou Gehrig, a Quiet Hero* (1942); Ray Robinson, *Iron Horse: Lou Gehrig in His Time* (1990); *The Sporting News Baseball Register, 1942* (1942).

La Vern J. Rippley

GERMAN-AMERICAN ATHLETIC CLUB. The German-American Athletic Club (GAAC) was founded in 1884 primarily for men interested in wrestling and weight lifting. Elected president of the GAAC in 1910, Dietrich Wortmann had previously achieved athletic recognition as a wrestler. The club, which had a strong ethnic identity, disbanded in 1917 in reaction to the anti-German sentiments aroused by World War I. Wortmann revived the club in 1928, and it merged with the German Athletic Club. The club bought a German American landmark, the "Scheffelhalle," as a clubhouse; Wortmann apparently provided much of the funding. Many of the club's active members had been born in Germany, including Paul de Bruyn, who won the Boston Marathon in 1932. German-Jewish relations in New York City had traditionally been amicable, and the club accepted Jewish members of German background, including the great long-distance running coach Max Silver and the marathon runner Bill Steiner. Under Silver's coaching, the club was a metropolitan and national power in the marathon in 1933 and 1934.

In early 1935, in a letter to *Deutscher Weckruf und Beobachter*, the American Nazi German-language newspaper, GAAC officials stated their support for Nazi Germany. One by one, over the next few months, the Jewish athletes left the club. Dietrich Wortmann was one of the signers of the letter, which named Patrick Walsh, president of the Metropolitan Amateur Athletic Union (AAU), Charles H. Diehm, vice president of the Metropolitan AAU, and Avery Brundage, president of the American Olympic Association, as friends. This conflict over relations with Nazi Germany took place within the larger conflict over American participation in the 1936 Olympic Games in Munich. Wortmann was one of the Metropolitan Association delegates sent to the December 1935 national Amateur Athletic Association convention. This convention voted to table a resolution to boycott the 1936 Olympics; the vote of the Metropolitan AAU was overwhelmingly in favor of participation.

The German-American Athletic Club continued after World War II. In 1948 Dietrich Wortmann was elected president of the Metropolitan Association of the AAU, and Charles H. Diehm returned as secretary-treasurer.

SELECTED BIBLIOGRAPHY: Stanley Frank, "German-American AC Heils Athletes but Not Hitler: Jewish Members Play a Big Part," *New York Post*, 2 January 1935, 18; "Leaders of German-American AC, Key Men in Olympics Committee, Are Termed Pro-Nazi," *Columbia Daily Spectator*, 1 December 1935, 1, 4; *New York Times*, 16 October 1949, 10.

Pamela Cooper

GERMANS. Sports for German Americans rest on a 150-year-old tradition called turnerism, a label that describes a movement begun in Germany's capital city of Berlin by Friedrich Ludwig "Turnvater" Jahn, who built the first *Turn-platz* (exercise field) on the Hasenheide (literally, "rabbit mesa") in 1811. Oc-cupied at the time by the French under Napoleon, Germany would experience no rebirth, in the view of Jahn, unless its people trained to become both phys-ically healthy and mentally acute. His intent was for Germans to acquire qual-ities that would foster organizational and patriotic ideals for achieving liberty on the personal as well as the federal levels. Because of the turners' ardent devotion to individual and democratic goals, however, conservative leaders like Austria's Metternich, the prince who dominated Europe following the Napo-leonic era by advocating a return to the status quo, suppressed the liberal and nationalistic turner movement. Athletic exercises were declared illegal even as turnverein (athletic societies) were disbanded, with the result that Jahn himself served a five-year jail sentence. Despite such efforts, the turner spirit remained alive and thoroughly liberal in politics. University students with their *Burschen-schaften* (fraternities) agitated steadily for radical reform and were among the most influential assemblages in the revolution of 1848. In large numbers, turners flocked to the black-red-gold banner of the 1848 revolution (since World War II, the identical colors of the flag for the Federal Republic of Germany) to fight with leaders like Franz Sigel and Friedrich Hecker in Baden or at the barricades in Dresden, Frankfurt, and Berlin. Although these revolutionaries for a demo-cratic society were defeated when the insurrection collapsed, many avoided prison terms by taking refuge in the United States.

Flight and prison terms for the insurgents after 1848 notwithstanding, Jahn's principles of physical training had already preceded them to the United States by a quarter century when, in 1824, German immigrants Karl Beck and Karl Follen began teaching at historian George Bancroft's Round Hill boys' school in Northampton, Massachusetts. On the turner model Beck established a gym-nasium, offered classes according to the Jahn theory of physical education, and immediately translated the *Deutsche Turnkunst* (Art of German Gymnastics) into English for use by wider English-speaking audiences. Regardless of their efforts, however, German-style sports made little headway in America before the arrival of the transplanted refugees. Suddenly, around 1850 turnverein sprang up across the German belt of ethnic communities, often exemplifying the liberal-radical-reformer ideals associated with the *Freie Gemeinde* and the *Freimännervereine*, which promoted free thought and especially abolition. As a result, thousands of turners who had sought to advance their political agenda back in Europe by their activism in the United States volunteered to form entire companies in the Union Army.

The first *Turnergemeide* in the United States was organized in Cincinnati in 1848 and by 1850 had its own exercise yard and Turner Hall, followed in 1851 by a library, male chorus, and a monthly publication. Philadelphia soon followed suit when immigrants from Germany in 1849 began exercises in a Quaker meet-inghouse converted to a Turner Hall. Almost immediately this society exhibited a problem for the turners that continued for decades. Instead of pulling together for their ideals of mental and corporeal training, political radicalism frequently infected the parent group with schism. In the City of Brotherly Love, the socialist membership quickly split off to form a new turner group called the *Sozialer Turnverein*, which then brought suit against the parent society for ownership of half the property. In the same year of 1849, the like-minded *Sozialdemokratische Turnverein* opened in Baltimore, gaining 278 members within the first year, enabling it to outnumber all the other seventeen Turner groups then existing. In Maryland, where slavery was legal, this new society vigorously fought Nativists, enlisting its abolitionist allies coupled with its obstreperous *Turnerzeitung* (turner newspaper) with such sweeping success that in 1860 it became headquarters for the national turner fraternity.

New York's turners organized in 1848 at a meeting in Hoboken but soon suffered the predictable split of a *Sozialistischer Turnverein* offshoot. From the beginning, when moderates still prevailed, fencing instructor Franz Sigel had been advocating a more revolutionary, socialistic program. Soon other turner groups formed in Brooklyn. In 1850 the movement took root in Milwaukee, where three years later August Willich founded a social turnerverein for which by way of exception membership was limited exclusively to forty-eighters who had fled persecution in Germany during that year of revolution. Societies quickly formed likewise in the Wisconsin cities of Madison, Fond du Lac, LaCrosse, and elsewhere. In Davenport, Iowa, a *Sozialistischer Turnverein* commenced in 1852, when Schleswig-Holstein civil war veterans drilled wearing the colorful uniforms from their Danish-German conflict. Soon there were turner societies in St. Louis, Peoria, and Chicago, which in 1857 boasted twenty-six separate turner clubs. By 1856 turner fellowships had been initiated in twenty-six states, including at Sacramento and on the California coast. Even southern states whose ideology the turners opposed had their share: at Louisville, New Orleans, Mobile, and Charleston.

In most cases, turner membership as a whole during these early decades subscribed to the thesis that turnerism was a friend of progress and the enemy of "all special privilege, ecclesiastical despotism and political corruption." Among the members who fought clericalism and politics as usual were atheists, communists, pantheists, ardent nationalists, sober, middle-of-the road reformers, and cosmopolitans who championed the brotherhood of man regardless of race, class, creed, or national origin. Envisioning the ancient Greeks as their prototypes, the turners insisted on complete harmony between mind and body through physical and mental activities, the well-being of the majority, the highest endeavors to educate men physically, ethically, intellectually, and culturally. Thus, considerable sums of money were spent on gymnasiums and equipment. Also, a lot of energy was expended in calisthenics, acrobatic tumbling, and workouts on the bars, which promoted physical fitness for individuals through the life cycle. Although not in equal amounts, money was also expended on libraries, singing societies, debate matches, lectures, dramatic performances, and the advancement of free public schools where physical education but not religious instruction would be integral to the curriculum. More isolated were calls from turners or their leaders to gather funds and material support for liberal movements in Europe (e.g., Garibaldi in Italy), to send veterans of the 1848 revolutions back to garner individual freedoms in the old fatherland, and repeatedly to "carry the red flag of socialism" back for a rebirth on the European continent.

Emphasizing perhaps too zealously the radical liberal element in politics, the turners demonstrated an irrepressible love for pageantry, parades, public celebrations, and naive student romanticism, which many never outgrew. Annual *Turnfeste* offered ever more lavish and pretentious gymnastic spectacles coupled with torchlight processions, brilliant fireworks displays, noisy shooting, and hilarious singing, as opposed to earlier calls for the socialistic use of government for the betterment of humankind. Bugle calls and drum ruffles heralded spectacular exhibitions of acrobatics and physical strength. On occasion street celebrations were spiced with human pyramids shouldered by the strongest and most skillful turners, which, when exhibited together with German women athletes who appeared in bloomers, attracted and, on occasion, also shocked American onlookers.

During the Civil War, owing to the departure of most members for the front, the turner movement declined. When it picked up again after the war, the character of broad American support shifted away from the socialistic cause to one of calm, if self-serving, respect when veterans prominently displayed their medals and proclaimed their devotion to the American cause against slavery and for the republic. Thus, turners now had considerable success introducing physical education into the public schools of the nation, which, however, had the unanticipated outcome of reducing the need for physical training facilities maintained by the turner societies outside the schools. Basking in their success, by 1876 national membership in the turners stood at 14,000, all of whom theoretically had access to their central library of some 30,000 volumes. In 1890 the turners numbered over 30,000 mortals who had access to more than 160 gymnasiums and who supposedly were reaching an estimated 400,000 participants by their offering of physical activities. At the World's Fair in Chicago in 1893 the turners gave daily exhibitions of their work for thousands of spectators to whom they generously distributed their pamphlets. By 1948, when the organization celebrated its centennial, it boasted a membership of 25,000 in ninety-eight societies but has been declining since.

Its achievements over a century of time lay, however, not in its large numbers but in its advocacy for the rights of women, labor reforms, the eight-hour workday, factory safety, and child labor laws as well as the need for a political party that would foster their goals. Partly, these aspirations were achieved by the Progressives, especially in states like Wisconsin, Minnesota, and North Dakota, where their ideals were enacted by the likes of Governor and then Senator Robert LaFollette, Governor Floyd Olson in Minnesota, and the Non Partisan League in North Dakota. Always active on behalf of sports and physical education, the turners also worked on behalf of progressive income taxes, the direct election of the president, public ownership of utility companies, and the concept that the walls of the state university should be the borders of the state, in other words, the concept of university extension programs.

Although the turner movement was routed as a result of World War I animosity toward everything German, decades earlier turners were beginning to be attacked from within their own ranks for playing "pseudomilitary games," "student drinking," and their "phalanx of liberty" that had become little more than "philistines in uniform." Friedrich Hecker in St. Louis called on his fellow turners to reinvent the turnverein as a "carrier, developer and apostle of the free spirit," urging its members to take part in public affairs and to champion reform instead of acting like "tin soldiers" who are replaced in their boxes once the Turner Hall closes for the night. Others rightly alleged that the movement had abandoned its socialistic principles in favor of recreation and social affairs. Romantic jackets, ribbons, and uniforms became more comforting than waging radical politics, propounding social action, or even engaging in physical recreation. Opposition to Sunday closing laws and alcoholic prohibition seemed to satisfy any bent left for the political arena. As breweries contributed funds for turner construction projects, the ground floor barroom and restaurant became more important to the turner societies than their gymnasium. Still, during the years from 1896 through the mid-twentieth century, turner clubs placed various of their members on the Olympic teams of the United States, notably, in 1924, 1932, 1936, and 1948.

Even though gymnastics and the mandatory offering of physical education in public schools became the outstanding contribution of the German turner to American life, it was the sport of baseball that attracted German Americans most and in which the largest number of German sports enthusiasts indulged and excelled. As with any "minority" seeking to wear badges of assimilation, the Germans identified with their ethnic representatives on the athletic fields. In turn, individual prowess in sports lifted the self-esteem of the group that vicariously "beat off" the competition and shared the prestige enjoyed by the majority. Prizefighting worked for the Irish. Finns were great hockey players, the game of golf was dominated by English and Scotch men, while today African Americans excel at basketball and other sports as their means to gain recognition.

No longer do Germans seek out their own as the athletic heroes of their ethnicity, especially not in one particular sport, but formerly they most frequently claimed their champions on the baseball diamond—not just Babe Ruth* and Lou Gehrig,* but spicy characters like John Peter "Honus" Wagner,* also known as the "Flying Dutchman" because of his speed and his Pennsylvania German origin, who never batted under .300 while he played shortstop for a host of major league teams. George Edward "Rube" Wadell excelled as a left-handed pitcher who in minor league exhibitions was wont to make his fielders sit down and then proceed to strike out all batters who came to the plate. Frank Frisch,* the "Fordham Flash," was born to immigrant Franz Frisch and Katherine Stahl Frisch at New York in 1898 and attended Fordham, where he played baseball and football. Later with the New York Giants he established his great reputation as a switch-hitter. Henry Knight "Heinie" Groh gained fame at third base and as a right-hander who had whittled out from a Spalding his own cudgel that lasted him a career. California-born Emil Frederick Meusel, despite his German origins, bore the nickname "Irish" for his ruddy complexion in center field, while his brother Robert William Meusel acquired fame for a career averaging .76 runs driven in per game. Raymond William "Cracker" Schalk was one of the game's durable all-time catchers for the Chicago White Sox and the New York Giants.

Other German baseball notables include Michael Jack Schmidt, the right-hander with three consecutive home run titles who was voted Most Valuable Player in 1980, 1981, and 1986. Likewise, Albert Fred Schoendienst,* the son of a coal miner-farmer father, enjoyed fame as a second baseman for the St. Louis Cardinals. Buffalo-born Warren Edward Spahn, whose unusual World War II army career led to a Purple Heart and battlefield commission at the Remagen Bridge on the Rhine, hurled his way to fame over a twenty-one-year period as a left-hander for the Milwaukee Braves and others. Daniel J. Staub was an outstanding hitter who amassed over 4,000 bases. Who can forget Charles "Casey" Stengel? Born of Irish German parentage in 1890 at Kansas City, he was a man gifted with Teutonic syntax and Celtic garrulity, in addition to a second nickname, "Dutch," and records at bat and in the outfield for the Brooklyn Dodgers before ending his career as a manager of various teams. Not as colorful or as well remembered is George Trautmann, who, following his baseball career as a hurler, acceded to turner principles by his postgraduate study in physical education at Harvard. He then distinguished himself in administrative positions across a wide spectrum of sports, including baseball, notably, in Columbus, Ohio. Likewise, Harold Arthur Trosky was of German ancestry with the name Harold Arthura Troyavesky, starring as a first baseman with the Cleveland Indians.

Among the few great baseballers actually born in Germany was Christian Frederick Wilhelm von der Ahe (b. at Hille, Germany, in 1851). His fame, however, issued not for his role as a player but as a saloon keeper who founded the Sportsman's Park Association, which developed into a first alternative to the National League. Later, in 1883, he hired Charles Comiskey* to manage his St. Louis Brown Stockings, and he also became manager of the Cincinnati Red Stockings. George Martin Weiss counts among the baseball administrators, managing first the Baltimore Orioles and then the New York Yankees. Also in the ownership class was August Adolphus "Gussie" Busch of St. Louis, the son of the Anheuser-Busch cofounder, who purchased the St. Louis Cardinals in 1953 to block the team's departure for Milwaukee. Though his lifestyle resembled a Rhineland baron of old, devoted to hounds, horses, and magnificent entertainments on his Grant's Farm estate in St. Louis, Busch spent millions to hire new players and for purchasing Sportsman's Park, which he refurbished into Busch Memorial Stadium in downtown St. Louis (1966), the last major sports complex to be constructed with private funds. Also in the ownership category was the German Jewish American Barney Dreyfuss.* He came to America in 1881 and eventually became owner of the Pittsburgh Pirates in 1899. His teams won six pennants and two championships under his tutelage.

Of the thousands of lesser known, inconspicuous sports heroes of German heritage and ancestry, many distinguished themselves in athletic activities other than baseball. Few of these "unsung" stars made it into record books. For instance, there was basketball star Christian Steinmetz, who averaged 25.7 points per game for the University of Wisconsin's early varsity team, scoring 50 points in one contest. The Buffalo Germans* were one of the most celebrated early barnstorming teams of the pre–World War I era, earning induction into the Naismith Memorial Hall of Fame as a club. Johnny Weissmuller* was the first American to win five gold medals in Olympic Games and dominated the swimming scene throughout the 1920s. From 1932 to 1948 he acted in films as Tarzan. Often ethnicity was overshadowed by great writers who coined such titles and nicknames as the "Four Horsemen" of Notre Dame, among whom was a German named Stuhldreher, though none of them gained the fame of their Norwegian coach Knute Rockne.* Following the two world wars in which the United States opposed Germany, Germans as an ethnic group in American sports dissipated. Certainly, no team any longer wanted to be known as "the Germans" as the Notre Dame teams are still described as the "Fighting Irish." However, scholars have rightly used sports like baseball as an indicator of the extent to which a specific nationality became acculturated in America. For example, the assimilation-resistant Russian Germans of North Dakota were "rabid" baseball fans from their early days of settlement through the entire twentieth century, suggesting how quickly such groups acclimated themselves to the American scene.

Following World War II, sports in America rapidly escalated into school, university, national, and professional status (to the demise of local community teams), which brought with it a diminishing factor of ethnicity except for people of color. Beginning with Jackie Robinson* and continuing into the present, the sports avenue has proven to be a thoroughfare to success and respect for minorities. Nowhere, however, does there appear to be any other nationality or race contribution that parallels the way the Germans, through a century and a half, impacted American sports history with their turnverein movement.

SELECTED BIBLIOGRAPHY: Robert K. Barney, "German Turners in American Domestic Crisis," *Stadion* 4 (1978): 344–357; Robert K. Barney, "America's First Turnverein: Commentary in Favor of Louisville, Kentucky," *Journal of Sport History* 11 (Spring 1984): 134–137; Robert K. Barney, "Knights of Cause and Exercise: German Forty-Eighters and Turnvereine in the United States during the Antebellum Period," *Canadian Journal of History of Sport* 13, No. 2 (December 1982): 62–79; Erich Geldbach,

"The Beginnings of German Gymnastics in America," *Journal of Sport History* 3 (Winter 1976): 237–272; Wendy Gray and Robert Knight Barney, "Devotion to Whom? German-American Loyalty on the Issue of Participation in the 1936 Olympic Games," *Journal of Sport History* 17 (Summer 1990): 232–244; Mary Lou LeCompte, "German-American Turnvereins in Frontier Texas, 1851–1880," *Journal of the West* 26 (January 1987): 18–25; Henry Metzner, *A Brief History of the American Turnerbund* (1924); Robert J. Park, "German Associational and Sporting Life in the Greater San Francisco Bay Area, 1850–1900," *Journal of the West* 26 (January 1987): 47–64; Horst Ueberhorst, *Turner Unterm Sternenbanner* (1978); Horst Ueberhorst, *Turner und Sozialdemokraten in Milwaukee: Funf Jahrzehnte der Kooperation, 1910–1960* (1980); Horst Ueberhorst, "Turners and Social Democrats in World War I: Division and Decline of the Social Democratic Party," *Canadian Journal of History of Sport* 18 (May 1987): 76–85; Ralf Wagner, "Turner Societies and the Socialist Tradition," in Hartmut Keil, ed., *German Workers' Culture in the United States, 1850 to 1920* (1988), 221–239.

La Vern J. Rippley

GERULAITIS, VITAS (26 July 1954, Brooklyn, NY–18 September 1994, Long Island, NY). A tennis player, he was born to a Lithuanian family that emigrated to the United States in the late 1940s. The son of Vytautas and Aldona Gerulaitis, his father had been the men's tennis title holder in Lithuania (1938–40). His father began training him at the age of nine. Later, the Lithuanian women's tennis champion Veronica Sciukauskaite-Schmidt, a U.S. resident, was his instructor at the West Side Tennis Club in Forest Hills, Queens. By 1970, at age sixteen, Gerulaitis placed ninth in junior men's at the U.S. Open. A graduate of Archbishop Molloy High School in New York in 1972, he received a John Jay scholarship to attend Columbia University, but he dropped out in April 1973 to pursue a tennis career. He won the 1973 Davis Cup junior men's doubles title. In 1975 the young Gerulaitis was ranked fifteenth in the world after he won the men's doubles at Wimbledon. Gerulaitis played on U.S. men's teams in 1977 and 1978 in the Davis Cup competition. In 1977 he won the Australian Open and the Italian Open and ranked fourth in the world. He then went on to win the World Championship Tennis Masters tournament in Dallas in 1978. He lost to Bjorn Borg at the English Open (1978) and won the Italian Open (1979) for the second time. In 1979 he lost the U.S. Open championship to John McEnroe. Gerulaitis' last professional wins were at the Canadian Open in 1980 and at the Molson Tennis Challenge (Toronto, Canada) in 1981. After retiring from professional competition in 1984, he became a respected television commentator for tennis tournaments. Personable and well liked by his peers and his fans, he also distinguished himself as a humanitarian. Gerulaitis devoted much of his spare time to conducting free tennis clinics for poor urban youth in New York's public parks. His life came to a sudden and tragic end at age forty through accidental death by carbon monoxide poisoning in a friend's cottage on a Long Island estate the night before a charity tennis match.

SELECTED BIBLIOGRAPHY: R. Bellamy, "Vitas: In Sight of the Summit," *World Tennis* 27 (April 1980): 34–36; B. McDermott, "It's *Veni, Vidi, Vici* for Vitas," *Sports*

Illustrated 47 (15 August 1977): 24; *New York Times*, 20 September 1994, D23; M. Smilgas, "Vitas Gerulaitis Is Known as a Hustling Tennis Player," *People* 10 (3 July 1978): 32–34.

Sigitas Krasauskas

GIAMATTI, A. BARTLETT (4 April 1938, Boston–1 September 1989, Martha's Vineyard, MA).

Scholar, educator, college president, and baseball commissioner, he was the grandson of an Italian immigrant who worked as a laborer in New Haven, Connecticut. His father, Valentine Giamatti, spoke no English in the first grade but eventually graduated from Yale and earned a Ph.D. from Harvard. His mother was Mary Clayburgh Walton. He graduated from Yale College magna cum laude in 1960 and, just four years later, was awarded the Ph.D. in comparative literature from Yale University. He joined the Yale faculty as assistant professor of English in 1966, and at age thirty-three he attained a full professorship in English and comparative literature. He became Yale's nineteenth president on 1 July 1978. At thirty-eight, Bartlett Giamatti was the youngest Yale president in 200 years. As he struggled to balance the university's budget, Giamatti did not neglect academic matters, such as the grading system, the curriculum, and the proper place of athletics at Yale. Seven years at Yale took their toll on him physically, especially as he grappled with tough questions concerning the size of the faculty and staff and their compensation. Medical tests revealed that during the unrest and strikes on campus he had suffered a mild heart attack. In February 1985, after the Yale disputes had been resolved, Giamatti announced his resignation, to be effective in June 1986. Soon thereafter he was the unanimous choice to be the new president of the National League. Ever the idealist, Giamatti hoped to purify the game of baseball, to clean up the national pastime. In January 1989 he realized his childhood dream when he became commissioner of major league baseball. The untimely death of this "Renaissance Man," teacher and scholar, Ivy League president, baseball commissioner, and wonderful human being was shocking and devastating. His book *Take Time for Paradise* voices his undying conviction: "To know Baseball is to aspire to the condition of freedom."

SELECTED BIBLIOGRAPHY: *Current Biography* (1978); A. Bartlett Giamatti, *A Free and Ordered Space: The Real World of the University* (1988); A. Bartlett Giamatti, *A Great and Glorious Game* (1998); James Reston, Jr., *Collision at Home Plate* (July 1991); Allon Schoener, "Commentary," in *The Italian Americans* (1987); *New York Times*, 6 March 1983, VI-42, 28 April 1985, IV-9, 2 September 1989, I-1, 5 September 1989, I-18, 6 September 1989, II-10.

Margherita Marchione

GIBSON, ALTHEA (25 August 1927, Silver, SC–).

An African American tennis player, she is the oldest of five children of Daniel and Annie Gibson. She and her family moved from South Carolina to Harlem during the depression, when sharecropping was no longer economically viable. While in Harlem Daniel earned a living working in a garage. A 1952 graduate of Florida A&M University, Gibson is often remembered for her tennis excellence, yet she also competed successfully in professional golf. In 1947 Gibson won the all-black American Tennis Association* (ATA) singles tennis title and defended that honor for ten consecutive years. In 1950 she became the first black, male or female, to play in the U.S. Lawn Tennis Association (USLTA) national championships at Forest Hills, where she lost in the second round. The following year she became the first black player to compete in the championships at Wimbledon. In 1957 she won titles at both Wimbledon and Forest Hills while earning a number two world ranking. Gibson was named the Associated Press 1957 Female Athlete of the Year, yet another first for an African American. She won the same award in 1958 and again captured the singles titles at Wimbledon and the USLTA nationals. Late in 1958 she left tennis amateur ranks in favor of a $100,000 contract to perform exhibition tennis matches before and during halftime of Harlem Globetrotters* basketball games. Gibson also played on the Ladies Professional Golf Association (LPGA) tour; in 1964 she became the first African American to hold an LPGA player card. She played seven years before retiring from touring full-time. Gibson also pursued careers as a tennis teaching professional, sport administrator, singer, and actress. In 1971 she earned a place in the International Tennis Hall of Fame.

SELECTED BIBLIOGRAPHY: Robert Condon, *Great Women Athletes of the Twentieth Century* (1991); Althea Gibson, *I Always Wanted to Be Somebody* (1958); Janet Woolum, *Outstanding Women Athletes: Who They Are and How They Influenced Sports in America* (1992).

Mary G. McDonald

GIBSON, JOSHUA ("Josh") (21 December 1911, Buena Vista, GA–20 January 1947, Pittsburgh). An African American baseball player, he was the son of Mark and Nancy (Woodcock) Gibson. His father was a sharecropper in Georgia who moved to Pittsburgh in 1921 and relocated his family three years later after he found work in that city's Carnegie-Illinois Steel mill. Gibson attended Allegheny Pre-Vocational School in Pittsburgh through the ninth grade. As a teenager he excelled in both track and field and baseball and worked at several jobs to help support his family. He began his career as a hard-hitting catcher with the hometown sandlot Pittsburgh Crawfords* in 1928. He jumped to the rival Homestead Grays* in 1930, but a larger paycheck lured him back to the Crawfords in 1932. Now one of the stars of black baseball, he became the second highest paid player in the Negro National League.* Gibson rejoined the Grays in 1937, but that summer he also participated in a baseball tournament in the Dominican Republic, catching for a team sponsored by that nation's dictator, Rafael Trujillo. He spent the remainder of his sixteen-year career with the Grays, with the exception of two seasons (1940–41) with Veracruz of the Mexican League. Throughout his career he also excelled on barnstorming tours in

Latin America and in the Puerto Rican Winter League. A powerful batter who was known for his tape-measure home runs in major league ballparks and his consistently high batting average, he was respected by many white stars who played against him in exhibition games. Excluding his record in Mexico and Puerto Rico, in 501 games in the Negro Leagues he compiled a batting average of .362, with 146 home runs. Although he continued to perform brilliantly during the 1940s, he suffered from headaches, dizziness, and occasional bouts of disorientation and incoherence. His tragic and untimely death in 1947 occurred just a few months before Jackie Robinson* broke the racial barrier in major league baseball. A star who led his teams to many league titles in the United States and Mexico, he was elected to both the National Baseball Hall of Fame and the Mexican Baseball Hall of Fame in 1972.

SELECTED BIBLIOGRAPHY: William Brashler, *Josh Gibson* (1978); John Holway, *Josh and Satch* (1991); Robert W. Peterson, *Only the Ball Was White* (1970); James A. Riley, *The All-Time All-Stars of Black Baseball* (1983); Rob Ruck, *Sandlot Seasons: Sport in Black Pittsburgh* (1987).

George B. Kirsch

GIBSON, ROBERT (9 November 1935, Omaha, NE–   ). An African American baseball player, he was known as "Bob," "Hoot," and "Gibby." He was the seventh son of Pack and Victoria Gibson. His father was a millworker who died of pneumonia a month before Gibson's birth. His mother worked in a laundry. After starring in basketball and baseball at Omaha Technical High School from 1949 to 1953, Gibson accepted a scholarship to play basketball at Creighton University—rejecting an offer to play baseball for the Kansas City Monarchs. He was Creighton's first star black athlete, breaking numerous scoring records during his career. In 1957 he signed as a pitcher with the St. Louis Cardinals (National League [NL]) and played basketball with the Harlem Globetrotters.* Gibson's major league baseball career peaked in the mid-1960s. A force on the mound, he set numerous records in his World Series appearances in 1964, 1967, and 1968, including eight consecutive complete games pitched, seven consecutive victories, seventeen strikeouts in a game (1968), and three complete-game wins in a World Series (1967). His 1.12 earned run average (ERA) in 1968 was the lowest ever for a pitcher with at least 300 innings pitched. In his seventeen-year career with the Cardinals, Gibson compiled a 251–174 record, with fifty-six shutouts, 3,117 strikeouts, and a 2.91 ERA. His two Cy Young Awards (1968, 1970), NL Most Valuable Player (1968), and nine Gold Gloves earned him election into the Hall of Fame in 1981. A fierce competitor who overcame injuries, Gibson's career symbolizes the rise of the black athlete in the 1960s and early 1970s. After his retirement he pursued business interests in Omaha, Nebraska.

SELECTED BIBLIOGRAPHY: Bob Gibson, with Lonnie Wheeler, *Stranger to the Game: The Autobiography of Bob Gibson* (1994); Bob Gibson, with Phil Pepe, *From*

Ghetto to Glory: The Story of Bob Gibson (1968); David Halberstam, *October 1964* (1994); Steve Rushkin, "The Season of High Heat," *Sports Illustrated* 79 (19 July 1993): 30–37.

David R. McMahon

GLICKMAN, MARTY (14 August 1917, Bronx, NY–   ). A track athlete and sportscaster, he is of Jewish heritage. His parents, Harry and Molly Glickman, immigrated to the United States from Iasi, Romania. His father was a cotton goods salesman and then owned his own business, which he lost during the depression. His mother was a seamstress, then a foreman in the garment business. When Glickman was seven, his family moved to Brooklyn. He excelled at football and track at James Madison High School. Glickman qualified for the 1936 Berlin Olympics in the 4-by-100-meter relay. He and fellow Jewish teammate Sam Stoller were taken off the relay team by Olympic track coach Lawson Robertson and replaced by Jesse Owens* and Ralph Metcalfe on the pretense that the German team was holding unnamed world-class sprinters in reserve for the relay race. Glickman later charged that this unprecedented replacement was directed by Olympic czar Avery Brundage, whom he characterized as "an American Nazi." He starred in track and football at Syracuse University, where he graduated with a B.S. in political science in 1939. He served in the U.S. Army Air Corps as an officer in World War II. Glickman established his reputation as the erudite radio broadcasting voice of the New York Knicks, Rangers, Giants, and Jets. According to his own accounts, he broadcast 2,000 radio re-creations of baseball games, 3,000 basketball games, 1,000 football games, 2,100 track meets, and 15,000 harness races during his versatile fifty-year career. He was also a pioneer in cable television sports broadcasting for Home Box Office. In his autobiography, he claimed to be the first athlete to make a career in that field. He stated that his "broadcast goal was to take the listener into the announcers' booth and have him/her not only see the game in the mind's eye but also feel the game the way the spectator in the stands sees and feels the game."

SELECTED BIBLIOGRAPHY: Marty Glickman, *Fastest Kid on the Block* (1996); Stanley Meisler, "National Perspective; Olympics; Nazi Games Exhibit Details Discrimination, Deception; Two American Jews Were Booted off Track Team, Apparently to Spare Hitler Embarrassment," *Los Angeles Times*, 23 July 1996, A5; "1936 Jewish Olympian Remembers Berlin Experience, Interview with Marty Glickman," *All Things Considered*, National Public Radio, 30 July 1996.

Richard FitzPatrick

GOLDBERG, MARSHALL (24 October 1917, Elkins, W. Va.–   ). A football player of Jewish heritage, he is the son of Sol and Rebecca Goldberg. His father owned a movie theater. Goldberg attended Elkins High School and was captain of the football, basketball, and track teams. He was a star running back for the University of Pittsburgh. In 1936 Pittsburgh had an 8–1–1 record for the season and beat Washington 21–0 in the Rose Bowl. In 1937 Pittsburgh's record was

9–0–1 and was named national champion, and Goldberg earned All-American honors. In 1938 Pittsburgh's record was 8–2. Goldberg teamed with John Chickerneo, Harold Stebbins, and Dick Cassiano in a group named the "Dream Backfield." Goldberg again made All-America. He played professionally with the Chicago Cardinals in 1939–42 and 1946–48. In between those terms he was a lieutenant in the U.S. Navy, serving in both the Atlantic and Pacific theaters in World War II. In 1941 and 1942 he led the National Football League in kickoff returns. He left football and founded the Marshall Goldberg Machine Tool Company in Chicago. Goldberg was elected to the College Football Hall of Fame in 1958.

SELECTED BIBLIOGRAPHY: Alison Danzig, *The History of American Football* (1956); John D. McCalym and Charles H. Pearson, *College Football U.S.A., 1869–1973* (1973); Howard Roberts, *The Story of Pro Football* (1953).

Pat Harmon

GOLF. Golf came to the United States in the late 1880s and developed into an important participant and spectator sport during the half century before 1930. The game arrived in America with a decidedly Scottish image. While Americans of Scottish origins were important in launching the game, golf's roots in Scotland and its image as the game of moral, religious, and parsimonious Scots were equally important. Upper-class Americans took to the game as one that built character and did not undermine Protestant values, largely because of its Scottish origins. Because the game was played at private country clubs, it was seen during its early years as the special game of the white, Anglo-Saxon upper classes. However, from the very beginning, other ethnic groups have occupied important places within the world of golf. Over the last century conflict between the white dominant classes and less privileged ethnic groups has been unusually sharp as more and more Americans sought access to public and private courses and to closed competitions.

The Scottish influence on American golf was strong at many of the early private clubs. St. Andrews Golf Club, founded in 1888 and often referred to as the "mother club," was the product of Scots in America who wished to play their native game. Notable in this group was John Reid,* a native of Dunfermline, Scotland, who had earned a small fortune in the iron industry in New York. Often called "the father of American golf," he induced a small group of his friends to join together into a club that established a crude course in 1888. As time passed, interest grew, and the club moved to better sites, finally coming to rest in Mt. Hope, New York. Another founder-father of American golf was Charles B. Macdonald,* a Chicagoan and second-generation Scottish American. The driving force behind the Chicago Golf Club, he distinguished himself as a prominent player, golf course architect, and critic of new trends in the game.

As golf developed in the 1890s, it tended to draw Scots out of Scotland who saw the opportunities offered by the growing number of American clubs. Americans needed course designers, club makers, instructors, and greenkeepers. The first of this group was Willie Dunn from Musselburgh, who was lured to the United States by an offer from a group of rich New Yorkers who wished to build a course on Long Island. The result was the Shinnecock Hills Golf Club, completed in 1891. Most important, in this group of Scots and a few Englishmen was the twosome of Donald Ross and Tom Bendelow, who designed hundreds of courses. Ross was responsible for the growth of golf at Pinehurst, North Carolina, which today has a reasonable claim to the title of golf capital of America. The Scottish designers and professionals who came to America between 1890 and 1920 deeply imbued American golf with Scottish tone and traditions.

In the twentieth century, the game has lost much of this Scottish tradition. Golf has become Americanized as new technology has allowed construction of courses far from seaside links land, where the Scots feel the game must be played. Even so, the game, at the level of myth and image, remains Scottish in the minds of many. Minority Americans of various sorts took to golf in the early years, but they were vastly outnumbered by the more affluent. Some ethnic Americans have first embraced golf as an economic opportunity. At Shinnecock Hills, the local tribe of Native Americans, the Shinnecocks, have been associated with the club as builders of the course, caddies, and greenkeepers. Most notable, early on, was John Shippen,* a player of mixed African American and Shinnecock heritage. Shippen was so adept at the game that he became Willie Dunn's assistant in the pro shop. An excellent player, he competed in the 1896 U.S. Open over the objections of the other professionals and finished in a tie for fifth. Shippen eventually became the professional at Shady Rest Golf and Country Club* in Scotch Plains, New Jersey, one of the very few black clubs prior to World War II. Shady Rest began its history as a black club in 1921 and came to an end in 1963, when it became a public course.

Golf offered ethnic and less affluent Americans access to the game through the job of caddie. Affluent country clubs allowed hundreds of young people onto the grounds in order to have workers to carry their golf bags. From this opening individuals such as Gene Sarazen* (born Saraceni, the son of Italian immigrants) developed into notable professionals. The slowly growing number of public courses also increased access to the game of golf.

In the South, however, segregation was generally applied to public golf courses, severely limiting the access of African Americans to golf. Given these limits, it is remarkable that African Americans have made substantial contributions and have founded several organizations that promoted the sport. In addition to Shippen's pioneering role, George Grant, a dentist from Boston, designed the first golf tee registered by the U.S. Patent Office in 1899. Dewey Brown and Joseph Bartholomew became notable club designers during the 1920s and 1930s. In 1925 black golf enthusiasts also established the U.S. Colored Golfers Association. Renamed the United Golfers Association* in 1928, it became the dominant force in golf for African Americans until the desegregation of public courses and organizations like the Professional Golfers' Association.

In June 1990 the issue of racial discrimination against African Americans in private golf clubs received national attention. The Shoal Creek Country Club of Birmingham, Alabama, was hosting a Professional Golfers' Association Tournament, and the club's founder, Hall W. Thompson, admitted during a pretournament press interview that his club excluded blacks from membership. While Thompson subsequently apologized for his remarks and claimed he was quoted out of context, the ramifications of these comments had far-reaching effects not only in the world of tournament golf but in race relations throughout America. Following the publication of Thompson's statements, the African American community reacted immediately and decisively. As a direct result of its protests, the Professional Golfer's Association (PGA) of America and its brother organization, the Professional Golfers' Tour, subsequently adopted new policies regarding the criteria for selection of tournament sites, barring from consideration any club that discriminated on the basis of race or sex. Many designated tournament courses actively sought out and offered membership to select minorities throughout the country. Several clubs refused to change policies and, as a result, were not considered as sites for upcoming PGA tournaments. The PGA of America, an association made up of the nation's club professionals, itself had a "Caucasian clause" in its constitution until 1961 and was particularly sensitive to the resulting criticism. In November 1990, the U.S. Golf Association (USGA) adopted similar rules for selection of venues for its thirteen tournaments, eliminating any club that discriminated against minorities or women.

The aftermath of the Shoal Creek incident continues to focus attention on race relations throughout the country. While many of the clubs involved in both PGA and USGA tournaments sought out and accepted minority members, many African American leaders continue to complain that these clubs offer "token" memberships and are not really making any legitimate commitment to integration. As a result of the questions raised regarding discrimination in country clubs, many states are considering or have adopted legislation that has opened investigation of the tax status of private clubs in an effort to force them to adopt more inclusive membership practices.

Since the 1960s the growth of ethnic participation in the game of golf has grown slowly. Professionals such as Lee Elder* and Calvin Peete* (African Americans) and Lee Trevino* and Nancy Lopez* (Hispanics) have breached the barriers imposed by the various professional organizations. Until recently, participation by ethnic groups among the approximately 25 million American players was small. Like many sports, golf has become increasingly international. Today, the average American player routinely sees Japanese and other international players compete for major championships. Nothing however, can match the influence of Tiger Woods.* His amazingly successful amateur career and astonishing record as a young professional have spawned a vast public debate about race and golf. The debate has many facets, not the least of which is the discussion of his multiethnic background. Woods is African American, Asian American, Native American, and white. No golfer and perhaps no athlete has induced so much discussion of ethnicity and sport since Jackie Robinson.* While it is too early to accurately assess his impact on participation, Woods seems to have done much to lure young players from many ethnic groups into the game.

Golf, over its history in the United States, has sharply reflected the dominance of white, affluent Protestants. As a sport largely played at expensive private clubs, less affluent groups were effectively handicapped in taking up the game. Desegregation and the rapid growth of public and daily fee courses since World War II have slowly opened avenues for increased participation by other less affluent groups.

SELECTED BIBLIOGRAPHY: "Black-and-White Issue Comes to the Fore," *USA Today*, 26 July 1990, Sports Section, 1; Jaime Diaz, "Bias at Private Club: A Test for Pro Golf," *New York Times*, 28 July 1990, 1; "Golf's Country Club Dilemma," *U.S. News and World Report* (20 August 1990): 60; Herb Graffis, *The PGA: The Official History of the Professional Golfers' Association of America* (1975); Charles B. Macdonald, *Scotland's Gift—Golf* (1928); H. B. Martin, *Fifty Years of American Golf* (1936); William C. Rhoden, "Golf Strikes a Sensitive Nerve," *New York Times*, 5 August 1990, Section 8, 1; Calvin H. Sinnette, *Forbidden Fairways: African Americans and the Game of Golf* (1998); Herbert Warren Wind, *The Story of American Golf* (1956).

Richard J. Moss

GONSALVES, WILLIAM ADELINA ("Billy")

GONSALVES, WILLIAM ADELINA ("Billy") (10 August 1908, Fall River, MA–17 July 1977, Kearny, NJ). A soccer player, he was the son of textile worker Augustine and Rose (Fraitas) Gonsalves, Portuguese immigrants from the Madeira Islands. Gonsalves grew up in Fall River, Massachusetts, where his long career began at the age of fourteen with the local Pioneer, Charlton Mill, and Liberal Clubs and eventually led to a professional contract with the Boston Wonder Workers of the American Soccer League. Considered by his peers to be the finest American-born player of his or any other day, Gonsalves was a big man with tremendous shooting power, and he quickly made his presence felt in a Boston team full of experienced Scottish professionals. After two seasons in Boston, Gonsalves went home to Fall River to become part of one of the greatest American club teams of all time. In 1930 he was a member of the successful U.S. World Cup team in Montevideo and led Fall River to the U.S. Open Cup championships of 1930 and 1931. In 1932 Gonsalves moved on to play for New Bedford Whalers, then Stix, Baer, and Fuller of St. Louis and St. Louis Central Breweries. In each case he led his team to the national championship, and in the process he won six national championship medals in a row. In 1934 he was back in the national team playing in the World Cup in Italy before going on to win two more national championships with Brooklyn Hispano in 1943 and 1944. He was inducted into the National Soccer Hall of Fame in 1950.

SELECTED BIBLIOGRAPHY: Bob Broeg, "Gonsalves: 'No Equal' in American Soccer," *St. Louis Post-Dispatch*, 25 June 1973, 2B; Eric Charleston, "Billy Gonsalves: Not Just Any Old Man," *United States Soccer Monthly* 1 (December 1974): 26–29; Tony Cirino, *U.S. Soccer vs. the World* (1983); Peter L. de Rosa, "William Gonsalves," in David L. Porter, ed., *Biographical Dictionary of American Sports: Outdoor Sports* (1988); Bill Graham, *U.S. Annual Soccer Guide and Record* (1948–49).

Colin Jose

GONZALES, RICHARD ALONZO ("Pancho") (9 May 1928, Los Angeles–3 July 1995, Las Vegas). A tennis player, he was the son of Mexican immigrants Manuel A. and Carmen (Alire) Gonzalez. His father fitted furniture and painted movie sets. His mother was a seamstress in a garment factory who came from a wealthy family that lost everything during the Mexican Revolution. Growing up in a poor barrio in Los Angeles, Gonzales was encouraged by his mother to take up a "a gentleman's game." While once a conscientious student who attended Manual Arts High School, he began cutting classes to observe others play in order to pick up basic strokes. Becoming a self-taught player, Gonzales quickly became the top-ranked boy in southern California. He enlisted in the navy and, upon his return, became the Southern California Men's Singles Champion. Gonzales possessed one of the greatest serves the game has ever seen. Yet, he also had amazing touch, which helped to balance out his power game. Entering the amateur ranks in 1948, Gonzales burst onto the scene, winning back-to-back U.S. singles titles at Forest Hills in 1948 and 1949. During this time he also won men's doubles titles at Forest Hill and Wimbledon. In what is considered by many to have been a questionable move, Gonzales turned professional at age twenty-one. In the era prior to open tennis, a professional could not participate in what we consider today to be the grand-slam tournaments. However, Gonzales was a champion on the professional tour, winning the London title four times (1950–52, 1956) and the U.S. Pro title eight times (1953–59, 1961). When the Open era began in 1968, Gonzales was forty years old but still one of the top-ranked players in the world. However, the years of professional touring had taken an obvious toll on his game. Yet, in 1969, Gonzales won one of the longest matches in Wimbledon history, a five-hour-and-twelve-minute marathon against Charlie Pasarell. His passion for the game coupled with his modesty off the court helped to pave the way for other Latino Americans players such as Pancho Segura* and Mary Joe Fernandez.

SELECTED BIBLIOGRAPHY: Pancho Gonzalez, *Man with a Racquet* (1959); Pancho Gonzalez and Dick Hawk, *Tennis* (1962); Will Grimsley, *Tennis: Its History, People and Events* (1971); Jack Kramer and Frank Deford, *The Game* (1979); *New York Times*, 21 September 1949, 46, 5 July 1995, D-9; *Newsweek* 32 (2 August 1948): 70.

Thomas Cesa

GOTTLIEB, EDWARD (15 September 1898, Kiev, Russia–7 December 1979, Philadelphia). A basketball coach and executive, he was the son of Jewish immigrants Morris and Leah Gottlieb. After his graduation from South Philadelphia High School in 1916 Gottlieb went on to the Philadelphia School of Pedagogy. After school Gottlieb organized the South Philadelphia Hebrew Association's team. The Philadelphia SPHAS,* as they became known, were a Jewish barnstorming team that earned money and helped to arouse national interest in basketball. Gottlieb parlayed this interest into the formation of the Basketball Association of America (BAA) in 1946, which merged into the National Basketball Association (NBA) in 1949. Gottlieb was owner and coach of one of the league's original teams, the Philadelphia Warriors. He earned the nickname "the Mogul" as a do-everything, hands-on owner—hiring the players, coaching, and making all of the day-to-day decisions required to run his team. Gottlieb also helped to organize the league, serving on its Rules Committee and acting as its schedule maker. With Gottlieb as coach, the Warriors won the NBA's inaugural championship in 1950. During the nine years in which he coached the team, Gottlieb compiled a record of 263–318 before replacing himself in 1955 with George Senesky. He paved the way for the westward expansion of the NBA when he sold the Warriors to San Francisco in 1962. One of the concepts for which Gottlieb is known is the idea that stars make the NBA. Many owners tried to downplay the importance of individual players, afraid that it would only cause those players to make higher salary demands and that it would cause tension between the star and the other players on the team. Contrary to this philosophy, Gottlieb saw that star players would be a stadium draw (something that was of utmost importance in the early days of the NBA). With this mentality, he made Wilt Chamberlain* the team's territorial selection in 1955 while Chamberlain was still in high school. When Chamberlain joined the Warriors, Gottlieb went out of his way to encourage Wilt to score. Hall of Fame coach Pete Newell said of Gottlieb, "Eddie Gottlieb symbolized those owners of the 1950s. Those guys were street fighters. One minute, they were ready to kill each other. Then they'd calm down, shut the door, put their heads together and come up with the rules and ideas that made basketball a great game." For all that he did for the league, Gottlieb was elected to the Hall of Fame in 1971 as a "general contributor."

SELECTED BIBLIOGRAPHY: Ralph Hickok, *New Encyclopedia of Sports* (1977); Peter Levine, *Ellis Island to Ebbets Field* (1992); Ronald L. Mendell, *Who's Who in Basketball* (1973); *Philadelphia Inquirer*, 8 December 1979, C1, C4.

Zachary Davis

GRAZIANO, ROCKY (1 January 1921, New York City–22 May 1990, New York City). An Italian American prizefighter, he was born Thomas Rocco Barbella, son of New Yorkers Nick and Ida (Scinto) Graziano and grandson of Neapolitan immigrants. Rocky experienced an extremely difficult, hunger- and poverty-filled childhood. His father was a professional boxer and longshoreman. Rocky was a robber, a hustler, and a gang leader who reached only the seventh grade in school. Sentenced for his many crimes, he served time at the Catholic Protectory, Coxsackie, New York City Reformatory, Tombs Prison, and Rikers Island. Gradually, a new person emerged: boxer Rocky Graziano. The ex-con pounded his way up the pugilistic ladder during the 1930s and 1940s: Metropolitan Amateur Athletic Union (AAU) Welterweight Champ, four-round pro fights, six-round semifinals, and Main Events. During World War II, Private Graziano argued with an officer, went absent without leave (AWOL), and served his punishment on the boxing squad at Ft. Leavenworth, Kansas. Soon after his release he returned to professional boxing and eventually won the Middleweight Championship of the World in 1947, when he defeated Tony Zale.* Rocky lost the rematch in 1948 but did not quit boxing until he suffered defeats from Sugar Ray Robinson* and Chuck Davey in 1952. His career ended with a record of 67–10–6, including fifty-two knockouts, a record that merited election to the Boxing Hall of Fame in 1971. In the 1950s he took up acting, becoming a regular on *The Martha Raye Show*, playing her boyfriend "Goombah" (1955–56). In 1956, his autobiography, *Somebody Up There Likes Me* (1955), became a movie starring Paul Newman. He made films with Frank Sinatra and Ronald Reagan.

SELECTED BIBLIOGRAPHY: Ira Berkow, "Leave Your Worry on the Doorstep," *New York Times*, 26 May 1990, Sec. 1, p. 41; Lester Bromberg, "2d Avenue's Prize Stock Merchant," *Saturday Evening Post* 219 (20 July 1946): 24, 121–122; Rocky Graziano, with Rowland Barber, *Somebody Up There Likes Me* (1955); Rocky Graziano, with Ralph Corsel, *Somebody Down Here Likes Me Too* (1981); John Lardner, "The Rock Moves Up," *Newsweek* 28 (28 July 1946): 80; Alex McNeil, *Total Television: A Comprehensive Guide to Programming from 1948 to 1980* (1980).

Philip M. Montesano

GREEKS. The earliest record of organized Greek American ethnic sports participation dates back to circa 1906. Greek immigrants, like other newcomers, viewed sports as a means of preserving their group identity and providing pleasure while they were away from home.

According to most credible sources, the earliest Greek American sports organization in the United States was the Greek-American Sports Club (S. C.). There is no official record or other information as to the exact year of its founding. However, it is believed that it was organized in the early twentieth century, around 1906 or 1908. Soon after, another Greek American sports organization was founded in New York. Its name was Hermes Sports Club; it is believed to be the first Greek American sports club to have started a soccer team. The two clubs merged around 1930 under the name Greek-American Hermes S. C. After World War II, however, only the "Greek American" regrouped and continued functioning. The Hermes organization never resumed its activities. It was officially dissolved in May 1988, when its remaining officials, headed by club president George Hatzelis, donated all of its funds (amounting to $23,755.54) to St. Michael's Home for the Aged, a Greek American institution located in Yonkers, New York.

Greek American ethnic sports differed greatly before and after World War II. Before the war Greek Americans participated mostly in track, wrestling, and weight lifting. After the conflict they played only soccer. Since the same trend appeared in Greece, it is fair to conclude that Greek American ethnic sports followed the line of sports expression in Greece itself. Before the war, Greek Orthodox churches in America made their basement gymnasiums available to Greek immigrants to train in wrestling and weight lifting. After the war, the churches made their gyms available only to their own youngsters, mainly for basketball.

Many prewar Greek American athletes belonging to the Greek-American S. C. or Hermes S. C. participated and excelled in wrestling and track-and-field competitions. Jim Londos was a world-famous Greek American professional wrestler, while Chris Soukas excelled as an amateur wrestler in the United States. Panagiotis Trivoulidis won the Boston Marathon in 1926. Dimitrios Tofalos, an Olympic gold medalist in the Athens intermediate Olympics of 1906, later migrated to America and trained Greek American athletes in New York.

Soccer emerged on the Greek American soccer scene during the 1920s. Hermes S. C. organized the first team. After they merged with the Greek-American S. C., more good players arrived from Greece and joined the club. Among them were goalkeeper Leonidas Koulouridis, center-back Orestis Kalafatis, and Tom Komninos. Games were played mainly in Central Park in Manhattan and Van Cortlandt Park in the Bronx.

It is said that the Greek-American Hermes Soccer Club was playing somewhere in Brooklyn on 7 December 1941, when the news came that Japanese planes had attacked the American fleet at Pearl Harbor. The game was discontinued, and the players left for home worrying if they would be drafted to fight in the war. Sure enough, they all were. Therefore, no Greek American sports activities were recorded during the war.

A soccer enthusiast named Thomas Laris and a sportswriter named Panos Kolimparis are believed to be the two people most responsible for reorganizing the Greek-American Sports Club after the war. It all started in the autumn of 1946, when Laris gathered a group of youngsters and formed a team named for the club. He was the first president and also the team's first coach. However, he stayed with the team for only about three years. Around 1950 he organized another club, which he named the Hellenic S. C. For the next twenty-five years, the arch rival Greek-American S. C. and the Hellenic S. C. were the two dominant Greek soccer clubs in New York. Both teams played in the then-powerful German American Football (Soccer) Association.

Between 1965 and 1970 the Greek-American S. C. reigned over American soccer. It became a powerhouse by importing players from Greece who were coached by a Greek American, Alkis Panagoulias. The team captured consecutive U.S. Open Challenge Cup titles in 1967, 1968, and 1969. It also won the cup in 1974. Panagoulias later became the coach for Greece's national team. He also coached the U.S. national team.

In 1963, two other Greek American soccer clubs were formed in New York: Doxa in the Washington Heights area of Manhattan and Nea Ellas in Astoria. In 1971 Olympiakos was formed in Jamaica, Queens. In 1973, Hermes S. C. was formed in Astoria, New York. Later, Nea Ellas changed its name to N.Y. Atlas. In New Jersey, the New Jersey Nationals were formed, while Panhellenic had existed in Stamford, Connecticut, for many years.

At the same time, other Greek American soccer clubs were founded in different areas of the country. The best known of these were the Olympiakos of Chicago and the Greek-Americans of San Francisco.

In 1974 a very energetic and gifted Cypriot American named Philip Christopher started the Pancyprian Athletic Association, which emerged as the new powerhouse of Greek American soccer. The Pancyprian Freedoms, as they were named later on, imported the former captain of the Greek National Team, Mimis Papaioannou. On the strength of his talents as a player and later on as a player-coach, they won the U.S. Open Challenge Cup in 1980, 1982, and 1983. The Pancyprian Freedoms were always made up of mainly Cypriot players, many of whom the club assisted financially with their tuition at American colleges and universities. Besides winning three U.S. Open Challenge Cups, the Pancyprian Freedoms represented the United States in the Confederation of North, Central American and Caribbean Association Football (CONCACAF) championship and played against such world-famous clubs such as Atlante of Mexico. Later on, another Cypriot American club was formed. It called itself "Eleftheria," which means freedom (freedom for Cyprus).

In 1978 the Hellenic American Soccer League (HASL) came into existence, comprising clubs other than the already existing ones. In 1984 all Greek American soccer clubs in New York, New Jersey, and Connecticut joined the newly formed HASL. Between 1984 and 1990 the league had at least twenty-five Greek American soccer clubs from the tristate area. The Greek-American S. C. and the New York Atlas S. C. merged in 1990. The Hellenic S. C. ceased to exist in 1980.

During the 1990s immigration from Greece practically stopped. This caused many clubs either to disappear or to reduce their activities. As of 1997 the Hellenic American Soccer League numbered only four semipro Greek American soccer clubs (Hermes, Long Island Stars-Hercules, N.Y. Greek-American Atlas, and Pancyprian Freedoms) and five amateur clubs. With the exception of the Pancyprian Freedoms, the semipro clubs had few or no Greek American players on their rosters. Other clubs, such as Doxa and Olympiakos, had only junior players. Hermes and N.Y. Greek-American Atlas also had junior teams in addition to their regular men's teams. "Eleftheria-Pancyprians" was an organization of boys' and junior soccer teams that operated under the auspices of the

Pancyprian Athletic Association. N.Y. Greek American Atlas, Olympiakos, and Pancyprian Freedoms also fielded teams with players over thirty years of age as well.

From 1946 to the present, millions of dollars were spent to support Greek American soccer teams. A major portion of this money went toward payments to non-Greek American players to play for Greek American clubs. This money was raised through public functions such as annual dances and yearbook sales. Very little money, however, was raised through ticket sales at the games. Much of the money came out of the pockets of the officials running the clubs. It is unfortunate that no effort was made to use this money to build a soccer field for the Greek American clubs. Clubs struggled week after week to secure fields on which to play their games. Several times Greek government officials promised to help buy a field, but this promise was never fulfilled.

The Greek Orthodox Church in America has provided its youth with the opportunity to engage in an annual basketball championship involving teams from different churches. In addition, annual "Olympic Games" are organized in various areas. Not all churches are obligated to participate, and not all do. Some of the best basketball players in Greece have been acquired from Greek Orthodox parishes in America. The best ever was Nick Gallis, a former native of New Jersey.

SELECTED BIBLIOGRAPHY: Charles C. Moskos, *Greek Americans: Struggle and Success*, 2d ed. (1989); Theodore Salutos, *The Greek in the United States* (1964); Alice Scourby, *The Greek Americans* (1977).

Nicholas Notaridis and Nick Koliarakis

GREENBERG, HENRY BENJAMIN ("Hank") (1 January 1911, New York City–4 September 1986, Beverly Hills, CA). A baseball player, he was the son of Jewish immigrants. His father (David) owned a garment manufacturing company, and his mother (Sarah Schwartz) was a homemaker. His parents, both born in Romania, met in New York. He was a graduate of James Monroe High School in the Bronx, New York, and attended New York University. Prior to his career there had been other good Jewish players, but he was baseball's first great Jewish star. Greenberg was a big, right-handed, slugging first baseman for the Detroit Tigers. He led the league in home runs four times, including 1938, when he hit fifty-eight, challenging Babe Ruth's* record of sixty. He also led the league in runs batted in four times and in 1937 drove in 183, one shy of Lou Gehrig's* American League record and the third best mark of all time. He was chosen for the All-Star squad each year for the period of 1937 to 1940. He led the Tigers to four pennants and two World Series triumphs. Greenberg was selected the Most Valuable Player in the American League in 1935 and 1940. His playing career was limited by more than four years of military service, injuries, and early retirement, yet he amassed 331 home runs. He returned to the Tigers in the middle of the 1945 season and hit a home run in his first game.

In the final game of that season Greenberg hit a grand-slam home run in the ninth inning to win the pennant. His last season was spent with the Pittsburgh Pirates. After his playing career ended, he was part owner and held front office positions first with the Cleveland Indians and then the Chicago White Sox. Greenberg was not an observant Jew and had no use for any organized religion. However, he did have a strong Jewish feeling and never played on Yom Kippur, the holiest day of the year for Jews. He was a source of great pride and inspiration to Jewish Americans. He was elected to the Baseball Hall of Fame in 1956, the first Jew selected.

SELECTED BIBLIOGRAPHY: Ira Berkow, *Hank Greenberg: The Story of My Life* (1989); "Hank Greenberg," in Martin Appel and Burt Goldblatt, *Baseball's Best: The Hall of Fame Gallery* (1977); "Hank Greenberg," in Mike Shatzkin, *The Ballplayers* (1990).

Randy B. Klipstein

GREENLEE, WILLIAM AUGUSTUS (1897, Marion, NC–10 July 1952, Pittsburgh). An African American baseball entrepreneur, he was the son of a masonry contractor and the illegitimate daughter of a prominent white man. Greenlee dropped out of college and headed to Pittsburgh during the Great Migration of 1916. He worked in various jobs until he joined the army during World War I. After being wounded, Greenlee returned home and took advantage of the new opportunities presented by Prohibition in bootlegging and numbers racketeering. In the 1920s Greenlee opened a series of clubs, including his most famous establishment, the Crawford Grill, and became the benefactor of local black businesses and social causes. In 1930 Greenlee bought the Pittsburgh Crawford* Giants, or the Crawfords, a black sandlot team, in order to extend his political influence and launder his numbers money. But he quickly realized the entertainment value and profit potential of black baseball. He salaried his players, recruited superior talent, and constructed Greenlee Field, one of the few independent, black-owned ballparks in the nation. Greenlee emerged as an effective sports promoter and inherited the mantle of leadership of black baseball from Rube Foster.* In 1933 he revived the Negro National League* and served as its president until 1939. As an owner, he stimulated park attendance through raffles and door prizes and, as league president, initiated the East-West All-Star Game. The problems that Greenlee sought to reform through the Negro National League, especially stadium availability, rowdyism, high travel expenses, player defections, and scheduling, persisted and contributed to the decline of both the league and Greenlee's own team. With the decline of his numbers game, Greenlee sold off his own players, closed the park that bore his name, and in 1939 sold the team. But the franchise folded before the new owners could field a team. Over the next few years, Greenlee promoted his stable of boxers, who included John Henry Lewis, the first African American light-heavyweight champion, but he failed to obtain a new franchise for his Crawfords in the Negro

202 GREER, HAROLD ("Hal")

Leagues. In 1945, with the backing of Branch Rickey of the Brooklyn Dodgers, Greenlee reentered black sport by establishing the U.S. League, which proved a miserable failure and lasted only two seasons. The U.S. League and later the integration of baseball weakened and ultimately destroyed black control over black baseball. Greenlee returned to running the Crawford Grill, which was destroyed by fire in 1951, and during the last years of his life witnessed the decline of his numbers business and became embroiled in income tax problems.

SELECTED BIBLIOGRAPHY: Robert Gardner and Dennis Shortelle, *The Forgotten Players: The Story of Black Baseball in America* (1993); Mark Ribowsky, *A Complete History of the Negro Leagues* (1995); Rob Ruck, *Sandlot Seasons: Sport in Black Pittsburgh* (1987).

Larry K. Menna

GREER, HAROLD ("Hal") (26 June 1936, Huntington, W.Va.–). An African American basketball player, he was the son of William Garfield Greer, a railroad machinist. Greer's mother died when he was young. His father remarried, and he was raised by his father and stepmother, Tula Greer. He and his family were excellent athletes at the segregated Huntington Douglass High School. Hal led Douglass to the West Virginia Athletic Union (segregated schools) high school championships in 1951 and 1953. In the fall of 1954, soon after the *Brown v. Board of Education* Supreme Court decision, Greer was recruited to play basketball at the nearby previously all-white Marshall University. He was in the first class to have African American undergraduate students at Marshall. As the first black basketball player at Marshall he led his team to the 1956 Mid-American Conference Championship, an 18–5 record and a National Collegiate Athletic Association (NCAA) bid. In 1958 he averaged 23.6 points per game as Marshall led the nation in scoring with an average of 88 points a game. Greer began his fourteen-year National Basketball Association (NBA) career in 1958–59 with the Syracuse Nationals. At 6' 2" and 176 pounds, he quickly became a starting guard and excellent scorer. In 1963 the Syracuse franchise moved to Philadelphia and became the 76ers. With the addition of Wilt Chamberlain* the 76ers won the NBA championship in 1967 with Greer averaging 22.1 points per game. Greer played in eight NBA All-Star Games and was named the Most Valuable Player (MVP) of the 1968 game when he scored 21 points. He was best known for using a jump shot as his foul shot. Greer retired from the NBA following the 1972 season, having played 1,084 games and scored 21,369 points for a 19.7 per game career average. In 1981 the city of Huntington renamed the street that runs through Greer's old neighborhood and past Marshall University as Hal Greer Boulevard.

SELECTED BIBLIOGRAPHY: Dana Brooks, "Harold 'Hal' Greer," in *The Twentieth Century: Great Athletes* (1992); Zander Hollander, ed., *The Modern Encyclopedia of Basketball* (1973); David S. Neft, Roland T. Johnson, Richard M. Cohen, and Jordan A.

Deutsch, *The Sports Encyclopedia: Pro Basketball* (1995); Hal Greer Folder, Marshall University Sports Information Office, Huntington, W.Va.

C. Robert Barnett

GRIFFITH-JOYNER, DELOREZ FLORENCE ("FloJo") (21 December 1959, Los Angeles–21 September 1998, Mission Viejo, CA). An African American track star, she was the seventh of eleven children of Florence, a seamstress, and Robert Griffith, an electronics technician. She began racing when she was seven years old. She graduated from Jordan High School in Los Angeles in 1978, attended California State University at Northridge for two years, and earned a degree in psychology from the University of California at Los Angeles (UCLA) in 1983. Griffith-Joyner dominated sprinting in 1988, setting numerous world records and winning four Olympic track medals in Seoul, South Korea. While reporters focused intensely on her flashy, one-legged track suits and long, brightly painted nails, the athletic achievements of Florence Griffith-Joyner cannot be discounted. After winning National Collegiate Athletic Association (NCAA) titles in the 200 meters and 400 meters, Griffith-Joyner earned an 1984 Olympic silver medal in the 200-meter run in her native Los Angeles. During the 1988 Olympic trials she beat the existing world record in the 100 meters four times and also set an American record in the 200 meters. In Seoul, South Korea, she earned an Olympic record in the 100 and broke the world record in the 200 meters. She won a third gold in the 4×100-meter relay and a silver medal as a member of the U.S. 4×400-meter relay team. In recognition of these achievements in 1988 Griffith-Joyner was the recipient of the Jesse Owens Award as the top track-and-field athlete, the Sullivan Award as the top amateur athlete in the United States, and the 1988 Associated Press Female Athlete of the Year Award. In February 1989 Griffith-Joyner retired from track and field to pursue career options as a model, actress, clothing designer, and product endorser. She also served as cochair of the President's Council on Physical Fitness and Sports and coached children on behalf of the Florence Griffith-Joyner Youth Foundation. In 1995 she was inducted into the U.S. Track and Field Hall of Fame. She made a brief, aborted attempt at a comeback prior to the 1996 Olympics, this time in the 400 meters. Before her untimely death (probably due to a seizure and heart failure) she had vowed to compete in the marathon at the 2000 Olympic Games in Sydney, Australia.

SELECTED BIBLIOGRAPHY: Robert Condon, *Great Women Athletes of the Twentieth Century* (1991); "Flojo Announces Retirement," *Track and Field News* 42 (April 1989): 58; Jon Hendershott, "Griffith Moving to Center Stage," *Track and Field News* 40 (December 1987): 26–27; Seig Lindstrom, "Flo: All Dressed Up, 100 Meters to Go," *Track and Field News* 41 (September 1988): 27; *New York Times*, 22 September 1998, C-23; "Nobody but Flo," *Track and Field News* 42 (February 1989): 8–9; Howard Willman, "What's Griffith's Best Race?" *Track and Field News* 37 (December 1984): 26.

Mary G. McDonald

GUYON, JOSEPH (26 November 1892, White Earth Indian Reservation, MN–27 November 1971, Louisville, KY). A Native American football player, his father, Charles M. Guyon, and his mother were members of the Chippewa tribe. Guyon's Indian name was Ogee-Chidea, meaning "brave boy." His football career had a dual path. He played college football at two institutions, Carlisle Indian School in 1912–13 and Georgia Tech in 1917–18. He played for two famous coaches, "Pop" Warner at Carlisle and John Heisman at Georgia Tech. He alternated at two positions, making the Parke Davis All-America team as a tackle in 1913 and the Frank Menke All-America team as a halfback in 1918. After college he turned to pro football and played in the National Football League, 1920–25 and 1927. He starred for the New York Giants in 1927, when they won the league championship. Guyon also played professional baseball in the minor leagues. After his retirement he was employed by the government in Indian education affairs, worked as a bank security officer, and was a high school football coach in Louisville. He was elected to the Pro Football Hall of fame in 1966 and the College Football Hall of Fame in 1971.

SELECTED BIBLIOGRAPHY: Alison Danzig, *The History of American Football* (1956); *Atlanta Journal*, 15 December 1971; John D. McCallum and Charles H. Pearson, *College Football U.S.A., 1869–1973* (1973); John Steckbeck, *Fabulous Redmen* (1951).

Pat Harmon

H

HALAS, GEORGE S. ("Papa Bear") (2 February 1895, Chicago–31 October 1983, Chicago). A college and professional football player, coach, and owner, he was the son of first-generation Bohemian immigrants Frank J. and Barbara (Poledny) Halas. The elder Halas operated a grocery store and a saloon. Within their west side Chicago neighborhood the Bohemian community revolved around St. Vitus Catholic Church and the Sokol (social and athletic center). George graduated from Crane Tech High School in 1913 and earned a B.S. in civil engineering in 1918 from the University of Illinois, where he excelled as a three-sport athlete. In 1920 as a player/coach of the Decatur Staleys, he attended the initial organizing meeting of the APFA (American Professional Football Association) in Canton, Ohio. At Halas' suggestion the organization was renamed the National Football League (NFL) in 1922. He became co-owner of the Staleys that year, moved them to Chicago, and renamed them the Bears. Halas would coach the Bears for forty seasons in several stints (1920–29, 1933–42, 1946–55, 1958–67), winning eight NFL championships (1921, 1932, 1933, 1940, 1941, 1943, 1946, 1963). Halas made the Bears an expression of his personality, the "Monsters of the Midway," a rough, tough outfit that hammered its opponents into submission. Halas' adaptation of the T formation was adopted by the rest of the league and became the basic offensive formation at all levels of football. As an inventive coach and shrewd entrepreneur, Halas made numerous other contributions to pro football. His signing of University of Illinois halfback Harold "Red" Grange provided the NFL with its first superstar and brought much needed attention to pro football, providing credibility and financial stability. His other innovations included daily practice sessions, using classroom instructions and game films, broadcasting games on the radio, using spotters in the stands to suggest plays, hiring full-time assistant coaches, coast-to-coast barnstorming tours, and using a tarpaulin on the field for protection against bad weather conditions. He was elected to the Pro Football Hall of Fame as a charter enshrinee in 1963.

SELECTED BIBLIOGRAPHY: Myron Cope, ed., *The Game That Was: The Early Days of Pro Football* (1970); Frank Deford, "I Don't Date Any Woman under 48," *Sports Illustrated* 47 (5 December 1977): 36–38; Ray Didinger, "George Halas: He Invented Pro Football," *Football Digest* 13 (February 1984): 32–35; George S. Halas, "My Forty Years in Pro Football," *Saturday Evening Post* 230 (23 Nov. 1957): 34–35; George Halas, with Gwen Morgan and Arthur Veysey, *Halas by Halas: The Autobiography of George Halas* (1979); Jerry Kirshenbaum, "Papa Bear," *Sports Illustrated* 59 (14 November 1983): 17; Robert W. Peterson, *Pigskin: The Early Days of Pro Football* (1997); George Vass, *George Halas and the Chicago Bears* (1971); Richard Whittingham, *The Chicago Bears* (1986).

Dennis Ryan

HARLEM GLOBETROTTERS. Originating in the mid-1920s as the all-black Savoy Big Five in Chicago's Savoy Ballroom, the Harlem Globetrotters became the world's most popular basketball team. Their rise to fame began in 1926, when Abraham M. Saperstein* began booking the Savoy team in games around Chicago. He expanded the club's barnstorming schedule in 1927, and over the next few years the team increased its touring to the Midwest and then the far West, eventually playing over 150 games a year during the depression decade of the 1930s. After a series of name changes Saperstein finally titled his squad the Harlem Globetrotters, even though the team came from Chicago and never came close to New York City for its games. Although during its formative period the club's players warmed up in a circle and showed off their fancy ball-handling and passing skills, the team competed seriously and won the vast majority of its contests. During these years a few of the Globetrotters entertained the spectators with such crowd-pleasing tricks as spinning the ball on their fingertips or concealing the ball from their opponents. The Globetrotters gained the respect of the professional basketball establishment when they finished third in the first invitational World Tournament in Chicago in 1939, losing to the eventual champion, the New York Renaissance* team, in the second round. The following year the Globetrotters were champions of the World Tournament, defeating both the Renaissance five and the Chicago Bruins of the National Basketball League. The club remained successful during the 1940s, with a banner year in 1947–48 that included a fifty-two-game winning streak and a split in a two-game exhibition series against the powerful Minneapolis Lakers.

As professional basketball opened its doors to African Americans during the late 1940s and early 1950s, Saperstein realized that he no longer had a monopoly of the most talented black players. Choosing not to seek entry for his team into the new National Basketball Association, he decided to alter the club's format. He transformed the Globetrotters from a serious, competitive, and entertaining team to one that featured fancy passes, trick shooting, clownish behavior, and comedy routines. The change was complete by 1951, when the Globetrotters embarked on their first world tour, playing 108 games against an all-star group of collegians. Since then the Globetrotters have recruited a new generation of stars, including Marques Haynes,* Reece "Goose" Tatum, Meadowlark Lemon, and Curly Neal. Under new ownership after Saperstein's death in 1966, the club continued to thrive. In the mid-1980s it added two women—Lynette Woodard and Jackie White.

During the Globetrotters' formative years the players frequently encountered racial discrimination, especially in finding adequate lodging during their long tours. Although Saperstein labored for equal treatment and respect for his men, there was little he could do to counter the racism of the era. Through his team he provided a means for showcasing black basketball talent. While some viewed the Globetrotters' clownish antics and comedy acts as demeaning to blacks, few could doubt that they contributed significantly to the later success of African Americans in the sport.

SELECTED BIBLIOGRAPHY: Arthur R. Ashe, Jr., *A Hard Road to Glory: A History of the African-American Athlete since 1946*, vol. 3 (1988); *Harlem Globetrotters 1976: Fiftieth Anniversary Issue* (1975); Robert W. Peterson, *Cages to Jumpshots: Pro Basketball's Early Years* (1990); Josh Wilker, *The Harlem Globetrotters* (1997); George Vecsey, *Harlem Globetrotters* (1973).

George B. Kirsch

HARTACK, WILLIAM J., JR. ("Bill") (9 December 1932, Ebensburg, PA–). One of America's greatest all-time jockeys, he is the son of William Hartack, Sr., a Slovak immigrant coal miner in Black Lick Township. He graduated valedictorian of his high school class. Hartack was one of two jockeys ever to win five Kentucky Derbies. From 1955 to 1957 he won more races than any jockey in America. He also earned the most prize money, winning an amazing $3,060,501 in 1957, a record that lasted a decade. His victorious horses in the Kentucky classic included Iron Liege (1957), Venetian Way (1960), Decidedly (1964), Northern Dancer (1964), and Majestic Prince (1969). Hartack also won the Preakness on three occasions with the horses Fabius (1956), Northern Dancer (1964), and Majestic Price (1969). In 1960, he also captured the Belmont Stakes trophy with his horse Celtic Ash. Although none will deny his claim to be one of the finest riders, Hartack acquired a reputation for pugnacity with his agents. When riding for the renowned Calumet Farms in the 1950s, he disagreed with both trainers and managers over technique. He preferred to take the lead in a race and hold it, regardless of instructions. Disputes led to his departure from Calumet Farms. Hartack made no effort to make his ethnicity public. He shunned his earlier connections with Slovak Americans and his native Cambria County. He established an enviable reputation as an outstanding athlete but always was a very difficult person when it came to financial negotiations. Hartack continued to race as late as 1978–81, when he headed for the tracks of Hong Kong. Following his retirement, he continued his career in the racing business by serving as both an official and a commentator for televised races. Hartack's achievements earned him a place in history and are chronicled at the National Horse Racing Hall of Fame.

SELECTED BIBLIOGRAPHY: Ralph Hickock, *A Who's Who of Sports Champions* (1995); Joe Hirsch and Gene Plowden, *In the Winner's Circle* (1974); Joseph Krajsa, ed., *Slovaks in America: A Bicentennial Study* (1978).

Michael J. Kopanic, Jr.

HARTUNG, JAMES NICHOLAS (7 June 1960, Omaha, NE–). A gymnast of Czech ancestry, he entered Sokol classes in his native city at the age of six. He quickly demonstrated his talent, winning one gymnastic meet after another, both in the Sokol and the Amateur Athletic Union (AAU). He won first place in the 1977 Sokol *slet* in Chicago and also at the next *slet* in Fort Worth in 1981. In 1975 and 1976 he won First Place All-Around in the AAU Junior Olympics. Enrolling in the University of Nebraska in 1979, he easily made the varsity gymnastic team, and with the help of his coaches there he was named National Collegiate Athletic Association (NCAA) All-Around Champion in 1980 and 1981, while his team at the University of Nebraska captured the NCAA Team Championship from 1979 through 1982. Current NCAA records list James Hartung with twenty-two All-American Awards and seventeen individual records. In addition, he never placed lower than third in the AAU Championships between 1978 and 1984 and won first place in 1981. He was a member of four U.S. gymnastic teams at World Championships in 1978, 1979, 1981, and 1983. He placed second All-Around in the 1980 Olympic tryouts in 1980 and fourth in the 1984 tryouts. He was a member of the U.S. gymnastic team that won the gold medal at the Los Angeles Olympics in 1984, contributing to their success with a fifth place in the vault and a ninth place All-Around. Hartung was an assistant coach for the U.S. team at the 1989 World Championship and is an internationally certified judge for gymnastic competitions. At the same time, he maintains his membership in the South Omaha Sokol Club, which, he says, concerns more than gymnastics; rather, it is about life overall.

SELECTED BIBLIOGRAPHY: *Centennial of the Sokols in America, 1865–1965* (1965); A. B. Frederick, *Roots of American Gymnastics* (1995); Richard Edd Laptad, *A History of the Development of the United States Gymnastics Federation* (1972); Minot Simons, *Women's Gymnastics: A History* (1995).

Vladislav Slavik

HAVLICEK, JOHN (8 April 1940, Lansing, OH–). The best-known Czech American basketball player, he is the son of Frank Havlicek, an immigrant from Czechoslovakia, and Amanda (Turkal) Havlicek, the daughter of a Yugoslavian coal miner. His parents owned a grocery store in Lansing, and their son John earned All-State honors in both football and basketball at Bridgeport High School. He was an All-American in basketball at Ohio State in 1962. He and his teammate Jerry Lucas led Ohio State to three straight National Collegiate Athletic Association (NCAA) tournament finals, winning in 1960. After his college career he was drafted by the Cleveland Browns of the National Football League (NFL), the Boston Celtics of the National Basketball Association (NBA), and the Cleveland Pipers of the new American Basketball League. After being cut by the Browns, he began an illustrious career with the Celtics in the 1962–63 season. He played for six NBA championship teams in this first seven years, starring as a "sixth man" and popularizing that role in professional basketball. Later in his career he played for two more championship teams before retiring after the 1977–78 season. In 1974 he was named the Most Valuable Player in the playoffs. Nicknamed "Hondo" and renowned for his tireless energy and constant motion, he was the first NBA player to score 1,000 or more points for sixteen consecutive seasons. He was also an excellent defensive player who was named eight times to the NBA all-defensive team. An NBA All-Star thirteen times, in his sixteen seasons Havlicek played 1,270 regular season games and scored 26,395 points, an average of 20.8 per game. He had 8,007 rebounds and 16,119 assists. He was elected to the Naismith Memorial Basketball Hall of Fame in 1984.

SELECTED BIBLIOGRAPHY: Curry Fitzpatrick, "It's the End of a Long, Long Run," *Sports Illustrated* 48 (10 April 1978): 28–30; Mark Goodman, "Fond Farewell to Hondo Havlicek," *Sport* 66 (May 1978): 53ff; John Havlicek and Bob Ryan, *Hondo: Celtic Man in Motion* (1977); Tom Henshaw, *Boston Celtics: A Championship Tradition* (1974); Herman L. Masin, "Here Comes Hondo!" *Senior Scholastic* 94 (14 March 1969): 19.

Miloslav Rechcigl, Jr.

HAWKINS, ABE (?, Donaldsonville, LA–1867, Donaldsonville, LA). He was a slave jockey whom researchers now credit with developing the high, crouching, monkey-on-a-stick "American seat" heretofore considered the original technique of white rider Tod Sloan. Hawkins was raised on thoroughbred breeder Duncan Kenner's plantation. He first gained fame riding at the Metairie Race Course near New Orleans in the 1850s. After emancipation he went north, successfully riding in St. Louis, Paterson, New Jersey, Long Island, and Saratoga. After the Civil War ended, Hawkins and Kenner corresponded, Hawkins offering his considerable earnings to Kenner, whose fortunes had suffered during the war, and Kenner offered Hawkins a home, should he need it, at Ashland. Hawkins developed a lung disease in 1867, returned to Ashland, and was buried in a tomb overlooking the track there.

SELECTED BIBLIOGRAPHY: Alexander Mackey-Smith, *The Race Horses of America 1832–1872: Portraits and Other Paintings by Edward Troye* (1981); Myra Lewyn, "Abe Hawkins—Jockey," New Orleans Fairgrounds Race Course, New Orleans, LA (1996).

Lynn S. Renau

HAYES, ELVIN ("The Big E") (7 November 1945, Rayville, LA–). An African American collegiate and professional basketball player, he is a graduate of Eula Britton High School in Rayville. An All-American in high school, he led his team to fifty-four consecutive victories. When he enrolled at the University of Houston, he joined his teammate Don Chaney as the first African American athletes to compete for the Cougars. In college he was an All-American and *The Sporting News'* Player of the Year in 1968. The highlight of his college career was a Houston victory over the University of California at Los Angeles (UCLA) on 20 January 1968, which ended the Bruins' consecutive games winning streak at forty-seven. His individual duel with Lew Alcindor (later, Kareem Abdul-Jabbar*) in that game was memorable, but Alcindor and his UCLA teammates eliminated Houston from the National Collegiate Athletic Association (NCAA) tournament in both 1967 and 1968. In 1968 Hayes joined Alcindor and several other African American basketball players to protest racial discrimination in the United States by boycotting the Olympic Games in Mexico City. Hayes also had a sterling professional career. Drafted by the San Diego Rockets of the National Basketball Association (NBA) in 1968, he remained with that franchise after it relocated to Houston in 1971. Traded to the Baltimore (later, Washington) Bullets in 1972, he achieved his greatest performances during his nine years with that club. He helped the Bullets reach the NBA finals three times, including a championship over Seattle in 1978. He returned to the Rockets for three seasons before retiring in 1984. When he left the NBA, he ranked first among the league's all-time leaders in games and total minutes played and third in scoring and rebounds. He was elected to the Naismith Memorial Basketball Hall of Fame in 1990.

SELECTED BIBLIOGRAPHY: Arthur R. Ashe, Jr., *A Hard Road to Glory: A History of the African-American Athlete since 1946*, vol. 3 (1988); Elvin Hayes, *They Call Me the Big E* (1978); John Papanek, "The Big E Wants an MVP," *Sports Illustrated* (16 October 1978): 46–50ff.

George B. Kirsch

HAYES, ROBERT ("Bob") (20 December 1942, Jacksonville, FL–). An African American track and football star, he is the son of John Hayes, shoeshine parlor owner, and Mary Hayes, a maid. Raised in poverty in a Jacksonville ghetto, as a youth Bob worked in his father's shoeshine parlor until he was eighteen. He was a schoolboy sensation in the sprints, high jump, and long jump at Matthew Gilbert High School, where he also played football. After his graduation in 1960 he enrolled with a football scholarship in Florida A&M University, an African American institution in Tallahassee. Although he competed on the gridiron for Florida A&M, he gained national and world fame through his performance in the 100-yard and 100-meter dashes. He captured three consecutive national Amateur Athletic Union titles and set a world record time of 9.1 seconds for 100 yards in 1963. Hayes was labeled "the world's fastest human" after his world record-setting gold medal victories in the 100-meter race and the 400-meter relay at the 1964 Olympic Games in Tokyo, Japan. After completing his intercollegiate football career, he signed a two-year contract with the Dallas Cowboys of the National Football League. Although previously most track stars had been unable to make a successful transition to professional football, Hayes' athletic instincts and talents and his blinding speed made him a valued member of the Cowboys from 1965 to 1974. He retired after the 1975 campaign, which he spent with the San Francisco Forty-Niners. His reputation suffered considerably after he pleaded guilty to drug charges in 1979. He was paroled after serving ten months of a five-year sentence. He was inducted into the National Track and Field Hall of Fame in 1976.

SELECTED BIBLIOGRAPHY: Mal Florence, "And Then There Was Bob Hayes," *Los Angeles Times*, 25 July 1984, sec. 8, 16, 23; Bob Hayes, with Robert Pack, *Run, Bullet, Run: The Rise, Fall, and Recovery of Bob Hayes* (1990); David Lipman and Ed Winks, *The Speed King: Bob Hayes of the Dallas Cowboys* (1971).

George B. Kirsch

HAYNES, MARQUES OREOLE (3 October 1926, Sand Springs, OK–   ). A star basketball player for the Harlem Globetrotters,* he was the fourth child of Matthew and Hattie Haynes of Tulsa, Oklahoma. Marques excelled in sports by following the example of his older siblings. His father, a domestic worker, left the family when Marques was four years old. After a slow start, he starred in basketball at Booker T. Washington High School, leading his team to a state championship in 1942, his senior year. A four-year starter at Langston University, an all-black college, Haynes earned a bachelor's degree in industrial education in 1946. At Langston he lifted his team to victory in an exhibition game against the Harlem Globetrotters. The Globetrotters took note; in 1946 he signed with the Kansas City Stars, an affiliate of the Globetrotters, and in 1947 he was promoted to the main squad. While a Globetrotter, Haynes showcased his amazing ball-handling skills, turning down offers to play in the National Basketball Association (NBA). Some have regarded him as the most influential dribbler in the first 100 years of the sport, inspiring superstars like Earvin "Magic" Johnson.* In 1953 Haynes left the team over contract disagreements with owner Abe Saperstein.* Haynes struck out on his own with the Fabulous Magicians, proving a black man could run his own team. Haynes played for the Globetrotters again, but on his own terms and only after Saperstein's death. Haynes also amassed wealth through business interests.

SELECTED BIBLIOGRAPHY: Nelson George, *Elevating the Game: Black Men and Basketball* (1992); David L. Porter, ed., *Biographical Dictionary of American Sports: Basketball and Other Indoor Sports* (1989), 119–120; Robert W. Peterson, *Cages to Jump Shots: Pro Basketball's Early Years* (1990); George Vecsey, *Harlem Globetrotters* (1973); Josh Wilker, *The Harlem Globetrotters* (1997).

David R. McMahon

HENDERSON, EDWIN (24 November 1883, Washington, DC–3 February 1977, Tuskegee, AL). An African American physical educator, coach, athletic administrator, civil rights activist, and historian of African American athletes, he was the son of parents of mixed blood. His father (William) was a government worker, and his mother (Louisa) was a housewife. A graduate of M Street School (now Dunbar High School), Minor Normal School, Howard University (B.A.) and Columbia University (M.A.), Henderson introduced basketball and organized the public school athletic league in Washington, D.C.'s, segregated school system. He cofounded the Washington, D.C., Pigskin Club and established such organizations as the Inter-Scholastic Athletic Association of Middle Atlantic States, Eastern Board of Officials, Washington, D.C., chapter of the American Alliance for Health, Physical Education, Recreation, and Dance (AAHPERD), and the Falls Church, Virginia, branch of the National Association for the Advancement of Colored People. He was a member and frequent officeholder in a number of other professional organizations, including the Committee for Coordinating Recreational Plans in the District of Columbia, Joint Army and Navy Committee on Recreation, National Council on Physical Fitness of the Federal Security Agency, and the District of Columbia's 12th Street Branch of the Young Men's Christian Association. Henderson also fought throughout his life against various forms of racial discrimination. He waged battles against Jim Crow transportation facilities in Virginia, led campaigns to eliminate segregated recreational and organized sport programs in both Washington, D.C., and at the regional levels, and fought to prohibit southern states from excluding African Americans from membership in local AAHPERD chapters. Henderson was, moreover, a prolific writer. He published numerous articles on African American athletes in well-known journals. He wrote several book chapters on African American athletes and coedited the frequently cited *Official Handbook: Inter-Scholastic Athletic Association of Middle Atlantic States*. Perhaps most important, Henderson wrote the first books on the history of African Americans in sport. The books, *The Negro in Sports* (1939, 1949) and *The Black Athlete: Emergence and Arrival* (1968), are still standard reference works for scholars interested in the subject. Henderson's achievements did not go unrecognized. He was honored by organizations representing all races and professional interests. He was given the Young Men's Christian Association (YMCA) Distinguished Service Award, received a Presidential Citation and honor award from AAHPERD, was appointed honorary president of the North American Society for Sport History, and in 1974 was selected as a charter member of the Black Athletes Hall of Fame.

SELECTED BIBLIOGRAPHY: Leon N. Coursey, "The Life of Edwin Bancroft Henderson and His Professional Contributions to Physical Education" (Ph.D. diss., Ohio State University, 1971); James H. M. Henderson and Betty F. Henderson, *Molder of Men: Portrait of a "Grand Old Man"—Edwin Bancroft Henderson* (1985); Greg Stuart, "The Beginning of Tomorrow," *Black Sports* (February 1972): 62–67; David K. Wiggins, "Edwin Bancroft Henderson, African American Athletes and the Writing of Sport History," in David K. Wiggins, *Glory Bound: Black Athletes in a White America* (1997), 221–240.

David K. Wiggins

HENIE, SONJA (8 April 1912, Oslo, Norway–12 October 1969, Paris, France). A figure skater, she was the daughter of Norwegians Selma and Hans Wilhelm Henie. Her father was an Oslo fur wholesaler and a European cycling star. Sonja Henie is known for revolutionizing figure skating by creating the idea of free skating, a series of moves and turns that flow smoothly from one to the other. Henie won gold medals in three consecutive Olympic Games (1928, 1932, 1936). She was given her first pair of skates at age six, and she participated in ballet and dance lessons. At the age of ten she won the 1923 National Figure Skating Championship of Norway. The following year she competed in her first Olympic Games in Chamonix, France, and finished last. Judges thought her style was out of the ordinary and her skirt too short. From 1927 to 1936, Sonja won ten consecutive World Figure Skating Championships. Henie garnered enormous attention, and audiences loved her. Upon completion of the 1936 games she began touring North America with her own ice show. At a Los Angeles show she attracted the attention of a movie studio executive and signed a five-year film contract. Between 1936 and 1939 she made six films for 20th Century Fox. Henie became one of the most popular actresses in Hollywood at that time. She became an American citizen in 1941, and her primary residence was in the United States from the late 1930s to the 1950s. She contributed greatly to the popularity of figure skating in the Winter Olympic Games.

SELECTED BIBLIOGRAPHY: Furman Bisher, "Figure Skating's One and Only Goddess of the Ice," *Atlanta Constitution*, 17 February 1994, sec. C, p. 6, c. 1; Robert J. Condon, *Great Women Athletes of the 20th Century* (1991); Sonja Henie, *Wings on My Feet* (1940); Richard Strait and Leif Henie, *Queen of Ice Queen of Shadows* (1985).

Shawn Ladda

HERMAN, PETER (12 February 1896, New Orleans–13 April 1973, New Orleans). A prizefighter, as a boy Peter Gulotta lived along the Mississippi River, where his Italian father was a "banana carrier." At age twelve, Pete found work as a barbershop bootblack. During lunch, Pete left the barbershop to watch boxing at a local athletic club. A friend invited him to spar; he liked boxing and soon turned professional using the name Pete Herman. In 1914, Herman suffered his one and only knockout at the hands of Frankie Burns. That same year, he went on to defeat Eddie Campi and Young Zulu Kid. By February 1916, Herman had earned a title bout against world bantamweight champion Kid Williams. The fight ended in a draw; Williams retained the title. A January 1917 rematch ended with Herman's winning the bantamweight title. Throughout his career, Herman fought top fighters like Little Jack Sharkey, Young Chaney, Joe Lynch, Johnny Buff, Kid Regan, Johnny Ertle, and Jimmy Wilde. In December 1920, Herman lost the bantamweight title to Lynch, regained it in a July 1921 rematch, and then lost it on 23 September 1921 to Buff. Herman ended his career in 1922 with a victory over Roy Moore in April. Repeated punches to the head damaged Herman's vision and eventually left him blind. In spite of his handicap, Herman successfully operated a café in the French Quarter of New Orleans. During his boxing career Herman's record included nineteen knockouts, sixty-nine wins, eight draws, eleven losses, and sixty-one no decisions. These statistics merited his induction into the International Boxing Hall of Fame in 1997.

SELECTED BIBLIOGRAPHY: Peter Arnold, *All-Time Greats of Boxing* (1993); Peter Heller, *"In This Corner . . . !" Forty World Champions Tell Their Stories* (1973); John D. McCallum, *An Encyclopedia of World Boxing Champions since 1882* (1975); *New York Times*, 26 July 1921, 11 and 27 July 1921, 11 and 24 September 1921, 8 and 15 April 1973, 61.

Philip M. Montesano

HIRSCH, MAXIMILIAN (30 July 1880, Fredericksburg, TX–2 April 1969, New Hyde Park, NY). The son of German Jewish immigrants Jacob and Mary Hirsch, his father was a postmaster who had fought for the Union in the Civil War. At the age of twelve Hirsch hopped a train to Maryland and was off to the races. He rode sixty winners in four years as a jockey. His first major stakes success as a trainer came in the 1915 Dwyer with Norse King, and four years later he purchased Grey Lag as a yearling for $10,000. He sold him for $60,000. His first champion as a trainer was Sarazen in 1924, and he was followed by Assault, Bridal Flower, But Why Not, High Gun, and Gallant Bloom. From the 1930s to the end of his life Hirsch trained for the powerful King Ranch stable of Robert Kleberg, Jr. For King Ranch Hirsch turned Assault from a gimpy little colt into a Triple Crown winner; he also won the Kentucky Derby and the Belmont Stakes with sore-legged Middleground. He selected High Gun as a $10,200 yearling and developed him into a champion, winner of the Belmont Stakes, Dwyer, Manhattan Handicap, and Jockey Club Gold Cup. The last race in which he entered a horse was run only hours before his death. The horse was Heartland, and she won. Moreover, despite a lifetime of success, Hirsch's last year was statistically his best, as he led New York trainers in 1968 with earnings of more than $900,000. Over his sixty-nine-year career (1900–69) he saddled more than 100 stakes winners. He was inducted into the National Thoroughbred Racing Hall of Fame in 1959.

SELECTED BIBLIOGRAPHY: David Alexander, "Max Hirsch 1880–1969," *Thoroughbred Record* 189 (12 April 1969): 1078–1080; *American Bloodstock Review* 1 (2 August 1941): 10–14; *Blood-Horse* 95 (5 April 1969): 1144–1145; Bob Cooke, "Max Hirsch Belonged," *Horsemen's Journal* 33 (April 1982): 42–46; "Max Hirsch," National Museum of Racing Press Release, 3 August 1959; William Leggett, "Some Moments for Max," *Sports Illustrated* 10 (25 June 1959): 45; Lexington, Kentucky *Herald-Leader*, 31 July 1966, 24.

Courtesy of the National Thoroughbred Racing Hall of Fame

HOCKEY. Canadians played a major role in virtually all early U.S. ice hockey activities. While it has not been definitely established where and when the first formal game of ice hockey was played in the United States, records indicate that by the season of 1894–95 the game was being played on an organized basis in Baltimore, Maryland, and Hallock and Minneapolis, Minnesota, and at the St. Paul's School in Concord, New Hampshire. The game may have been played earlier in Baltimore and St. Paul, Minnesota, but the evidence is inconclusive. Baltimore is credited with building the first indoor arena in North America with artificial ice. The first recorded game at this facility was played on 26 December 1894, when Johns Hopkins University and the Baltimore Athletic Club tied 2–2. Canadian Sam Mitchell was Hopkins' captain fourteen months later when they again played a 2–2 game, this time against Yale on 1 February 1896, in what is regarded as the first intercollegiate game in the United States.

The University of Minnesota organized a team in 1895, mainly through the efforts of H. A. Parkyn, a Toronto native and quarterback on the Minnesota football team. This team played the Winnipeg Victorias in Minneapolis on 18 February 1895. On 23 January 1896 teams from St. Paul, Minneapolis, and Winnipeg held a four-team international tournament in St. Paul. This may have been the first international tournament ever played in the United States.

The St. Paul's School, which had been playing ice polo in the 1880s and early 1890s, changed to ice hockey rules for the season of 1894–95. Faculty member James Conover had been instrumental in introducing ice sports at the school after he had made a trip to Montreal to purchase equipment. Coach Malcolm K. Gordon subsequently played a key role in the early development of ice polo and ice hockey at the prestigious New Hampshire school. Gordon is also remembered as the coach of the legendary Hobey Baker, who went on to star at Princeton University.

Previous to this time a game similar to ice hockey, known as ice polo, had been played on a formal basis in New England and areas of the upper Midwest as early as 1883. Minnesota held statewide tournaments in ice polo starting in 1887. The famous early All-American Yale football player Pudge Hefflefinger of Minneapolis participated in these tournaments.

The New York Hockey Club, composed entirely of Canadian residents, introduced the game to New York City during the season of 1895–96. In that initial season the club played the Montclair, New Jersey, Athletic Club, Baltimore Athletic Club, and two teams from Montreal.

The Amateur Hockey League, composed of four teams from New York City, was formed in November 1896 and played their first league schedule in 1896–97. Many league games were played at the famous St. Nicholas Arena, which opened in March 1896. During the period 1900–17 this venue was a mecca for the high society of New York as they gathered to cheer for Yale, Dartmouth, Princeton, and the St. Paul's School. The Amateur Hockey League flourished through the years, adding teams from Boston, and operated through the 1917 season. Just to the south in Baltimore, an amateur league was functioning by the mid-1890s.

In the collegiate ranks, following Minnesota and Johns Hopkins' lead, in 1896 Yale, Cornell, and the University of Maryland started hockey. Thereafter, within a few years, Harvard, Brown, Columbia, and Dartmouth were competing. Yale became interested in the sport after some of their students visited Canada in 1895 and came back to organize a team that played during the season of 1895–96. The Intercollegiate Hockey League was formed for the season of 1899–1900 with Yale, Harvard, Brown, Princeton, and Columbia. This was the first intercollegiate league to operate in the United States. By the early 1900s amateur hockey was being played in Boston, Philadelphia, Pittsburgh, St. Louis, Duluth, Minnesota, and many small communities in northern Michigan and Minnesota. Within the next decade the amateur game spread to Cleveland, Chicago, Detroit, Buffalo, New York City, New Haven, Connecticut, and San Francisco. Secondary school hockey was played as early as 1902 in Minneapolis, St. Paul, and New York City and within a decade had appeared in Cleveland, Buffalo, Boston, Pittsburgh, Baltimore, and other cities in New England and the Midwest.

During the period immediately preceding World War I interest in the sport grew rapidly, particularly in the upper Midwest and Boston areas. These areas, close to Canada, have historically produced most American players. During this period Duluth, Minnesota; Cleveland; St. Paul; Calumet and Sault Ste. Marie, Michigan; Pittsburgh; and Boston iced strong amateur teams. These cities, along with others, formed the U.S. Amateur Hockey Association (USAHA) at a meeting in Philadelphia on 25 October 1920. The newly organized USAHA affiliated itself with the Amateur Athletic Union (AAU) and the Canadian Amateur Hockey Association (CAHA).

Hockey during World War I and through the season of 1919–20 was under the control of the International Skating Union (ISU). It was under the auspices of this group that the first U.S. Olympic Team was organized and sent to Antwerp, Belgium, to compete in the 1920 Winter Games. The American team of eleven players included four Canadians: Herb Drury, Joe and Larry McCormick, and Frank Synott, who were playing on teams in the USAHA. This resulted in a protest from the Canadian press regarding their eligibility, but they were allowed to compete for the United States.

The USAHA was the governing body of amateur hockey in the country through the season of 1925–26, after which it disbanded. Until the AAU assumed control for the season of 1930–31, the sport was not under the control of a national body. This led to problems selecting and organizing a team for the 1928 Winter Olympic Games scheduled for Amsterdam, the Netherlands. The final outcome was that the United States did not participate. In the mid-1930s key enthusiasts in the United States realized that however competent the AAU was in its own field, it could not give its customary efficiency to an alien sport such as ice hockey. An organization exclusively devoted to ice hockey was needed to govern the sport on a national basis. Thus, at a meeting in New York on 29 October 1937, the Amateur Hockey Association of the United States (AHAUS) was formed. Thomas F. Lockhart of New York City was elected president, and Philip E. Thompson of Atlantic City, New Jersey, was selected as secretary-treasurer. A working agreement with the CAHA was effected. Charter league members of the AHAUS were the Eastern Amateur Hockey League, the International Hockey League (Minnesota/Michigan teams); the New York Metropolitan League; and the Michigan-Ontario League.

In February 1947 at a meeting in Prague, Czechoslovakia, the AHAUS was elected to membership in the International Ice Hockey Federation. It sent the first team under its sponsorship to the 1948 Winter Olympic Games in St. Moritz, Switzerland. Since this date the AHAUS (now USA Hockey) has continued to be the governing body of amateur hockey in the United States. Naturalized Canadians have played significant roles at all levels of USA Hockey. Most notable among these have been Winnipeg, Manitoba, native Robert Fleming, longtime chairman of the International Committee; Murray Williamson, also a Winnipeg native, who coached both the 1968 and 1972 U.S. Olympic Teams; and Art Berglund, USA Hockey's director of national teams and international activities, a Fort Francis, Ontario, native.

In the 1920s amateur hockey, especially in high schools and colleges, showed significant growth. Many educational institutions in the East, upper Midwest, and, to a limited extent, California added hockey to their athletic programs. Such colleges as Marquette (Milwaukee), Minnesota, Michigan Mines, St. Mary's (Winona, Minnesota), Eveleth Junior College (Minnesota), Wisconsin, Southern California, and Loyola (Los Angeles) iced strong teams that were able to compete with the leading eastern schools. The sport continued to prosper during the 1930s until it was interrupted by World War II.

In the late 1940s and early 1950s many colleges added hockey to their programs, and since then the sport has continued to grow and display a high caliber of play. By the late 1990s there were 146 National Collegiate Athletic Association (NCAA) colleges (124 men, twenty-two women) playing hockey on a varsity basis. Canadian influence on college hockey in the United States has been considerable. Prior to the University of Minnesota's victory in the 1974 NCAA tournament only Boston College's 1949 victory was accomplished with an all-American roster. Until Minnesota's victory it could be accurately stated that the NCAA tournament was played to determine the best Canadian college team in the United States. While Canadian influence has diminished since that time, it is still significant. Lake Superior States' (Michigan) 1992 victory was accomplished with a predominantly Canadian lineup, while in 1995–96 Canadians constituted 38% of all Division I rosters. While the 1994 winner of the Hobey Baker Award for college hockey's most outstanding player was an American, eight of the ten finalists were from Canada. When the NCAA announced its fiftieth anniversary college hockey team in February 1997, thirteen of the twenty-one players selected (62%) were from Canada.

High school hockey is played on a school-sponsored varsity level on approximately 700 teams (boys and girls) across the United States, numbering some 28,000 players. About 45% of these teams are located in the traditional hockey states of Massachusetts and Minnesota. The sport is also a significant activity at select private (preparatory) schools, principally in the Northeast.

The first national youth hockey tournament for boys under high school age was held in 1949 under the sponsorship of the AHAUS. Presently, national tournaments in eighteen different classes are held annually under the guidance of USA Hockey. In the past decade youth hockey has displayed considerable growth and is presently played in virtually every state. The 1995–96 season saw over 435,000 players as members of 27,825 teams competing in formal programs in the United States.

The first professional league in the world, predating those later formed in Canada, was the International Hockey League, which initiated operations for the season of 1904–5 with four cities from the United States and one from Canada. Instrumental in forming the league was Dr. John L. "Doc" Gibson, a Canadian dentist from Kitchener, Ontario, who starred for the Portage Lake (Michigan) team. Other league members were Calumet, Sault Ste. Marie, and Pittsburgh and Sault Ste. Marie, Ontario. This league, composed almost entirely of Canadian players, operated through the season of 1906–7 and disbanded because of exorbitant operating costs. The quality of play was the best in North America at that time, and many players later became outstanding performers in the National Hockey Association and the National Hockey League (NHL). Several were admitted to the Hockey Hall of Fame: William "Riley" Hern, Bruce and Hod Stuart, Fred "Cyclone" Taylor, and Gibson himself.

Portland became the first American city to enter a major hockey league when they joined the Pacific Coast League (PCL) for the season of 1914–15. Seattle followed by entering the league for the 1915–16 season, and Spokane joined for the 1916–17 campaign. Along with the NHL, the PCL, which operated from 1912 through 1926, was considered a major league and played off against the NHL champion for the Stanley Cup. Seattle (with an all-Canadian club) was the first U.S. city to capture the Stanley Cup when they defeated the Montreal Canadiens in 1917.

Boston became the first American city to secure a franchise in the NHL when they entered the league for the 1924–25 season. Within the next few years, New York (two teams), Detroit, Chicago, Philadelphia, and Pittsburgh joined the league, requiring it to be divided into two divisions. The NHL became a six-team league for the 1942–43 season and operated under that format until the expansion to twelve teams and two divisions for the 1967–68 season. Since then additional franchises have been awarded. From the entry of the NHL into the United States in 1924 until the early 1970s, player and coaching personnel were overwhelmingly Canadian. While there was a scattering of Americans playing in the NHL in the 1920s, 1930s, and 1940s, by the 1950s they had disappeared. The situation started to change in the 1970s as both Americans and Europeans began to make their presence felt. Both these groups are now well represented in the NHL, but as the 1996–97 season got under way, Canada still provided 62% of all player personnel, with Europeans (20%) and the United States (18%) supplying the rest of the manpower.

While there have been only a few black Canadian and African American hockey collegiate and professional hockey players, in recent decades their numbers have been slowly increasing. Henry Beckett of Springfield College was the first African American to compete at the intercollegiate level (1903–6), and after World War II Lloyd Robinson of Boston University became the first American-born black to compete in the NCAA playoffs. Arthur Dorrington, born in Nova Scotia, became the first black professional hockey player in the United States in 1950, when he skated for the minor league Atlantic City Seagulls of the Easter League. Willie O'Ree was a black native of Frederick, New Brunswick, who became the first of his race to play in the NHL, competing for the Boston Bruins in the 1957–58 and 1960–61 seasons. Over the next four decades about thirty more hockey players of African descent competed for NHL teams. Perhaps the most celebrated black Canadian hockey star is Grant Fuhr. An adopted son of a Canadian couple, during the 1980s he became the goaltender for the Edmonton Oilers, leading his team to five Stanley Cup championships. In the 1990s he also starred for the St. Louis Blues.

By the late 1920s four minor professional hockey leagues were operating, with most of the franchises being located in American cities. Those operating were the International and the Canadian-American Leagues, both composed of cities located in the eastern United States and Canada, the American Hockey Association in the Midwest, and the Pacific Coast Hockey League. During the past seventy years these original leagues have made many changes in names and member cities. In the late 1980s and first five years of the 1990s there was major expansion among hockey's minor leagues. While there are no formal levels as in minor league baseball, it can be reasonably concluded that the present American and International Leagues operate at the highest level, the East Coast, Colonial, and Central Leagues somewhere in the middle, while the Western Pro and West Coast Leagues would form a third level. Player and coaching personnel are predominantly Canadian, but as in the NHL, Americans and Europeans form significant minorities.

During early 1972 the World Hockey Association (WHA), comprising twelve cities in the United States and Canada, was formed with the intention of challenging the NHL as a second major league. The effort was the only serious threat ever posed to the NHL, and it ultimately failed. However, four WHA teams joined the NHL for the 1979–80 season: Edmonton Oilers, Winnipeg Jets (now Phoenix Coyotes), Quebec Nordiques (now Colorado Avalanche), and the Hartford Whalers (now Carolina Hurricanes). Perhaps more significantly, the league acquired the services of one of its greatest all-time players, Brantford, Ontario, native Wayne Gretzky. Gretzky has gone on to star for NHL teams in American cities Los Angeles, St. Louis, and New York. Gretzky is probably the ultimate example of Canadian influence on hockey played in the United States, though Gordie Howe* and Bobby Orr* would also rate very high.

The 1920 Winter Olympics were the first and last Olympic competition in which seven-man hockey was played. By 1924 the six-man game was in vogue, and Canadians Herb Drury and Frank Synott once again played for the United States at Chamonix, France. Thereafter, the Canadian influence on U.S. National/Olympic teams waned until the 1960s. The 1962 National team had five naturalized Canadians on the squad, while the 1967 team had four and was coached by Winnipeg native Murray Williamson. Naturalized Canadians Bill Reichart and Lou Nanne were key members of the 1964 and 1968 Olympic teams, respectively, while Williamson coached the latter. Williamson also coached the 1972 silver medal-winning team at Sapporo, Japan. Naturalized or dual-citizenship Canadians were in much evidence on the U.S. entry in the first Canada Cup Tournament held in 1976. The team, the first to compete internationally solely with professionals, had four such players, including Nanne. Canadian Bob Pulford coached the team. Thereafter, the participation of these players became less common until the 1996 World Cup of Hockey, the successor to the Canada Cup. The United States stunned the hockey world by defeating Canada two games to one as dual-citizen Brett Hull played a key role in the victory.

SELECTED BIBLIOGRAPHY: "Artificial Ice: A Tie Hockey Game at the Opening of the North Avenue Rink," *Baltimore Sun*, 27 December 1894, n.p.; Arthur R. Ashe, Jr., *A Hard Road to Glory: A History of the African-American Athlete since 1964*, vol. 3 (1988); Bloomberg Wire Service, "Dryden, Chelios Head NCAA 50th Anniversary Team," *New York Post*, 25 February 1997, 87; Donald M. Clark, "Brief History of Ice Hockey in United States," *Amateur Hockey Association of the United States (AHAUS) Guide* (1974–75), 59–60; Donald M. Clark and Mark Schroeder, eds., *USA Hockey Team Results Book: Olympic and World Championship Competition 1920–1986* (1986); John Davies, *The Legend of Hobey Baker* (1966); Editorial Staff, minor hockey league statistics, *Hockey News* 19 (1997): 45; Michael Faber, "Giant Sucking Sound," *Sports Illustrated* (20 March 1995): 105–110; Mike Klingaman, "Hopkins' Hockey Roots," *Baltimore Sun*, 1 February 1996, 1–2; Kerby W. Meyers, college hockey team rosters, *Drop the Puck* (1995–96), 8–63 and (1991–92), 8; *New York Times*, 30 November 1997, NJ-26, 19 January 1998, C-9; Office Staff, NCAA Sponsorship List 1996–97; Office Staff, USA Hockey Registered Teams and Players 1995–96.

Donald M. Clark and Roger A. Godin

HOLMAN, NATHAN ("Nat") (19 October 1896, New York City–12 February 1995, New York City). A basketball player and coach, his parents, Louis, owner of a small grocery store, and Mary (Goldman), a housewife, were Russian Jewish immigrants. A graduate of New York City's High School of Commerce, Holman received a diploma from the Savage School of Physical Education. During World War I, he served in the navy. After exhibiting excellence in basketball, soccer, baseball, and football as a schoolboy athlete, Holman emerged as the preeminent professional basketball player of his generation. From 1917 to 1930, he played for teams in Bridgeport, Scranton, Germantown, (Pennsylvania), Albany, New York, Cleveland, Syracuse, Chicago, and other cities in diverse leagues and barnstorming competition. The 5' 11" Holman led New York's Original Celtics, the era's dominant team, from 1921 to 1928. A brilliant shooter and playmaker, he helped to devise the pivot play. Holman's professional career overlapped with his remarkable tenure as varsity basketball coach at City College of New York (CCNY). During Holman's thirty-seven seasons coaching CCNY (1919–52, 1955–56, and 1959–60), his teams won 421 games against only 190 losses. Holman's 1949–50 squad won both the National Collegiate Athletic Association (NCAA) and National Invitational Tournament (NIT) championships, an unequaled accomplishment. Tragically, several members of this championship team were involved in a point-shaving scandal, leading to Holman's suspension, followed by exoneration, for "conduct unbecoming a teacher." Basketball Hall of Famer, a progenitor of the "New York Style" game, coach of teams with a strong Jewish presence, and promoter of Israeli basketball, Holman was an icon to many New York Jews.

SELECTED BIBLIOGRAPHY: Stanley Cohen, *They Played the Game* (1977); Sam Goldpaper, "Nat Holman Is Dead at 98; Led CCNY Champions (obituary)," *New York Times*, 13 February 1995, B7; Peter Levine, *Ellis Island to Ebbets Field: Sports and the American Jewish Experience* (1992); Charles Rosen, *Scandals of '51: How the Gamblers Almost Killed College Basketball* (1978). Nathan "Nat" Holman File, Naismith Memorial Basketball Hall of Fame.

William M. Simons

HOLMES, LARRY (3 November 1949, Cuthbert, GA–   ). An African American heavyweight boxing champion, he is the son of John Holmes, a sharecropper and construction worker, and Flossie Holmes. His family moved to Easton, Pennsylvania, in the mid-1950s, where Larry attended school until the seventh grade. He began his career as an amateur boxer at St. Anthony's Youth Center in Easton and turned professional in 1973. He rapidly progressed from a sparring partner for Muhammad Ali* to a contender for the heavyweight crown. His victory over Ken Norton on 9 June 1978 earned him the World Boxing Council's (WBC) version of the title. He became the premier heavyweight in the world after Ali, the World Boxing Association's champion, retired in 1979. Holmes successfully defended his WBC belt seventeen times over the next five years, with dramatic wins over Earnie Shavers, Renaldo Snipes, Gerry Cooney, and others. Perhaps his most emotional victory was an eleven-round destruction of Ali in 1980, after the former champion tried an ill-fated comeback. After breaking his ties with promoter Don King,* Holmes relinquished his claim to the WBC title in 1983, but the new International Boxing Federation recognized him as its champion. After successfully defending that crown three times, Holmes was finally defeated by light-heavyweight champion Michael Spinks in 1985. Holmes retired after a second (and controversial) loss to Spinks, but he returned to the ring in the late 1980s and early 1990s, only to lose to Mike Tyson* and Evander Holyfield. During the late 1990s he continued to fight, even as he approached the age of fifty. Although he dominated the heavyweight division between 1978 and 1985, he did not attain the worldwide fame of Ali, in part because he never defended his title abroad and in part because he did not engage in racial or political issues.

SELECTED BIBLIOGRAPHY: William Nack, "Champ Who Would Be Champ," *Sports Illustrated* 53 (22 September 1980): 74–78; William Nack, "A Classic Confrontation," *Sports Illustrated* 56 (7 June 1982): 42–50; Pat Putnam, "Doom in the Desert," *Sports Illustrated* 53 (13 October 1980): 34–40; Pat Putnam, "Night They Called It a Daze," *Sports Illustrated* 55 (16 November 1981): 32–36.

George B. Kirsch

HOLZMAN, WILLIAM ("Red") (10 August 1920, New York City–13 November 1998, West Hempstead, NY). A collegiate and professional basketball player and coach, he was born on the Lower East Side of Manhattan, the son of Jewish immigrants. His father, Abraham, was a tailor and a native of Russia who discouraged his boy from participating in sports. His mother, Sophie, was from Romania. Holzman moved with his parents to the Ocean-Hill Brownsville section of Brooklyn when he was four years old. There "Roita" (Yiddish for "Red") attended Franklin K. Lane High School, where he was a star athlete. He accepted a basketball scholarship to the University of Baltimore but left after six months because of homesickness. He transferred to the City College of New York, where for two seasons he became an All-American playmaking guard under the legendary coach Nat Holman.* After graduating in 1942, he enlisted in the navy; his three years of military service consisted mainly of playing basketball to entertain and lift the morale of American servicemen. After World War II Holzman had a nine-year career in professional basketball, eight of which he spent with the Rochester Royals. Lester Harrison, the Jewish owner of the Royals, originally signed Holzman as a substitute bench player whose role was mainly to attract Jewish fans to games. But after a stellar performance in a game against the Sheboygan Redskins, Holzman joined the club's starting lineup. He helped guide the Royals to championships of the National Basketball League in 1946 and the National Basketball Association (NBA) in 1951. He began his head coaching career with the Milwaukee (later, St. Louis) Hawks in 1953 and remained with the Hawks until he was replaced in 1957. He moved on to the New York Knickerbockers, for whom he worked in several positions until he took over the job as head coach from Dick McGuire in December 1967. He achieved his greatest success with the Knicks, winning two NBA titles (1970 and 1973) over a ten-year span that ended when he was fired in 1977. Although he returned as the Knicks' head coach for a second term from 1978 to 1982, he could not bring the team back to the level of its prior glory years. Among his honors are his selection as NBA Coach of the Decade for the 1970s by the professional basketball writers and his election as a coach into the Naismith Basketball Hall of Fame in 1986.

SELECTED BIBLIOGRAPHY: Red Holzman, with Leonard Lewin, *The Knicks* (1971); Red Holzman, *Red on Red* (1987); Red Holzman and Harvey Frommer, *Holzman on Hoops* (1991); *New York Times*, 15 November 1998, 46, Sec. 8-1, 12, 16 November 1998, D-3.

George B. Kirsch

HOMESTEAD GRAYS. An African American baseball club, the team was one of the premier nines of black baseball from the 1920s to the late 1940s. It originated in 1900 in a group of young black ballplayers in Homestead, Pennsylvania, near Pittsburgh, who called themselves the Blue Ribbons. In 1910 the club was reorganized and renamed the Homestead Grays by a few players who worked in the Homestead Steel Works. During World War I Cumberland Posey* became the team's captain and then its manager. By the early 1920s he had become its owner, and he turned the Grays into a successful professional outfit by recruiting top talent and expertly promoting the team as an independent barnstorming nine that enjoyed great popularity among Pittsburgh's black community. Posey agreed to join the American Negro League (ANL) in 1929, but the Grays returned to barnstorming for the next two years when the ANL collapsed after only one season.

Over the next two decades the Homestead Grays retained their privileged place in the world of black baseball, both as a barnstorming nine and as a member of various professional leagues. In 1932 Posey formed and enrolled his team in the East-West League, but the circuit did not last through that summer. Now challenged on his home turf by the upstart Pittsburgh Crawfords,* Posey and the Grays rebounded and ultimately became the most dominant team in black baseball from 1937 to the late 1940s. Following the example of his rival Gus Greenlee,* Posey raised cash to finance his team by recruiting a partner who was a principal banker for Homestead's numbers rackets.

After joining the revived Negro National League* (NNL), the Homestead Grays dominated their competition, winning the NNL pennant every year except two from 1937 through 1948 and also capturing several Negro Leagues' World Series titles with victories over the champions of the Negro American League. Although their roster experienced considerable turnover during this era, they reigned supreme because at one time or another the club featured such stars as Josh Gibson,* James "Cool Papa" Bell,* Buck Leonard,* and lesser-known players such as Ray Brown, "Smokey" Joe Williams, and Oscar Charleston. The combination of Norman "Jelly" Jackson at shortstop and Matthew "Licki" Carlisle at second base anchored the defense. In the batting order, the ferocious combination of Gibson and Leonard—known together as the "Black Babe Ruth" and the "Black Lou Gehrig"—supplied the prowess at the plate.

Beginning in 1939 and continuing through World War II, the Grays played their home games at both Pittsburgh's Forbes Field and Griffith Stadium in Washington, D.C. Griffith Stadium was the Washington Senators' home field, and the Grays played there when the white major league team was on the road. The Homestead Grays attracted more fans to Griffith Stadium than the Senators, who were perennial cellar-dwellers. After World War II the Grays failed to win the NNL crown in 1946 or 1947. Although they rebounded with a league title and a Negro World Series triumph over the Birmingham Black Barons in 1948, by that year both the Homestead Grays and the Negro Leagues were approaching extinction because of the integration of major league baseball by Jackie Robinson* of the Brooklyn Dodgers in 1947. But during its glory years no team in black baseball was more celebrated than the Homestead Grays.

SELECTED BIBLIOGRAPHY: Robert Gardner and Dennis Shortelle, *The Forgotten Players: The Story of Black Baseball in America* (1993); Robert Peterson, *Only the Ball Was White* (1970); Mark Ribowsky, *A Complete History of the Negro Leagues* (1995); Donn Rogosin, *Invisible Men* (1983); Rob Ruck, *Sandlot Seasons: Sport in Black Pittsburgh* (1987).

Vernon Andrews and George B. Kirsch

HOWE, GORDON ("Gordie")

HOWE, GORDON ("Gordie") (21 March 1928, Floral, Saskatchewan, Canada–   ). A hockey player, he is the son of Albert Howe, a laborer from Minnesota, and Kathleen Schultz, a second-generation German Canadian. He starred for the Detroit Red Wings (1946–71) and Hartford Whalers (1979–80) of the National Hockey League (NHL) and the Houston Aeros (1973–77) and New England Whalers (1977–79) of the World Hockey Association. Howe's longevity in such a physically demanding sport was unprecedented, as was his excellence. Known for his adroit scoring touch, tireless skating, and physical toughness, Howe led the Red Wings to four Stanley Cups (1950, 1952, 1954, 1955). He was the league's Most Valuable Player and scoring champion six times. Howe was named to an incredible twenty-one All-Star teams, an NHL record. Upon retirement in 1980, Howe held numerous NHL records, including most career games played (1,767), goals (801), and points (1,850). He was inducted into the Hockey Hall of Fame in 1972. In addition, in 1973 with Houston he became the only player in pro hockey history to play on a line with his sons (Mark and Marty). He received the Lester Patrick Award from the NHL in 1967. Howe played a major role in the transformation of hockey from a Canadian game to a North American game.

SELECTED BIBLIOGRAPHY: Richard Bak, *Detroit Red Wings: The Illustrated History* (1997); Gordie Howe and Colleen Howe, *And . . . Howe* (1995); Morgan Hughes and Joseph Romain, *Hockey Legends of All Time* (1996); Roy MacSkimming, *Gordie: A Hockey Legend* (1994); Jim Vipond, *Gordie Howe Number 9* (1968).

Dennis Ryan

HUNGARIANS. The over 100-year process of mass migration from Hungary to the United States can be broken down into three distinct waves. The first great exodus was the "labor migration" of the period from 1890 to 1914, when 1.5 million Hungarians crossed the ocean to the New World in hopes of finding prosperity. About a third of them were ethnic Hungarians; the remaining million were members of Hungary's various ethnic minorities. Most of these newcomers were country folks, peasants, and craftsmen. Itinerant craftsmen had always popularized sports in the Hungarian countryside, and they remained true to this tradition in their new homeland as well. Bowling as a recreation started the same year as the first Hungarian pubs opened (1887). Joseph Schuster, a carpenter, organized one sport club after the other for the various ethnic groups from Hungary. Lou Daro was the first Hungarian to achieve popularity and amass a considerable fortune through sports in the United States. Both men started their sports careers in Hungarian circuses as strongmen, wrestlers, and boxers.

Beginning in the 1920s, when the Hungarian immigrants were ready to think of the United States as home, they started to set up Hungarian houses, workers' homes, and athletic clubs, as well as their own bowling and soccer teams. Fraternal organizations took an active part in promoting the sport activities of young Hungarians, in hopes of securing their loyalty to the ethnic community. By the 1930s, second-generation Hungarians came to favor American football and baseball. The outstanding achievements of some of them began to make news in the sports sections of the leading American papers. Examples are the Redskins' Andy Farkas and Andrew J. Kantor of the Big Ten Championship Baseball Team. Among the earliest native Hungarians who achieved fame in fencing in the United States was Nickolas Muray, national sabre champion in 1927–28 and a member of the U.S. Olympic team in 1928 and 1932. Helena Mroczkowska was U.S. women's foil champion four times between 1940 and 1948.

At the end of World War II, another mass of Hungarians fled to the West in an effort to escape the battle zone and the invading Red Army. Most of them returned to their homes once the fighting was over, but over 100,000 displaced persons—mostly from the upper and middle classes—sought refuge elsewhere. Some 16,000 of them wound up in the United States. Among them were some athletes who had already made a name for themselves. A number of these people became trainers or managers in their various fields and would contribute substantially to a number of U.S. Olympic victories. Hungarian Olympic champion George Jekelfalussy Piller worked as a fencing coach in California. Lajos (Louis) Csiszar was head fencing coach at the University of Pennsylvania, the U.S. Olympic team in 1956, and the Pan-American Games. Tibor Nyilas, a seven-time American sabre titlist, was a member of the U.S. Olympic fencing team in 1948, 1952, 1956 and 1960, and of the Pan-American team in 1951, 1955, and 1959. Geza (Gene) Gazdag was founder and president of the Vanderbilt Athletic Club in New York. Tibor Machan, an oarsman, European champion, and collegiate world champion, was head coach for the U.S. Olympic rowing team at the 1964 Tokyo Olympics. Perhaps the best known of the second generation is Joseph William Namath, the controversial football personality and celebrated quarterback of the New York Jets. The captain of the U.S. volleyball team at the Seoul Olympic Games was the second-generation Hungarian Karch Kiraly.

The third wave of Hungarian emigration came in the aftermath of the crushed 1956 revolution. Forty thousand people, mostly young college students and skilled workers, arrived in the United States between November 1956 and March 1957. The overwhelming show of sympathy and support for the Hungarian refugees enabled them to continue their education, find gainful employment, and assimilate quickly and easily. By the early 1960s, some of the older athletes had embarked on highly successful training and coaching careers. Csaba Elthes, a professional fencing master, trained the U.S. fencing teams for a number of Olympic and Pan-American Games in the 1960s and 1970s. Five-time national fencing champion Alex Orban was a member of the U.S. Olympic fencing team in Mexico in 1968 and in Munich in 1972 (sabre). Paul Pesthy was a four-time member of the U.S. Olympic pentathlon and épée fencing teams and a four-time winner of the U.S. épée championship. Csaba Miklos Pallaghhy was American sabre team champion from 1958 to 1962, and Pan-American sabre team champion in 1963. Thomas George Kovacs was a member of the U.S. national relay swimming team in 1961 and 1962. Water polo player Ervin R. Vegh was a four-time U.S. champion. Peter Gogolak developed the soccer style of place kicking in American football at Cornell during the early 1960s, and he brought his innovation to the pro ranks while playing in the National Football League. His brother Charles starred at Princeton using the same technique. Larry Csonka,* who excelled as a running back for the Miami Dolphins and the New York Giants, is also of Hungarian descent. Bela Karolyi, a Hungarian ethnic from Romania, became celebrated for his training of American female national and Olympic champions and medalists in gymnastics since 1981. Mihaly Igloi, who became an American citizen in 1963, coached many of the world's greatest middle-distance runners, including such outstanding American milers as Jim Beatty and Dyrol Burleson. Since the 1950s Hungarian coaches and players from this relatively small ethnic group have made outstanding contributions to the American world of sports.

SELECTED BIBLIOGRAPHY: *Hungarica Biographical Information*, National Szechenyi Library, Hungarica Documentation, Budapest, Hungary; *New York Times*, 7 January 1998, A-17; Julianna Puskas, *Ties That Bind, Ties That Divide: 100 Years of Hungarian Experience in the United States* (1998); Tibor Szy, ed., *Hungarians in America: A Biographical Directory of Professionals of Hungarian Origins in the Americas* (1966); Edmund Vasvari Collection: Hungarian Sportsmen in the United States, microfilm, Hungarian American Foundation, New Brunswick, NJ.

Julianna Puskas

HURLING (*ioman* in Irish Gaelic). This fifteen-a-side stick-and-ball game is often described as Ireland's national sport. Players use a 3.5-foot stick with a rounded, three-inch blade (the hurry or *caman*) to drive a hard ball between two uprights, scoring three-point goals (when the ball passes under an eight-foot crossbar) or single points (when the ball passes over it). The ball may be handled before being struck, and the long drives resulting from this tactic are one of the game's characteristic features. Players may also make solo runs by balancing the ball on the blade of the hurry. A women's version of hurling, called *camogie*, is played in Ireland.

The origins of hurling are commonly traced to pre-Christian Irish culture—though it must be remembered that the Irish Gaelic annals and sagas alluding to the game were committed to writing only in the Middle Ages. Still, it is clear that hurling has a very long history in the southern provinces of Munster and Leinster. By the seventeenth and eighteenth centuries it enjoyed the patronage of local gentry, who arranged and supervised matches and often gambled on the outcomes. But in the nineteenth century the game went into deep decline, due to the withdrawal of landlord patronage and the dislocating effects of the famine. When the Gaelic Athletic Association* (GAA) was established in 1884, one of its main objectives was "to bring the hurling back to Ireland" both as nationalist symbol and as alternative to "Anglicized" sports like cricket and soccer. Under a code of rules devised by GAA founder Michael Cusack the game was developed at club, county, and provincial levels. Today it remains under GAA administration, standing second in popularity to Gaelic football* among sports of Irish origin.

Forms of hurling have been practiced in the United States since the mid-nineteenth century, though the sport has never gained currency outside Irish American communities. The earliest references to organized clubs, in San Francisco (1853) and New York (1857), predate the Civil War. Two decades later the sport was exhibited at the inaugural field day of the Irish Athletic Club of Boston, though a president of the club later recalled that "in the light of a proper introduction of the game of hurling it was a failure" because of the participants' inexperience. Still, the game's literary pedigree made it uniquely appealing to a generation powerfully concerned with the preservation of Gaelic culture, and the 1880s and 1890s witnessed its steady growth. Particularly influential was the game's codification by the GAA in Ireland, relayed to American clubs through hurling exhibitions by Irish athletes in ten eastern cities in 1888.

In the twentieth century this early promise has been only partially fulfilled, for hurling in the United States has never really developed at the grassroots level. The sport has come under the auspices of American affiliates of the GAA, and elite play has long been dominated by athletes newly arrived from Ireland. Formerly these were immigrants, but today their visits tend to be fleeting, as they are paid to perform for Irish American communities in Boston, Philadelphia, Chicago, San Francisco, and, above all, New York. In the 1950s Gaelic Park in the Bronx was home to sixteen hurling teams, all stocked with players from Ireland. By the summer of 1995 that number was down to five, leaving the future of hurling in America very much in doubt.

SELECTED BIBLIOGRAPHY: Maurice Dinneen, "The Game of Hurling," *The Gael* 20 (1901): 290–292; Tom Humphries, *Green Fields—Gaelic Sport in Ireland* (1996); Raymond Smith, *The Hurling Immortals* (1969); Kevin Whelan, "The Geography of Hurling," *History Ireland* 1 (1993): 27–31; Ralph C. Wilcox, "The Shamrock and the Eagle: Irish Americans and Sport in the Nineteenth Century," in George Eisen and David K. Wiggins, eds., *Ethnicity and Sport in North American History and Culture* (1994).

George Rugg

I

ICE SPEED SKATING. The origins of ice speed skating in North America were rooted in the coldest part of the Little Ice Age, which gripped Northern Europe around A.D. 1300–1700. This introduction of a European and Scandinavian ice-skating culture to North America primarily developed as a result of the creative energies of Dutch merchants who used skates to transport products along frozen canals. The Dutch taught the British to skate the "roll" before the British introduced the long-distance skill to America.

Although a crude form of bone ice skating existed in pre-Christian Scandinavia, the modern iron-blade skate is attributed to Holland from a fourteenth-century woodcut portraying the social life of skating's patron saint, Lydwina of Schiedam. Races using crude iron design from Scandinavia are written about as early as A.D. 200, but North American reports did not become official until 1879, when British and American skating officials formed the first national governing bodies in an attempt to control outrageous claims on world speed records. The International Skating Union was not formed until 1892, largely due to the arrival of the first "official" male (amateur) world champion from North America. He was a non-Scandinavian Irishman named Joseph F. Donoghue,* who trained on the frozen uppers of the Hudson River in Newburgh, New York. Women did not have a world championship until 1936, when it was won by Kit Klein from the United States, even though Dutch women raced in the early 1600s.

U.S. national speed skating champions from the early eighteenth century were found along the upper Hudson and in Illinois, with wild claims for glory emanating from Wisconsin, Michigan, Indiana, and northern Ohio. The Irish race-walker/pedestrian (professional) John Ennis from Chicago held the speed skating distance record for 100 miles, while Donoghue's oar-maker father Tim, Sr., was the unchallenged (pro) short-distance champ for twenty years between the 1860s and 1880s. Charles F. June, a Hudson River boat captain, claimed the title of national champion prior to 1860 and was an outstanding backward racer. In the period of 1815–20, Jacob June, John Decker, and Negro Charles Payne were said to be the fastest speed skaters "in these parts" of the Hudson. In the remote areas of North America many incredible skating feats were reported, which led to the "official" 1879 verification effort to approve "genuine" world records. Native American Indian speed skater Gabriel Acquin's seventy-three-mile performance on the St. John River in New Brunswick was the "most remarkable feat . . . ever recorded" in the *London Field* (19 December 1863); these vaguely scientific reports would eventually lead to the age of standardized "records" at the more easily verifiable shorter distances. In 1881 John Ennis responded to a Vienna Skating Society invitation for him to attend a race in Austria; he wrote in *The Spirit of the Times* that the distances are "too short to attract the fastest American skaters who are accustomed to longer contests." He was willing to attend only if $1,000 was offered for an attempt to skate 600 miles in seventy-two hours, twelve hours a day, for six successive days, and he also volunteered to make a match against any man or against any six men, each of whom would travel twelve hours, with their total score added up against him. In the winter of 1876–77 Ennis had skated a six-day match versus Eugene St. Clair Millard of Cincinnati, Ohio, waiting half the time for good ice and doing only 500 miles.

Questionable and "unscientific" speed skating results from seventeenth-century Holland and early eighteenth-century Britain (each used totally different track structures) led to much of the bureaucratic control that originated in New York City and London in 1879. Besides attempts to control speed standards, there was an effort to control and regulate amateurs and professionals. Prior to 1879 racing events were primarily professional money events with prizes and purses being offered to the skaters. In 1883, Axel Paulsen, the well-known figure and speed skater, sailed from Norway and toured Canada by railroad promoting his patented "tube" speed skates; and again in 1884 in Brooklyn, New York, he dominated the first intercontinental skating race. This event excited interest in the New York area as Axel (known for creating the 1 1/2 "axel" jump in figures) challenged the young Donoghue to set new speed standards for the sport.

Between 1884 and 1900 Scandinavian skating clubs from Minneapolis and professional skating hustlers from Norway and Canada were largely responsible for most of the speed skating frenzy that spread along a line of northern regions to New Brunswick. Since these speed skating "professionals" came to America to promote the sport and themselves, it created some difficulty for New York officials who were instrumental in the development of amateur athletics in the United States. William B. Curtis, a founder of the New York Athletic Club in 1868 and a dedicated open river skater who was also known as the "father of amateur athletics" in America, helped develop Donoghue as the first "amateur" World Champion from North America. After Donoghue's amateur reign from 1888 to 1893, there was not a world champion speed skater from North America until the arrival of Wisconsin's Eric Heiden in 1977. While Donoghue trained on the frozen Hudson River before the climate warmed, and the Hudson no longer froze, Heiden took advantage of America's first long-track artificial rink built in 1964 near Milwaukee to make his mark.

North America's first artificial ice rink was built in 1879 at New York City's original Madison Square Garden (Gilmore's Garden), but the major spread of indoor ice technology in New York City did not occur until the mid-1890s, when the rising sport of ice hockey also began to compete for ice space. By 1900, at the tail end of the Little Ice Age, the era of open river speed skating had faded and was later replaced by artificial long-track ovals in 1964 and by the even tighter short-track oval around 1975.

SELECTED BIBLIOGRAPHY: John M. Heathcote and Charles G. Tebbutt, *Skating, Figure Skating, Curling, Etc.* (1892); John J. Nutt, *Newburgh: Her Institutions, Industries and Leading Citizens* (1891); J. Van Buttingha Wichers, *Schaatsenrijden* (1888).

Paul J. DeLoca

IRISH. It remains a mystery why the relationship between sport and the Irish American people has received such scant attention in the literature, while ethnic groups that are smaller and seemingly less significant to sports have been placed on a veritable American athletic pedestal by scholars and chroniclers alike. One might speculate that the Gaelic denizens' prominent role in the construction of America's political, labor, temperance, and religious traditions of the nineteenth century has diminished the importance of their seemingly trivial athletic pursuits. Or perhaps it was the oftnoted relationship drawn between Irish American notoriety in the professional sports (particularly prizefighting) arena and perpetuating the stereotype of the illiterate, drunken, brawling, male Irish buffoon that convinced observers (both middle-class "lace curtain" Irish Americans and others) to generally ignore their athletic accomplishments. Nevertheless, such sporting personalities as Casey, Comiskey, Connolly, Corbett, Flanagan, Kelly, O'Leary, McGrath, McGillicuddy, Morrissey, O'Reilly, Ryan, and Sullivan together with community-based, college, and professional teams bearing such names as Celtics, Emeralds, Fenians, Irish, Hibernians, and Shamrocks clearly attest to the centrality of this nation's Irish athletic heritage and will, forever, be assured their place in the annals of American sport. Indeed, one need only read the Irish American press of today and yesteryear to recognize the central role that sport has played and continues to play in the early assimilation of Irish immigrants into the nineteenth-century American mainstream, their social amelioration, and the continued preservation of Irish native culture and identity throughout America's Gaelic enclaves.

It is claimed that the first Irishman stepped ashore in the New World in 1492. During the past 500 years millions of Erin's sons and daughters have crossed the Atlantic in search of personal and religious freedom and economic opportunity. Throughout the colonial period the majority of Irish immigrants were Protestant merchants who found much in common with other settlers. However, as Ireland's small farm economy found itself unable to sustain the nation's population growth during the first half of the nineteenth century and driven further by English landlords and a series of famines, a massive Gaelic wave of mostly poor, illiterate, rural Catholics began to arrive on the quays of America's northeastern seaports. Accounting for about half of the total number of immigrants to America during the nineteenth century, Irish Americans, finding their geographical mobility limited by poverty, frequently clustered in inner-city enclaves where they found employment as longshoremen, factory workers, and domestics. Later, with westward expansion, Irishmen joined the ranks of canal and railroad workers, leading to the establishment of Irish American communities across the country. Today, one in five Americans claims Irish ancestry.

Facing poverty, ill health, and anti-Irish bigotry, these immigrants, generally speaking, achieved quite remarkable success. They were instrumental in transforming the Roman Catholic Church from a small, often despised sect to the largest organized religion in America. They were active in establishing and organizing the American labor movement and in providing public services for the emerging industrial city (including police forces and fire companies), and they led democratic inroads into American urban politics. Above all, Irish immigrants paved the way for more ready acceptance of later nineteenth- and early twentieth-century immigrants to the New World. Yet all this was accomplished with a certain degree of resentment commonly directed at the Irish immigrants' innate clannishness. Their eagerness to establish fraternal benevolent organizations (the earliest of which was the Charitable Irish Society of Boston, 1737), immigrant aid societies (such as the Irish Emigrant Society of New York, 1841), socioreligious and temperance groups, and political groups (such as the Fenian Brotherhood, 1858, and the Clan Na Gael, 1867), along with their desire to proudly display their Gaelic allegiance on St. Patrick's Day (through parades first held in Boston, 1737, and New York City, 1762) frequently rekindled past animosities in the minds of Anglo-American xenophobes and challenged the notion of an American "melting pot."

Sport, being part and parcel of the immigrants' cultural baggage, first found its place at the assemblies of a rapidly multiplying number of benevolent, cultural, militia, political, and religious associations in America throughout the second half of the nineteenth century. Most often billed as the "Irish National Games," members competed in footraces, hurdling, and jumping events as well as throwing the light and heavy stones, boat races, and target shoots. By 1871, members of the Clan Na Gael Association of New York were joined at their second annual picnic by representatives from other cities as the native sports of Gaelic football and hurling were included on the program. In 1871 a reporter for the *Irish World* explained: "The object of these associations is not dissimilar to that of the German Turnverein. It aims at the physical, social, and intellectual elevation of the Irish in America. It promotes a love of literature and social life in its clubrooms and in its gymnastic exercises it helps develop the Irish muscle." By 1878 this event was attracting more than 13,000 participants.

It would not be long before a host of Irish American athletic clubs would spring up supporting both native (Gaelic) and domestic (American) sports. Irish American militia groups had long sponsored shooting teams. From the Irish Dragoons (of New York), to the Hibernian Rifles (San Francisco), League of St. Patrick (San Francisco), Green Isle (New York), Shamrock (New York), and Celtic (New York) clubs, immigrants flocked to join, for, as the *Irish World* stated in 1897, "[i]n Ireland the people are denied by law the right to bear arms; [whereas] in the United States it is deemed a patriotic duty in citizens to enroll themselves in military organizations." Once more and despite this twist of democratic rhetoric, the formation of such clubs prompted words of consternation from Americans who continued to condemn foreign-born militia groups for fostering divided loyalties.

Likewise, traditional Gaelic sports began to witness an increase in popularity. In 1881 a reporter for the *Boston Pilot* noted, "A large number of the Irish people in Boston are becoming interested in the exhibition of the games and pastimes of their ancestors." Considered the most ancient of Irish sports, hurling* ("Caman" in Celtic and "Iomain" in Gaelic) is a stick-and-ball game most closely resembling lacrosse. The earliest reference to organized hurling in the United States cites the formation of a club in San Francisco in 1853. It was another four years before the Irish Hurling and Football Club was formed in New York City. During the next thirty years the New York, Emmet, Wolfe Tone, Brooklyn, Geraldine, and Men of Ireland teams promoted the game in New York, while, following the sport's first formal introduction to New England by the Irish Athletic Club of Boston in 1879, the Boston and Shamrock hurling clubs remained the most prominent organizations. In 1888, the Gaelic Athletic Association's* tour of North America (which brought more than fifty Irish athletes to the United States for the purpose of competing in hurling and track-and-field events held in New York, Boston, Philadelphia, Newark, and Paterson, New Jersey, Providence, Rhode Island, and Lowell, Massachusetts) provided an impetus to the sport's growth and popularity. One correspondent later noted with some degree of optimism: "Since the Gaelic Invasion of America . . . hurling has taken a firm root on American soil, and the present series of games at the magnificent grounds at Celtic Park for the James R. Keane Cup are certain to arouse an amount of interest and enthusiasm, and to make the Irish national pastime extremely popular with the exiled Gaels of Greater New York."

Gaelic football* did not appear to share the same widespread following that hurling claimed. The earliest account of an organized team appeared in New Orleans in 1859, where the game was first promoted by Irish fire companies and later by clubs bearing such nationalistic appellations as Erin Go Bragh and Faugh a Ballagh. In Philadelphia the leading clubs were the Red Branch Knights and the Irish Nationalists, while San Francisco boasted the Emmets, Parnells, and Geraldines. By 1899 the Dunn Trophy was donated to the Greater New York Irish-American Athletic Association (GNYIAAA) "intended for the encouragement of the Gaelic football game and amateur sports for which Ireland was noted."

Evidence demonstrates that sport clearly played a significant role in the preservation of culture and promotion of Irish identity within immigrant communities. The first Gaelic Athletic Association in America was organized in
Chicago in 1890. Three years later the association claimed fifteen clubs (including ten football teams and five hurling teams) with a membership of 2,000.
In Boston a group of Irish Americans actively sought to organize a Gaelic
Athletic Union in 1895. According to the *Boston Journal*, the new association
was aimed at "those interested in the revival of Irish sports." Control of Gaelic
football and hurling in New York later shifted from the Irish-American Athletic
Association to the Irish Counties Athletic Union, formed in 1904. Today, both
native sports are practiced by Irish American clubs across the United States; the
most active location is Gaelic Park in the Bronx, New York. Yet the manner in
which sport was used to reinforce cultural identity represents but one part of
the story.

Irish immigrants were all too well aware of the impact that a modern, organized sporting bureaucracy could have on their traditional native pursuits. Indeed, the dominant values and practices of the Amateur Athletic Association of
England had become the single most important determinant in the establishment
of the Dublin-based Gaelic Athletic Association in 1884 by Michael Cusack and
Maurice Davin. Nevertheless, an ocean apart, Irish Americans early recognized
the promise that participation in the popular sports of their new home might
bring in regard to more ready acceptance and even socioeconomic advancement.

It has long been argued that, throughout history, pugilism has found its
greatest appeal among oppressed minorities, promising a rapid escape from poverty and discrimination. This is certainly true in the case of the nineteenth-
century Irish American. The names of Sam O'Rourke, Cornelius Horrigan, John
C. "Benecia Boy" Heenan, James "Yankee" Sullivan, and John Morrissey* fill
the antebellum annals of the American ring. Toward the end of the nineteenth
century, Paddy Ryan, Jake Kilrain, John L. Sullivan,* and "Gentleman Jim"
Corbett* each provided testimony to the Gaels' continued affinity for the sport.
Yet, it should be noted that support for the Irish Americans' avidity for the ring
was far from unanimous. As early as 1871 the *Irish World* reminded its readers,
"The Irish, from their connection with the English, have unfortunately acquired
some of the barbarous habits and customs of the Saxons, as they did their
language. But Irishmen even in the prize ring are not wholly lost to honor. The
genuine Celt fights not for money, but for fame—such poor fame as it is—and
he could never forget his manhood so far as to make himself, like the Saxon
villain, a bull-terrier gladiator for the sport of a blackleg nobility." To set the
blame on English soil was not to be unexpected, but still questions surrounding
the moral virtue and worthwhile qualities of prizefighting could not be ignored.
As J. C. Furnas has pointed out, "The rugged young men who survived [bare-
knuckle fights] did their share to give the Irish a bad name by being usually
either Irish or of second generation Irish stock."

Pedestrianism also offered poor Irish immigrants the opportunity to reap sizable financial rewards. While Edward Payson Weston is most often remembered as America's nineteenth-century "Champion Pedestrian of the World," the comparable achievements of Daniel O'Leary have frequently gone unnoticed. His professional career commenced with the defeat of Weston in a 200-mile race in 1874. He went on to beat Weston in a six-day walking event the following year and in a six-day rematch in London in 1877. In 1878 he became the first winner of the Astley Belt, the initial competition for which was described by a reporter in the *Irish World* as ". . . being an international match, the honor of old England was at stake and a score of the very best legs in Britain were put on the track to keep the belt from getting into the hands of a Yankee and an Irishman. Parliament had officially adjourned to derive pleasure from the spectacle and give cheer to the noble Britons." In 1879 he established the O'Leary Belt Race for the Championship of America.

Although the professional rowing fraternity of the northeast wherrymen was a world apart from the crew life of America's most prestigious universities, it appears that professional rowing matches were afforded some degree of legitimacy by mainstream American society. Irish Americans took to rowing with great vigor, forming clubs such as the Maid of Erin, Young Men's Catholic Lyceum, St. Mary's Temperance Society, and St. James Young Men's Catholic Total Abstinence in Boston and similarly throughout most cities of the northeastern states. Challenges frequently appeared in the Irish American press of the day with stakes set at anywhere between $250 and $1,000 a side and crowds of 30,000 or more in attendance. Following the Saratoga Regatta of 1874 the *Irish World* published a story entitled "Irish American Muscle in the Ascendant," in which the reporter concluded: "And thus did Irish-American muscle bear off the palm in every contest of this the most important day of the regatta. This result should give an impetus to athletic organization among our men. Of all healthful exercises, rowing is most to be encouraged, and there is not a more legitimate sport than boat-racing."

Rowing also provided a glimpse at the role played by sport in the process of cultural conflict and accommodation. The annual encounter between the *Maid of Erin* and *Harvard* crews mirrored the fundamental cleavage between Yankee Puritans and Irish Catholics in Boston. Yet perhaps such contests served as a cathartic outlet. The words of a ballad written by the Reverend William R. Huntingdon of the Harvard class of 1859 ("Songs of the Harvard versus Fort Hill Boy Rowing Match of 1858," *Harvard Magazine*, July 1858), offers disguised satisfaction at his boat's victory over the Irish-crewed *Fort Hill Boy*. Mocking all that was Irish—the accent, the dialect, the self-confidence—the writer goes on to question the trustworthiness of the losing crew whose payment of bets was dependent upon victory.

By 1870 baseball had emerged as America's "national pastime," and Irishmen flocked in droves to the diamond. Irish teams with Gaelic names sprang up across the country. It was, however, the professional players who won the baseball laurels for the Irish American. Carl Wittke suggested: "The Irish adopted the national pastime of baseball with greater immediate success than any other immigrant group. . . . The reputation of Irish ballplayers was so great that others frequently took Irish names to help them in their baseball careers." By 1872 a correspondent for *The Sporting News* claimed that one-third of major league players were of Irish extraction. By the turn of the century another observer noted, "All the prominent clubs of last year were captained by Irish Americans," including Kelly (Brooklyn), Delehanty (Philadelphia), Collins (Boston), Donovan (St. Louis), Doyle (Chicago), Gleason (Detroit), McGraw (Baltimore), and Duffy (Milwaukee). Today, a stroll through the Baseball Hall of Fame in Cooperstown, New York, reminds us of the deep presence and significant contribution made by Irish professional baseball players. Foremost of the Gaelic American ballplayers was Michael Joseph Kelly,* the son of an Irish immigrant paper maker from Troy, New York. Making his debut with the Olympic Club of Paterson, New Jersey, in 1877, he went on to record a superlative professional career with the Buckeye Club of Columbus, Ohio, the Cincinnati Red Stockings, and the Chicago White Stockings. His subsequent "sale" to the Boston Red Stockings in 1887 was unprecedented in the sport and brought the "Ten Thousand Dollar Beauty" immediate renown.

Although Irish American interest in track and field might be viewed as a logical extension of their deep-held affinity for pedestrianism, the two sports possessed separate and unique characteristics. Footraces, hurdling, jumping, and throwing events (which had long been part of native celebrations in rural Ireland) were soon included in Gaelic events in America. As James Brendan Connolly* (the first modern Olympic victor) recalled: "There was a summertime living in those days for professional athletes. Caledonian and Hibernian organizations . . . were keeping alive the athletic customs of their forbears [*sic*] in Scotland and Ireland. Field days were held regularly for money prizes, and dated to make a workable circuit for the athletes." Yet the most significant contribution of Irish Americans to the sport was reserved for the highly respected, organized, and amateur track-and-field competitions that emerged in the final decade of the nineteenth century. Due in large part to the exclusionary policies and practices of the New York Athletic Club (opened in 1868 and frequented by Astors, Belmonts, Roosevelts, Vanderbilts, and others of New York Knickerbocker society) and the Boston Athletic Association (a favored haunt of those of Brahmin pedigree), Irish Athletic Clubs were formed in both cities during 1879. Later changing their names to Irish-American Athletic Clubs* (the New York club's emblem was a green fist set against a background of green shamrock inserts traversed by a diagonal band of red, white, and blue), they became powerful forces in international track and field. Beginning with the first modern Olympic Games in Athens in 1896, Irish Americans were to dominate international track-and-field competition for more than twenty years with Connolly, Sweeney, Kilpatrick, Cregan, Flanagan, Mitchell, McGrath, McDonald, and Ryan (the latter five behemoths better known as the "Irish Whales"*) becoming household names within worldwide athletic circles.

Clearly, sport has represented a most significant chapter in the lives of Irish Americans during the past century and one-half, as Gaelic denizens and their descendants secured a place in sport history, first, by embracing the popular pursuits of the American athletic arena and, second, through contributing to a Gaelic revival, in part accomplished through the practice and promotion of indigenous games. Today the tradition continues as Gaelic names remain etched in the corridors of the nation's sporting halls of fame, and their legacy is remembered in the image of Notre Dame's Fighting Irish and the Boston Celtics.

SELECTED BIBLIOGRAPHY: Arthur Daley, "The American Irish in Sports," *The Recorder* 34 (1973): 43–100; Marcus de Burca, *Michael Cusack and the GAA* (1989); Michael Funchion, ed., *The Group Irish-American: Irish American Voluntary Organizations* (1983); Michael T. Isenberg, *John L. Sullivan and His America* (1988); W. F. Mandle, *The Gaelic Athletic Association and Irish Nationalist Politics, 1884–1924* (1987); John Boyle O'Reilly, *The Ethics of Boxing and Manly Sports* (1888); Steven A. Riess, *City Games: The Evolution of American Urban Society and the Rise of Sports* (1989); Steven A. Riess, "Race and Ethnicity in American Baseball, 1900–1919," *Journal of Ethnic Studies* 4, No. 4 (Winter 1977): 39–55; William V. Shannon, *The American Irish* (1963); Ralph Wilcox, "The Shamrock and the Eagle: Irish-Americans and Sport in the Nineteenth Century," in George Eisen and David Wiggins, eds., *Ethnicity and Sport in North American History and Culture* (1994), 55–74; Carl Wittke, *The Irish in America* (1956).

Ralph C. Wilcox

IRISH-AMERICAN ATHLETIC CLUB. An Irish-American Athletic Club (IAAC), founded in Manhattan in 1879, held track meets and social events for several years before disappearing from public view. Two of its members won national distance-running titles in 1879 and 1880. The modern Winged Fist club, with Patrick J. Conway as founding president, was granted a charter as the Greater New York Irish Athletic Association (GNYIAA) on 7 October 1897. Its mission, according to Conway, "was to develop athletics among the Irish race and promote Gaelic sports, such as football and hurling." For $9,000 the founders purchased land in Laurel Hill, an isolated section of Queens adjoining Long Island City. With an additional $48,000 the GNYIAA built Celtic Park as its field.

Although the GNYIAA rented Celtic Park to groups for a variety of popular events, including Gaelic sports, its focus was on track and field. Swedish-born Ernie Hjertberg became coach and began building it into a national track power, rivaling the established athletic clubs. John Flanagan won the club's first individual national title in the hammer throw in 1901. The County Limerick native revolutionized the event; other weightmen, the so-called Irish Whales,* joined him. Many worked for New York City's Police Department. But Hjertberg also recruited outstanding non-Irish runners, including Jews. The club's breakthrough came in 1904, when it defeated the rival New York Athletic Club for the national outdoor title. At that summer's Olympic Games, GNYIAA athletes won four gold medals: Flanagan in the hammer throw, Martin Sheridan in the discus throw, and Meyer Prinstein* in the long and triple jumps. In 1906 the club, now renamed the IAAC, began a string of eight successive team victories at the outdoor nationals (with the exception of 1909, when it didn't enter).

In 1909 Scottish-born Lawson Robertson, age twenty-five, an IAAC sprinter-jumper, was appointed team coach. His tenure marked the club's heyday. With wit, gaiety, and kindness he molded a collection of temperamental and wild stars into one of the great teams in track history. They formed the core of the winning U.S. team at the 1912 Stockholm Olympics and continued to set world records thereafter. "Robby" expected versatility in his athletes; but as was common in that era, his approach to training was casual. His world record holders included the newer generation of Whales (Pat McDonald, Matt McGrath, and Pat Ryan) and "Peerless Mel" Sheppard and Abel Kiviat,* as well as the Italian Emilio Lunghi in the middle distances; the distance runner Hannes Kolehmainen, the first Flying Finn; the triple jumper Dan Ahearn; and many others. The team dominated the outdoor nationals of 1911–14. After finishing second in 1915 and again winning the team tide in 1916, the IAAC faded. Robertson left for the University of Pennsylvania in 1916; then the club stopped competing during World War I. An unsuccessful postwar reorganization effort, combined with friction with the new Gaelic Athletic Association* about events at Celtic Park, doomed the club in the 1920s. It was formally dissolved in 1930, and Celtic Park was sold to the City and Suburban Homes Company for $500,000. The Celtic Park Apartments were built on the site in 1931.

In its brief lifetime during track's watershed era, the IAAC was the seedbed of enduring developments. Providing opportunity for elite athletes of immigrant and working-class backgrounds, it helped to break the hold of the wealthy on amateur sport. It trained many for victory in the Olympic Games. From its ranks were recruited the first professional coaches for national track teams abroad, as well as for U.S. Olympic teams.

SELECTED BIBLIOGRAPHY: "Athletics on Sunday," *New York Tribune*, 19 June 1910; "Paid $9,000 in 1897 for Celtic Park," *New York Times*, 28 June 1931; Melvin W. Sheppard, "Spiked Shoes and Cinder Paths: An Athlete's Story," *Sport Story Magazine* (1924), Part I-XI; Earl Eby, "There Was but One Robby . . . ," *Franklin Field Illustrated* (1953); Bill Mallon and Ian Buchanan, *The United States' National Championships in Track and Field Athletics, 1876–1985* (1986).

Alan S. Katchen

IRISH WHALES. During the late 1800s and early 1900s a group of Irish American athletes known as the "Irish Whales" dominated the hammer throw event in national and international track-and-field meets. The throwing of the hammer is an ancient Celtic sporting event whose origins have been traced to the Tailteann Games held in Tara, Ireland, from 2000 B.C. to A.D. 1169. The Tailteann Games were inaugurated as a tribute to honor the beloved Queen Tailte. King Lughaidh summoned "all the men of Eire" to partake in the amiable competition between rival Celtic tribes on the royal plains of County Meath. Competitors would propel a stone affixed to a handle for the longest distance. Eventually, the sledgehammer would be the accepted instrument used in such competitions. Irish folklore attributes the survival of the hammer throw to the Irish migrant workers shipped from Ireland to England for iron mining. The men were chosen specifically for their large physique needed for strenuous labor. The miners worked long hours under harsh conditions. During their rest time they used sledgehammers provided by their employers to engage in impromptu contests. Through these hammer throws, the Irish miners clung to their Celtic heritage, believing that their performance on the field reflected their prowess in the mines.

The English universities of Oxford and Cambridge incorporated the hammer throw into their athletic programs on 5 March 1864. William Curtis of the New York Athletic Club introduced the hammer throw in the United States and became the first American champion in that event in 1876. The Irish Whales— John J. Flanagan, Matthew J. McGrath, and Patrick J. Ryan—were the most celebrated hammer throwers during its golden age, which dated from the 1890s to the 1920s. George Underwood, a sports reporter for a New York daily, coined the phrase "Irish Whales" during the 1908 Olympics in describing the athletes' gargantuan physiques.

Flanagan, McGrath, and Ryan were all natives of Ireland who earned fame in the United States through their triumphs in a field event that was deeply embedded in Celtic tradition. Flanagan, born in 1873 in County Limerick, is revered as the "father" of the modern hammer throw both for his remarkable athletic achievements and also for his innovations in hammer-throwing technique and equipment design. After winning national titles in Ireland and England, he migrated to the United States in 1896, joining both the New York City Police Department and also the elite New York Athletic Club. In addition to winning three consecutive Olympic gold medals (1900, 1904, and 1908), he earned nine national championships and seven other titles in the United States. He also set thirteen world records. McGrath was born in County Tipperary in 1878, journeyed to New York City in 1897, and became a dedicated member of the police force. During his long athletic career, which spanned 1902–35, he acquired seven American titles, broke two world records, and competed in an unprecedented five Olympic Games. He captured the silver medal in 1908, set a world mark in 1911, and carried off the gold medal in 1912 at Stockholm, setting a new Olympic record. Ryan was born in 1887 in County Limerick, began competing in 1902 in Ireland, and came to New York City in 1910. Unlike Flanagan and McGrath, Ryan was not employed in the New York City Police Department but rather worked as a construction laborer. He set a new world record in 1913 (which stood for an unprecedented twenty-five years) and won a gold medal at the 1920 Olympic Games in Antwerp.

The stereotype of the "Irish cop" derives in part from the mythlike characters of the Irish Whales. While Flanagan and McGrath gave their time and energies to serve on the New York City police force, all of the Irish Whales used their talent to elevate their fellow Irishmen. The Irish press heralded their achievements, and Irishmen living in the slums made the weekly pilgrimages uptown to cheer on their heroic throwers.

SELECTED BIBLIOGRAPHY: Bob Considine and Fred G. Jarvis, *A Portrait of the New York Athletic Club* (1969); Ken Doherty, *Track and Field Omnibook* (1976); Bill Mallon and Ian Buchanan, *Quest for Gold: The Encyclopedia of American Olympians* (1984); T. H. Nally, *The Aonac Tailteann and the Tailteann Games: Their Origins, History and Ancient Associations* (1922); Cordner Nelson, *Track and Field: The Great Ones* (1970).

Margaret Mary Hennessey

IROQUOIS NATIONALS LACROSSE CLUB. Organized in 1983 by representatives of the Six Nations that constitute the Iroquois confederation (Haudenosaunee), this club was the first all-Indian sports team to achieve full national recognition by other countries. Its principal founders were Oren Lyons,* a faithkeeper of the Onondaga Council and a former Syracuse University player, and Rick Hill and Wes Patterson from the Tuscarora. Originally launched to compete in a tournament in Baltimore, the club's goal was to gain official recognition from the non-Indian lacrosse community and a berth in lacrosse's World Cup games. The creation of the Iroquois Nationals in part reflected the growth of Indian activism during the 1970s and 1980s, but it also marked a continuation of the time-honored Native American tradition of assembling talented teams for major games.

The Iroquois Nationals club faced many financial and political hurdles during its formative years. Lyons acted as the team's main coach and spokesperson, and he and his associates met resistance from corporations in their campaigns to raise funds for uniforms, equipment, travel, and other expenses. Club officers recruited the premier Iroquois players from high school and colleges, but they had to journey long distances for practice sessions. In the fall of 1985 they toured England, winning three of five games and playing the English national team to a tie. In 1986 they played a match against the Australian national team.

By 1990 the club had finally gained recognition from the International Lacrosse Federation, and the players were able to travel to Perth, Australia, for the World Cup competition using Haudenosaunee passports. A high point of that tournament was the playing of a traditional Indian Flag Song and the raising of a purple flag with Indian insignia to symbolize Iroquois sovereignty. But the Australia experience was not entirely positive, because the Iroquois athletes did encounter some resistance from the U.S. team. Several of the American players resented the Iroquois presence in the World Cup and disliked their style of play. Kent Lyons, an Onondaga, recalled subtle racial slurs directed against the Iroquois team, prompted in part by their use of Tuscarora-made wooden sticks. Although the Iroquois squad was unable to win a match in Australia, the players viewed their expedition as a successful symbolic victory because of their acceptance by the International Lacrosse Federation. The club strengthened its position in the lacrosse community by participating in the 1994 World Cup in England. The achievements of the Iroquois Nationals also led to the creation of a Junior Nationals squad, composed mostly of Indian high school students. In the 1998 International Lacrosse Federation's World Championship at Baltimore the Iroquois Nationals finished fourth, behind the United States, Canada, and Australia.

SELECTED BIBLIOGRAPHY: Doug George-Kanentiio, "The Iroquois Nationals: Creating a Sports Revolution for American Indians," *Akwesasne Notes* 1, No. 2 (1969): 94–95; Thomas Vennum, Jr., *American Indian Lacrosse: Little Brother of War* (1994).

George B. Kirsch

ITALIANS. They are images that we have all seen, read about, and talked about: quarterback Joe Montana being swarmed by a Dallas Cowboy onrush and yet somehow finding Dwight Clark in the back of the end zone with what football historians have termed "the Catch"; Joe DiMaggio,* the Yankee Clipper and fifty-six consecutive-game-hitting-streak "phenom," gripping Marilyn Monroe as gracefully as any bat; pitcher Ralph Branca giving up the shot-heard-round-the-world to Bobby Thompson as the Giants win the Pennant; and believing in miracles as Mike Eruzione captains the 1980 Olympic Hockey Team to a gold medal. These are the moments that have become an indelible part of our national culture and lexicon. When we think of Montana, DiMaggio, Branca, and Eruzione, we think of them not as Italian Americans but simply as Americans—which is indicative of both just how fully Italian Americans have assimilated themselves into the mainstream and how extraordinary their influence has been on our sporting lives.

Indeed, their influence has been extraordinary, and yet in typically Italian American fashion, it has come quietly—so quietly, in fact, that we often take the results for granted, as if they had always existed. Yet, where would the success of today's college basketball tournament be without the incredible upsets of coach Jim Valvano's* North Carolina State team over Houston in the 1983 championship game or coach Rollie Massimino's Villanova quintet over Georgetown in the 1985 championship game? How would Muhammad Ali* have captured the nation's imagination without the support and sagacity of his trainer, Angelo Dundee? How colorless would our language be without the additions of baseball's Yogi Berra*?

What would become of our sporting life if Italian Americans had never participated? Green Bay would probably not have a football franchise today, if coach Vince Lombardi* hadn't turned it into "Title Town" with five championships in the 1960s. The national Olympic program for gymnastics would never have achieved its current success, without "only you, Mary Lou" Retton catapulting to a perfect ten at the 1984 Summer Games. Baseball legend George Ruth* would have gone without a nickname, had not his teammate Ping Bodie

(Francesco Pezzolo) dubbed him the "Bambino," otherwise known as the "Babe."

The Italian immigrants who came at the turn of this century naturally brought with them a love of their native pastimes, chief among them soccer, bocce, cycling, and cards. Recreation normally came on Sundays and could be found at either of two places—a local club, the Unione Sportiva Italiana in Manhattan being one of the first organized; or more prevalently, a "neighborhood house," a public facility designed to help assimilate the immigrants. Assimilate they did, quickly adopting the national pastime of baseball as their own.

The first-known Italian American in professional baseball was Louis Pisano (who went by the name of Buttercup Dickerson), a left fielder on the 1878 Cincinnati Red Stockings. The first major league star was Tony Lazzeri,* second baseman for the powerhouse 1927 Yankees. Lazzeri fought a great deal of prejudice: he was known as the "push 'em up wop" because of his resiliency after getting hit by so many pitches. Throughout this century, there have been countless Italian American ballplayers: big (like Ernie Lombardi*) and small (like Phil "Scooter" Rizzuto*), inspiring (like Roy Campanella,* who was also half black) and enigmatic (like Billy Martin), and some who even turned into fine managers (like Tommy Lasorda).

But then, above all, sails the Yankee Clipper. He is not just a great player from the 1940s; he is, unabashedly, a hero. Heroes have to be aptly named, and his has an alliteration and rhyming cadence that conjure up that graceful swing— Joltin' Joe DiMaggio. Baseball heroes need legendary statistics, and his stand among the greatest of all time: a lifetime batting average of .325; voted the American League's Most Valuable Player three times (1939, 1941, 1947); carried his team to ten World Series, winning all but one; played in eleven All-Star Games. He probably could have accomplished even more, had he not lost three years to service in World War II. Heroes need defining moments. DiMaggio's came in 1941, when he waged onward with a hit in fifty-six consecutive games—a record that has never been approached since, let alone surpassed. Heroes also need adversaries, by which to measure their greatness. DiMaggio found his Achilles in the Boston Red Sox's reluctant warrior Ted Williams. Heroes must have a sense of magnanimity. DiMaggio displayed his through the archetypal Italian American image, the family. Never did he flash a bigger smile then when standing with his brothers, Dom and Vince, themselves professional ballplayers. As a king needs a kingdom, so, too, do heroes. DiMaggio was never lacking for fans, including legions of Italian Americans throughout the country. In fact, many of today's prominent Italian American sports journalists and commentators trace their love of sports back to their fathers cheering on DiMaggio. In the end, heroes do not die, for their legends are continually retold, sealing a permanent mark upon our national conscience. DiMaggio has had not just one but two hit songs written about him. The first came in 1941, as Les Brown's band celebrated DiMaggio's hit streak: "From coast to coast that's all you'll hear of Joe the one-man show. He's glorified the horsehide steer, Joltin' Joe DiMaggio. Joe, Joe DiMaggio, we want you on our side." The second came in 1968—seventeen years after DiMaggio retired—as songwriter Paul Simon tried to describe shattered innocence. In one simple phrase, Simon captured just what the Yankee Clipper means to America: "Where have you gone Joe DiMaggio? A nation turns its lonely eyes to you."

One year after DiMaggio retired, an Italian American by the name of Rocky Marciano* (Rocco Marchegiano) would win the world heavyweight championship. He would hold the title until 1956, retiring a perfect 49–0, the only heavyweight champion never to lose a professional bout. Like most Italian Americans, Marciano was small—just 5'11" and 185 pounds. He didn't have a great deal of speed or grace. Fighters like Jersey Joe Wolcott and Archie Moore pounded on Marciano, but they couldn't beat him. He was too strong and tough, the by-product of his dedication to training. Marciano could also punch, and his punches were devastating. He won forty-three of his forty-nine fights by knockouts.

One can't help think of Marciano without thinking of Sylvester Stallone's film character in the "Rocky" series. While not directly based on Marciano, the character was no doubt inspired by him. Although many Italian American boxers have been nicknamed "Rocky," including noted champion Rocky Graziano* (Rocco Barbella), Marciano transformed the nickname into a persona. Marciano was not just called "Rocky"; he was a rock. He might not have had incredible skills, but he had incredible power. No matter who the opponent was, the rock of that power would not be broken. So, in writing a script about an underdog Italian American boxer whose only assets are strength and courage, how could Stallone choose any other name besides "Rocky"? Through Marciano's legacy and through the success of the movie series, "Rocky" now stands with only "Ali" as the American archetypal names for boxing.

Though baseball and boxing rank high, Italian Americans have made their greatest collective contribution to professional football. The 1958 championship game is considered to be one of the most important in National Football League history, as it consummated the relationship between football and television viewers. Running back Alan "the Horse" Ameche provided the game's most vivid image, as he rumbled forward into the end zone and straight on to America's living room, giving Baltimore an overtime victory against New York.

Coach Vince Lombardi and Green Bay dominated the 1960s, punctuated with victories in the first two Super Bowls. Sportswriters have argued whether Lombardi actually said, "Winning isn't everything; it's the only thing." It doesn't matter whether Lombardi said it or not (in fact, he did). Our national lexicon attributes it to him, because it is so easy for us to imagine his saying it. The aura of Lombardi wasn't that of a coach, but a general. He didn't coax his players; he commanded them. He didn't just have an iron-clad commitment to winning; he refused to fail. Perhaps lesser-known words describe his spirit best:

"Any man's finest hour is when he has worked his heart out in a good cause and lies exhausted on the field of battle victorious." Indicative of Lombardi's legacy, the Super Bowl trophy is now named in his honor.

The 1970s belonged to Pittsburgh. Their team had a ferocious defense, winning four Super Bowls. But the image most remembered came from one miraculous play in a 1972 playoff game against Oakland. In the game's final seconds, Pittsburgh running back Franco Harris (the real workhorse of that great team) scooped up a deflected pass and rushed into the end zone for the winning score. Harris' "Immaculate Reception" gave Pittsburgh its first playoff victory in franchise history but, more importantly, propelled the team toward its championship years.

In 1977 the DiBartolo family acquired the San Francisco 49ers. Then a league also-ran, the 49ers would become a powerhouse in the 1980s and 1990s, winning five Super Bowls. Among its many offensive weapons, the 49ers featured quarterback Joe Montana. A three-time Super Bowl and two-time league Most Valuable Player, Joe Cool is remembered not for the many dominating victories but rather for the way, time and again, he would lead his team to a fourth-quarter comeback, with his short timing passes smartly dissecting the opponent's "prevent" defense.

Italian Americans have championed college football as well. Six have won the Heisman Trophy, sport's most famous prize given to the best college football player: Angelo Bertelli (Notre Dame, 1943), Alan Ameche (Wisconsin, 1954), Joe Bellino (Navy, 1960), John Cappelletti (Penn State, 1973), Vinny Testaverde (Miami, 1986), and Gino Torretta (Miami, 1992).

No Italian American, however, has had more success in college football than Penn State's head coach Joe Paterno.* He has won more games than any other active coach in division I-A; he has captured the national championship twice and had an unbeaten team voted out of the championship four other times; his teams have gone undefeated for the regular season a record seven times; and he has won every major bowl. But beyond his record of compiling football victories, Paterno is a success because he has won while stressing academics, graduating his players, and preparing them for their lives ahead. Since he first accepted an assistant coaching position in 1950, he has in many ways been Penn State. Typical of his involvement with the university, he led the fund-raising efforts for a new campus library—the same library that the trustees decided should bear his name.

Paterno embodies an Italian American trait rarely portrayed in the media: intelligence. Paul Tagliabue,* the current commissioner of the National Football League (NFL), was previously a very successful attorney. In fact, in defending the NFL, he limited an antitrust lawsuit brought by the U.S. Football League to a mere three dollars in damages.

In addition, before serving as commissioner of major league baseball, Bart Giamatti* was a Renaissance scholar, author, professor, and president of Yale University. Giamatti was genuinely a fan's commissioner, for he was baseball's number one fan. Although he inherited several crises upon taking office, his tenure was defined by an overwhelming desire to protect the interests of the average gamegoing family. His untimely death deprived baseball of a moral vision far beyond the context of owners, players, and skyrocketing salaries. It is no coincidence that within a few years of his death, baseball had fallen into total chaos, with even the World Series canceled.

Besides baseball, boxing, and football, Italian Americans have excelled in every other aspect of our sports and games. Mario Andretti,* a name synonymous with auto racing, is the only driver ever to win the sport's three major events: the Daytona 500 stock car (1967), the Indianapolis 500 (1969), and the Grand Prix (1978). In 1940, John Mariucci, with the Chicago Blackhawks, became the first American to play in the National Hockey League; Mariucci would later be inducted into the sport's Hall of Fame in 1973. Swimmer Matt Biondi set several world records and earned eleven career Olympic medals, including eight gold. Eddie Arcaro* jockeyed 4,779 horses into the winner's circle in thoroughbred racing. Golf has enjoyed the prowess of Gene Sarazen* (Eugene Saraceni) and Ken Venturi; figure skating has seen the triumphs of Brian Boitano and Linda Fratianne; wrestling has wrangled with Bruno Sanmartino and Antonio Rocco; and, in basketball, coach Lou Carnesecca* turned the men's program at St. John's University into a national power. Bowling has had many Italian American champions, including Jimmy Smith, the first inductee into the sport's Hall of Fame; Hank Marino, voted the greatest bowler in the first half of this century; and Johnny Petraglia, who in the 1970s became one of only two players to have ever won the Tournament of Champions title, the Professional Bowlers Association National Championship, the U.S. Open, and the World Open. Phil Ferrari became the first American-born player to win the U.S. bocce singles championship (1993), a title previously held by Italian nationals. In 1991, at the age of thirteen, Dean Ippolito became the youngest person ever to win the U.S. amateur chess championship, and Eric Greco is one of today's best young players in bridge.

No sport, however, has ever been so dominated by one individual as when Willie Mosconi* held a pool cue. Mosconi won the pocket billiards world championship fourteen times between 1941 and 1957 and set an amazing world record when he sank 526 consecutive balls—the equivalent of clearing thirty-five tables straight. His legendary battles with Minnesota Fats were frequently televised, but while Fats was more colorful than Mosconi, he was never his equal in ability. In fact, the film *The Hustler* was based loosely on the life of Fats; yet, when it was produced, Mosconi and not Fats served as the technical adviser, doubling for the actors to create all the trick shots. Typical of Italian American sportsmen, Mosconi was a very humble and simple man. He lived with his wife in the same house for more than thirty years. Like the rest of America, he kept his pool table in the basement, and it was only there that the rows of towering trophies gave testament to his life's work.

Italian Americans have also been sports inventors. In the area of physical fitness, Charles Atlas (Angelo Siciliano) created "Dynamic Tension," a strengthening program that turned ninety-seven-pound weaklings into strongmen the world over. Subscribers to the program included Joe DiMaggio and Rocky Marciano. In the 1940s, Frank Zamboni devised a tractor that would quickly produce a clean sheet of ice at his skating rink. Fifty years later, the Zamboni machine still efficiently swipes the ice as well as entertaining fans between periods at a hockey game. In addition, while serving as the longtime trainer for the Princeton University football team, Edward Zanfrini (along with team physician Dr. Harry McPhee) invented the neck "doughnut," a gadget attached to the shoulder pads that has protected many a player from pinched nerves in the neck and shoulder.

However, the most important innovations have come in basketball. Hank Luisetti* started the one-handed basketball shot while an All-American at Stanford University in 1938. Luisetti, a member of the Basketball Hall of Fame, was also the first collegiate player to score fifty points in a game. Moreover, Dan Biasone created the twenty-four-second shot clock. In the late 1940s, Biasone became the first Italian American to own a basketball franchise when he purchased the Syracuse Nationals.

Today, Italian Americans continue their prominence in sports. Baseball has stars like catcher Mike Piazza and manager Joe Torre; football has quarterback Dan Marino,* one of the most prolific passers in professional history. Rick Pitino, P. J. Carlissimo, Mike Fratello, and John Calipari have proven themselves able basketball coaches. Fred Couples is a top player on the golf tour, Jennifer Capriati on the tennis tour. Donna Lopiano serves as president of the Women's Sports Foundation. Jerry Colangelo, once the youngest general manager in the National Basketball League, now owns three sports franchises in Phoenix, Arizona—the Suns in basketball, the Diamondbacks in baseball, and the Coyotes in hockey.

SELECTED BIBLIOGRAPHY: Carmelo Bazzano, "The Italian-American Sporting Experience," in George Eisen and David K. Wiggins, eds., *Ethnicity and Sport in North American History and Culture* (1994), 103–116; Lawrence DiStasi, *The Big Book of Italian American Culture* (1990); Willie Mosconi, *Mosconi on Pocket Billiards* (1959); Michael O'Brien, *Vince: A Personal Biography of Vince Lombardi* (1987); Rick Reilly, "Sportsman of the Year/Not an Ordinary Joe," *Sports Illustrated*, (22–29 December 1986): 64–71; Everett M. Skehan, *Rocky Marciano: Biography of a First Son* (1977); See also the archives of the National Italian American Foundation, Washington, DC. For more information on this subject, contact George R. Randazzo, founder and president of the National Italian American Sports Hall of Fame, at 2625 North Clearbrook Drive, Arlington Heights, IL 60005; Anthony Valerio, comp., *Bart: A Life of A. Bartlett Giamatti, by Him and about Him* (1991); Richard Whittingham, *The DiMaggio Albums*, vols. 1 and 2 (1989).

Ciro C. Poppiti

IVAN, THOMAS NATHANIEL ("Tommy") (31 January 1911, Toronto, Ontario, Canada–24 June 1999, Lake Forest, IL). One of the National Hockey

League's (NHL) most respected men, Ivan coached the Detroit Red Wings (1947–54) and served as general manager of the Chicago Blackhawks (1954–77). During Ivan's tenure with the Red Wings the team won three Stanley Cups (1950, 1952, 1954) and six consecutive regular season championships. Ivan exhibited a quiet and dignified demeanor, providing a healthy contrast to fiery general manager Jack Adams. In 1954 Ivan sought a new challenge as general manager of the chronically weak Blackhawks. Through the implementation of an extensive farm system to develop prospects (a tactic learned under Jack Adams*) and the acquisition of key players in trades, Ivan guided the team first to respectability, then to dominance. His efforts culminated in a long-awaited Stanley Cup victory for the Hawks in 1961, their first since 1938. For the next decade the Hawks were perennial contenders and box office successes, making the Stanley Cup finals four times and playing to sold-out crowds in the raucous Chicago Stadium. In 1975 Ivan was enshrined in the Hockey Hall of Fame as a builder and received the Lester Patrick Award from the NHL in honor of his outstanding service to hockey in the United States. A naturalized U.S. citizen and a dedicated supporter of college hockey, he was one of the first NHL managers to regularly tap this source for talent. In addition, Ivan managed the American squad for the 1976 Canada Cup, organized the 1978–79 Olympic Hockey Festival, and served as chairman of the U.S. Hockey Hall of Fame.

SELECTED BIBLIOGRAPHY: Richard Bak, *Detroit Red Wings: The Illustrated History* (1997); Paul R. Greenland, *Hockey Chicago Style: The History of the Chicago Blackhawks* (1995); Gerald Pfeiffer, *The Chicago Blackhawks: A Sixty-Year History 1926–1986* (1986); Bob Verdi, "Dean of NHL General Managers," *The Hockey News* 25, No. 12 (24 December 1971): 3; Bob Verdi, "Ex-GM Ivan Looks Back on Good Hockey Life," *The Hockey News* 30, No. 37 (September 1977): 8.

Dennis Ryan

J

JACKSON, REGINALD MARTINEZ (18 May 1946, Wyncote, PA–). An African American baseball player, he is the son of a semipro baseball player and Philadelphia tailor and dry cleaner, Martinez Jackson. His grandmother on his father's side was of Spanish descent; his mother is Clara Jackson. An outstanding athlete at Cheltenham Township High School, Reggie accepted a scholarship to play football at Arizona State University (ASU) under Frank Kush. Jackson quit football at ASU and took up baseball instead. In 1966 the Kansas City A's (American League [AL]) drafted him as the second player selected overall that year. Reggie remained with the A's when they relocated to Oakland and helped them win three consecutive World Series from 1972 to 1974. Traded to the Baltimore Orioles (AL) in 1976, the following year he became a free agent acquisition for the New York Yankees. Earning the nickname "Mr. October," Jackson compiled a .357 career World Series batting average and batted in 1,702 runs in his twenty-one-year career as an outfielder for Oakland, Baltimore, New York, and California. At his retirement his 563 career home runs was sixth best, and he was the all-time strikeout leader with 2,597. A brash and daring athlete, he later succeeded as a black entrepreneur, earning more money off the field than on. He was inducted into the National Baseball Hall of Fame in 1993.

SELECTED BIBLIOGRAPHY: Maury Allen, *Mr. October: The Reggie Jackson Story* (1981); Reggie Jackson, *Reggie: The Autobiography*, 2d ed. (1984); "Slugger Reggie Jackson Enters Hall with Grace," *Jet* 84 (16 August 1993): 51.

David R. McMahon

JACOBS, HIRSCH (8 April 1904, New York City–14 February 1970, Miami, FL). A thoroughbred horse trainer, he was the son of Jack Jacobs and of Jewish descent. Savvy, skill, and attention to detail enabled Jacobs to rise from being trainer of a claiming stable to the luxury of raising his own champions to train. He was the leading trainer in the United States eleven times in twelve years, beginning in 1933. After claiming Stymie for $1,500, he developed the horse into a popular New York campaigner and the leading money earner of his day. From that foundation, he and partner Isidor Bieber developed a breeding operation that produced forty-seven stakes winners. The partners were America's leading breeders for four years in the 1960s. The transition from a day-to-day trainer of a stable to breeder of the ultimate in fashionable pedigrees recalled the career of John Madden a half century earlier. With astute acquisitions such as that of Searching for $15,000, Jacobs built an operation that produced Hail to Reason (champion two-year-old and later America's leading sire); Affectionately (a champion runner and dam of Horse of the Year Personality); Priceless Gem (winner of the Futurity and dam of French champion Allez France); plus other champions he bred, owned, and trained, Straight Deal and Regal Gleam. Over his forty-five-year career he saddled winners of a record 3,596 races. He was inducted into the National Thoroughbred Racing Hall of Fame in 1958.

SELECTED BIBLIOGRAPHY: *Blood-Horse* 96 (21 February 1970): 652–58, 101 (27 January 1975): 506; Arnold Kirkpatrick, "Hirsch Jacobs," in William Robertson and Dan Farley, eds., *Hoofprints of the Century* (1976); Betty Moore, "Hirsch Jacobs Was 'Greatest Horseman,' " *Morning Telegraph*, 10 August 1970; *New York Times*, 14 February 1970, 27; Tom O'Reilly, "Hirsch Jacobs 'Winningest' Trainer," *Daily Racing Form*, 2 May 1959.

Courtesy of the National Thoroughbred Racing Hall of Fame

JACOBS, MICHAEL STRAUSS

JACOBS, MICHAEL STRAUSS (10 March 1880, New York City–24 January 1953, Miami Beach, FL). The son of Polish Jewish immigrants, his father (Issac) was a tailor, and his mother (Rebecca) was a homemaker. Mike dropped out of school after the sixth grade and later joined Tex Rickard in the sports promotion business. Although he made something of a name for himself as copromoter (with Rickard) of the Jack Dempsey*–Georges Carpentier boxing match in 1921, he became most famous as the promoter who signed African American heavyweight prizefighter Joe Louis* in 1935. Risking white scorn for promoting a black fighter, Jacobs nonetheless saw Louis' great potential as a boxer and helped guide him to a heavyweight championship. Over the next fifteen years he promoted all of the Brown Bomber's bouts and played a critical role in Louis' success. He used his money and position to establish virtually total control over boxing in New York City, much to the dismay of some critics, like journalist Damon Runyon, who accused him of stifling the careers of young fighters. He certainly made a lot of money on Louis, allegedly amassing a fortune of over $10 million. However, by promoting this talented African American heavyweight, Jacobs helped open the way for other black athletes.

SELECTED BIBLIOGRAPHY: Anthony Edmonds, "Michael Strauss Jacobs," in John A. Garraty, ed., *Dictionary of American Biography*, supplement 5, *1951–1955* (1977),

359–360; George Field and Earl Brown, "The Boxing Racket," *Life* 20 (17 June 1946): 102–104ff; Budd Schulberg, "Champions for Sale: The Mike Jacobs Story," *Colliers* 125 (15 April 1950): 18–19ff, (22 April 1950): 30–31ff, (29 April 1950): 24–25ff, (6 May 1950): 30–31ff, (13 May 1950): 24–25ff.

                                                                      Anthony O. Edmonds

JAI ALAI. The origins of jai alai are obscure, but paintings found in Egyptian pyramids depict a primitive form of the game played thousands of years ago. There is also evidence that a forerunner of modern jai alai existed in ancient Greece. The sport as it is now known was invented by Basque peasants in the Pyrenees Mountains of France and Spain during the seventeenth century. Originally, it was a group of games called *pelota vasca* (Basque ball). Later it became synonymous with the merry festival, or *jai alai*, that often accompanied the performances, and this name was adopted for the sport. The most daring of these games—*cesta punta*—evolved into the game played in America. According to the *Guinness Book of World Records*, jai alai is the world's fastest ball game. The ball often attains speeds in excess of 160 miles per hour. Eventually, jai alai spread beyond the Pyrenees and was played throughout Spain, Mexico, the Philippines, and Cuba, where it arrived in 1898. Introduced into Latin America during the last decade of the nineteenth century, the game became a national pastime in many countries of that region.

Jai alai resembles handball but is far more difficult and challenging, requiring special, highly developed talents, as well as equipment unique to the sport. For fans, the added excitement of pari-mutuel wagering makes jai alai one of the most enjoyable spectator sports. The object of the game is to amass a given number of points by forcing the opponent to miss the ball or hit it out of bounds. The ball, *orpelota*, is caught and propelled with a glovelike, scoop-shaped wicker basket, the cesta, which is strapped to a player's wrist. Jai alai matches are usually played in a large auditorium known as a fronton; the court on which the game is played is called the *cancha*. The round-robin form of play is used in the United States. It is known as quiniela play. Jai alai games are played either by single contestants or two-man teams. As a player or team wins points, he stays on the court to face the next one up in order. Most games are seven points with points doubling after all teams (usually eight) have played one round. This is called "spectacular" scoring. Designated games may be played to more points. The first team (or singles player) to gain seven points wins the game. Second, third, and fourth (required in superfecta games played to nine points) go to the teams with the next highest number of points. Ties require playoffs. Overseas the form of play usually is the *partido*, contested between two teams of two players. In Spain, for example, a *partido* runs twenty-five to forty points, and play may last an hour. Betting occurs on each point as well as the game itself.

Jai alai was introduced into the United States in 1903 as an exhibition at the St. Louis World's Fair. In 1924 jai alai was introduced in Florida at the present site of the Hialeah Race Track. The first facility was destroyed by a hurricane, and the existing Miami jai alai fronton, which is owned by World Jai Alai,* was opened in 1926. Pari-mutuel wagering on the games was legalized in the 1930s. Throughout the United States the only other exhibitions of jai alai were found in New Orleans from 1925 to 1928 at Rainbow Gardens, as part of Mann's Million-Dollar Night Club in Chicago from 1927 to 1929, and at the Hippodrome in New York in 1938.

Pedro Mir, the pioneer of jai alai in the United States, came to the United States in 1923 from Havana, Cuba, at the age of twenty-three. Mir is the author of many of today's rules of play. He retired from the game at the early age of twenty-eight, having won numerous singles and doubles championships in Miami, Chicago, New Orleans, Mexico, Peru, Belgium, and Spain. He then served as an ambassador for the game, acting as player-manager, chief judge, and matchmaker at the Miami jai alai fronton from 1933 to 1975.

For many years, Miami jai alai remained the only place in the country where the ancient sport was firmly established, but its success and popularity eventually prompted the opening of nine additional frontons in Florida, with those in Tampa and Ocala also owned by World Jai Alai. Presently, only the World Jai Alai frontons in Miami, Tampa, and Ocala as well frontons in Dania, Fort Pierce, Orlando, and Palm Beach remain operating in Florida. There is currently one fronton in the state of Connecticut, Milford Jai Alai, as well as one in Rhode Island, Newport Jai Alai. Internationally, jai alai is played today in Spain, France, Italy, Mexico, Indonesia, Venezuela, and the Philippines. Though the game's birthplace is the Basque country, there are more jai alai frontons in Florida than any place in the world.

The world governing body is the Federacion Internacional de Pelota Vasca, founded in Madrid in 1929. Since 1952, the federation has sponsored World Championships every four years in either South America, France, or Spain.

SELECTED BIBLIOGRAPHY: Jose M. Goitia, *Jai Alai: The Other Side of the Screen* (1983); Kath Lindsay, "Pioneer Jai-Alai Player to Be Honored at a Dinner," *Miami Herald*, 17 December 1978, 10N; Miami Jai-Alai Press Kit, Miami, FL, The ABC's of World Jai-Alai, Miami, Florida.

James R. Varella

JAPANESE. Japanese began to immigrate in small numbers to the United States in the late nineteenth century. As early as 1850, Americans, especially on the West Coast, had already begun to express concern about the influx of another Asian group, the Chinese. Formalized in the Chinese Exclusion Acts (1882), these sentiments were well established when the Japanese began to arrive at Angel Island in San Francisco Bay. By the turn of the century, the number of immigrants from Japan was only 10,000. The "Gentlemen's Agreement" of 1907 affirmed the ongoing antipathy of Californians to immigration from Japan. Among its other clauses, this diplomatic agreement between the U.S. and Japanese governments restricted the further immigration of Japanese males. The Alien Land Act (1913) further limited the rights of the issei—the first-generation Japanese to arrive in the United States. The National Origin Act (1924) imposed another impediment by restricting the immigration of Japanese women to the United States. The children of the issei born in America were called the nisei. The issei, who wanted to perpetuate their values, language, and heritage in their children, fostered a variety of institutions with that intention. One was the *gakuen*, or language school. These performed a significant part in the lives of nisei in the early 1930s and were one of the initial sites of sponsored sports for the nisei. Other institutions that were important in solidarity of community were the Buddhist temples or Christian churches that the Japanese Americans attended. While the *gakuen* offered recreational activities that focused primarily upon the nisei, the temples and churches sponsored activities for both the issei and nisei. These activities ranged from sewing and knitting classes to musical groups and athletic activities. The 1932 Olympic Games, held in Los Angeles, were a time of intense pride for the Japanese immigrants who followed the successes of Japanese athletes, particularly in swimming, in their community newspapers, such as Los Angeles' *Rafu Shimpo*.

Following the bombing of Pearl Harbor in December 1941, the lives of the Japanese residing on the West Coast of the United States were changed irrevocably. In mid-February 1942 President Franklin Delano Roosevelt signed Executive Order 9066 removing all Japanese and Americans of Japanese descent into assembly centers and internment camps. With an inordinate amount of leisure time, sport programs, which had been established prior to World War II in the Japanese communities, thrived in the camps. These included traditional Japanese activities such as karate, judo, and sumo, which the issei favored, as well as American sports, enjoyed mostly by nisei, such as baseball, softball, basketball, volleyball, football, and tennis.

Two organizations that were developed to foster Japanese American sport in the Los Angeles area were the Women's Athletic Union for women and for men the Japanese Athletic Union. Both were established in the late 1920s. Leagues were conducted in basketball, softball, and volleyball for young women and football, baseball, track, and basketball for young men. Following World War II, the reconstituted Women's Athletic Association was formed but made little progress in reorganizing leagues.

Baseball was played by the Japanese before they emigrated to the United States. In 1934, more than 70,000 spectators attended a game between American and Japanese baseball stars at Tokyo's Meiji Shrine Stadium. Upon their arrival in America, many immigrants established leagues and continued to play baseball. In the 1920s leagues were established for play among only Japanese. Some teams were organized that played in mixed Japanese and non-Japanese leagues (i.e., the Los Angeles Nippon team). In the 1930s, nisei became involved with the sport. During the internment, baseball was an immensely popular sport. Teams were organized for all age groups within the camps, and some leagues were fiercely competitive. Following World War II some leagues were reestablished, but never on the scale that they had achieved before the war.

Softball was played by young Japanese American women beginning in the 1920s in the Los Angeles area. Originally, teams were organized around *ga-kuens*, but leagues were soon established. By the mid-1930s, a seventeen-team league was running in Los Angeles. Following the war, the popular leagues were reestablished but never on the same scale as during the prewar years.

Basketball was a sport that was a favorite among both men and women. For women, leagues were sponsored by the women's Athletic Union and for men by the Japanese Athletic Union. This was the most prevalent recreational sport for women. During the internment, basketball continued in popularity for both men and women, with outdoor facilities in abundance. Following the internment, league size diminished, but play continued.

Japanese Americans have continued to participate in a number of other recreational sports throughout their history in America. Among the most popular are tennis, golf, and volleyball.

The notable contributions that Japanese Americans have made to U.S. sport history include the introduction of martial arts, especially judo and karate, to the United States. The survival of the Japanese community through their internment during World War II and their continued participation in sport are perhaps their most significant contribution to U.S. sport history.

SELECTED BIBLIOGRAPHY: Kevin Gray Carr, "Making Way: War, Philosophy and Sport in Japanese Judo," *Journal of Sport History* 20 (1993): 167–188; Roger Daniels, *Asian America: Chinese and Japanese in the United States since 1850* (1988); Samuel O. Regalado, "Sport and Community in California's Japanese American 'Yamato Colony,' 1930–1945," *Journal of Sport History* 19 (1992): 130–143; Alison M. Wrynn, "The Recreation and Leisure Pursuits of Japanese Americans in World War II Internment Camps," in George Eisen and David K. Wiggins, eds., *Ethnicity and Sport in North American History and Culture* (1994).

Alison M. Wrynn

JENKINS, CLARENCE R. ("Fats") (10 January 1898, New York City–6 December 1968, Philadelphia). An African American who excelled in basketball and baseball, he was the older of two sons born to Charles B. and Nellie Jenkins. He attended Commerce High School in New York City. A small, lean athlete, he acquired the name "Fats" from his larger and younger brother, Harold. Jenkins played professionally with the New York Renaissance Five* and several Negro League* baseball teams. His basketball career began at the age of fourteen, when he joined an amateur team, St. Christopher, sponsored by the St. Phillip's Episcopal Church. Jenkins turned professional in 1922 and played two years for the McMahon Brother's Commonwealth Five. In 1924 he joined the New York Renaissance team in Harlem, which was owned and managed by Robert L. Douglas.* Jenkins served as captain of the barnstorming Rens in the 1930s, leading his team to an eighty-eight-game winning streak in 1932–33 and the first World Professional Championship in 1939. As an outfielder and southpaw, Jenkins played for several black baseball teams between 1920 and 1938, mainly the New York Black Yankees and the Harrisburg Giants. Jenkins represented the East team in 1933 and 1935 in the All-Star Negro League Games. In the 1940 season, Jenkins served as the manager for the Brooklyn Royal Giants. Following his retirement from sports, Jenkins became a businessman and a boxing referee.

SELECTED BIBLIOGRAPHY: Dick Clark and Larry Lester, eds., *The Negro Leagues Book* (1994); Robert Peterson, *Only the Ball Was White* (1970); David L. Porter, ed., *Biographical Dictionary of American Sports: Basketball and Other Indoor Sports* (1989); Susan J. Rayl, "The New York Renaissance Professional Black Basketball Team, 1923–1950" (Ph.D. diss., Pennsylvania State University, 1996); James A. Riley, *The Biographical Encyclopedia of the Negro Baseball Leagues* (1994).

Susan Rayl

JENKINS, FERGUSON (13 December 1943, Chatham, Ontario, Canada–   ). A baseball player from Canada of African descent, he is the son of Ferguson Holmes Jenkins, a chef, and Delores Louise Jenkins. As a student at Chatham High School he played baseball and basketball and also excelled in ice hockey. After declining offers to play professional hockey, he signed with the Philadelphia Phillies, reaching the major leagues late in 1965. After being traded to the Chicago Cubs early in the 1966 season, he blossomed into a star pitcher, winning twenty games for six consecutive years with the Cubs. After a mediocre campaign in 1973 he was traded to the Texas Rangers. He spent the next eight years with the Rangers and the Boston Red Sox before closing out his career with two final seasons back with the Cubs. He was known as a tireless control pitcher who completed nearly half of his starts over his nineteen seasons (267 out of 594), while amassing 284 victories against 226 defeats. He became the first pitcher in the major leagues to strike out more than 3,000 batters (3,192) while walking fewer than 1,000 (997). Although Jenkins' reputation suffered in 1980 for his arrest and conviction for possession of drugs, that same year his native country granted him its highest civilian award, the Order of Canada, for his humanitarian work. After his retirement in 1984 he became a rancher in Guthrie, Oklahoma, where he also served as a pitching coach for Oklahoma City's minor league club. Later he was a pitching instructor with the Cincinnati Reds and the Cubs. He was elected into the National Baseball Hall of Fame in 1991.

SELECTED BIBLIOGRAPHY: *Chicago Cubs Vineline* 2 (March 1987): 24–25, 5 (February 1990): 12, 6 (February 1991): 11; Eddie Gold and Art Ahrens, *The New Era Cubs* (1985); William Humbar, "Ferguson Jenkins, CM, Comes to Cooperstown," *Baseball Research Journal* 20 (1991): 12–13.

George B. Kirsch

JEREMIAH (YEREMIAN), EDWARD JOHN (4 November 1905, Worcester, MA–7 June 1967, Hanover, NH). An Armenian American hockey coach, Jeremiah was a graduate of Dartmouth College, class of 1930. After earning his degree he played five years of professional hockey with New Haven and Boston of the Canadian-American League, the New York Americans and Boston Bruins of the National Hockey League, and Cleveland of the International League. Jeremiah's hockey coaching career began the following year, when he led the Boston Olympics, a farm team of the Boston Bruins, to the National Amateur Athletic Union Championship in 1935–36. In the fall of 1937 he took charge of a deteriorating hockey program at his alma mater. He proceeded to gain a championship in his first year and became a fixture for three decades. Under his direction Dartmouth's hockey teams dominated the Ivy League by taking the next five titles in a row, winning thirty-five games while losing only three and tying one. His clubs compiled a record of 308 victories, 247 defeats, and twelve ties. In seven of his first nine years as coach Jeremiah's teams won the Pentagonal League hockey championship, and from 1942 to 1946, interrupted by the war years of 1944 and 1945, they won a record forty-six consecutive games without a defeat. He took Dartmouth to the National Collegiate Athletic Association (NCAA) Tournament Finals in both 1948 and 1949, losing to a Canadian-dominated Michigan team in the 1948 finals and bowing to Boston College in a heartbreaking decision a year later. Dartmouth won Ivy League titles in 1959 and 1960. In 1964 he coached the U.S. Olympic hockey team to a fifth-place finish in the Olympic Games in Innsbruck, Austria. In 1951 Jeremiah was the first recipient of the Spencer Penrose Coach of the Year Trophy. That same year he was selected Hockey Coach of the Year by the American Hockey Coaches Association. He was awarded the Lester Patrick Trophy Award in 1965 and was selected as a charter member of the U.S. Hockey Hall of Fame in 1973. In 1952 Jeremiah was a member of the important U.S. Olympic Ice Hockey Selection Committee as well as being Chairman of the NCAA Eastern Hockey Selection Committee. Jeremiah was the author of *Ice Hockey* and *Heads-Up Hockey* and edited the hockey section for the *Encyclopedia Britannica*.

SELECTED BIBLIOGRAPHY: Arra S. Avakian, *The Armenians in America* (1977); Richard N. Demirjian, *Armenian-American/Canadian WHO's WHO of Outstanding Athletes, Coaches and Sports Personalities, 1906–1912* (1989).

Richard N. Demirjian

JEWS.

While historically stereotyped as physically weak and unfit, Jews played a prominent role in American sports as participants, fans, communicators, and entrepreneurs. Sport enabled Jews to acculturate (but not necessarily assimilate), while often promoting a sense of peoplehood. It gained participants self-esteem and respect from peers and the core society, countered stereotypes, and promised social mobility.

Jews are an ethnic group and a religious faith, although one may belong to the former without the latter. The immigrant Jewish sporting experience was more a product of regional ethnic culture than religious beliefs, which were not inherently antiathletic. Mid-nineteenth-century Western European Jews came from modern countries where physical culture was popular and frequently arrived with some familiarity with exercise or athletics.

The first major Jewish American sportsmen were English immigrants and their sons, mainly boxers who maintained a proud Anglo Jewish pugilistic tradition dating to champion Daniel Mendoza (1792–95). The most notable prizefighting newcomer was "Young" Barney Aaron, American lightweight champion in 1857.

Midcentury German Jewish immigrants were typically emancipated individuals whose recreation was similar to that of other Germans. Some were turners who joined turnvereins in America. These gymnastics clubs were open to all German men and promoted German culture, political activism, respect for working-class concerns, and physical education. Shortly after the Civil War, Jews were elected president of the leading Chicago and Milwaukee turner units. The most prominent athlete among these newcomers was Philo Jacoby, whose rifle victory at the 1868 Berlin Shooting Championships was the first international title for an American individual.

Second-generation German Jews fully participated in the post–Civil War sporting culture. Daniel Stern, a founder of the New York Athletic Club (NYAC) in 1868, won the first American amateur walking championship in 1876. In the 1880s Lon Myers* of Richmond was the preeminent American runner, holding every national record from fifty yards to the mile. Brooklynite Lipman Pike, of Dutch descent, became in 1866 one of the first professional baseball players. In 1871 Pike was player-manager for Troy in the first pro league, the National Association of Professional Base Ball Players, and later starred in the National League. German Jews who achieved renown in football included Lucius Littauer, player (1875, 1877) and coach (1881) at Harvard, and Princeton quarterback Phil King, second-team All-American in 1890.

Well-to-do second-generation German Jews organized ethnic sports associations to maintain their ethnic identity. The Young Men's Hebrew Association* (YMHA) was started in 1854 by Baltimoreans to stimulate moral recreation, sociability, physical fitness, and spirituality. By 1900 there were 100 Y buildings in German Jewish neighborhoods, serving 20,000 members, with gymnasiums and other athletic facilities.

German Jews formed status-oriented athletic and country clubs in response to discrimination and to separate themselves from Russian Jews. In 1906 prosperous New York Jews, including Bernard Baruch, formed the City Athletic Club because clubs like the NYAC were anti-Semitic. Chicago's luxurious Lake Shore Country Club included Leonard Florsheim, Modie Spiegel, and Julius Rosenwald. There they enjoyed expensive sports like golf and tennis, their wives socialized, and their offspring met potential spouses.

A few fabulously wealthy German American Jews played a prominent role in thoroughbred racing, particularly financier August Belmont,* the first Jew in the New York Yacht Club and the initial president of New York's prestigious American Jockey Club (1865). His Nursery Stud was one of the finest in the world, and his stable led the nation in earnings in 1889 and 1890. Belmont encountered considerable discrimination and anti-Semitism but mixed in elite society and was disowned by the Jewish community. No Jew was admitted to the prestigious Jockey Club (1894) until Harry F. Guggenheim in 1951.

Jewish newcomers were also sports entrepreneurs. Swiss immigrant John M. Brunswick designed in 1845 what became the standard billiard table. His Brunswick Billiard Manufacturing Company became one of the leading sporting goods firms in the world. German Jewish businessmen were very involved in professional baseball to make money and demonstrate civic spirit, especially in Cincinnati, which had an influential Jewish community, and southern cities, where they wanted to gain recognition as public-spirited citizens. The most important were immigrant Barney Dreyfuss,* who owned major league franchises in Louisville and Pittsburgh from 1888 to 1931, and Andrew Freedman,* a Tammanyite who owned the New York Giants (1895–1902). He was one of the most hated owners ever, going through sixteen managers in eight years. Freedman used political connections to push around other owners and encouraged rowdyism on the field, fought with fans, ballplayers, umpires, and sportswriters, and was miserly with his employees.

Two million Eastern European Jewish immigrants arrived in the United States between 1882 and 1914 from the static premodern shtetl. These newcomers looked and dressed differently, were strictly orthodox, spoke Yiddish, and were stereotyped as weak, unhealthy, unfit, and unaccustomed to "manly" labor. They were unfamiliar with physical culture, then largely unknown in Eastern Europe, and saw sports as strange, foolish, time-wasting, and often dangerous distractions that pulled sons from study or work and encouraged behavior that drew them away from a strict upbringing.

Despite parental opposition or, at best, indifference, Russian Jewish sons became big sports fans, having identified sport with American society. They followed their sports heroes in the press and eagerly participated in sports, especially those that fitted their environment and required little space, equipment, or schooling. Talented athletes became neighborhood heroes and gained admiration from the broader society and respect for the ethnic group. Playing sport provided a means to display manliness, which among the working class was less a matter of character (being a mensch) than of strength, courage, and virility.

Opportunities for inner-city youth were abetted by settlement houses that built gyms to get them off the streets and into productive recreation. German Jews generously supported settlement houses like New York's Educational Alliance (1892) to help coreligionists adjust to urban America and sustain their Judaic heritage. By 1910 there were at least seventy-five Jewish settlements and community centers and another fifty that mainly catered to a Jewish clientele. Sponsors believed that adult-directed sport helped Americanize second-generation

Russian Jews, raised moral standards, improved health, and eliminated the canard that Jews lacked physical courage. The major male settlement sports were basketball, boxing, wrestling, and track, and basketball was the major sport for young women.

Inner-city Jews were especially successful in boxing, a useful skill to master. The "tough Jew" who stood up for himself and his coreligionists against Polish, Italian, or Irish thugs became a neighborhood hero. Amateurs had lots of chances to fight at smokers and local boxing gyms for prizes or badges that they turned into cash; the best amateurs became professionals. Jews were among the most successful fighters in America, especially in the interwar era, and built on their fistic success to gain prominence in the business aspects of pugilism.

Heavyweight contender Joe Choynski in the 1890s was the first Eastern European Jew to achieve renown in the ring. There were Jewish champions by the early 1900s, starting with Chicago bantamweight Harry Harris (1900), whose family came from England, and San Francisco's Abe Attell,* featherweight champion from 1904 to 1912. There were three other Jewish champions in the 1910s, most notably, Benny Leonard,* lightweight titlist from 1917 to 1925, considered one of the finest all-time ring generals.

In the 1920s Jews were a dominant group in boxing, constituting one-sixth of all champions, and by the end of the decade had the most contenders. There were seven Jewish American titleholders in the 1930s, most notably, Barney Ross,* who held the light and middleweight championships simultaneously. He was an important hero who the public believed was showing Hitler that Jews could not be pushed around.

The Jewish eminence in the ring declined rapidly after the depression, largely because of their economic success. However, Jews remained very prominent outside the ring as trainers (Ray Arcel had twenty-one champions), managers (Joe Jacobs, Sam Pian), promoters (Mike Jacobs,* who nearly monopolized title fights [1937–49], and writers (Nat Fleischer,* founder of *Ring Magazine* [1922]).

Inner-city life also fostered interest in basketball. Jewish youth played regularly in school yards, settlement houses, and churches. Jews dominated eastern high school and college basketball in the interwar era and made New York the mecca of the game. From the first All-American poll in 1929 through 1964, there was at least one Jewish All-American except in 1935, 1951, and 1952. City College of New York (CCNY) was a national powerhouse during Nat Holman's* thirty-eight-year regime, with eight All-Americans and a roster that was typically 80% Jewish. In 1950 CCNY became the only school to win both the National Invitational Tournament and National Collegiate Athletic Association championships in the same season. New York basketball was de-emphasized following the uncovering of a point-shaving fix in 1951.

The best Jewish basketball players have been professionals since the early 1900s, such as settlement alumni Barney Sedran* and Max Friedman,* teammates on the "busy Izzies" of the University Settlement House. Sedran made up to $12,000 during his fifteen-year career when most players got $15–$75 a game. In 1921 they played with Nat Holman on the New York Whirlwinds, a weekend team organized by Tex Rickard, who was promoting pro basketball at Madison Square Garden. Holman later played for the New York Original Celtics, the best pro team of the 1920s. One of their main rivals was the Philadelphia SPHAs* (South Philadelphia Hebrew All-Stars), led by Eddie Gottlieb,* which won six American Basketball League (ABL) championships and the first Basketball Association of America crown (forerunner of the National Basketball Association, [NBA]) in 1946–47. The ABL was heavily Jewish as late as 1945–46, when it was nearly 45% Jewish. The best Jewish player in the NBA was Adolph Schayes,* a 6'8" New York University (NYU) alumnus, who played from 1949 to 1964. He was an All-Star for twelve straight years and established many records, including most points (19,249), games played (1,059), and consecutive games (764). During this era there was a sharp decline in Jewish basketball players, and they virtually disappeared by the mid-1960s. This reflected Jewish migration out of the inner city and social mobility.

Jews played a major role in the business side of basketball, back to Frank Basloe, who organized a pro squad in 1903 in Herkimer, New York, and Chicagoan Abe Saperstein,* who organized the Harlem Globetrotters* in 1926. The NBA's first president was Maurice Podoloff (1949–63), with franchises owned by Ben Kerner (St. Louis Hawks), Max Winter (Minneapolis Lakers), Eddie Gottlieb (Philadelphia Warriors), and Walter Harrison (Rochester Royals). David Stern, currently NBA president, is a Jew, and several owners, most notably Jerry Reinsdorf (Chicago Bulls) are Jewish.

Jews in the early 1900s also excelled in track, which did not require a lot of space for training, sophisticated equipment, or highly technical coaching. Youth competed at settlement houses, YMHAs, and school associations, especially New York's Public Schools' Athletic League (1903), which promoted interscholastic competition and sports for all to improve health and character. They had important role models like Myer Prinstein,* who won four gold medals and one silver medal in the long jump and triple jump in the 1900, 1904, and 1908 Olympic Games. Yet Prinstein, Abel Kiviat* (1,500-meter world record holder and silver medalist at the 1912 Olympics), and other Jewish stars were barred from elite track clubs and competed for lower-status clubs.

The first Jewish American Summer Olympians (1896–1936) won twenty-six medals, mainly in track and boxing, compared to ninety-seven for European Jews; in 1932 Irving Jaffee won two golds in speed skating. The Americans were predominantly second-generation, from working- or lower-middle-class backgrounds, while the Europeans were mainly assimilated middle- and upper-middle-class fencers and gymnasts.

Prior to the 1936 games a broad-based movement emerged to protest Nazism. Several Jewish athletes boycotted the games, although six Jewish Americans went to Berlin. Marty Glickman* and Sam Stoller, scheduled to run in the 400-meter relay, were dropped from the squad in a controversial decision.

Second-generation Russian Jews were originally less prominent in sports that were expensive, required a lot of space, or advanced education. However, by the 1920s, as families became more assimilated and moved to better neighborhoods, and boys stayed in school longer, they achieved success in football. By 1929 over 500 Jews were playing college football, most notably, Benny Friedman,* All-American quarterback at Michigan (1925–26) and later a National Football League (NFL) star. In 1936 alone, there were twenty-five Jews in the NFL. Two of the top rookies in 1939 were halfback Marshall Goldberg* from Elkins, West Virginia, and quarterback Sid Luckman* from Brooklyn. Through 1993 151 Jews played in the NFL (nearly three-fourths before 1950).

Jews remained underrepresented in baseball. Successful players in the early 1900s were mostly from outside New York City. They encountered a lot of discrimination and often adopted pseudonyms. Anti-Semitism was bolstered by the general perception that Arnold Rothstein had fixed the 1919 World Series. In the 1920s several teams sought Jewish players to draw Jewish fans. Andy Cohen started for the Giants in 1928 and immediately became a big local hero. The principal Jewish star was Bronxite Hank Greenberg,* a tough, powerful man who did not play on Yom Kippur. He batted .313 during his career, had fifty-eight homers in 1938 and a league record 183 runs batted in in 1937, and led the Detroit Tigers to four pennants.

Jews have played a prominent role in the turf. In the 1920s newly rich Eastern European Jews entered racing, most notably, Chicagoan John D. Hertz, whose Count Fleet won the Triple Crown in 1943. Hertz and other Jews ran major tracks. Chicagoan Benjamin Lindheimer's syndicate bought Washington Park in 1935 and Arlington in 1940. Jews were also jockeys, trainers, and gamblers. The most outstanding Jewish trainers were Max Hirsch* of Fredericksburg, Texas, whose horses won over $15 million in purses, and New Yorker Hirsch Jacobs,* who won over $11 million in purses and captured more races than any other trainer. Jews even achieved distinction as jockeys, particularly sixteen-year-old Walter Miller, who in 1906 won 388 races, a record unmatched until 1950. Several well-known bootleggers were originally bookmakers, including Rothstein and Max "Boo Hoo" Hoff. Meyer Lansky subsequently unified American bookmaking operations through the racing wire, controlled in the 1930s by Moe Annenberg.

The most prominent Jewish women athletes were L. T. Neuberger, who won seven U.S. table tennis titles from 1951 to 1961, discus thrower Lillian Copeland,* silver and gold medalist at the 1928 and 1932 Olympics and world record holder in the javelin, discus, and shot put, and basketball Hall of Famer Nancy Lieberman.* Jewish women who promoted women's sport included Senda Berenson,* modifier of rules for women's basketball (1895), Charlotte Epstein,* mother of American women's swimming, who helped make it an Olympic sport (1920), and Gladys Medalie Heldman, editor and publisher of *World Tennis Magazine*, originator of the Virginia Slims professional tour (1971).

Jewish women participated in sport often under the auspices of Jewish organizations that sought to maintain their femininity and Jewish identity. Highly assimilated middle- and upper-class Jewish women participated in the more prestigious sports at high schools, colleges, and country clubs. Sheltered immigrant daughters relied on settlement houses, YWHAs, and summer camps established by philanthropists.

Since World War II Jewish participation in the major sports has declined, although Jewish influence as sports entrepreneurs has increased, especially in team sports. There have been few boxers, although Mike Rossman and Saoul Mamby won championships in the 1970s and 1980s. There has been a sharp decline in football and basketball players, but the number of baseball players remained stable. Sandy Koufax* of the Dodgers was the preeminent pitcher since the war.

Jews dominated the minor sports of ping pong and handball. Jewish men won every men's singles title between 1945 and 1964 save twice and every women's singles championship except two between 1947 and 1957. One-third of all U.S. Handball Association members were Jews, led by Vic Hershkowitz and Jimmy Jacobs, who collectively took fifty-seven national titles from 1950 to 1963.

Since the 1960s, Jews were particularly successful in individualistic upper-middle-class sports like tennis, swimming, and gymnastics, reflecting their higher socioeconomic status, migration to suburbia, and structural assimilation. Their families stress education, live where sport achievement is not all-consuming, and don't need to become tough heroes.

Prominent Jewish American athletes in these sports include Mark Spitz* (swimming), Brian Gottfried, Harold Solomon, Brian Teacher, and Eliot Teltscher (tennis), Marshall Holman and Mark Roth (bowling), Mitch Gaylord and Kerri Strug (gymnastics), and Amy Alcott (golf). Mathieu Schneider has excelled in hockey.

Jews are particularly prominent as sports communicators. Since the 1950s top baseball scribes included Roger Kahn, Dick Young, Milt Gross, Leonard Koppett, and Jerome Holtzman, while novelists Mark Harris, Norman Mailer, Bernard Malamud, and Philip Roth have written on sport. Jewish prominence in broadcasting began with Bill Stern in the 1930s, who was followed by Marty Glickman,* Mel Allen,* Howard Cosell,* and Marv Albert.

SELECTED BIBLIOGRAPHY: Ken Blady, *The Jewish Boxers Hall of Fame* (1988); Allen Bodner, *When Boxing Was a Jewish Sport* (1997); Hank Greenberg, *Hank Greenberg: The Story of My Life*, Ira Berkow, ed. (1989); Peter Levine, *Ellis Island to Ebbets Field: Sport and the American Jewish Experience* (1992); Bernard Postal, Jesse Silver, and Roy Silver, *Encyclopedia of Jews in Sports* (1965); Steven A. Riess, ed., *Sports and the American Jew* (1998).

Steven A. Riess

JOHNSON, EARVIN, JR. ("Magic") (14 August 1959, Lansing, MI–   ). An African American basketball player, he is the son of Earvin, Sr. (an automobile factory worker), and Christine Johnson. In 1977 as a senior at Everett

High School he spearheaded his squad to a 27–1 record and a state champion-ship, showcasing his extraordinary talents in scoring, rebounding, assists, and steals. His two years at Michigan State University were spectacular, as he closed out his college career in 1979 with a sparkling victorious performance in the National Collegiate Athletic Association (NCAA) championship game against Larry Bird's Indiana State squad. By the time he entered the National Basketball Association (NBA) with the Los Angeles Lakers that fall he was much cele-brated for his ball-handling wizardry, his offensive and defensive skills, and especially his cheerful and engaging personality. Nicknamed "Magic," at 6' 9" he was unusually tall for a guard, and he astounded spectators with his pinpoint (and often "no look") passes and his clutch shooting. Playing with Kareem Abdul-Jabbar,* he helped the Lakers win five NBA titles (1980, 1982, 1985, 1987–88); he was the league's Most Valuable Player in 1987, 1989, and 1990. During the 1980s Johnson, Larry Bird, and Michael Jordan* were chiefly re-sponsible for the phenomenal rise in popularity of the NBA in the United States, and all three capitalized on their fame by signing lucrative contracts for com-mercial endorsements. But the sports world was stunned in 1991 when Johnson announced that he had tested positive for the human immunodeficiency virus (HIV). He announced his retirement from the NBA, but he returned to the court to star on the U.S. "Dream Team" that won the basketball gold medal at the 1992 Olympics in Barcelona, Spain. He later returned to the Lakers for brief stints as a player and a coach, and he also worked as a television color com-mentator. In 1992 he served as a presidential adviser on AIDS, and he became outspoken on the need for AIDS education and safe sex.

SELECTED BIBLIOGRAPHY: Sally B. Donnelly and Dick Thompson, "It Can Happen to Anybody, Even Magic Johnson," *Time* 138 (18 November 1991): 26–27; Bill Gutman, *Magic: More than a Legend* (1992); James Haskins, *"Magic": A Biography of Earvin Johnson* (1982); Earvin "Magic" Johnson and Richard Levin, *Magic* (1983).

George B. Kirsch

JOHNSON, JOHN ARTHUR ("Jack") (31 March 1878, Galveston, TX–10 June 1946, Raleigh, NC). An African American prizefighter, he was the son of Henry Johnson, a former boxing slave who became a school janitor, and Tiny Johnson. As a boy Johnson attended elementary school for a few years and worked at menial jobs while he developed his skills as a boxer. In 1903 he won the unofficial black heavyweight championship. He attained national notoriety on 26 December 1908 in Australia, when he defeated Canadian boxer Tommy Burns to become the first black heavyweight champion of the world. While Burns was not a popular nor highly regarded champion, Johnson's defeat of a white fighter during a period when social Darwinism was widely espoused an-gered many white Australians. Many Americans also dismissed Johnson's ac-complishment and called for former white heavyweight champion Jim Jeffries to come out of retirement to defeat Johnson and reclaim the title for the white race. On 4 July 1910 more than 20,000 fans—including over 100 correspondents and writers from the United States, Europe, and Australia—watched as Johnson smiled, played with, and taunted Jeffries before knocking him down—the first fighter to ever do this to Jeffries—and out. Rioting broke out all over America, resulting in injury to many and death to a few, and some cities banned the showing of the film of the fight. Many African Americans considered the fight's result to be uplifting; Johnson had knocked down another wall of segregation and had defeated white supremacy (at least in the ring). Johnson further antagonized whites by his ostentatious lifestyle. During a time when African Americans were expected to show deference toward whites, Johnson flaunted his wealth by displaying expensive cars, clothes, and diamond rings to a resentful white public. However, the social violation that most incensed whites was his penchant for dating and marrying white women. Governors and other politicians denounced Johnson's relationships with, and marriages to, white women. However, the government charged Johnson with a violation of the Mann Act, arguing he had transported a woman, Belle Schreiber, from Pittsburgh to Chicago in August 1910 for the purpose of prostitution and debauchery. Johnson admitted sending Schreiber money, although he denied it was for immoral purposes. Johnson was found guilty of violating the Mann Act, fined $1,000, and sentenced to one year in prison. He fled America for Europe. After two years in exile, Johnson agreed to meet Jess Willard in a fight for the heavyweight title in Havana, Cuba. Johnson lost in the twenty-sixth round to a younger, much bigger fighter in a match that Johnson claimed was fixed. While some believe Johnson was the greatest boxer ever, it is undeniable that he was one of the most important figures in the history of American sport. His win over Jeffries signaled an end to unchallenged notions of white supremacy in the ring. He paved the way for Joe Louis,* Floyd Patterson,* Sonny Liston,* and others to fight for the heavyweight title, although many who followed him would be careful to cultivate an image of acquiescence, one that runs counter to the image many observers had of Johnson. Johnson was a black champion in many ways.

SELECTED BIBLIOGRAPHY: Finis Farr, *Black Champion: The Life and Times of Jack Johnson* (1965); Al-Tony Gilmore, "Jack Johnson and White Women: The National Impact," *Journal of Negro History* 58 (January 1973): 18–38; Al-Tony Gilmore, *Bad Nigger!: The National Impact of Jack Johnson* (1975); Othello Harris, "The Role of Sport in the Black Community," *Sociological Focus 30*, No. 4 (1997): 311–319; Jack Johnson, *Jack Johnson: In the Ring and Out* (1992); Jack Johnson, *Jack Johnson Is a Dandy: An Autobiography* (1969); Randy Roberts, *Papa Jack: Jack Johnson and the Era of White Hopes* (1983); Howard Sackler, *The Great White Hope; A Play by Howard Sackler* (1968); William H. Wiggins, Jr., "Jack Johnson as Bad Nigger: The Folklore of His Life," *The Black Scholar* 2 (January 1971): 35–46; William H. Wiggins, Jr., "Boxing's Sambo Twins: Racial Stereotypes in Jack Johnson and Joe Louis Newspaper Cartoons, 1908–1938," *Journal of Sport History* 15 (Winter 1988): 242–254.

Othello Harris

JORDAN, MICHAEL JEFFREY (17 February 1963, Brooklyn, NY–   ). An African American basketball player, he is the son of Dolores Jordan (a bank worker) and James Jordan (a factory supervisor and electrical engineer). Jordan was raised in Wilmington, North Carolina, where he attended Laney High School. He was recruited by Dean Smith at the University of North Carolina at Chapel Hill, for whom, as a freshman, he scored the winning basket in the 1982 National Collegiate Athletic Association (NCAA) Championship game against Georgetown. Following his junior year at North Carolina, Jordan entered the National Basketball Association (NBA) draft and was selected third by the Chicago Bulls. Before starting his NBA career, he starred on the U.S. Olympic basketball team that won the gold medal at the 1984 Summer Olympics in Los Angeles; he also signed a revolutionary endorsement deal with Nike. Jordan has had a staggeringly successful career in the NBA, winning six NBA Championships with the Chicago Bulls (1991–93, 1996–98), the last three of which followed his temporary retirement from the game and brief flirtation with minor league baseball. He also repeated his gold medal-winning success with the U.S. Olympic basketball team at the 1992 Summer Olympics in Barcelona. Among other records and accolades, through the 1997–98 season Jordan held the highest career points per game average with 32.0, with ten scoring titles. He was chosen the NBA Most Valuable Player (MVP) on five occasions, winning the NBA Finals MVP in every series in which he played. As well as being arguably the greatest basketball player of all time, Jordan is one of the most marketed and highest-profile figures on the globe. As such, he is the prototypical African American sport celebrity against whom all others are destined to be compared. He announced his second retirement in January 1999.

SELECTED BIBLIOGRAPHY: Henry Louis Gates, Jr., "Net Worth," *The New Yorker* (1 June 1998): 48–61; Bob Greene, *Hang Time: Days and Dreams with Michael Jordan* (1992); David Halberstam, "A Hero for the Wired World," *Sports Illustrated* 75 (23 December 1991): 76–81; David Halberstam, *Playing for Keeps: Michael Jordan and the World He Made* (1999); Walter Iooss and Mark Vancil, *Rare Air: Michael on Michael* (1993); Michael Jordan, *For the Love of the Game* (1998); Mitchell Krugel, *Jordan: The Man, His Words, and His Life* (1994); Gene Martin, *Michael Jordan: Gentleman Superstar* (1987); Jim Naughton, *Taking to the Air: The Rise of Michael Jordan* (1992).

David Andrews

JUDO. This martial art developed in Japan in the late nineteenth century under the tutelage of Dr. Jigoro Kano, utilizing elements of Jujitsu. It was introduced to the United States by Yoshiaki Yamashita, a student of Kano's, in 1902. Individual dojos began to form along the West Coast of the United States and in Hawaii following Yamashita's visit. Although women were encouraged to participate in practicing judo, they were not included in competitions. After Dr. Kano visited the United States in 1932 during the Los Angeles Olympics as honorary president of the Japanese Amateur Athletic Association, four black-belt associations were formed in southern California, northern California, Seattle, and Hawaii. These were patronized almost exclusively by Japanese Americans. Although the practice of judo continued in the internment camps on a limited basis, it was viewed with suspicion, and the U.S. government sought to limit its practice. U.S. championships, which were first held in 1953, were won almost exclusively by Americans of Japanese descent for the first decade of competition. Also in 1953 the National Collegiate Judo Association was formed. Judo became an official Olympic sport for men at Tokyo in 1964 and for women at the Barcelona Games in 1992.

SELECTED BIBLIOGRAPHY: Pat Harrington, *Judo* (1992).

Alison M. Wrynn

K

KAHANAMOKU, DUKE (24 August 1890, Honolulu, HI–22 January 1968, Honolulu, HI). A Hawaiian swimmer and surfer, he was named after his father, who, in turn, had been named after Alfred, the duke of Edinburgh, who visited Hawaii in 1869. A full-blooded Hawaiian who grew up in Waikiki, Kahanamoku first attracted attention outside the islands as a competitive swimmer who won three gold medals and two silver medals for the United States at the 1912 Stockholm Olympics. Kahanamoku was also a skilled and joyful surfer who brought his knowledge of the sport to California and Australia. Indeed, to many followers of surfing, Kahanamoku taught the world to surf, and, to many, he symbolized the sport until his death in 1968. Nevertheless, as a competitive swimmer, Kahanamoku remained one of the best in the world throughout the 1910s. World War I prevented him from repeating his Stockholm feats. However, at the age of thirty, Kahanamoku won a gold medal in the 1920 Olympics. Kahanamoku spent many years shuttling between Honolulu and Los Angeles, where he carved out a movie career of sorts playing Polynesian "natives." In Honolulu he became known as an unofficial greeter to well-heeled tourists, but he was not so well heeled himself, as he operated a gas station there. He transformed his notoriety into political capital as he was elected to several terms as sheriff of Honolulu County as both a Republican and a Democrat.

SELECTED BIBLIOGRAPHY: Douglas Booth, "Ambiguities in Pleasure and Discipline: The Development of Competitive Surfing," *Journal of Sport History* 22 (Fall 1995): 189–206; Ben Finney and John Houston, *Surfing: The Sport of Hawaiian Kings* (1966); Sandra Kimberley Hall and Greg Ambrose, *Memories of Duke: The Legend Comes to Life* (1995).

Joel S. Franks

KANSAS CITY MONARCHS. Founded by a white businessman, J. L. "Wilkie" Wilkinson, the Monarchs were perhaps Negro baseball's premier franchise. Its talented roster, which included some future major leaguers, attracted the black community's support, making it one of black Kansas City's most important social institutions. The team affiliated with the Negro National League* (NNL) from its inception in 1920 until 1931, when it began play as independents, barnstorming from 1932 to 1936. In 1937 the Monarchs joined the Negro American League (NAL). The NAL struggled after integration, a signal that black baseball was doomed. Yet the Monarchs' list of achievements remains impressive. They were the champions of the first Negro World Series in 1924 and again in 1942. They earned pennants numerous times during the years of the Negro Leagues: from 1923 to 1925; in 1929 and 1937; and from 1939 to 1942. Like most teams they struggled during the war years as their best players were called to service. After the war, agitation increased for the integration of major league baseball. The pathbreaker was one of their own, Jackie Robinson,* who integrated baseball in 1947 after playing for the Monarchs in 1945. Thereafter, recruiting players and attracting fans became more difficult, and the quality of play declined. Wilkinson sold the team to Tom Baird after the 1948 season. Baird sold the franchise after the 1955 season to a black businessman, Ted Raspberry, from Grand Rapids, Michigan. Raspberry's hopes of maintaining black baseball were never realized as interest continued to decline—but the Monarchs, now no longer based in Kansas City, continued to play into the early 1960s.

In their heyday, the Monarchs represented the creativity and culture of African Americans in baseball. As one of the most traveled teams in professional sports, they entertained thousands of baseball fans in rural areas across the Midwest. They also incubated players for the majors, such as Jackie Robinson and Ernie Banks.* Even Satchel Paige's* debut in the majors followed a long stint with the Monarchs. The Monarchs showcased the talents of some of the best Negro League players ever, including James "Cool Papa" Bell* and Chet Brewer. Most importantly, the Monarchs were a well-run organization, a model for black baseball in an era when segregation had forced the separation of whites and blacks in baseball.

SELECTED BIBLIOGRAPHY: Janet Bruce, *The Kansas City Monarchs: Champions of Black Baseball* (1985); James A. Riley, *The Biographical Encyclopedia of the Negro Baseball Leagues* (1994), 456; Maury White, "Remarkable Iowan Pioneered Black Teams, Women Players," *Des Moines Register*, 21 August 1994, 11D.

David R. McMahon

KARATE. This martial art was introduced to the United States in 1927 at a public demonstration at the Young Men's Christian Association (YMCA) in Honolulu, Hawaii. Kensu Yabu from Japan gave karate lessons to Okinawan immigrants in Hawaii during 1927. Karate had originated on the island of Okinawa as a variation of the Chinese style of fighting called *kempo*, combined with an unarmed form of combat called *te*. It was especially popular among immigrants from the Okinawan area of Japan during the 1920s, as it had been passed from generation to generation as a family art. The first karate school in the United States was opened in Hawaii in 1933 by Zuiho Mutsu and Kamesuke Hagaonna in Honolulu at the urging of Thomas Miyashiro, who had studied with Yabu. The students were mostly Japanese Americans. Dr. James M. Mitose, a *kibei* (an individual born in the United States but educated in Japan), was responsible for the growth of interest in kempo-karate just prior to World War II. He opened the Official Self-Defense Club in Honolulu in 1942 for teaching "the true meaning of self-defense." His classes were attended mostly by Westerners. In the 1950s, nisei and sansei (third-generation Japanese Americans) began the expansion of karate practice in Hawaii.

SELECTED BIBLIOGRAPHY: Bruce A. Haines, *Karate's History and Traditions* (1987).

Alison M. Wrynn

KEEFE, TIMOTHY JOHN ("Sir Timothy") (1 January 1857, Cambridge, MA–23 April 1933, Cambridge, MA). A baseball player, he was the son of Irish immigrants Patrick (a builder) and Mary Leary Keefe. Tim received a high school education before pitching in the major leagues from 1880 to 1893 for the Troy Trojans, New York Metropolitans, New York Giants, and Philadelphia Phillies. In 1888 he won a record nineteen consecutive games. The next year he became baseball's first "holdout," as he demanded $5,000 annually from the Giants and prevailed. Keefe umpired in the National League from 1894 to 1896 before working in real estate and coaching baseball for Harvard, Princeton, and Tufts. He was secretary of "the Brotherhood," the players union that spawned the Players League revolt of 1890. He founded a sporting goods company in 1889 and provided the official ball for the Players League. He designed the Giants uniforms in 1888. Keefe was known as a right-handed control pitcher, a student of the game, and an early practitioner of the change-up pitch. He won 342 games, the eighth highest total ever. He was named to the Baseball Hall of Fame in 1964.

SELECTED BIBLIOGRAPHY: Lee Allen and Thomas Meany, "Tim Keefe," *Kings of the Diamond* (1965); Lowell Reidenbaugh, "Tim Keefe," *Baseball's Hall of Fame: Cooperstown: Where the Legends Live Forever* (1993).

Timothy J. Wiles

KEELER, WILLIAM HENRY ("Willie") (3 March 1872, Brooklyn, NY–1 January 1923, Brooklyn, NY). An Irish American, Keeler was the son of a streetcar operator on the DeKalb Avenue line in Brooklyn. At 5' 4-1/2" and 140 pounds, the diminutive baseball player earned the nickname "Wee Willie" and has the distinction of being the smallest player enshrined in the National Baseball Hall of Fame in Cooperstown (1939). Keeler's major league career began in 1892 with the New York Giants and continued until 1910. An outfielder and utility infielder, Keeler was an integral part of the most powerful teams and played for the foremost managers in baseball, including Ned Hanlon at Baltimore and Brooklyn, John M. Ward and John J. McGraw* at the Polo Grounds, and Clark Griffith at Hilltop (Yankees). Keeler's prowess at the plate is often compared to that of Ty Cobb. He hit successfully in forty-four straight games, had a .432 batting average in 1897 (third highest in major league history), and hit .345 lifetime (fifth highest in major league history). An accomplished bunter and noted place hitter, Keeler is credited with originating the "Baltimore chop." As an Oriole, he and teammate McGraw developed and refined the hit-and-run play. Keeler's bat control was such that he rarely struck out and is credited with playing in excess of 100 games during the 1906 season before fanning. During an interview with a newspaper reporter Keeler explained his batting strategy as "keep your eye clear and hit 'em where they ain't." This often repeated comment has become a part of the American lexicon and is now applied to numerous situations both on and off the baseball field.

SELECTED BIBLIOGRAPHY: Mike Shatzkin, ed., *The Ballplayers: Baseball's Ultimate Biographical Reference* (1990); John Thorn, *A Century of Baseball Lore* (1974); Biographical Files, National Baseball Hall of Fame Library, Cooperstown, NY.

Gregory S. Harris

KELLEY, JOSEPH JAMES ("Joe") (9 December 1871, Cambridge, MA– 14 August 1943, Baltimore). A baseball player of Irish descent, the 5' 11", 190-pound Kelley was a player, manager, scout, and coach in professional baseball from 1891 to 1926. Kelley began his professional baseball career with Lowell of the New England League as a pitcher, going 10–3 in 1891. On days Kelley did not pitch he spent time in the outfield, stealing twenty-one bases and hitting .331. By the end of the season he signed a contract with the Boston Beaneaters of the National League (NL), starting his career as a major league outfielder. For the next sixteen years Kelley compiled a .317 lifetime batting average (going eleven consecutive years with a .300 or better average), belted 2,222 hits (including 356 doubles), struck out only 163 times, and stole 443 bases. By 1892 Kelley had brought his leadership abilities to the Baltimore Orioles (National League [NL]), helping transform them into league champions. With the Orioles, Kelley was always among the NL leaders in slugging percentage and stolen bases. On 3 September 1894, as a member of the Baltimore Orioles (NL), Joe accomplished an on-field feat that has never been duplicated in the history of baseball. During a doubleheader, Kelley had nine consecutive hits. He was posthumously elected to the National Baseball Hall of Fame in 1971.

SELECTED BIBLIOGRAPHY: Craig Carter, ed., *Daguerreotypes, the Complete Major and Minor League Records of Baseball's Greats*, 8th ed. (1990), 150–151; Craig Carter, *The Sporting News, 1997 Edition, Complete Baseball Record Book* (1997), 19; Peter Filichia, *Professional Baseball Franchises: From the Abbeville Athletics to the Zanesville*

Indians (1993), 15, 25; Lowell Reidenbaugh, "Joe Kelley," in his *Baseball's Hall of Fame: Cooperstown: Where the Legends Live Forever* (1993).

Scot E. Mondore

KELLY, GEORGE LANGE ("High Pockets") (10 September 1898, San Francisco–13 October 1984, Burlingame, CA). The son of James and Mary (Lange) Kelly, George came from paternal Irish ancestry and maternal German stock. He left Polytechnic High School in his senior year to pursue a professional baseball career. Acquired by the New York Giants in 1915, Kelly became their regular first baseman in 1920. He led the National League in runs batted in (RBIs) with 94 in 1920 and 136 in 1924. He established a major league record by hitting seven home runs in six consecutive games from 11 July through 16 July 1924. Kelly hit over .300 for six straight seasons and compiled a career .297 batting average. He coached the Cincinnati Reds from 1935 through 1937 and the Boston Braves from 1938 through 1943. From 1946 to 1954 George scouted for various major league teams while working in the off-season as a ground transport dispatcher at San Francisco International Airport until he retired in 1960. Kelly was known as a consistent hitter and outstanding first baseman. He was inducted into the National Baseball Hall of Fame in 1973.

SELECTED BIBLIOGRAPHY: Harry T. Brundidge, "George Kelly's Story of 40 Years in Game," (Newspaper unknown), 8 January 1958; Hall of Fame Biographical Files; Lowell Reidenbaugh, "George Kelly," in *Baseball's Hall of Fame: Cooperstown: Where the Legends Live Forever* (1993).

Jill E. Renwick

KELLY, MICHAEL JOSEPH ("King") (31 December 1857, Troy, NY–8 November 1894, Boston). A baseball player, he was the son of Irish immigrants Michael and Catherine (Kylie), who survived the Irish famine of the 1840s by escaping to America. Kelly began his career in 1878 with the Cincinnati National League team. In sixteen years of professional baseball he played for seven teams in three different leagues, and he retired with a lifetime batting average of .308. Kelly was known as an outstanding and daring ballplayer, but he also had a charming personality and a friendly attitude toward the fans, which helped him become known as the "King of Baseball." Chicago fans once threatened to boycott their team's games when Kelly was sold to Boston. He was immortalized in the song "Slide, Kelly, Slide," which became the country's first hit recording after it was released on an Edison cylinder. Although ghostwritten, his 1888 autobiography was the first to be published by a ballplayer. Additionally, young boys are reported to have approached him with paper and pencil seeking autographs, thereby establishing this behavior as a cultural phenomenon. He is considered to be the first American athlete to achieve matinee idol status. Following his career, he took to the vaudeville stage as a singer-dancer-actor, becoming the first American athlete to successfully enter the theater. Kelly was elected to the Baseball Hall of Fame in 1945.

SELECTED BIBLIOGRAPHY: Marty Appel, *Slide, Kelly, Slide: The Wild Life and Times of Mike "King" Kelly—Baseball's First Superstar* (1996); John L. Evers, "King Kelly," in Mike Shatzkin, *The Ballplayers* (1990), 561–562; Mike Kelly, *Play Ball: Stories of the Ball Field* (1888); Michael Joseph Kelly, Research File, National Baseball Hall of Fame Library (October 1996).

James L. Gates, Jr.

KEMP, RAY (7 April 1907, Rassing, PA–   ). An African American football player, his father (Ona) was a coal miner-farmer, and his mother (Hattie Perkins) was a housewife. Kemp was raised in, and played high school football in, Cecil, Pennsylvania, a small coal mining town east of Pittsburgh. He was a college and professional football player in the 1920s and 1930s. Following a year of working in the coal mines Kemp enrolled at Pittsburgh's Duquesne University in 1927. There he played football for Elmer Layden—one of the famous Notre Dame "Four Horsemen." At that time few African Americans were members of integrated teams, even in the North. Kemp had no African American teammates during his last three years at Duquesne, when he was in the starting lineup. He received honorable mention on some 1931 All-American teams. In 1932 Kemp helped Layden coach at Duquesne and played for the semipro "J. P. Rooneys," a team owned by Art Rooney. The following season Rooney purchased a National Football League (NFL) franchise for Pittsburgh and called his new team the Pirates. The squad consisted of holdovers from the Rooneys (including Kemp) and some NFL castoffs. Twelve African Americans had played in the NFL from the beginning of the league through the 1932 season. But in 1933 Kemp and Joe Lillard of the Chicago Cardinals were the only two African Americans in the league. He was released following the third game of the season but was rehired for the final game against the New York Giants. Ironically, Kemp started and played most of that game for the Pirates, but it proved to be his last as a player. In 1934 he was offered the football coaching position at Bluefield (West Virginia) State College. That season he led the Blues to a 8–0–1 season in what proved to be his first season of a successful thirty-nine-year career as a coach, athletics director, and teacher at Bluefield, Lincoln (Missouri) University, and Tennessee State University. In 1934 the NFL entered a period of segregation when Lillard was not rehired by the Cardinals, nor were any African Americans signed by other teams. The league remained segregated until the 1946 season.

SELECTED BIBLIOGRAPHY: C. Robert Barnett, "The First Black Steeler," *Pittsburgh Courier*, 27 August 1983; David Neft, Richard M. Cohen, and Jordan A. Deutsch, *Pro Football: The Early Years, an Encyclopedic History, 1895–1959* (1978).

C. Robert Barnett

KETCHEL, STANLEY (14 September 1886, Grand Rapids, MI–15 October 1910, Conway, MO). A Polish American boxer, he was the son of Thomas Kiecal and the former Julia Oblinski, who worked in the farms and furniture factories of Grand Rapids. He had a career record of fifty-two wins, four losses, four draws, and four no decisions. He left home around the age of twelve to pursue a life of adventure in "the Wild West." He eventually found work as a waiter in a hotel in the rowdy mining town of Butte, Montana, as a bouncer and fighter. He launched his professional boxing career at the age of sixteen. Stan Anglicized his last name and quickly became a fan favorite as he knocked out thirty-five of his first forty foes. Ketchel received no formal boxing training, but at 5' 9" and 154 pounds he fought with a fearsome intensity that earned him the nickname of "the Michigan Assassin." Outside the ring Ketchel was a colorful character, a fun-loving prankster who wore western garb and carried a blue-barreled revolver. When he beat Mike "Twin" Sullivan in February 1908, he assumed the vacant world middleweight championship. In September 1908 Ketchel lost his title to Billy Papke, in part because he was knocked down by a vicious right to the face by Papke when the champion extended his glove to shake hands at the opening bell. After that bout, fighters started the custom of shaking before the bell. Two months later Ketchel handily won the rematch to become the first middleweight to regain the title. He fought frequently and often took on heavier opponents, even knocking out light-heavyweight champion Jack O'Brien. His most famous bout came against the first African American heavyweight champion, Jack Johnson.* Despite being outweighed by about forty pounds, Ketchel fought fearlessly until he was knocked out by Johnson in the twelfth round by a vicious blow that left some of Ketchel's teeth embedded in Johnson's glove. In the fall of 1910, while Ketchel was in training on a ranch in Conway, Missouri, he was shot and killed by a hired hand, Walter Dipley. Dipley was found guilty of murder, and Ketchel's body was returned to Grand Rapids for burial in a Polish cemetery, which virtually the entire town attended.

SELECTED BIBLIOGRAPHY: Nat Fleischer, *The Michigan Assassin* (1946); Jack Johnson and Damon Runyon, *Jack Johnson: In and Out of the Ring* (1927); Gilbert Odd, *Encyclopedia of Boxing* (1983); Peter Walsh, *Men of Steel* (1993).

Thomas M. Tarapacki

KING, DON (20 August 1931, Cleveland, OH–   ). An African American boxing manager and promoter, he was raised in a working-class area of Cleveland where violence and crime were endemic. From an early age he was involved in gambling operations, and at age twenty-three and thirty-five King was implicated with gambling-related homicides. He was convicted in the second incident and served more than four years in prison. In any assessment of his impact on boxing as a bizarre, eccentric promoter, part genius and part villain, King can be compared only to the legendary Tex Rickard. One of King's most celebrated extravaganzas was his political tour de force "the rumble in the jungle"—the 1974 Muhammad Ali*–George Foreman* fight. Their arena was the sweatbox of Kinshasa, Zaire, Africa, and King adroitly maneuvered Zaire dictator Mobutu Sese Seke to "front up" with a guarantee of $10 million to host the championship fight. Following the successful sports drama in the Third World King staged the "thrilla in Manila" with Muhammad Ali and Joe Frazier.* King has enjoyed phenomenal success in promoting world championship fights. His "grand slam of boxing" on 20 February 1992, the Julio Caesar Chevez–Greg Haugen fight staged in Mexico City, attracted a world record boxing crowd of 132,274. Despite ongoing pressure from a variety of law enforcement groups, King's greatest debacle may be the disastrous Mike Tyson*–Evander Holyfield 1997 title fight. Critics will continue to point to the manner in which King, buoyed by money, pay-per-view audiences, and astronomic contracts, steered Tyson as if he was a puppet, not a protégé. King was inducted into the International Boxing Hall of Fame in 1997.

SELECTED BIBLIOGRAPHY: Richard Hoffer, "Feeding Frenzy," *Sports Illustrated* 87 (7 July 1997): 32–38; Leigh Montville, "Don King," *Sports Illustrated* 81, No. 12 (19 September 1994): 137; William Nack, "The Long Count," *Sports Illustrated* 87, No. 12 (22 September 1997): 72–87; Randy Roberts, "The Politics and Economics of Televised Boxing," in Elliott J. Gorn, ed., *Muhammad Ali: The People's Champ* (1995); Jeffrey T. Sammons, *Beyond the Ring: The Role of Boxing in American Society* (1988); *When We Were Kings* (film, 1997); materials received from the International Boxing Hall of Fame, Canastota, NY.

Scott A.G.M. Crawford

KIVIAT, ABEL RICHARD (23 June 1892, New York City–24 August 1991, Lakehurst, NJ). A track-and-field athlete, he was the son of Jewish immigrants from Bialystok, Poland. His father (Morris) was a rabbinical student-turned-peddler who, with his mother (Zelda), owned a clothing store on Staten Island. While still attending Curtis High School, he became a middle-distance runner for the Irish-American Athletic Club* (IAAC) in 1909 and later its captain. Only 5'4" and slightly bowlegged, Kiviat won the Metropolitan New York and Canadian one-mile championships that summer and then anchored the IAAC four-mile relay to a world record. From 1910 to 1915 he was a leading miler, winning the Baxter Mile four times (1910–13) and setting an indoor record of 4:18.2 on a flat floor track. He was the national outdoor mile champion in 1911, 1912, and 1914. In 1912 he lowered the world 1,500-meter record three times in thirteen days, and his final time of 3:55.8 was unbroken for five years. At the Stockholm Olympics in 1912 he lost a memorable 1,500-meter race to Britain's Arnold Jackson, nipping Norman Taber of the United States for the silver medal in track's first photo finish. Kiviat was an extraordinarily versatile runner, winning nine national titles and setting indoor records at 600, 880, and 1,000 yards. He performed the unmatched feat of winning the 600 and 1,000 at the indoor nationals in both 1911 and 1913. Outdoors, he anchored the IAAC's 4 × 880-yard relay to a world record in 1910 and won the 1913 U.S. cross-country championship. He was suspended by the Amateur Athletic Union in 1915 for allegedly demanding seventy-five dollars in expense money. Reinstated before the 1924 Olympics, a leg injury in the 3,000-meter steeplechase trials ended his career. Kiviat served about thirty years as a deputy clerk of the U.S. District Court in Manhattan. A man of humor and charm, he spoke frequently to youth and community groups. Proud of his traditional Jewish upbringing, he was inducted into the International Jewish Sports Hall of Fame in Israel and provided a model of physical accomplishment for Jewish youth. Subsequently, he served for decades as a press steward at major meets. He was rediscovered at age ninety as the oldest living Olympic medalist and jogged one kilometer in the 1984 torch relay. He was elected to the National Track and Field Hall of Fame in 1985.

SELECTED BIBLIOGRAPHY: Lewis H. Carlson and John J. Fogarty, *Tales of Gold* (1987); Alan H. Feiler, "The Durability of the Long Distance Runner," *Baltimore Jewish Times* 190, No. 9 (29 December 1989): 46–49; Gardner Nelson and Roberto Quercetani, *The Milers* (1985); William Simons, "Abel Kiviat Interview," *Journal of Sport History* 13, No. 3 (1986), 235–266.

Alan S. Katchen

KOUFAX, SANFORD ("Sandy") (30 December 1935, Brooklyn, NY–   ). Considered one of baseball's best left-handed pitchers, he is of Jewish ancestry, the son of Jack and Evelyn Braun. After his parents divorced, his mother, an accountant, married Irving Koufax, an attorney. Koufax played baseball and basketball in Brooklyn school yards and Jewish community clubs. His basketball talent earned him a scholarship to the University of Cincinnati in 1953. While a student there, he impressed baseball scouts with his pitching prowess, and he signed a professional contract with the Brooklyn Dodgers in 1954. Koufax pitched for the Brooklyn and Los Angeles Dodgers from 1955 through his retirement in 1966. Through the 1961 season, he was known primarily as a strikeout pitcher with raw talent. In his first major league start during the 1955 season, he struck out fourteen Cincinnati Reds. In the five seasons after 1961, Koufax dominated the National League. He led the league in earned run average every season and continually ranked among the leaders in wins. Koufax led the Dodgers to world championships in 1963 and 1965 and the National League pennant in 1966. Koufax accomplished this success despite pitching in severe pain as result of an arm injury he suffered in 1963. In 1966 Koufax had one of his best seasons and won the Cy Young Award. This was his third such honor, having previously won in 1963 and 1965. Despite tremendous success on the pitching mound, Koufax retired after the 1966 season to prevent permanent damage to his arm. Five years later, he became the youngest man enshrined into the Baseball Hall of Fame. He also threw four no-hitters, a record that was later broken by Nolan Ryan. Koufax would not pitch during the Jewish high holidays of Rosh Hashanah and Yom Kippur in late September and early October. During the 1965 World Series versus Minnesota, Koufax sat out the first game because of this conflict. Although Don Drysdale lost game one and Koufax lost game two, Koufax picked up wins in the fifth and seventh game, bringing the title to

Los Angeles. After baseball, Koufax served as an instructor, real estate salesman, and NBC Sports broadcaster.

SELECTED BIBLIOGRAPHY: Peter Levine, *Ellis Island to Ebbets Field* (1992); David L. Porter, ed., "Koufax, Sanford 'Sandy,' " *Biographical Dictionary of American Sports: Baseball* (1987); Joel Zoss and John Bowman, *Diamonds in the Rough: The Untold History of Baseball* (1996), 129; various items from Sanford Koufax, players file at the National Baseball Hall of Fame Library including articles (many undated) on his career.

Corey Seeman

KRIZ, FRANK (?, 1893, New York City–?1955, New York City). He was the son of Czech immigrant parents. He began gymnastic training at the Bohemian Gymnastic Association Sokol of New York City when he was eight years old. Encouraged by his instructor at the Sokol, Joseph Gregor, he began competition at age nineteen and dominated all the meets he entered, both Sokol and Amateur Athletic Union (AAU), until he was thirty-five years old. He won the AAU All-Around Championship in 1922 and 1924, and he took first place for the vault in 1918 and 1922, the parallel bars in 1922, and the horizontal bar in 1924. Frank Kriz represented the United States at the Olympic Games in 1920, 1924, and 1928, winning first place at the Olympic tryouts in 1920 and 1924. At the 1924 games in Paris he won the vault with the incredible score of 9.98, and placed sixth in the rope climb with a time of 8 and 2/5 seconds. His final score of 100.293 was nineteenth all-around, far ahead of the other Americans, even though he was thirty-one years old at the time. Frank Kriz worked as a fireman in New York City. He built a horizontal bar behind his firehouse so that he could practice in his spare time. He was posthumously inducted into the U.S. Gymnastics Hall of Fame in 1959.

SELECTED BIBLIOGRAPHY: *Centennial of the Sokols in America, 1865–1965* (1965); A. B. Frederick, *Roots of American Gymnastics* (1995); Richard Edd Laptad, *A History of the Development of the United States Gymnastics Federation* (1972).

Vladislav Slavik

KRZYZEWSKI, MICHAEL (13 February 1947, Chicago–). A second-generation Polish American, his father (William) was an elevator operator, and his mother (Emily) was a maintenance worker at the Chicago Athletic Club. A graduate of Weber High School in Chicago, he went on to college at West Point, where he played point guard on Army's team. After graduation Krzyzewski coached basketball at Army-based teams outside the United States, later coaching at the prep school and collegiate levels. Since 1981 he has been the head coach at Duke University in Durham, North Carolina. There "Coach K" achieved national recognition both for himself and the program that he has built into a national powerhouse. The Blue Devils were the premier college basketball team of the late 1980s and early 1990s, as Krzyzewski brought Duke to seven Final Fours in nine years (including five straight from 1988 to 1992), a streak matched only by the great John Wooden-led University of California at Los

Angeles (UCLA) squads of the 1960s and 1970s. Highlighting this run of greatness were the back-to-back national championships that Duke won in 1991 and 1992. Krzyzewski's 1986 team also set a national record by notching thirty-seven victories in a single season. Under his guidance Duke has been noted for its particularly high academic and personal standards for its players. Krzyzewski has garnered four National Coach of the Year awards (1986, 1989, 1991, 1992) and in 1992 was also named Sportsman of the Year by *The Sporting News*, the first college basketball coach ever to receive that honor.

SELECTED BIBLIOGRAPHY: *Duke Basketball Media Guides*; John Feinstein, *A March to Madness* (1998); Jennifer Frey, "Don't Cry for Mike Krzyzewski—He Knows That It's a Wonderful Life," *Washington Post*, 15 March 1998, D-4; Robert Lipsyte, "All Coaches Who Can, Just Do It," *New York Times*, 25 April 1993, S-9.

Zachary Davis

KWAN, MICHELLE (7 July 1980, Torrance, CA–   ). A figure skater, she is a first-generation Chinese American. Her father, Daniel, is from the Canton region of China; her mother, Estella, is from Hong Kong. Both Michelle and her older sister Karen began skating lessons when Michelle was five years old after watching their brother play ice hockey. Kwan turned professional at age twelve, becoming the youngest senior competitor at the U.S. Nationals in almost twenty years. In 1993 she won first place in women's singles at the Olympic Sports Festival. In 1994 she became the youngest medalist ever at the U.S. National Figure Skating championships. Kwan was first alternate to the 1994 Winter Olympic team during the Nancy Kerrigan/Tonja Harding controversy. In 1994 she finished fourth at the World Championships at the age of fourteen. In 1995 Kwan finished second at the National Championships and once again finished fourth at the World Championships. In 1996 she won the U.S. Women's National Figure Skating Championships and the World Championships. At the 1997 National Championships, Kwan placed second. She also received the silver medal at both the 1997 World Championships and the 1998 Winter Olympics at Nagano, Japan.

SELECTED BIBLIOGRAPHY: Susan Bickelhaupt, "Gold Not Kwan's Only Goal," *Boston Globe*, 19 April 1998, E-19; Filip Bondy, "Seeking a Perfect 6 at a Precocious 12," *New York Times*, 21 January 1996, B13; Kimberly Gatto, *Michelle Kwan: Champion on Ice* (1998); Randy Harvey, "Kwan Can Tell You That All That Glitters Is Not Gold," *Los Angeles Times*, 7 April 1998, C-2; Michelle Kwan, *Michelle Kwan: My Book of Memories* (1998); Jere Longman, "At 18, Kwan Idling at the Crossroads," *New York Times*, 29 July 1998, 4; Linda Shaughnessy, *Michelle Kwan: Skating Like the Wind* (1997).

Alison M. Wrynn

L

LACROSSE. Lacrosse was the most important and widespread indigenous stickball game played by American Indians when Europeans first arrived in the New World. Played by men in a variety of forms mostly east of the Mississippi River, lacrosse was one of the world's first team sports. Its distinguishing feature was the use of a netted racquet to retrieve the ball from the ground and throw, catch, and carry it into or past a goal. The cardinal rule in all varieties of lacrosse was (and remains today) that the ball, with few exceptions, must not be touched with the hands.

Early data on lacrosse (beginning in the 1630s) are scant and often conflicting, informing us mostly about team size, equipment used, the duration of games, and dimensions of playing fields. The oldest surviving sticks (museum specimens) date only from the first quarter of the nineteenth century, and the first detailed reports on Indian lacrosse are even later. The anthropologist James Mooney (among the Eastern Cherokee) was the first in 1888 to document the game with a camera. Earlier artistic renderings, such as George Catlin's of Choctaw lacrosse (1834), have been shown to be fanciful and unreliable representations.

An accurate reconstruction of lacrosse's history is probably impossible. As can best be determined, the distribution of lacrosse shows it to have been played throughout the eastern half of North America, mostly by tribes in the St. Lawrence Valley, in the southeast, and around the western Great Lakes. On the basis of the equipment (principally the sticks) and their handling techniques, it is possible to discern three basic forms of lacrosse—the southeastern, Great Lakes, and Iroquoian. Among southeastern tribes (Cherokee, Choctaw, Creek, Chickasaw, Seminole, and others), a double-stick version of the game is still played. A two-and-a half-foot stick is held in each hand; the soft, small deerskin ball is retrieved and, with the wrists locked, cupped between the sticks. Great Lakes players (Ojibwe, Menominee, Winnebago, Santee Dakota, and others) used a single three-foot stick terminating in a round, closed pocket about three to four inches in diameter. The pocket was scarcely larger than the ball, which was usually made of wood, charred and scraped to shape, although hard clay balls have been documented. With the stick clamped over it, a ground ball was retrieved with a quick twist of the wrist, which nonnative players later called "the Indian scoop." The northeastern stick, found among Iroquoian (Mohawk, Seneca, Onondaga, etc.) and New England tribes, is the progenitor of all present-day sticks. The longest of the three—usually more than three feet—it was characterized by its shaft's ending in a sort of crook; giving rise to the folk etymology that the game was named after a bishop's crosier (*crosse*). The northeastern stick was characterized by a large, flat triangular surface of webbing extending as much as two-thirds the length of the stick; where the outermost string met the shaft, it formed the pocket of the stick.

Lacrosse appears to have been given its name by early French settlers in Canada, using the generic term for any game played with a curved stick and a ball. Native terminology, however, tends to describe more the technique of the game. In the mid-nineteenth century, English-speaking Montreal amateur athletes adapted the Iroquois game they were familiar with and attempted to modernize it with a new set of rules. The game became quickly popular in Canada, where today, together with hockey, it is officially recognized as one of the country's two "national sports." Canada began to export lacrosse throughout the English Commonwealth (Australia, for instance), as nonnative teams traveled to Europe for exhibition matches against Iroquois players. These tours were partly an attempt to stimulate emigration to Canada. The game spread to the northeastern United States (mostly through upstate New York) following the Civil War.

Beyond its recreational function, lacrosse traditionally played a more serious role in Indian culture. Its origins are rooted in the legends of those tribes playing it, and the game continues to be used to cure illness and is surrounded with rituals and ceremonies that are ancient and fundamental to the traditional lifestyles of Native Americans. Among some peoples (mostly southeastern tribes) game equipment and players are still ritually prepared by venerated religious leaders, and team selection and victory are often considered supernaturally controlled. With the Iroquois, the origins and purpose of lacrosse are spiritual. It is first and foremost a medicine game, to serve individuals, nations, and the Haudenosaunee (Six Nations confederacy). The game's entertainment value and its role in settling tribal disputes are secondary functions. Among southeastern peoples lacrosse primarily served spiritual purposes, but at times it also provided a surrogate for war. The game also permitted the players to vent aggression, and territorial disputes between tribes were sometimes settled with a game.

Native forms of lacrosse declined in many areas by the late nineteenth century. This was due, in large part, to the policy of the U.S. government, which aimed to destroy Native American language and culture in order to convert Indians to Christianity and appropriate their land. As traditional Indian culture was eroding, lacrosse came under increasing attack from both government officials and missionaries. They claimed that the sport encouraged excessive violence and interfered with church attendance. They also believed that the traditional custom of wagering on matches had a detrimental effect on the already impoverished Indians.

At the same time, the spread of nonnative lacrosse from the Montreal area eventually led to its position today worldwide (especially in Australia, Japan, and Germany) as one of the fastest growing sports, with more than half a million players. It is controlled by official regulations and played with manufactured rather than hand-made equipment—the aluminum shafted stick with its plastic head, for example, and hard rubber ball. Meanwhile the traditional Great Lakes game died out by 1950, but the Iroquois and southeastern tribes continue to play their own forms of lacrosse. During the 1980s and 1990s the Iroquois Nationals Lacrosse Club* gained recognition from the International Lacrosse Federation and competed in World Cup tournaments. Ironically, the field lacrosse game of nonnative women today most closely resembles the Indian game of the past, retaining the wooden stick but lacking the protective gear and demarcated sidelines of the men's game.

SELECTED BIBLIOGRAPHY: Stewart Culin, *Games of the North American Indians*, in *Twenty-fourth Annual Report of the Bureau of American Ethnology, 1902–1903* (1907); James Mooney, "The Cherokee Ball Play," *American Anthropologist* 3 (1890): 105–132; North American Indian Travelling College, *Tewaarathon: Story of Our National Game* (1978); Thomas Vennum, Jr., *American Indian Lacrosse: Little Brother of War* (1994).

Thomas Vennum, Jr.

LACY, SAMUEL H. (23 October 1903, Mystic, CT–   ). An African American sportswriter, Lacy was born in Connecticut but moved with his parents, Rose and Sam, to Washington, D.C., when he was only two years old. His mother was a Shinnecock Indian. Sam grew up just five blocks from Griffith Stadium, and he graduated from Henry Armstrong High School after starring in basketball, football, and baseball. He went on to Howard University to complete his education. Lacy began his journalism career in 1930 at the *Washington Tribune*. He moved on to the *Chicago Defender* in 1940 and finally settled in as the sports editor for the *Afro-American* in Washington, D.C., in 1944. Lacy wrote a weekly column called "A to Z" from 1944 to 1991. He is best known for his efforts in the fight to integrate major league baseball. He worked with fellow reporter Wendell Smith to set up tryouts for Negro League* players. He also fought to integrate the hotels where the players stayed and wrote articles in support of integration in other sports as well. Lacy served on a Major League Committee of Baseball Integration with Branch Rickey, Larry MacPhail, and Joseph Rainey. In 1948 Lacy became the first black admitted to the Baseball Writers Association. His contributions to sportswriting were recognized in 1984 with his election to the Maryland Media Hall of Fame and in 1985 with his induction into the Black Athletes Hall of Fame in Las Vegas. In 1991 Lacy received the Lifetime Achievement Award from the National Association of Black Journalists. He was also a recipient of the Red Smith Award for lifetime achievement from the Associated Press Sports Editors, and in 1998 he was inducted into the writer's wing of the National Baseball Hall of Fame.

SELECTED BIBLIOGRAPHY: "Black Sportswriter Broke Journalism Barriers," *Hagerstown Herald Mail*, 25 August 1991; Alex Dominguez, "First Black Baseball Writer Blazed Trail for Others to Follow," *Chicago Sun-Times*, 3 November 1991, 20; Barry Horn, "Sportswriter Lacy Still Going Strong at 94," *Houston Chronicle*, 26 April 1998, 9; Mark G. Judge, "Writing the Good Fight," *Washington City Paper*, 17 May 1991, 28–30; Samuel Lacy Papers, National Baseball Hall of Fame, Cooperstown, NY.

Leslie Heaphy

LAJOIE, NAPOLEON ("Larry") (5 September 1874, Woonsocket, RI–7 February 1959, Daytona Beach, FL). A baseball player, he was the son of French Canadian immigrants. His father (Jean Baptiste) was a laborer, and his mother (Celina) was a homemaker. He had almost no formal education. Lajoie joined the Philadelphia Phillies in 1896 after playing minor league baseball for only three months. He soon proved to be an exceptional ballplayer, a graceful fielder, and one of the game's greatest hitters. In 1898 he switched from first base to second base, the position he played for the rest of his career. Dissatisfied with his salary, Lajoie jumped in 1901 from the Phillies, where he was earning $2,400 a year, to Connie Mack's* Athletics, the Philadelphia team in the new American League. Mack offered him a four-year contract for $24,000, and Lajoie became the new league's first star. An injunction prompted his trade to Cleveland in 1902, where his excellent play continued for a dozen years. So popular was he in Cleveland that the team was nicknamed the Naps from 1905 to 1914. Lajoie managed the Naps for five seasons while he was still a player, but he never was a member of a pennant-winning team. He is remembered as one of the best second basemen ever, with his .422 batting average in 1902 being the highest ever recorded in the American League. He was elected to the Baseball Hall of Fame in 1937.

SELECTED BIBLIOGRAPHY: John McCallum, "Nap Lajoie, The Fabulous Frenchman," *Inside Baseball* (December 1952): 46–47, 74–77; J. M. Murphy, "Napoleon Lajoie: Modern Baseball's First Superstar," *The National Pastime* 7 (1988): 1–79; "Napoleon Lajoie," in Martin Appel and Burt Goldblatt, *Baseball's Best: The Hall of Fame Gallery* (1977).

Steven P. Gietschier

LAMOTTA, JAKE (10 July 1921, New York City–   ). A prizefighter, he is the son of Giuseppe, a native of Italy, and Elizabeth, his Italian American mother. LaMotta's education came informally through street fighting, robbing, and hustling, which brought him to the State Reform School in Coxsackie, New

York. Upon release, LaMotta boxed as an amateur before turning professional. From 1941 to 1954, he fought 106 bouts with eighty-three wins, nineteen losses, and four draws. His fight with Billy Fox in November 1947 created his "bad guy" image. LaMotta threw the fight but explained to a Senate committee years later that he took a dive "for a shot at the middleweight championship." On 16 June 1949 he got his shot and won the middleweight championship of the world by defeating Marcel Cerdan. LaMotta lost the title in February 1951 to Sugar Ray Robinson and eventually retired from boxing in 1954. The ex-boxer soon purchased a Miami Beach cabaret. In 1957, while running it, he was arrested and jailed for aiding a fifteen-year-old prostitute at his Miami Beach bar. LaMotta denied the charges but served his sentence. In the mid-1950s Rocky Graziano* introduced him to acting on the Martha Raye television show. This led to his appearance in nineteen films. LaMotta's autobiography, *Raging Bull* (1970), became an acclaimed film starring Robert DeNiro (1980). LaMotta was inducted into the International Boxing Hall of Fame in 1990.

SELECTED BIBLIOGRAPHY: Jake LaMotta, with Joseph Carter and Peter Savage, *Raging Bull: My Story* (1970); *New York Times*, 15, 18, 19, 20, 21, 22 November 1947 and 18 December 1947, 45 and 20 March 1957, 20 and 15 June 1960, 1, 52 and 16 June 1960, 42; Robert A. Nowlan and Gwendolyn Wright Nowlan, *The Films of the Eighties* (1991); James B. Roberts and Alexander G. Skutt, *The Boxing Register International Boxing Hall of Fame Official Record Book* (1997).

Philip M. Montesano

LAPCHICK, JOSEPH (12 April 1900, Yonkers, NY–10 August 1970, New York City). A basketball player and coach, he was the son of immigrant parents from Slovakia, Joseph and Frances (Kassik) Lapchick. His father was a policeman. Lapchick reached a height of 6' when he was only twelve years old and attracted the attention of professional basketball scouts while he was still a teenager. Like many Slovak youth, he left high school to contribute to the family income and worked as a machinist. He grew to a height of 6'5" and became one of the all-time great Slovak American basketball stars during the 1920s and 1930s. As a young man he moved from team to team in several leagues in search of the highest bidder because no seasonal contracts existed. Finally, in 1923 he stuck with one team for the season—the "Original Celtics," the first professional team to issue season contracts. With Lapchick's height, the Celtics dominated the American Basketball League (ABL) because a jump ball was called after every field goal, and the Celtics could usually retain possession. The Celtics proved so dominant that the league forced the team to dissolve itself. Lapchick next played with the Cleveland Rosenblums, who took the next two ABL championships. After a season with the Toledo Red Men, Lapchick rejoined a reorganized Celtics team for six more seasons before retiring in 1936. Afterward Lapchick continued his basketball career in coaching at St. John's University in New York City. Two of his early teams (1943 and 1944) won the National Invitational Tournament (NIT). When he returned to college hoops in

1957, his teams won two more NIT tournaments in 1959 and 1965. Lapchick ended his collegiate coaching career with 335 wins and only 129 losses. He also coached the New York Knickerbockers from 1948 to 1956, compiling a record of 326 victories and 247 losses. In 1966 his achievements earned him a place in the Basketball Hall of Fame.

SELECTED BIBLIOGRAPHY: Ralph Hickock, *A Who's Who of Sports Champions* (1995); Joseph Krajsa, ed., *Slovaks in America: A Bicentennial Study* (1978); John D. McCallum, *College Basketball, U.S.A. since 1892* (1978).

Michael J. Kopanic, Jr.

LATZO, PETER (1 August 1902, Colerain, PA–7 July 1968, Atlantic City, NJ). A prizefighter, he was the son of Carpatho-Rusyn immigrants. Latzo grew up in Taylor, southwest of Scranton. A gifted athlete who probably could have played professional baseball, he emulated his older brother and became a fighter at age sixteen. Most of his early bouts were in Scranton and Wilkes-Barre, Pennsylvania. "Pete" Latzo was world welterweight boxing champion from 20 May 1926 to 3 June 1927. He won the title in Scranton, Pennsylvania, with a ten-round decision over Irish American Mickey Walker. Once a child-laborer in the anthracite mines, Latzo became the third Slavic American champion in boxing history. Latzo belonged to the Greek Catholic Union, a Carpatho-Rusyn gymnastics and sports society. Interestingly, a New York sportswriter praised him for using his real name, although, like many boxers, he had earlier assumed an Irish one. "Our Champion" was the appellation the Sokol newspaper gave him following his title victory. However, he lost his third title defense to Joe Dundee at New York's Polo Grounds.

SELECTED BIBLIOGRAPHY: Bob Burill, comp., *Who's Who in Boxing* (1974); John D. McCallum, comp., *The Encyclopedia of World Boxing Champions since 1912* (1975); *Philadelphia Inquirer*, 21 May 1926, 24.

Richard Renoff

LAZZERI, ANTHONY MICHAEL ("Poosh 'Em Up") (6 December 1903, San Francisco–6 August 1946, San Francisco). A baseball player, he was the son of Italian American boilermaker Augustin and Julia Lazzeri. Tony left St. Theresa's Catholic School at the age of fifteen. He became an ironworker and played minor league baseball for Salt Lake City in the Pacific Coast League in 1922. Signed by the New York Yankees in 1926, he played in the major leagues from 1926 to 1939, earning All-Star recognition in 1933 and remaining with the Yankees until 1937. Despite having epilepsy, the hard-hitting second baseman was a vital link for a team that won six American League (AL) pennants and five World Series titles. For his major league career he batted .292 with 1,840 hits, 178 home runs, and 1,191 runs batted in (RBIs). He drove in 100 or more runs seven times and hit .300 or better five times. In 1936 Lazzeri set the AL single-game record with eleven RBIs, including two grand-slam home runs, a record at that time. His major league career ended in mid-1939 after short stints with the Brooklyn Dodgers and New York Giants. Lazzeri managed Toronto from mid-1939 through 1940. He returned to the minor leagues as a player and then manager during the early 1940s. After leaving baseball, Lazzeri retired to San Francisco with his wife, Maye, and ran a tavern until his death. Although not flashy, Lazzeri was known for his consistent play and leadership abilities. He was named to the Baseball Hall of Fame in 1992.

SELECTED BIBLIOGRAPHY: Mark Gallagher, "Tony Lazzeri," *The Yankee Encyclopedia* (1990); Frank Graham, *The New York Yankees: An Informal History* (1943); *New York Times*, 9 August 1946; David L. Porter, "Tony Lazzeri," *Biographical Dictionary of American Sports* (1987).

Dan Bennett

LEBOW, FRED (3 June 1932, Arad, Romania–9 October 1994, New York City). A promoter of road racing, he was born Fishel Lebowitz, the son of Orthodox Jews. His father was a produce merchant in Romania. During the Nazi invasion the family was split up and hidden by friends; when the Soviets occupied Romania, most of his relatives went to Israel. Fred wandered around Europe, became an Irish stateless citizen, and migrated to the United States. In Manhattan he attended the Fashion Institute of Technology; in Brooklyn he was a Talmudic scholar; in Cleveland he was a salesman and part-owner of a comedy club. After returning to New York City, he got a job in the garment industry. Lebow began jogging in the late 1960s and joined the New York Road Runners Club (NYRRC) in 1969. He and the NYRRC's president (Vincent Chiapetta) organized the first New York City Marathon, a modest Central Park event that had 126 finishers in 1970. An average runner, Lebow emerged as a superb race organizer, expanding the New York City Marathon and initiating the Mini-Marathon, a long-distance race exclusively for women. In 1972 he was elected president of the NYRRC; within a few years this position became his full-time job. In 1976 Lebow organized the first citywide New York City Marathon, which started on the Verrazzano-Narrows Bridge and covered all five boroughs. Lebow enhanced the prestige of this event by using "under-the-table" cash incentives to recruit world-class runners in the days before such payments to athletes were legitimated. He aggressively promoted the New York City Marathon, attracting sponsors who were willing to support the event because of its appealing demographic group of young, upwardly mobile professionals who ran marathons. He drew increasing numbers of entrants by enhancing the race experience with numerous amenities. Most importantly, Lebow engaged the whole city in the marathon by calling for thousands of volunteers and modifying the race to accommodate slow runners. The size and financial impact of the New York City Marathon eventually turned the NYRRC into a modern business enterprise.

SELECTED BIBLIOGRAPHY: Pamela Cooper, *The American Marathon* (1998); George Hirsch, "The Visionary," *Runner's World* (January 1995): 55–58; Fred Lebow, with

Richard Woodley, *Inside the World of Big-Time Marathoning* (1984); *New York Times*, 10 October 1994, B-8.

Pamela Cooper

LENDL, IVAN (7 March 1960, Ostrava, Czechoslovakia–   ). A tennis player, his father, Jiri Lendl, and his mother, Olga Lenlova, were both nationally ranked tennis players in Czechoslovakia. Jiri was a lawyer who became president of the Czech Tennis Federation in 1990. Ivan showed considerable athletic prowess from a very early age. He turned professional in 1979 after having won the French, Italian, and Wimbledon Junior titles in 1978. In 1980 he led Czechoslovakia to its first Davis Cup victory. Although Lendl held the number one world ranking for 270 weeks—longer than any other competitor since computer rankings were established in 1973—he never achieved the celebrity status of contemporaries John McEnroe and Jimmy Connors. His upbringing in a dreary industrial town in communist Czechoslovakia undoubtedly contributed to his low-key personality and quiet demeanor—in sharp contrast to the fiery temperaments of McEnroe and Connors. He was admired by many knowledgeable tennis fans for his relentless and tireless right-handed baseline play. Over his fifteen-year career Lendl was in nineteen grand-slam finals and won eight. He had his most success in the U.S. Open, where he appeared as a finalist eight consecutive years (1982–89) and won three titles. Perhaps his greatest single grand-slam victory was in the 1984 French Open final, when he rallied from two sets down against John McEnroe to win in five. His career was also notable for his inability to win at Wimbledon despite being a two-time finalist there. By the time Lendl retired in 1994 because of a bad back, he had accumulated ninety-four professional titles, more than any man in the Open era other than Jimmy Connors. He settled in the United States in 1984 and became a U.S. citizen in 1992. After retiring from competition, he became an avid golfer with numerous business interests.

SELECTED BIBLIOGRAPHY: Bud Collins, *My Life with the Pros* (1989); Alan Greenberg, "Though Great, Lendl Was Easy to Pick On," *St. Louis Post-Dispatch*, 25 December 1994, 1F; Ivan Lendl, *Ivan Lendl's Power Tennis* (1986); Jon Wertheim, "Catching Up with . . . : Tennis Champion Ivan Lendl," *Sports Illustrated* (14 July 1997): 5.

Richard FitzPatrick

LEONARD, BENNY (7 April 1896, New York City–18 April 1947, New York City). A prizefighter, he was born Benjamin Leiner, the son of Yiddish-speaking Russian immigrants. Probably the most popular Jewish fighter of the twentieth century, his accomplishments in the ring and for charities (Jewish and Catholic) contributed much to combating anti-Semitism. Leonard grew up on the Lower East Side, where ethnic boundaries were clearly defined, and Jewish, Italian, and Irish kids often fought over turf and bragging rights. Despite his Orthodox Jewish parents' disapproval of fighting, his uncle took him to a gym to learn self-defense. His earnings soon overcame his parents' objections, enabling them to move uptown, to Harlem. Known as a "scientific" fighter who could outthink any opponent, in 1917 he beat Freddy Welsh for the lightweight title. He retired undefeated as a champion in 1925. Leonard's Jewishness was an important aspect of his identity as a fighter. Some of his most exciting, profitable fights were ethnic battles against Irish boxers. He was also unusual for his era in being willing to defend his title without regard to any color line. After retirement, Leonard became part owner of a hockey team in Pittsburgh and various other businesses. The 1929 stock market crash wiped him out, and he returned to boxing in 1931, retiring for good after being knocked out by Jimmy McLarnin, only his fifth loss in 209 fights. He later taught boxing at City College and at a Jewish summer camp for recreation and self-defense, established to prepare for rising anti-Semitism in Europe. During World War II he taught self-defense for the U.S. Maritime Service. He died in the ring in 1947 while officiating a fight.

SELECTED BIBLIOGRAPHY: Ken Blady, *The Jewish Boxers' Hall of Fame* (1988); Nat Fleischer, *Leonard the Magnificent* (1947); Peter Levine, *Ellis Island to Ebbets Field: Sport and the American Jewish Experience* (1992); *New York Times*, 19 April 1947, 15.
Marc Singer

LEONARD, RAY CHARLES ("Sugar Ray") (17 May 1956, Wilmington, SC–). An African American boxing champion, he was the fifth of seven children born to Gertha Leonard, a nurse, and Cicero Leonard, a supermarket manager, who raised him in Palmer Park, Maryland. Leonard attended Parkdale High School there, and he enjoyed a distinguished amateur boxing career climaxed by a gold medal triumph in the light-welterweight division at the Montreal 1976 Olympics. Throughout his career Leonard retained his fiscal independence and economic freedom. His manager (Mike Trainer) also had the Midas touch. Leonard's boyish charm, quicksilver moves, and television appeal made him a box office sensation. He seemed to be at ease as both celebrity figure and modern-day gladiator. On 30 November 1979 Leonard won the World Boxing Council (WBC) section of the world welterweight championship by defeating Wilfred Benitez.* On 20 June 1980 Panamanian Roberto Duran lured Leonard into a slug-and-wallop brawl and took over the world championship. Six months later Leonard reverted to his easy and elegant boxer, not bruiser, role and regained his crown. On 16 September 1981 Ray knocked out Thomas "Hit Man" Hearns, the World Boxing Association welterweight champion. A year later a detached retina forced Leonard to retire temporarily from boxing. In May 1984 Leonard launched a comeback with a narrow twelve-round victory over Marvin Hagler for the world middleweight championship. However, his quick feet and fast hands were those of thirty-year-old, not a twenty-year-old fighter. On 9 February 1991 Leonard lost to a journeyman boxer, Terry Norris, and then retired. Over his career he grossed over $100 million in earnings. He was *Ring* magazine's Fighter of the Year in 1979, 1981, and 1987 and *Sports*

Illustrated's Sportsman of the Year in 1981. In the 1990s he dabbled at tele-vision commentating and fighter management. In 1991 a *Los Angeles Times* story based on court documents revealed that Leonard had admitted that over a three-year period he had physically abused his wife and had used cocaine and alcohol. Boxing fans remember him for his imitations of Muhammad Ali, his razzle-dazzle, his choirboy smile, and also his toughness and his determination to win. He was inducted into the International Boxing Hall of Fame in 1997.

SELECTED BIBLIOGRAPHY: M. Messner and W. Solomon, "Sin and Redemption: The Sugar Ray Leonard Wife-Abuse Story," in M. Messner and D. Sabo, eds., *Sex, Violence and Power: Rethinking Masculinity* (1994); William Nack, "Sugar Ray Leon-ard," *Sports Illustrated* 81 (19 September 1994): 128; Joyce Carol Oates, "Interview," *Playboy* 40 (November 1993): 63–76; John Robertson, "Sugar Ray Leonard," in David L. Porter, ed., *African-American Sports Greats: A Biographical Dictionary* (1995); ma-terials received from International Boxing Hall of Fame, Canastota, NY.

Scott A.G.M. Crawford

LEONARD, WALTER FENNER ("Buck") (8 September 1907, Rocky Mount, NC–   ). An African American baseball player, he is the son of John Leonard, a railroad worker, and Emma Leonard. Leonard's father died when he was eleven years old, and he dropped out of school at fourteen to help support his family. Decades later he earned a high school equivalency degree after his playing days were over. As a young man he repaired air brakes for a railroad company and also played baseball for local black teams. After losing his job in 1933, he joined clubs in Baltimore and Brooklyn. The following year he signed with Pittsburgh's Homestead Grays,* beginning a long association with the team that dominated the Negro National League* during the late 1930s and 1940s. A slick fielding and hard-hitting first baseman, he became celebrated as the "black Lou Gehrig."* He and his teammate Josh Gibson,* known as the "Thun-der Twins," starred for the Grays in their regularly scheduled league games, barnstorming contests, Negro League All-Star events, and exhibition matches against white major leaguers. A recent statistical compilation lists his lifetime batting average over 462 league games as .328. After the Grays folded in 1950, Leonard played in Mexico for five more years, retiring at the age of forty-eight. During the 1940s the Grays played many of their home games in Washington's Griffith Stadium, and Leonard was one of several black ballplayers interviewed by the Senators' owner as a possible candidate for playing in the major leagues. But nothing resulted from that overture, and when Jackie Robinson* broke the racial barrier in the major leagues in 1947, Leonard was too old for consider-ation. After his retirement Leonard worked at a variety of jobs outside baseball and also as vice president of the Rocky Mount team in the Carolina League. His election to the National Baseball Hall of Fame in 1972 and the revival of interest in the Negro Leagues brought him renewed fame and popularity as an elder statesman and promoter of the national pastime.

SELECTED BIBLIOGRAPHY: A. J. Carr, "Buck Leonard, Lou Gehrig of Black Baseball," *The Sporting News* (4 March 1972); John Holway, *Voices from the Great Black Baseball Leagues* (1975); Robert W. Peterson, *Only the Ball Was White* (1970); James A. Riley, *The Biographical Encyclopedia of the Negro Baseball Leagues* (1994).

George B. Kirsch

LEWIS, FREDERICK CARLTON ("Carl") (1 July 1961, Birmingham, AL–). An African American track-and-field star, he is the son of William Lewis and Evelyn (Lawler) Lewis. His parents, both excellent athletes at Tuskegee Institute, became high school teachers after graduation. In 1963 the Lewis family relocated to Willingboro, New Jersey, near Philadelphia, where Carl grew up in a middle-class community. Coached by his parents, in 1979 Carl set a national high school record in the long jump while a senior at Willingboro High School; he also won a bronze medal at the Pan-American Games that year. Ranked fifth in the world in his event, he accepted a track scholarship at the University of Houston, where he became an intercollegiate national champion in the 100 meters and the long jump. He dropped out of college in 1982 to join the Santa Monica Track Club. He achieved worldwide fame at the 1984 Olympic Games in Los Angeles when he won gold medals in the 100 meters, 200 meters, long jump, and 400-meter relay—thereby matching Jesse Owens' feat in the 1936 Berlin Games. In the 1988 Olympic Games in Seoul, South Korea, Lewis finished second in both the 100 meters and 200 meters but was awarded the gold medal in the 100-meter race when Ben Johnson was disqualified for failing a drug test. Four years later at the Barcelona Olympic Games he added another gold medal in the long jump and also anchored the U.S. team to victory in the 400-meter relay. In 1991 he also set a world record for 100 meters with a time of 9.86 seconds. In 1996 at the Atlanta Olympics he won a fourth gold medal in the long jump, giving him a record-tying nine Olympic titles over four games. Although Lewis was one of the world's premier track athletes during the 1980s and early 1990s, he did not achieve the same level of celebrity status attained by other black sports stars of that era—perhaps because of his outspoken personality or because of rumors that he had used performance-enhancing drugs. He was more successful in earning product endorsements in Europe and Asia than in the United States.

SELECTED BIBLIOGRAPHY: Nathan Aasend, *Carl Lewis: Legend Chaser* (1985); Lewis H. Carlson and John J. Fogarty, *Tales of Gold* (1987); Roy Conrad, "Carl Lewis Aiming for Very Top," *Track and Field News* 32 (August 1979): 53; Steve Klots, *Carl Lewis* (1995); Yvonne Lee, "Lewis Still No. 1 American," *Track and Field News* 42 (January 1989): 11; Carl Lewis, with Jeffrey Marx, *Inside Track: My Professional Life in Amateur Track and Field* (1990); Bert Rosenthal, *Carl Lewis: The Second Jesse Owens* (1984).

George B. Kirsch

LIEBERMAN-CLINE, NANCY (1 July 1958, Brooklyn, NY–). A basketball player, she grew up in Far Rockaway, New York, in a nonobservant Jewish family with her mother, Renee, and brother Cliff. Renee was divorced from Jerry Lieberman, a building contractor, early in Nancy's life. In her junior year in high school (1975), she played for the U.S. team in the Pan-American Games. A year later at the age of seventeen Nancy was the youngest member of the silver medalist U.S. Olympic basketball team. After being heavily recruited, Lieberman chose Old Dominion University and majored in marketing. While at Old Dominion she was a four-time All-American and won the Wade Trophy (best collegiate female basketball player) twice. Nancy was also a member of two collegiate national championship teams, in 1979 and 1980. Lieberman had hoped to play in another Olympic Games, but the 1980 games were boycotted by the United States. Nancy then went on to play in the short-lived Women's Professional Basketball League with the Dallas Diamonds. She also played on the Washington Generals, the chief opponent of the Harlem Globetrotters.* In 1986 Nancy became the first woman to play men's professional basketball when she joined the Springfield Fame of the U.S. Basketball League. Lieberman was inducted into the Naismith Basketball Hall of Fame in 1996. Later she played for the Phoenix Mercury of the newly formed Women's National Basketball League (WNBA) and was the coach of the Detroit Shock for the 1998 WNBA season.

SELECTED BIBLIOGRAPHY: Joan S. Hult and Marianna Trekell, *A Century of Women's Basketball: From Frailty to Final Four* (1991); Joe Layden, *Women in Sports* (1997); Nancy Lieberman-Cline, *Lady Magic: The Autobiography of Nancy Lieberman-Cline* (1992); Nancy Lieberman, *Basketball My Way* (1982); Robert Slater, ed., *Great Jews in Sport*, rev. ed. (1992).

Shawn Ladda

LIPINSKI, TARA (6 June 1982, Philadelphia–). A Polish American figure skater, she is the daughter of Jack Lipinski, an oil company executive, and the former Patricia Brozyniak, a legal secretary. An active youngster, Lipinski started roller-skating at the age of three. At the age of nine she won a gold medal in the Roller Skating Nationals. She first tried ice skating at age six, and when she showed potential, her parents took her for lessons at the University of Delaware. In 1991 Jack Lipinski's company transferred him to Texas. Tara went with him, but she did not have access to high-level coaching and facilities. She and her mother moved to Delaware in 1993, while her father remained in Texas. The family was usually reunited on weekends. Two years later Tara and her mother moved to the Detroit area to train under the highly regarded coach Richard Callaghan. Despite her youth and small stature, Tara emerged as a top figure skater and became the first skater to land the tricky triple loop-triple loop in competition. In 1996 Tara began the year by winning a bronze medal at the U.S. Figure Skating Association (USFSA) Championship after Nicole Bobek dropped out due to injury. In the World Championship that year, she finished fifteenth. Also that year, Tara won a bronze medal in Skate Canada, a bronze at the Trophee Lalique in Paris, and a silver at the Nations Cup in Germany. In 1997, the 4' 8" seventy-five-pound skater won the USFSA Championship and then became the youngest skater to win the International Skating Union Championship in Canada. She went on to the World Championships in Switzerland and skated two flawless programs to become the youngest world champion ever. In the 1998 U.S. Nationals Tara fell in her short program, but a strong long program allowed her to finish second to Michelle Kwan.* At the Nagano 1998 Winter Olympics Tara took the ice and outskated Kwan with a stunning performance that combined technical mastery and artistry. At fifteen, she was the youngest figure skater ever to win Olympic gold. Shortly after Nagano, Tara announced that she was turning professional and would likely not be eligible to compete in another Olympics.

SELECTED BIBLIOGRAPHY: Susan Elia, "Tara Lipinski: Triumph on Ice," *Dance Magazine* 72 (July 1998): 86, 88; Nadya Labi, "Back on Top," *Time* (2 March 1998): 66–68; Tara Lipinski, as told to Emily Costello, *Tara Lipinski: Triumph on Ice* (1997); Jere Longman, "Prodigy's Dream Has a Price," *New York Times*, Current Events Edition, 11 October 1994, B-9; Mark Starr, "Tara's Joy," *Newsweek* (2 March 1998): 62–64; Tom Wheatley, "Texan, 12, Is Gold Plated," *St. Louis Post-Dispatch*, 4 July 1994, C-1.

Thomas M. Tarapacki

LISTON, CHARLES (8 May 1932, Pine Bluff, AR–30 December 1970, Las Vegas). An African American prizefighter who was also known as "Sonny," he was one of twenty-five children fathered by Tobe Liston, a farmer. His mother, Helen (Baskin) Liston, had eleven children. As a child Liston did agricultural labor and had little formal schooling. Although he won amateur boxing titles and even the heavyweight championship, he seemed unable to put a life of petty crime behind him. The press and public derided him for his criminal record— he once did time in the Missouri State Penitentiary for attempted robbery. He seemed to be the champion nobody wanted. He won the title by defeating Floyd Patterson* in 1962 and beat him again in their 1963 rematch. He lost to Cassius Clay in 1964 and was defeated by the same boxer, now Muhammad Ali,* in a 1965 rematch. Both fights were controversial. In the first bout, Liston failed to answer the bell in the seventh round; in the second match, Ali felled Liston with a punch ringside observers said did not land. After his loss to Ali he fought mostly undistinguished opponents, losing a North American Boxing Federation title fight to Leotis Martin by a knockout in 1969. He won fifty of fifty-four professional bouts, thirty-nine by knockout. His career was marred, however, by his criminal record and alleged connections with organized crime. Sadly, he died of a drug overdose.

SELECTED BIBLIOGRAPHY: Arthur R. Ashe, Jr., *A Hard Road to Glory, A History of African-American Athletes since 1946*, vol. 3 (1988); Gerald Early, *The Culture of Bruising* (1994); David L. Porter, ed., *Biographical Dictionary of American Sports: Bas-*

ketball and Other Indoor Sports (1989), 427–428; A. S. Young, *Sonny Liston, The Champ Nobody Wanted* (1963).

David R. McMahon

LITHUANIANS. Lithuanian emigration to the United States occurred in three distinct historical phases. The first wave of Lithuanian emigrants left their homeland, primarily for economic reasons, beginning in 1868, a time when Lithuania was under czarist rule. The second wave of emigration in the years following World War I from an independent, but economically fragile, Lithuanian republic was similarly motivated by economic factors. This period of emigration peaked between 1926 and 1930 and continued to a lesser degree after that. The last major wave of emigration was motivated by the political conditions of Soviet rule, which began during the latter years of World War II.

The United States became the primary destination for most of the Lithuanian emigrants. It is estimated that as many as 400,000 Lithuanians settled in the United States in the period between 1868 to 1926 and that an additional 100,000 arrived between 1926 and 1940. These two waves constituted the "old" immigration of Lithuanian people who found a new home in the United States.

As Lithuanian American communities became established in various centers across the United States, these newcomers increasingly began to organize themselves around their cultural life as they gradually took steps to integrate themselves into the wider American society. In the freedom of the United States, Lithuanian cultural life began to manifest itself in the publication of books and the organization of groups for music, drama, and literature, as well as sports, many of which had been forbidden by the czarist government of their homeland.

Modern sports and the organization of sports clubs and athletic associations were virtually unknown to the Lithuanian immigrants during their early period of settlement in the United States. Although a significant number of these early immigrants took part in sporting activities in their leisure time, these were mostly informal games and competitions that were pursued for recreational purposes. As sporting activity was generally viewed as attractive and edifying for young people, as well as an effective vehicle for the preservation of language and cultural values, a more formal approach to the creation of sports clubs began to emerge over time wherever there were sufficient concentrations of Lithuanian immigrants.

These newcomers were essentially unaware of what constituted organized sport, including the aims and the philosophy behind modern sporting activity. They initially lacked the foresight to see the importance of systematic athletic training or the necessity of encouraging their youth to expand their interests to include activities from the diversity of athletic opportunities that were available in the modern sports arena. Their view of organized sports, including rigorous training programs specifically designed for preparation in competitive events, was narrowly focused on displays of physical strength rather than on the principles and techniques of modern athletic competition. This was particularly evident in their preference for weight lifting, wrestling, and boxing.

The first sports club to be established outside Lithuania was the "Lietuviu Atletu Klubas" (Lithuanian Athletic Club or LAK). This club was formed in Brooklyn, New York, in 1902 and continues to exist to the present day. Its founders initially maintained their traditional approach to competitive activities by placing primary importance on the cultivation of sports that focused on physical strength. In conjunction with organizing sports activities, this new club also sought to involve Lithuanian youth and the newly arrived immigrants in the cultural life of the expanding ethnic community. This club played a very important role in the resettlement of Lithuanians throughout the United States by not only helping them through the hardships of immigration but also assisting them to successfully integrate into American life.

The more significant of the early Lithuanian sports clubs, such as White Clover, Brighton Park, White Rose, and White Stars, were all founded in Chicago. Chicago was the host city for the largest of the Lithuanian American communities in the United States. The White Stars club, which continued to exist for a number of years after World War II, was one of the first clubs to expand into a wider range of sports that included basketball, baseball, golf, and bowling, in addition to the more traditional endeavors such as weight lifting. Other Lithuanian sports clubs were established in Grand Rapids, Cleveland, Detroit, Boston, Rochester, Worcester, Waterbury (Connecticut), and other American cities. The first Lithuanian-American Sports Federation, which most of these clubs joined, was founded in 1914.

After World War I, American-born athletes of Lithuanian descent became more active in popular American sports, including basketball, track and field, tennis, golf, softball, baseball, and football. Many American-born Lithuanian youth were drawn into sports through their participation in college athletics or American-based sports organizations and clubs.

As greater numbers of American-born Lithuanian youth began to participate in mainstream sports, they undertook systematic training to develop their athletic potential. In this fashion, they began to move beyond the traditional ethnic approach to sporting activities practiced by an earlier generation into the world of modern sports.

The involvement of Lithuanian Americans in mainstream sports began in earnest in the 1930s and became large-scale during the 1940s. Embracing a modern orientation toward competition, many of these athletes became widely known for their accomplishments. Their skill helped to raise the level of achievement among the growing number of Lithuanian American teams, which had a positive impact on American sports as a whole.

Every larger Lithuanian community had its notable wrestlers, boxers, golfers, and basketball players who won fame in competitions with other ethnic teams, in national and international competitions, and at the Olympic Games. Boxing, with its emphasis on physical strength and endurance, had long been a favored sport among Lithuanian immigrants. It was not a tremendous surprise to the Lithuanian immigrant community when Jack Sharkey took the world heavyweight title in 1932.

Many players of Lithuanian descent were on state college football teams by 1930. Five such teams selected distinguished Lithuanian athletes as team captains (Worcester, Lawrence College, Haverhill, Lexington, and Pittsburgh). The Lawrence College team partially attributed its success to its six American-born Lithuanian players.

Many competitions among Lithuanian sports teams were staged in basketball, volleyball, and a growing number of other sports. A number of well-known men's and women's basketball teams played for the Lithuanian Athletic Club (LAK) between 1928 and 1938. In 1931 LAK played against the Hartford Lithuanians, state champions at the time, and won. Teams made up of players of Lithuanian origin often ended up as state champions or first-place holders in competitive athletics. At the end of the sport seasons "All-American" teams often included well-recognized names of Lithuanian American athletes.

The third wave of Lithuanian emigration was launched in 1944, when about 70,000 Lithuanians fled their country. This last wave, in contrast with the previous two, included many professionals, businessmen, academics, and students and also brought about 80% of Lithuania's sporting elite out of their homeland. These refugees escaped primarily into Allied-controlled Germany, where they lived temporarily in refugee camps until 1949, when most of them resettled in the United States.

While in German refugee camps, Lithuanian groups established a structured organization for the maintenance of culture, language, and education. Among these activities, traditional folk dance and sporting events were popular vehicles to maintain ethnic and cultural ties. At least twenty-eight sports clubs were created by the Lithuanian refugees in the American, French, and British zones of postwar Germany. These clubs helped to create an ethnic network for the Lithuanians scattered in various refugee camps. The competitions sponsored by these clubs were not limited to the Lithuanian refugee groups; rather they also played against teams made up of U.S. servicemen as well as various national teams of Western Europe. The activity of these refugee camp clubs was overseen by the Lithuanian Sports and Physical Education Committee. This committee, along with its organizers and most of the athletes it represented, moved to the United States in 1949. In 1951, the year of its first annual sports tournament in Toronto, the membership of this committee was still rather limited, but it quickly grew to number between thirty and forty clubs from the United States and Canada. The committee, which changed its name in 1965 to Siaures Amerikos Lietuviu Fizinio Auklejimo ir Sporto Sajunga (Lithuanian Athletic Union of North America or SALFASS), continues to host an annual tournament, which athletes of Lithuanian origin regard as their most important event in North America.

Better experienced and much more informed in a broad range of athletics, training techniques, and competitive sports than the older immigrants, the "new" immigrants of the third wave of Lithuanian emigration added significantly to the sporting activity of Lithuanian American communities. Many of the older ethnic sports clubs had been on the decline as American-born Lithuanian youth were drawn to more diverse sports than those practiced in these clubs. The third wave of Lithuanian immigrants included a large number of seasoned and accomplished athletes with organizational abilities and experience who established new sports clubs based on modern athletic practice in Lithuanian American communities. As a result, Lithuanian Americans are no longer as active in boxing, wrestling, or weight lifting, long the mainstay of traditional ethnic sports. Although athletes and teams from this latest group of newcomers won fame in mainstream American sports, the contributions of the previous Lithuanian immigrant groups must not be overlooked. In the spirit of athletic competition Lithuanian Americans will continue to strive for excellence and to provide a positive contribution not only to sporting life in America but to the fabric of a young nation that has given many immigrant populations a new homeland.

SELECTED BIBLIOGRAPHY: K. Cerkeliunas, P. Mickevicius, and S. Krasauskas, *Iseivijos Lietuviu Sportas 1944–1984* (1986); Jonas Jakubs Jakubauskas, *Amerikos Lietuviu Sporto Istorija: Sports History: Lithuanians in America* (1966); Sigitas Krasauskas, *Vejas: Siaures Amerikos Lietuviu Krepsino Rinktines Isvyka i Lietuva* (1989); H. Sadzius, ed., *Kuno Kulturos ir Sporto Istorija* (1996).

Sigitas Krasauskas

LITWACK, HARRY (20 September 1907, Galicia, Austria–7 August 1999, Huntingdon Valley, PA). A Jewish basketball player, he was the son of a shoe repairman, Jacob Litwack, and Rachel (Rech) Litwack. After arriving in Philadelphia with his family from Poland at the age of five, he graduated from South Philadelphia High School in 1925. Litwack went on to play at Temple University, from which he graduated in 1930. He captained the Owls for the final two years of his college career. He played for seven seasons as a leader of the Philadelphia SPHAS.* After spending a year coaching high school, Litwack headed the freshman team at Temple, where he compiled a 181–32 record. At the same time, he was serving as an assistant coach for the Philadelphia Warriors under Eddie Gottleib.* Litwack became the head coach for the Temple Owls in 1953, a position he would hold for the next twenty-one years. During that time, Litwack compiled a 373–193 record for his team, leading Temple to the National Invitational Tournament (NIT) championship in 1969. Litwack's teams had winning records for twenty of those twenty-one seasons and won as many as twenty-seven games in both 1956 and 1958. Temple finished in third place in the National Collegiate Athletic Association (NCAA) tournament in both of those years. Litwack was widely acclaimed as "a fine gentleman of basketball." He was elected to the Basketball Hall of Fame as a coach in 1975.

SELECTED BIBLIOGRAPHY: Zander Hollander, ed., *The Modern Encyclopedia of Basketball* (1979); Peter Levine, *Ellis Island to Ebbets Field* (1992); *New York Times*, 9 August 1999, B-7.

Zachary Davis

LOMBARDI, ERNEST NATALI ("Schnoz"; "Lumbering Lom") (6 April 1908, Oakland, CA–26 September 1977, Santa Cruz, CA). A baseball player of Italian descent, Lombardi was a catcher in major league baseball from 1931 to 1947. The 6'3", 230-pound Lombardi started his professional career with the Brooklyn Dodgers, and one year later he was the backstop for Cincinnati Reds pitchers, where he would stay for the majority of his career. In 1938 Ernie Lombardi caught both of Johnny Vander Meer's no-hitters, won the National League batting title with a .342 average, and earned himself the Most Valuable Player award. During his career he compiled a lifetime batting average of .306. He won a second National League batting title in 1942 with the Boston Braves. Lombardi left major league baseball in 1947. After his baseball career he tried committing suicide in 1953 and later worked as a press box attendant for the San Francisco Giants. He was elected to the Baseball Hall of Fame in 1986.

SELECTED BIBLIOGRAPHY: Jeanine Bucek, ed., *The Baseball Encyclopedia, the Complete and Definitive Record of Major League Baseball* (1996), 1279–1280; *New York Times*, 28 September 1977, B-2; Lowell Reidenbaugh, "Ernie Lombardi," *Baseball's Hall of Fame: Cooperstown: Where the Legends Live Forever* (1993); James K. Skipper, Jr., *Baseball Nicknames* (1992), 164; Jack Zanger, *Great Catchers of the Major Leagues* (1970), 128.

Scot E. Mondore

LOMBARDI, VINCENT THOMAS (11 June 1913, Brooklyn, NY–3 September 1970, Washington, DC). A football player and coach, he was the son of Enrico "Harry" Lombardi and Matilda Izzo Lombardi. His father, a native of Salerno, Italy, worked as a butcher and wholesale meat store owner on the Lower East Side of Manhattan and in Brooklyn. Lombardi's high school education included three years at Brooklyn's Cathedral College of the Immaculate Conception Preparatory Seminary and his senior year at St. Francis Prep in Brooklyn, where he played football well enough to earn a scholarship to Fordham University. An above-average student academically, he became a regular guard on the football team in his senior year and was a member of a line widely heralded as the "Seven Blocks of Granite." From 1939 to 1946 he taught physics, chemistry, Latin, and physical education and coached football and basketball at St. Cecilia High School in Englewood, New Jersey. In 1947, he was hired as an assistant football coach at Fordham and then as an assistant at the U.S. Military Academy under famed head coach Col. Earl "Red" Blaik in 1949. He moved to the pro ranks in 1954, serving as assistant coach for offense for the New York Giants. In 1959 he was hired as head coach and general manager of the Green Bay Packers. His first season brought the Packers their first winning record in twelve seasons. The following year, they played (but lost) in the National Football League (NFL) championship. They went on to win titles in 1961, 1962, 1965, 1966, and 1967, including the first two Super Bowls, closing out the 1966 and 1967 seasons. Lombardi retired as Packers coach in 1968, remaining with the team as general manager for one year. He returned to coaching the following year with the Washington Redskins and, as he had done in Green Bay, guided them to a winning season after years of substandard performance. His players described him as a master motivator who brought out one's best qualities. Not all of his characteristics and techniques were welcomed—he was often labeled authoritarian, volatile, and brutal. But his consistent focus on developing character and strengthening will brought him phenomenal respect. During his years with the Packers and Redskins he was frequently invited to speak to business and civic groups on leadership, motivation, discipline, and patriotism. Lombardi reportedly encountered considerable anti-Italian bigotry, particularly as a youngster, and he got into a number of fights in retaliation. He endured ethnic slurs even late in his career when a major magazine article condemned his coaching style, referring to him as "Mussolini" and "Mafia leader." Along with fueling emotional turbulence, these experiences might help to explain his support for civil rights issues expressed in public speeches, interviews, and community service (the last including work in defeating housing discrimination against black players in Green Bay). He became widely admired by members of his ethnic community. Throughout his life he served the Catholic Church in various capacities. He was enshrined in the NFL Hall of Fame in 1971, and his name was given to the trophy awarded to the winner of pro football's Super Bowl.

SELECTED BIBLIOGRAPHY: Jerry Kramer, *Lombardi: Winning Is the Only Thing* (1974); James D. Whalen, "Lombardi," in David L. Porter, ed., *Biographical Dictionary of American Sports: Football* (1987); Jerry Kramer, *Distant Replay* (1985); Jerre Mangione and Ben Morreale, *La Storia: Five Centuries of the Italian American Experience* (1992), 372, 383; David Maraniss, *When Pride Still Mattered: A Life of Vince Lombardi* (1999); Michael O'Brien, *Vince: A Personal Biography of Vince Lombardi* (1987); George Pozzetta, "The Italian Americans," in Rudolph Vecoli, ed., *Gale Encyclopedia of Multicultural America*, vol. 2 (1995), 779.

Joel Wurl

LOPEZ, ALFONSO RAMON ("Al")

LOPEZ, ALFONSO RAMON ("Al") (20 August 1908, Tampa, FL–). A Hispanic baseball player, he was the son of Modesto and Faustina Lopez, who emigrated from Spain, first to Cuba and eventually to Key West and then Tampa, Florida. His father worked in the cigar factories of Ybor City, the Spanish-speaking area of Tampa where the family lived. Al Lopez spoke only Spanish until midway through elementary school. He attended high school in Tampa but began playing professional baseball at age sixteen and did not graduate. He was a baseball catcher with the Brooklyn Dodgers, Boston Braves, and Cleveland Indians and manager for the Indians and the Chicago White Sox. Lopez played professionally first with minor league teams in Tampa (1925–26) and Jacksonville, Florida (1927), and Macon, Georgia (1928). After three games in 1928 with the Brooklyn Dodgers, he was sent to Atlanta the next year. He then caught for Brooklyn for the next six years before being traded to Boston. He played four seasons with Boston, one split between Boston and Pittsburgh, six with the Pittsburgh Pirates, and one with the Cleveland Indians. Lopez played on All-Star teams in 1934 and 1941 and at the end of his playing career in 1947 had caught a record 1,918 games. The next year Lopez began managing a minor league team in Indianapolis, and after a pennant win and two second places, he was named manager of the Cleveland Indians. Lopez had winning seasons in all his six years with Cleveland, including the American League pennant in 1954. In 1956 he became manager of the Chicago White Sox, and after two seasons of second-place finishes, in 1958 he was named Manager of the Year. His White Sox team won the American League pennant the next year. Lopez stayed with Chicago for the 1960–65 and 1968–69 seasons. After retirement he lived in Tampa, where he was honored with a life-size statue and a ballpark that bears his name. He is fondly remembered in Chicago as the last manager to take one of the city's teams to a World Series. In 1977 he was inducted into the National Baseball Hall of Fame as a manager.

SELECTED BIBLIOGRAPHY: Gerard A. Brandmeyer, "Baseball and the American Dream: A Conversation with Al Lopez," *Tampa Bay History* 3 (1981): 48–73; "Al Lopez," in *Great Athletes* (1992); David L. Porter, ed., *Biographical Dictionary of American Sports—Baseball* (1987); John Thorn and Pete Palmer, eds., *Total Baseball*, 3d ed. (1993).

Richard V. McGehee

LOPEZ, NANCY (6 January 1957, Torrance, CA–   ). A golfer, she is the daughter of Mexican-heritage parents. Her father (Domingo) owned the 2nd Street Auto Body Shop in New Mexico, and her mother (Marina) was the family's primary caretaker and bookkeeper for her father's shop. A graduate of Roswell, New Mexico, Goddard High School, Lopez accepted a scholarship to the University of Tulsa, where she won the intercollegiate golf title and was named collegiate athlete of the year. During her first year on the Ladies Professional Golf Association (LPGA) tour (1978), Lopez won nine tournaments, including an unprecedented five in a row, and was named Rookie of the Year, Golfer of the Year, and Female Athlete of the Year. She also was Rolex Player of the Year (1978, 1979, 1985, 1988) and Vare Trophy Winner (1978, 1979, 1985). In 1985, Lopez set an all-time record at the Henredon Classic, recording a twenty-under-par tournament total (268), including twenty-five birdies. Up to 1998 Lopez has amassed forty-seven LPGA victories and in 1987 became the youngest inductee to enter the LPGA Hall of Fame. In 1996 Lopez played in eighteen LPGA events, posting five top-ten finishes. Lopez's status in the LPGA is unparalleled, and her success in this mainstream sport has been recognized as a source of pride for all Latinos/as. Some have suggested that Lopez is to the Latino community what Muhammad Ali* was to the African American community—a symbol of pride and perseverance.

SELECTED BIBLIOGRAPHY: R. Chabran and R. Chabran, eds., "Lopez, Nancy," *The Latino Encyclopedia*, vol. 3 (1996), 915–916; R. Chavira, "Three to Cheer," *Neustro* 1 (August 1977): 34–35; "Her Drive to Win," *Nuestro* 2 (September 1978): 22–23, 26; R. Nagel and S. Rose, eds., *Hispanic American Biography* (1995).

Katherine M. Jamieson

LOUIS, JOE (BARROW) (13 May 1914, Lafayette, AL–12 April 1983, Las Vegas). An African American prizefighter, he was the son of Mun Barrow, a farmer, and his wife, Lillie, a homemaker. Joe Louis Barrow was probably the most famous boxer of the 1930s and 1940s. After his mother's divorce and remarriage, the family moved to Detroit in 1924, where the young Louis liked neither his school nor the violin lessons his mother forced on him. He was fascinated by prizefighting, however, as he watched boxers go through their paces at a local gymnasium. In 1932 he became an accomplished amateur boxer, and under the tutelage of African American businessmen John Roxborough and Julian Black and trainer Charles "Chappie" Blackburn,* Louis turned professional in 1934. In 1935 Mike Jacobs,* a noted New York boxing promoter, added young Louis to his stable of fighters. After capturing the world heavyweight championship from James Braddock in 1937, the "Brown Bomber," as sportswriters dubbed him, defended that title a record twenty-five times during the next twelve years, including a stunning one-round knockout of German Max Schmeling in 1938. Louis retired as champion in 1949. After an unsuccessful comeback, he spent the last part of his life battling financial problems, mental illness, and other personal difficulties. When he died in 1983, he was an official "greeter" at a Las Vegas casino. Although no doubt a highly skilled fighter, Louis was even more important as a racial symbol. Hoping to overcome the negative image generated by Jack Johnson,* Jacobs and Roxborough convinced Louis that he should behave in a dignified, even docile fashion outside the ring. Although some southern newspapers attacked the notion of a black champion, most white Americans praised the young Detroiter, especially after his defeat of Schmeling in 1938. They viewed Louis' victory as a triumph of American democracy over Nazi totalitarianism. The image of Louis in the eyes of his fellow blacks was more complicated. Some approved of his efforts to placate whites, while most hailed his accomplishments because they seemed to expand the scope of African American participation in American life. Supporters especially applauded his attempts to desegregate facilities on military bases during World War II. On another level, some black intellectuals, most notably, Richard Wright, wrote that Louis' victories over white boxers provided a vicarious thrill to blacks who could not openly challenge white racism. Thus, Joe Louis became that unusual race hero who could appeal to both whites and African Americans. After Franklin Roosevelt, Louis was perhaps the most admired American of his time.

SELECTED BIBLIOGRAPHY: Richard Bak, *Joe Louis: The Great Black Hope* (1998); Joe Louis Barrow, Jr., and Barbara Munder, *Joe Louis: 50 Years an American Hero*

(1988); Anthony O. Edmonds, *Joe Louis* (1973); Joe Louis, *My Life Story: An Autobiography* (1996); Chris Mead, *Joe Louis: Black Hero in White America* (1985); Jeffrey T. Sammons, *Beyond the Ring: The Role of Boxing in American Society* (1988).

Anthony O. Edmonds

LUCKMAN, SIDNEY (21 November 1916, Brooklyn, NY–5 July 1998, North Miami Beach, FL). A football player, he was the son of a Jewish immigrant, Meyer Luckman. He attended Erasmus High School in Brooklyn, where he stood out as a genuine triple-threat back. He entered Columbia College in 1936, where he played for an outstanding coach, Lou Little. A tailback on a Lions team with a losing record, he demonstrated his overall talents in all dimensions of the game (he once punted for seventy-two yards), but he excelled as a passer. Columbia has had many outstanding college passers, but Luckman is still regarded as the best to have played there. In 1939 he was chosen by George Halas* of the Chicago Bears to become that team's first T formation quarterback, and on his Pro Football Hall of Fame enshrinement plaque he is described as a suberb signal caller and the first great T formation quarterback. Halas regarded him as the team leader and stated that Luckman *never* made a wrong play call. His own idol, growing up, was Benny Friedman,* the University of Michigan quarterback. Constantly compared with the great Washington Redskins quarterback Sammy Baugh, Luckman's most celebrated game was his victory over the Washington Redskins in the 1940 championship game, which his Chicago Bears won by the still startling score of Bears 73, Washington 0. During World War II Luckman served in the U.S. Merchant Marine, which gave him an opportunity to play some league weekend games. He was elected to the All-NFL (National Football League) team five times and was chosen the Most Valuable Player in 1943, during which year he managed to throw seven touchdown passes in one game and five in the title game. Plagued by a shoulder injury, Sid permanently retired from professional football in 1950. Subsequently, Sid coached football for the U.S. Merchant Marine Academy for many years.

SELECTED BIBLIOGRAPHY: Michael L. Lablanc, ed., *Football, Professional Sport Team Histories* (1994), 105, 246–249; *New York Times*, 6 July 1998, B8; David L. Porter, ed., *Biographical Dictionary of American Sports: Football* (1987); Robert Slater, *Great Jews in Sport*, rev. ed. (1992).

Lawrence Huggins

LUISETTI, ANGELO JOSEPH ("Hank") (16 June 1916, San Francisco–   ). A star basketball player, he was the only child of Steven and Amalia (Grossi) Luisetti and grew up in the Italian section of Telegraph Hill near North Beach. His father was a dishwasher who eventually owned his own Italian restaurant in downtown San Francisco. He graduated from Galileo High School and, in 1934, enrolled at Stanford on a scholarship. There he became the most heralded basketball player of his era as he was selected three-time All-American and two-time College Player of the Year. Luisetti was a skilled passer and dribbler but was famous for his one-handed shooting style, unique in an era of the two-handed set shot. He led Stanford to consecutive Pacific Coast Championships. Beginning his career as a center, he moved to guard and later played forward, perfecting the one-handed shot. As a handsome 6'3" star on the West Coast, Luisetti achieved greater fame when he played at Madison Square Garden. During the 1937–38 season he scored fifty points (still a Stanford record) against Duquesne. Despite his offensive ability, he was a team player. He set a college season scoring record with 1,596 points, an average of sixteen and one-half points per game. After graduating from Stanford in 1938 with a business degree, Luisetti played and coached club and Amateur Athletic Union (AAU) basketball teams. He became sales manager of an auto dealership and in 1958 served as president of a regional travel agency until his retirement in 1981. During World War II he served in the navy. Luisetti is a member of Stanford's Sports Hall of Fame and the Naismith Memorial Basketball Hall of Fame.

SELECTED BIBLIOGRAPHY: Gary Cavalli, *Stanford Sports* (1982); Mike Douchant, *Encyclopedia of College Basketball* (1995); John D. McCallum, *College Basketball, U.S.A., since 1892* (1980); Sandy Padwe, *Basketball's Hall of Fame* (1970).

Frank J. Cavaioli

LYONS, OREN R., JR. (5 March 1930, Cattaraugus Indian Reservation, Gowanda, NY–   ). A Native American Indian lacrosse goalie and official, he is the son of Oren R. Lyons, Sr., of the Eel Clan of the Onondaga Nation and Winnifred Gordon Lyons of the Wolf Clan of the Seneca Nation. He was raised according to the traditional customs and heritage of the Iroquois Confederation on the Onondaga Reservation in northern New York state, where he attended the reservation school. He played both field and box lacrosse for the Onondaga Athletic Club from 1945 through 1954, which won the championship of the North American Lacrosse Association from 1950 through 1954. In 1950 and 1954 Lyons was named outstanding goalie of that league and captured the Oren Lyons Sr. Cup. In 1958 he earned his undergraduate degree from the Syracuse University College of Fine Arts. At Syracuse Lyons earned third-team All-American honors in 1957 and 1958 as cocaptain and goalie, and he led his team to an undefeated season during his junior year. After graduation he played for the New York Lacrosse Club, the New Jersey Lacrosse Club, and the Onondaga Athletic Club, and he also served as chairman of the Iroquois Nationals Lacrosse Club.* Between 1958 and 1969 he pursued a career in commercial art in New York City, becoming the art and planning director of Norcross Greeting Cards. He exhibited his own paintings widely and earned a reputation as a noted Native American artist. Lyons was *condoled* (installed) into the Onondaga Council of Chiefs as a Faithkeeper of the Turtle Clan in November 1967. This was done through the ancient customs and laws of the Haudenosaunee, also known as the Six Nations Iroquois Confederacy. He was later adopted into the Onondaga Nation in July 1972, again through the customs and laws of the Haudenosaunee.

He is respected throughout North America as a leading spokesman for the rights of Native American peoples and an expert on environmental and interfaith issues and Native American traditions, law, and history. Professor of American studies and director of the Native American studies program at the State University of New York at Buffalo (SUNY), Lyons is the editor of *Daybreak*, a national Native American magazine, and also author, editor, and illustrator of numerous publications. Named Man of the Year in Lacrosse for 1989, he was inducted into the Lacrosse Hall of Fame in 1993.

SELECTED BIBLIOGRAPHY: *Congressional Record* 138, No. 134 (26 September, 1992); Robert Lipsyte, "R.I.P., Tonto," *Esquire* (February 1994): 39–45; Robert Lipsyte, "A Goalie Keeps Faith for an Iroquois Nation," *New York Times*, 29 January 1993, B14; Oren Lyons, Jr., "Land of the Free, Home of the Brave," *Northeast Indian Quarterly* (1988): 18–20; Oren Lyons, John Mohawk, Vine Deloria, Laurence Hauptman, Howard Bereman, Donald Grinde, Jr., Curtis Berkey, and Ronald Venables, eds., *Exiled in the Land of the Free: Democracy, Indian Nations, and the U.S. Constitution* (1992); Paul Schenider, "Respect for the Earth," *Audubon* (March–April 1994): 110–115.

George B. Kirsch

M

MACDONALD, CHARLES BLAIR (14 November 1856, Niagara Falls, Ontario, Canada–21 April 1939, Southampton, NY). A pioneer and promoter of early American golf, he was the son of Godfrey and Mary (Blakewell) Macdonald, both of whom were naturalized U.S. citizens. His father was a successful businessman and a native of Scotland; his mother was born in Canada. Macdonald received his early education in Chicago before traveling to Scotland in 1872 to live with his grandfather and study at the university at St. Andrews. He learned to play and love golf while a student there. After his studies he moved back to Chicago in 1874, and over the next two decades he played golf only during his business trips to England. After John Reid* and other easterners had popularized golf in the United States during the late 1880s and early 1890s, Macdonald decided to promote the sport among his friends and associates in Chicago. In 1893 he was the guiding force behind the construction of the Chicago Golf Club. In the 1890s Macdonald was one of the founders of the U.S. Golf Association. He won the first U.S. Amateur Championship in 1895, but he was quickly surpassed by a rising generation of much better players. He was particularly expert on the issue of rules, often insisting that American golf follow the pattern set down, over the ages, by Scotland. Macdonald also earned a lasting reputation as a course architect. His best work included the course at the Chicago Golf Club, the Mid-Ocean Club course on Bermuda, and the National Golf Links of America in Southampton, New York. He was fond of using famous Scottish and English designs as models for holes on his American courses. In 1928 Macdonald published *Scotland's Gift—Golf*, which remains one of the richest sources of insight into the early days of American golf. He made his living as a stockbroker and, true to his rigid definition of amateurism, never earned a penny from his involvement with golf.

SELECTED BIBLIOGRAPHY: Charles B. Macdonald, *Scotland's Gift—Golf* (1928); H. B. Martin, *Fifty Years of American Golf* (1936); *New York Times*, 22 April 1939, 17; Herbert Warren Wind, *The Story of American Golf* (1948).

Richard J. Moss

MANLEY, EFFA (27 March 1900, Philadelphia–18 April 1981, Los Angeles). Co-owner of the Newark Eagles, a Negro National League* team, from 1935 to 1948, she was the illegitimate daughter of Bertha Ford Brooks, a white seamstress, and John M. Bishop, a white wealthy financier who had a seat on the New York Stock Exchange. Manley's racial heritage, like so much of her life, was filled with controversy. Since her white mother had two marriages to black men and six racially mixed children, and since she grew up in a black community and culturally always identified with African Americans, people assumed that she was a light-skinned black. But although both of her parents were white, Manley was one of the most colorful and influential people in Negro baseball during the 1930s and 1940s. In an era when women were second-class citizens, and blacks had few, if any, rights, she managed to become a respected force not only in the Negro Baseball Leagues but also in the black Civil Rights movement. When her husband, Abe Manley, acquired the Brooklyn Eagles franchise in 1935, Effa immediately took over the day-to-day operations of the team. She did this so that Abe could concentrate on recruitment. To improve the Brooklyn Eagles' financial position, in 1936 Abe negotiated with the owner of the Newark Dodgers, a black semipro team, to buy the franchise. In 1936 he moved the Brooklyn Eagles to Newark, and they officially became the Newark Eagles. Effa took an active part not only in the Newark Eagles but in all Negro National League affairs. With Abe she attended all league meetings and voiced her concerns. At times her unsolicited advice was not appreciated by some of the other owners, particularly because she was a woman. Although the other owners may have complained, they respected her financial judgment. Effa handled all the finances of the Negro National League when Abe was officially the treasurer. During her later years she devoted herself to keeping the history of Negro baseball alive and to gaining recognition for many of its ballplayers. In 1976 she published her book, *Negro Baseball: Before Integration*, and she wrote numerous letters to both the Baseball Hall of Fame and *The Sporting News*, trying to gain recognition for the Negro Baseball Leagues and its players. When the Hall of Fame finally recognized eleven black players, she begged it to enshrine others. In 1985, four years after her death, the National Baseball Hall of Fame Museum added an exhibit on black baseball, with her picture prominently displayed.

SELECTED BIBLIOGRAPHY: Effa Manley, with Leon Hartwick, *Negro Baseball: Before Integration* (1976); James Overmyer, *Effa Manley and the Newark Eagles* (1993); James A. Riley, *The Biographical Encyclopedia of the Negro Baseball Leagues* (1994).

Gai I. Berlage

MANNING, GUSTAVE RANDOLPH (3 December 1873, Lewisham, England–1 December 1953, New York City). He was the first president and for many years an influential member of the governing body of soccer in the United States. He arrived in New York City in 1905 with his wife, Louella, an American girl from Kansas, and a medical degree from Freiberg University in Germany, and he went into practice. In 1912 he was elected president of the newly formed American Amateur Football Association (AAFA), and in 1913 under his leadership the AAFA sought affiliation with the Fédération Internationale de Football Association, the governing body of world soccer. Another group, the American Football Association, also sought affiliation, but Manning's group won recognition. Eventually, through Manning's conciliatory efforts the two groups merged to form what is today the U.S. Soccer Federation. During World War I he enlisted in the U.S. Army and rose to the rank of colonel. He served as chairman of the Foreign Relations Committee of the U.S. Football Association from 1913 to 1948. He received national attention in the news media when he was the first to resign from the American Olympic Committee as a protest against the Olympic Games being awarded to Japan in 1940 while that country was at war with China. He was inducted into the National Soccer Hall of Fame in 1950.

SELECTED BIBLIOGRAPHY: Bill Graham, ed., *North American Soccer Guide* (1954–55); *Soccer America* (9 July 1981).

Colin Jose

MANUSH, HENRY EMMETT ("Heinie") (20 July 1901, Tuscumbia, AL–12 May 1971, Sarasota, FL). A baseball player, his father (George) was a German immigrant and an upholsterer, and his mother (Catherine) was a homemaker of German and English descent. He left Massey Military Academy at age seventeen to work as a pipefitter. Manush signed with the Detroit Tigers after playing industrial league baseball in Utah. In 1923 manager Ty Cobb recognized his hitting talent and installed him in left field. Manush hit .334 as a rookie and won the American League batting title in 1926. A line-drive hitter who learned to hit to all fields, he compiled a .330 batting average over seventeen seasons, four times getting more than 200 hits and six times more than forty doubles. Manush was traded to the St. Louis Browns in December 1927 and to the Washington Senators in the middle of the 1930 season. He finished his major league playing career in 1939 after stints with the Boston Red Sox, Brooklyn Dodgers, and Pittsburgh Pirates. Manush managed in the minor leagues for five years and then scouted and coached intermittently for several teams until 1962. He was elected to the Baseball Hall of Fame in 1964.

SELECTED BIBLIOGRAPHY: "Hall of Famers Goslin and Manush Dead," *The Sporting News* (29 May 1971): 35; Harry T. Brundidge, " 'Heinie' Manush Made Good on Home Town Team When He Was Only 13," *St. Louis Star*, 17 May 1929, 3; "Heinie Manush," in Martin Appel and Burt Goldblatt, *Baseball's Best: The Hall of Fame Gallery* (1977).

Steven P. Gietschier

MARATHON. Soon after its introduction in 1896, marathon running in America became the event of lower-middle-class and working-class men, many of whom belonged to ethnic sports clubs. The Boston Marathon, the oldest continuous marathon in the United States, was started in 1897 by the Boston Athletic Association, but organizations such as the Highland Club of Roxbury, an Irish enclave, were more likely to contribute participants. Along with the Irish, Native Americans were among the first ethnic groups to have a strong presence in the marathon.

In 1908, John J. Hayes, an Irish American New Yorker, won the Olympic marathon in an intensely disputed finish over the Italian runner Dorando Pietri. Four months after the Olympics, Pietri and Hayes met in a professional marathon in Madison Square Garden. The Garden was packed with fans of both ethnicities who expected to see their cultural honor defended on the field of sport. Such Irish–Italian competition was displayed in many of the eight professional marathons held in the New York City area during the next seven months. French and Native American runners also entered the professional marathons, which were perceived as representational sport.

Amateur marathon participation in 1909 also reflected ethnic identification. The finishers lists of many of these marathons show mostly Irish surnames; Italians were often the second most numerous group. Some apparently German American runners are listed, as well as a number of Jewish runners. A few African Americans entered the marathon, as well as French Canadians working in America.

The open nature of the marathon, a new event held on the roads, lent itself to a great democracy of participation. Before World War I, the many "hyphenated" Americans in the marathon had given the event a blue-collar identity it would hold until the late 1960s. The marathon was also established as an East Coast, urban event, another connection to high ethnic participation. In the years before World War I, a substantial number of the top finishers of the Boston Marathon had Irish last names. The Boston Marathon would retain an Irish identity well after World War II.

The Auto City Marathon in Detroit began in 1920 and continued under the auspices of the local Irish American Athletic Club. Although Finns were a small group in America, there were many Finnish runners in American long-distance races during the 1920s. New York City area marathons reflected the Italian American presence in the event and in the overall population. On Columbus Day, 12 October 1925, the village of Port Chester, north of New York City in Westchester County, started a marathon that would continue through 1941. The running of a marathon from New York City to Port Chester on Columbus Day acknowledged the Italian American contribution to Port Chester and to American culture in general. But Columbus Day, an expression of Italian American pride, is a patriotic American celebration. This marathon symbolized the Americanization of ethnic groups during the 1920s.

During 1928 a number of marathons were held throughout the United States in preparation for the upcoming Olympic Games. The ethnic balance of the marathon had remained; the winners were often of Irish, Italian, Finnish, or Native American descent. A Jewish runner won the 1928 Port Chester Marathon.

The Jewish presence in the marathon reached a peak in the early 1930s, when the great marathon coach Max Silver put together a winning team of long-distance runners for the German-American Athletic Club, guiding them to victory in the 1935 Amateur Athletic Union national marathon championship. When the club's leadership revealed Nazi sympathies later in 1935, the team dispersed, many to the Millrose Athletic Association. Top-level runners could always find club affiliation, but Jewish runners newly entering competition had few choices. Harlem's New York Pioneer Club* (NYPC) welcomed white as well as black runners, and many young Jewish runners joined the Pioneers during and immediately after World War II.

The New York Pioneer Club was very successful in the marathon, winning the team title in the AAU national marathon championships in 1954 and 1955 and taking the 1955 Boston Marathon team trophy. Theodore Corbitt was a member of the NYPC when he became the first African American Olympic marathoner. Corbitt later became the first president of the New York Road Runners Club, organizers of the New York City Marathon and other long-distance events.

Nat Cirulnick, a Jewish runner who had belonged to the Pioneer Club, also served as New York Road Runners Club president. Other presidents of the New York Road Runners Club in the 1960s were Aldo Scandurra and Vincent Chiapetta. Most people, when they think of the New York City Marathon, remember Fred Lebow,* the Romanian Jewish immigrant who guided the event to five-borough glory and international fame.

The "marathon boom" of the 1970s brought participatory running to the upper middle class, and the marathon runner has since been stereotyped as a college-educated, upwardly mobile individual. Yet the marathon was for many years the sport of working-class, often ethnic men. Their ethnic conflicts determined the nature of the sport in its early years. More importantly, the need of ethnic youth for a sport club that would welcome all participants regardless of athletic ability paved the way for the Road Runners Club of America and laid the organizational foundation for the marathon boom.

SELECTED BIBLIOGRAPHY: Jesse P. Abramson, "Democratic Ideal: The Pioneer Club," *Amateur Athlete* (September 1945): 11, 15; Pamela Cooper, *The American Marathon* (1998); Tom Derderian, *Boston Marathon: The History of the World's Premier Running Event* (1993); Stanley Frank, *The Jew in Sport* (1936); David E. Martin and Roger W. H. Gynn, *The Marathon Footrace: Performers and Performances* (1979).

Pamela Cooper

MARCIANO, ROCKY (1 September 1923, Brockton, MA–31 August 1969, Newton, IA). Born Rocco Francis Marchegiano, he was a world champion

heavyweight boxer. The son of Italian immigrants, his father (Pierino) worked in a shoe factory. His mother's maiden name was Pasqualena Picciuto. Rocky was a high school dropout, became a street fighter, and turned to boxing to overcome poverty. While serving in the army from 1943 to 1946, Rocky successfully participated in boxing tournaments and refined his skills. In 1948, at 185 pounds and 5'11", he turned professional, changed his name to Marciano, won his first eleven fights by knockouts, and the following year won thirteen more, eleven by knockouts. On 23 September 1952 the "Brockton Blockbuster" knocked out Jersey Joe Wolcott for the world heavyweight championship. He successfully defended his crown in a rematch with Wolcott and five more times against Roland LaStarza, Ezzard Charles (twice), Don Cockell, and Archie Moore. Marciano retired in 1956 as the only undefeated heavyweight champion in the world. He had won all of his forty-nine professional fights, forty-three by knockouts. He is a member of *Ring* magazine's Boxing Hall of Fame and the International Boxing Hall of Fame. After his retirement he appeared on television, the lecture circuit, and at clubs. He died in a plane crash on his way to Iowa to make a personal appearance.

SELECTED BIBLIOGRAPHY: Bill Libby, *Rocky: The Story of a Champion* (1971); William Nack, "The Rock," *Sports Illustrated* 79 (August 1993): 52–68; Everett M. Skehan, *Rocky Marciano: The Biography of a First Son* (1977).

Frank J. Cavaioli

MARICHAL, JUAN ANTONIO SANCHEZ (20 October 1937, Laguna Verde, Dominican Republic–   ). A baseball player known as "the Dominican Dandy," he was the son of Francisco Marichal and Natividad Sanchez, both of whom were involved in small-scale ranching and farming in the banana-producing area of the northern border of the Dominican Republic near Haiti. Marichal began playing baseball when he was six and at age ten decided he would become a pitcher. He quit high school after the eleventh grade and played amateur and professional baseball. Still in his youth, he developed a high leg kick, which was to become his trademark. He signed a professional contract with the San Francisco Giants in 1958 and made his major league debut in 1960. During the next ten years with the Giants he won more than twenty games in a season on six occasions. After fourteen years with the Giants, he finished his career with the Boston Red Sox and Los Angeles Dodgers in 1974 and 1975. His career record is 243 victories and 142 losses, a winning percentage of .631, with an earned run average of 2.89. Along with Bob Gibson* and Sandy Koufax,* Marichal was one of the three dominant major league pitchers of the 1960s. In 1983 he became the first Dominican inducted into the Baseball Hall of Fame in Cooperstown, New York. Following his playing career, Marichal worked as scout for the Oakland Athletics until 1995.

SELECTED BIBLIOGRAPHY: Hector J. Cruz, *Juan Marichal: La Historia de Su Vida* (1983); Charles Einstein, "The Juan Marichal Mystery," *Sport* (June 1963): 49; Charles Einstein, "Juan Marichal at the Crossroads, *Sport* (April 1968): 58.

Milton Jamail

MARINO, DANIEL CONSTANTINE, JR. (15 September 1961, Pittsburgh–   ). A football player, he is the only son of Daniel and Veronica Kolczynski Marino. His Italian American father drove a truck for a newspaper. His mother is of Polish descent. Marino grew up in a middle-class, Italian Irish neighborhood and attended St. Regis Catholic parochial school. Young Dan played quarterback on the school's football team, which his father coached. He is a graduate of Pittsburgh's Central Catholic High School. As a freshman at the University of Pittsburgh in 1979 he led his team to five straight victories, which included the defeat of Pittsburgh's arch rival, Penn State, and a win over Arizona in the postseason Fiesta Bowl. By the beginning of his senior year Marino was recognized as the best quarterback in college football. Soon after earning his bachelor's degree in 1983, he signed a four-year, $2 million contract with the Miami Dolphins. Over the next several years he amassed an incredible array of records. He was the first quarterback in the history of the National Football League (NFL) to have four 4,000-yard seasons (1984–86 and 1988). As the quarterback of the Miami Dolphins he rose to National Football League superstardom faster than any signal caller before him. He is also credited with being largely responsible for shifting the emphasis in professional football from the run to the pass. Thanks to his extraordinarily strong arm, coupled with his lightning-fast release, his passing efficiency rating was one of the highest in the league's history. During his career he donated time to the Leukemia Fund and to posters for the American Library Association aimed at encouraging and promoting reading. He was also active in the Miami chapter of the National Italian-American Hall of Fame.

SELECTED BIBLIOGRAPHY: Pete Axthelm, "The Year of the Rookie," *Newsweek* 102 (14 November 1983): 79; *Current Biography* (1989); H. Daniels, "One on One . . . Dan Marino," *Sport* 82 (December 1991): 20; Rick Reilly, "Well, Look Who's Back," *Sports Illustrated* (14 January 1991): 21–22; Rick Telander, "His Time Is Passing," *Sports Illustrated* 75 (4 November 1991): 38–43.

Margherita Marchione

MARTIN, SYLVIA WENE (?1930, Philadelphia–   ). A bowler, Martin was born to Jewish parents who ran the family grocery store. At the age of seventeen, her brother and sister took her with them to a bowling alley. Her brother claimed she was too short (4'11") to play, and she was relegated to scorekeeper. The next night Sylvia's mother took her to bowl. Six years later, Sylvia was the first woman to bowl a perfect 300 game in sanctioned East Coast play. She was also the first woman to bowl more than one 300 game in the same season. Martin set a Women's International Bowling Congress (WIBC) national record while averaging 206 in the 1952–53 season. Martin averaged 206 the next season and 208 the following year. In 1955 and 1960 she won the Bowling Proprietors Association of America All-State Individual Match Game title and was named for both years the Woman Bowler of the Year by the Bowling Writers Association of America. Martin and her partner, Adele Isphording, won the 1959

WIBC doubles title. Other honors include Pennsylvania Sports Woman of the Year (1961), Philadelphia's Outstanding Athlete (1963), Women's International Bowling Congress Hall of Fame (1966), and Jewish Sports Hall of Fame, Israel (1979).

SELECTED BIBLIOGRAPHY: Ethel Cooper, "Dalton and Wene—Perfect Games," *The Woman Bowler* 15 (1951): 12; Phyllis Hollander, *American Women in Sports* (1972); Sylvia Wene Martin, *The Woman's Bowling Guide* (1959); Robert Slater, ed., *Great Jews in Sport*, rev. ed. (1992).

Shawn Ladda

MAYS, WILLIE HOWARD (6 May 1931, Westfield, AL–). An African American baseball player, he is the son of William and Ann Mays. His father was a steel mill worker. After his parents divorced, he lived with his aunt, Sarah. He attended Fairfield Industrial High School and joined the Birmingham Black Barons of the Negro National League* at the age of seventeen. Two years later, in 1950, the New York Giants bought his contract from the Black Barons, and in 1951 he reached the major leagues and won the Rookie of the Year Award. He played for the New York Giants (San Francisco Giants after 1957) through 1972. He finished his career with the New York Mets in 1973. During his twenty-one-year career he won four National League home run crowns (1955, 1962, 1964, 1965) and one batting title (1954). He was named the Most Valuable Player in the National League in 1954 and 1965 and appeared in twenty-four All-Star Games and four World Series. He ended his career with 3,283 hits, which included 660 home runs, which ranked him third on the all-time home run list. He was the first player in the National League to hit 600 home runs. His career batting average was .302. Although probably best remembered as a home run hitter, he was almost flawless as a center fielder, winning twelve consecutive Gold Glove Awards, 1957 through 1968. In 1979 he was elected to the National Baseball Hall of Fame in his first year of eligibility.

SELECTED BIBLIOGRAPHY: Donald Dewey and Nicholas Acocella, *The Biographical History of Baseball* (1995); Charles Einstein, *Willie Mays: My Life in and out of Baseball* (1972); Alan Minsky, *Home Run Kings* (1995); Lou Sahadi, with Willie Mays, *Say Hey* (1988); Mike Shatzkin, *The Ball Players* (1990).

Clyde Partin

McCOVEY, WILLIE ("Stretch") (10 January 1938, Mobile, AL–). An African American baseball player, he is the son of Frank McCovey, a railroad worker, and Ester (Jones) McCovey. As a youth he excelled in baseball, football, and baseball on his hometown's playgrounds and also worked to help support his family. At sixteen he dropped out of school and journeyed from Mobile to Los Angeles. A tryout with the New York Giants earned him a minor league contract, and during the late 1950s he moved up from Class D to Triple A with Phoenix of the Pacific Coast League. He reached the major leagues with the (now San Francisco) Giants in July 1959. During the early 1960s he was pla-tooned with Orlando Cepeda at first base and also played outfield. By 1965 he had established himself as a feared home run hitter, and for the next decade he was one of the game's greatest stars. His twenty-two seasons included nearly three years with the San Diego Padres (1974–76) and a few games with the Oakland Athletics (1976). A highlight of his career was his National League Most Valuable Player award for 1969. He retired in 1980 with 521 home runs and was elected to the National Baseball of Fame in 1986. During the racial turmoil of the 1960s he did not become personally involved with militant pro-tests, but he did eventually support charitable organizations, including his own Willie McCovey March of Dimes Annual Charity Golf Tournament.

SELECTED BIBLIOGRAPHY: Charles Einstein, *Willie's Time* (1980); Arnold Hano, *Willie Mays* (1970).

George B. Kirsch

McGILLICUDDY, CORNELIUS ALEXANDER ("Connie Mack") (22 De-cember 1862, East Brookfield, MA–8 February 1956, Germantown, PA). A baseball player, manager, and owner, he was the son of Irish immigrants. His father (Michael) worked in cotton mills and shoe factories, and his mother (Mary) was a homemaker. He left school as a teenager for a job in a shoe factory. Mack was a catcher for the Washington Senators between 1886 and 1889. After a year in the Players League, he played with the Pittsburgh Pirates from 1891 to 1896 and became playing manager in 1894. After being fired in Pittsburgh, his friend Ban Johnson, presiding over the Western League, asked him to manage the Milwaukee club. When Johnson decided to turn the Western League into the American League, he awarded the Philadelphia franchise to Mack. Mack became manager of the Athletics in 1901. Remembered for wearing street clothes on the bench and waving his scorecard to give directions, he built and dismantled great teams during his fifty years as manager of the Athletics. He won four pennants and three World Series between 1910 and 1914 but sold his stars in 1915. The pennant returned to Philadelphia between 1929 and 1931, and world championships came in 1929 and 1930, but again he broke up the team. Mack retired from managing after the 1950 season, leaving a record of nine pennants, five World Series titles, and first place among managers in total games (7,878), wins (3,776), and losses (4,025). He was elected to the Baseball Hall of Fame in 1937.

SELECTED BIBLIOGRAPHY: "Connie Mack," in Thomas Aylesworth and Benton Minks, *The Encyclopedia of Baseball Managers* (1990); "Connie Mack," in Martin Appel and Burt Goldblatt, *Baseball's Best: The Hall of Fame Gallery* (1977); "The Legend of Connie Mack," *Philly Sport Magazine* (August 1989): 52–62; Ken Smith, *Baseball's Hall of Fame* (1972).

William Francis

McGINNITY, JOSEPH JEROME ("Iron Man") (19 March 1871, Rock Island, IL–14 November 1929, Brooklyn, NY). A baseball player, he was the son of an Irish coal miner who died young. He went to work in the mines while a teenager. His work hardened him, and he took up the game of baseball as a hobby. He played unorganized ball in the Illinois area and eventually was discovered by professional scouts while playing in the Oklahoma Indian Territory. He did not move into the major leagues until 1899, when he was twenty-eight years old. As a rookie with the Baltimore Orioles in 1899 he led the team with twenty-eight victories, and over the next ten years as a major leaguer he earned his "Iron Man" moniker because of his ability to pitch both games of a doubleheader. While his career was relatively short, he did win 246 games in only ten seasons. He twice surpassed the thirty-game mark, winning thirty-one in 1903 and thirty-five in 1904. After his retirement he served the Brooklyn Dodgers as a coach and scout. McGinnity was elected to the Baseball Hall of Fame in 1946.

SELECTED BIBLIOGRAPHY: "Joe McGinnity," in Mike Shatzkin, *The Ballplayers* (1990); Joseph Jerome McGinnity, Research File, National Baseball Hall of Fame Library (October 1996).

James L. Gates, Jr.

McGRAW, JOHN JOSEPH ("Little Napoleon") (7 April 1873, Truxton, NY–25 February 1934, New Rochelle, NY). A baseball player and manager, his father (John) was an Irish immigrant who had served in the Union Army during the Civil War and later was employed as a railroad maintenance worker in upstate New York. McGraw survived a difficult childhood with an abusive father to become one of the most dominant figures in American baseball history. McGraw's playing career began in 1891 with the Baltimore Orioles and ended in 1906 with the New York Giants. During those sixteen years he compiled a career batting average of .334 and developed a reputation as an arrogant and abusive individual who would stop at nothing to win a game. His knowledge of the rules and ability to handle difficult ballplayers made him managerial material. In 1899 he became a player-manager and remained in that capacity for the last eight years of his career. McGraw always seemed to be involved in some controversy. He once refused to be transferred from Baltimore to Brooklyn; he refused to allow his team to play the American League champions in the 1904 World Series; he once agreed to a contract only after the reserve clause had been removed; and it is reported that he was prepared to sign black ballplayers to his squad. Following his playing career, McGraw managed until 1932. During his managerial tenure the Giants dominated the National League, winning ten pennants and three World Series. He was elected to the Baseball Hall of Fame in 1937.

SELECTED BIBLIOGRAPHY: Charles C. Alexander, *John McGraw* (1988); Frank Graham, *McGraw of the Giants: An Informal Biography* (1944); "John McGraw," in Mike Shatzkin, ed., *The Ballplayers* (1990); John J. McGraw, *John J. McGraw: My Thirty Years in Baseball* (1995); John Joseph McGraw, File, National Baseball Hall of Fame Library (October 1996).

James L. Gates, Jr.

McLAUGHLIN, JAMES (22 February 1861, Hartford, CT–19 January 1927, New Orleans). A jockey, he was an orphan of Irish descent and the father-in-law of Hall of Fame jockey Tommy Burns. He came to the races under Bill Daly, and the Dwyer Brothers bought his contract at sixteen. He was the leading rider in races won four consecutive years (1884–87). McLaughlin won the Belmont Stakes six times, with Forester (1882), George Kinney (1883), Panique (1884), Inspector B. (1886), Hanover (1887), and Sir Dixon (1888). He also won the Kentucky Derby on Hindoo in 1881 and the Preakness on Tecumseh in 1885. Hindoo, Inspector B., and Sir Dixon were among the four Travers winners he rode. Miss Woodford gave McLaughlin the first of his three victories in the Alabama Stakes, the first of four triumphs in the Ladies handicap, and the first of two wins in the Monmouth Oaks. McLaughlin won eight Ridal Handicaps, three Flash Stakes, and four Juvenile Stakes. His 1886 Juvenile win on Tremont was one of thirteen races he won on the colt that year. He also captured the Withers, Sapling, and Dixie Handicap on Hanover and the Belmont Futurity on His Highness. His career lasted seventeen years (1876–92), and he was inducted into the National Thoroughbred Racing Hall of Fame in 1955.

SELECTED BIBLIOGRAPHY: *American Turf* (August 1949); *Blood-Horse* (29 April 1967, 9 June 1984); *New York Times*, 20 January 1927, 18; *Turf and Sport Digest* (January 1935); Walter S. Vosburgh, *Racing in America, 1865–1921* (1934); Lyman Horace Weeks, *The American Turf* (1898).

Courtesy of the National Thoroughbred Racing Hall of Fame

MEXICANS. Writer Gloria Anzaldua has described the experiences of Americans of Mexican ancestry in terms of crossing cultural borderlands. Indeed, while Americans of Mexican ancestry have not discovered any magical melting pot in the United States, they have discovered opportunities to cross borderlands separating them from the dominant Anglo society. Sport has helped provide them with such opportunities. Nevertheless, Mexican Americans have also for decades endured and struggled against the forces of racial oppression and class exploitation. They have therefore used sport to develop and sustain a sense of community in the face of Anglo domination. Sadly, however, sport has also been a site of racial oppression and class exploitation of Mexican Americans.

In the area of the United States that once belonged to Spain and then became a part of Mexico in the 1820s, sport evolved around the horse. For example, in Mexican California a society had developed largely based on ranching. Consequently, sport among the *Californios* was closely connected to an economy that vitally needed workers who were skilled horse riders. The beach bordering Santa Barbara was the site of horse races, attracting enthusiastic spectators and bettors. For many of the Anglos who visited Mexican California, horse racing and festive rodeos signified that the *Californios* were far too lazy to exploit California properly. Aggravating Anglo hostility was the fact that most of the *Californios* and other Spanish-speaking residents of North America were mestizos and mestizas—people of mixed Native American and European ancestry.

After the United States won the Mexican War, it gained control of California, Arizona, New Mexico, Nevada, Colorado, and Utah, as well as the expanded borders of previously annexed Texas. While the war-ending Treaty of Guadalupe Hidalgo promised that the rights of the new American residents would be respected, the conquered regions' Mexican population generally found itself under siege. For example, in the 1850s Anglo Protestants in California were able to ban Mexican sporting pastimes that had typically taken place on Sunday—the Protestant Sabbath.

In the latter decades of the nineteenth century, however, people of Mexican ancestry participated in sports associated with Anglos. The extent of this participation is difficult to determine since these people might have had Anglo fathers and were often identified as Spanish. In baseball, for example, Vincent Irwin played professionally in California during the late 1870s and early 1880s. He then became the first major league player of Mexican ancestry when he joined the Providence Grays in 1882. Interestingly, Irwin played under his mother's surname, Nava. Another distinctive athlete of Mexican ancestry was Juagarina. A splendid all-around athlete, Juagarina was a woman who engaged in competitive sword contests and boxing matches. Her defeated opponents were often male.

The twentieth century offered powerful inducements to Mexican immigration to the United States in the form of job opportunities in agriculture, transportation, industry, and domestic service. It also offered people of Mexican ancestry race-based discrimination in the form of segregated housing and schooling, while the jobs many of them performed satisfied Anglo stereotypes of them as racially fit for only "stoop labor." Meanwhile, when the economy plummeted, and their labor seemed unnecessary, they were often told to "go back to where you came from." Frequently, legal authorities forced them to cross southward into Mexico.

Athletic clubs helped sustain Mexican American communities through the bad and not-so-bad times. Mexican American mutual aid societies or *mutualistas* often sponsored baseball teams. In the 1920s a *mutualista* from Santa Barbara was represented by one of the finest amateur nines in California. In the 1930s and 1940s the Mexican Athletic Club in San Francisco sponsored soccer and basketball teams. At about the same time Mexican American women joined community-based softball teams.

This was all going on at a time when Mexican Americans typically encountered segregated recreational facilities. One of the biggest concerns of pre–World War II community activists was to end the segregation of swimming pools in addition to other public facilities. The League of United Latin American Citizens (LULAC) was frequently successful in protesting recreational segregation.

Individual athletes also sustained community pride. In southern California, Joe Rivers (Ybarra), Bert Colima, and Manuel Ortiz were Mexican American boxers and heroes during the first half of the twentieth century. During the 1930s professional wrestler Vincent Lopez was also popular in southern California Mexican American communities.

These and other prominent Mexican American athletes often did more than represent their community strivings. They crossed cultural boundaries and won the respect of non-Mexican American athletes. Indeed, Mexican American athletes continue to do so. In the 1950s there was no more exciting tennis player than Los Angeles–born Richard "Pancho" Gonzales.* Other more recent and noteworthy "crossover athletes" have been golfers Lee Trevino* and Nancy Lopez.* Gonzales, Trevino, and Lopez have, in their own ways, shown that tennis and golf do not necessarily belong to privileged Anglos. Much the same thing could be said regarding Rudy Galindo, a champion, working-class, Mexican American ice skater in the 1990s.

College and professional football have offered athletes of Mexican ancestry opportunities to gain fame and make money. Joe Kapp quarterbacked his University of California eleven to a Rose Bowl in the late 1950s and several years later led the Minnesota Vikings to a Super Bowl. Tom Flores was a standout quarterback for the College of the Pacific in Stockton, California. But few had heard of him until he starred for the Oakland Raiders in the 1960s. He subsequently coached the Oakland and then Los Angeles Raiders, whose quarterback was Jim Plunkett. The son of an Anglo father and Mexican American mother, Plunkett won the prestigious Heisman Trophy while quarterbacking Stanford to a Rose Bowl championship in the early 1970s. He then played several years for the New England Patriots and San Francisco 49ers before leading the Raiders to two Super Bowl championships in 1981 and 1984.

Despite the past and present Mexican American athletic success stories, Mexican Americans who want to emulate Jim Plunkett or Nancy Lopez or simply want to have fun still encounter rough and well-guarded terrain while crossing the cultural borderlands. The fact that many Americans of Mexican ancestry are neither economically privileged, Anglo, nor male means they possess insufficient access to appropriate training for high-level competition and insufficient enjoyment of recreational facilities. Indeed, despite the achievements of Gonzales, Lopez, and Galindo, we are not likely to see barrio kids flocking to American tennis courts, golf courses, and ice skating rinks.

SELECTED BIBLIOGRAPHY: Susan K. Cahn, *Coming on Strong: Gender and Sexuality in Twentieth-Century Women's Sport* (1994); Albert Camarillo, *Chicanos in a*

Changing Society: From Mexican Pueblo to American Barrio in Santa Barbara and Southern California, 1848–1930 (1979); Mario T. Garcia, *Mexican Americans: Leadership, Ideology and Identity, 1930–1960* (1989); Douglas Monroy, *Thrown among Strangers: The Making of Mexican Culture in Frontier California* (1990); George Sanchez, *Becoming Mexican American: Ethnicity, Culture, and Identity in Chicano Los Angeles, 1900–1945* (1993).

Joel S. Franks

MEYERS, JOHN TORTES ("Chief") (29 July 1880, Riverside, CA–25 July 1971, San Bernardino, CA). A baseball player, he was the son of noted Santa Rosa Mission Cahuilla basket maker Felicite Tortes and German American Indiana native John Mayer [*sic*], a veteran of the Civil War. He was the first great American Indian catcher at the major league level. A lifetime .291 hitter, he was a fierce competitor with a rifle arm and became two-time National League Most Valuable Player (MVP) runner-up (1911–12). He was already a twenty-six-year-old veteran of nine semipro seasons in 1906, when he was signed to a professional contract by Harrisburg, Pennsylvania, manager "Sliding Billy" Hamilton. After a strong showing in 1908 at St. Paul, Meyers went to the majors for good in 1909 with the New York Giants. His otherwise stellar career suffered nominally from the disappointment of never having been on a World Series winner, as he lost four times (three times with the Giants and once with Brooklyn). He still holds the series record for most assists in a six-game series (twelve). In the characteristic Indian way, Meyers tended to understate the racism he experienced during his career, but he once remarked that Indians in organized baseball were sometimes made to feel like "foreigners."

SELECTED BIBLIOGRAPHY: Henry C. Koerper and Gerald A. Smith, "The Catcher Was a Cahuilla: A Remembrance of John Tortes Meyers, 1880–1971," unpublished manuscript; Lawrence S. Ritter, *The Glory of Their Times* (1966).

Joseph M. Giovannetti

MIKITA, STANLEY (20 May 1940, Sokolce [Sokolcany], Slovakia–   ). A hockey player, he was raised in Slovakia as Stanislav Groth. His father was a textile worker, and his mother tilled the soil. His uncle and aunt from Canada, Mr. and Mrs. Joseph Mikita, adopted him after visiting Slovakia. Stan took his uncle's surname and went on to star in amateur hockey on a variety of boys' teams in Saint Catherines, Ontario. In November 1958, the Chicago Black Hawks asked him to take a temporary replacement job for three games in the pros. When he returned to his junior squad, the TeePees, he won the league scoring championship with ninety-seven points (thirty-eight goals and fifty-nine assists), despite playing in only forty-five games due to a broken wrist. The next season Mikita joined the Chicago Blackhawks' training camp. Although lacking in size, Mikita made up for it with his hard work and aggressive play. Montreal fans nicknamed him "Le Petit Diable" (the little devil). His play became smarter and more gentlemanly with time. He won the Lady Byng Trophy for sports-manlike conduct in 1967. Mikita played twenty-two years as a professional with the Chicago Blackhawks. His awards included the Ross Trophy for fifty assists in the 1963–64 season, when he also finished second with thirty-nine goals, beaten only by his fellow teammate Bobby Hull, who had forty-three. In 1964–65 Mikita again won the Ross Trophy with eighty-seven assists. In 1966–67 he became the first player to win the Triple Crown, with a record-setting sixty-two assists and tying Hull's ninety-seven points. He took home the Lady Byng Trophy, the Ross Trophy as best scorer, and the Hart Trophy, which recognized him as the National Hockey League's (NHL) Most Valuable Player. That year he was the first team NHL All-Star center, and he achieved that honor again in 1967–68. The following year he ranked fourth in scoring with a total of ninety-seven points. His career peaked in the late 1960s, and repeated injuries hampered his scoring. A bad back also plagued him, and in 1973 he broke his heel. A serious head injury forced him to wear a special helmet designed especially for him. He eventually went into the business of manufacturing helmets in the Chicago area. Over his career he scored 541 goals and 926 assists. He averaged more than a point per game in a truly outstanding career. The author of two books about hockey, he led the NHL in scoring four times. He is enshrined in the Hockey Hall of Fame.

SELECTED BIBLIOGRAPHY: Ralph Hickock, *A Who's Who of Sports Champions* (1995); *Jednota*; Joseph Krajsa, ed., *Slovaks in America: A Bicentennial Study* (1978); Stan Mikita, *I Play to Win* (1969); Stan Mikita, *Inside Hockey* (1971); "The Slovaks" (videotape), *The Columbus Legacy* (1992); M. Mark Stolarik, *The Slovak-Americans* (1988).

Michael J. Kopanic, Jr.

MILLER, CHERYL DEANNE ("Silk") (3 January 1964, Riverside, CA–   ). An African American college, Olympic, and professional basketball player, sportscaster, and head coach, she was the third child of Saul and Carrie Miller. A member of an athletically talented family, she graduated from Riverside Polytechnic High School and the University of Southern California (USC). She gained the nickname "Silk" due to her style of play. In high school Miller averaged 32.8 points per game and led her team to a 132–4 record between 1979 and 1982. In her senior year she became the first woman to dunk a basketball in regulation play. For four consecutive years, she was named to the *Parade* All-America Team, Amateur Athletic Union All-American, consensus All-American, and All California Interscholastic Federation as the Most Valuable Player (MVP). At USC, Miller's superior play continued as she led her team to two national titles in 1983 and 1984. She set several school records for most points, rebounds, and free throws. She also received several honors, including Naismith All-American (1982–86), Eastman Kodak All-American

(1982–86), West Coast Athletic Conference All-Conference Team (1982–85), National Collegiate Athletic Association (NCAA) tournament MVP (1982–84), and the Broderick Award as the Female College Basketball Player of the Year (1986). USC retired her uniform jersey in 1986. Miller was a member of the 1983 Pan-American, 1984 Olympic, and 1986 Goodwill Games gold medal teams. She joined *ABC Sports* as a commentator in 1988 and returned to USC in 1993, where she served as head coach for two years. In 1995 Miller was inducted into the Basketball Hall of Fame, and in 1997 she was named the head coach of the Phoenix Mercury team of the newly organized Women's National Basketball Association.

SELECTED BIBLIOGRAPHY: "Basketball Hall of Famers Savor Their Inductions," *Jet* 88 (5 June 1995): 48; "Cheryl Miller Succeeds as USC Coach in Her First Year," *Jet* (4 April 1994): 48; David L. Porter, ed., *Biographical Dictionary of American Sports: Basketball and Other Indoor Sports* (1989); Janet Woolum, *Outstanding Women Athletes: Who They Are and How They Influenced Sport in America* (1992).

Susan Rayl

MILLER, LEON A. (15 July 1895, Cherokee, NC–11 August 1961, New Hyde Park, NY). A Native American Indian lacrosse player, official, and coach, he attended Cherokee Indian School from 1905 to 1909 and the Carlisle Indian School from 1910 to 1916, from which he received an M.E. degree. At Carlisle he was a teammate of Jim Thorpe* and a member of the varsity lacrosse, track, and football teams. After graduation Miller served as an army captain in World War I and later worked as an engineer at the Ford Motor Company in Highland Park, Michigan. During the 1920s he played football briefly on Thorpe's Indian All-Stars and was a professional lacrosse player and official. In 1932 he became head lacrosse coach at the City College of New York (CCNY), a position that he held until 1960. At CCNY he became an associate professor of health and physical education and also served as assistant football coach for three years and head coach for 1943–44. During his years at CCNY he wrote many newspaper articles about lacrosse and worked for several years as the assistant editor of the sport's *Intercollegiate Guide*. He also was a member of the New York Lacrosse Club. A banker and member of the American Stock Exchange, he was also respected as a leader in Indian councils and was a government adviser on Indian affairs. In honor of his decades of staunch support and development of lacrosse in the United States Miller was inducted into the Lacrosse Hall of Fame in 1961.

SELECTED BIBLIOGRAPHY: *New York Times*, 14 August 1961, 25; Archives of the Lacrosse Hall of Fame, Johns Hopkins University, Baltimore.

George B. Kirsch

MILLS, BILLY (30 June 1938, Pine Ridge Indian Reservation, SD–   ). A track athlete, his father (Sydney) was a farmer and boxer, and his mother (Grace) was a homemaker. Mills, an Oglala Sioux, completed high school at Haskell Institute and graduated with a physical education degree from the University of Kansas. He has also been awarded three honorary doctorates. Billy was one of the top milers in the United States coming out of high school and among the best cross-country runners in the country while in college. Mills won a gold medal in the 10,000-meter race at the 1964 Olympics, setting an Olympic record and becoming the first American ever to win this event. In 1965 he set a world record for six miles. Mills has been inducted into several Halls of Fame, including the U.S. Olympic Hall of Fame and the U.S. Track and Field Hall of Fame. He was awarded warrior status by the Lakota following his Olympic win and was recognized as one of 100 golden Olympians at the 1996 Olympic Games. Mills cowrote the autobiographical movie *Running Brave*, as well as the book *Wokini*. He is national chairman of Running Strong for American Indian Youth and a board member on the Native American Sports Council and the Wings of America Running Program. He is also a motivational speaker for corporate America. Mills continues to use running as a catalyst for increasing Native American athletes' self-esteem and pride in their heritage. His work with Native American sport organizations, combined with his motivational writing and speaking engagements, makes him an important role model for both Indian and non-Indian youth.

SELECTED BIBLIOGRAPHY: Billy Mills, with Nicholas Sparks, *Wokini: Your Personal Journey to Happiness and Self-Understanding* (1990); Billy Mills and Patricia Mills, *Running Brave* (Englander Productions, 1983); Joseph B. Oxendine, *American Indian Sports Heritage* (1988).

Victoria Paraschak

MIX, RONALD J. ("Ron")

MIX, RONALD J. ("Ron") (10 March 1938, Los Angeles–   ). A college and professional football player, he was the second son of tailor Sam Mix, a Russian Jewish immigrant who came to the United States at the age of thirteen, and Daisy (Koskoff). He graduated from Hawthorne High in 1956 and the University of Southern California in 1960, garnering All-America honors as an offensive tackle during his senior year. Later that year, Mix joined the Los Angeles Chargers for the inaugural season of the American Football League (AFL). He was named an all-AFL performer in each of the next nine seasons, helping the Chargers (who moved to San Diego in 1961) to five AFL championship games. At 6'4" and 255 pounds, Mix was one of the largest men in the league at his position, yet he possessed amazing speed and agility; his ability to make one block at the line of scrimmage and another in the secondary was unmatched. Known as the "Intellectual Assassin" because he balanced a violent on-field persona with scholarly pursuits off the field, Mix retired in 1969 to pursue a law degree, which he completed in 1970. In 1971 he was enticed to return to football by the Oakland Raiders of the National Football League (NFL) and played for two final seasons before beginning his law practice. As one of only a few Jewish players in the league, Mix was proud of his religious heritage. He was inducted into the Jewish Sports Hall of Fame in Netanya, Israel, in 1980. In 1979, Mix was recognized for his outstanding career with induction into the Professional Football Hall of Fame.

SELECTED BIBLIOGRAPHY: Tom Bennett, ed., *The NFL's Encyclopedic History of Professional Football* (1977); Denis J. Harrington, *The Pro Football Hall of Fame: Players, Coaches, Team Owners and League Officials, 1963–1991* (1991); Jack Horrigan and Mike Rathet, *The Other League* (1970); Ronald Mendell and Timothy Phares, *Who's Who in Football* (1974); David Neft and Richard Cohen, *The Football Encyclopedia* (1991).

Dennis Ryan

MOLINEAUX, TOM (23 March 1784, Georgetown, VA–14 August 1818, Galway, Ireland). An African American prizefighter, he was the first American Negro to fight in a major championship bout, which took place in December 1810 in England. Born a slave, his master, Algernon Molineaux, took Tom and his family to live in Richmond, Virginia. Boxing apparently got passed down to young Tom. Evidence indicates that Molineaux's father (Zachariah) and his grandfather had been notable boxers among the plantation slaves. Stories have it that Molineaux gained his freedom through his pugilistic prowess. In 1809 Molineaux was living and working around the Catherine Markets in New York City, challenging and defeating all comers in boxing. After traveling on a merchant ship to England, where the fight game was flourishing, Molineaux was taken in tow by Bill Richmond, one of the famous fighters of his day. A squarely built, rugged young man, Molineaux achieved immediate success in England. He scored eight rapid victories, mostly by knockout, and prepared for a showdown with the British champion Tom Cribb on 10 December 1810. The fight would be held under "London Prize Ring Rules," which meant bare-knuckle fighting. In a great struggle, Molineaux was the victim of biased judging. Time in the twenty-eighth round was extended past the legal limit of thirty seconds for Cribb to recover, and Molineaux became weakened later in the forty-fourth round. Cribb was declared the victor. Molineaux and Cribb would meet again on 28 September 1811, with Cribb claiming the title after eleven rounds. Molineaux never recovered from the injustice of the first encounter with Cribb. He died destitute, alcoholic, and despondent at the age of thirty-four.

SELECTED BIBLIOGRAPHY: Arthur R. Ashe, Jr., *A Hard Road to Glory: A History of the African-American Athlete, 1619–1918*, vol. 1 (1988); Edwin Henderson, *The Black Athlete: Emergence and Arrival* (1968); R. S. Rinnert, *African American Answer Book— Sports* (1995); R. S. Rinnert, *Book of Firsts: Sport Heroes* (1994).

C. Keith Harrison

MOORE, ARCHIBALD (13 December 1913, Benoit, MS–9 December 1998, San Diego). An African American prizefighter, he was born Archibald Lee

Wright, the son of Tommy Wright, a day laborer, and Lorena Wright. Although he maintained that he was actually born in 1916 in Collinsville, Illinois, his mother and other family members have confirmed the earlier date. He took his last name from his uncle and aunt, Cleveland and Willie Moore, who raised him after his parents separated. As a youth in St. Louis, he attended Lincoln High School, but he became involved in petty theft and spent twenty-two months in a reform school. He learned to box as a young man and turned professional in either 1935 or 1936. His long career of over 200 fights lasted nearly thirty years, ending in 1963. During the 1930s and 1940s he fought first as a welterweight and then as a light-heavyweight, but an ulcer ailment and poor management delayed his chance for a championship until he was thirty-nine years old. On 17 December 1952 he won the light-heavyweight title by a unanimous decision over Joey Maxim. Although he held that belt for nine years, he lost two memorable bouts for the heavyweight crown to Rocky Marciano* and Floyd Patterson.* In November 1962, as he approached his forty-ninth birthday, he was knocked out in the fourth round by Cassius Clay (later, Muhammad Ali*), as Clay was rising through the ranks of the heavyweight contenders. In his last years as a boxer he became celebrated for his remarkable longevity and his dietary secrets, which he claimed he learned from an Australian aborigine. After he retired, he worked in youth programs and as a trainer and adviser for boxers. He was elected to the International Boxing Hall of Fame in 1990.

SELECTED BIBLIOGRAPHY: Frank Deford, "The Ageless Warrior," *Sports Illustrated* 70 (8 May 1989): 103–109; Sid Friedlander, "The Archie Moore Story," *New York Post* (26–30 January 1959); Irv Goodman, "Archie Moore's Secret of Perpetual Youth," *Sport* 26 (May 1959): 23, 82–85; Archie Moore and Leonard B. Pearl, *Any Boy Can: The Archie Moore Story* (1971); *New York Times*, 10 December 1998, B16.

George B. Kirsch

MORALES, PABLO (5 December 1964, Chicago–). Son of Cuban émigré parents, Pedro and Bianca Morales, he was a champion swimmer. In the 1984 Olympic Games at Los Angeles Morales won a gold medal in the 4 × 100-meter medley relay and two silver medals. At that time he was attending Stanford University, earning a degree in 1987. At Stanford he won eleven individual college championships and received the university's Al Masters Award, in recognition of the highest all-around athletic, leadership, and academic performance. Although he was the world record holder in the 100-meter butterfly in 1988, Morales failed to qualify for that year's Olympic team. He began law school at Cornell University but interrupted his career to participate in the 1992 Barcelona Olympics, winning the 100-meter butterfly and swimming the butterfly leg on the world record-setting 4 × 100-meter medley relay. In 1992 he was voted the U.S. Olympic Committee's Sportsman of the Year and was a finalist for the Sullivan Memorial Award. After completing Cornell Law School, he began the practice of law in northern California.

SELECTED BIBLIOGRAPHY: "Bravo, Pavlo," *Sports Illustrated* 77 (3 August 1992): 34; Tom Weir, "Tragedy Often Dilutes Joyful Olympic Tears," *USA Today*, July 1992.

Richard V. McGehee

MORGAN, JOE (19 September 1943, Bonham, TX–   ). An African American baseball player, he moved from Bonham to Oakland, California, in the late 1940s with his parents. Shortly thereafter Morgan became fascinated with baseball by going to Pacific Coast League games with his father. As a Little Leaguer he idolized Jackie Robinson* and Nellie Fox, both second basemen. He tried out for professional teams while still attending Castlemont High School in Oakland. Initially rejected primarily because of his diminutive size (5'7", 155 pounds), he enrolled in Oakland City College in 1961. As a freshman he signed his first professional baseball contract with the Houston Colt .45s. After two seasons in the minor leagues, during which he earned the Texas League's Most Valuable Player award in 1964, he reached the major leagues with Houston in 1965 and was named the *Sporting News'* National League Rookie Player of the Year. In 1966 he became the first Houston player named to the National League All-Star team but was unable to play due to injury. After the 1971 season he was traded to the Cincinnati Reds in an eight-man deal. Along with players like Pete Rose, Johnny Bench, and Tony Perez, Morgan was a part of the "Big Red Machine" that eventually won the World Series in 1975 and 1976. He was the National League's Most Valuable Player in 1975 and 1976, won a Gold Glove for fielding excellence in 1973–76, and earned a position on the All-Star team each year from 1973 to 1979. In 1979 he declared for free agency and signed with the Houston Astros. During the 1981 strike-shortened season he moved to the San Francisco Giants and was named the *Sporting News'* National League's Comeback Player of the Year in 1982 after several injury-hampered seasons. Turning down an offer to manage the Houston Astros after the 1982 season, he signed with the Philadelphia Phillies in 1983 and helped lead them to the World Series, which they lost to the Baltimore Orioles. He finished his career after playing two seasons back in his hometown with the Oakland Athletics. Known for his ability to excel in all facets of the game, the Hall of Famer finished his career with 274 home runs, 1,177 runs batted in, and 697 stolen bases. Possibly best known as a student of baseball who understood the intricacies of the game, he became a popular commentator for nationally televised baseball games after his playing career.

SELECTED BIBLIOGRAPHY: Nathan Aaseng, *Little Giants of Pro Sports* (1980); Marshall Burchard, *Joe Morgan* (1978); Joel H. Cohen, *Joe Morgan: Great Little Big Man* (1978); *Current Biography Yearbook* (1984); David Falkner, *Joe Morgan: A Life in Baseball* (1993).

Troy D. Paino

MORRISSEY, JOHN (12 February 1831, Templemore, Tipperary, Ireland–1 May 1878, Saratoga, NY). Bare-knuckle prizefighter, gambler, and politician, he was the only son of Timothy Morrissey, a laborer who took his family from Ireland to Canada when John was a young boy. After three months the Morrisseys settled in Troy, New York, where John spent only one year in public school. He did not learn how to read or write until he was nineteen years old, when he taught himself. At age twelve he began his working career in a wallpaper factory, moving on to a job in an iron works before landing a position as a deckhand on a Hudson River steamer. As a young man he earned a reputation as a rowdy, tough gang leader by winning many brawls in saloons and on the streets of Troy. After a brief early stay in New York City he journeyed to California in 1850 in search of gold and the chance to fight Tom Hyer for the prizefighting championship of the United States. He found neither fortune nor fame in California, but on 12 October 1853 at Boston Four Corners, New York, he defeated Yankee Sullivan in thirty-seven rounds for $2,000 and a claim to the heavyweight title. In his last fight he conquered John C. Heenan on 20 October 1858 at Long Point, Canada, for $2,500 a side. Retiring from the ring, he devoted the rest of his life to operating gambling businesses, speculating in investments on Wall Street, and serving as a congressman and state senator from New York. After beginning his career as an operator of betting parlors during the 1850s, he launched his major casino in 1862, when he built a gaming house in Saratoga, New York. He then became one of the founders of the Saratoga Racetrack, which began operations in the summer of 1863, in the midst of the Civil War. Morrissey counted several leading turfmen among his associates, including John R. Hunter and William R. Travers. Although he put up most of the money, he refrained from adding his name to the list of socially prominent incorporators of the Saratoga Association for the Improvement of the Breed. During the 1860s and 1870s he became a flamboyant and controversial character in New York state politics. A Democrat affiliated with Tammany Hall in New York City, he served two terms in the U.S. House of Representatives (1867–71) and was elected to the New York state Senate in 1875 and 1877.

SELECTED BIBLIOGRAPHY: Elliott J. Gorn, *The Manly Art: Bare-Knuckle Prizefighting in America* (1986); W. E. Harding, *John Morrissey, His Life, Battles, and Wrangles* (1881); *New York Times*, 2 May 1878, 1–2; A. J. Weise, *History of the City of Troy* (1876).

George B. Kirsch

MOSCONI, WILLIE (21 June 1913, Philadelphia–16 September 1993, Haddon Heights, NJ). A pool player of Italian ancestry, his father, Joseph William Mosconi, was an ex-prizefighter who owned a gym and pool tables. His mother, Helen (Reilly), was a homemaker. Willie attended Barrett Junior High School and South Philadelphia High before enrolling in, but not completing, Banks Business College. After a short stint as an upholsterer, Mosconi turned to pool for his livelihood. Induction into the military during World War II came in March 1945, when Mosconi was thirty-one. After the war Mosconi resumed his championship play and won nineteen titles. From 1941 to 1957 Mosconi established these records: an average of 18.34 balls per inning (1950); a run of 526 straight balls (1954); and 150 consecutive balls sunk in one inning (1956). In 1957 he suffered a stroke that required several years of rehabilitation. A recovered Mosconi returned to action in 1961. That year, he taught pool techniques to Paul Newman and Jackie Gleason, stars of the movie *The Hustler* (1961). In the 1970s and 1980s, he dueled Minnesota Fats (Rudolf Wanderone) in televised pool matches. In the 1980s he taught pool in his own Superior Billiard Academy in Philadelphia, on *Pocket Billiards* on ESPN, and for the equipment manufacturer World of Leisure. Upon his death in 1993 he left behind his fundamentals for success at pool: proper cue grip, good table stance, a good bridge, smooth stroke and follow-through, careful cueing of the ball, and precision in hitting the object ball.

SELECTED BIBLIOGRAPHY: Charles Moritz, ed., "Willie Mosconi," *Current Biography Yearbook* 1963 (1964), 281–283; Willie Mosconi, *Willie Mosconi on Pocket Billiards* (1959); Willie Mosconi and Stanley Cohen, *Willie's Game: An Autobiography* (1993); Steve Rushin, "Willie Mosconi," *Sports Illustrated* 79 (27 September 1993): 44–45.

Philip M. Montesano

MOSES, EDWIN (31 August 1955, Dayton, OH–   ). An African American track athlete, he specialized in the 400-meter intermediate hurdles. His father, Irving Moses, was an elementary school principal and science teacher; his mother, Gladys Moses, was a curriculum supervisor for the Dayton school system. As a teenager Edwin was bused to the predominantly white Fairview High School, where he ran the 120-yard high hurdles and the 440-yard race on the track team. After graduating in 1973, he enrolled in Morehouse College in Atlanta, Georgia, on an academic scholarship. A double major in physics and mechanical engineering, he graduated in 1978 with a 3.57 grade point average. Specializing in the 400-meter intermediate hurdles, Moses steadily improved his times in that event, and he earned international recognition with his world record-setting gold medal victory at the 1976 Olympics at Montreal, Canada. Over the next twelve years he dominated his race at national and international track meets. Although he missed the 1980 Olympics due to the American boycott of the Moscow Games, he captured a second gold medal in the 1984 Los Angeles Games. While he set four world records during his career, perhaps his most remarkable achievement was his streak of 122 consecutive victories from 1977 to 1987. He retired after finishing third at the 1988 Olympics in Seoul, South Korea. Moses applied his scientific training to his performance in his event, perfecting a technique in which he took only thirteen strides between each of the ten hurdles. He was the recipient of the Sullivan Award in 1983, and *Sports Illustrated* selected him as its Sportsman of the Year in 1985.

SELECTED BIBLIOGRAPHY: Jon Hendershott, "Edwin Moses, *Track and Field News* 29 (September 1976): 33–34, Jon Hendershott, "An Artist in Solitude," *Track and Field*

News 32 (March 1980): 8–13; Dave Johnson, "Edwin Moses," *Track and Field News* 36 (December 1983): 66–67; Frank Litsky, "Loss by Moses Brings a Sense of Relief," *New York Times*, 23 June 1987, A25–A28; Edwin Moses, with Jon Hendershott, "Boycott Changed Everything," *Track and Field News* 33 (January 1981): 6–8; Cordner Nelson, *Track's Greatest Champions* (1986).

George B. Kirsch

MOTLEY, MARION (5 June 1920, Leesburg, GA–27 June 1999, Cleveland OH). An African American football player, his father (Shakeful) was a foundry worker and his mother was Blanche (Jones) Motley. A graduate of Canton (Ohio) McKinley High School, he attended the University of Nevada-Reno but was best known as a professional football player with the Cleveland Browns from 1946 through 1954 and as one of four African American players to reintegrate professional football in 1946. Although he was an outstanding high school fullback, during the early 1940s Motley played in relative obscurity at the University of Nevada-Reno because few colleges recruited black players. After joining the navy he played the 1945 season for coach Paul Brown at the Great Lakes Naval Training Center, which beat Notre Dame 39–7 in the final game of the season. In 1946 Motley and Bill Willis joined the Cleveland Browns, coached by Paul Brown in the newly organized All-American Football Conference (AAFC). That year African Americans Ken Washington* and Woody Strode joined the National Football League's (NFL) Los Angeles Rams. Motley was a 6'2", 235-pound fullback with sprinter speed, and Willis was a speedy guard. They became dominant players on one of professional football's premier teams. The Browns won all four AAFC championships before the league folded in 1949. When the Browns joined the NFL, they played in four straight championship games, winning in 1950. Motley sat out the 1954 season with a knee injury and finished his career in 1955 with the Pittsburgh Steelers. An excellent runner and blocker, Motley was the all-time leading rusher in the AAFC and All-NFL in 1950 and led the Browns to eight championship games in eight seasons. He was inducted into the Pro Football Hall of Fame in 1968. Motley and Willis understood the need for dignity and decorum, and their success and the championships of the Browns ensured the smooth, but slow, reintegration of professional football after 1946.

SELECTED BIBLIOGRAPHY: Paul Brown, with Jack Claby, *PB: The Paul Brown Story* (1979); David Neft, Richard M. Cohen, and Jordan A. Deutsch, *Pro Football: The Early Years, an Encyclopedic History, 1895–1959* (1978); *New York Times*, 28 June 1999, B–7; Beum Riffenburgh, *The Official NFL Encyclopedia* (1986).

C. Robert Barnett

MURPHY, ISAAC (16 April 1861, Frankfort, Fayette County, KY–12 February 1896, Lexington, KY). Born Isaac Burns, he was one of the first African American jockeys. After his father (James) died, his mother moved to Lexington to live with her father, Green Murphy, the town's bell ringer and crier for auctions.

At the peak of his career he was making as much as $10,000 a year. The irony about Murphy's career is that if he had been born in the twentieth century, he would not have had the same opportunity to become a jockey, because racism barred blacks from the sport after 1900. Born in the heart of horse country, Murphy rode his first major race astride Lady Greenfield at Louisville in 1878; he achieved national prominence as jockey for the Hunt Reynolds Stable of Lexington. In 1884 he rode to victory in the most famous of American races, the Kentucky Derby, aboard Buchanan. Then in 1890 and 1891, he had successive triumphs in the Kentucky Derby on Riley and Kingman. His three Kentucky Derby triumphs stood as a record until it was tied in 1930 by Earle Sande and then broken by Eddie Arcaro with his fourth win in 1948. At the end of his career Murphy branched out as an owner but never found a successful horse. He suffered from weight problems, chronic alcoholism, and the effects of racial discrimination. He died from pneumonia at the age of thirty-five, leaving a career mark of 628 wins out of 1,412 races (44%). The National Museum of Racing Hall of Fame selected Murphy as the first jockey to earn membership in 1955; the following year he was selected to the Jockey Hall of Fame at Pimlico Race Track, Maryland.

SELECTED BIBLIOGRAPHY: Arthur R. Ashe, Jr., *A Hard Road to Glory: A History of the African-American Athlete, 1619–1918*, vol. 1 (1988); Edwin Henderson, *The Black Athlete: Emergence and Arrival* (1968); R. S. Rinnert, *African American Answer Book-Sports* (1995); David K. Wiggins, "Isaac Murphy: Black Hero in Nineteenth Century American Sport, 1861–1896," *Canadian Journal of History of Sport and Physical Education* (May 1979): 15–23; A. S. "Doc" Young, *Negro Firsts in Sports* (1963).

C. Keith Harrison

MUSIAL, STAN (21 November 1920, Donora, PA–   ). A baseball player, he is the son of Lukasz Musial, a Polish-born millworker, and Mary Lancos Musial. A natural athlete, young Stan received early gymnastic training at the local Polish Falcon Club. After graduating from Donora High School in 1938, he rejected a basketball scholarship from the University of Pittsburgh (over the objections of his father) to sign a professional baseball contract as a pitcher with St. Louis. Stan was considered a top prospect as a pitcher, but in 1940, while in the minors, he injured his shoulder in a fall. He was regarded as a good hitter, however, and was switched to the outfield. A year later he was a late-season call-up for the Cardinals and hit .426 in a dozen games. He became a regular in 1942 and the following season won his first batting title. Brooklyn fans gave Stan his nickname, "the Man," following his extraordinary performances against the Dodgers in Ebbets Field. Musial played well at home and on the road; his 3,630 career hits were equally divided between home and the road. He was a St. Louis Cardinal for his entire career, and he helped the team gain three World Series Championships. An outstanding outfielder, Stan switched to first base late in his career and was the first man to play 1,000 games at two different positions. By the time he retired in 1963, Musial had played in 3,026 games, scored 1,949 runs, driven in 1,951 runs, hit 475 home runs, and posted a .331 career batting average. He held seventeen major league, twenty-nine National League, and nine All-Star Game records. A twenty-four-time All-Star, he won seven batting titles and was named the National League's Most Valuable Player in 1943, 1946, and 1948. He was elected to the Baseball Hall of Fame in 1969, his first year of eligibility. After his retirement Musial remained with the Cardinals as general manager and senior vice president. He was also active in Polish American causes, including the effort to establish Little League baseball in Poland in the 1980s.

SELECTED BIBLIOGRAPHY: Furman Bisher, "Get Any Hits, Stan?" *Saturday Evening Post* 236 (25 May 1963): 30; Bob Broeg, *The Man Stan: Musial, Then and Now* (1977); Jerry Lansche, *Stan the Man Musial: Born to Be a Ballplayer* (1994); Stan Musial, as told to Bob Broeg, *Stan Musial: "The Man's" Own Story* (1964); Timothy M. O'Leary, "Last Time Around with Stan," *Sports Illustrated* 19 (7 October 1963): 20–25; Harry T. Paxton, "A Visit with Stan Musial," *Saturday Evening Post* 230 (19 April 1958): 32–33ff; John Reddy, "Stan, the Incredible Durable Man," *Reader's Digest* 82 (April 1963): 175–180.

Thomas M. Tarapacki

MYERS, LAURENCE ("Lon") (16 February 1858, Richmond, VA–15 February 1899, New York City). Descended from a Jewish immigrant family with roots in colonial New York City and Richmond, Virginia, he was the first American to achieve international fame as a track star. The son of Solomon H. Myers, a clerk in a Richmond business, he was a member of the first graduating class of Richmond High School. Myers was sickly as a youth and took up athletics as a means to overcome his chronic ill health. A bookkeeper of short stature and slight build (5'7-1/2" and 114 pounds), Myers created a sensation in the world of track and field in 1879 when he broke the world record for the 440-yard run with a time of 49-1/5 seconds, becoming the first person to break fifty seconds at that distance. During his amateur career, which lasted until 1885, he was sponsored by the Manhattan Athletic Club. He set numerous American and world records at distances ranging from fifty yards to one mile. In 1884 Myers weathered a controversy over charges brought against him accusing him of violating the amateur code by accepting a salary from the Manhattan Athletic Club, for running a skating rink, for receiving payment for judging a professional race, and for editing a sporting paper. Although he was cleared of all the charges in 1884, in 1886 he finally declared himself a professional, primarily to compete against the celebrated English champion long-distance runner W. G. George. He retired in 1888 after several victories over George in New York City and Sydney, Australia.

SELECTED BIBLIOGRAPHY: *New York Times*, 17 February 1899, 5; *Spirit of the Times*, (23 and 30 July 1881): 680, 708; Joe D. Willis and Richard G. Wettan, "L. E. Myers, World's Greatest Runner," *Journal of Sport History* 2 (Fall 1975): 93–111.

George B. Kirsch

N

NAGURSKI, BRONKO (3 November 1908, Rainy River, Ontario, Canada–7 January 1990, International Falls, MN). A football player, he was born Bronislav Nagurs'kyj, the son of Ukrainian immigrants (father, Michael). His parents moved the family from Rainy River to nearby International Falls when he was a small boy. There they managed a small grocery store. Bronko competed in several sports in high school at International Falls and at Bimidji, Minnesota. After graduation in 1926, he enrolled at the University of Minnesota, where he played end, tackle, and fullback on the Gopher football team. The 6'2", 225-pound Nagurski earned a reputation in college as a rugged tackler on defense and a punishing, unstoppable force as a ball carrier on offense. In his senior year (1929) at Minnesota, he was named All-American at both the tackle and fullback positions. He went on to become a legendary fullback and linebacker for George Halas'* Chicago Bears during 1930–37 and 1943. Nagurski played a major role in the Bears' domination of the National Football League (NFL) during his nine-year career, which included three league championships and a combined record of 79–20–12. His official individual rushing statistics were not impressive by contemporary standards (4,031 yards, 4.4-yard average), but his performance on both offense and defense was exceptional enough to merit All-Pro honors from 1932 through 1934. He retired before the 1938 season when Halas refused to raise his salary from $5,000 to $6,000, but five years later he agreed to return for one more season and helped lead the Bears to another NFL title in 1943. Midway through his career with the Bears, he took up professional wrestling to augment his income and continued earning a living on the wrestling circuit after his retirement from football through the 1950s. After quitting wrestling, Nagurski returned to International Falls, where he owned and operated a gasoline station and occasionally served as a fishing guide. His accomplishments were sufficient to earn him charter membership in the College Football Hall of Fame in 1951 and the NFL Hall of Fame in 1963. In 1995 the Football Writers

Association of America honored him posthumously by giving his name to the trophy for college football's defensive player of the year.

SELECTED BIBLIOGRAPHY: James D. Whalen, "Nagurski," in David L. Porter, *Biographical Dictionary of American Sports: Football* (1987); "Bronko Nagurski's Family History Recalled," *The International Falls Daily Journal* 71 (1990): 1–5; "Nagurski," in Danylo Husar Struk, ed., *Encyclopedia of Ukraine*, vol. 3 (1993); Paul Zimmerman, "The Bronk and the Gazelle," *Sports Illustrated* (11 September 1989): 128; Nagurski Biographical File, University of Minnesota Archives.

Joel Wurl

NAISMITH, JAMES (6 November 1861, Almonte, Ontario, Canada–28 November 1939, Lawrence, KS). The inventor of basketball, he was one of three children born to John Naismith, a farmer of Scottish Presbyterian stock, and Margaret (Young) Naismith. Naismith received a high school diploma in 1883 and earned a bachelor's degree in philosophy in 1887 from McGill University in Montreal. His love of sports led him to a career in physical education, but he also wished to pursue theological studies. In order to combine these two interests he enrolled at the Young Men's Christian Association (YMCA) Training School in Springfield, Massachusetts. In December 1891, a class assignment challenged Naismith to invent an indoor gymnasium game to be played during the winter months. He sought to create a team game that avoided the violent body contact prevalent in football. The game he designed, basketball, was first played with a soccer ball and two peach baskets as goals. Naismith elevated the goals to reward finesse and agility over brute strength. His game spread rapidly around the country and throughout the world, carried by the graduates of the YMCA school. In 1898 Naismith went to the University of Kansas, becoming director of chapel and physical education, as well as the school's first basketball coach. Naismith coached the varsity team from 1899 to 1909, amassing a 53–55 record. From this point on, he would have very little to do with the game he had created. In many ways, he was displeased at what the game had become. Naismith abhorred the "win at all costs" attitude prevailing in college basketball. True to his YMCA background he saw sport primarily as a tool to promote physical fitness and moral behavior, and he was distraught to see it promoting "un-Christian" elements like raucous crowds and unsportsmanlike play. Naismith was ordained as a minister in 1916 and became a naturalized U.S. citizen in 1925. He remained at Kansas as professor of physical education until retiring in 1937. His last interaction with basketball came at the 1936 Olympics, where he was honored at the first Olympic basketball tournament. He was elected as a charter member of the Naismith Memorial Basketball Hall of Fame in 1959, to be located in Springfield, Massachusetts—a fitting tribute to the man who invented the game.

SELECTED BIBLIOGRAPHY: Frank Cosentino, *Almonte's Brothers of the Wind: R. Tait McKenzie and James Naismith* (1996); John Dewar, "The Life and Professional

Contributions of James Naismith" (Ed.D. diss., Florida State University, 1965); Ronald L. Mendell, *Who's Who in Basketball* (1973); Grace Naismith, "Father Basketball," *Sports Illustrated* 2 (31 January 1955): 64–65; James Naismith, "Basket Ball," *American Physical Education Review* (19 May 1914): 339–351; James Naismith, *Basketball: Its Origin and Development* (1941); *New York Times*, 28 November 1939, 25; Sandy Padwe, *Basketball's Hall of Fame* (1970); *Springfield (Massachusetts) Sunday Republican*, 14 April 1968; Bernice Larson Webb, *The Basketball Man: James Naismith* (1973).

Dennis Ryan

NATIONAL INDIAN ATHLETIC ASSOCIATION. Locally organized all-Indian competitions have been an ongoing feature of Native sport across North America; however, it was 1973 before an umbrella organization was formed to provide all-Indian competitions at the national level. In 1973 Ron Johnson and Satch Miller sent out letters to individuals they thought might be interested in forming a national all-Indian basketball organization. A group of about thirty people, representing eighteen different reserves, met in May to discuss this organization. Some participants pointed out the need to organize a number of sports, not just basketball. Thus, the National Indian Activities Association (NIAA) was formed as a multisport organization providing national (i.e., North American) all-Indian championships, with Ron Johnson as its first executive director. This organization hoped to showcase Native athletes through national Indian competitions while helping Native youth develop pride in their heritage.

NIAA-sponsored events began with a national men's basketball championship in 1974 and quickly expanded to include women's basketball, fast-pitch softball, and golf. Activities have varied somewhat depending on the interest of the organizers; for example, competitions have also been held in slow-pitch softball, bowling, boxing, tennis, and volleyball. An Indian participation base is enforced—all competitors must be at least one-quarter Indian. A grievance board is set up at all championships to deal with any concerns over the eligibility of particular athletes.

Initially, the NIAA received federal funding from the U.S. government, with additional dollars generated through participant entry fees. Board members were elected from designated regions, and qualifying competitions were encouraged prior to national championships. This format did not last; federal funding ceased in 1980, the board became a small, fairly consistent group of individuals, and the format for the championships became largely invitational.

When federal funding ended, Satch Miller continued coordinating NIAA events in a volunteer capacity. He became interim president in 1984 and has remained president of the organization since that time. In 1990 Kugie Louis became a volunteer executive director. He registered the association as a non-profit charitable organization and renamed it the National Indian Athletic Association. He remains the executive director today, working with the volunteer Executive Board. Yearly sports championships occur in basketball, fast-pitch and slow-pitch softball, golf, and boxing. All of these championships except boxing include both male and female competitions. Funding for NIAA activities comes from participant entry fees and occasional contributions from corporations. Sports clinics as well as youth and education conferences have been held in conjunction with some championships. Recreation workshops also began in 1994; two conferences per year now provide training in Native recreation.

There is little public knowledge about the involvement of Native athletes in mainstream sport; even less is known about all-Indian endeavors in sport and recreation. This association is one example of Native organizers striving to increase an awareness of athletic opportunities among Native peoples while also fostering self-esteem and a positive Native identity among the participants. Elements of the sacred circle are promoted: family, identity, spirituality, and health; thus, a holistic approach is taken toward sport competition. By promoting athletic competitions in this format, the organizers hope to increase sports consciousness among participants in a manner consistent with traditional Native values.

SELECTED BIBLIOGRAPHY: Kugie Louis, Executive Director of the National Indian Athletic Association, 4084 Ibex Street NE, Salem, OR 97305, (503)- 390-4245; Joseph B. Oxendine, *American Indian Sports Heritage* (1988).

Victoria Paraschak

NATIVE AMERICANS. Native Americans are the original (or indigenous) peoples of North America. Archaeological evidence suggests they were in North America at least 15,000 years ago, actively participating in various "indigenous" physical activities that reflected their understanding of the world. Europeans, who arrived in North America 500 years ago, created the United States in 1776. The federal government has tried to assimilate Native peoples into Euro-American (or "mainstream") life. Government–Native relations thus have played an important role in shaping the physical activities of Native peoples. Native participants have embraced many mainstream sporting activities while also maintaining aspects of indigenous physical activities.

Native peoples played physical activities for enjoyment but also connected them to many parts of Native life (i.e., religious, political, economic, and social). Indigenous physical activities included games of chance as well as games of skill. Games of chance used dicelike implements or involved hiding, then guessing where a marked item was located. Other indigenous activities were primarily skill-based. Games requiring physical skills were usually self-testing and involved physical strength, endurance, or speed. Running, swimming, wrestling, boxing, pulling and pushing activities—all are included in this category. Another group of activities, involving equipment, required hand-eye coordination. Archery, spear throwing, snowsnake, and hoop and pole are examples of this type of activity. Occasionally, activities also involved animals, such as horse racing or dogsled racing.

Ball games, which involved equal-sized teams competing against each other, were a very popular and widespread type of physical activity. These activities involved heavy gambling and lots of people, both as participants and as spectators. While *tewaarathon* (or lacrosse*) is the best known of these activities, there were many other ball games as well. Some games (e.g., the Meso-American ball game) were played inside a court structure. Other games (such as shinny) used sticks to hit or propel the ball. Rules sometimes demanded that only the feet or hands propel the ball. (Kickball is an example of the first type.) Usually a single ball was thrown toward the goal, although occasionally two balls were joined together by a thong and thrown (as in double ball). Both men and women enjoyed participating in physical activities; however, many of the activities were segregated by sex (e.g., double ball and shinny were most often played by women, while lacrosse and hand games were usually all-male activities).

Along with these games there were other physical activities, such as sun dances and potlatches, which occurred as an integral part of Native religious ceremonies. The powwow, another form of indigenous physical activity, is a summer gathering many centuries old. Its contemporary form emerged in warrior organizations on the plains. Tribes from Oklahoma and Nebraska shared this activity with the Sioux in the early 1870s, and it was often combined with the ghost dance until that dance was banned by the government in 1893. Warrior societies diminished in number following the end of Indian wars, and the powwow continued primarily as a social show dance.

Several indigenous physical activities have disappeared from Native culture over the years. However, some of these activities continue today and have begun to resemble mainstream sports. Examples of present-day events where indigenous physical activities remain the major focus include snowsnake competitions (most popular among the Iroquois), hand games (e.g., among the Bannock-Shoshone), stickball leagues (e.g., among the Mississippi Chocktaws), Inuit games (among Alaskan Inuit), and powwows (across North America). "American" sports that incorporate indigenous activities include dogsled racing, rodeo,* lacrosse, swimming, archery, running, boxing, and wrestling.

American government policy, beginning in 1871, operated under the philosophy that Native peoples could be legislated into becoming white Americans. For example, religious freedom was denied, dances and ceremonies were banned as pagan and immoral, and Native schoolchildren were punished for speaking their own language. These actions by government agents were intended to undermine the foundations of Native life.

The federal government became involved in Native education in the 1870s, and in 1879 an off-reservation boarding school was begun at Carlisle, Pennsylvania. These training schools for Native youth were designed to prepare children for life off the reservation, both in terms of vocational training and "proper" social behavior. Behaviors that were traditionally Native (such as indigenous sports) were banned, and in their place rigid exercise programs were established. As well, boys were encouraged to participate in mainstream sport activities, such as football, baseball, basketball, and track and field. These residential schools soon produced talented male Native athletes who went on to compete against some of the best universities in the United States in the early 1900s.

Despite attempts by government and education officials to eliminate them, for a variety of reasons indigenous activities continued to be practiced by Native peoples. In some areas, Native individuals secretly persisted with their traditional ceremonies. Other Native groups were encouraged by non-Native entrepreneurs to demonstrate indigenous games and ceremonies because of the entertainment value they provided white Americans, who were intrigued by "exotic" Native peoples and their indigenous activities. These demonstrations occurred within the context of Wild West shows, as well as within sport.

Wild West shows began in 1882 with Buffalo Bill's first event in North Platte, Nebraska. Other organizers offered similar shows, and these events, which began in the western United States, eventually spread east as far as New York. Native participants were integral to these touring shows, reenacting famous battles and demonstrating indigenous dances, games, and riding skills. For example, pow-wow participants were encouraged to "dance fancier" for the audience's entertainment. Rodeos eventually emerged out of these events and fairs, with special races designated for Native riders (e.g., for "Squaws"), who were rarely allowed to compete in open events. Often, organizers stipulated that Native participants had to camp on the rodeo grounds and "act Native" if they wished to compete. Only a few of the Native rodeo competitors went on to compete in mainstream rodeo—the best-known males were Jackson Sundown and Tom Three Persons, while females included Emma Blackfox, Good Elk, and Princess Redbird.

Organizers from the St. Louis World's Fair arranged for a more "scientific" display of Native physical skills just prior to the 1904 Olympics. Individuals from thirteen tribes around the world, without previous training, participated in Anthropology Days (eighteen events over two days). Although they were supposedly demonstrating their "natural" physical talents, the Native participants instead ended up as a sideshow for the non-Native spectators.

Sport organizations occasionally treated Native participants differentially. For example, in snowshoeing, organizers assumed that Native athletes would be superior and thus created separate events for Native athletes. The "open" races were understood to be only for white members from other clubs. Eventually, this assumption was formalized; the category was replaced with "Open Race (Indians excepted)." Media, beginning in the 1870s and continuing into the early years of the twentieth century, added after Native competitors' names "(Indian)" to distinguish their achievements from others in society.

Lacrosse, another physical activity indigenous to Native Americans, was "reinvented" by non-Natives as a mainstream North American sport. Although Native lacrosse teams were integral to, and successful in, amateur lacrosse competitions, George Beers, a non-Native Canadian, created formal rules in 1867 outlining how to play the game "properly." By 1880, Native athletes were banned, by race, from playing in amateur lacrosse championships, supposedly to help destroy professionalism and undesirable behavior on the playing field. Native teams subsequently established their own Indian Championship of the World, and some athletes who could pass for non-Natives also continued to play. However, they were effectively removed as a Native presence from representation in amateur lacrosse.

During this assimilationist period, indigenous physical activities were being actively suppressed by government and educational institutions, although they were encouraged by non-Native entrepreneurs. Meanwhile, sport and education officials facilitated male Native participation in select, "legitimate" sports. The range of physical activities that was acceptable for Native peoples was very limited. Although some Native peoples continued to practice their indigenous activities, they did so at their own peril; these activities had clearly been defined as inappropriate and illegal by the dominant, non-Native society.

During the first six decades of the twentieth century, Native peoples from different tribal backgrounds began to join together on issues facing all Native Americans. This unification was aided by Indian residential schools' policy, since Native students were sent there regardless of tribal background. Participation in the world wars similarly brought Natives from across the United States together. World War I sparked the beginnings of a national sense of Native political self-awareness, or "pan-Indianism." Native Americans were given the federal vote in 1924 as an acknowledgment of gratitude for Native participation in World War I. In 1934 the federal government passed the Indian Reorganization Act, recognizing for the first time that there could be an alternative to assimilation. A sense of Pan-Indianism also began to emerge through Native involvement in physical activities.

Male Native athletes, many of whom attended Carlisle Indian School or the Haskell Institute, successfully competed with non-Native athletes in the first half of the twentieth century, especially in the sports of football, baseball, basketball, and track and field. Jim Thorpe* was the best known of these athletes. He won two events, the pentathlon and the decathlon, at the 1912 Olympics and went on to play professional baseball and football. Frank Pierce was, however, the first Native American to compete in the Olympics, running the marathon in both 1904 and 1908. Other Native Olympians include Frank Mt. Pleasant (1908 marathon), Louis Tewanima (1908, marathon; 1912, 10,000-meter run), Jesse Renick (1948, basketball), and Billy Mills* (1964, 10,000-meter run). Native athletes also competed successfully in professional sport—both baseball and football. Charles A. "Chief" Bender,* who pitched for the Philadelphia Athletics, for example, was elected to the Baseball Hall of Fame, while Joseph N. Guyon* was inducted into the National Professional Football Hall of Fame. The success and recognition of these athletes in American society contrast with the relative absence of traditional dance ceremonials and with the minor place of powwows in American life during this time.

The prominence of Native athletes in mainstream sport diminished after 1930. With the closing of many of the residential schools, Native athletes had minimal opportunities for developing sports skills. Few athletes had access to, or felt comfortable within, mainstream schools or sports leagues. Powwows, however, became more popular. Many powwows were held to honor Native "veteran warriors" who were returning to their reserves from the world wars. Cash prizes were offered as part of some powwows beginning in the 1950s, and the pow-wows took on a more intertribal nature beginning in the 1960s, although they were, and are still, organized by particular tribes.

During the 1960s the movement among Native peoples for self-determination continued to grow. During the Civil Rights movement Native peoples took a renewed pride in their heritage. As Native pride increased, so did their interest in representing that pride through select cultural practices—most often those that originated in Native culture. Billy Mills also helped focus national attention on Native athletes in sport when he won the 10,000-meter race at the 1964 Olympics.

By 1968 President Johnson had openly confirmed his support for Native self-determination. President Nixon concurred in July 1970. Benefits to Native peoples in sport were quick to follow. The American Indian Athletic Hall of Fame was formed in 1972 at Haskell Indian Junior College, with the support of the commissioner of the Bureau of Indian Affairs. As of 1995, seventy-six athletes had been inducted (three were women). The next year the National Indian Activities Association was formed to provide all-Indian championships in basketball (and eventually in other sports as well, such as softball, golf, and bowling). This association received federal funding until 1980. The Indian National Finals Rodeo began, with federal funding, in 1976. This competition brings together contestants from various regional Indian rodeo organizations to compete for world championships. The 1970s was clearly a time when the federal government acknowledged the legitimacy of Native athletes and financially assisted them to organize sports and honor outstanding Native athletes.

More recently, Native organizers have helped Native athletes to participate in sport through a variety of organizations. The Wings of America Running Program, for example, began in 1986 as a race for Native high school cross-country runners. The best male and female competitors received funding to attend the U.S. Junior National Cross-Country Championships. Native athletes have been very successful at the national level and are often able to obtain university scholarships through this process.

Native organizers also formed the Native American Sports Council in 1994 to help Native athletes succeed in the Olympic system. This council is recognized by the U.S. Olympic Committee and by every national sports governing body. It has sponsored training camps in team handball and in distance running, using the Olympic training sites in Colorado. It has also funded Native athletes who are working to make national teams.

Native peoples continue to participate in Native cultural practices. The sun dance and the potlatch, for example, have reemerged as contemporary ceremonials. Powwows have continued to grow in popularity; over 100 powwows are held annually in North America. These powwows often provide a unique site for the experiencing and symbolizing of Pan-Indianism, thereby representing a united group of First Nations peoples.

Participation in all-Native sport also continues to grow. The North American Indigenous Games have been held every two years since 1990. These games, which are restricted to people of Native heritage, involve participants from both Canada and the United States. Although mainstream sports are the focus of this competition, participants return home with a renewed pride in their Native roots.

Native athletes have also successfully asserted their right to compete as a distinct nation in the sport of lacrosse. The Iroquois Nationals,* first formed in 1983, is composed of players from the various Six Nations. In 1990 the International Lacrosse Federation granted the Iroquois nation status, and they competed in the world championships in Australia, using their Haudenosaunee passports. They are the first Native sports team to achieve full national recognition by other countries. The movement to acknowledge Native teams in international lacrosse has continued to expand. In 1996 the Iroquois Junior Nationals competed in the World Junior Lacrosse Championships. There is also an Iroquois National Women's Lacrosse Team—and the Iroquois Nationals are trying to secure the 2002 World Championships on Iroquois territory, possibly in Syracuse or Buffalo.

One political issue that Native peoples have recently tackled is the use of inappropriate Native images in North American sport. The American Indian movement, for example, has protested the inappropriate use of Native mascots, gestures, logos, and slogans. While professional teams such as the Washington Redskins, the Atlanta Braves, and the Cleveland Indians have resisted pressures to change their names, states such as Wisconsin have ruled that the use of Native names in public school sports settings may be discriminatory. Through this protest of Native mascots, Native peoples and their supporters are slowly altering the images that exist in society concerning Native peoples. These successes and the positive involvement of Native peoples in all-Indian activities in sport, powwows, and dance ceremonials enable them to take control of some of the negative representations that still exist and reshape them to promote pride in their status as the indigenous peoples of North America.

No history of a nation is complete without the inclusion of its indigenous peoples. Yet Native peoples are largely invisible in American sports history. Their indigenous activities continue to be a unique aspect of American culture. These activities have persisted, even though non-Natives, for many years, have intentionally tried to replace them with mainstream physical activities. A select group of primarily male Native athletes has done extremely well in mainstream sport; they deserve recognition for their accomplishments and serve as role models for all Americans. Native organizers also provide alternative avenues for physical expression through all-Indian sport competitions and indigenous activities such as powwows, indigenous games, and religious ceremonials. These activities, together, represent the broad spectrum of interests held by Native peoples as they advance, as a nation, into the twenty-first century. The history of Native peoples in American sport thus provides all Americans with an example of the struggles marginalized groups face in order to ensure enjoyment through sport and physical activities for their peoples.

SELECTED BIBLIOGRAPHY: Kendall Blanchard, "Traditional Sports, North and South America," in David Levinson and Karen Christensen, eds., *Encyclopedia of World Sport: From Ancient Times to the Present* (1996), 1075–1083; Stewart Culin, *Games of the North American Indians* (1907, reprint 1992); Joseph B. Oxendine, *American Indian Sports Heritage* (1988, reprint 1995); Victoria Paraschak, "Racialized Spaces: Cultural Regulation, Aboriginal Agency and Powwows," *Avante* 2 (1996): 7–18; Victoria Paraschak, "Native American Sporting Competitions," in David Levinson and Karen Christensen, eds., *Encyclopedia of World Sport: From Ancient Times to the Present* (1996), 679–683; William K. Powers, "Powwow," in Mary Davis, ed., *Native America in the Twentieth Century: An Encyclopedia* (1994), 476–480; Thomas Vennum, Jr., *American Indian Lacrosse: Little Brother of War* (1994).

Victoria Paraschak

NAVRATILOVA, MARTINA (18 October 1956, Revnice, Czechoslovakia–). A tennis player, she was born Martina Subertova to Miroslav Subert and Jana Subertova. She changed her name after she was adopted by her stepfather and first coach, Miroslav Navratil. Her grandmother was a nationally ranked tennis player; her mother was an accomplished skier. By the time she was ten years old, growing up in communist Czechoslovakia, Martina had become committed to a career in tennis. Navratilova was the national champion in Czechoslovakia from 1972 to 1975. She first came to the United States in 1973 at the age of sixteen. She immediately became a factor in women's tennis, although, in her early years, she was known more for her problems with her weight and her emotional temperament. In a career that can be described only in superlatives, she captured 165 titles—more than any other professional tennis player. Among Martina's many accomplishments were eighteen singles grand-slam titles, which included a record-setting nine Wimbledon championships. She was also a peerless doubles player, winning 165 doubles titles, 109 of them consecutively with her partner, Pam Shriver. Her contests with Chris Evert created one of the epic rivalries in all sports. After losing twenty-one of her first twenty-five matches against Evert, Navratilova dominated their series with an overall 43–37 lead by the time Evert retired. The left-handed Navratilova was renowned for her superb conditioning and aggressive serve-and-volley play. She was number one in the world rankings for a total of 332 weeks and remained a top-ranked player until her retirement at the age of thirty-eight in 1994. In 1981 she became a U.S. citizen. A few days later, Navratilova publicly revealed that she is a lesbian, the first major professional athlete to do so. Since her retirement, she has been an advocate for gay rights, animal rights, and environmental causes. In 1997 she was the captain of the U.S. Federation Cup team.

SELECTED BIBLIOGRAPHY: Adrianne Blue, *The Lives and Times of Martina Navra-tilova* (1995); Martina Navratilova, with George Vecsey, *Martina* (1985); "Martina Na-vratilova," *Sports Illustrated* (19 September 1994): 80; "The Lioness in Winter," *Time* (30 November 1992): 62.

Richard FitzPatrick

NEGRO LEAGUES AND NEGRO NATIONAL LEAGUE, 1920–60. For sixty years (1887–1947), African Americans could not play major league base-ball because of the existence of a color line. Instead, they formed their own professional leagues to give young black males the chance to develop their skills. The Negro Leagues operated in the East, South, and Midwest from 1920 through 1960, with their strongest years stretching from 1920 through 1947. The leagues began a slow, but inevitable, decline after Jackie Robinson* joined the Brooklyn Dodgers in 1947. The door to the major leagues had been opened, and others would follow Robinson through the crack, pushing it open wider and wider. By 1960 the Birmingham Black Barons realized the audiences were no longer there, and they called it quits, ending the existence of the Negro Leagues after forty years.

The Negro Leagues officially began in 1920, but African Americans were not new to the game then. Since the end of the Civil War blacks played profes-sionally but not in large numbers. They competed among themselves and oc-casionally on minor league squads, since no written rule excluded them (except from 1867 to 1871). The existence of Jim Crow attitudes throughout the United States, however, made it difficult for the two races to play on the same teams, especially after 1887. Adrian "Cap" Anson of the Chicago White Stockings refused to let his team play the Newark Little Giants because they were using a black pitcher named George Stovey. This marked the beginning of the color line, held in place by an unofficial gentlemen's agreement until 1945, when Branch Rickey signed Robinson to his minor league affiliate, the Montreal Roy-als. No white owners wanted to challenge the rule for fear of losing money and support.

The color line did not go completely unchallenged throughout the years, how-ever. A few owners tried to sign light-skinned black players and Cubans on their teams, with limited success. When Frank Thompson founded the first all-black professional team in 1885, the Cuban Giants, he tried to pass them off as Cubans by having the players speak gibberish on the field in hopes of convincing fans they were speaking Spanish. Giants manager John McGraw* tried to pass off Charlie Grant as Chief Tokohama, but his plan was uncovered before Grant could play a single inning. Other black players spent their careers jumping from one minor league squad to another, including John "Bud" Fowler, who began play in 1878 with a team from Lynn, Massachusetts. Fowler played for about twenty different clubs in a career that spanned the years from 1878 to 1899. Players constantly moved because of the pressure teams suffered if they had black athletes on their rosters. Moses Fleetwood Walker* is best known for his year with the Toledo team in 1884 since they belonged to the American Association, a major league, making Walker the first black in the major leagues. Walker also played for many other teams during his career before giving it up and writing a book entitled *Our Home Colony*, about race relations in America.

There were also a few attempts before 1920 to establish black leagues, but none lasted beyond a week or two. The earliest attempt occurred in the South in the 1880s but never really got off the ground. Another group tried unsuccessfully in 1910, but the league folded without playing any games. A lack of financial support, effective leadership, and suitable ballparks, combined with existing racial attitudes, all made it difficult for black teams to succeed.

By the end of World War I things were beginning to change. Sports were becoming increasingly popular as a big business, as training for military personnel, and for physical education programs in schools. The introduction of the radio in the 1920s helped increase people's awareness of athletics as events that could now be broadcast to larger audiences. Within the black community changes were also taking place as families migrated in large numbers to the North. This movement created growing markets for black businesses, including baseball. At the same time the Harlem Renaissance encouraged pride in African American identity and achievements. This atmosphere helped Andrew "Rube" Foster* pull together a group of interested businessmen, sportswriters, and attorneys to establish the first Negro National League (NNL) in Kansas City in 1920. There was no other alternative for blacks if they wanted to play baseball than to form their own separate leagues.

Foster became the new league president, serving until he became ill in 1926. Foster's own team, the Chicago American Giants, became one of the original entrants, along with the Detroit Stars, the Kansas City Monarchs,* the Indianapolis ABCs, the Dayton Marcos, and the St. Louis Giants. Although not all of these teams remained permanent members of the league, they did get it started. Dayton became the first team to be replaced during that first season. Franchise fees were set at $500 per team in 1920. The fees were to cover such costs as umpires, stadium rentals, and equipment and maintenance expenses, which generally included booking fees. Booking agents played an important role in the success of the Negro Leagues. Men such as Foster, Abe Saperstein,* and Nat Strong helped ball clubs book their opponents and find stadiums for them to play in. In return they received a percentage for every game they booked. For league contests the amount of money was dictated by the league, but for barnstorming games the fees were worked out on an individual basis.

Barnstorming was essential to all Negro League clubs. Their schedule might include sixty to eighty league contests but they played over 200 games a year, the rest being barnstorming games. Traveling across the country playing any opponents who could pay expenses was necessary to a team's survival. All open dates between league contests were filled in order to meet team expenses. This meant clubs spent a lot of time on the move traveling from one small town to the next. Travel was not always easy for the Negro League clubs because of the existing Jim Crow codes in various parts of the country. Sometimes teams had trouble finding places to eat and sleep, so they were forced to sleep on the bus. In some cities they had to go to the back door of a restaurant in order to be served, or they sent in a light-skinned player to bring out food for the rest of the team. Bus drivers who were white were also helpful because they could get service for the team whenever it was necessary.

The NNL lasted from 1920 through 1931 before folding due to financial woes. Attendance at games dropped in the early years of the depression, but expenses continued to mount. The league also had trouble after Foster left the helm, and it never really recovered from that loss.

The NNL was not the only Negro League that existed, however. In 1923 a second major Negro League was added on the East Coast known as the Eastern Colored League. Ed Bolden of Hilldale, Pennsylvania, founded this league in order to cut down on travel expenses for those teams on the eastern seaboard. In addition, the Negro Southern League started operating in 1920 under the direction of former player Sol White and continued through the 1940s as a minor league system. Many of the best Negro Leaguers got their start down south before moving up to join well-known clubs such as the Kansas City Monarchs, the Homestead Grays,* and the Pittsburgh Crawfords.*

In 1932 the East-West League opened for one season before giving way to the second NNL in 1933 under the leadership of Pittsburgh's Gus Greenlee* and the Negro American League (NAL) led by H. G. Hall in 1937. The last two leagues to be founded were the West Coast Baseball Association in 1945 and 1946 and the U.S. League (USL) in 1945. Branch Rickey had a hand in establishing the USL in hopes of finding the right player to integrate the major leagues.

In addition to regular league play the Negro Leagues established a World Series in 1924 and an East-West classic in the 1930s. The World Series gave teams bragging rights in the Negro Leagues but did not truly create a world champion since the winner represented only part of the professional ranks of baseball. The Homestead Grays, Kansas City Monarchs, and Pittsburgh Crawfords seemed to dominate the series, winning on multiple occasions. The East-West game developed as the showcase for the best players in the Negro Leagues. Each year at Comiskey Park in Chicago the best players performed before crowds ranging in size up to 50,000 fans. White owners, managers, and scouts came out to watch these games and marveled at the talent assembled on the field. It was here the fans got to see players such as Satchel Paige,* Doubleduty Radcliffe, Hilton Smith, Cannonball Redding, Josh Gibson,* Newt Allen, Judy Johnson, and Cool Papa Bell* display their skills.

After 1947 the leagues slowly began losing teams and fans. By the mid-1950s the number of entrants had dwindled to four clubs. Three women (Toni Stone,* Connie Morgan, and Peanut Johnson) were even signed to play with the Indianapolis Clowns and Kansas City Monarchs. While they were signed, in part, to encourage better attendance, they could also play. Infielder Toni Stone even made the All-Star team one year.

As the leagues declined, numerous black ballplayers got the opportunity to play at the minor and major league levels. Willie Mays* and Hank Aaron* got their start in the Negro Leagues but spent the majority of their careers in the formerly all-white major leagues. The Negro Leagues filled a need at a time when the United States was not yet ready to end segregation, and they disappeared when the hole no longer needed filling.

SELECTED BIBLIOGRAPHY: Dick Clark and Larry Lester, eds., *The Negro Leagues Book* (1994); Leslie Heaphy, "Shadowed Diamonds: The Growth and Decline of the Negro Leagues" (Ph.D. diss., University of Toledo, 1995); Jerry Malloy, Intro., *Sol White's History of Colored Baseball* (1995); Robert Peterson, *Only the Ball Was White* (1970); James A. Riley, *The Biographical Encyclopedia of the Negro Leagues* (1994); Donn Rogosin, *Invisible Men* (1983).

Leslie Heaphy

NEW YORK PIONEER CLUB. The New York Pioneer Club (NYPC) was started in 1936 by three Harlem businessmen: Robert Douglas,* owner of the Renaissance Ballroom; William Culbreath, a trainer at New York University; and Joseph J. Yancey.* The club was originally the New York Olympic Club, a track club for Harlem men and boys who did not have the experience or membership fees that would get them membership in one of the city's competitive clubs.

The NYPC would accept any athlete who wanted to join. They had no clubhouse; in winter, the NYPC trained in the 369th Army Anti-Aircraft Artillery Armory at 142nd Street and Fifth Avenue. In warm weather, the members ran at McCombs Dam Park in the Bronx, where white runners saw the group and began training with them. In 1942 the members changed the club's constitution so that white athletes could become official members. The club's mission was to encourage higher education and foster a better racial understanding through the medium of education and sport.

By 1945 the NYPC had won a substantial number of individual metropolitan and national Amateur Athletic Union (AAU) championships, as well as team awards. The club also emphasized deportment, polite speech, and proper dress. The club helped the needier members, paying for clothes and haircuts. The founders had university friends to whom they could suggest candidates for college scholarships.

Civil rights were an important part of the NYPC agenda. In 1946 the NYPC decided that its members would not attend the upcoming AAU national track-and-field championships in San Antonio, Texas, the first major open meet to be held in the South, because black athletes were not permitted to stay at the same hotels as white athletes. This type of social segregation also appeared at the 1950 AAU nationals held at the University of Maryland. As an integrated group, the team could not stay together at any hotel in Maryland nor at the University of Maryland dormitories. The NYPC 800-meter runner Roscoe Lee Browne arranged lodging for them at Lincoln University in Pennsylvania, where he was teaching. The NYPC commuted to the nationals from Pennsylvania.

The NYPC started sending athletes to the Olympic Games in 1948. By 1956 there were six Pioneers in the Olympics, in 1956 there were nine, and Pioneer representation in the games continued. During the 1990s the NYPC functioned under the coaching and management of Edward Levy. An all-male club for years, the New York Pioneers began admitting women in 1991.

The New York Pioneer Club is significant not only in its contribution to the Civil Rights movement but also in its contribution to the democratization of sport, particularly running. The huge open fields of today's marathons and other road races owe much to Joe Yancey's acceptance of all boys as potential athletes.

SELECTED BIBLIOGRAPHY: Jesse Abramson, "Democratic Ideal: The Pioneer Club," *Amateur Athlete* (September 1945): 11, 15; Pamela Cooper, *The American Marathon* (1998); Theodore Corbitt, "Testimonial to a Pioneer: Joseph J. Yancey," *Road Runners Club New York Association Newsletter* 65 (1975): 10.

Pamela Cooper

NEW YORK (HARLEM) RENAISSANCE. An all-black professional basketball team that started playing games in New York City's Harlem Renaissance Casino in 1923, the Harlem "Rens" was organized by Robert L. Douglas,* a Caribbean immigrant. The squad won an amazing 2,318 games against only 381 losses during the 1920s and 1930s. Their games in Harlem were as much a social event as an athletic one. Men and women from the community would show up to watch the Rens play and then dance afterward to the music of Count Basie or Jimmy Lunceford.

During its first few years the Rens played only in New York City. By the late 1920s they were traveling throughout the state and across the Northeast, South, and Midwest. While traveling throughout the country they typically encountered fan abuse, exclusion from certain athletic halls, and less pay than their generally inferior white opponents. Because integrated competition at the professional level was not prohibited at the time, the Rens developed rivalries with two legendary white teams: the Original Celtics of New York, coached by future St. John's and Knicks' coach Joe Lapchick,* and the Philadelphia SPHAS.*

Before going on a temporary hiatus during World War II, the Rens established itself as the best professional team in the United States. During the 1930s Douglas gathered some of the best basketball talent found anywhere. Led by Wee Willie Smith, an aggressive 6'5" center from Cleveland, future Hall of Famer Charles "Tarzan" Cooper,* and Fats Jenkins, James Pappy Ricks, Eyre Saitch, Bill Yancey, and Johnny Holt, the 1932 to 1936 edition of the Rens went 473–49 against other professional club teams around the country. In 1939 they won a national professional tournament organized and played in Chicago, defeating the all-white Oshkosh, Wisconsin, All-Stars, 34–25, in the championship game.

A financial success for almost two decades under the leadership of Douglas, the Rens proved that a black professional basketball team could thrive without exploiting white racism by demanding that its players act like clowns for white entertainment. Ironically, the success of Douglas and the Rens helped nurture an audience and develop players for the Harlem Globetrotters,* a team of the same era that did capitalize on racist stereotypes of African Americans.

SELECTED BIBLIOGRAPHY: Arthur R. Ashe, Jr., *A Hard Road to Glory: A History of the African-American Athlete, 1919–1945*, vol. 2 (1988); Nelson George, *Elevating the Game: Black Men and Basketball* (1992); Robert W. Peterson, *Cages to Jump Shots: Pro Basketball's Early Years* (1990); Susan J. Rayl, "The New York Renaissance Professional Black Basketball Team, 1923–1950" (Ph.D. diss., Pennsylvania State University, 1996).

Troy D. Paino

NISHKIAN, BYRON LEVON (28 January 1916, San Francisco–6 June 1987, San Francisco). A skier of Armenian descent, he participated in a variety of sports in high school and college. He learned to ski at Yosemite, California, where the first ski school in the western United States was established. He served as president of the Yosemite Winter Club and U.S. Ski Association and was a member of the Olympic Ski Committee, State of California Olympic Advisory Committee for Squaw Valley (1959–60) Organizing Committee, 1960 Winter Olympic Games, Squaw Valley, and was president of the Far West Ski Association (1959–61). He had the distinction to serve on the Federation of International Skiing (FIS) Eligibility Committee (1961–87), where he helped formulate rules for many international ski races. He also served on the U.S. Olympic Ski Games Committee from 1962 to 1968. He was the president of the U.S. Ski Association from 1965 to 1968. Nishkian also was elected a member of the Martini Rossi International Sports Club, an organization that has long been identified with the support of skiing and other sport activities. In 1975 Nishkian organized the FIS Congress in San Francisco and was elected to the U.S. National Ski Hall of Fame, Ishpeming, Michigan, in 1976. He was the deputy chief of protocol for the 1980 Winter Olympic Games in Lake Placid and served as the official U.S. representative at several World Ski Championships. Nishkian was the recipient of numerous awards from the U.S. Congress and the California State Senate for his contributions to world peace and friendship through competitive sports, especially skiing. Nishkian took over the firm his father had established in 1919 and was responsible for design of many prominent buildings. The firm spent 10% of its engineering time and talent designing ski facilities and resorts. Nishkian designed, owned, and was president of Alpine Meadows Ski Area, California.

SELECTED BIBLIOGRAPHY: Arra S. Avakian, *The Armenians in America* (1977); Richard N. Demirjian, *Armenian-American/Canadian WHO'S WHO of Outstanding Athletes, Coaches, and Sports Personalities* (1989).

Richard N. Demirjian

NITSCHKE, RAYMOND E. (29 December 1936, Elmwood Park, IL–8 March 1998, Venice, FL). A college and professional football player, he was the son of Robert and Anna Nitschke. His father, a surface line worker of German ancestry, died when Nitschke was three years old. His mother, of Danish descent, passed away when he was fourteen. He later stated that he vented his anger over losing his parents on the kids in his neighborhood. A star athlete in baseball, basketball, and football at Proviso High School in Maywood, Illinois, he was an All-State quarterback and received a football scholarship at the University of Illinois. There he switched to fullback, excelling as a blocking back and occasional ball carrier during his college career (1954–57). Drafted in the third round by the Green Bay Packers in 1958, he became a middle linebacker. After a slow start in the National Football League (NFL) due to injuries and military service, he rose to stardom under the coaching of Vince Lombardi.* During the 1960s he earned All-Pro honors from 1964 to 1966 and helped the Packers capture five NFL titles (1961–62; 1965–67) and two Super Bowl trophies following the 1966 and 1967 seasons. He was also the Most Valuable Player (MVP) in the Packers' championship game victory over the New York Giants in 1962. An intense competitor who was revered for his ferocious tackling and his overall toughness, he kept close ties with the Packers after his retirement in 1972. He later published a pro football newsletter and became an executive for a midwestern trucking company. Nitschke was elected to the Pro Football Hall of Fame in 1978.

SELECTED BIBLIOGRAPHY: George Allen, with Ben Olan, *Pro Football's 100 Greatest Players* (1982); *New York Times*, 9 March 1998, A-17; Ray Nitschke, with Robert W. Wells, *Mean on Sunday* (1973); Mike Tully, *Where Have They Gone?: Football Stars* (1979).

George B. Kirsch

NORRIS, JAMES D., JR. (6 November 1906, Chicago–25 February 1966, Chicago). The son of James Norris (wealthy businessman, hockey team owner) and Ethel Dougan, immigrants from Canada, he attended Cornell University. Norris, Jr., was an influential and powerful owner of hockey teams and stadiums, being associated with National Hockey League (NHL) Stanley Cup champions in Detroit (1936, 1937, 1943) and Chicago (1961). Though better known as the man who controlled professional boxing in the 1950s as president of the International Boxing Club, Norris' real passion was hockey. Along with his father he co-owned the Detroit Red Wings from 1933 until 1952, when he took over the floundering Chicago Blackhawks franchise with partner Arthur Wirtz. In 1954 Norris wrested coach Tommy Ivan* away from Detroit to serve as general manager for the Hawks. Norris pumped money into the farm system, which under Ivan's direction produced such excellent young players as Bobby Hull, Stan Mikita,* and Pierre Pilote. These youngsters combined with key players added in trades spurred the Hawks to a Stanley Cup triumph in 1961, their first in twenty-three years. Throughout the 1960s the Hawks were one of the league's most successful teams—both on the ice and at the box office. Much of the credit for the revival went to the ownership of Norris; local columnist Bill Gleason referred to him as "the man who restored hockey in Chicago." In 1962 Norris was elected to the Hockey Hall of Fame in the builders category, joining his father in this capacity. In recognition of his outstanding service to hockey in the United States Norris posthumously received the Lester Patrick Award from the NHL in 1972.

SELECTED BIBLIOGRAPHY: "James Norris Rites on Saturday," *Chicago Sun Times*, 26 February 1966; Paul R. Greenland, *Hockey Chicago Style: The History of the Chicago Blackhawks* (1995); Ken McKenzie, "Jim Norris Built Hawks into NHL Power," *The Hockey News* 16, No. 28 (13 April 1963): 2; Gerald Pfeiffer, *The Chicago Blackhawks: A Sixty-Year History 1926–1986* (1986).

Dennis Ryan

NORWEGIANS. Not surprisingly, Norwegian Americans have excelled most notably at winter sports. The most significant contribution to America has unquestionably been the introduction of skiing. "Ski" is the Norwegian word for snowshoe. Though an ancient practice, skiing was not a sport until the modern era. In the 1830s, wooden skis were introduced near Telemark, Norway. By the 1870s Norwegian towns had ski festivals with cross-country skiing and jumping. Norwegians spread skiing around the world as they migrated to Australia and the United States. In America, skiing initially took hold in the California Sierras, when Norwegian emigrants headed there searching for gold. In 1853 the first "ski runs" were held in Onion Valley, California; however, it is not known whether these were ski races as we think of them today or snowshoe events. The first competition in which we have evidence of actual skiing was held in 1885 at the Norwegian Ski Club of Minneapolis. By this time, Norwegians were spreading the art of skiing throughout America to such diverse (although all cold) states as Maine, Michigan, Wisconsin, New Hampshire, and Minnesota. The following year, Norwegian Americans held ski races in Red Wing, Minnesota, and Eau Claire, Wisconsin. By 1890, there were many Norwegian-established ski clubs in the upper Midwest. In 1904 the National Ski Association was established in Ishpeming, Michigan. Since that day, Norwegian Americans have continued to excel in skiing.

Other winter sports that have become popular among talented Norwegian Americans are figure skating, speed skating, dog sled racing, and the luge. One notable Norwegian speed skater was Axel Paulsen, who popularized the sport while touring the United States during the 1880s. Perhaps the Norwegian who was most famous in America for participation in a winter sport was Sonja Henie.* Although figure skating was introduced to America by the English, Henie stole Americans' hearts and popularized figure skating when she won gold medals at the Olympics in 1928, 1932, and 1936. Skating in many American movies made Henie the first international skating star, and she did more to spread the sport throughout the United States than any other person.

Norwegian Americans, however, have also excelled at many nonwinter sports. They are largely responsible for any following that bandy has in the United States. They have also triumphed at the biathlon. However, this immigrant population has also excelled at that most "American" of sports, football. One of America's most beloved football heroes hailed from Norway: Hall of Famer and football genius Knute Rockne.* Rockne first rose to national prominence in 1913, when he contributed significantly to Notre Dame's surprising 35–13 defeat over Army. This game established Notre Dame as a football power. The year 1913 was one of three seasons that Rockne played as starting end at Notre Dame. He then served four seasons as assistant coach and thirteen seasons as head coach before tragically dying in a plane crash. The charismatic Rockne was involved in a fascinating confluence of sports, ethnicity, and American identity at Notre Dame, of which his Norwegian heritage was perhaps the smallest piece. By establishing itself as a major football power, Notre Dame was demonstrating to the country that a Catholic school could succeed at something quintessentially American. One of the reasons that Notre Dame's 1913 victory against Army was so startling was that a Catholic school was not merely beating any old team in any old sport—it was beating the team that represented the American armed forces in that sport that is most fundamentally militaristic. For Notre Dame, as for Knute Rockne, football was not just a sport; it was an entree into the realm of the truly American.

Norwegian Americans have contributed to American sports in two primary ways. First, they have been a bulwark of winter sports in America. Most importantly, Norwegians introduced skiing, but they also have been dedicated in their pursuit of other winter sports. Second, they provide a fascinating example of how sports serves as a vehicle for the assimilation of an immigrant community into the United States.

SELECTED BIBLIOGRAPHY: E. John B. Allen, *From Skisport to Skiing: One Hundred Years of an American Sport, 1840–1940* (1993); Wallace Francis, *Knute Rockne* (1960); Theodore M. Hesburgh, *God, Country, Notre Dame* (1990); Helen M. White, "Ski-Sport Heroes from Norway," in Helen M. White, *The Tale of a Comet and Other Stories* (1984).

Lauren F. Winner

O

OLAJUWON, HAKEEM ABDUL (21 January 1963, Lagos, Nigeria–). An African American collegiate and professional basketball player, he is the son of Salaam and Abike Olajuwon, who owned a cement business in his native city in Africa. He first competed in basketball in 1978, while he was a student at the Moslem Teachers College in Lagos. Guy Lewis, basketball coach at the University of Houston, recruited him from Nigeria in 1980 as a tall (6' 10") athlete with raw talent and great potential. At Houston Olajuwon developed into one of the finest college performers in the United States. Nicknamed "the Dream," he led the Cougars into the National Collegiate Athletic Association (NCAA) final four tournament three times, losing the championship game in 1983 on a last-second basket by North Carolina State University. An All-American selection in 1984, he finished first in the NCAA's Division I in field goal percentage and rebounds and blocked shots per game. Named the Southwestern Conference's Player of the Decade for the 1980s, he also enjoyed great success in the ranks of professional basketball. Selected by the Houston Rockets as the first pick overall in the 1984 National Basketball Association's (NBA) draft, he holds the league record for most blocked shots, is a six-time member of the All-NBA first team, and became the first foreign-born player to earn Most Valuable Player (MVP) honors (1994). When the Rockets won the NBA championship in 1994 and 1995, he was MVP of the final round each time. He also became the third player in NBA history to compile at least 10,000 points, 5,000 rebounds, and 1,000 steals, assists, and blocked shots. Although Olajuwon became an American citizen in 1993, he did not sever all of his ties to his African homeland and heritage. Fluent in four Nigerian dialects as well as French and English, he is a devout observer of Islam and operates an export sporting goods business to Nigeria.

SELECTED BIBLIOGRAPHY: John Capouya, "Beers with Akeem Olajuwon," *Sport* 79 (April 1988): 21–23; Lianne Hart, "With 'Twin Towers' Ralph Sampson and Akeem Olajuwon, Houston Rockets to the Top of the NBA," *People Weekly* 22 (17 December

1984): 144–146; Jackie MacMullan, "Dream Season," *Boston Globe*, 12 January 1994, 49, 53; Jack McCallum, "A Dream Come True," *Sports Illustrated* 76 (22 March 1993): 16–21; Hakeem Olajuwon, with Peter Knobler, *Living the Dream* (1996); Renee D. Turner, "The House Akeem Olajuwon Helped Design," *Ebony* 47 (March 1991): 46–48, 50.

George B. Kirsch

O'REILLY, JOHN BOYLE (28 June 1844, Dowth, Ireland–10 August 1890, Hull, MA). An editor, lecturer, writer, and poet, he was one of his era's most influential commentators on Irish American acculturation. He was also an important advocate of athletics and physical conditioning. O'Reilly received some initial education from his parents, William (a schoolmaster) and Eliza, but he left home at age nine to work as a printer's apprentice. He came to America in 1869 as a fugitive from the British penal colony in Western Australia, where he had been consigned for recruiting Irishmen in the British army to the militant Fenian cause. In America his views moderated, and as editor of the Irish Catholic weekly Boston *Pilot* (1870–90) he won respect among immigrants and "natives" alike by urging the retention of an Irish cultural identity while emphasizing the obligations of American citizenship. O'Reilly was equally passionate arguing the moral worth of amateur athletics. He was himself an expert canoeist and an able boxer, swimmer, and fencer. His most extended statement on the strenuous life, *Ethics of Boxing and Manly Sport* (1888), is at once a boxing instructional, a program of diet and exercise, and an account of the author's canoeing voyages. It also includes a section on "Ancient Irish Athletic Games, Exercises, and Weapons"—for O'Reilly believed Gaelic sporting traditions to be as crucial to Irish American ethnic consciousness as language and literature. In 1879 he helped found the Irish Athletic Club of Boston as a means of nurturing traditional games, and he instituted the John Boyle O'Reilly Hurling Cup to encourage the revival of that quintessentially Irish sport.

SELECTED BIBLIOGRAPHY: William Leonard Joyce, *Editors and Ethnicity. A History of the Irish-American Press, 1848–1883* (1976); Francis G. McManamin, *The American Years of John Boyle O'Reilly, 1870–1890* (1976); John Boyle O'Reilly, *Ethics of Boxing and Manly Sport* (1888); James Jeffrey Roche, *Life of John Boyle O'Reilly* (1891).

George Rugg

O'ROURKE, JAMES HENRY (1 September 1850, Bridgeport, CT–8 January 1919, Bridgeport, CT). A baseball player, "Orator Jim" O'Rourke was a player, manager, team owner, and league president over the course of his career. His parents, Hugh O'Rourke and Catherine O'Donnell, emigrated from County Mayo, Ireland, in 1845. James was the first in the major leagues to play 100 games at six different fielding positions. During the off-season he earned a law degree from Yale, and he had a reputation for verbosity. O'Rourke began his professional career in 1872 with the Middletown (Connecticut) Mansfields. In 1873 he signed with the legendary Boston Red Stockings. Manager Harry

Wright wanted O'Rourke to change his name to play in anti-Irish Boston, but James refused. He earned the first official hit for the National League in 1876 and helped the team to five pennants. In 1879 he jumped to Providence after a dispute with Boston management. His departure is often cited as one of the factors that prompted the infamous reserve clause added to player contracts, in use until 1974. The clause allowed teams to retain players for an additional year beyond their contract even if contract terms were not settled and was interpreted by owners to mean they held the rights to a player in perpetuity. O'Rourke went on to achieve pennant wins with Providence (1879) and the New York Giants (1888–89). Like many of his contemporaries he jumped to the protest Players League in 1890. He later returned to the Giants and retired in 1893. In 1904, he visited the Polo Grounds and helped the Giants to yet another pennant. His combined average for the National and Players Leagues was .310. After retirement O'Rourke organized, played for, managed in, and acted as president of the Connecticut League until 1914. He was elected to the National Baseball Hall of Fame in 1945.

SELECTED BIBLIOGRAPHY: Harold Seymour, *Baseball: The Early Years* (1960); Bernard Crowley, lecture given at Bridgeport, CT, Library, 1991 (video collection, National Baseball Hall of Fame Library, Cooperstown, NY); O'Rourke file, National Baseball Hall of Fame Library, Cooperstown, NY.

Lesley L. Humphreys

ORR, ROBERT GORDON ("Bobby") (20 March 1948, Parry Sound, Ontario, Canada–   ). He is the son of Douglas Orr, a second-generation Irish Canadian employed at an explosives plant, and Arva, a waitress. While starring for the National Hockey League's (NHL) Boston Bruins (1966–75) and Chicago Blackhawks (1975–1978), Orr revolutionized the role of the defenseman. Not content with the traditional focus on defending, he utilized exceptional speed and stickhandling ability to spring forward into the attack and create scoring opportunities for his team. Orr and Phil Esposito* led the Bruins to Stanley Cup triumphs in 1970 and 1972, with Orr claiming the Conn Smythe Trophy as playoff Most Valuable Player (MVP) on each occasion. Over the course of his short tenure in the league, Orr accumulated two Art Ross Trophies (scoring champion), three Hart Trophies (regular season MVP), and a record eight consecutive Norris Trophies (best defenseman), as well as numerous league scoring records. His brilliant career was curtailed by a series of debilitating knee injuries that forced his retirement from the game in 1978. In 1979 Orr became the youngest man ever enshrined in the Hockey Hall of Fame and received the Lester Patrick Award from the NHL in recognition of his outstanding contribution to hockey in the United States. Orr was instrumental in establishing the sport in the six American cities to which the NHL expanded in 1966, his charisma and skill attracting spectators, television viewers, and media interest. Orr revitalized hockey in Boston and is revered there, as evidenced by a 1979 vote that named him the city's all-time most popular athlete.

SELECTED BIBLIOGRAPHY: Deidra Clayton, *The Life and Times of R. Alan Eagleson* (1982); Jim Devaney, *The Bobby Orr Story* (1973); Stan Fischler, *Bobby Orr and the Big Bad Bruins* (1969); Morgan Hughes and Joseph Romain, *Hockey Legends of All Time* (1996); Harry Sinden and Dick Grace, *The Picture History of the Boston Bruins* (1976).

Dennis Ryan

ORTÍZ, CARLOS (9 September 1936, Ponce, PR–   ). In a land of thirty-four world boxing champions, among the best is Carlos Ortíz. Together with Sixto Escobar, world bantamweight champion on three occasions (1934, 1935, and 1938) and José Luis "Cheguí" Torres,* light-heavyweight champion in 1965 (and silver medal at the Olympics of 1956 for the United States), Ortíz is part of the first golden era of Puerto Rican boxing history. He spent his early years in the city of Mayagüez, Puerto Rico, until his family moved to New York, where he learned the art of boxing. At a time when one world boxing organization reigned, Ortíz won the World Junior Welter Title in 1959 and the World Lightweight Title in 1962 and 1965. He lost the lightweight title in 1967 after successfully defending it twice in that same year. Ortíz fought on eleven more occasions, losing only in the last fight in 1972, thus ending an extraordinary career of eighteen years of professional boxing. As a champion he reigned for nearly a decade, defeating the best in his division.

SELECTED BIBLIOGRAPHY: Comisión de Boxeo y Lucha Libre Professional de Puerto Rico, *Portraits of Champions* (1997); Emilio E. Huyke, "Boxeo," *Colecciones Puertorriqueñas, Los Deportes en Puerto Rico* (1968), 107–124; Jaime Varas, "Boxeo," *La Gran Enciclopedia de Puerto Rico, Tomo 11, El Deporte en Puerto Rico* (1976), 149–201.

Raúl Mayo-Santana

OWENS, JAMES ("JESSE") (12 September 1913, Oakville, AL–31 March 1980, Tuscon, AZ). An African American track-and-field athlete, he was the son of Henry and Mary Emma (Alexander) Owens. His parents were poor cotton sharecroppers with a large family who moved to Cleveland, Ohio, when Jesse was nine years old. As a youth and then a schoolboy at Cleveland's Fairmount Junior High School and East Technical High School he won interscholastic national titles in 1933 in the 100-yard dash (tying the world record at 9.4 seconds), the 200-yard dash, and the broad jump. His decision to attend Ohio State University was controversial because of that institution's prior record of racial discrimination. He did not earn a college degree. He achieved one of the greatest single-day performances in the history of his sport on 25 May 1935 at the Western Conference Track and Field meet at Ann Arbor, Michigan. In less than one hour he set world records in the broad jump, 220-yard dash, and 220-yard low hurdles, and he tied the world mark for the 100-yard dash. One year later he reached the pinnacle of world fame at the 1936 Olympic Games at Berlin, Germany. Adolf Hitler and his Nazi regime hoped to use that Olympic competition to showcase German and Aryan athletic superiority, but Owens' four gold medals (in the 100- and 200-meter dashes, long jump, and 4×100 meter relay) instead demonstrated the domination of a black American. While Owens became the first person to win four gold medals in the Olympics, his achievement was soon marred by controversy. He and Ralph Metcalfe's participation in the relay came at the expense of two Jewish athletes (Marty Glickman* and Sam Stoller) who had been dropped from the event, possibly because of anti-Semitism by American Olympic officials. Yet Owens' spectacular success made him a hero in both the white and black communities in the United States, as his victories promoted both American patriotism and the racial integration of sports. Shortly after the Olympics the Amateur Athletic Union banned Owens from future amateur competition because he had refused to complete a European tour sponsored by the U.S. Olympic Committee. During the late 1930s he struggled to earn an income by racing against humans, horses, dogs, and automobiles, and he suffered further humiliation through racial discrimination, business failures, and bankruptcy. During World War II he performed public relations work for the U.S. government. Despite his poor treatment by the Amateur Athletic Union after the 1936 Olympics, by the 1950s he was traveling hundreds of thousands of miles a year making speeches and raising funds for the U.S. Olympic Committee. In the 1960s he opposed civil rights activism in general and black power movements in sports. He had no sympathy for the proposed black boycott of the 1968 Olympics in Mexico City. While he later became more sympathetic to the plight of African American athletes, he never fully embraced the black nationalist agenda in sports. He was inducted into the National Track and Field Hall of Fame in 1974 and the U.S. Olympic Hall of Fame in 1983.

SELECTED BIBLIOGRAPHY: William J. Baker, *Jesse Owens: An American Life* (1986); Myron Cope, "The Amazing Jesse Owens," *Sport* 37 (October 1964): 60–63, 98–99; Norman Katkov, "Jesse Owens—the Ebony Express," *Sport* 16 (April 1954): 28–31; Richard Mandell, *The Nazi Olympics* (1971); Jesse Owens, with Paul Neimark, *Blackthink* (1970); Jesse Owens, with Paul Neimark, *I Have Changed* (1972); Jesse Owens, with Paul Neimark, *Jesse: The Man Who Outran Hitler* (1978).

James R. Coates, Jr., and George B. Kirsch

P

PAGE, ALAN (7 August 1945, Canton, OH–). An African American football player, he is the son of Howard and Georgianna (Umbles) Page. He excelled in football and academics at Canton Central High School, graduating in 1963. A standout at defensive end at Notre Dame, he was named consensus All-American in 1966 and received a B.S. degree in political science in 1967. After graduating from college, Page played most of his career as a defensive tackle for the Minnesota Vikings. He was an integral part of the vaunted front four known as the "Purple People Eaters." He obtained a law degree from the University of Minnesota in 1978. Released by the Vikings, Page subsequently starred for the Chicago Bears, their Central Division rivals, from 1978 to 1981. Few National Football League (NFL) players will ever match Page's long list of accomplishments. As a player he saw action in four Super Bowls, was named Rookie of the Year in 1967 and Most Valuable Player in 1971, and played in nine Pro Bowls. In 1988 he was inducted into the Pro Football Hall of Fame. After retiring from football, Page practiced law and served as a popular judge on Minnesota's state supreme court.

SELECTED BIBLIOGRAPHY: Pat Harmon, biographical sketch of Alan Page for the College Football Hall of Fame, in a letter to David R. McMahon, 29 January 1997; Alan C. Page, "The Obligation to Educate Our Children," *Vital Speeches of the Day* 62 (1 May 1996): 421–424; David L. Porter, ed., *African-American Sports Greats: A Biographical Dictionary* (1995), 242–244.

David R. McMahon

PAIGE, LEROY ROBERT ("Satchel") (7 July 1906, Mobile, AL–5 June 1982, Kansas City, MO). An African American baseball player, he was one of eleven children born to John and Lulu Paige. His father was a gardener, and his mother was a washerwoman. He earned his nickname as a young boy by carrying bags at the nearby railroad depot. His career included stints with practically every Negro American and Negro National League* team, scores of semipro teams in Canada, Central and South America, and three major league teams, the Cleveland Indians, St. Louis Browns, and Kansas City Athletics. He learned to play baseball at a reform school where he was sent following his arrest for stealing toys. By 1926 Paige began pitching for the Chattanooga Black Lookouts, a semipro team in the Negro Southern League; he made his black major league debut the following year with the Birmingham Black Barons. During the next few years Paige jumped from team to team, often in pursuit of better-paying offers, when in 1931 he joined the Pittsburgh Crawfords.* During the 1940s he played with the Kansas City Monarchs,* which won the Black World Series in 1942 against the Homestead Grays.* Nearing what he thought was the end of his career, he was offered a spot on the roster of the Cleveland Indians by legendary owner Bill Veeck during the club's pennant drive in 1948. Paige made his major league debut at the age of forty-two. After spending three successful seasons with the St. Louis Browns, during which time he was named to the 1952 American League All-Star Team, Paige made his last major league appearance in 1965 with the Kansas City Athletics after a twelve-year absence from the major leagues. While it is impossible to compile an accurate record of Paige's career statistics, it has been estimated that he pitched in approximately 2,500 games with 2,000 victories, 300 shutouts, and fifty-five no-hitters. Officially, he posted 123 wins against seventy-nine defeats in the Negro Leagues,* the second highest lifetime victory total for that league, and the most strikeouts, 1,177 in 1,584 innings. In the majors, he compiled a 29–31 won-lost record and a 3.29 earned run average (ERA) at an age when most players had long since retired. The most legendary African American player of his era, in 1971 Paige became the first Negro Leaguer to be inducted into the Baseball Hall of Fame.

SELECTED BIBLIOGRAPHY: LeRoy (Satchel) Paige, *Maybe I'll Pitch Forever* (1961; reprint 1993); John B. Holway, *Josh and Satch: The Life and Times of Josh Gibson and Satchel Paige* (1991); Mark Ribowsky, *Don't Look Back: Satchel Paige in the Shadows of Baseball* (1994).

Larry K. Menna

PARKER, FRANK A. (13 February 1916, Milwaukee, WI–24 July 1997, San Diego). A tennis player, he was born Franciszek Andrezej Piakowski to Polish immigrants Paul and Anna Piakowski. At the age of ten he became a ball boy at a tennis club to help support his family, which was impoverished by the death of his father when Frank was very young. At the Town Club, Parker was discovered by Mercer Beasley, a well-known coach who set out to mold the raw talents of the youth into championship form. Under Beasley's tutelage, Parker amassed a number of impressive junior championships. He first broke into the top ten among American men in 1933, and at seventeen he won the national clay-court championship. Parker lived with Beasley's family as his coach moved to coaching assignments, first in New Orleans, then in Lawrenceville, New Jersey, where Frank attended prep school and, subsequently, nearby Princeton University. The affiliation with Mercer Beasley ended in 1938, when Beasley's wife, Audrey, divorced him and married Parker, who was more than twenty years her junior. Audrey Parker became her husband's tennis adviser and trainer; she died in 1971. Parker was ranked among the top ten Americans between 1933 and 1950. During this long tenure, he distinguished himself as a two-time U.S. national singles champion in 1944 and 1945 (while a sergeant in the U.S. Army Air Force). He was the French singles titlist in 1948 and 1949 and was a major contributor to two Davis Cup championships for the United States. Parker was known for a solid all-around game and superb conditioning. He retired after a short run in the professional circuit in the early 1950s. Subsequently, he worked as a sales manager for a paper products firm in Chicago. He was inducted into the International Tennis Hall of Fame in 1966.

SELECTED BIBLIOGRAPHY: Richard Goldstein, "Frank Parker, U.S. Tennis champion, 81" (Obituary), *New York Times*, 28 July 1997, A15; Stan Hart, *Once a Champion: Legendary Tennis Stars Revisited* (1985); "Parker, Frank," *Current Biography* (1948), 486–488.

Richard FitzPatrick

PARSEGHIAN, ARA (21 May 1923, Akron, OH–   ). One of the most celebrated of Notre Dame's football coaches, he was the son of Armenians Michael and Amelia Parseghian. His father was a banker in Akron, and his parents named him after Ara the Beautiful, king of Armenia. He graduated from Akron South High School in 1941. A 1949 graduate of Miami University of Ohio, he earned a bachelor of arts in education and biological sciences and a master of arts in educational administration. After being named All-Mid-American Conference (1946–47), Captain (1947), and Little All-American (1947), Parseghian embarked on a career in professional football. He played offensive and defensive halfback for the Cleveland Browns in 1948 and 1949 until an injury cut short his career. He returned to his alma mater and compiled a won-lost record of 39–6–1 between 1951 and 1955. His teams were Mid-American Conference Champions in 1954–55 and had an undefeated won-lost record of 9–0 in 1955. He moved on to Northwestern University, Evanston, Illinois, where he coached from 1955 to 1963 with a won-lost record of 36–35–1. Particularly noteworthy was that he defeated Notre Dame four straight years between 1959 and 1962. The next year he moved on to take the head coaching job at South Bend. When he arrived from Northwestern, the Irish had just experienced five losing seasons. Nine of his teams were among the nation's top ten in the wire service polls. In his eleven years at Notre Dame (1963–1974) his won-lost record was 95–17–4. The Fighting Irish won undefeated national championships in both 1966 and 1973. Between 1951 and 1974 Parseghian's overall collegiate won-lost record was 170–58–6. He was elected to the College Football Hall of Fame in 1980.

SELECTED BIBLIOGRAPHY: Terry C. Bender and Larwence W. Stiles, *Major College Football* (1983); William B. Furlong, "Ara's New Era," *Saturday Evening Post* 237 (28 November 1964): 72–75; Tom Pagna, *Notre Dame's Era of Ara* (1976).

Richard N. Demirjian

PASO FINO. The sport of Paso Fino horses is autochthonous from Puerto Rico and has its origins dating back to the fifteenth century. It consists of the union between rider and horse into one elegant entity competing in forms, pace, and gait. It evolved matching the topography of the island, which is mountainous over short distances. The horses developed were of medium-size build, with well-defined muscles and a wide chest allowing for a fine-paced ride with elastic, smooth high-stepping. This "fine-paced," short, quick, and rhythmic movement led to the name of the sport and horses. In past centuries owners of Paso Fino horses sent their pride mounts to the capital of San Juan during the festival of the patron saint to participate in "Las Carreras de San Juan" (the races of San Juan). At one time Paso Fino races were prohibited by the Spanish governor at the request of the bishop of the Catholic Church because competitions tended to end late at night with extensive parties. The sport continued clandestinely in the haciendas of wealthy owners who loved the Paso Fino. In 1943 the Asociación de Dueños de Caballos de Sillas was organized, and their first formal competition was held in the Las Monjas racetrack in Santurce. At this time these tracks were used for both horse racing and other sports like track and field and Paso Fino. The Horse Show Association of the United States recognized this first Paso Fino organization in 1944. Twenty years later the entity was transformed into the Federación del Deporte de Paso Fino. The sport organization has had an official autonomy ever since, evolving with different identities. Paso Fino competitions are divided into three main events: Beautiful Forms, Fine Pace, and Gait ("Andadura"). Some of the notable horses include the famous Dulce Sueño, a champion in Paso Fino in 1948 and stallion of twenty of the first twenty-three champions; Cebuco, the champion of the Beautiful Forms event seven times; and Canela, who in 1975 won the highest titles of Paso Fino and Beautiful Forms for the fourth time. The sport has extended to other countries in the Americas, including some states in the United States. It was declared the national sport of Puerto Rico by the Olympic Committee and the governmental sports authority in 1966. In the Central American and Caribbean Games (CAC) in San Juan, Puerto Rico, of the same year, Paso Fino was presented as an exhibition and impressed the CAC leadership as the most beautiful show ever presented of a national sport. As a sport of elegance and tradition it continues today to be a source of national pride to owners, breeders, trainers, riders, spectators, and the people of Puerto Rico.

SELECTED BIBLIOGRAPHY: Emilo E. Huyke, "Paso Fino," *Colecciones Puertorriqueñas, Los Deportes en Puerto Rico* (1968), 362–366; Jaime Varas, "Paso Fino," *La Gran Enciclopedia de Puerto Rico, Tomo 11, El Deporte en Puerto Rico* (1976), 253–262.

Raúl Mayo-Santana

PATERNO, JOSEPH VINCENT (21 December 1926, Brooklyn, NY–). A football coach, he is the son of Angelo Lafayette Paterno and Florence de la Salle Paterno. His mother's family was from Naples, and his father's was from Calabria, to which it had emigrated from Albania. His father attended law school and worked in the New York City courts. Joe was the eldest child and graduated from Brooklyn Prep, a Jesuit high school where he developed a love for learning. He then matriculated at Brown University to play football under coach Rip Engle. After graduation from Brown in 1950 he served as an assistant to Engle and then succeeded him as head coach after Engle's retirement. Known as a demanding, no-nonsense football coach, this attitude has been extended to the academic performance of his players, and during his tenure more than 90% of Penn State players have graduated with earned degrees. Under Paterno's leadership Penn State has won national championships and/or been in contention for them virtually every year during his coaching tenure. Under his tutelage, Penn State has appeared in many national postseason bowl games, and Paterno has won Coach of the Year Awards from several professional and writers' associations.

SELECTED BIBLIOGRAPHY: Thomas Granger, "Joe Paterno: The Lion in Autumn," *Saturday Evening Post* 255 (October 1983): 61–63, 98, 100; Mervin D. Hyman and Gordon White, Jr., *Joe Paterno: Football My Way* (1978); R. Mendell and T. B. Phares, *Who's Who in Football* (1974); J. Paterno, with B. Asbell, *Paterno by the Book* (1989); James A. Peterson and Dennis Booher, *Joe Paterno: In Search of Excellence* (1983).

Lawrence Huggins

PATRICK, JOSEPH LYNN (3 February 1912, Victoria, British Columbia, Canada–26 January 1980, St. Louis). A hockey player, coach, and manager, he was the son of third-generation Irish Canadian Lester Patrick (influential National Hockey League [NHL] coach and general manager) and Grace Patrick. Over a twelve-year playing career with the New York Rangers he was a two-time All Star, a scoring champion, and a vital contributor to the 1940 Stanley Cup championship team. Following his playing career Patrick went into coaching, first with the Rangers (1948–50) and then with the Boston Bruins (1950–54), serving also as general manager (1950–65). Patrick's greatest accomplishments came with the expansion St. Louis Blues, for whom he served as vice president from 1967 until 1977. He hired Scotty Bowman* to coach and manage the team, and together they built a squad that went to the Stanley Cup finals in each of its first three seasons of play. In 1980 Patrick was inducted into the Hockey Hall of Fame. Patrick's commitment to promoting hockey in the United States was impressive. He strove to facilitate an increase in the number of American players in the NHL in order to stimulate more interest among American fans. During the 1960s he espoused the idea that colleges could produce good professional players, setting an example as one of the first executives to consistently sign these athletes to play for his teams. Much of the credit for the improvement in American collegiate hockey must go to Patrick and others like him who advocated giving American-born players the chance to prove themselves in the NHL. In 1989 Patrick posthumously received the NHL award named for his father, in recognition of his meritorious service to the sport of hockey in the United States.

SELECTED BIBLIOGRAPHY: Roger Barry, "Lynn Sees American Colleges as NHL Source of Supply," *The Hockey News* 14 (25 May 1961): 4; Frank Boucher, *When the Rangers Were Young* (1973); Brian Macfarlane, *The Rangers* (1997); Harry Sinden and Dick Grace, *The Picture History of the Boston Bruins* (1976); Eric Whitehead, *The Patricks: Hockey's Royal Family* (1980).

Dennis Ryan

PATTERSON, FLOYD (4 January 1935, Waco, NC–   ). An African American boxer, he was the son of Thomas Patterson, a railroad laborer, and Anabelle Patterson, a domestic and factory worker. Extremely withdrawn as a boy and often truant from school during his early childhood in Brooklyn, New York, in 1945 his mother committed him to the Wiltwyck School for emotionally disturbed children in upstate New York. At the Wiltwyck School he became literate and learned to box. There he was discovered by Cus D'Amato, who became his manager. After returning to Brooklyn, he attended Alexander Hamilton High School before dropping out to get a job. As an amateur fighter he trained in D'Amato's Gramercy Park Gym, and at the age of seventeen he won the gold medal in the 165-pound middleweight class at the 1952 Olympic Games in Helsinki. He immediately turned professional and won thirty-five out of his next thirty-six bouts. On 30 November 1956 Patterson captured the heavyweight crown with a fifth-round knockout of an aging Archie Moore. On 26 June 1959 he lost his title to Ingemar Johansson, but he avenged that defeat with a sixth-round knockout of Johansson the following year. In 1962 and 1963 he suffered two first-round knockouts by Sonny Liston.* During the next few years he kept his fighting career alive with several victories over lesser opponents, but he lost two more title bouts, to Muhammad Ali* in 1965 and to Jimmy Ellis in 1968. He retired after another loss to Ali in 1972. One of the lightest of all the heavyweight champions (never weighing more than 200 pounds for a fight), he was known for his "peek-a-boo" style of keeping his gloves high in front of his face. During the 1960s Patterson's boxing career became embroiled in the racial politics of the Civil Rights revolution and the black power movement. A popular champion during the early 1960s, he was a moderate on racial issues who was soon labeled as an accommodationist and "Uncle Tom" by more radical black activists. His humiliating losses to Liston severely damaged his reputation, but he then tried to redeem himself in his title match against Ali in 1965. Although some writers viewed that fight as a contest between Patterson's faith in Christianity and Ali's conversion to Islam, the real issue was racial. Ironically, Patterson became a symbol of middle-class America and a black "white hope" against Ali, who threatened mainstream society with his black power ideas. After his retirement Patterson served for seven years on the New York State Athletic Commission (NYSAC), and in 1985 he was named director of New York state's off-track betting. In 1995 Governor George Pataki appointed him chairman of the NYSAC. He was inducted into the International Boxing Hall of Fame in 1991.

SELECTED BIBLIOGRAPHY: W. C. Heinz, "The Tenderhearted Champ," *Saturday Evening Post* 230 (27 July 1957): 25; Floyd Patterson, with Milton Gross, *Victory over Myself* (1962); Gilbert Rogin, "The Invisible Champion," *Sports Illustrated* (16 January 1961): 50–58; Jeffrey Sammons, *Beyond the Ring: The Role of Boxing in American Society* (1988); Gay Talese, "Portrait of the Ascetic Champ," *New York Times Magazine* (5 March 1961): 32.

George B. Kirsch

PAYTON, WALTER (25 July 1954, Columbia, MS–1 November 1999, Barrington, IL). An African American football player, he was the son of Alyne Payton and Peter Payton. His father worked for a firm that manufactured packs and parachutes for the U.S. government. As a teenager his physical build did not clearly set him apart as a potential football player. Even at his Chicago Bears peak he was a modest 5' 10" and an unimpressive 202 pounds. After a late start in football—his junior year at Columbia High School—he blossomed at Jackson State University. His teammates nicknamed him "Sweetness," and throughout his career in the National Football League (NFL), 1975–87, he epitomized grace and elegance. There were occasions when his athletic presence seemed ethereal. He was a consummate mover of unparalleled grace. In 1974 Payton was named "College Player of the Year" by *The Football Roundup*. He became the leading career scorer in National Collegiate Athletic Association (NCAA) history with 464 points. At Jackson State Payton was a versatile player who scored sixty-six touchdowns. He kicked field goals, punted, and caught passes as if he were a wide receiver. His special teams statistics were phenomenal—forty-three yards per kickoff return. He graduated with a degree in communications and special education. Payton started 172 of 178 games for the Chicago Bears. He had one streak of 156 consecutive contests. He retired following the 1987 season. In 1985 Payton became the first NFL player to total more than 2,000 yards in three consecutive seasons. Over his career he scored 125 touchdowns and logged 21,803 combined yards (including 16,726 yards rushing). This surpassed Jim Brown's legendary feat by a whopping 6,344 yards. He entered the Pro Football Hall of Fame in 1993. An astute businessman, Payton was very active in civic and charity events and owned, among other real estate ventures, a restaurant in Schaumburg, Illinois. In auto racing he joined up with Indy Car's Dale Coyne to form the Payton-Coyne Racing Team.

SELECTED BIBLIOGRAPHY: Stan W. Carlson, "Walter Payton," in David L. Porter, *African-American Sports Greats: A Biographical Dictionary* (1995), 251–253; Materials received from Saleem Choudhry, Pro Football Hall of Fame Library-Research Center, Canton, OH; *New York Times*, 2 November 1999, C23.

Scott A.G.M. Crawford

PEETE, CALVIN (18 July 1943, Detroit–   ). An African American golfer, he was one of nineteen children. He moved with his parents, Dennis and Irenia (Bridgeford) Peete, to Pahokee, Florida, where he grew up. His father was a farm laborer. He succeeded in his sport despite the most unlikely personal background for a professional golfer. After Peete dropped out of high school, he made his living selling trinkets and wares to migrating farmworkers who followed the seasonal crops of fruits and vegetables from North Florida. On one of his trips north to Rochester, New York, Peete played some golf and took a serious interest in the game. His game quickly improved, even though he was hampered with a deformed left arm—he could not fully straighten it—as a result of a childhood accident. Within two years he was playing scratch golf (zero handicap) but had no aspirations to become a professional golfer since he had no idea that a black man could earn a living playing golf. In 1968 he watched Lee Elder* compete against Jack Nicklaus in a televised golf tournament, the American Golf Classic. At that time Elder was the most promising black professional on the Professional Golfers' Association (PGA) Tour, and his loss in a playoff to the most renowned golfer of all times motivated Peete to renew his commitment to golf. Peete didn't earn his PGA playing card until 1971, and over the next three years he struggled to maintain his eligibility to compete on the PGA Tour, finishing 96th, 105th, and 108th on the PGA Tour money earnings list. In 1978 the thirty-five-year old Peete won his first tournament, the Greater Milwaukee Open. In 1982 he became the second black multiple winner on the PGA Tour when he won the Greater Milwaukee Open, the Anheuser-Busch Classic, the BC Open, and the Pensacola Open. His third place finish in the 1982 PGA Championship demonstrated his ability to compete at the highest level of the sport. Through 1984 Peete earned almost $1.25 million, by far the most money earned in such a short period by an African American playing golf. He was honored by *Golf Digest* magazine as the "Most Improved Player of 1983," and he was named to their All-American Team. The Golf Writer's Association awarded him the prestigious "Ben Hogan Award." Despite his unorthodox swing, Peete distinguished himself as the most consistent striker of the golf ball in professional golf, regularly leading all other professionals in the category of driving accuracy (the ability to land the first shot on the fairway) and greens in regulation. The PGA requires its members to have graduated from high school in order to compete in the Ryder Cup matches (the prestigious biennial competition featuring the best American professionals against the best European professionals). Peete passed the high school equivalency examination in 1982 and was selected as a member of the 1983 U.S. Ryder Cup team. Despite his accomplishments on the professional golf tour, Peete did not convert his success into significant commercial gain. Unlike white golf professionals with similar tour statistics, he received no major national commercial endorsements or advertising contracts.

SELECTED BIBLIOGRAPHY: Jamie Diaz, "Big Role Model, Barren Stage," *New York Times*, 4 May 1990, B1; David MacDonald, "Golf's Most Unlikely Star," *Reader's Digest* 123 (October 1983): 169–170, 173–174; Barry McDermott, "Long Shot Out of a Trap," *Sports Illustrated* 52 (24 March 1980): 26–31; Barry McDermott, "Call It a Major Win, for Peete's Sake," *Sports Illustrated* 62 (8 April 1985): 40–42, 47; Barry McDermott, "Peete. . . . But No Repeat," *Sports Illustrated* 64 (20 January 1986), 36–37; Kenny Moore, "His Was Great Act of Faith," *Sports Illustrated* 58 (25 April 1983): 36–38, 43–45; "Something Had to Be Done," advertising supplement, *Golf Illustrated* (September 1991); Carolyn White, "Peete: 'There May Be No Blacks in Tour in 3 to 5 Years,' " *USA Today*, 5 April 1990, 6E.

Larry Londino

PEP, WILLIE (PAPALEO) (19 September 1922, Middletown, CT–). A boxer, Guglielmo Papaleo grew up in Connecticut with his Sicilian-born parents, Mary, a factory worker, and Sal, a construction worker. Childhood pictures show Papaleo in boxing gloves at ages five and nine. In 1938 he won the Connecticut State Amateur Flyweight Championship, dropped out of high school, and changed his name to Willie Pep. The next year, he won the Connecticut State Amateur Bantamweight Championship. After sixty-five amateur bouts, Pep fought his first professional match in July 1940. Fifty-four victories later on 20 November 1942, Pep defeated "Chalky" Wright for the World Featherweight Championship. From 1943 to 1966, Pep defended his crown against challengers Sal Bartolo, "Chalky" Wright, Phil Terranova, Jack Leslie, and Humberto Sierra. He served in both the navy (1943–44) and the army (1945). He lost the championship to "brawling" Sandy Saddler on 29 October 1948. A Pep-Saddler rematch occurred in New York on 11 February 1949; Pep regained the featherweight title. On 8 September 1950, Saddler won another rematch. Pep fought Saddler again on 26 September 1951 and lost. In March 1966, Pep fought his last fight; he had won 230 bouts, lost eleven, fought one draw, and knocked out sixty-five opponents. In the 1970s and 1980s Pep worked for the state of Connecticut in the Athletic Division's Boxing Office. Pep was inducted into the International Boxing Hall of Fame in 1990.

SELECTED BIBLIOGRAPHY: Ronald K. Fried, *Corner Men: Great Boxing Trainers* (1991); *New York Times*, 12 February 1949, 12 and 9 September 1950, 12 and 27 September 1951, 41 and 28 September 1951, 35; Willie Pep, with Robert Sacchi, *Willie Pep Remembers . . . Friday's Heros* (1973); James B. Roberts and Alexander G. Skutt, *The Boxing Register International Boxing Hall of Fame Official Record Book* (1997); Jim Shea, "Make Believe a Cop Is Chasing You," *Sports Illustrated* 73 (16 July 1990): 8–10.

Philip M. Montesano

PÉTANQUE. This is one of several variants of the French game of *boules*. These are mostly target-ball games having the same object as bocce (Italy) and lawn bowls (Great Britain), that is, to place one's *boules* closer to a small target ball (the "jack") than those of the opponent.

The game of *boules* as played in the south of France came to be known as the *jeu provençal*. Early in this century (ca. 1907), *pétanque*, in turn, distinguished itself from the *jeu provençal*, which is still played in the south and known as *la longue*. The new elements introduced by *pétanque* were (1) a requirement that each player keep both feet on the ground, within a "throwing circle" drawn on the ground, from which all balls must be thrown and (2) a shorter playing distance with the jack beginning the round six to ten meters from the throwing circle.

One element retained from the *jeu provençal* is the concept of playing on open terrain of virtually any surface condition instead of in an enclosed and groomed "alley." The same *boules* are used in both *pétanque* and the *jeu provençal*. With the introduction in the 1930s of hollow steel *boules* (replacing solid boxwood balls armor-plated with nails) the sport had reached its modern form.

The rules originally varied from one place to the next. They were first codified in 1927. In 1945 the Fédération Française de Pétanque et Jeu Provençal (FFPJP) was founded. The introduction in France of paid vacation time and postwar mobility spread the "little game" of the southern provinces to the rest of France. The Fédération Internationale de Pétanque et Jeu Provençal (FIPJP) includes member federations in forty-three countries, has 600,000 members, and has organized a World Championship annually since 1959.

Pétanque is played in the United States wherever recent immigrants from France, particularly those from the south of France, have settled. Following World War II there was an influx of French into the San Francisco Bay Area, and *pétanque* became a vehicle for social interaction at gatherings of the newly arrived. In 1959 the first *pétanque* club in the United States, La Boule d'Or, was organized by Jean Bontemps, an importer from Provence. In 1960 La Boule d'Or was host to an international tournament on their home terrain in San Francisco's Golden Gate Park. Participants came from Quebec, France, and Tunisia. In 1973 Bontemps moved to the Washington, D.C., area. There he met Alfred Levitt, a painter from New York. Levitt had been teaching art in St. Remy de Provence, where he developed a love for *pétanque*. In New York, Levitt founded the club La Boule New Yorkaise, which met to play *pétanque* in Washington Square. Levitt contacted the FIPJP and with their blessing founded the Federation of *Pétanque*, U.S.A. (FPUSA) in 1973. Its purpose is "to build a national body of Federation-affiliated clubs and individuals dedicated to spreading, practicing and enjoying *Pétanque*." Levitt was president of the FPUSA for its first ten years.

There are currently twenty-six member clubs of the FPUSA, with the greatest number (twelve) located in California. As a member federation of the FIPJP, the FPUSA participates in the World Championships held by that organization: Senior, held every year and open to men and women, and Women's, held every other year. FPUSA clubs and competitions are dominated by French-born players. More recently, other immigrant groups have brought *pétanque* with them to the United States, from homelands that had previously been part of the French empire. For example, *pétanque* is played in the Vietnamese and Cambodian communities.

Americans with no cultural connection to France are increasingly taking an interest in the game. This is often the result of spending vacation time in France and coming home with *boules* and the desire to recapture the atmosphere of the games they saw abroad. The possible addition of *pétanque* to the roster of Olympic Games (a matter that the FIPJP has been pursuing) could significantly increase the exposure and recognition of *pétanque* as a sport in the United States.

SELECTED BIBLIOGRAPHY: Articles of Association of La Boule d'Or; Constitution of the FPUSA; Jean-Michel Izoird, *La Pétanque* (1997).

Frank Pipal

PHILADELPHIA SPHAS. A premier basketball club from the late 1920s to the mid-1940s, the Philadelphia SPHAS originated as a Jewish grade school team called the Combine. As teenagers most of these boys competed for the South Philadelphia High School five, and in 1917 the team earned the endorsement of a social club, the South Philadelphia Hebrew Association, from which it acquired its name. The following year Eddie Gottlieb* took charge of the squad, which broke its affiliation with the social club but retained its name. Under Gottlieb's coaching by the late 1920s the SPHAS had won three championships in their local Philadelphia league and had defeated several of the nation's best professional teams, including the Original Celtics and the New York Renaissance.* Gottlieb also signed up two non-Jews, but he maintained his club's Jewish identity by using the name "Philadelphia Hebrews." Gottlieb then entered his team in the American Basketball League (ABL) for two seasons, 1926–28, under the name of the "Philadelphia Warriors." After four years in the Eastern League the team joined the revived ABL with an all-Jewish roster in 1933 and won the league title. It remained entirely Jewish from then on. Over the next dozen years the SPHAS (sometimes using the name Hebrews) won six more ABL crowns. The SPHAS also played games outside the league schedule, mostly barnstorming along the eastern seaboard, with annual Christmas trips to the Midwest. Gottlieb also allowed his men to earn extra cash by playing for teams in minor local leagues.

The Philadelphia SPHAS were proud to showcase their Jewish identity, and they became the darlings of the Jewish community of their home city and of Jews across the country. With uniforms embroidered with the six-pointed Star of David and the Hebrew letters *samech, pey, hey,* and *aleph,* the players openly announced their ethnic affiliation to promote themselves and their club. During their glory years the team's home court was the Broadwood Hotel, and the dances that followed their contests made their games highlights of the social season for the city's Jews. The success of the SPHAS on the court signified the ongoing assimilation of Jews into the mainstream of American society. But when the SPHAS competed on the road, they sometimes encountered anti-Semitic taunts and even attacks with beer bottles, lighted cigarettes, and pricks from women's hat pins.

The SPHAS competed in the ABL through 1945, but when the Basketball Association of America began its first season in 1946, Eddie Gottlieb formed a new club, the Philadelphia Warriors, which joined the new circuit as a charter member. Although a barnstorming club used the name "SPHAS" during the late 1940s, the original team had long since passed into basketball history. Its achievements reflected the important contribution that Jewish coaches and players made to the early growth of the sport in the United States.

SELECTED BIBLIOGRAPHY: John Devaney, *The Story of Basketball* (1976); Joe Jares, *Basketball: The American Game* (1971); Peter Levine, *Ellis Island to Ebbets Field: Sport and the American Jewish Experience* (1992); James Naismith, *Basketball: Its Origin and Development* (1941); Robert W. Peterson, *Cages to Jump Shots: Pro Basketball's Early Years* (1990).

George B. Kirsch

PINCAY, LAFFIT, JR. (29 December 1946, Panama City, Panama–   ). The son of a jockey (Laffit Pincay, Sr.) and Rosario Pincay, he was brought from Panama by Fred Hooper to ride in the United States in 1966 at the age of nineteen. He won four Eclipse Awards as the nation's outstanding jockey of 1971, 1973, 1974, and 1979. He led all riders in money won six times and in 1971 led in number of wins. Big for a jockey at 5'1" and 117 pounds, he was a strong rider who could keep unruly colts to their task, yet had the hands to coax the best from two-year-old fillies. In a close finish, his peers conceded that Pincay could make the difference at the wire. Riding mainly in California, he was called east to win the Belmont Stakes three times, on Conquistador Cielo in 1982, on Caveat in 1983, and on Swale in 1984; to win the Beldame Stakes on champions Gamely in 1968–69, Susan's Girl in 1972, Desert Vixen in 1974; and to win the Jockey Club Gold Cup in 1979 with Affirmed, which he stated was the best race and the best horse he ever rode. Other champions with which he won stakes were John Henry, Landaluce, Genuine Risk, Althea, Perrault, Cougar, It's in the Air, Autobiography, Heavenly Cause, Heartlight No. One, and Chinook Pass. Between 1966 and 1984 his mounts earned more than $92 million—and only Bill Shoemaker's victories were worth more. During that period his mounts won 5,996 out of 26,778 races (22.4%). He was inducted into the National Thoroughbred Racing Hall of Fame in 1975. In December 1999 he set a new record for total career victories.

SELECTED BIBLIOGRAPHY: *Blood-Horse* (4 August 1975); *Horseplayer Magazine* (May 1994); *Jockey News* (February/March 1997); Ron Smith, *The Sporting News Chronicle of Twentieth Century Sport* (1992); Michael Watchmaker, "Horse Racing," in *Athletics* (1985).

Courtesy of the National Thoroughbred Racing Hall of Fame

PITTSBURGH CRAWFORDS. An African American baseball team, the club became one of the most formidable nines of the Negro Leagues* during the 1930s. The Crawfords originated in the 1920s as a racially mixed group of amateur sandlot ballplayers in Pittsburgh's Hill District. They named themselves after a local bathhouse, and by the late 1920s the club had evolved into an all-black nine that often drew over 3,000 spectators to their home games at Ammon Field. Their fans viewed them as black Pittsburgh's team, since all of their players were either born in Pittsburgh or had moved there with their families.

In 1930 William "Gus" Greenlee* purchased the Crawfords and began their transformation into one of the most powerful black teams in the nation. Now a successful barnstorming club, their arch rivals were Pittsburgh's Homestead Grays,* who were owned by Cumberland Posey* and had already established themselves as one of the premier black clubs in the United States. Like many other black baseball entrepreneurs, Greenlee financed his club with profits acquired from the numbers rackets in his town. In order to showcase his baseball team, in 1932 he invested $100,000 in Greenlee Field, which became one of the finest independent ballparks in the country and one of the few that were controlled by a black owner. After his team finally defeated the Homestead Grays, Greenlee sought admission in Posey's East-West League. Rebuffed by Posey, in 1933 Greenlee decided to resurrect the Negro National League. Led by five future Hall of Fame players (James "Cool Papa" Bell,* Oscar Charleston, Josh Gibson,* Judy Johnson, and Satchel Paige,* the Crawfords won the Negro National League Championship in 1935. Although in both 1933 and 1936 the Crawfords attracted over 200,000 spectators to their games, the team was not a financial success. In part this was a result of the club's high payroll, with the largest salaries going to the nine's greatest stars—Paige and Gibson. Paige joined the Pittsburgh Crawfords in 1931 and became a popular gate attraction. Gibson was one of the best power hitters of the Negro Leagues. With a talented supporting cast, these two players made the Crawfords the most talked about team in the Negro Leagues. But their success turned out to be short-lived, because disappointing attendance at Greenlee Field and the failure of the club to turn a profit contributed to the demise of the team after the 1938 season. But although the Pittsburgh Crawfords played only six seasons in the Negro National League, their achievements as a famed sandlot and barnstorming club generated great pride in their hometown's black community. As a black-owned club they also provided an important early example of an African American sports franchise.

SELECTED BIBLIOGRAPHY: James Bankes, *The Pittsburgh Crawfords* (1991); Robert Gardner and Dennis Shortelle, *The Forgotten Players: The Story of Black Baseball in America* (1993); Robert Peterson, *Only the Ball Was White* (1970); Mark Ribowsky, *A Complete History of the Negro Leagues* (1995); Donn Rogosin, *Invisible Men* (1983); Rob Ruck, *Sandlot Seasons: Sport in Black Pittsburgh* (1987).

                                                    Vernon Andrews and George B. Kirsch

POLES. For Polish Americans, more than most ethnic groups in the United States, sports was a powerful force in shaping the development of the community. With their mobility restricted by discrimination and stereotyping as well as by their own language and culture, Polish Americans used sports to break down the barriers to their advancement in American society.

Poles were not a large part of the early immigration to North America. They were not highly motivated to emigrate until the seventeenth century, when the nation began to experience a gradual and irreversible decline marked by a series of political crises, military setbacks, and territorial partitions. Insurrections and other political developments produced spurts of emigration. At the time of the American Civil War there were approximately 30,000 Poles in the United States, mostly political refugees attracted by America's democratic ideals.

In the mid- to late nineteenth century Polish immigration increased dramatically when various far-reaching political, social, and economic changes altered the economy and drove large numbers of peasants to leave their homeland *za chlebem*, "for bread." During this period of mass migration, lasting from 1870 until 1920, over 2 million Poles, mostly peasants, came to America.

Most of the Poles who came here during the mass migration had worked on farms in their homeland, as had their ancestors before them. They had very little formal education and few skills and had little to offer except their strength and stamina. In large part they obtained unskilled and semiskilled work in the factories, mills, and slaughterhouses of large northeastern and midwestern industrial cities, such as Chicago, Detroit, Cleveland, and Buffalo and in small mining towns of Pennsylvania and Ohio. They lived frugally with other Poles in insular enclaves, usually centered around a Roman Catholic church.

The rise of modern sports coincided with this influx of Polish immigration, but initially sports had little impact upon American *Polonia* (the term given to communities of Poles living outside Poland). Cultural and language differences created barriers to participating in such unfamiliar sports as football and baseball. In addition, the occupations that most of the Polish immigrants held required very long hours of hard physical labor that tended to discourage participation in sports.

True to their peasant origins, the Poles were strong, dedicated, and disciplined workers more than willing to do the most difficult and dangerous jobs for the lowest wages and were preferred by many employers. However, except for these blue-collar industrial jobs, their opportunities were very limited due to the stereotyping and discrimination that existed, as well as the Poles' own long-held beliefs and behaviors that tended to discourage their upward mobility.

The first Polish American to become prominent in sports was Oscar Bielaski, the American-born son of a Polish political émigré. Bielaski learned baseball as a drummer boy with the Union Cavalry during the American Civil War. After the war he became a clerk in Washington and continued to play baseball. At the time the sport was dominated by men from the older immigrant groups, such as English, Irish, and Germans. Bielaski first played professionally for the Washington Nationals of the National Association in 1872; he later was a member of the Chicago White Stockings, who won the first-ever National League pennant in 1876.

Shortly after the turn of the century, the first Polish American "superstar" appeared on the sporting scene. Stanley Ketchel,* born Stanislaw Kiecal in Grand Rapids, Michigan, won the middleweight boxing championship in 1908. The colorful and hard-hitting fighter was immensely popular, especially in *Polonia*. Ketchel, shot to death in 1910 at the age of twenty-four, is still considered among the best middleweights of history.

In the first two decades of the twentieth century, many working-class ethnics developed a significant level of participation in sports, but Poles had little presence. As in the cases of Bielaski and Ketchel, it was typically the children of Polish immigrants who were drawn to sports. As natives of the United States, they learned the intricacies of American athletics at an early age. They also viewed them as a means to attain financial security, as well as a way to become assimilated into the American "melting pot."

But their parents' financial concerns, particularly their desire to gain home-ownership, caused them to encourage their children to go to work at an early age rather than pursue a sports career on the professional or collegiate level. Stan Coveleski,* the Hall of Fame pitcher who was the hero of the 1920 World Series, worked as a coal miner at the age of twelve. His long hours left him little time for organized ball, but he would spend his evenings throwing stones at tin cans. Coveleski's reputation for amazing accuracy in that pursuit led to a pro contract. "There was nothing strange in those days about a 12-year-old Polish kid in the mines for 72 hours a week at a nickel an hour," he later recalled. "What was strange was that I ever got out."

By the early 1900s baseball was already called "the Great American Pastime," and immigrant children viewed it as an avenue to social and economic mobility and a way to gain acceptance into mainstream American society. Unlike many other professions at that time, baseball was considered by many to be the epitome of the ideals of democracy and equality upon which the nation was founded. The widely held belief of the time was that baseball was one enterprise in which any man (unless his skin was black) would be evaluated solely on the basis on his performance, not on where his parents came from.

The economic boom following World War I provided the working class with leisure time, and Polish Americans began playing sports, especially baseball, in large numbers. Not only was baseball "America's game," but it was popular in the areas where most Poles settled, the urban industrial centers of the Northeast, and it was inexpensive to play.

Following World War I Polish Americans encountered strong "antiforeign" sentiment that was exacerbated by the dramatic decline in industrial jobs during the Great Depression. The Poles, never fully accepted by mainstream America, were now regarded with a great deal of hostility and resentment and were viewed as a threat to the nation.

Polish Americans started to appear on major league baseball rosters with greater frequency in the 1910s and 1920s, though they often used Anglicized names. They included Walter "Whitey" Witt (born Wladislaw Wittkowski), Al Simmons* (Aloysius Szymanski), and Jack Quinn (John Paykos). In the 1930s and 1940s Polish Americans had a sizable representation on major league rosters. By the time of World War II they included some of the game's top stars, such as Stan Musial,* George "Whitey" Kurowski, Hank Borowy, Ted Kluszewski, Steve Gromek, and Eddie Lopat.

If baseball provided Polish Americans with their first significant opportunity beyond farms and factories, football helped *Polonia* define itself. Their dominance in football gave Polish Americans a positive identity in mainstream America and gave *Polonia* national recognition. In addition, unlike baseball, professional football did not have a system of minor leagues to develop talent. Football players were recruited from the colleges, thereby exposing many young Polish American athletes to a new array of educational and social experiences.

In its early days organized football was mostly played by local athletic clubs and universities, so Polish Americans had little presence since they generally did not have the connections to get into the athletic associations or the money or inclination to go to college. Eventually, the sport's popularity spread beyond the clubs and colleges, and around the turn of the century semipro teams were sponsored by churches, companies, and many small communities. Working-class Polish Americans then started to play the sport in significant numbers. The very qualities that made Poles excellent industrial workers—strength, durability, persistence, dedication—made them well suited for the rugged physical aspects of football. In addition, the high degree of teamwork and coordination required by the sport was similar to that of the close-knit village community in Poland and the ethnic enclave in America. Polish American parents were beginning to realize that their children's future success was dependent on their pursuing higher education, and they knew that the only way they could go to college was to earn an athletic scholarship.

Football grew in popularity in the early part of the twentieth century, and Polish Americans began to display a talent and passion for the sport. Polish names started appearing on the rosters of the top college football teams. In 1904 University of Pennsylvania guard Frank Piekarski became the first Polish American to be named an All-American. Before long, Polish athletes enrolled in Notre Dame, the nation's most prominent Catholic University. Joe Pliska was a halfback on Notre Dame's first undefeated team in 1913, and in 1917 Fighting Irish center Frank Rydzewski earned All-American recognition. Notre Dame was known as the "Fighting Irish" because it was dominated by Irish Americans in its early days, but in the 1920s and 1930s so many Polish athletes filled the rosters that Notre Dame Coach Knute Rockne* once commented: "If I can't pronounce a player's name, he must be good!"

In subsequent years Polish Americans like Bill Osmanski, Ed Danowski, Alex Wojciechowicz,* Ed and Dick Modzelewski, and Frank Gatski appeared frequently on pro football rosters. Polish Americans had such a significant presence in football that they became closely identified with the sport, and that continues today, when that presence is greatly diminished. When the Chicago Bears faced the Los Angeles Rams in the 1985 National Football Conference championship game, Bears head coach Mike Ditka* made headlines when he referred to his squad as "a Grabowski team" and called the Rams "a Smith team." The Bears, who went on to win Super Bowl XX, did not have a large number of Polish players. Ditka's point in calling his players "Grabowskis" was that they were hardworking overachievers who epitomized tough, determined, aggressive football.

While most of *Polonia* took great pride in the accomplishments of their sports heroes and their reputation for strength and toughness, it was not until relatively recently that Polish Americans developed any significant national presence in any other field of endeavor. The result was that the athletic image was the only one that many Americans had of Polish Americans. Some Poles resented the "jock" stereotype, arguing that it contributed to the "Polish joke" phenomenon of the 1960s.

Although football and baseball were the preferred sports of Polish Americans, they had a presence in nearly every sport, even "country club" sports like tennis that did not attract large numbers of working-class ethnics. Tennis great Frank (Piakowski) Parker* and golf champions Ed Furgol and Bob Toski were among the Polish Americans who rose from blue-collar roots to excel in sports that were inaccessible to most working-class ethnics.

Sports also impacted average Polish Americans, whose lives were enriched by participation in athletics. Polish organizations attracted new members through sports, especially younger men and women. The best known was the Polish Falcons* of America, founded in 1887 to promote "a sound mind in a sound body." Various other organizations, including hundreds of clubs and church groups, used sports to promote ethnic solidarity.

Although women's involvement in sports was severely restricted for many years, Polish American women were among the pioneers. Although women did not have equal status with men, they traditionally held a valued place in the community, often working in the fields and factories shoulder-to-shoulder with their male counterparts. Many outstanding women athletes emerged from *Polonia*, including track great Stella (Walasiewicz) Walsh,* basketball record-setter Carol Blazejowski,* and a number of members of the groundbreaking All-American Girls Baseball League.

The height of Polish American prominence in sports was probably the post–World War II era. In 1946 Stan Musial won the National League Most Valuable Player award, and he and rookie standout Whitey Kurowski led the St. Louis Cardinals to victory in the World Series. Notre Dame's Johnny Lujack and Leon Hart won college football's top honor, the Heisman Trophy, in 1947 and 1949, respectively, and Vic Janowicz of Ohio State won that award in 1950. Tony

Zale,* "the Man of Steel," reigned as middleweight boxing champion for most of the 1940s. Frank Parker* was one of the top tennis players in the world and was ranked number one in 1948. Future Football Hall of Famer Alex "the Great" Wojciechowicz led the Philadelphia Eagles to National Football League championships in 1948 and 1949.

Polonia was transformed dramatically following the war, as the suburbanization of America gradually broke down the old ethnic communities. Polish Americans continued to be active in sports, but increased educational opportunities and other changes decreased their dependence on athletics as a means of launching themselves beyond a blue-collar existence.

After World War II there were periods of increased emigration of Poles, especially during the late 1940s. But not only were these immigrations much smaller than that of the pre–World War I period of mass migration, the new immigrants were better educated and more mobile. They made important contributions, particularly in coaching Olympic sports in which Americans did not have a high level of expertise. Eddie Borysiewicz and Janusz Peciak, who in the 1980s coached the U.S. cycling and pentathlon teams, respectively, were among the most prominent.

Over the past century *Polonia* has made some remarkable gains, especially in light of its modest beginnings and the many impediments to its progress. In *Ethnic America*, Thomas Sowell pointed out that in the 1920s the average IQ of a Polish American was 85, well below the national average of 100. By the 1970s, the IQ level had risen an amazing 24 points to 109. Census figures also show that Polish Americans have exceeded the national family income average index and have ranked ahead of the Italian, German, and Anglo-Saxon ethnic groups, among others. Although traditional Polish peasant culture discouraged education and ambition, Polish Americans have made great advances, and sports certainly played a role in those advancements.

Polonia's sports heroes include not only great athletes but also coaches like Mike Krzyzewski* of the Duke basketball team and Ted Marchibroda of the National Football League (NFL) Baltimore Ravens, as well as top management people like Florida Marlins' general manager Dave Dombrowski and Los Angeles Lakers general manager Mitch Kupchak.

If sports today plays a lesser role in *Polonia*'s economic and social status, it may be taking on an even greater role in sustaining the viability of the Polish ethnic community. As the use of the Polish language and customs declines, sports and athletics have increased value as a unifying force, particularly among the younger and more assimilated Polish Americans who may not observe Polish holiday traditions and probably do not belong to Polish cultural societies. For them, the Polish American tradition of sports is perhaps the strongest link to their ethnic identity.

Sports has strengthened the bonds between "old *Polonia*" (descendants of the pre–World War II immigrants) and "new *Polonia*" (post–World War II émigrés and their children). As with most ethnic groups, there are differences between people who arrived during various periods of immigration. For Polish immigrants this is especially true because of the vast political and social changes that have taken place in Poland over the past century. One of the strongest common bonds between "old *Polonia*" and "new *Polonia*" is sports. This is demonstrated by the creation of various new Polish American sports organizations, particularly the ones that foster ties between the United States and Poland. Although its role is changing, sports continues to be a vital force in the ongoing evolution of *Polonia*.

SELECTED BIBLIOGRAPHY: John D. Buenker and Lorman A. Ratner, *Multiculturalism in the United States* (1982); Thomas Sowell, *Ethnic America* (1981); Thomas M. Tarapacki, *Chasing the American Dream: Polish Americans in Sports* (1995); David Q. Voigt, *American Baseball*, vol. 2 (1983); Joseph A. Wytrywal, *America's Polish Heritage: A Social History* (1961).

Thomas M. Tarapacki

POLISH FALCONS. Since its establishment in the United States in 1887, the Polish Falcons of America has been committed to sports, physical fitness, and physical education. The Falcons were created as a physical education association promoting both the health of young Polish immigrants and also their patriotic identification with the Polish homeland and its struggle for independence. The Polish Falcons of America is a direct outgrowth of a similar organization that was established in Poland in 1867. The activities of the Falcons have always been centered on the Latin maxim "mens sana in corpore sano" (healthy mind in a healthy body).

The first Nest (club) in the United States was organized by Felix Pietrowicz on 12 June 1887 in Chicago, who became the group's secretary. Frank Stefanski was chosen the first president. By 1894 there were twelve Nests in the United States. On 7 January of that year, representatives from four of these Nests, all from Chicago, met and decided to incorporate and form a national organization. A charter was granted the group on 1 May 1894 under the name "Alliance of Polish Turners of the United States of America." Thus came into existence the only Polish organization in America dedicated to physical culture and athletics.

The national headquarters returned to Chicago in 1905 after delegates to the Seventh Convention agreed to join the Polish National Alliance (PNA) as an autonomous department. The decision to merge with the PNA eventually led to a split at the Ninth Convention in 1909 in Cleveland, Ohio. A dissident group of delegates created the "Free Falcons" with Emil Elektorowicz as president. At a Convention held in December 1912 in Pittsburgh, the reunification of the two groups was accomplished, thanks in part to the efforts of Dr. Theophil A. Starzynski. A new national headquarters was established in Pittsburgh.

Dr. Starzynski was unanimously elected president of the Falcons that year and was active both here and abroad, preparing the Falcons for any emergencies that might arise. During the years 1913 to 1917 he organized Officers Training Schools in Cambridge Springs, Pennsylvania, and Toronto and Camp Borden, Canada, where hundreds of Falcon members were trained as officers. These later served in the Polish army in France and in Poland. When the United States entered the war in 1917, many became officers in the U.S. Army. In addition, many Nests organized military exercises, which sometimes substituted for the traditional physical fitness programs prior to World War I.

As a result, the Falcons had 12,000 well-trained and disciplined members ready for army duty. Of these, 7,000 answered President Woodrow Wilson's first call for volunteers when war was declared against Germany. About 50,000 other Poles followed in their footsteps by volunteering before the draft. The rest, numbering 5,000, patiently awaited the opportunity to volunteer in the long-heralded Polish Volunteer Army proposed by the famed Polish pianist Ignacy Jan Paderewski at a Special Convention of the Polish Falcons called by Starzynski on 3 April 1917 in Pittsburgh.

Although circumstances prohibited the formation of this army, one was subsequently created by a special decree of the president of France. This Polish army in France was formally organized on French soil, and the American government later authorized the recruiting of volunteers in America for it. These men were trained in Canada, fought in France and in Poland, and greatly contributed to the liberation of Poland.

The Falcons admit as members individuals who at the time of application for membership are of good moral character and are physically and mentally sound and by birth or descent of Polish or Slavic nationality or judged supportive of the purpose and ethnic heritage of the Polish Falcons of America. Today there are more than 29,000 Falcon members across the country. Members currently belong to more than 100 subordinate lodges called "Nests," which are divided into eleven districts. One of the main purposes of the Polish Falcons is the promotion, development, and maintenance of physical fitness programs, along with social, cultural, and educational activities. Members of all ages are encouraged to join these programs and to share the camaraderie of being a Falcon member.

After World War I, sports again became the primary focus of the organization. Activities such as mass calisthenics, marching, drills, and especially gymnastics were all part of the program. Track-and-field events, as well as baseball, basketball, and cycling, were also added to the program. Physical education classes are conducted by many Falcon Nests throughout the country. Typical sports and athletic programs of the Falcons include gymnastics, exercises, group drills, marching, mass calisthenics, volleyball, basketball, softball, table tennis, golf, and bowling. National bowling, golf, volleyball, and softball tournaments are held annually, as well as tournaments in Falcon districts. Biennially, competitions, or Zlots, are held in various sports by some of the districts in conjunction with the district conventions. Quadrennially, a National Zlot is held in conjunction with the National Convention. At the next National Zlot scheduled for July

2000 in Chicago, championships will be decided in various sports, including gymnastics, track and field, drilling, basketball, and volleyball. National competitions are also held in Polish folk dancing. The Falcons strive to channel youthful energy into wholesome, fun-filled activities that build stamina and confidence while fostering new friendships.

Many Nests have their own buildings or Falcon Halls. Some Nests are owners of the buildings in common with other organizations, and some even have their own bowling alleys. Other cultural and social activities, such as folksinging and dancing, choirs, and amateur theater supplement the physical education and athletic activities of the Nests. One of the highlights of the Falcons sports programs was the establishment of the Polish American Olympics in Pittsburgh in 1936. Among the thousands of men and women who have participated in the Falcons sports programs are Olympic medalist Stella Walsh* and baseball great Stan Musial.*

SELECTED BIBLIOGRAPHY: Donald E. Pienkos, *One Hundred Years Young: A History of the Polish Falcons of America, 1887–1987* (1987); Thomas M. Tarapacki, *Chasing the American Dream: Polish Americans in Sports* (1995).

Timothy L. Kuzma

POLO. Of all American sports, polo is perhaps the most firmly associated with a particular ethnic identity—WASP (white, Anglo-Saxon Protestant)—and a particular class—the wealthy. Although the latter's hold on the sport has diminished somewhat in the last half century, the former's has hardly wavered. Polo is a straightforward game—it is played in teams and on horseback, and the object is to hit a ball with a mallet into a goal. Polo can be played both indoors and outdoors.

Although there are many American polo players, most Americans associate the game primarily with England. Perhaps the premier polo image is that of Prince Charles astride his horse. It is no surprise, then, that while polo originated in central Asia, it eventually spread to England: taking hold in Persia from the sixth century B.C.E through the first century C.E., polo spread to Arabia and then to Tibet ("polo" is the Balti word for ball), then to China and Japan, and finally to India, where the British adopted the sport. British men first played the game in Assam, and in 1859 the first European polo club was established. It is important to note the late date of polo's adoption by the "Brits"—not quite a century and a half ago. Despite polo's relatively recent appearance in England, one of the appeals of polo in England and America is that it is an old tradition. Like so many Anglo-American traditions, the "traditional" quality ascribed to polo is an invention.

In 1876 James Gordon Bennett, a New York City sportsman and newspaper publisher, witnessed his first polo match in England and decided to introduce the sport in America. Before returning to the States, he purchased mallets and balls, which were used in the first American polo games, informal exercises in

New York later that year. In 1877 Jerome Park racetrack for polo was established in Westchester County, New York, and later that year the Westchester Polo Club was also established. In 1881 the Meadow Brook Club on Long Island was founded. A mere five years after the importation of polo to the States, the sport was well ensconced as an ornament of the Anglo upper class.

It is noteworthy that polo first took hold in the American Northeast. There, in the late nineteenth century, the Anglo Protestant population was feeling besieged by immigration and was struggling with the conundrums that increasing industrialization brought. They latched onto polo as a symbol of the dominance of moneyed, Anglo cultural power. Polo remained in their provenance for many decades.

The most obvious reason that polo has remained one of our least democratic sports, remaining in the hands of a small elite, is that it is expensive. As with any equestrian sport, polo demands that its players be able to keep ponies. In the second half of the twentieth century, polo has spread a little to non-WASP members of the upper class. One significant impetus to this spread has been American universities. Polo has, of course, not established itself at most colleges in the country, but at those where it has become popular, access to polo has been offered to students who otherwise would never have had the chance to play. The significance of polo in American culture is that it is one of many symbols that highlight the Anglo elite's attempts to protect a "traditional," Anglo cultural identity for America and to adopt customs that were inaccessible to the masses. Polo also points to the confluence of class and ethnicity—the WASPs who so enthusiastically adopted polo could do so only because of their wealth, and it was the very question of wealth—not of some more vague concept of ethnicity—that prevented the sport from becoming more widespread in America.

SELECTED BIBLIOGRAPHY: Newell Bent, *American Polo* (1929); John Lloyd, *The Pimm's Book of Polo* (1989); Frank Milbum, *Polo, the Emperor of Games* (1994); Ami Shinitzky and Don Follmer, *The Endless Chukker: 101 Years of American Polo* (1978).

Lauren F. Winner

POSEY, CUMBERLAND WILLIS, Jr. ("Cum") (20 June 1890, Homestead, PA–28 March 1946, Pittsburgh). An African American professional basketball and baseball player, manager, and owner, he was the son of Cumberland W., Sr., a riverboat engineer and later a manager, banker, and real estate entrepreneur, and Anna Stevens, a teacher who was the first black graduate of Ohio State University. Posey graduated from Homestead High School and attended Pennsylvania State College, the University of Pittsburgh, and Duquesne University. He married Ethel Truman in 1913, and they had five daughters. Posey organized and played for the Monticello Rifles basketball team in the Pittsburgh area in 1909. In 1913 he organized the Loendi Big Five, a professional team that dominated the black basketball world until the 1920s. Loendi played their home games at Pittsburgh's Labor Temple, defeating black and white teams alike and gaining crowds of 5,000. A slender man at 5'9" and 145 pounds, Posey joined the Homestead Grays* baseball team in 1910 as an outfielder and in 1912 became the booking agent. Between 1919 and 1935 he served as the manager for the Grays. As owner of the team during the 1930s until his death Posey arranged for the Grays to use Forbes Field when the Pittsburgh Pirates were out of town, and he put all of his players on salary. He gained a reputation for raiding players such as "Smoky Joe" Williams, Josh Gibson,* and Satchel Paige* from rival teams. The Grays won nine consecutive National Negro League (NNL) pennants and two Negro World Series titles. Posey also served as NNL secretary and wrote a column for the *Pittsburgh Courier*.

SELECTED BIBLIOGRAPHY: David L. Porter, ed., *Biographical Dictionary of American Sports: Baseball* (1987); Susan J. Rayl, "The New York Renaissance Professional Black Basketball Team, 1923–1950" (Ph.D. diss., Pennsylvania State University, 1996); Rob Ruck, *Sandlot Seasons: Sport in Black Pittsburgh* (1987).

Susan Rayl

PRINSTEIN, MEYER (?1880–10 March 1925, New York City). A track star who won four gold medals at the Olympic Games and was a world record holder in the broad jump, he was of Russian Jewish heritage. With a height of 5' 7-3/4" and a weight of 145 pounds, he was a compact, but powerful, horizontal jumper and also a successful sprinter. Competing for Syracuse University during the late 1890s, in 1898 he set U.S. and world records in the long jump. After yielding his world record to his arch rival Alvin Kraenzlein of the University of Pennsylvania, Prinstein regained it in 1900 with a leap of 24' 7-1/4" in 1900. At the 1900 Olympic Games at Paris Prinstein and Kraenzlein got into a heated dispute over the issue of Sunday competition. The American contingent had protested the scheduling of events on the Sabbath, and although Prinstein as a Jew had no religious objection to competing on Sunday, he respected the wishes of his observant Protestant teammates. After French officials insisted that ten finals would be held on Sunday, the Penn delegation broke ranks with the men from Princeton and Syracuse and allowed each athlete to decide the matter according to his own conscience. Kraenzlein chose to compete and won the gold medal in the broad jump, thereby infuriating Prinstein, who honored his commitment to his teammates and stayed on the sidelines. Prinstein did gain some consolation by winning the gold medal in the triple jump at the Paris Olympics. He later took top honors in the triple jump and the broad jump at the 1904 Olympics in St. Louis and the broad jump in the 1906 Olympics at Athens. After earning a bachelor's degree from Syracuse in 1901, Prinstein competed for the celebrated Irish-American Athletic Club* until 1910. Later in his life he practiced law until his untimely death due to heart disease.

SELECTED BIBLIOGRAPHY: John Kiernan and Arthur Daley, *The Story of the Olympic Games: 776 B.C. to 1964* (1965), 31–36; Bill Mallon and Ian Buchanan, *Quest for Gold: The Encyclopedia of American Olympians* (1984); Cordner Nelson, *Track's*

Greatest Champions (1986); *New York Times*, 11 March 1925, 16; Bernard Postal, Jesse Silver, and Roy Silver, *Encyclopedia of Jews in Sports* (1965); David Wallechinsky, *The Complete Book of the Olympics*, rev. ed. (1988).

George B. Kirsch

PROVAZNIK, MARIE (née KALOUS) (24 October 1890, Prague, Czechoslovakia–11 January 1991, Schenectady, NY). Her father (Václav Kalous) supervised the construction of iron bridges, and her mother (Marie née Klement) was a housewife. She received her education at Minerva, a college preparatory school for girls, and Charles University Institute for Teachers of Physical Education. Provaznik taught girls secondary physical education in Prague, was professor at Charles University Institute for Physical Education, and served on the advisory committee in the Ministry of Public Health as head of the Department of Girls' and Women's Physical Education. She also served as the director of women's training in the Czechoslovak Sokol Organization, a national gymnastic and physical education organization. Marie was a dynamic and innovative teacher. She brought girls' and women's gymnastics and physical education in Czechoslovakia to a level of excellence previously considered unattainable. She was a leader in the use of film and radio for physical education instruction and promotion. In 1920 the Fédération Internationale de Gymnastique (FIG) was formed. Marie helped to lay the foundation for the Women's Technical Committee and held various offices. Under her leadership the Czechoslovak Sokol Organization developed the uneven parallel bars and high balance beam and introduced them into women's international competition. She was chief organizer of women's gymnastic competition at the 1948 London Olympic Games. Provaznik defected to the United States after the London Olympics following the communist takeover of Czechoslovakia in February 1948. Marie accepted a part-time teaching position at Panzer College of Physical Education and Hygiene, East Orange, New Jersey, where she participated in the teacher training program, demonstrated modern educational gymnastics in public schools, gave displays at professional conventions, and took part in clinics and workshops. She was active in Czechoslovak Sokol Abroad and worked with the American Sokol Organization* and Sokol USA. In addition she organized Relief for Sokols in Exile to aid Czechoslovak refugees and regularly spoke on the Voice of America.

SELECTED BIBLIOGRAPHY: Peter Paul Dusek, Jr., "Marie Provaznik: Her Life and Contributions to Physical Education" (Ph.D. diss., University of Utah, 1981).

Peter P. Dusek, Jr.

PUERTO RICANS. As an ethnic group and nationality, Puerto Ricans have a unique position among the peoples of the United States. They hold U.S. citizenship, but the Commonwealth maintains an autonomous Olympic identity. As such, some Puerto Rican athletes who have been raised in the United States and who have participated in sports in Puerto Rico have represented the island in international competitions. Also, other athletes have grown up in Puerto Rico and have later competed in and for the United States. This has led to two types of problems. First, the difference in language and culture has created many challenges in adaptation for athletes who were raised in one environment but lived and competed in another. The other difficulty arises when an athlete who was raised in Puerto Rico and competed in both countries chose to represent the United States internationally. In that case the question of the nationality of that individual becomes problematical. But even in those cases those athletes generally affirm their Puerto Rican identity.

The two sports that have had the most prominent worldwide Puerto Rican participation, champions, and record holders have been boxing and baseball. In boxing Puerto Rico has produced thirty-four international champions in many weight classes. The first "golden era" began with the championship of Sixto Escobar on 26 June 1934 in the bantamweight division. He won the title on two other occasions. He was followed by the legendary Carlos Ortíz,* who won the championship in both the junior welter- and lightweight divisions and overall was a champion for nine years (1959–67). José Luis "Chegüí" Torres* won the silver medal for the United States in the 1956 Olympics and won the light heavyweight title in 1965. Another "golden era" was marked by the first occurrence, around 1975–76, of four simultaneous Puerto Rican champions: Alfredo Escalera, Angel Espada, Wilfredo Benítez,* and Esteban de Jesús. Benítez holds the distinction of being the youngest-ever boxing champion, capturing his crown at the age of seventeen. Additionally, four boxers won championships in three different weight classes: Benítez, Wilfredo Gómez, and Wilfredo Vázquez. Also the flamboyant Héctor Camacho won a championship on five different occasions over thirteen years. Referee Waldermar Schmidt had a distinguished career, working many championship fights.

In baseball Puerto Rico has produced many major league stars, and for more than sixty years it has hosted a winter league that has served as a launching pad for future stars from both the island and the United States. The winter league has hosted legendary players from the Negro Leagues,* such as Josh Gibson,* as well as many Hall of Famers, such as Willie Mays.* The first Puerto Rican to play in the major leagues was pitcher Hiram Bithorn, who won eighteen games for the 1943 Chicago Cubs. Luis Rodríguez Olmo also entered the major leagues in 1943 for the Dodgers and was among the first to jump to the Mexican League in 1946 for a higher salary. These groundbreakers led the way for the great Roberto Clemente,* who played eighteen years for the Pittsburgh Pirates, amassing 3,000 hits, four batting titles, one World Series Most Valuable Player (MVP), a league MVP, and election to the Hall of Fame. Orlando Cepeda followed Clemente, winning the Rookie of the Year, one home run and two runs batted in (RBI) titles, and one MVP. Although he has not yet gained admission, he has all the credentials to be in the Hall of Fame. In addition, other major leaguers who became legendary performers in the winter league are Rubén Gómez, Juan "Terín" Pizarro, and Víctor Pellot Power. During the late 1990s

Puerto Rican stars in the major leagues included Juan González, Iván Rodríguez, Edgar Martínez, and Roberto and Sandy Alomar. In amateur baseball, famous players were Luis R. Colón, Jesús Feliciano, José E. Marrero, Luis A. Mercado, Nestor Morales, Rogelio Negrón, Mariano Quiñones, and Guillermo Rosado. César "Coca" González, who played in the 1940s and 1950s, was a standout for a generation, winning six batting championships in twelve years and retaining his amateur status despite many professional offers.

The Puerto Rican women's national softball team has been very successful in international competitions. Among its greatest stars were Ivelisse "Tata" Echevarría and Betty Segarra. Echevarría was a right-hand pitcher and strong hitter of the women's national softball team between 1977 and 1996, with an interruption of five years (1989–93) because of a sports lesion in her right shoulder. At the Central American and Caribbean Games (CAC), the women's softball team won a silver medal in 1978 and two gold medals in 1982 and 1993. At the level of the Pan-American Games, the team won two silver medals in Indianapolis (1987) and Mar del Plata, Argentina (1995). A gold medal in the American Pre-Olympic Tournament made possible their dream of competing in the 1996 Olympic Games in Atlanta. Ivelisse pitched three no-hitters in the Pan-American competitions (one in Caracas and two in Indianapolis). At the 1982 CAC games in Havana she won the batting title. In the Women's Softball World Championship in New Zealand (1986) she was classified as one of the three best pitchers of the world.

Basketball is a highly popular participatory and spectator sport on the island. At the Pan-American Games the national basketball team has won one gold, four silver, and two bronze medals; twelve medals at the Central American and Caribbean Games, a fifth place at the 1964 Olympics; and a fourth place at the 1990 World Championship. In 1959 Juan "Pachín" Vicéns was selected as the best amateur basketball player in the world at the World Championship in Chile. Beginning at the age of fifteen, he starred for the Ponce Lions team in the Puerto Rican Superior Basketball league, where he played for sixteen years (1950–66). He was the first Puerto Rican player to reach the mark of 5,000 points, with a lifetime average of 17 points per game. He also played college basketball in the United States at the University of Kansas, where he earned a B.S. degree. Other notable athletes include Raúl "Tinajón" Feliciano, Johnny Báez, Teo Cruz, Raymond Dalmau, Georgie Torres, Mario Morales, and José "Piculín" Ortíz; coaches Julio Toro, Flor Meléndez, and Carlos Morales and referee Calvin Pacheco.

In track-and-field athletics Puerto Rico has been most successful at the CAC and the Pan-American level. In men's pole vaulting Rolando Cruz finished in fourth place at the 1960 Olympics in Rome and became the first Puerto Rican to clear the heights of fourteen, fifteen, and sixteen feet. Other outstanding performers include Amado Morales (javelin), Elmer Williams (long jump), Arnaldo Bristol and Domingo Cordero (hurdles), Jorge González (marathon), and Angelita Lind and Ileana Hocking (women's middle-distance running). Twice a gold medalist in the 1,500 meters at the CAC games, Lind was a semifinalist in the 800 meters at the 1984 Olympics at Los Angeles. Ovidio de Jesús, runner and hurdler, was also a productive international winner.

Important figures in track and field were pioneer athlete Rebekah Colberg, Eugenio Guerra (an athlete, trainer, and leader), and Manuel González Pató, college trainer. Colberg participated in many athletic events and other sports, including the high jump, discus throw, javelin, tennis, basketball, and volleyball. A highly trained psychiatrist, she was the first female athlete to be inducted into the Puerto Rican Sports Hall of Fame, earning that honor in track and field and tennis. Guerra was a trainer at six CAC games and four Pan-American Games and was chief trainer in five Olympic Games (1948–64). He received the Olympic Order in 1994, an honor given by the International Olympic Committee. He earned election to the Puerto Rico Hall of Fame in track and field and softball.

Puerto Rico has also produced several famous swimmers and tennis players. The 1966 CAC games were called Anita Lallande's games because she swam to twelve medals, including ten gold. In men's swimming Fernando Canales competed for Puerto Rico, winning many medals in the CAC and Pan-American games; Jesús D. Vasallo held two world records competing for the United States; and Ricardo Busquets, a highly ranked National Collegiate Athletic Association (NCAA) swimmer, won a bronze medal in the 1997 World Championship in Australia. Tennis is led by Gigi Fernández,* who was a highly ranked singles player and one of the greatest doubles players in the world. She represented Puerto Rico in the 1984 Olympics (exhibition) and won two Olympic gold medals for the United States in doubles in 1992 and 1996. Charlie Pasarell, Jr., was the best male tennis player from Puerto Rico. A roommate of Arthur Ashe* at the University of California at Los Angeles, he was intercollegiate champion in men's singles and doubles and All-American for three consecutive years. He was also a member of the U.S. Davis Cup Team five times (1966–68, 1974–75).

Puerto Rican athletes have also excelled in a variety of other sports. In horse racing Angel Cordero, Jr.,* had an illustrious career. The winner of three Kentucky Derbys, two Preakness Stakes, and one Belmont Stakes, he captured the Eclipse Award for best jockey on two occasions. Two memorable horses should be mentioned: Camarero, who had a fifty-six-race undefeated streak, and Dulce Sueño, the stallion of twenty of the first twenty-three champions of the sport of Paso Fino. In golf Chi Chi Rodríguez* became a million-dollar winner as a professional with eight Professional Golfers' Association (PGA) victories. He remains active on the Senior tour. Other notables include Víctor Colón (gymnastics); Betsy Ortíz (tae kwon do); Luis Martínez, Lisa Boscarino, and Evelyn Matías (judo); Aníbal Nieves, José E. Betancourt (wrestling); Juan R. Torruella and Rosarito Martínez (sailing); María Cerra and Mirtheska Escanellas (fencing); William Padró and Juan Carlos Merheb (cycling); Lito Gotay (soccer); Jaime Almendro and Ashie González (bowling); Vivian Alberty (diving); Gloria Guzmán and Ralph Rodríguez (shooting); Julio Figueroa and Pilar Vázquez (volleyball); Gloria Rosa and María Reyes (archery). In weight lifting Fernando Luis Báez, the "little giant from Adjuntas," earned the first two gold medals (of a total of thirteen) for Puerto Rico at the Pan-American Games in Winnipeg, Canada (1967), and Cali, Colombia (1971). A participant in four Olympic Games, in 1964 he held a world record in the "military press," lifting in the bantamweight category. Also, the Young Men's Christian Association (YMCA) played an important historical role in sports promotion in Puerto Rico. Distinguished broadcasters and sportswriters include Pito Alvárez de la Vega, Héctor Rafael Vázquez, Manuel Rivera Morales, Emilio E. Huyke, Mario Rivera Martinó, and Joaquín Martínez Rousset. The inimitable Rafael Pont Flores was the sports editor of one of the important daily newspapers in Puerto Rico. Best known for his commentary on the Puerto Rican baseball league and the major leagues in the United States, he was elected to the Puerto Rican Professional Baseball Hall of Fame.

Sports in Puerto Rico have seen many great Olympic leaders, including the fathers of the Puerto Rican Olympic movement, Julio Enrique Monagas and Germán Rieckehoff-Sampayo. Rieckehoff, known as Don Germán, was an attorney, sports editor, founder and president of several Puerto Rican sports federations, president of the Puerto Rican Olympic Committee (1977–89), and member (1977–90) and honorary member (1990–97) of the International Olympic Committee (IOC). He was also the winner of the Olympic Order in 1991 and the Centennial Olympic Award in 1994 conferred by the IOC. Others who have contributed much to international sport are local and international basketball leader Genaro "Tuto" Marchand; Osvaldo Gil, a leader in amateur baseball; International Olympic Committee member Richard L. Carrión; Marimer Olazagasti, past secretary of sports and chairwoman of the 2004 Olympic ProSite Commission; and Héctor Cardona, the current president of the Olympic Committee and former president of the boxing federation. In Olympic competitions thus far all medals have been won in boxing: a silver medal by Luis F. Ortíz in the Los Angeles Olympics and bronze medals by Juan E. Venegas, Orlando Maldonado, Arístides González, Aníbal Acevedo, and Daniel Santos.

Puerto Rico also has three sports that are intertwined with the island's cultural heritage. Peleas de Gallos, or cockfighting, has a history covering two centuries. It was prohibited by the U.S. military government in 1899 but remained popular in clandestine gatherings. Finally bowing to popular demand, the ban was lifted by the designated civil governor in 1933. The game of Dominó, present in the island since the seventeenth century, has been a favorite in homes, parks, and clubs. A table game played with twenty-eight numbered tiles, it tests memory and arithmetic and strategic skill. It is played with four contestants in teams of two working in tandem, attempting to score points by one team member playing all his tiles first and this team receiving the total points on the remaining unplayed tiles. The sport of Paso Fino horses is the official national sport of Puerto Rico, dating from the fifteenth century. Autochthonous to the island, it has been extended to other countries in the Americas. It features rhythmic, harmoniously paced cadences, and elegant horse-and-rider competition involving three events: Beautiful Forms, Fine Pace, and Gait (Andadura).

SELECTED BIBLIOGRAPHY: Kenneth A. Brown, "Una leyenda llamada Roberto Clemente," *El Nuevo Día, Domingo Deportivo*, 28 September 1997, 4–11; Comisión de Boxeo y Lucha Libre Profesional de Puerto Rico, Portraits of Champions (1997); Frances Concepción and Aurea Echevarría, *Tres Mujeres Deportistas, un Discurso Patriarcal* (1997); Junior Cruz, *Sóftbol de Alto Nivel* (1983), 1–86; Miguel Andino Clemente Cruz, "Angel Tomás Cordero, Jr.," *Enciclopedia del Hipismo Puertorriqueño, Tomo I* (1981), 318–321; Silvio Echevarría, "Ivelisse Echevarría Echevarría," Presentación en el Centro Cultural Angel Pacheco Alvarado, 28 September 1996 (Portrait); Federación de Atletismo Aficionado de Puerto Rico, Prontuario, Campeonatos Nacionales (1997); Emilio E. Huyke, "Laureles de Puerto Rico," *Colecciones Puertorriqueñas, Los Deportes en Puerto Rico* (1968), 291–294; Enrique Montesinos, "Juegos Deportivos Centroamericans y del Caribe," in Carlos Uriarte González, ed., *Los Juegos Regionales más Antiguos* (1993), 422; Germán Rieckehoff, Expresiones Diversas de Germán Rieckehoff 1973–1983 (Collection of Manuscripts); Tomás Sarramía, "Junior Cordero," *Nuestra Gente* (1993), 65–66; Tomás Sarramía, "Chi Chi Rodríguez," *Nuestra Gente* (1993), 182–183; Jaime Varas, *La Gran Enciclopedia de Puerto Rico, Tomo 11, El Deporte en Puerto Rico* (1976), 352; Thomas E. Van Hyning, *Puerto Rico's Winter League* (1995).

Raúl Mayo-Santana

PYTHIAN BASE BALL CLUB. Founded in Philadelphia in 1867 by African Americans, the Pythians were an elite black sports association and one of America's most prominent black baseball clubs during the late 1860s. While its players ranked far below their white counterparts in social status, they were among the most successful within their city's African American community. Sixty-nine percent of them were mulattoes, and only one-quarter held unskilled or semi-skilled jobs. The Pythians had the leisure time and money to play baseball while most of their brethren suffered from poverty and racism, but a significant number of them also worked to improve the status of blacks in Philadelphia. Many were active in black social and civic organizations. A small minority of activists, including Jacob C. White, Jr., and Octavius V. Catto, had been active members of a committee to recruit blacks for the Union Army in 1863. White, the club's secretary, became principal of the largest and most advanced black public school in the city. He was a moderate on race questions, steadily pursuing a policy of accommodation with whites. Catto, who was more dynamic and militant, lived a short, but active, life as a star baseball player, teacher, and civil and voting rights advocate. Admitted to the city's prestigious Franklin Institute, he had just launched himself into national prominence when an assassin's bullet cut short his life in October 1871.

The Pythians, like most of the other early black baseball clubs, emulated the white associations in their organizations, social life, match play, intercity tours, and competition for state and national black championships. They issued and received formal challenges to compete against rivals from Camden, New Jersey,

West Chester, Pennsylvania, Washington, D.C., Brooklyn, and Harrisburg; and they, too, entertained their guests at lavish dinners. Their great success on the ball field was due in part to recruiting outsiders to bolster their first nines for special matches, just as many white clubs did, even though this was in violation of the rules of the National Association of Base Ball Players—which claimed authority as the sport's first governing body.

Like many of the other black clubs, the Pythians were on good terms with white teams and frequently obtained permission to use their grounds for feature contests. White umpires sometimes even officiated at their games. The Pythians enjoyed harmonious ties with Philadelphia's famed Athletics, who were generous with their facilities and support. But although white and black baseball players generally got along well, there was still much resistance among the white fraternity to the recognition of equality inherent in interracial competition. There were only a few matches between the Pythians and local white nines.

Although African American clubs such as the Pythians often shared playing fields and enjoyed good relations with white teams, they were denied equal representation in baseball gatherings, as they were excluded from Reconstruction-era politics in the North. The 1867 convention of the National Association of Base Ball Players flatly refused to admit clubs with black delegates, and state meetings followed the same segregationist policy. The Pythians sent an emissary to Harrisburg in 1867 to present the club's credentials to the Pennsylvania gathering, but he found that only a few friends from the Athletics and other clubs favored admitting the all-black Pythians. Supporters advised a discrete withdrawal to avoid humiliation, and the Pythian delegate concurred. Thus, while the Pythians and other African American clubs pioneered black baseball in the United States during the 1860s, they were not able to gain equal status in the nation's ballplaying fraternity.

SELECTED BIBLIOGRAPHY: George B. Kirsch, *The Creation of American Team Sports: Baseball and Cricket, 1838–72* (1989), 125–126, 148, 150–52, 166, 212; Harold Seymour, *Baseball: The People's Game* (1990), 533–539; Harry C. Silcox, "Philadelphia Negro Educator: Jacob C. White, Jr., 1837–1902," *Pennsylvania Magazine of History and Biography* 97 (January 1973): 75–98; Harry C. Silcox, "Nineteenth-Century Philadelphia Black Militant: Octavius V. Catto," *Pennsylvania History* 44 (January 1977): 53–76; Pythian Base Ball Club records, American Negro Historical Society Papers, Leon Gardner Collection, Historical Society of Pennsylvania.

George B. Kirsch

R

REID, JOHN (14 October 1840, Dunfermline, Scotland–7 October 1916, Yonkers, NY). Generally considered the "father of American golf," he was the son of Andrew and Helen (Arnot) Reid. Reid received his early education in Scotland and then emigrated to the United States in 1865, settling in New York City. A successful businessman, in 1887 Reid induced another Scottish American, Robert Lockhart, to bring some golf clubs and balls back from Britain on one of his regular trips abroad. On 22 February 1888 Reid and several others tried out the equipment in a field near Reid's home in Yonkers, New York. From this exhibition grew the modern game of golf in the United States. In November 1888 Reid and his group formed the St. Andrews Golf Club, perhaps the first and certainly one of the most important of the early clubs. After several moves, the club eventually settled in Mt. Hope, New York. In 1894 Reid was one of the founders of the U.S. Golf Association and its first vice president. He and Charles B. Macdonald* wrote the organization's constitution and bylaws. An active partisan of Scottish culture, Reid was also an avid collector and singer of Scottish folk songs. He was a member and president of the St. Andrews Society and the Burns Society.

SELECTED BIBLIOGRAPHY: Kathleen Doyle, "In John Reid's Cow Pasture," *American History Illustrated* 23 (Summer 1988): 34–35; Charles B. Macdonald, *Scotland's Gift—Golf* (1928); H. B. Martin, *Fifty Years of American Golf* (1936); Herbert Warren Wind, *The Story of American Golf* (1948).

Richard J. Moss

REYNOLDS, ALLIE PIERCE ("Superchief") (10 February 1915, Bethany, OK–27 December 1994, Oklahoma City, OK). A baseball player and a gifted all-around Indian athlete, he was the son of a fundamentalist minister, D. L. Reynolds. He was one-quarter Creek Indian, and he starred in track and football at Capitol High School in Oklahoma City. He was recruited to Oklahoma A&M on a track scholarship, but he also excelled on the gridiron as a running back and on the diamond as a no-hit pitcher. He graduated from A&M with a B.S. degree in social science. Although drafted by the New York Giants of the National Football League, he signed with the Cleveland Indians for $1,000. Three impressive seasons in the low minors brought the twenty-seven-year-old rookie to Cleveland in 1942. He posted a respectable 51–47 record for the Indians from 1942 to 1946 before the Indians dealt him to the Yankees. He helped New York win six world championships in seven years between 1947 and 1953. His superlative record with the Yanks of 7–2, 2.79 earned run average (ERA) in the World Series, and 131–60 during the regular season (.686 percentage) is usually overshadowed by his two no-hitters in 1951. Reynolds was equally effective starting or relieving for manager Casey Stengel, which Reynolds later felt shortened his career. He once unsuccessfully ran for chief of the Creek Nation. A Methodist, he was elected to the Oklahoma Sports Hall of Fame.

SELECTED BIBLIOGRAPHY: Bill Ballew, "Allie Reynolds: 'Superchief' Remembers His Days in the Majors," *Sports Collector's Digest* (10 August 1990): 250–251; Harry Molter, *Famous Athletes of Today* (1953); *New York Times*, 28 December 1994, D18.

Joseph M. Giovannetti

RHODES, TED (9 November 1913, Nashville, TN–4 July 1969, Nashville). An African American golfer, he grew up in Nashville, Kentucky, and began caddying at the age of twelve on two exclusive area golf courses, Bell Meade and Richland. He developed an intense interest in the game and studied the nuances of the golf swing while caddying for members of these clubs. The time came when Rhodes had developed his game to the point that he was good enough to play on the United Golfers Association* (UGA) circuit—the only available option open to African American players during this period—but he didn't have the resources to buy golf clubs. The story goes that George Livingstone, the longtime professional at Bell Meade, allowed him to pick out clubs to make a set from a barrel of clubs discarded by members. From this humble beginning, Rhodes fashioned a brilliant career as a professional golfer at a time when the opportunities for a black man to make a living playing golf were extremely limited. He became the first African American to compete against whites in a Professional Golfers' Association (PGA)–sponsored tournament, the 1946 Los Angeles Open, and won consecutive UGA national championships from 1949 to 1951. He would also play a prominent role in the eventual elimination of the clause in the constitution of the Professional Golfers' Association of America that prohibited non-Caucasians from attaining membership and thus eligibility to compete on the tour. In 1948, Rhodes and fellow black pros Bill Spiller and Madison Gunther were not allowed to play in the Richmond (California) Open. They filed a lawsuit against the PGA of America, which was settled out of court when the PGA pledged not to refuse playing privileges on the basis of race in the future. While these initial efforts by Rhodes and his colleagues did not end discrimination on the PGA tour, they led to the eventual elimination of the Caucasian clause in the PGA constitution in 1961.

SELECTED BIBLIOGRAPHY: "Joe Louis Barred from San Diego Open," *New York Times*, 14 January 1952, 25; "Joe Louis Insists on Entry in Golf," *New York Times*, 15 January 1952, 31; Bill Mardo, "Two Negro Golfers Sue PGA for $250,000," *Daily Worker*, 16 January 1948, back page; Bill Mardo, "Fight vs. Golf Jimcrow Won," *Daily Worker*, 26 September 1948, 10; "PGA Clears Way for Louis to Play in San Diego Open," *New York Times*, 16 January 1952, 30; Calvin H. Sinnette, *Forbidden Fairways* (1998).

                                                                                Larry Londino

RISKO, JOHNNY (? 1902, Bohunice, Slovakia [Austria-Hungary]–13 January 1953, Miami Beach, FL). A prizefighter, he was the son of Slovak immigrants whose family came to the Cleveland area when he was six. He acquired his nickname "the Baker Boy" from working at his family's west side bakery in Lakewood, Ohio (Cleveland's west side). He boxed professionally from 1924 to 1940. After World War I, perhaps nobody stirred more emotion among Slovak American boxing fans than Risko. During the 1920s and 1930s he acquired a reputation as a "spoiler," the underdog heavyweight boxer who put to rest the dreams of many potential champions. At 5'10" and weighing 188 pounds, Risko appeared a bit pudgy and never would impress an unsuspecting opponent with his stature. Risko turned professional in 1924, but an injury of his right shoulder in his fourth professional bout proved costly. He would never quite be the same again. After six months of recuperation, Risko reentered the ring and developed a terrific left hook to compensate for his right arm injury. Because of his startling tenacity when opponents were seemingly pounding him, Risko acquired other nicknames, such as "Cleveland's Rubber Man" and the "Trial Horse of Champions." His most famous bout took place in Cleveland against "the Fighting Marine," Gene Tunney,* in 1925. He lost a controversial twelve-round decision, which ultimately cost him a chance at the world heavyweight championship. Some say anti-Slavic prejudices of the era tipped the judge's decision in the direction of his Irish opponent. In such close fights, rematches were virtually mandatory, but in this case, Tunney refused to fight Risko again. Nonetheless, Risko went on to beat both Max Baer* and Jack Sharkey,* both of whom went on to become world heavyweight champions. By the time his professional career ended, Risko had fought 137 matches. Of these he managed twenty-two knockouts, won forty-four decisions, and lost thirty-six decisions. He himself suffered three knockouts. Risko spent his earnings with recklessness, and only his manager's foresightedness saved some of his earnings ($100,000) in a trust fund for his later life. After his retirement, Risko went into business for himself and ran a successful bar in Cleveland. He also served in World War II.

SELECTED BIBLIOGRAPHY: *Cleveland Plain Dealer*, 15 January 1953; Joseph Krajsa, ed., *Slovaks in America: A Bicentennial Study* (1978).

                                                                    Michael J. Kopanic, Jr.

RIZZUTO, PHILIP FRANCIS (25 September 1918, New York City–   ). A star baseball player, his parents were Philip and Rose (Angotti) Rizzuto. The son of an Italian New York trolley car conductor, he grew up as a Brooklyn Dodger fan. Enticed by the dream of playing baseball, Rizzuto quit Richmond Hill High School before he graduated. The school awarded him his diploma in 1948 in recognition of his success in life. After an initial tryout, Dodger manager Casey Stengel rejected the 5'6" Rizzuto as too short to play for his team. Yankee scouts, however, saw an aggressive quickness and signed him to a minor league contract in 1937. By 1940 he was playing shortstop for Kansas City in the American Association. That same year, the "Scooter" became Minor League Player of the Year, and the New York Yankees called him up to the majors in 1941. The young shortstop watched Joe DiMaggio's* fifty-six-game hitting streak in 1941 and played in his first All-Star game in 1942. Navy duty during World War II in New Guinea and Hawaii interrupted his baseball career from 1943 to 1945. Rizzuto returned to baseball in 1946, playing until his 1956 release. He was the American League's Most Valuable Player in 1950 and competed in five All-Star Games and nine World Series. An outstanding bunter, he compiled a lifetime batting average of .273 and a fielding percentage of .968. He was elected to the Baseball Hall of Fame in 1994. Rizzuto's second career as a broadcaster of Yankee games began in 1957. For forty years he entertained radio and television audiences with his commentary, mixing reports on the games with amusing anecdotes and announcements of birthdays and wedding anniversaries.

SELECTED BIBLIOGRAPHY: Tom Peyer and Hart Seely, eds., *O Holy Cow! The Selected Verses of Phil Rizzuto* (1993); Phil Rizzuto, *The October Twelve: Five Years of New York Yankee Glory, 1949–1953* (1994); "Scooter Spared," *Time* 37 (14 April 1941): 44; Gene Shoor, *The Scooter* (1982); John Thorn and Pete Palmer, eds., *Total Baseball*, 3d ed. (1993); Joe Trimble, *Phil Rizzuto* (1951).

Philip M. Montesano

ROBERTSON, OSCAR ("The Big O") (24 November 1938, Charlotte, TN–   ). An African American basketball player, he is the son of Mazell (Bell) Robertson. His father was a sanitation worker. His mother (a domestic and later a beautician) raised him in Indianapolis, where he learned to play basketball at a local Young Men's Christian Association (YMCA). He then starred in track and field, basketball, and baseball at Indianapolis' all-black Crispus Attucks High School. Selected three times to the All-State Indiana high school basketball team, he led his school to two state championships. Next Robertson became the first African American to play basketball for the University of Cincinnati. He excelled for the Bearcats, leading them to two third-place finishes in the National Collegiate Athletic Association (NCAA) tournament in 1959 and 1960 and setting fourteen NCAA scoring records while averaging 33.8 points per game over three seasons. During his schoolboy and collegiate years Robertson experienced several racist incidents. On one occasion a victory parade for his state championship high school team was relocated from the center of Indianapolis to a remote park on the edge of town because of fears of racial conflict. In 1959, when Cincinnati played a game at the University of Houston, Robertson had to stay at a black college, apart from his white teammates. After his graduation he was cocaptain of the U.S. Olympic basketball team that won the gold medal at Rome, Italy, in 1960. His fourteen-year career with the Cincinnati Royals and the Milwaukee Bucks from 1961 through 1974 was spectacular. The modern sport's first big guard (at 6' 5" and 210 pounds), he was the most versatile player of his era, a perennial league standout in scoring, assists, and rebounding. The National Basketball Association's (NBA) Most Valuable Player in 1964 and a member of the All-NBA team eleven times, he finally achieved his goal of winning an NBA championship with the Bucks (with Lew Alcindor, later Kareem Abdul-Jabbar,* as the team's center) in 1971. During his career he was an admirer of Jackie Robinson* and was outspoken in urging NBA clubs to sign more black players. Also active in union matters, he was elected president of the NBA Players Association in 1966. In that office he helped to establish collective bargaining with the owners. Robertson was elected to the Naismith Memorial Basketball Hall of Fame in 1979.

SELECTED BIBLIOGRAPHY: Arthur R. Ashe, Jr., *A Hard Road to Glory: A History of the African-American Athlete since 1946*, vol. 3 (1988); Phil Berger, *Heroes of Pro Basketball* (1968); Al Hirschberg, *Basketball's Greatest Stars* (1963); Edna Rust and Art Rust, Jr., *Art Rust's Illustrated History of the Black Athlete* (1985).

George B. Kirsch

ROBESON, PAUL LEROY (9 April 1898, Princeton, NJ–23 January 1976, Philadelphia). The son of a schoolteacher, Anna Louis Robeson (née Bustill), and a Protestant minister, William Drew Robeson, he was an African American collegiate and professional athlete, an acclaimed singer, and actor. A brilliant student and athlete at Somerville High School in New Jersey, he received an academic scholarship to Rutgers College, where he was elected to Phi Beta Kappa in his junior year and was selected valedictorian in his senior year. Robeson excelled in the college sports arena, earning twelve varsity letters in basketball, baseball, football, and track. He was also named an All-American in football in 1917 and 1918. Following graduation in 1919 Robeson earned a law degree at Columbia University, which he funded by playing professional football for the Akron Pros and the Milwaukee Badgers. While at Columbia he also took up amateur dramatics. After graduation in 1923 and following a brief and exceedingly unhappy stay at a New York law firm, Robeson embarked on a professional singing and acting career that, during the 1930s and 1940s, garnered him worldwide popular acclaim. In the reactionary post–World War II climate his sympathy for socialism and racial equality drew much criticism from the American establishment, which had a damaging impact on Robeson's career. In

1950 the federal government canceled Robeson's passport, which severely hurt his theatrical and musical career.

SELECTED BIBLIOGRAPHY: Martin B. Duberman, *Paul Robeson* (1988); Philip S. Foner, ed., *Paul Robeson Speaks: Writings—Speeches—Interviews, 1918–1974* (1978); Freedomways Associates, eds., *Paul Robeson: The Great Forerunner* (1978); Dorothy Butler Gilliam, *Paul Robeson: All-American* (1976); Paul Robeson, *Here I Stand* (1958); Marie Seton, *Paul Robeson* (1958).

David Andrews

ROBINSON, FRANK (31 August 1935, Beaumont, TX–   ). An African American baseball player, he is the son of Frank and Ruth (Shaw) Robinson. He attended school in Oakland, California, where he graduated from Mc-Clymonds High School. He was a baseball player for the Cincinnati Reds (1956–65), Baltimore Orioles (1966–71), Los Angeles Dodgers (1972), California Angels (1974), and Cleveland Indians (1974–75, 1976). He was named Rookie of the Year in 1956 while with Cincinnati and was the league's Most Valuable Player in 1961 while playing with Cincinnati and again in 1966 while he was with the Baltimore Orioles. He was also a Triple Crown winner in 1961. He is the only player ever to be named the Most Valuable Player in both of the major leagues. He was an All-Star selection for nine years and won a Gold Glove in 1958. He hit 586 home runs during his career, and he was named the 1966 World Series Most Valuable Player in the Orioles' four-game sweep over the Dodgers. He was the first player to hit 200 home runs in both leagues and the first player to hit All-Star Game home runs for both sides. He was also the first black manager in the major leagues, piloting Cleveland (1975–77), the San Francisco Giants (1981–84, first black National League manager), and then the Baltimore Orioles (1988–90). He was also a manager in the first major league game in history to feature a pair of black managers, 27 June 1989, Baltimore versus Toronto. He was a civil rights advocate and became one of the most outspoken critics of racist tactics in baseball.

SELECTED BIBLIOGRAPHY: Donald Druey and Nicholas Acocella, *The Biographical History of Baseball* (1995); Alan Minsky, *Home Run Kings* (1995); Frank Robinson, with Al Silverman, *My Life Is Baseball* (1968); Mike Shatzkin, *The Ballplayers* (1990).

Clyde Partin

ROBINSON, JACK ROOSEVELT ("Jackie") (31 January 1919, Cairo, GA–24 October 1972, Stamford, CT). An African American baseball player, he was the son of Jerry and Mallie Robinson. When he was a child, his mother moved the family from Cairo, Georgia, to a white neighborhood in Pasadena, California, after her husband had deserted the family. In high school, young Jackie lettered in four sports and later led his baseball team at Pasadena Junior College to the championship; in 1939 he entered the University of California at

Los Angeles (UCLA), where he became the first athlete in the history of the school to win letters in four sports in one year. After a short stint playing semipro football, Robinson decided to join the army after the attack on Pearl Harbor. While in the army he overcame severe racial discrimination in rising to second lieutenant and receiving an honorable discharge in 1944. After the end of the war, Robinson found himself without a college degree and in need of a job. Fortuitously, through an army buddy he received a tryout with the famed Kansas City Monarchs* of the Negro Leagues* and made the team in 1945. While with the Monarchs, Robinson was signed to a contract by Branch Rickey, general manager of the Brooklyn Dodgers, who had been hired to build the team into a pennant contender. Robinson possessed the personal fortitude, determination, and talent needed to weather the insults, jeering, race baiting, and physical threats that he would soon face in the difficult road ahead. In 1946 Robinson made his debut with triple-A Montreal Royals, won the International League batting title with a .349 average, and led his team to victory in the Little World Series. The following year he had the greatest impact of any player on the game of baseball and perhaps on the history of any sport when as a Dodger he became the first modern black player to play in the major leagues. Soon other African Americans followed him to the majors in both leagues. Robinson had a remarkable ten-year career. He received the first Rookie of the Year award in 1947 and was named the National League's Most Valuable Player two years later. He played in six consecutive All-Star Games from 1949 to 1954, set a National League record for double plays by a second baseman in 1950, and led the Dodgers to six National League pennants and one World series championship in 1955. He compiled a .311 lifetime batting average and set a major league record by stealing home nineteen times. In his first year of eligibility he was elected to the National Baseball Hall of Fame in 1962. Robinson broke new ground off the field as well as on it. In 1952 he became the first African American executive for a television or radio station. Rather than being traded to the New York Giants in late 1956, he chose instead to retire and became a vice president of personnel with the Chock Full O'Nuts Coffee chain. Once retired, Robinson sought other ways to bring about racial justice and equality that he had so nobly advanced on the baseball diamond. During the Civil Rights movement of the 1960s he promoted racial change by working with James Farmer of the Congress on Racial Equality and with Martin Luther King, Jr., and the Southern Christian Leadership Conference. For much of the 1960s he served on the Board of Directors of the National Association for the Advancement of Colored People (NAACP) and in 1964 helped established the Freedom National Bank, which until its closing in 1990 remained the only African American-owned and -operated bank in New York state. In politics, Robinson also worked for Nelson Rockefeller's presidential campaign in 1964 and later became special assistant of community affairs to the governor and state commissioner of boxing in New York.

SELECTED BIBLIOGRAPHY: Maury Allen, *Jackie Robinson: A Life Remembered* (1987); Harvey Frommer, *Rickey and Robinson: The Men Who Broke Baseball's Color Barrier* (1982); Jackie Robinson, *Baseball Has Done It* (1964); Jackie Robinson and Alfred Duckett, *I Never Had It Made: An Autobiography* (1972; reprint 1995); Rachel Robinson, with Lee Daniels, *Jackie Robinson: An Intimate Portrait* (1996); Jules Tygiel, *Baseball's Great Experiment: Jackie Robinson and His Legacy* (expanded ed., 1997).

Larry K. Menna

ROBINSON, SUGAR RAY (3 May 1921, Detroit–12 April 1989, Los Angeles). A world-champion African American boxer, he was born Walker Smith, Jr. His father worked at a construction company by day and held other jobs at night. His mother (Leila Hurst Smith) was a chambermaid and seamstress. He attended the Balch Grammar School in Detroit before his family moved to New York City. From a very early age his idol was the "Brown Bomber"—Joe Louis.* He began his professional career as a pugilist at fifteen. By borrowing a boxing identification card from a Detroit boxer called Ray Robinson, he was able to convince authorities that he was "of age" to fight for pay. More importantly, the moniker "Sugar" Ray Robinson was to become a perfect soubriquet for a boxer whom many view as the best middleweight of all time. A deliberate and disciplined amateur fighter, he won Golden Gloves titles in 1939 and 1940. After turning professional in 1940, he won his first forty bouts before losing to the indestructible Jake LaMotta* in February 1943. On 20 December 1946 Robinson won the first of his six world titles with a fifteen-round decision over Tommy Bell for the world welterweight title. By 1947 Robinson boxed at the middleweight level. His 14 February 1951 rematch with LaMotta had press headlines proclaiming "the St. Valentine's Day Massacre." A year later Robinson succumbed to heat exhaustion and battle fatigue in New York's Yankee Stadium in a surprise upset loss to Joey Maxim. At the end of 1952 Robinson retired but returned in 1955 to regain the world middleweight title by knocking out Bobo Olson. Throughout the late 1950s he retained, lost, and regained his middleweight crown several times, fighting Olson, Gene Fullmer, Carmen Basilio, and other contenders. He retired at the age of forty-four at the end of 1965. His career record shows 174 wins, nineteen losses, six draws, and two no-contests. After his retirement Robinson had some acting roles, owned a Harlem nightclub, and set up the Sugar Ray Robinson Youth Foundation. During his final years he suffered from Alzheimer's disease, heart problems, and diabetes. He was inducted into the International Boxing Hall of Fame in 1990.

SELECTED BIBLIOGRAPHY: R. Hickock, *The Encyclopedia of North American Sports History* (1992); *New York Times*, 13 September 1951, 1, 40 and 26 March 1958, 1, 45; John Robertson, "Sugar Ray Robinson," in David L. Porter, ed., *African-American Sports Greats* (1995); Sugar Ray Robinson, with Dave Anderson, *Sugar Ray: The Sugar Ray Robinson Story* (1969).

Scott A.G.M. Crawford

ROCKNE, KNUTE KENNETH (4 March 1888, Voss, Norway–31 March 1931, Bazaar, KS). A football player and coach of Norwegian descent, he was the son of Lars and Martha Rockne. His father, a machinist and carriage maker, won first prize with an exhibit at the Columbia Exposition in Chicago in 1893. He sent for his family, and the Rocknes settled in Chicago. Rockne attended school in Chicago, then worked five years as a postal clerk, saving money for college. He enrolled at Notre Dame in 1910 as a twenty-two-year-old freshman. He played end on the football team and was named to Walter Camp's third All-America team in 1913. He was captain of the football team, a pole vaulter on the track team, editor of the school yearbook, and an honor student with a 92.5 point scholastic average. He majored in chemistry, and he played the flute in the band. Upon his graduation Notre Dame hired him as chemistry instructor and assistant coach. He became head coach in 1918, and his leadership, charisma, and eloquent speaking ability made him the most famous name in American football history. In his thirteen years, 1918–1930, Notre Dame won 105 games, lost twelve, and tied five. His winning percentage, .881, is the highest on record. In five of his years—1919, 1920, 1924, 1929, 1930—Notre Dame had an undefeated record. His coaching technique was so powerful that some experts said he was ten years ahead of the game. In 1934, three years after his death, eighteen of his former players were head coaches at major schools, using the Rockne doctrine. Rockne's death in a plane crash was universally mourned. He was elected to the College Football Hall of Fame as a charter member in 1951.

SELECTED BIBLIOGRAPHY: Jerry Brondfield, *Rockne* (1976); Arthur Daley, *Knute Rockne* (1960); Robert Quackenbush and Mike Bynum, *Knute Rockne* (1988); Michael R. Steele, *Knute Rockne: A Bio-Bibliography* (1983); Francis Wallace, *Knute Rockne* (1960).

Pat Harmon

RODEO. Despite the popular belief that rodeo originated in informal contests among Anglo cowboys in the "Wild West" of the late 1800s, in truth it is a product of the cultural interaction of Hispanics, Anglos, Native American Indians, and African Americans. Contrary to the mythology of the American West, rodeo evolved from a variety of equestrian pastimes of Spanish and Mexican peoples in North America prior to 1850. There is also circumstantial evidence that Native American equestrian and hunting practices and customs may have influenced both Anglo and Hispanic cattlemen as they developed their contests during the late 1800s. Indians and African Americans were active participants during rodeo's formative years, and both groups sustained their role throughout the twentieth century.

Rodeo's main events include timed competitions in steer wrestling, calf roping, and barrel racing and also rough stock (bull and wild bronc)-riding. Bronc-riding contests and cowboy tournaments date from 1869 in the United States and became regular features of western life during the 1880s. Buffalo Bill Cody's Wild West shows of that decade included the first professional rodeo exhibitions, but the sport did not achieve a modern national organization until the 1930s.

The antecedents of rodeo (the word derives from a Spanish term for roundup) may be found in the *charreadas* of the Spanish empire in the New World, where Hispanic *charros* and *vacqueros* performed daring feats of riding horses and bulls, roping cattle, and wrestling with steers. After Mexico secured its independence from Spain in 1821, immigrants from the United States moved into that new nation's provinces of Texas and California. The newcomers worked in the cattle industry with the Hispanic residents and borrowed elements of their culture, including some of their equestrian pastimes. After the American victory in the Mexican War of 1846–48 and the annexation of the northern provinces of Mexico, the Anglos took control of cattle ranching. They also developed their roping and riding skills. Cody is credited with popularizing rodeo as a professional and commercial sport when he staged his first Wild West show in North Platte, Nebraska, on the Fourth of July, 1882. Between 1883 and 1916 Cody's show and many imitators toured North America and Europe, featuring buffalo hunts, Indian dances, mock attacks on stage coaches, Pony Express demonstrations, and "Cowboy Fun" exhibitions of acrobatic horseback and steer riding. Prominent in the latter events were Hispanic *vacqueros*, including superstar Antonio Esquivel from San Antonio. The most celebrated Hispanic performer in these shows was Vincente Oropeza, who billed himself as the "Premier 'Charro Mexicano' of the World." Oropeza introduced and popularized trick and fancy roping in the United States. In 1893 he became the star of Cody's new show, "Mexicans from Old Mexico," in which he concluded his act by spelling his name (one letter at a time) with the spinning rope. More recently, Mexican Americans also sponsored traditional Mexican-style *charreadas*. These festivals are team competitions in ten events, nine of which are for men only. These include horsemanship, bull tripping and riding, team roping, and bronc riding. In the women's event contestants engage in a form of sidesaddle team riding drill and are judged on general appearance, timing, and their ability to handle their mounts.

Native American Indians have contributed much to the development of rodeo in the United States through early influences and prominent performers. Although there is no concrete proof of a direct link between ancient Plains Indians sporting traditions and the first rodeos, there are striking similarities. Anthropologist Ian Dyck has noted these in the indigenous peoples' cattle-herding skills, human-bison-cattle contests, horse skills, human and horse versus bison-cattle contests, races, annual sporting gatherings, parades and finery, the use of charms, and the presence of clowns. Dyck concludes that it is likely that there was substantial cultural borrowing between western cowboys and Indians, with at least some of the initial transfer coming from Indians to cowboys.

After 1880 Indians performed at early Wild West shows and rodeos throughout North America. They competed in events reserved only for those who camped on the grounds, but many also entered other challenges. Tom Three Persons, Pete Bruised, Jim Wells, Fred Gladstone, Jim Gladstone, and Bud Longbrake have won championships in the United States and Canada. More recently, the All Indian Rodeo Cowboys Association sponsors competitions in ten regions across North America, while indigenous tribes participate in pageants and dances at shows held by the Professional Rodeo Cowboys Association (PRCA). At some of these festivals relay races with Indians riding horses bareback entertain audiences.

African Americans were also active in the early history of rodeo, as black cowboys showed off the skills they learned in the West of the late 1800s. Bill Pickett is credited with the invention of bulldogging or steer wrestling around 1900, while Jesse Stahl earned fame as a saddle bronc rider. Both have been elected to the Cowboy Hall of Fame in Oklahoma City. Although the Rodeo Cowboys Association (now the PRCA) never formally excluded blacks, prior to the 1960s racism and the lack of blacks among the professionals effectively kept them out of white competitions. During the 1940s and the 1950s African Americans formed the Southwestern Colored Cowboys Association, which provided a minor league for aspiring black contestants. With the advent of integration during the 1960s Myrtis Dightman became a contender for national honors as a bull rider. Often compared to Jackie Robinson,* in 1966 Dightman became the first black man to qualify for the National Finals Rodeo. In 1982 Charles Sampson became the first black cowboy to win a world championship, earning this distinction in the bull-riding event. Fred Whitfield took world titles in calf roping in 1991 and 1995. Recently, there have been several black cowboy organizations. During the late 1990s the Black World Championship Rodeo staged competitions in Harlem and Brooklyn in New York City, as well as a dozen other cities across the country.

Although at the end of the twentieth century Hispanics, Native American Indians, and African Americans collectively constituted a minority in the ranks of professional rodeo contestants, their continuing presence testified to the contribution of each group in the history of the sport in the United States. With Hispanic and Native American roots and a tradition shaped by Anglo and black western cowboys, rodeo is a truly hybrid, multicultural, American sport.

SELECTED BIBLIOGRAPHY: Ian Dyck, "Does Rodeo Have Roots in Ancient Indian Traditions?" *Plains Anthropologist* 41 (August 1996): 205–219; Gavin Ehringer, "Rodeo Arena: Saluting Black Cowboys," *Western Horseman* 58 (July 1993): 84–88; James F. Hoy, "The Origins and Originality of Rodeo," *Journal of the West* 18 (July 1978): 17–33; Mary Lou LeCompte, "The Hispanic Influence on the History of Rodeo, 1823–1922," *Journal of Sport History* 12 (Spring 1985): 21–38; Andy Newman, "Deep in the Heart of Brooklyn, Cowboys and Kosher Food," *New York Times*, 1 September 1997, B-1, 3; Wayne S. Wooden and Gavin Ehringer, *Rodeo in America* (1996).

George B. Kirsch

RODRIGUEZ, JUAN ("Chi Chi") (23 October 1935, Rio Piedras, PR–). A golfer born to a poor family in Puerto Rico, he is the son of Juan Rodriguez, a plantation worker, and Modesta Vila Rodriguez. Rodriguez began caddying at age six and learned his golf while working. Financial difficulties forced him to drop out of República de Colombia High School in San Juan when he was in the eleventh grade. As a professional golfer he entered the Professional Golfers' Association (PGA) Tour in 1960, won eight regular tour events, and earned more than $1 million. He joined the Senior PGA Tour in 1985 and captured twenty-two senior titles by the late 1990s, when his career earnings surpassed $6 million. In 1979 Rodriguez helped establish the Chi Chi Rodriguez Youth Foundation in Clearwater, Florida, as a school to serve disadvantaged inner-city children, in part through the medium of training in golf and other sports. Rodriguez was selected as the winner of Florida's 1997 Hispanic Achievement Award.

SELECTED BIBLIOGRAPHY: *Christian Science Monitor*, 15 May 1965, 14; Emilio E. Huyke, "Golf," *Colecciones Puertorriquenes, Los Deportes en Puerto Rico* (1968); Dan Jenkins, "Little Chi Chi's Other Side," *Sports Illustrated* 21 (10 August 1964): 34; Tomás Sarramía, "Chi Chi Rodriguez," *Nuestra Gente* (1993).

Richard V. McGehee

ROSEN, ALBERT LEONARD ("Al," "Flip") (29 February 1924, Spartanburg, SC–). A baseball player and executive, he is the son of Louis and Rose (Levine) Rosen. He was raised in Miami, Florida, by his mother and maternal grandmother, Gertrude Levine, after his parents' divorce. As a Jew who grew up in a Gentile neighborhood, he experienced anti-Semitism and learned to retaliate by becoming an accomplished boxer. He toyed with semipro softball throughout his teens and settled into baseball after high school. Rosen attended the University of Miami and the University of Florida prior to joining the navy during World War II. He returned to college to receive his degree from the University of Miami in business management in 1947. Immediately after graduating, he entered baseball with the Cleveland Indians farm team in Thomasville, North Carolina. Rosen joined the Indians in Cleveland in 1950. He set an American League (AL) rookie record with thirty-seven home runs in his freshman year. During his ten-year career with the Indians, Rosen was named to the AL All-Star Team four times. He earned a reputation as a tough competitor; he challenged all persons who taunted him for his Jewish heritage. Rosen ended his playing career in 1956 after a disappointing season the previous year. His career lifetime record included a batting average of .285, 192 home runs, and 717 runs batted in (RBIs). In 1978, George Steinbrenner hired Rosen as president of the New York Yankees. He then went on to work with the Houston Astros as general manager from 1980 through 1985 until the San Francisco Giants owner, Bob Lurie, took him on as president and general manager. Rosen enjoyed success in San Francisco when the Giants appeared in the 1987 National League Championship Series and the 1989 World Series.

SELECTED BIBLIOGRAPHY: Harry T. Paxton, "That Clouting Kid from Cleveland," *Saturday Evening Post* (11 August 1951): 25, 86–88; David L. Porter, "Al Rosen," in *Biographical Dictionary of American Sports: Baseball, 1989–1992 Supplement* (1992); Roger Kahn, "The Jewish Education of Al Rosen," *Cleveland Magazine* (n.d.), in Al Rosen file, Baseball Hall of Fame Library.

Jill E. Renwick

ROSENBLOOM, MAXIE (6 September 1904, Leonard's Bridge, CT–6 March 1976, South Pasadena, CA). A champion prizefighter, nightclub entertainer, and Hollywood actor, at the age of three he moved with his family to the heavily Jewish neighborhood of Manhattan's Lower East Side. As a boy he dropped out of school in the fifth grade and spent some time in a reformatory. Beginning his professional career in 1923 as a middleweight, he gained increasing national recognition with a string of victories culminating in a defeat of Jimmy Slattery in 1928 for a share of the light-heavyweight title. Rosenbloom earned the undisputed crown in that weight class with a victory over Lou Scozza in 1930 and retained that title until he lost a controversial decision to Bob Olin in 1934. Known as a skilled defensive boxer, his style of hitting mostly with open gloves earned him the nickname "Slapsie Maxie." Although pugilistic purists were critical of his technique, he compiled a career record of 210 wins, thirty-eight losses, and fifty-one draws or no decisions. His victory in 1933 over Adolph Heuser, Germany's light-heavyweight champion, probably influenced the new Nazi regime's decision to bar German athletes from competing against Jewish opponents, in order to avoid further embarrassing losses to supposed inferior races. After his retirement in 1939 he remained a celebrity as a popular comedian, often paired with Max Baer* in nightclub routines, and as a supporting actor in numerous films in which he portrayed punch-drunk fighters and thugs. He was inducted into the International Boxing Hall of Fame in 1993.

SELECTED BIBLIOGRAPHY: Francis Albertani, "Maxie Rosenbloom, Greatest Light Heavyweight Hebrew Prospect since Days of Battling Levinsky," *The Ring* 5 (September 1926): 16–17; Ted Carroll, "The Merry Madcaps," *The Ring* 26 (May 1947): 28–29, 36; Nat Fleischer, "The Fighter Who Doesn't Care," *The Ring* 9 (October 1930): 5, 49; C. Gillespie, "Maxie Leads 'Em All," *The Ring* 11 (June 1932): 6; Chris Greyvenstein, "Fists of Fame," *South African Boxing World* (June 1986): 8–10; *New York Times*, 8 March 1976, 28; Red Smith, "Slapsie Maxie: Exit Laughing," *New York Times*, 14 March 1976; Sam Taub, "Maxie Rosenbloom, Ring Comic, Dies at 72," *The Ring* (June 1976): 32–33, 56.

George B. Kirsch

ROSS, BARNEY (23 December 1909, New York City–18 January 1967, Chicago. The son of a Jewish Talmudic scholar and grocer, Isidore Rosofsky, an immigrant from Brest-Litovsk, Barnet David Rosofsky turned away from religious studies at the age of fifteen upon finding his father murdered in his grocery store on Maxwell Street in Chicago. He left Joseph Medill High School and drifted into street gangs, soon working as an errand boy for Al Capone, who apparently refused to let him into the mob because he thought it was inappropriate for a rabbi's son. Turning to boxing, he changed his name to Barney Ross so his mother (Sarah Rosofsky) would not find out he was dishonoring his father's memory by fighting. In 1929 he won the National Golden Gloves featherweight championship. Wearing a Jewish star on his trunks, he was often matched against Irish and Italian opponents in Chicago and became a popular ethnic symbol among Jewish fans. In 1933 he defeated Tony Canzoneri to gain both the world lightweight and junior welterweight titles. The following year Ross won the welterweight crown from Jimmy McLarnin, lost it back to him, and in 1935 regained the title. He ultimately lost it in 1938 to Henry Armstrong.* Ross, with his mother (and his rabbi), came to regard his success in the boxing ring as a way of combating Hitler and Nazi anti-Semitism. He donated much of his winnings in the ring to Jewish charities; he also developed a taste for the life of a playboy, gambling away what was left. In 1942, Ross joined the marines and won the Silver Star at Guadalcanal. His war injuries led to a $500-a-week morphine addiction; his triumph over drugs was the basis of the 1957 movie, *Monkey on My Back*. His life was also the subject of *Body and Soul* (1947).

SELECTED BIBLIOGRAPHY: Ken Blady, *The Jewish Boxers' Hall of Fame* (1988); Peter Levine, *Ellis Island to Ebbets Field: Sport and the American Jewish Experience* (1992); Steven A. Riess, "A Fighting Chance: The Jewish-American Boxing Experience, 1890–1940," *American Jewish History* 74 (1985): 223–254; Barney Ross and Martin Abrahamson, *No Man Stands Alone: The True Story of Barney Ross* (1957); "Ross, Ring Champion and War Hero, Is Dead," *New York Times*, 19 January 1967, 31.

Marc Singer

RUDOLPH, WILMA GLODEAN (23 June 1940, St. Bethlehem, TN–12 November 1994, Nashville, TN). An African American track athete, she was raised in rural Clarkesville, Tennessee, by railroad porter Ed Rudolph and his second wife, Blanche, a domestic worker. A 1963 graduate of Tennessee State University with a degree in elementary education, Rudolph was the first American woman to win three Olympic gold medals. As a child Rudolph contracted double pneumonia, scarlet fever, and polio, the sum of which left her weak with a paralyzed left leg. By age thirteen, however, Rudolph was starring on the Burt High School basketball team, thanks to medical treatments and massages performed by her mother and siblings. At the age of sixteen, she won a bronze medal in the 4×100-meter relay at the 1956 Olympics in Melbourne, Australia. In the 1960 Rome Olympics, she earned gold in the 100- and 200-meter dashes and joined her famed Tennessee State Tigerbelle teammates Barbara Jones, Lucinda Williams, and Martha Hudson to win the 4×100-meter relay. Rudolph was named the Associated Press Female Athlete of the Year in 1960 and 1961 and won the prestigious Sullivan Award as the top amateur athlete in 1961. In 1974 she was elected to the U.S. Track and Field Hall of Fame. After retiring from competition in 1962, Rudolph served as a teacher, NBC radio show cohost, goodwill ambassador to French West Africa, and coach at DePauw University in Greencastle, Indiana. Her autobiography, *Wilma*, was made into a television movie in 1977. In 1981 she started the nonprofit Wilma Rudolph Foundation to assist children. She succumbed to brain cancer at the age of fifty-four in 1994.

SELECTED BIBLIOGRAPHY: Tom Biracree, *Wilma Rudolph* (1988); Susan Reed and Jane Sanderson, "Born to Win," *People Magazine* 22 (1994): 62.

Mary G. McDonald

RUGBY. Rugby union has always been an ethnic game in the United States. Eclipsed by its homegrown cousin, American football, the English-born running-and-tackling sport has rarely attracted youngsters or the top-grade athletes, who take up the more popular gridiron game, basketball, or baseball. Thus, immigrant and expatriate players who learned to play rugby at an earlier age have been disproportionately influential. Similarly, because rugby is not played universally but rather in hotbeds and outposts, British-influenced college campuses and immigrant/expatriate communities have been very important in its propagation. In the 1980s and 1990s, however, American rugby has been newly infused with the spirit of Polynesian players, both as national-class players and as entirely ethnic teams.

Rugby arrived in the United States via the college campus, where Ivy League students copied nascent football games played by their British counterparts. The first recorded match of rugby union in North America was an 1876 intercollegiate contest between Harvard and McGill of Montreal, Canada. Soon the game spread to the West Coast's more distinguished schools, such as Stanford and California, where it was played fairly skillfully with the help of British, Irish, and sometimes Antipodean and South African athletes. When in the early twentieth century football was banned for a time on college campuses, rugby flourished; but during World War I its popularity waned because it was branded a "foreign" game. The Great Depression and World War II also acted as brakes on development, and professionalism remained out of the question as rugby's Victorian ethics meant the game remained staunchly amateur.

In 1920 and 1924 self-organized groups of college-age players represented the United States at the Olympic Games and managed to win gold medals (mostly because the world's powers did not enter teams). But while some of American rugby's regional authorities and local clubs date back to this time, the game did not establish a national governing body until 1975, meaning the U.S. rugby community didn't really develop an "American character" except as a counterculture activity. That image flourished in the 1960s and 1970s, when the game resumed growing, and it continues to find ready acceptance.

Meanwhile, players and coaches from the British Commonwealth exercised considerable influence, sometimes strictly because their background suggested knowledge of the game. British and Irish figures tended to be more prevalent on the eastern seaboard; New Zealanders, Australians, and South Africans were more important on the Pacific Coast; while the hinterlands rarely saw the "accents." Many were player-coaches, while others had a role in the actual foundation of club and college sides. Then, too, as rugby has a worldwide tradition of traveling abroad, those clubs that toured the United States were British or Antipodean, and those that went overseas tended to go to Britain or New Zealand.

One example is Massachusetts' Williams College, where an Englishman and a few students borrowed heavily in forming their club's crest. One of the founders of the Williams club wrote: "The claret-and-gold bars were the colors of the club, borrowed from . . . one of P. Pearson's old clubs in England. The Tudor rose is the logo for the English Rugby Union, and the red dagger and cross are the coat-of-arms for the city of London, where we played most of our matches [on a 1962 tour]." More evidence can be found in the high number of American teams called "Old Blue" or "Kansas City Blues" or another variation, typically referring to a local alma mater but in fact harking back to Oxford and Cambridge Universities, where those who represent the school in athletics are said to have won their "blue."

British-born Americans have also contributed meaningfully on a national level. For example, Keith Seaber's résumé includes a founding role in the United States of America Rugby Football Union (USARFU) and service as secretary and vice president. (The document that immediately preceded the USARFU's constitution is called the "Cambridge Agreement," after the English university town where an organizational meeting was held.) Later, English-born Ian Nixon represented the United States as its top referee and served two terms as president.

The 1975 birth of the USARFU brought about a sanctioned national team, and competition for roster places began to engender some nativism among those who thought the U.S. national team should feature "Americans." Others replied that those living in the United States long enough to meet international eligibility rules were in effect first-generation Americans and thus entitled to represent the United States.

At the same time, Polynesians began to enter the game on the West Coast and as Mormon converts living in Utah, representing a new kind of foreign influence and raising overtly racist stereotypes. While Commonwealth types often came to America in ones and twos and frequently worked in professional occupations, Tongans and Samoans tended to settle in groups and began as members of the working class. Polynesians made rugby a "family" game in that groups of relatives' families would often come to watch the day's activities. However, for many years Tongans in particular also conducted their own competitive leagues, outside USARFU's aegis. Part of the reason owes to American rugby's historic disorganization and part to the fact that American rugby typically requires players to foot the bill, accentuating the Polynesians' comparatively poor economic status and shutting the door on their ability to participate in national competitions. (The last also explains why black participation has been minimal.) However, as Polynesian players have been internationally regarded as explosive and violent, many American authorities were not anxious to extend their purview. Sporadic incidents of mass violence involving Polynesian clubs and spectators, sometimes when playing white teams and sometimes among themselves, cropped up in the 1980s and 1990s, feeding these stereotypes.

By the late 1990s resentment of the Commonwealth types was withering—although for purposes of encouraging native participation, the USARFU retained a rule limiting the number of noncitizens in a club side's starting fifteen. But Polynesian players remained suspect, so much so that America's leading rugby periodical continued to publish thinly disguised racist editorials. But as with all sports, there was no arguing with game results, and heavily Polynesian teams from California such as San Mateo did well in nationwide competitions, winning several titles. Surpassing earlier club-side greats like Roy Helu, players like Tongan-born Soane "Vuka" Tau and Vaea Anitoni,* the all-time leading try-scorer for the U.S. national side, earned international distinction and the U.S. rugby community's respect.

In the late 1990s, the "browning" of American rugby intersected with the coming of commercial management. International rugby's belated 1995 acceptance of professionalism—payment of players and coaches—meant that leading teams began borrowing heavily from established American sports, creating not only better organization for rugby's 40,000 participants but also a climate where opportunity costs were less steep. The game seemed on an upward curve, with Antipodeans and Polynesians helping to lead the way.

SELECTED BIBLIOGRAPHY: Eric Dunning and Kenneth Sheard, *Barbarians, Gentlemen, and Players: A Sociological Study of the Development of Rugby Football* (1979); Ed Hagerty, ed., *Rugby Magazine* (1976–); Paul Hogan, ed., *An Informal History of the Williams Rugby Football Club, 1959–1993* (unpublished, 1993); John Nauright and Timothy J. L. Chandler, eds., *Making Men: Rugby and Masculine Identity* (1996); John Talbot Powell, *Inside Rugby: The Team Game* (1976).

Kurt Oeler

RUSSELL, WILLIAM ("Bill") (12 February 1934, Monroe, LA–). An African American basketball player, he is the son of Charles and Katie Russell. At the age of five he moved with his family to Oakland, California, as his parents relocated to seek greater opportunity in a more racially tolerant environment. His mother died shortly thereafter. Although Russell's basketball skills developed slowly during his adolescence, by the time he graduated from McClymonds High School he was talented enough to earn a basketball scholarship to the University of San Francisco. During his final two years there he matured into a dominant center. He and his teammate K. C. Jones (a guard) led the Dons to fifty-five consecutive victories and two National Collegiate Athletic Association (NCAA) championships in 1955 and 1956. Before turning professional, he and Jones joined the 1956 U.S. Olympic basketball team, leading the squad to a gold medal in Melbourne, Australia. His participation in that Olympics was significant because there had been no black players on the Olympic quintet that won the gold medal at the 1952 games in Helsinki, Finland. Later in 1956 he signed a contract with the Boston Celtics, playing under coach Arnold "Red" Auerbach.* His thirteen-year pro career featured eleven National Basketball Association (NBA) titles, including eight in a row (1959–66), and five NBA Most Valuable Player awards (1958, 1961–63, 1965). Both in college and in the NBA his rebounding, defensive, and shot-blocking skills revolutionized basketball. During the 1960s he engaged in an intense court rivalry with Wilt Chamberlain,* winning the NBA final series in six out of the seven occasions when the two dominant centers faced each other. During his final two seasons (1967–69) Russell was the player-coach of the Celtics, becoming the first black man to manage an NBA team. After his retirement as a player he also coached the Seattle Supersonics and the Sacramento Kings and worked as a television sportscaster. Although as a young athlete he had expressed pride in representing his country at the 1956 Olympics, in the 1960s and 1970s he became very critical of American racial policies and practices. He personally objected to his election to the Naismith Memorial Basketball Hall of Fame in 1974; in his memoirs he expressed his desire "to separate myself from the star's ideas about fans and fans' ideas about stars."

SELECTED BIBLIOGRAPHY: Arthur R. Ashe, Jr., *A Hard Road to Glory: A History of the African-American Athlete since 1946*, vol. 3 (1988); John Capouya, "Bill Russell, Reconsidered," *Sport* 79 (January 1988): 33–38; Bill Russell, with Taylor Branch, *Second Wind: The Memoirs of an Opinionated Man* (1979); Bill Russell and William McSweeney, *Go Up for Glory* (1966); Edna Rust and Art Rust, Jr., *Art Rust's Illustrated History of the Black Athlete* (1985).

George B. Kirsch

RUTH, GEORGE HERMAN ("Babe")

RUTH, GEORGE HERMAN ("Babe") (6 February 1895, Baltimore–16 August 1948, New York City). A baseball player, he was of German descent, the son of George Herman Ruth, a driver and gripman on a cable car, later a lightning rod salesman and installer. His mother, Kate, was the daughter of German-born Catholics named Shamberger, though she had Americanized the name to Shamberg. For stealing money at a local saloon in 1902 Babe Ruth was sent to St. Mary's Industrial School for Boys in Baltimore, to which institution the court had committed him until the age of twenty-one. In and out of reform school over the next dozen years, Babe never enjoyed a home life, and thus his eight years with the Xaverian Brothers gave rise to the legend that Babe was an orphan. It is true that his mother died in 1910, when Ruth was eight, and his father failed to connect with the youth, with the result that the religious brothers became his surrogate parents. At St. Mary's, as nationally, baseball was the

great American pastime. Rough-and-tumble Babe loved it and thoroughly out-
played all other members of the forty-three intramural St. Mary's teams, made
up of youngsters from each dormitory, floor, and manual workshop. At the age
of seventeen Ruth topped everyone at the school, playing star roles on the
mound, at bat, as catcher, and at third base. At the age of eighteen Ruth signed
a contract with the Baltimore Orioles to earn $600 for the six-month season.
Thus began a career that catapulted him to fame, first with the Boston Red Sox.
In 1916 Ruth made history by pitching the longest-ever World Series game
(fourteen innings) against Brooklyn. By 1920 Babe was playing for the Yankees
with a $52,000 annual contract and a performance record that gained him a hold
on the baseball public so gripping that schoolboys and sports enthusiasts to this
day memorialize him as baseball's greatest legend. Helping create the myth were
sportswriters who gave Ruth names like the "Bambino," the "Sultan of Swat,"
the "King of Clout," the "Behemoth of Bust." Whenever Ruth was in the lineup,
he added fuel to the popularity fires as well as to the owners' coffers, for with
Babe in the lineup, tickets sales soared at Yankee Stadium, "the house that Ruth
built." During the Great Depression Babe's salary dipped, declining until in 1935
at $35,000 a year he retired to take miscellaneous administrative and honorary
positions. During World War II he made many personal appearances on behalf
of the war effort. The Babe led an undisciplined life until his death. Lying in
state in Yankee Stadium, 75,000 people filed past his coffin, and on 19 August
1948 Cardinal Spellman conducted his funeral service at St. Patrick's Cathedral.
German Americans welcomed the chance to recall and to imbibe the limelight
that his ancestry had cast over them in the post–World War II recovery period.

SELECTED BIBLIOGRAPHY: Robert Creamer, *Babe: The Legend Comes to Life*
(1974); Anna Rothe, ed., *Current Biography* (1944); Marshal Smelser, *The Life That
Ruth Built* (1975); Ken Sobol, *Babe Ruth and the American Dream* (1974); Kal Wagenheim, *Babe Ruth: His Life and Legend* (1974).

La Vern J. Rippley

S

SAMUELSON, JOAN BENOIT (16 March 1957, Cape Elizabeth, ME–).
A long-distance runner, she is the daughter of Andre and Nancy Benoit of
Franco-American descent. Both of her parents were talented athletes. Her father
owned a small chain of dress shops. Both she and her father are Bowdoin
College graduates, and her mother has an undergraduate degree from the College
of William and Mary. A talented all-around athete, Benoit began running more
steadily in her senior year of high school as rehabilitation for a broken leg she
sustained from her favorite sport of skiing. In her college junior year she spent
three semesters away from Bowdoin at North Carolina State University on an
athletic scholarship to train at a higher level. In 1979, a virtual unknown in the
sport, she won the Boston Marathon in 2:35:15. One of her running goals was
to break the elusive 2:20 barrier, which she nearly accomplished in the Chicago
Marathon in 1983 with a time of 2:21:21. Benoit focused her training on competing in the Olympic Games and won the 1984 Olympic Trials (2:31:04) in
Olympia, Washington, despite suffering a knee injury and undergoing arthro-
scopic surgery just seventeen days earlier. Benoit's victory in the 1984 Olympic
Games at Los Angeles (the first women's marathon) and her prowess in the
sport dramatically demonstrated that women were capable of running long-
distance events. During the late 1990s she continued to compete in masters
distance events.

SELECTED BIBLIOGRAPHY: Joan Benoit, *Running Tide* (1987); Philip Hersh, "Benoit
Samuelson Makes Run for Atlanta at 38," *Chicago Tribune*, 30 January 1996, sec. 4, p.
1, c. 1; Joan Samuelson, *Running for Women* (1995); Janet Woolum, *Outstanding Women
Athletes* (1992).

Shawn Ladda

SAPERSTEIN, ABRAHAM M. (4 July 1902, London, England–15 March
1966, Chicago). A basketball coach and manager of the Harlem Globetrotters,*

he was the son of Louis and Anna Saperstein. His father was a tailor; his parents were Jews who migrated from Poland to England shortly after their marriage. In 1905 the family moved to Chicago, where Saperstein graduated from Lakeview High School in 1916, earning fifteen varsity letters in basketball, baseball, track, and wrestling. He attended the University of Illinois in 1922–23 but did not earn a degree. He began coaching a Negro American Legion basketball team, the Savoy Big Five, in 1925. In 1927 he changed the team's name to the Harlem Globetrotters and took them on a barnstorming tour to raise money. Saperstein served as owner, coach, and team chauffeur in its original days. With only five players on the team, Saperstein, a 5' 3" Jew, often found himself forced to play as a substitute in some games in the team's first season. The team achieved great success, both early on as a "serious" team and later as the more lighthearted clownish team that became legendary. When Saperstein died in 1966, the team he created was worth more than $3 million. Saperstein was one of the first to treat blacks as equals, and his team also served as a showcase for what blacks could do to the sport. Saperstein is remembered as one of basketball's goodwill ambassadors, creating and running a team that brought out the joy and lighter side of the sport and at the same time breaking down racial barriers. Saperstein was inducted into the Naismith Memorial Basketball Hall of Fame in 1970.

SELECTED BIBLIOGRAPHY: *Harlem Globetrotters 1976 50th Anniversary Issue* (1975); Peter Levine, *Ellis Island to Ebbets Field* (1992); Robert W. Peterson, *Cages to Jumpshots: Pro Basketball's Early Years* (1990); Josh Wilker, *The Harlem Globetrotters* (1997); Abraham Saperstein file, Naismith Memorial Basketball Hall of Fame.

Zachary Davis

SARAZEN, EUGENE (27 February 1902, Harrison, NY–13 May 1999, Naples, FL). A golfer who was born Eugenio Saraceni, he quit grade school, caddied in local clubs, and, when he contracted pneumonia, turned to professional golf, a career that spanned more than half a century. His father had abandoned priesthood studies in Italy, migrated to the United States, became a carpenter, and opposed Gene's golf career. A squat 5'6", Sarazen was a fierce competitor who generated great power in his strokes. He achieved greatness as a golfer in the 1920s and 1930s, when the United States was overtaking British leadership. In 1922 he made his mark at age twenty by winning the U.S. Open in Skokie, Illinois, and the Professional Golfers' Association (PGA) Championship. He went on to win another U.S. Open ten years later and two more PGAs in 1923 and 1933. His other major championships were the 1932 British Open, 1935 Masters, and 1954 and 1958 PGA Seniors. He was on the Ryder Cup teams that won six championships (1927, 1929, 1931, 1933, 1935, 1937), among other major victories. Sarazen was the first player to win all four major golf tournaments—the grand slam. This durable athlete is a member of the PGA Hall of Fame and the PGA/World Golf Hall of Fame. He has designed golf courses and developed the popular sand wedge. He used his golf expertise in television as a commentator on Shell's film series *The Wonderful World of Golf*.

SELECTED BIBLIOGRAPHY: Bill Delaney, "Gene Sarazen," *Great Athletes—The Twentieth Century* (1992); Jerry Potter, "Sarazen Will Celebrate 90th Birthday on Course," *USA Today*, 27 February 1992, B-2; Gene Sarazen and Herbert Warren Wind, *Thirty Years of Championship Golf* (1950); Robert Sommers, *The U.S. Open* (1987).

Frank J. Cavaioli

SAVITT, RICHARD (4 March 1927, Bayonne, NJ–). A Jewish tennis player who was one of the premier players of the 1950s, he was the son of Morris Savitt, who owned a food brokerage firm. His mother was Kate Haberman Savitt. His family moved to El Paso, Texas, in 1943. There he excelled in basketball at El Paso High School. After serving one year in the U.S. Navy, he enrolled at Cornell University, where he played varsity basketball and was captain of the tennis team before graduating with a B.A. in economics in 1950. By 1950 Savitt had a national ranking of sixth among amateurs in the era before open tennis. He went on to become one of the dominating American men players of the 1950s. His greatest success was in 1951, when he won both the Australian and the Wimbledon singles championships, making him the second American to accomplish that double feat in the same year. Despite being the number one ranked American amateur after those victories in 1951, he was dropped from the U.S. Davis Cup team that faced Australia in the finals that summer. The legendary Australian Davis Cup captain, Harry Hopman, attributed the U.S. squad's loss in the closely contested final to Savitt's absence from the American team. Some of the accounts of the controversy suggest the decision to drop Savitt may have been motivated by anti-Semitism. Savitt was a stockbroker. In the 1990s he supported efforts to introduce tennis to new immigrants to Israel. He was inducted into the International Tennis Hall of Fame in 1976.

SELECTED BIBLIOGRAPHY: E. Digby Baltzell, *Sporting Gentlemen: Men's Tennis from the Age of Honor to the Cult of the Superstar* (1995); Richard Evans, ed., *Tales from the Tennis Court: An Anthology of Tennis Writings* (1983); Harry Hopman, *Aces and Places* (1957); "Linesmen Ready?," *Time* (27 August 1951): 62–69 (cover story); Alan Trengove, *The Story of the Davis Cup* (1985).

Richard FitzPatrick

SCHAYES, ADOLPH ("Dolph") (19 May 1928, New York City–). A basketball player, his father, Carl, was a truck driver for Consolidated Laundries, and his mother, Tina, was a housewife. Both were Romanian Jewish immigrants. A graduate of DeWitt Clinton High School and New York University, Schayes developed into an outstanding schoolboy basketball player. In 1948 he won the Haggerty Award, given to the top collegiate basketball player in the New York City area. Schayes spent nearly his entire sixteen-year professional basketball career with the Syracuse Nationals in the National Basketball League (1948/49) and National Basketball Association (NBA) (1949/50–1962/63). When the franchise, renamed the 76ers, relocated to Philadelphia for the 1963/64 campaign, Schayes served as player-coach for the season before retiring from active play.

A 6'8", 220-pound forward, he was perhaps the first big pro to play with the agility of a small man. He was a driving, slashing player with quick moves. Possessing a career average of 18.2 points per game, Schayes at one time held numerous NBA records, including most career points (19,249), most career rebounds (11,256), and most consecutive games played (764). As an NBA coach with the Philadelphia 76ers (1963–66) and the Buffalo Braves (1970–71) Schayes won 115 games and lost 172. He was chief supervisor of NBA referees from 1966 to 1969. Schayes coached the 1977 U.S. Maccabiah team, which included his son Dan, a future NBA player. A Naismith Memorial Basketball Hall of Fame inductee (1972) and officially designated (1997) one of the NBA's fifty greatest all-time players, Schayes was the preeminent Jewish basketball player in NBA history.

SELECTED BIBLIOGRAPHY: "Hall of Famer Schayes to Guide Cagers," *United States Committee—Sports for Israel, Inc. Newsletter* (April 1977): 6; Peter Levine, *Ellis Island to Ebbets Field: Sports and the American Jewish Experience* (1992); William Simons, "Interview with Adolph Schayes," *American Jewish History* 74 (1985): 287–307; George Vecsey, "At N.Y.U., a Night for Nostalgia," *New York Times*, 29 November 1983, B-10; Adolph "Dolph" Schayes File, Naismith Memorial Basketball Hall of Fame.

William M. Simons

SCHMIDT, MILTON C. (5 March 1918, Kitchener, Ontario, Canada–   ). A native of Canada of German descent, he was one of hockey's elite stars, combining skill, stamina, speed, and scoring ability. He played his junior hockey for Kitchener of the Ontario Hockey League, along with his boyhood friend Woody Dumart. Schmidt and Dumart made their National Hockey League (NHL) debuts with the Boston Bruins in 1936–37, and they were joined the following season by another childhood friend, Bobby Bauer. Together they formed one of hockey's most potent units, which became known as the "Kraut Line" because of their German ancestry. Highly respected by his teammates and opposing players, Schmidt was a big, strong, rugged, hard-hitting, playmaking centerman and a relentless checker. He became the Bruins' all-time scoring leader until his mark was surpassed by John Bucyk in 1967–68. The powerful Bruins captured the Stanley Cup in 1938–39 and 1940–41. The 1939–40 campaign was Schmidt's personal best. He was the league's scoring leader with fifty-two points in forty-eight games and was also selected to the All-Star first team. After serving three years in the Royal Canadian Armed Forces during World War II, he returned to the Bruins and continued to play top-notch hockey. The 1946–47 season was his most productive, as he scored twenty-seven goals and thirty-five assists for sixty-two points in fifty-nine games, placing fourth in the league scoring race. As the longtime team captain and inspirational leader for the Bruins, Schmidt set an excellent example of hard work and dedication for the younger players to follow, both on and off the ice. A tireless worker, he sustained many serious injuries during his long NHL career but somehow always managed to come back stronger than ever. He became the fifth highest point scorer in league history up to the close of the first four decades of the NHL's history (1956–57 season), and his total career 346 assists placed him sixth on the all-time list. Schmidt was four times an All-Star, making the All-Star first team three times. He was also the 1950–51 recipient of the Hart Trophy as Most Valuable Player to his team. Following the 1954–55 season Schmidt became the new Boston coach. He eventually became the Bruin's general manager from 1966 until 1974, playing a prominent role in the redevelopment of the Bruins organization during that era. Shrewd trades orchestrated by Schmidt helped build the Bruins back into a powerhouse club that won the Stanley Cup in 1969–70 and 1971–72.

SELECTED BIBLIOGRAPHY: Charles L. Coleman, *Trail of the Stanley Cup*, vols. 2, 3 (1969, 1976); *Hockey News* (1947–55).

Ray Mulley

SCHOENDIENST, ALBERT FRED ("Red") (2 February 1923, Germantown, IL–   ). A baseball player of German descent, his father (Joseph) was a coal miner and farmer, and his mother (Mary) was a homemaker. He left school at age fourteen and joined the Civilian Conservation Corps at sixteen. He was a baseball player for the St. Louis Cardinals and two other teams, a manager, and a coach. Schoendienst joined the Cardinals in 1945 after three seasons in the minor leagues and a short stint in the army. After a year in the outfield, he moved to second baseman and soon became a starter. Quickly developing into a fine defensive player and a solid, line-drive hitter, he led second basemen in fielding percentage seven times and batted .280 with seven seasons over .300. He made the National League All-Star team ten times and won the 1950 All-Star Game with a home run in the fourteenth inning. He played in three World Series, one with the Cardinals and two with the Milwaukee Braves. Diagnosed with tuberculosis late in 1958, he missed most of the following year but returned to play into 1963, his nineteenth season in the majors. Schoendienst managed the Cardinals from 1964 through 1976 and then briefly in 1980. His teams won two pennants and the 1967 World Series and compiled a 1,028–944 record. He coached with the Oakland Athletics and the Cardinals, who retired his number in 1996. Schoendienst was elected to the Baseball Hall of Fame in 1989.

SELECTED BIBLIOGRAPHY: Bob Broeg, "Red and Stan—Spirit of St. Louis," *The Sporting News* (7 October 1957): 3, 16; Al Hirshberg, *The Man Who Fought Back: Red Schoendienst* (1961); Jack Newcombe, "Red Schoendienst," *Baseball Best* (May 1953): 9–13; "Red Schoendienst: Returned by an Unbroken Promise," in David Craft and Tom Owens, *Redbirds Revisited: Great Memories and Stories from St. Louis Cardinals* (1990); J. Roy Stockton, "The Wonderful Schoendienst Story," *Sport* 7 (September 1949): 55, 91–93.

Steven P. Gietschier

SCHWARCZ, ERNO (27 October 1904, Budapest, Hungary–? July 1974, Flushing, NY). An Austrian international player, in 1929 he was considered to be the highest paid soccer player in the United States. He arrived in New York City in the spring of 1926 with the famous Vienna Hakoah team of Austria, a club made up entirely of Jewish players. That fall he was back in New York playing for the New York Giants in the professional American Soccer League.* A winger throughout most of his playing career, he played for the famous Hungarian club Ferencvaros before joining Hakoah and appeared for Hungary against Germany and Finland in 1922. Signed by the Scottish club Glasgow Rangers in the summer of 1928, he was prevented from playing in Britain by the labor contract law. In the fall of 1928 he was instrumental in bringing together all the former Hakoah players playing in the United States, and he formed the New York Hakoah Club, which won the U.S. Open Cup in 1929 by beating the Madison Kennel Club of St. Louis in the final. Starting in 1931, he became player-coach of the New York Americans and led them to the U.S. Open Cup final of 1933 only to lose to St. Louis Stix, Baer, and Fuller. In 1937 he coached the team to the Open Cup final again and claimed the national championship by beating St. Louis Shamrocks. In later years he was involved in the administration of the American Soccer League as its business manager.

SELECTED BIBLIOGRAPHY: Bil Graham, ed., *North American Soccer Guide* (1952–53); Mezo Laszlo, *Futball-Adatar* (1987).

Colin Jose

SCHWARZENEGGER, ARNOLD (30 July 1947, Graz, Austria–   ). One of America's most popular movie stars who parlayed bodybuilding into a film career, he is the younger son of Gustav and Aurelia (Jedmy) Schwarzenegger, whose name translates as "black plowman." A police chief in the neighboring village of Thal, Arnold's father was a strict disciplinarian but also an affectionate man who had a major impact on the boy in a poor family. Authority fascinated Schwarzenegger, as did bigness. Driven during his teens to attain his own "big physique," Schwarzenegger worked out in the gym and at home to become a Mr. Universe. After graduating from high school in 1965, he joined the Austrian army and credits the army's meat diet with his capacity to win the Junior Mr. Europe title in Stuttgart, Germany. To compete, however, he had gone absent without leave (AWOL) and for punishment spent a year in the stockade, all the while working out to become the "Leonardo da Vinci sculptor" of his own body. Success came in 1967, when at the age of twenty he advanced to victory as the youngest-ever Mr. Universe, a conquest that came on the heels of titles like Best-Built Man of Europe and International Powerlifting Champion. A year later he arrived in the United States, where along with a few losses he also triumphed over the competition in most professional bodybuilding contests. Retiring from the circuit in 1975, he earned a B.A. from the University of Wisconsin-Superior in 1980, was awarded contracts for a documentary film on bodybuilding in 1977, and over the years played roles in various films, sometimes using pseudonyms. With major roles in a dozen box office thrillers, Schwarzenegger became a naturalized American in 1983 and campaigned hard in 1988 for George Bush, who in 1990 appointed him chairman of the President's Council on Physical Fitness and Sports. At no time in his career has he outwardly harked back to his tiny Austria for inspiration and, except for his heavy German accent, manifests nothing to distinguish his ethnicity from his American stardom.

SELECTED BIBLIOGRAPHY: George Butler, *Arnold Schwarzenegger* (1990); Charles Gaines and Charles Butler, *Pumping Iron* (1991); Wendy Leigh, *Arnold, an Unauthorized Biography* (1989); Charles Moritz, ed., *Current Biography Yearbook* (1992); Arnold Schwarzenegger and Douglas Kent Hall, *Arnold: The Education of a Body Builder* (1977).

La Vern J. Rippley

SCOTS. Scottish immigrants and their descendants have exerted a major influence on the development of athletics in the United States. Their most significant contributions occurred in the middle and latter decades of the nineteenth century, primarily through curling, track-and-field games, and golf. The assimilation of the Scots into the mainstream of White, Anglo-Saxon Protestant (WASP) society in the twentieth century has diminished their role in American sports, and traditional Scottish pastimes have evolved in the United States to the point where their ethnic origins have become obscured. But the love of the Scottish Americans for sport still shines through in their devotion to curling matches and the traditional Highland games. Even golf still exhibits a Scottish tone, although much diminished from the late 1800s.

Scottish soldiers and immigrants brought curling to North America during the late 1700s. Although the game proved to be more popular in Canada than in the United States during the nineteenth century, curling did take root in American soil by the mid-1800s. The Orchard Lake Curling Club, the first of its kind in the United States, began play on Lake St. Clair near Detroit in 1832. The club in Milwaukee, Wisconsin, launched in 1845, is the oldest continuously operating organization in the nation. Clubs also appeared in Boston and New York City prior to 1860, and after the Civil War every major Scottish community had at least one curling association, and a few had many more. The New York City area numbered at least a dozen by 1869. Other American cities that sent curling teams to international matches against Canadian clubs during this period were Albany, Cleveland, Paterson (New Jersey), Buffalo, Jersey City (New Jersey), Milwaukee, and Detroit. Since the mid-1800s curling has thrived in the upper Midwest, Great Lakes, New England, and mid-Atlantic regions. The sport was also played in Alaska, Washington, California, Texas, Colorado, Nebraska, Kansas, Missouri, and North Carolina. At the end of the 1990s there were about 15,000 curlers enrolled in over 135 clubs. Most of the participants were of Scottish descent, but the sport also attracted enthusiasts from other ethnic groups, especially in small towns in rural regions.

The early history of track and field in the United States offers a prime example of a sport that retained a great deal of its Scottish ancestry but that also took on characteristics of both the English and the American WASP sporting traditions. Prior to the Civil War, the American sporting community patronized professional pedestrianism to a considerable degree, especially during the 1840s and early 1850s. After the war there was a revival of enthusiasm in the 1870s and 1880s for these long-distance running and walking contests, along with some interest in English collegiate track events. But the Scottish Highland (or Caledonian) games were by far the most important influence on the origins and early development of North American track and field.

Prior to the Civil War Scottish newcomers to the United States competed in Highland games. The Highland Society of New York held its "first Sportive Meeting" as early as 1836, and the St. Andrews Society of Detroit claims the honor of hosting the oldest ongoing Highland Games, dating from 1849. The 1850s witnessed the beginning of the more regular scheduling of athletic meets sponsored by Scottish Caledonian societies in the United States, which eventually numbered more than 100 by the later years of the century. These associations helped the members to preserve at least part of their cultural heritage. Scottish residents of Boston founded a society in 1853, and one of its founders stated that its purpose was to perpetuate "the manners and customs, literature, the Highland costume and the athletic games of Scotland, as practiced by our forefathers." In addition to sponsoring athletics, these organizations scheduled dinners, dances, and concerts that featured bagpipes.

Scottish residents of Gotham launched the New York Caledonian Club in 1856 and began sponsoring annual games the following year, charging an admission fee of twenty-five cents and awarding cash prizes to the victors of each event. These sessions marked a significant change in the development of commercialized sports in America because, previously, individual promoters had arranged events and had sought profit through gate receipts. The only major exception had been horse racing, where jockey clubs sometimes organized meetings. The new Caledonian model was soon followed by baseball and other athletic clubs. The Scottish games differed from pedestrian contests in that they featured a variety of track-and-field events, including short and long races, jumping, leaping, vaulting, and feats of strength such as putting the heavy stone and tossing the caber (heavy pole or log of wood). The festivities also included traditional songs and dances of the old country, such as the Highland fling and the broad sword dance, as well as such comical races as wheeling the barrow blindfolded and running in sacks. After the events the officers, members, and guests of the club gathered for a sumptuous feast, complete with speeches and toasts.

The Scottish populations of Philadelphia and Newark, New Jersey, followed the example of their compatriots in Boston and New York prior to the Civil War, and after peace returned, Caledonian clubs and games sprouted across the continent. In New York, initially, the games were open only to club members, but visitors from other societies were allowed to compete as honorary participants. But by the late 1800s the Scottish clubs across the country generally opened their meets to all comers, including Englishmen, Irish, Germans, African Americans, and others. In 1867 Caledonian clubs from Canada and the United States held an international meet at Jones' Woods in Manhattan; three years later delegates from clubs from both countries gathered to standardize the rules governing the events at the games. At that time they federated to form the North American Caledonian Association. By the 1870s that international body confirmed the nature of the Caledonian games as they had evolved in North America, with admission fees for revenue for sponsoring clubs, open competition, and cash prizes.

In addition to the Caledonians, the second party that was instrumental in creating early track-and-field athletics in the United States included upper-middle-class and affluent sportsmen who admired both the Caledonians and also the English collegiate and amateur athletic clubs that were founded during this era. One of the pioneer athletic clubs and ultimately the most influential was the New York Athletic Club (NYAC), which was incorporated with fourteen members in 1868. On 11 November of that year the NYAC held its first meet and began the process of formulating the rules for track-and-field competition that would become generally accepted by the late 1870s. The powerful influence of the local Scotsmen on New York City's fledgling athletic club is apparent in the special invitation and challenge it sent to the New York Caledonian Club to compete in its inaugural meet. Frederick W. Janssen, an early chronicler of American track and field, labeled this gathering "an International Match—America against Scotland." He noted that the result might have been foreseen: "America won the running and walking contests, while Scotland was successful with the hammer and shot and in pole-leaping, standing high jump and running long jump,—the games most common at Caledonian meetings."

A comparison of the events commonly included in the premier athletic meets of the 1880s and the 1890s with those contested in the Caledonian games shows many similarities but also a few significant differences. The amateur athletic clubs of the late nineteenth century retained most of the Scottish races and field games that tested speed, stamina, strength and leaping and jumping ability—the sprints and longer runs, shot put, hammer and weight throws, running broad jump, pole vault, and running high jump. The native-born sportsmen added a few more middle-distance races but dropped the caber toss, Highland songs and dances, and the comical wheelbarrow and sack races. The tug-of-war (the only team competition) remained a favorite in both types of meets, especially since it usually featured rival clubs or ethnic groups. During the 1880s amateur festivals sometimes also scheduled lacrosse, cricket, or baseball throws and bicycle races, but by the end of the century ball throwing had passed out of fashion, while the bicycling mania resulted in separate meets for cyclists.

The amateur athletic clubs broke with their Scottish predecessors in their policies toward admission fees, eligibility for competitors, and prizes. The most prestigious associations generally did not charge gate money and sometimes admitted spectators by invitation only. (The Amateur Athletic Union did collect admission fees for its annual national championships.) Furthermore, whereas the Caledonian clubs invited professionals to compete for cash, the amateur clubs (adopting the English practice) barred them from their meets and offered the victors only ribbons, medals, or trophies. The New York Athletic Club and the National Association of Amateur Athletes of America (N4A) banned those who had ever competed for money or against any professional for a prize or who had been employed in any form of athletics.

As the New York Athletic Club, its sister societies, and national organizations like the N4A and the Amateur Athletic Union sponsored numerous competitions, they gradually took control of track-and-field athletics. Officers of the Caledonian clubs witnessed the defection of some of their members to the ranks of their rivals, and they also saw their annual games wane in popularity. In New York City some of the younger Caledonians dropped out of the Scottish society and its meets because they did not want to jeopardize their amateur standing by competing against professionals. They founded the new Scottish-American Club of New York, and they adopted the amateur code of the New York Athletic Club and the N4A. Significantly, they did not require that members must be of Scotch birth or descent.

As the Scottish societies experienced dwindling gate receipts and occasional financial losses at their festivals, some among their ranks began to call for reform and a return to the practice of holding athletic exercises for Scotsmen only. In 1885 *The Scottish American Journal* argued that the societies should no longer depend on their annual games for financial assistance. It pointed out, "The novelty has worn off these festivals, similar sports can be seen everywhere at frequent intervals during the summer, and the pic-nic features, which used to be so enjoyable, have been abandoned." Eight years later the same newspaper lamented that after amateur and college athletic clubs copied the Caledonian gatherings, "the grand old games, full of health and pleasure, became the victims of scientific treatment." It especially criticized the tendency toward modernization: "Records (so-called) were established and measurements for stone and hammer throwing were got down to fractions of inches, and 'amateurs' went into training, and employed instructors and 'coaches,' organized clubs and gave public exhibitions—looking sharply after the gate money." It chastised the Scottish clubs for following the trend, opening up their games, and "adopting competitions which were no more Scotch than Portuguese." It explained: "We have even seen Indians, negroes, as well as men of all nationalities, appearing at 'Scottish' games, but the more such experiments were tried the more open were the Caledonian games to charges which have tended to degrade sports under other auspices." The editorialist concluded with a plea for a return to "the simple sports which used to be played on the village haugh, or country roadside, and which had neither records, nor infinitesimal measurements, nor 'stop' watches, as accessories." Above all, the Scottish games "should be confined to Scotch competitors, without "negroes, or Germans, or Indians, or Englishmen." In 1896 an early chronicler of the Scottish experience also noted that although the new athletic clubs had adopted the Scottish games and the laws that governed them, they had also pushed the Caledonians into the background and regarded their athletic records with suspicion. He also remarked on the practice of "traveling professional Caledonian athletes" who made the circuit of games each year." That led to the practice of open competition "without distinction of creed, nationality, or previous condition of servitude." He observed that in Philadelphia those who "went to see *Scotch* games saw a general scramble for the prizes by negroes, Irishmen, and Germans, as well as Scots."

Golf was another time-honored Scottish pastime that gained great popularity in the United States during the late nineteenth and early twentieth centuries. As was the case with the Caledonian games, golf initially appealed to the upper ranks of American society, who adapted it to suit their sporting needs. But its evolution in this country differed from track and field in its rate of growth among middle- and upper-class men and women, racial minorities, and immigrants, for while affluent females and many males of modest means joined in the golfing mania of the 1890s and the early 1900s, only a few African Americans, Native Americans, and European newcomers took up the sport. Golf was partially democratized prior to World War I, but it did not achieve mainstream status in the American sporting culture until after World War II.

Although there is considerable evidence that a few hardy sportsmen played golf in various towns and counties in colonial, Revolutionary, and nineteenth-century America, the modern era of the game in the United States dates from the late 1880s. Scottish immigrants and Scottish Americans pioneered the revival of the game. John Reid* (often called "the father of American golf") was a native of Dunfermline, Scotland, who had earned a small fortune in the iron industry in New York. In 1887 he asked Robert Lockhart, a friend and fellow native of his hometown, to buy a set of golf clubs and some balls for him on his next business trip to Britain. Lockhart complied by visiting Old Tom Morris at St. Andrews in Scotland and purchased the equipment, which Reid and a few of his friends tried out on his cow pasture in Yonkers, New York, on Washington's Birthday, 1888. On 14 November of that year these gentlemen founded the St. Andrews Golf Club.

Another founding father of American golf was Charles B. Macdonald,* a Chicagoan and second-generation Scottish American. The driving force behind the Chicago Golf Club, he distinguished himself as a prominent player, golf course architect, and critic of new trends in the game. In 1872, at the age of sixteen, he had journeyed to the land of his ancestors to stay with his grandfather at St. Andrews and attend college. There he took sufficient time away from his studies to become a proficient golfer, but upon his return to Chicago a few years later he devoted himself to business. He renewed his sporting career in the 1890s, just as the golfing craze was sweeping through the East. After a few frustrating defeats he finally won a major tournament when he captured the U.S. amateur championship in 1895. Over the next few decades Macdonald found himself fighting many changes to the rules that he considered objectionable. These included modifications that allowed the wiping of balls on muddy greens, the granting of improved lies under certain conditions, the abolition of the sty-mie, and even the passing of the tradition of wearing red coats during play. On the other hand, Macdonald did support limiting the number of clubs, the out-of-bounds rule, and the new rubber-cored ball. In his autobiography, written near the end of his long career in golf, Macdonald concluded that the changes wrought by Americans had not greatly violated the essence of the Scottish sport. He wrote that "it is really extraordinary how well the game has established itself in harmony with most that was best in it in its Scotch home."

As Reid, Macdonald, and other Scottish Americans pioneered golf in the United States, they welcomed professional players from their homeland and England who were eager to capitalize on the sudden boom in the demand for their sporting expertise in North America. In 1891 three prosperous Long Island gentlemen (W. K. Vanderbilt, Edward S. Mead, and Duncan Cryder) invited Willie Dunn to journey to Southampton to design a twelve-hole seaside links, which became Shinnecock Hills. Dunn employed 150 Indians from the nearby Shinnecock reservation and incorporated their ancestral burial mounds into his layout. In 1895 an English golf magazine reported that American entrepreneurs were offering experienced club makers passage to New York and fifteen dollars per week in wages. The following year John Dunn, a Scotchman, recounted that during a five-month stay in the States he taught novices every day from morning until night. He especially enjoyed his three-month visit with Willie Dunn at the "Millionaires Golf Club" at Ardsley, with its private railway station, dock for yachts, stables, and swimming pool. He concluded his tour with six weeks under more spartan conditions in Buffalo, teaching even through a Scottish mist and with snow on the ground. Before returning home he enjoyed the hospitality and festivities sponsored by the Buffalo Gordon Highlanders and the New York Caledonian Club. By the end of the decade the trickle of British professionals became a flood, as the number of new American clubs skyrocketed in the North-east and the West. R. B. Wilson, James Foulis, W. H. Way, the Smith family from Carnoustie, and many others flocked to the New World to seek their for-tunes as teachers and as prizewinners in open tournaments, "rashly imagining that they would pick up more gold than could be found even in the Klondike region." Although the rage for open tournaments soon faded, many newcomers did stay on as teachers, course architects, greenkeepers, and club makers.

Scottish Americans' two greatest gifts to the sporting culture of the United States were certainly track and field and golf. During the twentieth century both of these developed distinctive characteristics that deviated from their original Scottish forms. But even as track and field evolved as a mainstream American sport, the Scottish tradition of sponsoring athletic competitions and festivals did not die out. On the contrary, during the 1990s communities of Scotch men and women in forty-four states organized meetings that featured heavy weights events, tug-of-war, country dancing, sheepdog trials, fiddling, harping, pipe bands, drumming, and other ethnic activities. Golf, of course, remained a popular recreation for Scottish Americans, even as people of all nationalities, races, and religions took up the game. Curling, however, retained more of its flavor as an ethnic pastime enjoyed by a smaller number of devoted players.

SELECTED BIBLIOGRAPHY: Roland T. Berthoff, *British Immigrants in Industrial America, 1793–1850* (1958); Kathleen Doyle, "In John Reid's Cow Pasture," *American History Illustrated* 23 (Summer 1988): 34–45; H. B. Martin, *Fifty Years of American Golf* (1936); Charles B. Macdonald, *Scotland's Gift, Golf: Reminiscences* (1928); Gerald Redmond, *The Caledonian Games in Nineteenth Century America* (1971); Peter Ross, *The Scot in America* (1896); David B. Smith, *Curling: An Illustrated History* (1981); Tim Wright, *United States Men's Curling Championships. The First Thirty Years* (1986).

George B. Kirsch

SEDRAN, BERNARD ("Barney") (28 January 1891, New York City–14 January 1969, New York City). A pioneer of college and professional basketball, he was raised in the heavily Jewish blocks of Manhattan's Lower East Side. Beginning in 1903, he played for the "midget" team of the University Settlement House, which was coached by a Jewish immigrant from Austria. There he first joined with his longtime teammate Max "Marty" Friedman* as the two youngsters led their squad (the "busy Izzies") to settlement house and metropolitan Amateur Athletic Union championships. Although only 5' 4" tall, Sedran next became player-coach of the basketball team at New York City's DeWitt Clinton High School and starred for three seasons at the City College of New York, graduating in 1911. Nicknamed "the mighty mite of basketball," in 1912 he turned professional with the Newburgh Club of the Hudson River League. Over the next fifteen years his experience was typical of the barnstorming era of early professional basketball, as he competed for ten different teams in six leagues. A prolific scorer and a talented playmaker, he often spearheaded his squad to championships. Frequently paired with Friedman, the two were top gate attractions, celebrated as the sport's "Heavenly Twins." Although statistics remain incomplete for his era, he scored at least 3,324 points as a professional. After his retirement as a player he coached six teams, including the Wilmington Bombers (champions of the American Basketball League in 1941 and 1942), Kate Smith's Celtics, the Brooklyn Jewels, and the New York Gothams. Enshrined in the Naismith Memorial Basketball Hall of Fame in 1962, he was the smallest athlete to be inducted up to that date.

SELECTED BIBLIOGRAPHY: Peter Levine, *Ellis Island to Ebbets Field* (1992), 28–29, 54–55; *New York Times*, 15 January 1969, 47; Bernard Sedran file, Naismith Memorial Basketball Hall of Fame, Springfield, MA.

George B. Kirsch

SEGURA, FRANCISCO ("Pancho") (20 June 1921, Guayaquil, Ecuador–). A Hispanic American tennis player, he was born into a poor family of mixed Inca and Spanish ancestry. As a child he suffered from malaria and rickets; the latter illness inflicted him with a deformation that prompted the nickname "parrot foot." His father's job as a caretaker at an exclusive tennis club gave Pancho an opportunity to learn the game. As a youngster he was so weak that he had to use both hands for his forehand, but later he became renowned for that stroke. After achieving fame in Ecuador for his tennis, Pancho emigrated to the United States for the first time in 1940 as a nineteen-year-old. He so impressed observers that he was offered a tennis scholarship at the University of Miami in Florida, for which he won an unprecedented three consecutive national collegiate singles titles (1943 to 1945). Segura had a brief career as an amateur in that era before open tennis. After he turned professional in 1947, he built his reputation among peers and tennis fans because of his devastating two-handed forehand, his indefatigable court coverage, and his crowd-pleasing demeanor. Professional tennis at the time consisted of small groups of players barnstorming in one-night competitions from city to city for weeks and months at a stretch. Segura competed successfully against Pancho Gonzalez,* Bobby Riggs, Frank Parker,* and Ken McGregor, though Jack Kramer, who was the organizer and marquee player of the professional tour, dominated him. Segura won the U.S. Pro Championship singles title three times and its doubles title four times. In 1968, at the age of forty-one, he won an epic doubles match at Wimbledon with Alex Omeldo. The sixty-two-game first set was the longest in the tournament's history. He gained widespread recognition as the coach of Jimmy Connors in the late 1960s and early 1970s. Subsequently, he competed on the Grand Masters Tour and was the resident pro at the La Costa Hotel and Spa in California. He was inducted into the International Tennis Hall of Fame in 1984, and became a U.S. citizen in 1991.

SELECTED BIBLIOGRAPHY: E. Digby Baltzell, *Sporting Gentlemen: Men's Tennis from the Age of Honor to the Cult of the Superstar* (1995); Harry Hopman, *Aces and Places* (1957); Jack Kramer, *The Game: My Forty Years in Tennis* (1979); Robin Norwood, "Remembering When Tennis Was Wild and Wonderful," *St. Louis Dispatch*, 27 July 1997, 10D; Robert L. Riggs, *Court Hustler* (1973).

Richard FitzPatrick

SEIXAS, VICTOR E., JR. (30 August 1923, Philadelphia–   ). A world-class tennis player, he was the son of Vic Seixas, Sr., who was born in Brazil of Portuguese descent and came to the United States as a child. His mother, Anna Victoria Moon, was of Irish Protestant heritage. Vic, Sr., owned a successful wholesale plumbing and heating supply business. Vic, Jr., was raised as a Philadelphia gentleman. He attended the William Penn Charter School, where he excelled as a letterman in five sports, including tennis. He served in the U.S. Army Air Force as an officer during World War II and earned a B.S. in commerce in 1949 at the University of North Carolina, where he was on the varsity basketball team and was the captain of the tennis team. Seixas was one of the top-ranked American tennis players in singles and doubles from 1942 into the late 1960s, competing as an amateur before the advent of the open era in men's tennis. He played in the U.S. National Championships at Forest Hills a record twenty-eight times and was the singles champion in 1954. He won national titles on four different surfaces. He also won the Wimbledon singles championship in 1953. A durable Davis Cup campaigner for the United States throughout the 1950s, Seixas anchored the team that won the Cup from the Australians in 1954. While he competed as an amateur, Seixas supported himself as a stockbroker. In his fifties he joined the Seniors' Professional Tour. He received the William M. Johnston Award for sportsmanship from the U.S. Tennis Association in 1949 and was inducted into the International Tennis Hall of Fame in 1971.

SELECTED BIBLIOGRAPHY: E. Digby Baltzell, *Sporting Gentlemen: Men's Tennis from the Age of Honor to the Cult of the Superstar* (1995); Stan Hart, *Once a Champion: Legendary Tennis Stars Revisited* (1985); Vic Seixas, with Joel H. Cohen, *Prime Time Tennis* (1983).

Richard FitzPatrick

SELES, MONICA (2 December 1973, Novi Sad, Serbia–   ). A tennis player and daughter of Serbian immigrants, her father (Karolj) was a cartoonist, television director, and her coach. Her mother, Esther, was a computer programmer. Seles is one of the top female tennis players of the open era. Introduced to tennis at the age of seven, she took to the sport quickly, eventually developing her devastating and unorthodox two-handed ground strokes. After winning the European junior championship at the age of ten, she and her family moved to the United States to attend the Nick Bollettieri Tennis Academy in Florida. She began to play a short professional schedule in 1988, winning her first match in February at Boca Raton. By year's end, Seles was ranked eighty-eighth in the world. In 1989, now a full-fledged pro, she reached the semifinals of her first tournament in Washington, D.C. In only her second tournament, she defeated number one seed Chris Evert to win her first professional title in Houston. By the end of 1989 she was ranked sixth in the world. In 1990 she won six titles, beating top players such as Martina Navratilova* and Steffi Graf, propelling her to the number two ranking by year's end. The greatest of these victories was her 7–6 (8–6), 6–4 victory over Graf at the French Open, her first grand-slam title. With her victory at the 1991 Australian Open, Seles became one of the youngest players in tennis history to be ranked number one, ending Graf's 186 weeks at the top spot. Winning both the French and U.S. Open titles, Seles set new records for prize money acquired in one year. Her dominance continued in 1992 as she won her third straight French Open and second U.S. Open title. However, in early 1993, at a tournament in Hamburg, Seles was stabbed in the back by a deranged fan. As a result, Seles missed the remainder of the 1993 and the entire 1994 seasons. Yet, she made a triumphant comeback in 1995, winning her first tournament back at the Canadian Open, reaching the finals of the U.S. Open, and winning the Australian Open in 1996, a remarkable feat. She became a naturalized American citizen in 1994 and was one of the top female tennis players of the 1990s.

SELECTED BIBLIOGRAPHY: Liza N. Burby, *Monica Seles* (1997); Kristin S. Fehr, *Monica Seles: Returning Champion* (1997); Michael E. Goodman, *Monica Seles* (1997); Joseph Layden, *Return of a Champion: The Monica Seles Story* (1996); Suzanne J. Murdico, *Monica Seles* (1998); Monica Seles, *Monica: My Journey from Fear to Victory* (1997); Monica Seles, *Monica* (1996); Mark Stewart, *Monica Seles: The Comeback Kid* (1998).

Thomas Cesa

SHADY REST GOLF AND COUNTRY CLUB. The story of Shady Rest begins at the Westfield Country Club, which was established in 1900 and featured a nine-hole golf course north of the Westfield train line on Jerusalem Road in Scotch Plains, New Jersey. On either side of the club was an African American community of small houses, and the residents would routinely cut across the golf course to get to the train line or to socialize. Over a period of years, a "right of travel" evolved that later affected the legal rights of the all-white private club, and in 1921, when the Westfield Country Club considered plans to expand the course to eighteen holes, this legal condition undoubtedly influenced their decision. They chose instead to sell the club and merge with the Cranford Golf Club to form the Echo Lake Country Club in Springfield. The former Westfield club was mortgaged to the Progressive Realty Company, created by a group of prominent African Americans, and became the Shady Rest Golf and Country Club, considered the first African American golf and country club in the United States.

There were other black-owned and/or-operated golf courses before and during this period, but no other had combined golf with the clubhouse, restaurant, lockers, tennis courts, horseback riding, skeet shooting, croquet, and social activities that were available at Shady Rest and generally associated with country clubs of the era. Shady Rest was run by and for blacks and became an important social and economic institution in the local community and the New York metropolitan area.

In 1925 the first National Colored Golf Championship was held at Shady Rest. This championship was organized by a group formed earlier that year in Washington, D.C., called the U.S. Colored Golfers Association. B. C. Gordon, president of Shady Rest, was elected the president of the association. Two years later the group was renamed the United Golfers Association,* an organization that served as the governing body of black golf until desegregation opened up many public courses to blacks in the mid-1960s.

During that same year, 1925, a fight for control of Shady Rest erupted over mismanagement of the club's finances between forces representing a New York contingent headed by Henry Parker and a local group from New Jersey. After a court battle William Willis, Sr., assumed control of Shady Rest and ran it for the remainder of its history. In many ways he represented the struggle of African Americans entering the mainstream of middle-class America. But in the early 1930s Shady Rest was forced to change ownership and became the property of the township of Scotch Plains.

In 1963 the gentlemen's handshake between William Willis, Sr., and the township of Scotch Plains came to an end. Shady Rest became the Scotch Hills Country Club and was opened to the public. The opening up of athletic opportunities for African Americans played a major role in the demise of Shady Rest. Overall, the club was a symbol of black achievement during a period when African Americans were suffering even more than depression-era white Americans. The club offered the evolving black middle class a social and economic institution with access to activities not associated with a minority community. Shady Rest provided a forum for some of the most prominent African Americans of the period from all spheres of influence—Althea Gibson,* Ella Fitzgerald, W.E.B. Du Bois—and was the home of John Shippen,* the first American-born golf professional. It boasted a membership of working-class and professional men and women and their families, and it provided an atmosphere of civility and belonging in what could otherwise be a hostile and unfriendly world.

SELECTED BIBLIOGRAPHY: Arthur R. Ashe, Jr., *A Hard Road to Glory: A History of the African-American Athlete*, vol. 2 (1988); Larry Londino, "A Place for Us: The History of Shady Rest and America's First Golf Professional," television documentary sponsored by the PGA of America and Elder Sports Management Institute (1994); Larry Londino, "Shady Rest: Itself a Strong Ship," *Golf Journal* (Spring 1996); 16–17; Richard Porter Preiss, "Black Country Clubs along the East Coast," paper presented at the American Culture Association Convention, Atlanta (1986).

Larry Londino

SHARKEY, JACK (26 November 1902, Binghamton, NY–17 August 1994, Beverly, MA). Born Juozas Zukauskas to a family of Lithuanian immigrants, he gained recognition as a boxer while he served in the U.S. Navy. He turned professional in 1924 and changed his name to Jack Sharkey by combining the names of professional boxer Jack Dempsey and noted navy boxer Tom Sharkey. In fifty professional matches he compiled a record of thirty-five wins (fourteen by knockout), eleven losses, and four ties. On 27 July, 1927 Dempsey fought Sharkey before 75,000 fans and a $1 million gate for the right to challenge Gene Tunney.* Sharkey was leading but was knocked out by Dempsey when he lowered his hands to complain to the referee about a low blow. Sharkey's wins against Stribling, Loughran, and Scott in 1929 opened the door to the world championship. In a match against the German titleholder Max Schmeling in 1930 Sharkey hit Schmeling with a low blow in the fourth round. The referee awarded the match to Schmeling. In a second fight between Sharkey and Schmeling in 1932, lasting the full fifteen rounds, the decision was given to Sharkey. Primo Carnera fought Sharkey on 29 June 1933 for the heavyweight championship of the world. Sharkey had previously decisioned Carnera. Although Sharkey won the first five rounds, Carnera took Sharkey down in the sixth round. Sharkey ended his professional career in 1936 with a loss to Joe Louis.* He refereed professional boxing and eventually retired in 1952. Jack Sharkey was an American by birth and a celebrated American athlete, but he never forgot his Lithuanian heritage. He chose a career in boxing because he wanted to excel in a sport in which no other son of Lithuanian immigrant parents had reached a world-class level.

SELECTED BIBLIOGRAPHY: Peter Heller, *In This Corner: Former World Champions Tell Their Stories* (1973); Bert R. Sugar, ed., *1983 Ring Record Book* (1983).

Sigitas Krasauskas

SHIPPEN, JOHN (5 December 1879, Washington, D.C.–15 July 1968, Newark, NJ). An African American golfer and the longtime golf professional at the Shady Rest Country Club,* Scotch Plains, New Jersey, he was probably the first American-born golf professional. It is a verifiable fact that John Shippen was the first American-born golfer to lead a U.S. Open (1896). It is also possible that he was the first American-born player who fulfilled the definition for what we now consider a golf pro. He was the son of John Shippen, Sr., an African American Presbyterian minister who moved to the Shinnecock Indian Reservation on Long Island in 1888. His mother was Eliza Spotswood Shippen, a Shinnecock Indian. It is likely that both of his parents were descendants of slaves. The young John Shippen became a caddie at the Shinnecock Hills Golf Course (one of the first in the United States), which was constructed near the reservation where Shippen lived. He developed an interest in playing the game and later gave lessons and served as an assistant to Scotsman Willie Dunn, who functioned as the golf professional at the Shinnecock club. Although the Professional Golfers' Association (PGA) of America wouldn't be established until 1916, John Shippen was the first American-born golfer to perform the duties of a golf professional. Shippen was good enough to compete in five U.S. Open Championships through 1913. Shippen's participation in the 1896 Open, held at Shinnecock Hills, sparked a racial controversy when a group of white players threatened to boycott the tournament if Shippen and Oscar Bunn, a Shinnecock Indian caddie, were allowed to play. However, Theodore Havemeyer, the president of the newly formed U.S. Golf Association, informed the disgruntled foreigners that Shippen and Bunn would play, and they did. Shippen was tied for the lead after the first eighteen holes, but during the second round he encountered one bad hole and eventually finished fifth. Shippen served as the greenkeeper and professional at Shady Rest from 1932 until the club was acceded to the township of Scotch Plains in 1964. When the U.S. Open was played at Shinnecock Hills in 1986, Shippen was remembered during the ABC telecast. Ironically, for many members of the former Shady Rest club, it was the first they learned of his accomplishments.

SELECTED BIBLIOGRAPHY: Ross Goodner, "Shinnecock Hills Golf Club, 1891–1966," printed by Shinnecock Hills Golf Club on occasion of the seventy-fifth Anniversary (1966); Guilford Jones, "Past Greats," *Black Sports* (July 1973): 64–67; Beverly Norwood, "86th United States Open Official Annual," U.S. Golf Association (1986); Calvin H. Sinnette, *Forbidden Fairways* (1998); Paul E. Sluby, Sr., "The Family Rec-ollections of Beulah A. Shippen and Mabel S. (Shippen) Hatcher: Roots in the Shinne-cock Indian Reservation," Long Island, NY, privately printed (1994); Peter F. Stevens, "In the Eye of the Storm," *Golf Journal* (June 1996); 12–15.

Larry Londino

SIFFORD, CHARLES (2 June 1923, Charlotte, NC–   ). He was the most prominent African American professional golfer between the end of World War II and 1970. He is the son of Roscoe Sifford, a laborer, and Eliza Sifford. He began caddying as a nine-year-old in Charlotte, North Carolina, and won a caddie tournament at an early age, shooting a score of 70. He subsequently moved to Philadelphia, where he continued to perfect his game, while teaching golf and working at other jobs. He played with, and taught, golf to singer Billy Eckstine, while he served as his professional chauffeur. After dominating the United Golfers Association* (UGA) Championship, winning a record five in a row between 1952 and 1956, he became the first black player to win a significant title in a predominantly white event, the Long Beach (California) Open in 1957. He came to prominence during the time when blacks were breaking the color barrier in other sports, but the golf establishment still clung to the old ways. Sifford bridged the gap between the time when blacks were excluded from play on the Professional Golfers' Association (PGA) Tour and were restricted to only black events and the UGA events and the eventual rescinding of the "Caucasian clause" from the PGA constitution in 1961, after which black professionals were granted the opportunity to play on the PGA Tour. Consequently, he endured the most blatant acts of discrimination on the professional golf tour. For example, in the 1969 Greater Greensboro (North Carolina) Open, Sifford, who was in contention to win the tournament, encountered racial heckling from a group of white men who had been drinking, which severely inhibited his chances for victory. Despite these incidents, Sifford became the first black player to win a nationally covered PGA event in golf's television age, the 1969 Los Angeles Open, and was one of the founding members of the PGA Senior Tour, where he continued to appear during the late 1990s.

SELECTED BIBLIOGRAPHY: Dick Edwards, "19 Years Is a Long Time to Be in the Rough," *Black Sports* (August 1973): 32–35, 52–53; Dan Jenkins, "Old Charlie Jolts the New Tour," *Sports Illustrated* 30 (20 January 1969): 16–17; William Johnson, "Call Back the Years," *Sports Illustrated* 30 (31 March 1969); Jim Murray, "As White as the Ku Klux Klan," *Los Angeles Times*, 6 April 1969; Charlie Sifford, with James Gallo, *Just Let Me Play: The Story of Charlie Sifford, The First Black PGA Golfer* (1992); "Top Negro Golfer," *Ebony Magazine* (June 1956): 61.

Larry Londino

SIMMONS, AL (22 May 1903, Milwaukee–26 May 1956, Milwaukee). A baseball player and the son of Polish immigrants, he briefly attended Stevens

Point Teachers College. Despite an unorthodox batting style, he developed into a lifetime .334 hitter who starred for Connie Mack's* great Philadelphia Athletics teams of the late 1920s and early 1930s. He was born Aloysius Szymanski and reportedly took his name off a billboard advertising a hardware store after being told that his long Polish name would not fit in a baseball box score. His nickname was "Bucketfoot Al," derived from his unusual batting style of striding toward third base, or "with a foot in the bucket." Although his batting technique was considered flawed, Simmons resisted efforts to change his style. He had such success as a hitter that no manager tried to change him. He turned pro with the Milwaukee Brewers in 1922 and hit .387 in his second season. Simmons led the league in hits with 253, still a record for a right-hander. Simmons was sold to the Philadelphia Athletics and led the As to a pennant in 1929. He hit thirty four home runs and a league-leading 157 runs batted in (RBIs), was named Most Valuable Player, and excelled in the World Series. In 1931 Simmons held out and did not sign a new contract until opening day. In all, Simmons hit better than .300 for eleven straight seasons. He hit .329 in four World Series and .462 in three All-Star Games. Best known for his hitting, he was an excellent outfielder who twice led the league in fielding. A leg injury prematurely ended his playing career in 1944 with Simmons just 73 short of the 3,000-hit plateau. He remained active in the sport, coaching in the major leagues and running a sandlot baseball program in New York City. Simmons was elected to the National Baseball Hall of Fame in 1953.

SELECTED BIBLIOGRAPHY: Martin Appel and Burt Goldblatt, *Baseball's Best: The Hall of Fame Gallery* (1980); Bill James, *The Bill James Historical Abstract* (1988); *Literary Digest* 116 (23 December 1933); 26; *New York Times*, 27 May 1956, I-88 and 28 May 1956, 31; Lowell Reidenbaugh, *Cooperstown: Where Baseball's Legends Live Forever* (1983).

                                                                                    Thomas M. Tarapacki

SIMMS, WILLIE (16 January 1870, Augusta, GA–26 February 1927, Asbury Park, NJ). An African American jockey born to former slaves, he began riding at East Coast tracks in 1887. He rode for many of the most prominent owners of the era, including Mike and Phil Dwyer, Richard (Boss) Croker, Pierre Lorillard, August Belmont, and James R. Keene. The leading rider in the United States in 1894 (228 winners out of 688 mounts), he won back-to-back Belmont Stakes on Commanche in 1893 and on Henry of Navarre the following year. Simms was aboard Dobbin when that horse finished in a dead heat in a match race with the previously unbeaten Domino in 1893. He was a two-time winner of the Kentucky Derby (Ben Brush in 1896 and Plaudit in 1898). Simms also captured most of the important fixtures in New York racing, including the 1897 Suburban Handicap, on Ben Brush; the 1895 Champagne Stakes, the 1894 Juvenile Stake, the 1893 Ladies Handicap, the 1893 and 1894 Lawrence Realization, the 1895 Jerome Handicap, and the 1894 and 1897 Dwyer Stakes. Dwyer and Croker took him to England in 1895, where he won two important races for owner Harry Reed. In England he introduced the American style of riding with short stirrups, later used with success by Tod Sloan, Johnny Reiff, and Danny Maher. In a fifteen-year career (1887–1901) he won 1,125 times out of a total of 4,532 mounts (24.8%). Simms wound up earning more money than the famed Isaac Murphy* ($300,000 to about $250,000). He was inducted into the National Thoroughbred Racing Hall of Fame in 1977.

SELECTED BIBLIOGRAPHY: *Blood-Horse* (8 August 1977): 3548; George Lambton, *Men and Horses I Have Known* (1924); *Thoroughbred Record*, 5 March 1927; Lyman Horace Weeks, *The American Turf* (1898).

Courtesy of the National Thoroughbred Racing Hall of Fame

SIMPSON, ORENTHAL J. (9 July 1947, San Francisco–). An African American football player and media celebrity, his father, Jimmy Simpson, was a bank custodian and a chef, and his mother, Eunice (Durton) Simpson, was a hospital orderly. They separated when Simpson was four years old. As a teenager he was the leader of a gang called the Persian Warriors. After some trouble with the law in 1961 Willie Mays* changed Simpson's career goals and convinced him that athletics could provide an escape route from the shiftless anomie of project life and gang subculture. At the Booker T. Washington Community Center Simpson succeeded in track and field, and at Galileo High School in Los Angeles he began his football career as a fullback. Next came two years at a junior college (City College of San Francisco) before Simpson achieved national glory in football at the University of Southern California (USC). While mostly remembered because of his football exploits, his real athletic forte was his blazing speed. In 1967 the Trojans were national track-and-field champions, and Simpson was a member of their world record-breaking 4 × 100-meters relay squad. Simpson graduated from USC with a major in sociology. After winning the Heisman Trophy in 1968, Simpson joined the Buffalo Bills and established numerous National Football League (NFL) records for most rushing attempts, most yards gained, and most touchdowns. He set an NFL record by scoring a touchdown in all of the regular season games in 1975. From 1972 to 1976 he was selected to play in the Pro Bowl. In the late 1970s he experienced injuries and was traded from the Buffalo Bills to the San Francisco 49ers. Following the path of other black football greats Woody Strode* and Jim Brown,* Simpson sought out a second career as a movie star. The vast majority of his movie roles were small parts of insignificant impact. Through a variety of prominent sports broadcasting positions and a burgeoning advertising career (especially in his tandem Hertz car commercial with golfing great Arnold Palmer), Simpson established himself as a congenial and trusted celebrity. His status was enhanced by a public manner that seemed collegial. All of this changed with the double slaying of Nicole Simpson (Simpson's second wife) and Ron Goldman. They were found slashed to death on 12 June 1994. After a long criminal trial the jury found Simpson not guilty (decision on 3 October 1995). A subsequent jury in a civil trial declared him responsible for the deaths of Simpson and Goldman (decision on 4 February 1997), and the Goldman/Simpson families were awarded vast compensatory damages totaling $25 million. Not only did the Simpson case dominate the field of mass media, but it eventually generated a maelstrom surrounding race and racism within American society.

SELECTED BIBLIOGRAPHY: Aaron Baker and Todd Boyd, eds., *Out of Bounds: Sports, Media, and the Politics of Identity* (1997), ix; Vincent Bugliosi, "Interview," *Playboy* 44, No. 4 (April 1997): 51–62, 174–177; Ellis Close, "Getting Past the Myths," *Newsweek* 129, No. 7 (17 February 1997): 37; Christopher Darden, "Justice Is in the Color of the Beholder," *Time* 149, No. 7 (17 February 1997): 39; "The Juice Squeezed," *The Economist* 324, No. 7903 (25 February–3 March 1995): 92; Douglass A. Noverr, "O. J. Simpson," in David L. Porter, ed., *African American Sports Greats: A Biographical Dictionary* (1995), 309–312; Rick Reilly, "Need a Fourth," *Sports Illustrated* 86, No. 13 (31 March 1997): 42–45; Harvey Marc Zucker and Lawrence J. Babich, eds., *Sports Films: A Complete Reference* (1987); Materials received from Saleem Choudrhy, Pro Football Hall of Fame Library, Canton, OH.

Scott A.G.M. Crawford

SKIING. Skiing is 4,000 years old in Scandinavia, associated with myth and legends, with god Ullr and goddess Skade as guardians. In the eighteenth century the only organized skiing was in the Norwegian army. In the latter part of the nineteenth century, when hundreds of thousands of Scandinavians were emigrating to the United States, skiing, judged Greenland explorer Dr. Fridtjof Nansen (1861–1930), was "perhaps of far greater national importance than is generally supposed."

Skiing was bound up with *Idraet*—always translated as sport but meaning more than merely building the body and mind, more than competitive endeavors. Via ancient outdoor sports whole communities and even the nation might be rejuvenated. These ideas were circulating as Scandinavians and particularly Norwegians settled in what was then the American Northwest, today's states of Iowa, Wisconsin, Michigan, and Minnesota, with odd pockets of immigrants elsewhere, notably, for skiing in New Hampshire, where one of two Nansen clubs was founded.

Early references to skiing—from 1841 on—all refer to the use of skis for hunting, getting supplies, and mail delivery, that is, for utilitarian purposes. When the immigrants formed clubs for ski-sport, from the 1880s on, they ensured their exclusiveness by writing into the constitutions that "the business meeting shall be in Norwegian. Any Scandinavian of good reputation . . . can be a member" (Berlin, New Hampshire). All the officers of the Aurora Club of Red Wing, Minnesota, were to be "Scandinavians or of Scandinavian descent." In some clubs there was a call for non-Scandinavian members, but when they joined in La Crosse, Wisconsin, for example, they were segregated as the "American faction."

About the turn of the century a different note was struck. Carl Tellefsen—Norwegian immigrant from Trondheim and president of the Ishpeming (Michigan) Ski Club—reminded his members in 1901 that "we are all Americans, not Englishmen, Swedes or Norwegians." He became the first president of the National Ski Association of America (NSA), founded in Ishpeming on 22 February 1905.

Of the National Ski Association's six officers, three were Norwegian immigrants. The association's annual journal, *The Skisport* (patently embracing *Ski-Idraet* in its title) ran a column entitled "Fra Kristiania," and when discussions of jumping styles came up, it simply reprinted the Norwegian rules in Norwegian and added in English at the bottom that they should be followed.

Early meets in the United States comprised both races across the countryside and jumping. Cross-country, so important in the old country, faded rapidly in the United States, first to much shorter courses and then simply deleted from the program; there was a lack of both participation and spectator interest. Jumping, on the other hand, thrived. The best "riders," as the contestants were called, formed a primitive professional circuit by 1907, the year they struck for higher prize money—much to the disgust of Tellefsen and the Norwegian secretary of the NSA, Axel Holter, who were both always keen to uphold the *Idraet* ideal.

Skiing spread to other areas of the United States, and non-Scandinavians took it up with enthusiasm. In New England skiing became popular among undergraduates, with Dartmouth College taking the lead. The jump remained the centerpiece of the carnival, but the Norwegian *Idraet* gave way to skiing as a bourgeois, manly leisure pursuit of the collegians who went on to join associations such as the Sierra Club and the Appalachian Mountain Club. Skiing became a social sport in the 1920s.

In the next decade a craze for downhill and the Austrian Arlberg technique in New England caused the second generation of the Norwegian American-dominated NSA to lose prominence to its eastern affiliate, the U.S. Eastern Amateur Ski Association. The Norwegian telemark technique was overtaken by the Alpine schuss, and *Idraet* could not compete with the amusement offered by social skiing. It appeared that the Norwegian sport had been eclipsed.

Although cross-country and jumping never disappeared, American skiing was heavily oriented to Alpine skiing until the 1970s. Coinciding with the beginnings of America's fitness boom, the unexpected silver medal of Bill Koch in the 1976 Olympic Games in the thirty-kilometer competition rekindled interest in cross-country skiing. Today, alongside the more glamorous (and expensive) events of Alpine skiing, cross-country, albeit on prepared trails, with participants dressed in special outfits and using high-tech equipment, enjoys a place in American skiing. Jumping has become a specialty of a few, largely because of the prohibitive insurance costs.

"Skiing," wrote a contributor to *Leslie's Magazine* 100 years ago, "is one of our foreign imports which is absolutely unobjectionable." Americans now enjoy it in all the snow-covered states, thanks to the initial Norwegian thrust.

SELECTED BIBLIOGRAPHY: E. John B. Allen, *From Skisport to Skiing: One Hundred Years of an American Sport, 1840–1940* (1993); E. John B. Allen, "The Modernization of the Skisport: Ishpeming's Contribution to American Skiing," *The Michigan Historical Review* 16 (Spring 1990): 1–20; Ake Svahnm, "Idrott und Sport. Eine semantische Studie zu zwei schwedischen Fachtermini," *Stadion* 5 (1979): 20–41; Helen M. White, "Ski-Sport Heroes from Norway," in Helen M. White, *The Tale of a Comet and Other Stories* (1984).

E. John B. Allen

SLOVAK CATHOLIC SOKOL. In the late nineteenth century, Slovak immigrants in America began to join fraternal organizations known as Sokols (Falcons), dedicated to building strong and healthy bodies for youth. Modeled on German gymnastic clubs, the Sokols grew into popular recreational and national fraternal societies. Thus, the Sokols were the first sports organization with a relatively wide appeal among Slovak immigrant families. Not only did the organizations become centers of recreation and social life, but they also worked closely with the Slovak national movement in America and at home in Slovakia. Sokols aimed to build character through athletics and to raise ethnic self-awareness among Slovak immigrants and their children.

The earliest Slovaks in America joined Czech Sokols because of the similarity in their languages and cultures. Czechs established their first Sokol organization in St. Louis, Missouri, in 1865, and other clubs soon followed in Chicago, New York, and other cities. As Slovaks came to America in larger numbers after 1870, some joined Czech Sokols out of a spirit of Pan-Slavic solidarity. Once their numbers warranted it, however, Slovaks founded their own Sokol groups. The first local "Slovak Sokol Society" started as a branch of the Czech Sokol in Chicago in 1892. A separate Slovak Gymnastic Sokol Union of America was formed in New York City in 1896.

After some controversy over the focus of its goals, the Slovak Sokol adopted the multiple aims of fostering national, cultural, and gymnastic education while also serving as a mutual aid fraternal society. It particularly targeted youth because they were most interested in sports. In 1905 the Slovak Sokol began publication of *Slovensky Sokol* and introduced standardized uniforms for official events.

The year also marked a watershed in another respect. At the Passaic, New Jersey, convention, the local Sokol requested that only those "affiliated with the Roman Catholic Church" be admitted. Fear of secular and anticlerical freethinkers as well as specific controversies over the distribution of communion with Slovak Lutherans had contributed to the rift. Catholic Slovaks, who were by far in the majority, complained that the group had adopted anti-Catholic programs.

When the central Sokol leadership refused to allow for a church-specific local club, lodges from Passaic and Hibernia, New Jersey, decided to found a separate Slovak Catholic Sokol. The majority of members originated from Spis County in east-central Slovakia and also felt a certain regional solidarity. The decision to leave the national Sokols led to a permanent split in the Slovak American Sokol movement. The new organization named itself the Slovak Roman and Greek Catholic Sokol Union of America, because it included both Roman and Byzantine rite Catholics. It worked closely with Slovak parishes, whose priests encouraged their parishioners to join only the Catholic Sokol. In 1933 the fraternal renamed itself the Slovak Catholic Sokol.

Following the split of the Slovak Sokol movement, the Catholic and secular Sokol held separate meetings, conventions, and biannual *slets*, festivals where members competed in gymnastic events. The Catholic Sokol adopted the slogan "A sound mind in a sound body" and chose the motto "For God and Nation" to symbolize the symbiosis of ethnicity and religion.

Membership in the Catholic Sokol grew quickly, reaching a total of 2,210 in 1910. After 1906, women were permitted to form in lodges, called Wreaths; the men's lodges were entitled Assemblies. To facilitate communication, the fraternal published *Katolicky Sokol* (Catholic Falcon) in 1910 as a supplement in *Slovak v Amerike*, the oldest continually published Slovak newspaper in the United States. A year later the fraternal issued its own paper, *Katolicky Sokol*, which has appeared as a weekly ever since. Although originally published in Slovak, most of the newspaper is now written in English. The Slovak Catholic Sokol eventually grew to become the third largest Slovak fraternal in the United States, with a total membership of over 35,000 by the 1930s.

In addition to sponsoring gymnastics, the Catholic Sokols gradually began to incorporate American sports in their clubs in the early twentieth century. Like other Slovak fraternals, it has provided a variety of insurance plans and student scholarships. It has also supported Catholic charitable institutions and parochial schools founded by Slovak Americans, such as Benedictine High School in Cleveland (a football and basketball powerhouse in the state of Ohio) and St. Cyril Academy for Girls in Danville, Pennsylvania. The heyday of Sokol activism occurred in the 1920s and 1930s. The Slovak Catholic Sokol participated in the 1929 gymnastic festival sponsored by the Czech Catholic gymnastic movement "Orel" (Eagle) in Prague, Czechoslovakia, and their twenty-one representatives returned with first-place honors. In 1935 an assembly of over 1,000 Catholic Sokol athletes celebrated the thirtieth anniversary of the fraternal's founding with one of its largest gatherings. After the war, the communist seizure of power diminished connections with their native Slovak homeland. Slovak Catholic Sokol membership peaked at over 45,000 following World War II as the fraternal experienced a postwar revival in interest. Slovak Sokol Days, such as those celebrated at Idora Park in Youngstown, Ohio, and other cities throughout the 1960s, featured gymnastic demonstrations by Sokol youths. In the 1970s membership began to taper off as the older generation passed away. Since then membership has gradually declined but recently stabilized at about 35,000.

To this day, the Slovak Catholic Sokol sponsors local and national sports activities and hosts annual national tournaments for bowling, golf, basketball, volleyball, and softball. During the 1990s, the Slovak Catholic Sokol continued to hold its annual summer *slets* such as the 1997 event in Kutztown, Pennsylvania. Although the membership has aged, the Slovak Catholic Sokol has been able, through its sports, to attract more youth than some of the other Slovak fraternals.

Since Slovakia became independent in 1993, the Slovak Catholic Sokol has continued its mission of promoting Slovak culture, the Catholic faith, Slovak independence, and sports among Slovak American youth.

SELECTED BIBLIOGRAPHY: Karol Bednar, "The Slovak Gymnastic Union Sokol in the U.S.A.," in *Panorama: A Historical Review of Czechs and Slovaks in the United States of America* (1970), 144–152; Thomas Capek, "Czechoslovaks in the United States," *Chicago Czechoslovak Exhibit* (1934), 25–127; Konstantin Culen, *Dejiny Slovakov v Amerike*, vol. 1 (1942); Stephanie O. Husek, "Slovak American Fraternal, Cultural, and Civic Organizations to 1914," in Joseph Krajsa, ed., *Slovaks in America: A Bicentennial Study* (1978), 23–38; "The Slovak Catholic Sokol," in Joseph Krajsa, ed., *Slovaks in America: A Bicentennial Study* (1978), 209–220; "Slovensky Katolicky Sokol," unpublished document, St. Andrew's Abbey (Cleveland, OH, undated); Daniel Tanzone, "Fraternalism and the Slovak Immigrant," *Jednota Annual Furdek* (1973): 15–29; Daniel Tanzone, "An Overview of Our 90 Years of Fraternal Service," in *Slovak Catholic Sokol. Souvenir Book Pamatnica* (1995); James J. Zatko, "Early Beginnings of Slovaks in America," *Slovakia* (1965).

                                                                          Michael J. Kopanic, Jr.

SLOVAKS. Slovaks first came to the United States in large numbers after the 1880s, when rural overpopulation and the prospect of well-paying jobs lured them to the "promised land" on the other side of the Atlantic. Most of the immigrants from Slovakia, which at the time lay in northern Hungary, came from the poorer eastern counties, which were mountainous and lacked fertile soil. The overwhelming majority of Slovaks lived in small rural villages and earned a bare subsistence-level living.

Sports had never exerted a mass appeal in the nineteenth century; Slovaks were too busy working and enjoyed little leisure time. In addition, the Hungarian government legally barred the formation of Sokol gymnastic organizations in Slovakia, viewing them as seditious cauldrons of nationalist sentiment. The free and widespread participation of Slovaks in the Sokols occurred not in Europe but in the more industrialized America.

The Slovak Sokol, meaning "Falcon" in Slovak, was founded in America as an offshoot of the older Czech organization during the 1890s. Sokols dedicated themselves to building strong and healthy bodies, insuring members, and promoting the national cause. Eventually, the Slovak Sokol movement split into two separate organizations, the original secular Sokol and a Slovak Catholic Sokol,* formed because of the large number of Slovak Catholics. Both organizations continue to function to this day and have increased communication with one another in the 1990s.

While the Sokols originally promoted gymnastics and track-and-field events, that changed after World War I. Sokols as well as other Slovak fraternals gradually sponsored more American sports to attract youth. The Sokols also sold insurance plans and later provided financial grants to qualified students.

In many ways, Slovak fraternals combined with American school athletic programs to heighten Slovak involvement in sporting activities. World War I increased the emphasis on the Americanization of immigrants, and sports provided one means to accelerate the process. With more leisure time in America, children and grandchildren of Slovak immigrants became more and more involved in sports on a mass scale. After the war, Sokols even spread to Slovakia because now these once-forbidden groups were permitted in independent Czechoslovakia. Huge gymnastic festivals, called *slets*, brought together Slovak and Czech Sokols from their own country, the United States, and other countries.

Other Slovak fraternals besides Sokols promoted athletic activities to attract young people and sell insurance, and they did so with a great deal of success. In the immediate post–World War I period, the Cleveland-based First Catholic Slovak Union (Prva katolicka slovenska jednota, usually just shortened as Jednota) devoted a sizable section of its newspaper's attention to boxing, baseball, and other sports in which Slovak Americans participated.

In the 1920s and 1930s a number of young Slovak American boys used boxing as a vehicle of social mobility by which they could earn fast money as well as achieve widespread recognition and fame. Joe Bosco from Barberton, Ohio, sometimes called the "Slovak Tex Rickard," was the first real Slovak boxing promoter. He was also the first American promoter to send his fighters to exotic far-off places such as South Africa, Japan, Jamaica, and other foreign boxing venues. Among his most famous finds was Frankie Wine (Vino), better known as the "Montana Mauler."

A number of prominent Slovak American boxers came from the Cleveland, Ohio, area, including the heavyweight "Rubber Man" Johnny Risko* and the fantastic featherweight Paul James Cvecka, better known by his ring name, Jimmy Vaughn. Pete Latzo (Laco) of Scranton, Pennsylvania, battled his way to win the World Welterweight Championship in 1926. Other prominent Slovak American boxers from the 1920s and 1930s included Joe Banovic of Binghamton, New York, Steve Hamas, "the Slovak Hurricane" from Passaic, New Jersey, George Poslpanka from Homestead, Pennsylvania, Al Hostak, the "Slovak Savage" from Seattle, and Steve Oswald from Milwaukee. In the 1940s, Joe Baksi from Kulpmont, Pennsylvania, represented Slovak Americans' last great hope for a heavyweight title, but he lost a 1945 round to future world champ Jersey Joe Walcott. All these pugilists ignited both local and ethnic Slovak pride.

Along with boxing, baseball became the rage among Slovak Americans. The ever-growing popularity of amateur baseball reached a fever pitch, and more youth actively participated. Fraternals expanded their sports programs and used them as a carrot to attract youth and keep them involved in Slovak American activities.

In the greater Pittsburgh district, the Catholic Jednota escalated its involvement in sports. Jednota founded its first baseball league in 1922, the zupa Ferdinand Juriga, named after the famous contemporary Slovak priest, politician, and writer. The trend spread quickly, and Jednota branches formed local leagues named after Slovak heroes across Pennsylvania, New Jersey, Ohio, Michigan, New York, and Illinois. At season's end, the districts chose All-Star teams, which played other Slovak American teams in other parts of the country for a national fraternal championship. During the long winters, fraternals even formed indoor baseball leagues.

Fraternals involved themselves in other American sports as well. Although not as popular as baseball, basketball also began in the 1930s. The Furdek district, located in the Cleveland area and named after the founder of the Catholic Jednota, Fr. Furdek, formed the first organized roundball loop, and this soon spread to other districts.

World War II marked a sharp dividing line in the evolution of sports among Slovak Americans. So many youth served in the armed forces that it disrupted fraternal sporting activities and caused a number of groups to discontinue their teams. While some revived after the war, the sports movement among fraternals had passed its peak. The war had accelerated further Americanization, while generational changes contributed to a gradual waning of separate ethnic sports participation. Postwar sports of Slovak Americans were concentrated more heavily in schools and in nonethnic leagues.

Among the nonethnic organizations that attracted Slovak American participation after the war were Little Leagues, varsity, and intramural leagues. Some athletes went on to play professional sports such as baseball, hockey, football, basketball, and boxing. Many of the hockey players, such as Stan Mikita,* emigrated from Slovakia and found success in the National Hockey League (NHL). Others who are less well known outside Slovak American circles continued to participate in Sokol gymnastics. For instance, Rudy Bachna became known for his gymnastic instruction at Kent State University and has taught a number of Olympic competitors.

Among the better-known Slovak Americans who went on to play professional baseball are Elmer Valo of the Philadelphia Athletics, Andy Pafko for the Chicago Cubs, George (Shotgun) Shuba of the Brooklyn Dodgers, Jack Kralick pitching for the Cleveland Indians, and Andy Kosco for the New York Yankees. Al Pilarcik, Al Kozar, and many lesser-known players in the history of baseball also had Slovak family origins.

Many Slovak Americans who played professional ball developed a reputation not as superstars but as reliable workhorses and loyal family men. Such is the case with Joe Orsulak, who compiled a solid record for the New York Mets, the Baltimore Orioles, and the Florida Marlins while coping with his wife's terminal cancer and a son who had open-heart operations.

American football grew in popularity in the post–World War II era, and it attracted talented Slovak athletes to both collegiate gridirons and those of the National Football League. Even in prewar America, boys of Slovak descent played football at campuses across the country, especially at Pennsylvania universities and at Catholic colleges such as St. Vincent, Catholic University, and Georgetown as well as at Carnegie Tech, Chicago, and elsewhere. In 1933, Joe "Muggsy" Skladany, an end at the University of Pittsburgh, was the first Slovak American to achieve All-American honors, while John Rokisky of Duquesne University repeated that feat in 1941. In 1938 no fewer than four Slovak Americans played in the All-Star Pro Game: halfbacks Andre Uram and Rudy Gmitro, both from the University of Minnesota, Frank J. Filchock, a quarterback from Indiana University, and George Karametic, halfback for Gonzaga University. Prominent postwar stars include Chuck Bednarik,* George Blanda,* Bernie Kosar, and many others. Dr. Paul Podmajersky played right guard on the Chicago Bears and then went on to serve as physician for the Sokol in the Chicago area.

Since the fall of communism and the lifting of travel restrictions, an increasing number of Slovak athletes have come to the United States to play hockey. For instance, Robert Dome from Skalica played for Utah, Long Beach, and Las Vegas in the International Hockey League. In 1997 the Pittsburgh Penguins chose him as a first-round draft choice in the NHL draft. Slovakia promises to be a continuing source of athletes for hockey.

After World War II, a few other sports became popular among Slovak American fraternals, especially bowling and golf. The change also reflected an accommodation to the older average age of fraternal members. Fraternals such as the National Slovak Society, the First Slovak Wreath of the Free Eagle, Jednota, and the Slovak Catholic Sokol have sponsored interstate bowling tournaments mostly in the states between New Jersey and Illinois. Although participation peaked in previous decades, the Slovak Sokols continue to use sports as a vehicle to attract members, continuing a proud tradition that has become identified with their national heritage.

SELECTED BIBLIOGRAPHY: Karol Bednar, "The Slovak Gymnastic Union Sokol in the U.S.A.," in *Panorama: A Historical Review of Czechs and Slovaks in the United States of America* (1970), 144–152; *Cleveland Yearbook* (1924); George Eisen and David K. Wiggins, eds., *Ethnicity and Sport in North American History and Culture* (1994); John McCallum and Charles H. Pearson, *College Football U.S.A. 1869 . . . 1973* (1973); Edward Minarcak, "The Steady Expansion of Baseball Activities in the Jednota," *Kalendar Jednota* (1933): 83–88; Edward Minarcak, "Sketching the 1936 Jednota Sport Enterprise," *Kalendar Jednota* (1933): 193–200; Stan Mikita, *I Play to Win* (1969); Andrew Pier, "Our Slovak Heritage in America," in Joseph Krajsa, ed., *Slovaks in America: A Bicentennial Study* (1978), 79–88; *Slovak Catholic Falcon* 86, No. 4283 (1996); Anna L. Sopoci, "The Slovak Gymnastic Union Sokol," copy sent by Daniel Tanzone; Mark Stolarik, *The Slovak Americans* (1988); Anthony X. Sutherland, "Tales from Our Jednota History," *Jednota Annual Furdek* 27 (January 1989): 241–284; Daniel Tanzone, "An Overview of Our 90 Years of Fraternal Service," in *Slovak Catholic Sokol. Souvenir Book–Pamatnica* (1995); David D. Van Tassel and John J. Grabowski, eds., *Encyclopedia of Cleveland History* (1987).

Michael J. Kopanic, Jr.

SLOVENIANS. Slovenians, of the westernmost Slavic nation, who number in their Alpine native land Slovenia only about 2 million souls, were for centuries a part of the Austrian empire and, after World War I, with the exception of the 1941–45 Axis-occupation period, the northermost province of Yugoslavia. This explains why they—including their athletes (among them the oldest Olympian gold medalist, the ninety-eight-year-old Leon Stukelj, who generated so much enthusiasm at the Atlanta Summer Olympic Games in 1996)—were almost unknown by their nationality or ethnicity as Slovenians but were referred to simply in terms of their citizenship as Austrians or Yugoslavs. Longing to assert their identity and achieve independence, they proclaimed the independent Republic of Slovenia on 25 June 1991 and subsequently gained international recognition. According to calculations by this author, based on the ethnically more precise 1910 U.S. Census and the subsequent population growth, the current number of Americans of Slovenian and mixed descent is at least 540,000.

Slovenian sport activities in America fall into three categories. "Private sports," spontaneous and unorganized, such as jogging, skiing, and skating, have been engaged in by individuals and families. The second category includes organized groups consisting exclusively or predominantly of Slovenian members such as Sokols, Orels, and clubs of bowlers, golfers, and so on. Finally, Slovenians participate in ethnically integrated American sports—American football teams, baseball leagues, and so on.

Within the second category, the Slovenian American Sokols (Falcons) were first established in Cleveland, Ohio, in 1893. They were soon followed by women's *Slovenske Sokolice* and by the Orels (Eagles) in several Slovenian American communities.

Slovenian American fraternal (self-help) organizations have always devoted a considerable portion of their activities and resources to numerous sports, especially to bowling, basketball, golf, *balina* (the Slovene version of bocce) and baseball, organizing numerous local, regional, and national tournaments.

After World War II the Slovenian anticommunist political immigrants established their own Slovenian sport clubs, like the Slovenian Gymnastic Union (Slovenska Telovadna Zveza), with many sportfests and competitions on local, national, and American Canadian levels. Former European Orel champions Ivo Kermavner and especially Janez Varsek devoted nearly every spare moment to transmitting some of their skills and enthusiasm to the young Slovenian generation. More recently, American and Canadian Slovenian skiing groups and competitions for all age groups have been organized.

Slovenians have also participated in the third mentioned category of ethnically integrated American mainstream sports. Judging by newspaper coverage, bowling has been the most popular participation sport in America. In 1975 John Bovitz, a notable Slovenian bowler and journalist in Minnesota, was elected president of the 4.3 million-member American Bowling Congress. Prominent Slovenian female bowlers include the sisters Stevie Rozman Balough and Sophie

Rozman Kenny, as well as Margie Slogar and Mary Doljack "Whitey" Primosh; the latter also played on world champion softball and basketball teams. Among several outstanding American male bowlers were Charles J. Lausche, Andrew E. Stanovnik, and Jim Stefanich, who won the 1967 Tournament of Champions.

Many Slovenians developed a great enthusiasm for American football. This is apparent from the large number of outstanding Slovenian high school and college football players, coaches, and stars. Among those who earned national distinction are Tony Adamle of Ohio State and the Cleveland Browns, his son Mike Adamle of Northwestern and the New York Jets and Chicago Bears, Andy Kozar of Tennessee and the Bears, Robert Anthony (Dick) Stanfel of the University of San Francisco and the Detroit Lions, and, more recently, Randy Gradishar of Ohio State and the Denver Broncos and Bob Golic of Notre Dame and the Cleveland Browns, where Bob Palcic is offensive line coach.

Numerous Slovenian Americans also fell in love with baseball and established many sandlot teams. Several players rose to the level of minor and major baseball leagues, among them Frank J. Lausche (who later chose politics over the offered position of baseball commissioner), Ernie Zupancic, John and Frank Doljack, Joe Kuhel (also manager of the Washington Senators), Al Milnar, Al Widmar, Walter Judnich, and Mark Petkovsek. Recently, John Smoltz of the Atlanta Braves has developed into one of the premier pitchers of the National League.

Ronald Tomsic gained national prominence when he played on the American Olympic basketball team that won the gold medal at the Summer Olympic Games in Melbourne, Australia, in 1956. Among the college basketball players, Arizona State University star Tony Cerkvenik was called by the legendary University of California at Los Angeles (UCLA) coach John Wooden "the greatest college rebounder I ever saw." Yul (Julko) Yost, a refugee from communist Yugoslavia, is the most prominent Slovenian volleyball player. A member of the national championship teams of Yugoslavia, Portugal, Puerto Rico, and the United States, he gained fame at the 1958 Amateur Athletic Union championship when he was clocked as "the most powerful volleyball hitter in the world."

Since the 1930s golf has become popular among Slovenian Americans of all social classes. The best known among the outstanding Slovenian amateur golfers was Ohio governor and U.S. senator Frank J. Lausche, and the most prominent Slovenian golf professional is Rudy Habjan, who was honored by the Professional Golfers' Association in 1965 as the Golf Professional of the Year. David Ogrin was a successful tour player in the 1980s and 1990s.

Skiing has gradually surpassed its recreational popularity, leading to nationally recognized achievements. William (Bill) Marolt won a number of national championships and became in 1979 the overall Alpine director, training the top American skiers for various competitions and the Winter Olympics. Bill's brother Bud has also served as ski school director of the popular Loveland Valley Ski School. Adolph M. Kuss became the cross-country coach for the

1964 U.S. Olympic team and the Nordic combined coach for the 1972 U.S. Olympic team, as well as a Nordic coach for the U.S. ski team from 1963 through 1972. Jim Grahek was selected as one of America's fourteen best ski jumpers, joined the Olympic ski jumping team, and was appointed the national head junior ski jumping coach in 1984. Slovenians also made their mark in the U.S. Collegiate Ski Association, where Vojko Lapajna won the 1992 giant slalom national championship, while Jani Grasic was the 1993 Combined National Champion.

In the 1930s Ann Govednik won some state and national swimming championships. She became the American champion in the 200-meter breaststroke in 1934, as well as a member of the U.S. Olympic team. Three other Slovenians, Joe Pucel, Leonard Klun, and Joe Grahek, nailed down the Minnesota State Diving Championships from 1932 to 1938. Slovenian immigrant Anton Cerer had been a member of the Yugoslav Olympic swimming team and competed with splendid results in the 1992 U.S. Masters at Indianapolis, where he won six gold medals in the seventy-five to seventy-nine-year category and established three new world records.

Another immigrant from Slovenia, Vicky Sega Foltz, was a three-time AACC (state college) champ in track and cross-country, 1979–80; Canadian and U.S. cross-country champion and world champion at four, five, and six miles and at 10,000 meters in 1970; world age group 35–40 gold medalist in marathon, cross-country, 10,000 meters and 5,000 meters, and World Road Race Champion in 1981.

In the sport of hot-air balloon piloting, Al Nels won the 1984 national championship. Professor Edo Marion, former Yugoslav fencing champion and participant in the 1936 Olympics at Berlin, served as Harvard University's fencing coach. Eddie Simms was Cleveland's and the U.S. Army's heavyweight boxing champion.

In car racing, the names of Don Yenko, Ernie Adamic and his brothers Ray and Al, and Joe Martincic stand out as winners of championships and numerous trophies, while sports cars designed by the Slovenian immigrant John Bucik appeared on the cover of several American magazines. Frank Brimsek became a hockey goalie legend, having played as goaltender with the Boston Bruins and Chicago Blackhawks. He won the Stanley Cup twice, as well as the Vezina Trophy as the National Hockey League's leading goalie, and was elected to the U.S. Hockey Hall of Fame in 1973.

Speed skaters Eric and Beth Heiden trace their maternal roots to Slovenia, while their father is of German origin. In February 1979, Eric Heiden won his eighth world championship. At the 1984 Olympic Winter Games in Lake Placid he won the unprecedented total of five gold medals. Eric's sister Beth won the world speed skating women's championship in February 1979 at The Hague and a bronze medal in 3,000-meter speed skating at Lake Placid Olympics. Nick J. Thometz was U.S. National Sprint Champion in 1984, 1985, and 1989 and a member of U.S. Olympic team in 1984, 1988, and 1992. He established a world record in 500-meter speed skating in 1987 and served as Olympic team coach in 1993–94 and national sprint team coach a year later. Since 1994 he has also been program director of U.S. speed skating.

Among weight lifters, Joseph H. Germ won the Ohio State Championship in the 132-pound. class in 1936 and the silver medal in Paris World Championships in 1937. Jeff Blatnick captured the gold medal in the superheavyweight division in Greco-Roman wrestling at the 1984 Summer Olympics at Los Angeles.

Peter Vidmar was the premier male gymnast in the Los Angeles Olympic Games, leading his teammates to his country's first gold medal in gymnastics and winning the silver medal in the individual all-around competition and the gold medal on the pommel horse.

Finally, it is difficult to imagine American sports without excellent sport facilities. Among these, the Three Rivers Stadium in Pittsburgh; Memorial Stadium in Austin, Texas; West Virginia Coliseum in Morgantown; Bowling Green, Kent State, Miami University, University of Michigan, and University of Wisconsin stadiums; Hiram Bithorn Stadium in Puerto Rico; and Robert F. Kennedy Stadium in Washington, D.C., were designed by Alexander Papesh (1928–71), the son of Slovenian immigrants and a partner of Osborn and Papesh Architects-Engineers, Inc. They represent another example of important Slovenian contributions to American sports.

SELECTED BIBLIOGRAPHY: Cecilia Dolgan, ed., *Slovenian National Directory* (1984); Edward Gobetz, ed., *Slovenian Heritage* (1981); Edward Gobetz, *Slovenia and Slovenian Americans* (1994); Archives of the Slovenian Research Center of America, Willoughby Hills, OH, 1951–97.

Edward Gobetz

SMITH, TOMMIE (6 June 1944, Clarksville, TX–   ). An African American track athlete, he is the son of James Richard Smith, a sharecropper and utility man, and Dora Smith, a domestic. When Smith was six years old, his father moved his family to Lemoore, California, near Fresno. As a boy Tommie picked cotton and gave his wages to his father. He excelled in athletics at Lemoore High School, and in 1963 he earned a scholarship to San Jose State College. Over the next few years he set world records for 200 meters and 200 yards. Although he decided not to follow the recommendation of Harry Edwards* to boycott the 1968 Olympic Games at Mexico City, he did express his feelings about racial injustice in the United States at the medal ceremony after he won the 200-meter event in the world record time of 19.83 seconds. He and bronze medal winner John Carlos* lowered their heads and raised black-gloved fists during the raising of the American flag and the playing of the national anthem. The U.S. Olympic Committee then suspended Smith and Carlos from the Olympic team and ordered them to return home. The International Olympic Committee also barred him from future Olympic Games. Smith graduated with B.S. degrees in social science and education from San Jose State in 1969. He later was a wide receiver for the Cincinnati Bengals for three years in the National Football League. After his retirement he became track coach and later was appointed athletic director at Oberlin College. In 1978 he took the position as track-and-field and cross-country coach at Santa Monica College. That year he was also elected to the National Track and Field Hall of Fame. Later in his life he worked as a sports therapist and was an innovator in the field of water therapy for purposes of rehabilitation. He also owned Calohtex, Inc. in Los Angeles.

SELECTED BIBLIOGRAPHY: Neil Admur, "Tommie Smith at 34: His Struggle Goes On," *New York Times*, 24 December 1978, D1, D4; Arthur R. Ashe, Jr., *A Hard Road to Glory: A History of the African-American Athlete since 1946*, vol. 3 (1988); Peter Axthelm, "Boycott Now—Boycott Later," *Sports Illustrated* 28 (26 February 1968): 24–26; Harry Edwards, *The Revolt of the Black Athlete* (1969); Edwin B. Henderson, ed., *International Library of Afro-American Life and History: The Black Athlete, Emergence and Arrival* (1976); "Radical Sprinters Back on Track," *Newsweek* 99 (8 March 1982): 12.

Earl Smith and George B. Kirsch

SMITH, WENDELL (27 June 1914, Detroit–26 November 1972, Chicago). An African American sportswriter, he grew up near the Ford family since his father worked as a chef for Henry Ford, Sr. He graduated from Southeast High School in Detroit, where he was an All-City basketball and baseball player. He attended West Virginia State College on an athletic scholarship, where he received a bachelor's degree in education in 1937. While there he captained the baseball and basketball teams as well as serving as sports editor for the school newspaper. After graduation Smith started his journalism career with the *Pittsburgh Courier-Journal*. By 1938 Smith was the sports editor for the *Courier-Journal* and later for the *Chicago American*. He also became a sportscaster for WGNTV in 1964. Smith also wrote a weekly column for the *Chicago Sun-Times*. He is best known for his labors in behalf of the integration of major league baseball. In 1945 he recommended Jackie Robinson* to Branch Rickey as the black baseball player who was most suitable to break the color barrier in major league baseball. He traveled with Robinson when he entered the major leagues, telling his story for the American public. Smith later ghostwrote Robinson's book, *My Own Story*. To honor Smith for his contributions he was posthumously awarded the J. G. Taylor Spink Award in 1993 and then was elected into the Writer's Wing of the Baseball Hall of Fame.

SELECTED BIBLIOGRAPHY: Jim Reisler, *Black Writers/Black Baseball: An Anthology of Articles from Black Sportswriters Who Covered the Negro Leagues* (1994); Tom Weir, "Smith a Baseball Pioneer Worthy of Honor," *USA Today*, 7 February 1994, 3C; David K. Wiggins, "Wendell Smith, the *Pittsburgh Courier-Journal*, and the Campaign to Include Blacks in Organized Baseball, 1933–1945," *Journal of Sport History* 10 (Summer 1983): 5–29; Wendell Smith Papers, at the National Baseball Hall of Fame, Cooperstown, NY.

Leslie Heaphy

SNYLYK, ZENON (14 November 1933, Putiatyntsi, Ukraine–). A stalwart soccer player in the United States, he is the son of Ukrainian immigrants Mykhailo Snylyk, an engineer, and Evstakhia (Klodzinska) Snylyk, a teacher. Snylyk was a two-time All-American for the University of Rochester (1954, 1955). In 1993 he was elected to that institution's Hall of Fame. He holds the national record for having been selected three consecutive times to U.S. Olympic soccer teams (1956, 1960, 1964). He starred with several Ukrainian clubs in the United States and was also a three-time member of the U.S. World Cup soccer squad. He currently leads Ukrainian soccer players with over ninety-two caps representing the U.S. in international matches. Snylyk also distinguished himself in tennis in local public tournaments and has earned regional rankings in his age group. He earned an M.A. in journalism from the University of Chicago in 1958 and was on the faculty at McGill University, 1959–60. During the 1990s he was the editor of the Ukrainian newspaper *Svoboda* in Jersey City, New Jersey.

SELECTED BIBLIOGRAPHY: Walter Dushnyk, *The Ukrainian Heritage in America* (1991); Vasyl Markus, *Ukraine—A Concise Encyclopedia* (1971); Dmtryo Shtohryn, *Ukrainians in North America* (1975).

Metodij Boretsky

SOCCER. Ethnic groups have long played a central role in the history of soccer in the United States, particularly in keeping the sport alive during the many decades when it was pushed to the fringes of American sports consciousness.

There is considerable debate as to how soccer arrived in the United States, which seems to have happened in the 1860s. It might have been brought by immigrants, but the more likely scenario is that it was brought back from England by American visitors, particularly as the sport did not become substantially established outside English schools and universities until 1870 or later.

All of that was during an era when a patchwork of similar, but not identical, games was being played at different schools and universities in England (common rules of soccer were not established until 1863). It is therefore difficult to say in individual cases whether a particular game played in an American city or university was soccer or not, but the first competition in the United States that is purported to have been a form of soccer was by the Oneida Football Club of Boston in 1862. The match between Rutgers and Princeton in 1869, which is often cited as the first American intercollegiate football game, was really a variant of soccer.

However, while it is not certain what role immigrant groups may have played in the arrival of soccer in the United States, it is clear that they were heavily involved in the growth of the sport. In the twentieth century, ethnic groups from the continent of Europe have played the largest role in American ethnic soccer. But in the latter part of the nineteenth century, the immigrants who fueled the initial growth of American soccer were most heavily from England, Scotland, and Ireland. Throughout the world, the leading factor in the spread of soccer away from its origins in England has been the presence of British workers, and this was as true in the United States as elsewhere.

Of the various areas that can claim to be original hotbeds of American soccer, perhaps the best early claim comes from the West Hudson area of northern New Jersey, centering on the cities of Kearny, Paterson, and Newark. There, textile industries drew thousands of British immigrants, particularly Scottish. By the final decades of the nineteenth century soccer was moving away from its upper-class origins and becoming a working-class sport in England, and the same thing was happening in the United States.

This area has continued through the decades to be a center of American ethnic soccer, particularly in the 1930s, when the Kearny Scots American and Kearny Irish American clubs were among the best in the country. Among the few players who were stars of the U.S. teams at both the 1990 and 1994 World Cup tournaments were two who grew up in Kearny, one the son of immigrants from Scotland and the other the son of immigrants from Italy.

Employment opportunities for immigrants made many other areas of the northeastern United States soccer hotbeds in the late 1800s and early 1900s. The employers included, most prominently, textile mills in Philadelphia and the Fall River, Massachusetts, regions and shipyards in the New York and Boston areas.

Fall River (a designation that in soccer nomenclature also includes the neighboring cities of New Bedford, Massachusetts, and Providence and Pawtucket, Rhode Island) enjoys a hallowed place in American soccer annals because of a series of strong teams over the years, beginning before the turn of the century. Perhaps the most famous of these came long after the British immigration of the 1800s. This was Ponta Delgada of Fall River, a team based in the area's large Portuguese community, which won several major championships in the late 1940s and contributed a number of players to the U.S. national team.

In addition, nineteenth-century immigration provided the impetus for soccer's growth in St. Louis, the home of many national champion teams over the years and the only city that can claim to have provided players for each of the five U.S. teams that have reached the World Cup tournament.

For much of the twentieth century St. Louis soccer has been based around commercial sponsors rather than ethnic organizations. But the reasons the sport first took hold there around the turn of the century are strongly connected to Irish immigration and the involvement of Catholic Church organizations.

By the period after World War I, the emphasis in American ethnic soccer had begun to turn away from the British and Irish immigrants to groups from Central Europe. The sport had by now become well established in Germany, Austria, Hungary, and elsewhere, and more immigrants from those countries were bringing an interest in the sport across the Atlantic with them. The 1920s did witness the brief establishment of a professional league, the American Soccer League* (ASL), that relied heavily on players from England, Scotland, and Ireland. However, it did not last much beyond the economic crash of 1929.

Six members of the U.S. team in the 1930 World Cup (which fared better than any American World Cup team since) were born in England or Scotland. But contrary to British popular myth, these were not British professional soccer players imported to America. Five of them had come to the United States as teenagers, as part of the sort of immigration movement that traditionally has fueled American soccer over the years. All six had earned their credentials as professional soccer players in the American Soccer League (ASL) of the 1920s. They were the beginnings of a long tradition of U.S. World Cup efforts benefiting from the talents of Americans who were born elsewhere. In 1994, when the World Cup was played in the United States, the American team included Tabere Ramos and Fernando Clavijo, both born in Uruguay; Frank Klopas, born in Greece; Roy Wegerle, born in South Africa; and Hugo Perez, born in El Salvador.

The German-American Soccer League of New York was also founded in the 1920s. This league (by no means limited to German teams or players) is perhaps the most prominent of the many ethnic leagues that emerged in American urban areas during the twentieth century. Others of particular significance have been the National Soccer League of Chicago and the Greater Los Angeles Soccer League.

While it would be a mistake to view teams or leagues with ethnic names as being restricted to players from a particular ethnic group, there was considerable ethnic connection in teams with German names like New York Eintracht and Los Angeles Kickers, Italian names like New York Colombo and Baltimore Pompeii, Greek names like New York Hellenic and San Francisco Greek-American, and Eastern European names like New York Hungaria and Chicago Slovak. A very frequent pattern was for the soccer team to be affiliated with an ethnic social club.

That immigration movements have been a major underpinning of American soccer is reflected in a statement by Walter Bahr, an American soccer hero of the 1940s and 1950s, that was quoted in a 1995 presentation at the National Soccer Hall of Fame. "After World War II," Bahr said, "ten of thousands of Ukrainians fled war-torn Europe to come to America. They had outstanding clubs in New York, Philadelphia, Newark and Toronto, and raised our soccer to new heights. After the Hungarian Revolution in 1956, we found Hungarian soccer clubs with top players taking the league and national titles. Every time there is an upheaval in the world, the soccer-playing immigrants come over and our soccer has benefitted."

A wider-based league than the heavily ethnic local leagues has been the ASL, which, although it went out of business as a professional league in 1931, was reorganized in 1933 as a semipro league and lasted until 1984. Many of the ASL's leading teams over the years were based around ethnic groups, with the list of ASL champions including such names as Kearny Scots-American, Brooklyn Hispano, Philadelphia Ukrainian Nationals, and New York Greek-Americans.

The effect of ethnic involvement has been much less significant in American collegiate soccer than in the club version of the sport, or at least less obvious. The most noticeable effect has been on the coaching side, rather than the playing side. Few foreign-born Americans have made a major impact on college soccer as players, but many have as coaches, perhaps most prominently Jimmy Mills of Haverford and Bill Jeffrey of Penn State, both born in Scotland; Steve Negoesco of the University of San Francisco, born in Romania; and Walt Chyzowych of Philadelphia Textile, born in Ukraine. American collegiate soccer has also benefited greatly from the playing talents of thousands of second- and third-generation Americans. Many outstanding American college players might never have set foot on a soccer field had they not grown up in homes where they were encouraged to play soccer by foreign-born parents or grandparents.

Crucial to the ethnic involvement in American soccer for much of the twentieth century has been the way that immigrants took leadership positions in the administration of the sport. Randolph Manning,* an Englishman educated in Germany, was the driving force in the creation of the U.S. Football Association (USFA), which was founded in 1913 as the governing body of the sport in the United States and still holds that role today, though its name now is the U.S. Soccer Federation (USSF). As influential in their day as Manning were Joseph Barriskill, born in Ireland, who was secretary of the USFA from 1943 to 1971, and Erno Schwarcz,* born in Hungary, who was business manager of the American Soccer League during much of the same era.

Presidents of the USFA came and went, but Barriskill, whose position involved overseeing the organization's day-to-day operations, was its real controlling hand for decades. Schwarcz, who originally came to America as a player on the Hakoah team from Austria that toured the United States in 1926 and 1927, was Barriskill's opposite number on the league side of the American soccer equation at midcentury.

But men like these also symbolized a problem that existed in an "ethnic" sport administered by people who loved the game and devoted countless hours to it but who were often not professional managers. American soccer might have died without the involvement of the ethnic groups, but any organization that relies as heavily on volunteer leadership as American soccer did for decades can be taking a risk.

This began to change significantly in 1984, when Werner Fricker* became president of the USSF. Fricker, born in Yugoslavia, was certainly from a strong ethnic and soccer background, but he also definitely was a professional manager, a very prosperous real estate developer in the Philadelphia suburbs. Among Fricker's many accomplishments at the USSF were the organization and administration of the campaign that culminated in 1988 with the selection of the United States by the Fédération Internationale de Football Association (FIFA) (the world governing body of soccer) as the host nation for the 1994 World Cup. This success, far and away the greatest achievement to that date by an

American soccer administrator, sowed the seeds of Fricker's downfall. In 1990 FIFA decided that running the World Cup was a job for the sort of executive who had made a success of the 1984 Olympic Games in Los Angeles. In that year Fricker was defeated for reelection as USSF president by a California lawyer, Alan Rothenberg, who was backed by FIFA.

However, the defeat of Fricker has not caused an end to ethnic involvement in American soccer but rather a change from the European orientation of the previous decades to a Latin orientation. Hispanic leagues have long been a major part of the ethnic soccer scene in the United States, especially in Florida and California, but rarely has the USSF paid as much attention to them as to the more traditional ethnic groups. Rothenberg made it a major program of his USSF presidency to tap the long-overlooked resource of the tremendous interest in soccer by many Hispanic Americans.

It is because of this that it appears that the last chapter of the story of ethnic involvement in American soccer has not been written. The eras when American soccer had a strong British and Irish flavor, when it had a strong Central European flavor, and when it had a strong Eastern European flavor do seem to be over. But in the 1990s, the era of a strong Hispanic flavor may be only beginning.

SELECTED BIBLIOGRAPHY: Nathan D. Abrams, " 'Inhibited but Not Crowded Out': The Strange Fate of Soccer in the United States," *The International Journal of the History of Sport* 12 (December 1995): 1–17; Tony Cirino, *U.S. Soccer vs. the World* (1983); Sam Foulds and Paul Harris, *America's Soccer Heritage* (1979); Andrei Markovits, "The Other 'American Exceptionalism': Why Is There No Soccer in the United States?" *The International Journal of the History of Sport* 7 (September 1990): 230–264; Len Oliver, "The Ethnic Legacy in U.S. Soccer," *Newsletter of the Society for American Soccer History* (Winter 1996, Spring 1996, and Summer 1996); J. C. Pooley, "Ethnic Soccer Clubs in Milwaukee: A Study in Assimilation," in M. Marie Hunt, ed., *Sport in the Sociocultural Process* (1972), 328–345.

Roger Allaway

SOCKALEXIS, LOUIS FRANCIS (24 October 1871, Old Town, ME–24 December 1913, Burlington, ME). A Native American baseball player, he was the son of Francis and Frances (Sockbeson) Sockalexis. Young Louis ignored his father's disdain for the "sport of the white man." Blessed with all the skills, Louis registered averages of .436 and .444 during two seasons of baseball at Holy Cross College (1895–96), where he also pitched three no-hitters. He also played briefly at Notre Dame. He captured the imagination of fans everywhere in his 1897 major league debut with the Cleveland Spiders of the National League when he homered twice against New York Giant great Amos Rusie. His average stood at .413 that May before his colossal fall from grace. An ankle injury and evidence that binge drinking was affecting his fielding put "Sock" on the bench for the latter part of 1897. Sockalexis finished that first season at

.338, with sixteen stolen bases and ten assists. He was used sparingly in 1898–99 and played two more seasons in the minors. Sockalexis' demise may have resulted from a combination of the overall dissociated, rowdy behavior of baseball in the "roaring nineties," poor personal choices, and an inability to deal with the legacy of 300 years of colonial oppression and institutionalized racism directed toward Indians.

SELECTED BIBLIOGRAPHY: Bud Leavitt, "Louis Francis Sockalexis," *Bangor Daily News*, 22–23 December 1979, 19–20; Harry Grayson, *They Played the Game* (1945).

Joseph M. Giovannetti

SOKOL USA (originally the Slovak Gymnastic Union Sokol). This organization celebrated its centennial in 1996, with a gymnastic festival called a "*slet*" in Philadelphia. The first Slovak Sokol club was founded in 1892 in Chicago, a second one appeared the following year in New York City, and a third in Bridgeport, Connecticut, in 1895. The latter two formed Sokol USA in 1896, which established a training schedule following that created by the founder of the Czech Sokol, Miroslav Tyrš, as well as a mandatory life insurance program for its members, which other immigrant fraternal organizations offered at this time. Some Sokol clubs, such as the one in Chicago, objected to the insurance program and refused to join. Nevertheless, at a time when expressions of ethnic pride were banned in Slovakia, Sokol USA flourished as a center for Slovak gymnastic and national culture. This effort was aided by the launching of a monthly paper, *Slovensky Sokol*, later renamed the *Sokol Times*.

In 1905, the Slovak Sokol club in Passaic, New Jersey, sought affiliation with the Roman Catholic Church, a bulwark of Slovak cultural identity. The request was denied by church authorities because the organization, following Tyrš' dictum, was open to all Slavs, regardless of religion. Because of this, the Passaic club seceded and formed the Slovak Catholic Sokol,* and several other Slovak Sokol clubs followed them. In addition to this dissension, the Slovak Sokol also faced the bitter opposition of the Hungarian government, which ruled over Slovakia at this time and banned the Sokol there. Because of this, Sokol USA was often short of instructors and had to educate newly arrived immigrants regarding its mission.

The creation of the new country of Czechoslovakia in 1918 improved the situation of the Slovak Sokol. In 1935 there were 208 Slovak Sokol clubs, only half of which went beyond insurance to offer gymnastic and sports activities, with a total membership of 12,359 adults and 7,195 juveniles. The Board of Instructors, led by the director of men, Karel Bednar, and the directors of women, Betty Klimow and Bessy Erhard, coordinated the gymnastic program, which included a system of gymnastic summer courses as well as traveling instructors to improve training in the individual clubs. Backed by the Czech Sokol organization, these efforts propelled Sokol USA to its highest level. In 1952 Sokol USA published their Sokol gymnastic manual, a translation of Tyrš' Sokol program, which has been revised and updated over the years.

Sokol USA had always been a center for progressive American Slovaks who supported cooperation with the Czechs. The editor of *Sokol Times*, Milan Getting, had been a moving force behind the Pittsburgh Agreement of 1918, which created the basis for a joint state of Czechs and Slovaks, and one of his successors, Karel Bednar, had opposed the Munich Agreement of 1938, which, by ceding Sudeten German territories to Nazi Germany, began the dismantling of the Czechoslovak state. In addition, American Slovaks had fought for the cause of Czechoslovak freedom in World War I and World War II.

Although Sokol USA has traditionally directed its efforts toward mass training, especially for children, it has also produced many talented gymnasts. Tom Balas was an alternate on the U.S. Olympic team in 1940, Ellen Babuska-Kovac won the New Jersey Amateur Athletic Union Championship in the years 1964 through 1969 and was named College All-American at the NCAA Championship in 1968, and Janet Bachna was manager of the U.S. women's gymnastic team at the Olympic Games in Rome in 1960 and was inducted into the Gymnastic Hall of Fame in 1966.

The fortunes of Sokol USA have declined since its high point in the 1930s. Especially since World War II, it has suffered from a lack of instructors, and current membership stands at 8,700 members, including juveniles, in eighty-two clubs, eleven of which offer gymnastic training. The organization runs one summer camp with gymnastic training for children and courses for instructors, holds gymnastic festivals (*slets*) every four years, and hosts popular golf and bowling tournaments. The organization is currently located in East Orange, New Jersey. Its leaders are elected every four years at a convention. Since 1994, Beatrice Walko has been president; Milan Kovac, secretary; Gail Wallach and David Walko, gymnastic directors; and Ellen Babuska-Kovac, editor of the club paper.

Sokol USA led the efforts to issue two U.S. stamps, one honoring Thomas Garrigue Masaryk, first president of Czechoslovakia in 1918, and the other commemorating the Sokol itself. Both appeared in the 1960s as part of the "Champions of Liberty" series. Over the last 100 years, Sokol USA has played a prominent role in shaping the character and fitness of thousands of immigrants and young Americans. As the dream of the original members became a reality, Sokol USA found its place in the mainstream of American society, devoting its efforts to improving the fitness of American youth.

SELECTED BIBLIOGRAPHY: *Centennial of the Sokols in America, 1865–1965* (1965); A. B. Frederick, *Roots of American Gymnastics* (1995); Richard Edd Laptad, *A History of the Development of the United States Gymnastics Federation* (1972); Minot Simons, *Women's Gymnastics: A History* (1995).

Vladislav Slavik

SPITZ, MARK A. (10 February 1950, Modesto, CA–   ). A swimmer of Jewish descent, he is the son of Arnold and Lenore Spitz; his father was a steel company executive. He began to swim when he was two years old, and by the age of ten he held seventeen national age group records. After winning four gold medals in 1965 at the Maccabiah Games in Tel Aviv, Israel, and five gold medals in 1967 at the Pan-American Games in Winnipeg, Canada, he was favored in four events in the 1968 Olympic Games in Mexico City. However, his performance fell short of expectations, as he took home gold medals only in relay events. In individual competitions he finished second in the 100-meter butterfly and third in the 200-meter freestyle. After graduating from Santa Clara High School in June 1968, he entered Indiana University in January 1969 as a predental student. During his collegiate career Spitz helped the Hoosiers capture the National Collegiate Athletic Association (NCAA) swimming championship every year, winning two NCAA and four Amateur Athletic Union individual swimming titles in 1971. That achievement earned him the 1971 James E. Sullivan Award as the nation's premier amateur athlete. After graduating from Indiana in 1972, Spitz gained worldwide fame at the Olympic Games in late August and early September. He finished first in the 200-meter butterfly, the 200-meter freestyle, the 100-meter butterfly, and the 100-meter freestyle, adding three more gold medals in relay events. Although journalists' accounts of Spitz's achievements included brief references to his Jewish heritage and the significance of his performance in a German city, most reports reflected a Cold War viewpoint by portraying him as an American hero who conquered his communist East German rivals. But the murder of eleven members of Israel's Olympic team by Arab terrorists on 5 September overshadowed Spitz's gold medals and records. Olympic officials, fearing that Spitz might also be a target of the terrorists, immediately flew him to London. Spitz then announced his retirement from competitive swimming. Although he had previously planned to enter dental school, he soon decided to cash in on the numerous lucrative offers he received for media appearances and commercial endorsements. In later years he pursued business interests, including real estate investments.

SELECTED BIBLIOGRAPHY: Joseph Bell, "Mark Spitz, What Now?" *Seventeen* 32 (May 1973): 140; Jerry Kirshenbaum, "On Your Mark, Get Set, Sell," *Sports Illustrated* (14 May 1973): 36; Peter Levine, *Ellis Island to Ebbets Field: Sport and the American Jewish Experience* (1992), 251–254; Susan Lydon, "All That Gold Waiting to Glitter," *New York Times Magazine* (11 March 1973): VI-4; *New York Times*, 29 August 1972, 28; *Newsweek* 100 (11 September 1972): 58; *Sports Illustrated* 32 (9 March 1970): 26.

George B. Kirsch

ST. GEORGE CRICKET CLUB. The St. George Cricket Club of Manhattan claimed to be the first regular cricket association in the United States governed by rules and regulations. It originated in two matches held in Brooklyn in the fall of 1838 between several sides of Englishmen resident in New York City and Brooklyn. The club was more formally constituted in 1839 and was finally christened on St. George's Day (23 April) in 1840 in the rear of a tavern on the old Bloomingdale Road in Manhattan. Its first members were mostly English import merchants and agents for British companies. The club's first professional was Sam Wright, a recent arrival from Sheffield and father of Harry and George Wright,* who later became famous in both cricket and baseball. Its first ground was on East Thirty-first Street, near First Avenue. In 1846 the team moved uptown to the Red House field on Third Avenue in Harlem. Five years later they relocated to Hoboken, New Jersey, where they remained until 1867, when they occupied a new field in Bergen Heights (Hudson City). In 1871 they moved back to Hoboken.

The members of the St. George club (the "Dragon Slayers") were mostly Englishmen residing in Manhattan or its vicinity who joined the organization for recreation, social status, and sociability. The association's roster included merchants, managers, professionals, and other solid citizens of the middle and upper echelons of society, along with a few prosperous skilled craftsmen. They were also typical of the ballplaying fraternity of that era in that they participated actively in the club's annual dinners and postgame parties after feature matches. At these all-male gatherings the guests would eat, drink, sing English songs, toast British and American officials, and tell stories.

During the antebellum years members of the St. George club promoted the English national game of cricket in the United States through arranging a series of international matches and through sponsoring annual conventions held in New York City. The international challenges began with several contests with Canadian clubs from Montreal and Toronto during the 1840s and 1850s, but the premier event was the visit of the celebrated All-England Eleven to Canadian and American cities in 1859. During the 1850s the Dragon Slayers also engaged in spirited and sometimes acrimonious rivalries with Philadelphia's Union Club and especially the New York Cricket Club. The feud between the St. George and the New York clubs was particularly bitter, and the bad feeling undermined the efforts of the delegates at the annual cricket conventions to popularize the sport in the United States.

The Civil War had a very damaging effect on early American cricket, but the men of St. George were able to keep their club alive throughout the conflict. After the return of peace in 1865 the Dragon Slayers renewed their matches with local and Philadelphia elevens and also sponsored two more visits of All-Star English elevens to the United States in 1868 and 1872. The club remained in a sound condition throughout the 1870s, but by then it had clearly lost its preeminent status in the world of American cricket to the Philadelphia clubs.

SELECTED BIBLIOGRAPHY: Melvin L. Adelman, *A Sporting Time: New York City and the Rise of Modern Athletics, 1820–70* (1986); George B. Kirsch, *The Creation of American Team Sports: Baseball and Cricket, 1838–1872* (1989); John I. Marder, *The International Series: The Story of the United States versus Canada at Cricket* (1968).

George B. Kirsch

STARGELL, WILVER DORNEL (6 March 1940, Earlsboro, OK–   ). An African American baseball player, he is the son of William and Verlene Stargell.

After participating in baseball, basketball, and football at Encinal High School in Alameda, California, Stargell attended Santa Rosa Junior College for one year before debuting with the Pittsburgh Pirates' minor league affiliate at San Angelo-Roswell (Sophomore League) in 1959. Three years later, Stargell earned a promotion to the Pirates, with his mammoth home runs soon popularizing the idea of "tape-measure" shots. In 1966, after two straight productive seasons, Stargell elevated his hitting further, establishing a career high with a .315 batting mark. In 1971 he enjoyed his finest season, breaking the major league record for most home runs in the month of April, setting career highs in home runs (forty-eight) and runs batted in (RBIs, 125), and helping the Pirates to the World Championship. Although Stargell possessed a powerful throwing arm, chronically sore knees necessitated his move from the outfield to first base on a full-time basis in 1975. Four years later, Stargell achieved his greatest fame when he led the Pirates to their second World Series title of the decade, while sharing National League Most Valuable Player (MVP) honors with the St. Louis Cardinals' Keith Hernandez. Saddled by injuries and increasing pain in his knees, Stargell became a part-time player over his final three seasons. He retired after the 1982 season. Stargell intimidated opposing pitchers with his large frame, his trademark "windmilling" of the bat in between pitches, and his massive uppercut swings. In the latter stages of his career he became known by the nickname "Pops," a tribute to his father-figure image and reputation for leadership, which he fostered by handing out gold stars to teammates as a reward for their contributions to Pirate victories. He played as an outfielder and first baseman for twenty-one major league seasons, compiling a .282 batting average, with 475 home runs (HRs) and 1,540 RBIs. Off the field, Stargell exhibited a sense of community involvement by serving as a national spokesman for the Sickle Cell Anemia Foundation. In 1988 Stargell gained baseball's ultimate honor—election to the National Baseball Hall of Fame.

SELECTED BIBLIOGRAPHY: Charles Feeney, "Mammoth HR Shots Are Stargell's Badge," *The Sporting News* (11 August 1979): 3; *Willie Stargell Day Program*, researched, written, and edited by Pirates' Publicity Office, 6 September 1982; *Willie Stargell's Personal Questionnaire*, National Baseball Hall of Fame Library, undated.

Bruce Markusen

STARK, ARCHIBALD MACPHERSON ("Archie") (21 December 1897, Glasgow, Scotland–27 May 1985, Kearny, NJ). The most prolific goal scorer in American soccer history, Stark attended St. Charles School in Glasgow before coming to the United States in 1910 to join his father. He made his U.S. soccer debut for West Hudson Juniors before signing professionally at the age of fourteen for the Scots-Americans of Kearny, helping them win the American Cup in 1913. Two years later he joined the Babcox and Wilcox team of Bayonne, New Jersey, before entering military service in World War I. Upon returning from France, Stark joined the Erie Athletic Association team of Kearny and then in 1921 the New York Football Club in the newly organized professional American Soccer League* (ASL). In 1924 he moved to the Bethlehem Steel Club, where he won national acclaim during the 1924–25 season, scoring 67 goals in forty-four league games. Stark totaled 309 goals in league competition for three different clubs between 1921 and 1931 plus scoring 15 in ASL Cup games and 29 in U.S. Open Cup games. With Bethlehem Steel he won the ASL championship in 1926–27 and the U.S. Open Cup in 1926, scoring a hat trick in the final. He played for the United States against Canada twice in 1925, scoring four times in the 6–1 American win at Ebbets Field in Brooklyn. In 1930 he went on tour to Europe as a guest player with Fall River and finished his playing career with the Irish-Americans of Kearny in the 1933–34 and 1934–35 seasons. He was inducted into the National Soccer Hall of Fame in 1950.

SELECTED BIBLIOGRAPHY: *Newark Star-Ledger*, 21 March 1978; Samuel T. N. Foulds, "Archibald Stark," in David L. Porter, ed., *Biographical Dictionary of American Sports: Outdoor Sports* (1988); 309–310; *United States Soccer Monthly* (May 1975).

Colin Jose

STONE, TONI (17 July 1921,? W.Va.–2 November 1996, Alameda or Oakland, CA). An African American baseball player, she was born Marcenia Lyle, the daughter of Boykin Free Lyle, a barber, and Willie Maynard Lyle, a beautician. She moved to St. Paul, Minnesota, at the age of six and began playing ball with the Girls Highlex Softball Club. A graduate of Roosevelt High School, her baseball name was Toni Stone. Her professional baseball debut came in 1947, when she barnstormed with the San Francisco Sea Lions, an integrated white and black semipro team. A few years later she deserted the Sea Lions to play for the Black Pelicans, a Negro minor league team in New Orleans. Shortly thereafter she switched teams again, this time to the New Orleans Creoles, another Negro minor league team that paid her $300 a month. Each time she switched she made more money. Stone's batting average of .265 with the Creoles is testimony to her skills as one of the best performers in the Negro Texas League. Her moment in history came in 1953, when she became the first woman to play for a major Negro League* club. Syd Pollock, owner of the Indianapolis Clowns, signed her to play second base for the Clowns, a team in the Negro American League. The Clowns, the baseball equivalent of the Harlem Globetrotters,* had a long history of mixing showmanship with baseball. Pollock no doubt hired Stone for her drawing power as a female player, but she was nevertheless an exceptional athlete. In her first season with the Clowns she played in 50 of the 175 games and had a batting average of .243. The highlight of the season came when she got a hit off the legendary Satchel Paige.* When Pollock hired Stone, he claimed that he had signed her to a $12,000 contract—thus paying his female "phenom" more than Jackie Robinson* made when he first signed with the Dodgers. He also maintained that her salary was based on her skills rather than her value as a gate attraction. How much he actually paid her is debatable. One writer claims that her actual salary was about $350 a month. Her career with the Clowns was short-lived. At the end of the 1953 season, Pollock sold her contract to the Kansas City Monarchs,* with whom she remained for one year. After Stone's professional playing days were over, she continued to play recreational ball with the California American Legion champs until she was sixty-two. She was inducted into the Women's Sports Foundation's International Women's Sports Hall of Fame in 1985.

SELECTED BIBLIOGRAPHY: Gai Ingham Berlage, *Women and Baseball: The Forgotten History* (1994); *New York Times*, 10 November 1996, 47; James A. Riley, ed., *The Biographical Encyclopedia of the Negro Baseball Leagues* (1994); *St. Paul Star-Tribune*, 5 November 1996, B-1, 7.

Gai I. Berlage

STRINGER, CHARLENE VIVIAN (16 March 1948, Edenboro, PA–   ). An African American basketball coach, she is the daughter of Charles Stoner, a full-time coal miner and part-time jazz musician, and Thelma Stoner. A 1970 graduate of Slippery Rock State University with a degree in physical education, Stringer is one of the most successful coaches in the history of college basketball and the first coach to lead a women's team to the National Collegiate Athletic Association (NCAA) Final Four while at two different institutions, Cheney State University in 1982 and University of Iowa in 1993. At the age of twenty-three, Stringer volunteered to coach the women's basketball team at the nation's first historically black college, Cheney State University. In 1982 Stringer led Cheney State into the NCAA Division I National Championship title game, eventually losing to Louisiana Tech, 76–62. While at the University of Iowa she led the Hawkeyes to a 269–84 record, seven Big Ten championships, and a final four appearance in 1993 and was named the National Coach of the Year three times. She also coached the U.S. national team to a bronze medal in the 1991 Pan-American Games in Havana, Cuba. In the summer of 1995, Stringer moved to Rutgers University, taking with her a career coaching record of 520 wins and 135 losses. At Rutgers, Stringer continued to field winning teams while playing an active role in the Black Coaches Association* (BCA).

SELECTED BIBLIOGRAPHY: Arthur R. Ashe, Jr., *A Hard Road to Glory: A History of the African-American Athlete since 1946*, vol. 3 (1988); Jane Burns, "Stringer Puts 500 Victories in Perspective," *Des Moines Register*, 21 January 1994, S1; Steve Harrison, "Strength Via Hope," *The Sporting News* 219, No. 1 (1995): 46–49; "Makeshift Lineup Reaps Milestone," *Des Moines Register*, 29 January 1994, S1.

Mary G. McDonald

STRODE, WOODY (1914, Los Angeles–1 January 1995, Glendora, CA). A football player and actor, he helped reintegrate professional football in 1946 and later was a character actor in numerous films. A native of Los Angeles, Strode graduated from Jefferson High School and University of California at Los Angeles (UCLA). He was a versatile athlete, participating in the shot put and later working as a professional wrestler, but he was most famous as an end on the UCLA football team in the late 1930s, when he was a teammate of both Ken Washington* and Jackie Robinson.* At 6' 3" and 205 pounds Strode was a fierce defensive end. He was named to the 1938 All Pacific Coast team and received some All-American mention. In 1946 Strode was signed by the National Football League (NFL) Rams, who had shifted from Cleveland to Los Angeles that season. The signing of Washington (a halfback) and Strode signaled the reintegration of African Americans into the NFL. That same year the Cleveland Browns of the new All-American Football Conference hired African Americans Marion Motley* and Bill Willis. Strode and Washington were signed because the Los Angeles Memorial Coliseum officials insisted that the Rams be integrated in order to use the facility. Strode played the following year in the Canadian Football League and then retired from football to work full-time as an actor. Ironically, Strode became better known as an actor than as an athlete.

SELECTED BIBLIOGRAPHY: David Neft et al., *Pro Football: The Early Years, An Encyclopedia History, 1895–1959* (1978); *New York Times*, 4 January 1995; *Time* (16 January 1995); A. S. Young, *Negro Firsts in Sports* (1963); Woody Strode file, the Pro Football Hall of Fame Library, Canton, OH.

C. Robert Barnett

SULLIVAN, JAMES EDWARD (18 November 1860, New York City–16 September 1914, New York City). An official of early American amateur athletics and an editor of sporting publications, he was the son of Irish immigrants Daniel and Julia (Halpin) Sullivan. His father was a foreman in the construction work of the New York Central Railroad, but Sullivan's public school education, his extensive reading, and his determination to succeed enabled him to rise to the ranks of the professional class. In 1878 he took a position in the publishing company of Frank Leslie. In 1889 he became business manager and editor of the *New York Sporting Times*, and in 1892 he was named president of the American Sports Publishing Company, owned by A. G. Spalding. As editor of hundreds of books in "Spalding's Athletic Library" he exerted an enormous influence on the growth of both amateur and professional sports in the United States, all the while advertising the sporting goods manufactured and sold through Spalding's business. A good all-around athlete, he never earned a major championship. He began his administrative career as vice president of the National Association of Amateur Athletes of America (N4A), but in 1888 he defected to the rival Amateur Athletic Union (AAU). He served as that organization's secretary (1889–96), president (1906–9), and secretary-treasurer (1909–14). During that era he became the most powerful man in American amateur athletics, vigorously promoting and enforcing a strict definition of amateurism (borrowed from the British model) that barred all those who earned money teaching or competing in sports from the AAU's meets. An active proponent of youth sports, he was one of the founders of New York City's Public Schools Athletic League and a supporter of public playgrounds and gymnasiums. Presidents Theodore Roosevelt and William Howard Taft appointed him as the chief American commissioner to the Olympic Games in 1908 and 1912, and he earned international honors for his contribution to the modern Olympic games.

SELECTED BIBLIOGRAPHY: John Lucas, "The Hegemonic Rule of the American Amateur Athletic Union 1888–1914: James Edward Sullivan as Prime Mover," *International Journal of the History of Sport* 11 (December 1994): 355–371; *New York Times*, 17 September 1914, 9; *Official . . . Handbook of the Amateur Athletic Union* (1914).

                                                                        George B. Kirsch

SULLIVAN, JOHN LAWRENCE (12 October 1858, Roxbury, MA–2 February 1918, Abingdon, MA). A prizefighter, his parents (Michael, a laborer, and Catherine) were Irish immigrants. His education ended with his graduation from grammar school around 1872. John L. Sullivan, the "Boston Strong Boy," was heavyweight boxing champion of the world from 1882 to 1892. In his teens Sullivan served brief apprenticeships in several trades and earned money playing baseball, but his strength and natural pugnacity soon led him to the ring. His success in both legal "exhibitions" and illegal prize bouts earned him an engagement with recognized champion Paddy Ryan in February 1882 at Mississippi City, Mississippi. Sullivan won easily. Over the ensuing decade Sullivan may have earned as much as $1 million, not by making formal title defenses (he did so only three times) but by touring and fighting four- or six-round exhibition bouts using padded gloves against all comers. On 8 July 1889 Sullivan defeated Jake Kilrain in seventy-five rounds at Richburg, Mississippi, in the last bare-knuckle championship fight and returned to touring. He finally lost his title by knockout to the younger and quicker James J. Corbett* in the first prizefight held under the Marquis of Queensberry rules (New Orleans, 7 September 1892). Sullivan was the greatest American sports celebrity of the nineteenth century. To working-class Irish Americans he could do no wrong, though many among the "lace-curtain" Irish saw his roistering and alcoholism as an embarrassment to the race. Ultimately, however, his popularity transcended class and ethnic boundaries.

SELECTED BIBLIOGRAPHY: Elliott Gorn, *The Manly Art: Bare-Knuckle Prize Fighting in America* (1986); Michael T. Isenberg, *John L. Sullivan and His America* (1988); John L. Sullivan, *Life and Reminiscences of a Nineteenth Century Gladiator* (1892).

                                                                        George Rugg

SUMO. This martial art has existed in Japan throughout its history. In 1907 *sumotori* Yokozuna Hitachiyama conducted a demonstration tour in Europe and the United States. During this tour he met President Theodore Roosevelt. A sumo demonstration was conducted later that year for President Roosevelt at the White House. In 1911 sumo made an appearance at the London World's Fair.

In 1914 a group of sumo champions conducted matches in Hawaii. In 1916 another group of *rikishi* (strength experts) performed in the United States. In 1921 a tour was conducted in both Hawaii and the United States. Sumo matches were popular among the Japanese American agricultural workers in California's Imperial Valley. Matches were held beginning in 1920 as part of larger celebrations. The issei encouraged the continuation of the sumo tradition in the internment camps during World War II when possible. Harley Ozaki (Toyonishiki) was the most successful Japanese American sumo competitor in Japan prior to World War II.

SELECTED BIBLIOGRAPHY: P. L. Cuyler, *Sumo: From Rite to Sport* (1979).

Alison M. Wrynn

T

TAGLIABUE, PAUL JOHN (24 November 1940, Jersey City, NJ–   ). A professional football executive, he is the son of Charles and Mary Tagliabue, who emphatically fostered the Italian work ethic in their close-knit family. His father owned a small business doing repair work at factories and loading docks on the New Jersey waterfront. The recipient of a basketball scholarship from Georgetown University in Washington, D.C., he was also an honors student as a government major, president of his senior class, and finalist for a Rhodes Scholarship. After graduating from Georgetown with honors in 1962, Tagliabue won the prestigious Root-Tilden Scholarship to the New York University School of Law, where he served as editor of the *Law Review*. He received his law degree in 1965. After working as a law clerk and policy analyst for the State Department, he became a senior partner at a powerful and prestigious law firm. In 1989 he succeeded Pete Rozelle as commissioner of the National Football League (NFL). In that office he was resourceful and knowledgeable as he supervised the league's expansion into international markets and negotiated television contracts and labor disputes. Responding to growing public concern, he also reformed and enforced the league's drug-testing policies, increased the emphasis on drug rehabilitation programs, and instituted tough new guidelines for steroid testing. He was also an outspoken supporter of hiring policies that would open up more NFL coaching opportunities to minorities.

SELECTED BIBLIOGRAPHY: Dave Anderson, "Tagliabue Has Only Begun to Rebound," *New York Times*, 29 October 1989, S5; *Current Biography* (1992); Peter Finch, "Tagliabue Is Everywhere But in the Huddle," *Business Week* (28 January 1991):72; Thomas George, "Tagliabue Is Elected NFL Commissioner," *New York Times*, 27 October 1989 B15–16; Robert Thomas, Jr., "Family Man, Sports Fan, NFL Chief," *New York Times*, 27 October 1989, B15–16; Rick Telander, "The Face of the Sweeping Change," *Sports Illustrated* 73 (10 September 1990): 38–42.

Margherita Marchione

TAYLOR, LAWRENCE (4 February 1959, Williamsburg, VA–   ). An African American football player, he is the son of Clarence Taylor, a dispatcher at the Norfolk News shipyards, and Iris Taylor, a schoolteacher. As a youth he concentrated on baseball, and he did not begin playing football until the age of fifteen. He was an All-American at the University of North Carolina and the Atlantic Coast Conference Player of the Year in 1980. By his senior year he had developed into a physically intimidating presence. At 6' 3" and 243 pounds he had the height and size of a basketball player along with incredible quickness. As a New York Giant in the National Football League (NFL) beginning in 1981 he was a fearsome competitor who relished the intensive cut-and-thrust of collision football. In 1982 Taylor reprised his title as Associated Press NFL Defensive Player of the Year. In 1986 he achieved his finest statistical season, capped by the New York Giants' first Super Bowl championship. His 20.5 sacks and 105 total tackles saw him at the acme of his professional powers. He was a unanimous selection as the NFL's Most Valuable Player. By 1990 Taylor had earned his tenth consecutive Pro Bowl appearance. A year later Taylor earned a second Super Bowl championship ring as the Giants bested the Bills 20–19 in Tampa, Florida. In 1991 Taylor's long run of Pro Bowl appearances was ended, in part, by reason of several injuries. Damage to his Achilles tendon threatened to terminate his playing career. His professional career had been placed in jeopardy several years earlier when, in 1988, NFL commissioner Pete Rozelle suspended him for thirty days for substance abuse. Taylor announced his retirement following the conclusion of the 1993 season. After retirement he participated in celebrity golf tournaments and also explored a number of other ventures, including professional wrestling. His personal and private life suffered considerably as a result of drug problems. He was elected to the Pro Football Hall of Fame in 1999.

SELECTED BIBLIOGRAPHY: Peter King, *Inside the Helmet: A Player's Eye View of the NFL* (1993); D. S. Neft, R. M. Cohen, and R. Korch, eds., *The Sports Encyclopedia of Pro Football* (1993); Ron Smith, ed., *The Sporting News—Chronicle of 20th Century Sport* (1992); Jim L. Sumner, "Lawrence Taylor," in David L. Porter, *African-American Sports Greats: A Biographical Dictionary* (1995); Materials received from Saleem Choudhry, Pro Football Hall of Fame Library-Research Center, Canton, OH.

Scott A.G.M. Crawford

TAYLOR, MARSHALL W. ("Major") (26 November 1878, Indianapolis–21 June 1932, Chicago). An African American bicycle racer, he was the son of Gilbert Taylor, who worked as a coachman for the Southards, a wealthy white family in Indianapolis. His mother was Saphonia Taylor. During the Civil War his father had fought with an all-black regiment for the North. Living amid privilege, Taylor received an education otherwise unattainable for African Americans at the time. But it was the bicycle the Southards gave him that most dramatically affected his life. He quit school after the eighth grade, got his first jobs in the newly established bicycle industry in Indianapolis, and began participating in the emerging sport of bicycle racing. Restricted from joining white bicycle clubs, he became a member of the all-black See-Saw Cycling Club in 1895, moved away from Indianapolis to Worcester, Massachusetts, and started winning amateur races on the East Coast. After dominating his amateur opponents, he began racing professionally in 1896. Overcoming the aggressive riding tactics of white riders and racist exclusionary policies of race organizers, Taylor by 1897 attained celebrity status for his accomplishments as a professional sprint cycling champion. At age twenty he broke the one-mile world record and established himself as one of the world's premier short-distance cyclists by winning the 1899 world championship. Having conquered all challenges in America, Taylor signed a contract with a French promoter in 1901 to race on the European tour. While in Europe he dominated his sport, and he did not face the racial hostility of fans, riders, and race organizers that existed in America. Exhausted after three years of constant training, racing throughout Europe and Australia, and the pressures of worldwide fame, Taylor retired from the sport in 1904. Bored, he returned to racing in Paris two years later at the age of twenty-eight. However, he never regained his championship form, and after four years of mediocre performances retired again at the age of thirty-two. Taylor's fifteen-year career as the only outstanding African American professional cycling champion was a powerful political statement for black achievement at the time. Though Taylor made a relatively nice living as a professional cyclist, making as much as $10,000 in a year, he died destitute and alone.

SELECTED BIBLIOGRAPHY: James C. McCullagh, *American Bicycle Racing* (1976); Andrew Ritchie, *Major Taylor: The Extraordinary Career of a Champion Bicycle Racer* (1988); Robert A. Smith, *A Social History of the Bicycle* (1972); Marshall W. Taylor, *The Fastest Bicycle Rider in the World* (1928).

Troy D. Paino

TENER, JOHN K. (25 July 1863, County Tyrone, Ireland–14 May 1946, Pittsburgh). He was a baseball player, National League president, U.S. Congressman, and twenty-sixth governor of Pennsylvania. Born in rural County Tyrone, Ireland, John was the son of George and Sarah Tener. When George Tener died in 1872, Sarah Tener took her family to Pittsburgh. Tener played sandlot baseball throughout his youth. In 1885 he signed with Haverhill (Massachusetts) of the New England League, and in 1888 and 1889 he pitched for the Chicago White Stockings, compiling a 22–20 record. Tener played on Spalding's 1888–89 World Tour, which included a return to his native Ireland. In 1890, his last year as a pitcher, he hurled for the Pittsburgh Players League Club (3–11, 7.31 earned run average [ERA]). After his playing career, Tener worked as cashier and president at the First National Bank in Charleroi, an industrial city near Pittsburgh. In 1908 he was elected to the U.S. House of Representatives as a Republican. After one term, he was elected Pennsylvania governor. In 1913

Tener accepted the position of National League (NL) president at no pay while he was still governor. He held the NL presidency part-time until January 1915, when his gubernatorial term ended. While NL president, Tener served on the National Commission and played a key role in the Federal League war of 1913–15. Tener held the office of the presidency until 1918. After baseball he returned to Charleroi's business community.

SELECTED BIBLIOGRAPHY: George C. Martinet, *Charleroi: The First 100 Years* (1990), 14, 15; Corey Seeman, Tener Family Papers [Archival Finding Aid], Pittsburgh (1993), 1–5.

Corey Seeman

TENNIS. Although tennis came to the United States in the 1870s as an English game favored by upper-class Americans, in the twentieth century it has become increasingly popular among African Americans, Native Americans, Eastern Europeans, Hispanics, and Asians. Recently, several of the world's greatest tennis stars have migrated to the United States and have become permanent residents or American citizens. The increasing number of public courts and programs in towns, schools, and colleges has opened up the sport to middle- and lower-class players from a variety of ethnic and racial backgrounds. As a result, the elite white, Anglo-Saxon Protestant tennis clubs no longer dominate the game to the extent that they did in the era prior to the 1960s.

During the late 1800s and early 1900s only financially successful African Americans had access to tennis courts and equipment. By 1890 several professional black families had built courts on their properties. While their numbers were few, these courts promoted the sport among the black well-to-do, which enabled their children to play collegiate tennis at such black colleges as Howard, Lincoln, and Tuskegee and even a few schools in the Ivy League. At the turn of the century, these same families also began to form tennis clubs, particularly along the East Coast in cities such as New York, Philadelphia, Atlanta, and Washington, D.C. They sponsored early interclub tournaments.

As a result of the increasing interest in the sport, these early clubs and their members united in 1916 to form the American Tennis Association* (ATA). The ATA worked on promoting the sport in the black community, developing tournaments, and encouraging juniors to play. In 1917, the ATA held its first national championships at Druid Hill Park in Baltimore. Its first national champions were Talley Holmes for the men's singles and Lucy Diggs Slowe for the women's singles. The ATA developed other great players in the coming years, such as Eyre Saitch on the men's side and Isadore Channels on the women's side. Yet, the most dominant player of this era was Ora Washington.* Between 1929 and 1937 she won a record eight ATA women's singles championships.

As a result of the Works Progress Administration during the depression years, many public courts were constructed. More courts were now accessible to blacks, and that produced a swarm of talented players. Leading the pack was Jimmy McDaniel, who, beginning in 1939, won four ATA singles championships. McDaniel is also known for participating in a singles match against tennis great Don Budge in 1940. This historic interracial match was won by Budge 6–1, 6–2, in Harlem, New York. Yet, the USLTA (United States Lawn Tennis Association), tennis' national governing body, still did not allow blacks to compete in their tournaments. Nonetheless, progress was made, albeit slowly. In 1948 a young Californian, Oscar Johnson, became the first black player to win a USLTA-sanctioned tournament. Johnson opened the door for other African American tennis players to compete in U.S. circuit tournaments. The two greatest champions of this era were Althea Gibson* and Arthur Ashe, Jr.* Gibson became the first black player of either sex to win major titles in tennis. She won the French women's title in 1956 and back-to-back Wimbledon and U.S. women's titles in 1957 and 1958, a truly remarkable accomplishment. Known for his disciplined mental approach to the game, Ashe remains the only African American male to win a major title. He won the first U.S. Open in 1968 and the Australian Open in 1970. However, his greatest victory came at Wimbledon in 1975, when he beat the heavy favorite, Jimmy Connors, in the final. In 1976 Ashe became the number one player in the world.

Since that time, black coaches, like John Wilkerson, have emerged and produced great talents. In Wilkerson's case, he brought black females Lori McNeil and Zina Garrison-Jackson from the Houston ghetto to winners' circles around the globe. Garrison-Jackson was the singles runner-up at Wimbledon in 1990. Another African American star, MaliVai Washington, also had a strong run at the All England Club in 1996, making it to the finals. "Phenoms" such as Venus and Serena Williams and Chanda Rubin are considered by many to be the future of American women's tennis.

Little is known about how tennis took root in the Native American community, but it reached new heights in popularity and participation among Indians during the tennis boom of the 1970s. Oklahoma was considered the first major hotbed for Native American tennis. In Lawrence, Kansas, Haskell Junior College (presently known as Haskell Indian Nations University) promoted the sport on the collegiate level among its predominantly Native American student body. However, the need to promote tennis on a national level became an important issue among the Native American tennis-playing population. Interest in the sport was not limited to Oklahoma and Kansas but reached Arizona, New Mexico, and California as well. In order to address these needs, Dr. George Bluespruce, Noah Allen, and Cecilia Firethunder formed the the North American Indian Tennis Association (NAITA). In 1976 the NAITA held the first National Indian Tennis Championships in San Diego. The championships were open to all tribes and to any player with a heritage at least one-quarter Native American. Allen became the first men's singles champion (1976), while Bluespruce became the second (1977). Firethunder went on to become the first president of the NAITA.

The NAITA has seen many great players throughout its history. Dwayne Begay was a five-time men's singles champion and during the late 1990s was nationally ranked in the men's 35 and over division for both singles and doubles. Russell Jilot also won the men's singles five times and added six men's doubles and two mixed doubles titles, making him one of the most diversified players in NAITA history. Pete Peterson won two men's singles titles and became one of the top three players in the Intermountain section of the USTA. Peterson is also the director of junior development with coaching guru Dennis Ralston at his club in Colorado Springs. However, the most dominant player in NAITA history is Dawn Allen. Between 1976 and 1991, Allen won fourteen women's singles titles, fourteen women's doubles titles, and eight mixed doubles titles. At one point in her streak, she had won the singles seven straight times and the women's doubles nine straight. Yet, her crowning achievement came in 1996, when she and Bluespruce became the first NAITA members to be elected to the American Indian Athletic Hall of Fame.

During the twentieth century American tennis players from a variety of ethnic backgrounds have distinguished themselves in the sport at the national and international levels. Prior to World War II the exclusive nature of the national tennis establishment and the upper-class clubs made it difficult for Jews, Eastern Europeans, Hispanics, and Asians to gain access to courts, instruction, and tournament competition. But over the past fifty years there has been greater opportunity for talented men and women of modest means to gain national recognition. Anti-Semitism within the Protestant establishment barred affluent Jews from membership in the most prestigious clubs, but a few become prominent players or officials. Richard Savitt* won both the Australian and Wimbledon singles titles in 1951, becoming the first Jew to win the English championship. Joseph F. Cullman III was the grandson of German Jewish immigrants. Long denied access to the amateur lawn tennis establishment, he played an important role in the era of open tennis, which began in 1968, when his Philip Morris company (he was chairman of the board) sponsored the first U.S. Open at Forest Hills. In 1990 he was elected to the Tennis Hall of Fame in Newport, Rhode Island.

American-born tennis champions of Eastern European, Latino, Middle Eastern, and Asian ancestry have made their mark on the sport in the United States, as have recent immigrants from several continents. Frank Parker* was a child of a poor Polish family who won several U.S. and French titles during the 1940s. Vitus Gerulaitus,* of Lithuanian extraction, was a premier player of the 1970s who took both the Australian and Italian crowns in 1977. Richard "Pancho" Gonzalez* was a Mexican American who achieved his greatest fame as a professional during the middle decades of the century. In 1989 Michael Chang,* son of Chinese immigrants, became the youngest grand-slam champion in tennis history when he won the French Open. Pete Sampras' father came from Greece, while Andre Agassi's* dad is an Armenian who was born in Iran. The list could go on.

Several tennis stars of the last sixty years were immigrants who became long-term residents or citizens of the United States. Francisco "Pancho" Segura* was born in Guayaquil, Ecuador. He won a scholarship to the University of Miami, won the U.S. intercollegiate championship three years in a row between 1942 and 1944, and later became an American citizen. Martina Navratilova* and Ivan Lendl* were products of Czechoslovakia. Navratilova is considered one of the greatest female tennis players of all time with eighteen grand-slam singles titles (nine Wimbledons, four U.S. Opens) to her credit. She once said: "I honestly believe I was born to be an American. This country was waiting for me. It would give me friends and the space and the freedom and the courts and the sneakers and the weight machines and the right food to let me become a tennis champion, to play the best tennis any woman ever played." Lendl, like Navratilova, believed in exhausting physical training off the court as well as on. His tireless work ethic lead him to three U.S. Open titles, a record eight U.S. Open final appearances, and an amazing total of 270 weeks at the number one ranking in the world. Monica Seles* immigrated from Yugoslavia and has won the U.S. Open, French Open, and Australian Open women's singles titles. One of America's greatest champions, John McEnroe, was coached by two immigrants, Harry Hopman from Australia and Tony Palafox from Mexico.

SELECTED BIBLIOGRAPHY: Arthur R. Ashe, Jr., *A Hard Road to Glory: A History of the African-American Athlete since 1945*, vol. 3 (1988); E. Digby Baltzell, *Sporting Gentlemen: Men's Tennis from the Age of Honor to the Cult of the Superstar* (1995); Robert Lipsyte, *Idols of the Game: A Sporting History of the American Century* (1995); *Wall Street Journal*, 11 September 1992, A18.

Thomas Cesa

THOMAS, DEBRA ("Debi"). (25 March 1967, Poughkeepsie, NY–   ). The first African American to figure prominently in figure skating, she is the daughter of Janice Thomas (a computer analyst) and McKinley Thomas. Raised in San Jose, California, Thomas attended San Mateo (California) High School, Stanford University, and the University of Colorado, balancing her academic and sporting careers at each institution. Her talent for skating was spotted at an early age, and at ten she embarked on a grueling training regimen under the tutelage of Alex McGowan. After years of slow, but steady, progress, Thomas' career really took off during her freshman year at Stanford, with victories at the 1985 National Sports Festival in Baton Rouge, Skate America International in Minneapolis, and the St. Ivel Skate International in England. The following year she experienced her greatest sporting triumphs, winning the 1986 U.S. Women's Figure Skating and the World Women's Figure Skating titles. After gaining significant financial backing from numerous corporate sponsors, she placed runner-up at the 1987 U.S. and World Championships and third at the 1988 Calgary Winter Olympics. Following a number of years on the professional ice-skating circuit, Thomas enrolled in the medical program at Northwestern University.

SELECTED BIBLIOGRAPHY: Lynn Norment, "Debi Thomas," *Ebony* 41 (May 1986): 147–148, 150; E. M. Swift, "Books or Blades, There's No Doubting Thomas," *Sports Illustrated* 64 (17 February 1986): 22–24, 29; E. M. Swift, "Another Miracle on Ice?" *Sports Illustrated* 64 (17 March 1986): 54–56, 58, 61; E. M. Swift, "Cashing in on the Collywobbles," *Sports Illustrated* 64 (31 March 1986): 28–30, 35.

David Andrews

THOMAS, ISIAH (30 April 1961, Chicago–). An African American basketball player and executive, he grew up in an inner-city Chicago ghetto family. His father, Isiah Lord Thomas II, was a foreman for the International Harvester Company and then lost his job, became a janitor, and left the family. In his gang-infested community his mother, Mary Thomas, struggled to support her children through jobs as a school worker and an employee of Chicago's Department of Human Services. As a boy Thomas was already a local star for his dribbling and shooting exhibitions at halftime at neighborhood games. His mother's courage and example motivated Thomas to earn a scholarship and become an honors student at St. Joseph's Prep in Westchester, Illinois, in suburban Chicago. His exploits in high school earned him All-American honors, and he accepted a scholarship to the University of Indiana, where his team captured a National Collegiate Athletic Association (NCAA) championship in 1976 under Bobby Knight. Thomas left college after his sophomore year for the National Basketball Association (NBA) draft and was the number one pick of the Detroit Pistons. He would finish his undergraduate degree in the off-season by correspondence classes; he eventually earned a diploma with a major in criminal justice in 1987. Meanwhile, he led the Pistons to victory in back-to-back championships in 1989 and 1990. The Detroit Pistons would fade soon after, but not Thomas. After his retirement he became vice president of operations for the NBA franchise Toronto Raptors, as well as part owner of the team. Next he became a color commentator for NBC sports.

SELECTED BIBLIOGRAPHY: Ira Berkow, "Isiah Thomas' Giant Step to the Pros," *The Complete Handbook of Pro Basketball* (1981); David Bradley, "The Importance of Being Isiah," *Sport* 79 (May 1988): 24–27, 29; *Gentlemen's Quarterly* 58 (February 1988): 190; Dennis Rodman, *Bad As I Wanna Be* (1996); *Sporting News* (28 March 1981): 35; Curry Kirkpatrick, "And a Little Child Led Them," *Sports Illustrated* 54 (6 April 1981): 15–19; William Nack, " 'I Have Got to Do Right,' " *Sports Illustrated* 66 (19 January 1987): 60–73; Isiah Thomas and Matt Dobek, *Bad Boys* (1989).

C. Keith Harrison

THOMPSON, JOHN (2 September 1941, Washington, DC–). An African American basketball coach, he is the son of John Thompson, a factory worker and mechanic, and Anna Thompson, a maid. Raised in a devout Roman Catholic family in the housing projects of the predominantly African American Anacostia section of Washington, D.C., he earned his high school degree from Archbishop High School. The 6' 10" Thompson received several college scholarship offers for basketball but settled on Providence College to appease his mother, who believed its Dominican priests would take care of her son. Named New England College Player of the Year during his senior year at Providence, he graduated with a degree in economics in 1964. Drafted in the third round by the Boston Celtics, he voluntarily left professional basketball after two unproductive seasons. He returned to Washington, D.C., where he worked as a social worker and teacher at Federal City College. While earning his master's degree in counseling in 1971 from the University of the District of Columbia, he started coaching high school basketball for St. Anthony's, a small Catholic high school on the northeast side of Washington. During his six years there he turned its basketball program into a national power. In 1972 he accepted an offer to coach the basketball team at Georgetown University, and he quickly transformed that school into a national basketball powerhouse. His teams of the mid-1980s, led by Patrick Ewing, made it to the national championship game three out of four years. Suffering heartbreaking defeats against the University of North Carolina in 1982 and Villanova University in 1985, the Hoyas won the national championship in 1984 by beating the University of Houston, 84–75. In addition to serving as assistant coach for Dean Smith's gold medal 1976 men's Olympic basketball team, he was the head coach for a disappointing bronze medal team in the 1988 Olympics. As a coach Thompson is known for his aggressive, full-court style of defense, the high graduation rate among his players, and the political stands he takes on behalf of underprivileged African American athletes. He publicly protested the implementation of new National Collegiate Athletic Association (NCAA) rules that set minimum academic standards for freshmen eligibility. He believed that the new regulations unfairly penalized minority students attending substandard high schools. He was a prominent leader of the Black Coaches Association,* which persuaded the NCAA to review academic standards and their impact on African American athletes.

SELECTED BIBLIOGRAPHY: Charles S. Farrell, " 'Big Four' Spread Influence of Black Coaches," *Black Issues in Higher Education* 11 (29 December 1994): 24–25; "John Thompson," *Current Biography* 50 (May 1989), 54–58; Jack Kroll, "Race Becomes the Game: A Defiant Coach Challenges the NCAA's Rule Book," *Newsweek* 113 (30 January 1989): 56; William C. Rhoden, "New Vistas for an Old Hoya," *New York Times*, 22 February 1992, B11; Leonard Shapiro, *Big Man on Campus: John Thompson and the Georgetown Hoyas* (1990); John Wideman, "Listen to the Drum," *Sports Illustrated* 61 (26 November 1984): 58.

Troy D. Paino

THOROUGHBRED HORSE RACING. Racing horses, simply defined, is the resolution of a disagreement between horsemen as to who has the fastest horse.

Thoroughbred racing, a highly formalized form of the sport, requires understanding the ethnic origins of the thoroughbred, an animal developed specifically for carrying a specified weight at high speed over a predetermined, measured course.

The thoroughbred traces its recorded history to the 1500s in England, when Elizabeth I (r. 1558–1603), building on the efforts of her grandfather, Henry VII (r. 1485–1509), developed a tax-supported breeding, stabling, and training facility at Tutbury near Staffordshire. On the advice of her bloodstock agent, Gervase Markham, Elizabeth added Arab stallions, "little Horses, verie swift," to the stud roster. Bred to native runners—the Irish Hobby and the Scottish Galloway—the result, over generations, was a light-boned, hot-blooded horse, ill suited in build or temperament for military, agricultural, or civilian use.

James I (r. 1603–25), Elizabeth's successor, supported both horse racing at home and colonization abroad. In 1607 an adventurous band of English aristocrats established Jamestown. The first shipment of horses, sent to Virginia in 1610, became part of the starving colonists' food supply. Horses were not imported again until 1618. The first boatload of Africans was brought ashore the following year. While the original status of these individuals is not clear, there is no question that, within decades of their arrival, Africans had been effectively enslaved.

In 1649, when the English Parliament convicted James' son, Charles I, of treason and beheaded him, there were 200 horses in Virginia. Twenty years later, equine population growth allowed Virginians to export their tough, fast, pony-sized animals to other New World settlements along the Atlantic coast and in Central America. Following Charles' death, Puritanical councils of state outlawed racing, but matches were held nonetheless. When the government retaliated by confiscating racehorses, pedigree records were lost.

Royalists returned long-exiled Charles II (r. 1660–85) to the throne in 1660. He was the last British monarch to jockey his own racehorses. The following year Charles married a Portuguese princess, whose dowry included the port of Tangier. North Africans were eager to rid themselves of Arabian stallions, which, because of religious constraints, they would not geld. Portuguese ships had long transported bloodstock and, occasionally, their African handlers north to European ports. Southbound Portuguese ships went to West Africa, which by 1700 was known as the Ivory, Gold, or Slave Coast. By then it was a well-established trade route. Rulers of West Africa's warring city-states traded gold, ivory, and prisoners of war—many of them cavalrymen—for Arabian horses, swords, and knives.

By the time Charles died, a hot-blooded horse, "thoroughly bred" for the sport of kings, had begun to emerge from British stud farms. Charles was followed by James II, who lost his crown during the Glorious Revolution of 1788–89. William and Mary took the throne, and they and their successor, Queen Anne, were avid racing fans. Queen Anne's contribution to the sport was Ascot, near Windsor Castle, which opened in 1711. It is no coincidence that all modern thoroughbreds trace their pedigrees to Barbary Coast stallions exported to England between 1662 and 1730. The two most potent—the Byerley Turk and the Darley Arabian—had a tremendous impact on the sport in America.

At Anne's death a German cousin inherited the throne. George I (r. 1714–27) disdained both his subjects and their love of racing. During the 1700s English racing lost, with one exception, direct ties to the Crown. After William Augustus, duke of Cumberland (1721–65), the obese and enormously unpopular third son of George II (r. 1727–60), was ousted from the army, he withdrew to Windsor Park. There he bred both Herod, descended from the Byerley Turk, and Eclipse, who carried the genes of the Darley Arabian. Cumberland assumed leadership of the Jockey Club, the organizational model for all American jockey clubs. These clubs, which sprang up first in the South, where horse racing was a deeply ingrained tradition, were aristocratic organizations whose membership rosters included only wellborn men wealthy enough to afford racing and the gambling that went with it. No jockey or individual associated with the daily care and maintenance of thoroughbreds was even considered for membership.

After Cumberland's death, Eclipse was bought by a well-to-do farmer who retired the unbeatable stallion to stud after only two years of racing. From 1771 on, he sired crop after crop of champions. By 1773 racing so dominated the English sporting scene that the Jockey Club authorized James Weatherby to publish an annual racing calendar. Eighteen years later Weatherby reluctantly published a thoroughbred genealogy, the *Introduction to a General Stud Book*, which Weatherbys still publish today.

Virginia colonists had no way of competing with English record keepers, nor had they any reason to do so. What they did have, by 1700, was the largest population of any American colony and an ever-growing enslaved Negro workforce with centuries-old expertise in breeding, breaking, training, riding, and shoeing hot-blooded horses. In 1730 Virginia planter Samuel Gist imported a twenty-one-year-old son of the Darley Arabian, the first recorded "thorough bred" sent to the colonies. By 1800 the Old Dominion state was the breeding ground from which both the thoroughbred and the quarter horse had emerged. What developed in the stable and at tracks was a working alliance between the elite inner circle of Anglo-Saxon masters and their African slaves—those who actually tended the horses. Otherwise, they did not fraternize.

Taking as edict the sentiments and writings of the Hon. Admiral Henry John Rous (1797–1877), the nineteenth-century English Jockey Club's perpetual leader, trainers were referred to as "training grooms," making it perfectly clear just how lowly their position was. Jockeys, called "boys" regardless of their age, were to be seen and not heard. English Jockey Club members controlled jockeys' livelihoods; disobedience meant lifelong banishment from racing, a decision from which there was no appeal. Slave owners could impose even harsher penalties on their "boys." Slavery was the beginning, turf historian Bernard Livingston noted, of a professional "serf" stratum in the burgeoning feudal structure of horse racing that developed in a manner unique to America.

Sketchy biographies of Negro horsemen have been gleaned from contemporary records, sporting journals, or newspaper obituaries. Austin Curtis (?–1809) was a freed black man and jockey-then-trainer for Willie Jones, a prominent North Carolina breeder. In racing circles one of the best-known personalities of the antebellum South was Charles Stewart. Stewart's recollections, published after the Civil War, are a fascinating account of his travels as exercise boy, jockey, groom, trainer, and stallion man for Col. William Ransom Johnson (1782–1849), the "Napoleon of the Turf." Stewart, a light-skinned Negro, may have had blood as well as bond ties to Johnson; by law and custom, masters had droit de seigneur over their female slaves. Talented slaves earned the money to buy their freedom. A jockey named Cato (c.1820–?) was manumitted the instant he won the 1839 Wagner-Grey Eagle match race held at the Louisville, Kentucky, Oakland Course.

After the Civil War black jockeys dominated southern racing. At the first Kentucky Derby at Churchill Downs in Louisville on 17 May 1875, thirteen of the fifteen jockeys were African Americans. From 1880 through 1905 black riders won sixteen Kentucky Derbies. The most prominent black jockey of this era was Isaac Murphy.* The first jockey to win the Kentucky Derby three times, he triumphed in numerous other prestigious races. Known for his charismatic personality as well as his riding ability, he died tragically of pneumonia at the age of thirty-six. Over his career he rode in 1,412 races, winning 628 times—a 44% winning record that has never been equaled.

Negro jockey Abe Hawkins,* trainer Ansel "Uncle Ansel" Williamson,* jockey-turned-trainer and bloodstock agent William Walker, Dudley Allen,* trainer and half owner of 1891 Kentucky Derby winner Kingman—all were, during their lifetimes, nationally known sports figures. Consigned to unmarked graves, their accomplishments were forgotten, except by southern racing historian Alexander Mackay-Smith, on whose pioneering work current research on African American contributions to the sport has heavily relied.

At the close of the nineteenth century thoroughbred racing was dominated by New York's "robber barons," the fabulously wealthy members of the Jockey Club, which they founded in 1894 to reign supreme over New York racing. They employed historians to write their version of thoroughbred history, refocused on themselves. Their fathers had paid genealogists to research their family trees as well, with instructions to "discover" medieval kings and European nobility among their ancestors. Carefully disseminated to the public, these ethnically edited genealogies established their lineage and birthright as participants in the sport of kings. It also set the standard of control by Anglo-Saxon thoroughbred sportsmen-owners, the ideal held to this day by the Jockey Club's membership.

A few ambitious and upwardly mobile Europeans made fortunes for themselves and their families, then entered the ranks of elite horsemen. In 1837 a brilliant young German financier emigrated to America, amended his family name—Schoenberg—and became August Belmont.* After making a fortune, he married Commodore Oliver Hazard Perry's Quaker daughter and got into racing.

Belmont's son, namesake, and an organizer of the Jockey Club, created Belmont Park in 1905. In 1989 William Leggett, senior writer for *Sports Illustrated*, extolled the elder Belmont's virtues in a five-page article written for *The Thoroughbred Record*. "Racing's Hall of Fame in Saratoga Springs," lamented Leggett, "does not list him as one of its four 'Exemplars of Racing,' an oversight as stunning as leaving George Herman Ruth* out of that brick building in Cooperstown." What Leggett failed to mention was that Belmont was a Jew in a century when signs warned Jews and Negroes not to enter the hotels at the upstate New York spa. Another famous family of the turf is that of Dutch buccaneer Cornelius Van Derbilt, whose descendants became Vanderbilts, marrying Anglo-American Whitneys for good measure before they took up thoroughbred racing.

The Gay Nineties saw unregulated speculation and gambling fever affect the economy as they never had before. As the southern plantation system, from which so many African American horsemen had come, contracted, and Ku Klux Klan activity forced talented blacks to migrate, their century of achievement drew to a close.

In the North a few Irishmen had achieved some prominence as trainers and jockeys during the antebellum era, and at the end of the nineteenth century others followed their example. At New York's Coney Island an Irishman named Bill Daly ran a school for jockeys—Irish immigrants' children and boys recruited from orphanages—whom he indentured, promising to make riders of them. By 1892 he had been arrested fifteen times for beating his charges with baling sticks and horsewhips, offenses for which he was never prosecuted. Race riding is a dangerous profession. Then, as now, the *average* career of a jockey spanned two years. Daly's "boys" were bodies on horses; no one cared where they came from. They were homeless and rootless, linked precariously to the bottom rung of racing's hierarchy by skill alone. At the end of their careers they either left the track or sank to the nameless status of groom or exercise rider.

Training thoroughbreds requires a unique blend of horse sense, savvy, and tenacity. Winning by besting one's competition, "getting his goat," is part of the game. No one ethnic group has dominated training in this century as Negro horsemen did in the last. A sample of names, the trainers of Triple Crown winners, reflects the profile of the American melting pot from 1919 to 1978: Guy Bedwell (1919), Sunny Jim Fitzsimmons (1930, 1935), George Conway (1937), Ben Jones (1941, 1948), Don Cameron (1943), Max Hirsch* (1946), Lucien Laurin (1973), Billy Turner (1977), and Laz Barrera* (1978).

Emerging from Central America in the 1960s, Hispanic jockeys made their mark on American racing, eclipsing the earnings records set by nineteenth-century Negro horsemen and the Iowa-born Irish Garner brothers and Eddie Arcaro,* Kentucky-born son of Italian immigrants, in the first half of the twentieth century. Laffit Pincay, Jr.,* and Angel Cordero* are both jockeys whose careers have spanned three-plus decades. Because of the voting process, recent immigrants have had a much easier time achieving Hall of Fame status than the men, especially African Americans, on whose skill, knowledge, and hard work the sport was founded.

Few sports have concealed their ethnic diversity more effectively than racing. From its royal beginnings racing has always been restrictive and hierarchical, denying multiculturalism as a way to preserve its image as "the sport of kings." Only recently, as a handful of track publicists attempt to mainstream a sport that has steadily lost market share since the 1970s, is research about racing's rich, ethnically diverse history being disseminated to the general public. Tradition-bound racing periodicals have chosen to ignore this trend. Turf writers are still more comfortable tracing a thoroughbred's pedigree than identifying the men and women who hold the industry together as anything other than "trainers," "grooms," or "jockeys."

SELECTED BIBLIOGRAPHY: Bernard Livingston, *Their Turf* (1973); Roger Longrigg, *The History of Horse Racing* (1972); Alexander Mackay-Smith, *The Race Horses of America 1832–1872: Portraits and Other Paintings by Edward Troye* (1981); Roger Mortimer, *The Jockey Club* (1958); Lynn S. Renau, *Racing around Kentucky* (1995).

Lynn S. Renau

THORPE, JAMES FRANCIS ("Jim") (28 May 1888, south of Belmont in Oklahoma Territory–28 March 1953, Lomita, CA). A Native American track athlete and baseball and football player, he was a member of the Sac and Fox tribe. Both his father (Hiram) and his mother (Charlotte) were farmers. Thorpe attended Haskell and Carlisle Indian schools. He made first team All-American honors in football in 1911 and 1912 while at Carlisle. In 1912 he won Olympic gold medals in both the pentathlon and the decathlon. These medals were revoked in 1913 because he had played semiprofessional baseball and thus did not qualify as an "amateur" for the Olympics. He played professional football and professional baseball until the mid-1920s. In 1950 the press named Thorpe the greatest football player and the best male athlete of the half century. Thorpe's amateur standing was reinstated in 1973, and in 1983 he was posthumously awarded replicas of his medals. Thorpe helped increase the popularity of professional football in its early years. He was the first president of the American Professional Football Association. He assembled the Oorang Indians, an all-Indian professional football team. He had bit parts in several movies, and in 1951 the movie *Jim Thorpe—All American* was released. The Most Valuable Player trophy for the National Football League was named the Jim Thorpe Trophy in 1955. Thorpe, who exemplified all-around athletic ability, remains the most prominent of all Native American athletes. The loss of his Olympic medals helps to highlight the amateur-professional dichotomy in place in the early 1900s; efforts by many individuals to have his medals restored indicate the high regard with which he was held in American society.

SELECTED BIBLIOGRAPHY: J. Newcombe, *The Best of the Athletic Boys: The White Man's Impact on Jim Thorpe* (1975); Joseph B. Oxendine, *American Indian Sports Her-*

itage (1988); Gene Schoor, with Henry Gilfond, *The Jim Thorpe Story* (1951); John S. Steckbeck, *Fabulous Redmen: The Carlisle-Indians and Their Famous Football Teams* (1951); Robert W. Wheeler, *Jim Thorpe: World's Greatest Athlete* (1979).

Victoria Paraschak

TORRES, JOSÉ LUIS ("Chegui") (3 May 1936, Playa Ponce, PR–   ). Torres joined the U.S. Army after high school graduation in 1954. He won the army and all services middleweight boxing championships. As a U.S. Olympian in 1956 he won the light-middleweight silver medal. Turning professional in 1958 under Cus D'Amato, Torres had compiled a 41–3–1 record when he retired from boxing in 1969. The high point of his professional career was winning the world light-heavyweight title from Willie Pastrano in 1965 (he lost the title to Dick Tiger the following year). Subsequently, Torres had a distinguished career as national Hispanic campaign chairman for Senator Robert Kennedy in the 1960s as well as similar positions for governors and mayors of New York City and the governor of Puerto Rico in the 1970s. He held other New York City and national political positions; was chairman of the New York Athletic Commission from 1985 to 1988; and was president of the World Boxing Organization from 1993 to 1995 (the first Hispanic and first professional boxer to hold this position). Torres was a newspaper columnist and also wrote biographies of Muhammad Ali* and Mike Tyson.* He was elected to the Boxing Hall of Fame in 1997.

SELECTED BIBLIOGRAPHY: Gigi Anders, "Honoring Hispanic Heroes: At Smithsonian, Five Get Heritage Awards," *Washington Post*, 16 September 1992, B-2; José Torres, *Sting like a Bee: The Muhammad Ali Story* (1971); José Torres, *Fire and Fear: The Inside Story of Mike Tyson* (1989).

Richard V. McGehee

TRACK AND FIELD. Track and field refers to footraces at distances up to 10,000 meters that are held on the track and to the jumping and throwing field events—high and long jumps, pole vault, shot put, javelin throw, hammer throw, and so on—held in the center of the track or on special grounds. Some would include events such as cross-country running, racewalking, and long-distance running as part of track and field.

Formal footraces appeared in the United States by the early nineteenth century, when they were held as side attractions to horse racing programs. A series of races at the Beacon Race Course in Hoboken, New Jersey, in 1844 gained the sport national attention. The entrants included Englishmen, Irishmen, and at least one Native American, as well as native-born local heroes Henry Stannard and John Gildersleeve, who won the first and second races, respectively. Sporting periodicals noted the issues of race and nationalism in these meets as they explained the excitement, in part, by the victories of white men over Indians and Americans over Englishmen.

A strong running tradition had long existed among many Native American nations. The Six Nations Confederacy, which in the nineteenth century centered around the Cattaraugus Reservation in Erie County, New York, produced athletes who competed in Albany, Buffalo, Boston, and New York City. Most of these runners, denied other economic opportunities, concentrated on winning cash prizes at country fairs and other exhibition races. Louis Bennett of the Seneca Nation won fame in Britain and the United States as the professional runner "Deerfoot," whose record for the one-hour run was not broken until 1953.

Field events such as high- and long-jumping, putting the stone, and throwing the hammer and other weights were practiced as part of the cultural celebrations of various American cities' Scottish Highland Societies. Scottish immigrants particularly interested in competition later organized the Caledonian Clubs; Boston had a Caledonian Club in 1853, and New York had one in 1856. By 1870 Caledonian Clubs flourished in many American cities, and Caledonian Games were held throughout the Northeast and in Detroit, Chicago, Milwaukee, and San Francisco. Although the Caledonian Clubs promoted Scottish ethnic identity, the Caledonian Games accepted all competitors. Native Americans entered the footraces, and African Americans also participated. The Caledonian Games were professional; that is, athletes competed for cash prizes.

Amateur athletic clubs began with the founding of the New York Athletic Club (NYAC) between 1866 and 1868. The NYAC's founding members were mostly of Anglo-Saxon heritage or scions of Scottish or German families that were well established in America. Among the last group were a few members of German Jewish descent. As the Irish became established in America, the NYAC accepted several Irish American athletes, including John Flanagan, the "father" of the modern hammer throw and the first of the famed "Irish whales."* These were large athletes who dominated the field events; several were members of the New York City Police Department, but not all gained admission to the exclusive NYAC.

Other sport clubs took up the ideals of amateurism to increase their competitive opportunities. Amateurism began as a social distinction, and members of early amateur clubs were usually middle-class or higher. Later, smaller amateur sport clubs did not impose financial or social restrictions on their members, and an athlete could find a place in one of these clubs on talent alone. The Amateur Athletic Union (AAU) was organized by a group of upper-status clubs in January 1888 and remained the governing body of American track and field for over ninety years. The AAU was closely connected to the NYAC, which came under criticism in the twentieth century for racial and religious bigotry.

During the late 1800s and early 1900s track-and-field enthusiasts from several ethnic groups founded amateur clubs. The Scottish-American Athletic Club broke off from the New York Caledonian Society in 1875 to provide amateur competitive opportunities for its members, who were not necessarily of Scottish ancestry. In 1878 the Irish-American Athletic Club* was organized in New York City as amateur but not upper status; by the early twentieth century, it was recruiting athletes who were not of Irish ethnicity. The Unione Sportiva Italiana, a sports club founded for Italian waiters, similarly accepted competent athletes of other ethnicities. The German-American Athletic Club* was organized in New York in 1884 for wrestling and weight lifting. The Finnish-American Athletic Club was founded in 1901. The Smart Set Club of Brooklyn, an African American club, encouraged track and field, staging a large indoor meet and entering relay teams in AAU competitions. The German-American Athletic Club retained a strong ethnic identity and became defunct in 1917 with the antagonisms surrounding the United States' entry into World War I on the side of England and France. New York's Irish-American Athletic Club also disbanded at this time, as an expression of patriotism.

Polish and Czechoslovakian sporting societies promoted ethnic allegiance along with athletics. The first Polish Falcons* appeared in Chicago in 1867, while the first Czechoslovakian Sokol began in St. Louis in 1865. Such ethnic societies received full membership in the AAU, and their athletes competed in AAU-sanctioned events. Many such small, neighborhood clubs represented ethnic groups and concentrated on footracing because they could not afford the facilities or grounds for other sports. In late nineteenth-century New York City, as many of the large, upper-status clubs failed through financial mismanagement, working-class clubs became increasingly important.

Ethnic clubs appeared during the early twentieth century throughout the United States. The Olympic Club in San Francisco, established in 1860 as a social club and athletic club, had dominated local sports through the 1910s. In the 1920s the Italian clubs Unione Sportiva Italiana, Virtus, and Sporting Italiana exerted an increasing influence, as did the Young Men's Christian Association and the Young Men's Hebrew Association.* Within a decade running events saw representatives of the Chinese Club, the Russian Club, and the Japanese American Club.

Settlement houses were a vehicle for late nineteenth- and early twentieth-century ethnic participation in sports, but, of course, these clubs were catalysts for Americanization rather than ethnic representation. For example, the Hudson Guild on West Twenty-Eighth Street in New York City was strongly Irish but also included Italian, Jewish, German, and Greek members who competed in track and field. Company teams similarly provided athletic opportunities to a diverse population. The Millrose Athletic Association was begun in 1908 by the employees of John Wanamaker's department store. The Millrose marathon team for the 1915 Panama Pacific Exposition marathon comprised Willie Kyronen, a Finn, Nick Giannakopulos, known as Nick the Greek, Charles Pores, a Jewish runner, and John Cahill; their coach was Olympian Melvin Sheppard.

As early as the 1890s track and field had become a mainstream sport in the United States, with athletes from a variety of social classes, nationalities, religions, and races competing at many levels. African Americans, Native American Indians, and working-class whites were permitted to compete at the Caledonian Games. But even though the most prestigious and exclusive athletic clubs banned nonwhites and charged membership fees that discouraged the enrollment of workers, they did allow talented white men from the lower to middle classes to represent their club in meets. Laurence Eugene "Lon" Meyers,* a Jew, became one of the first track superstars during the 1880s while a member of the elite Manhattan Athletic Club. During his illustrious amateur career (1878–85) he won fifteen American titles, as well as several English and Canadian championships. Between 1880 and 1885 he also held every American record at all distances from fifty yards to a mile.

During the early 1900s athletes from a wide range of ethnic and racial backgrounds won honors at the national and international level. The American victories at the Olympic Games in Stockholm in 1912 generated a great deal of speculation in the newspapers over the racial significance of the outcome. In an editorial *The Independent* cautioned against interpreting the results as a triumph for "the Anglo-Saxon race." It remarked: "The United States owes its supremacy over all other nations to the fact that it is a union of all races. The men in whom we take pride have not only English, Scotch, Welsh and Irish blood in their veins, but Scandinavian, Russian, German, Italian, Hawaiian, Indian and other blood as well. If the Old World claims all that she originally sent to us, America has still the Carlisle Indians, and among them James Thorpe,* the greatest all-around athlete of the world." *Harper's Weekly* described the U.S. contingent as a gathering of "lawyers, physicians, policemen, Indians, negroes, Hawaiians, college men, school boys, clerks, mechanics, and, in fact, entrants from every walk of life." It declared: "There was no class or color distinction on board the training ship or in the Stadium. Each man was an integral part of the team, bearing the American shield, with his work to do." While the upper-class definition of amateurism cost Jim Thorpe his medals after the Stockholm Olympics, it is still true that he had the opportunity to vanquish all of his competitors. It would take more than another half century before track and field would become truly democratized in the United States, but it is clear that it enjoyed great popularity among the masses of many nationalities and races prior to World War I.

Many factors contributed to the decline of ethnic clubs as a major influence in track and field. At the public school level, young athletes had alternative organizations, such as the Public Schools Athletic League (PSAL), created in New York City in 1903. Although PSAL was a private organization, it was supported by the New York City Board of Education. The PSAL started a section for girls in 1905. Within a few years the PSAL was so successful that seventeen other cities established similar programs. The gradual success of the modern Olympic Games in the twentieth century increased the importance of track-and-field competition. The university system, under the aegis of the National Collegiate Athletic Association, became the primary training program for track-and-field athletes after high school.

Ethnic clubs remained an important outlet for athletes beyond college age, for those who were unable to enter college, and for those whose high school facilities were inadequate. The New York Pioneer Club* of Harlem, founded in

1936, brought track and field to youth who had no other access to organized sport. Originally African American, the Pioneer Club became integrated and accepted men and boys from all over the New York City area, regardless of athletic ability.

African American men and women played an increasingly prominent role in track and field during the middle and later decades of the twentieth century. Jesse Owens* electrified the world with his stunning triple gold medal performance at the "Nazi" Olympics in Berlin in 1936. During the 1950s and 1960s many black athletes won Olympic and world championship titles; among the most prominent were Harrison Dillard, Milton Campbell, Lee Calhoun, Rafer Johnson, Ralph Boston,* and Bob Hayes.* The Civil Rights movement of these years generated a controversy over racial discrimination in American sports in general and track and field in particular. In 1968 Harry Edwards, a sociology instructor at San Jose State College in California, organized a successful boycott of the 100th anniversary games of the New York Athletic Club at Madison Square Garden in New York City. Although Edwards could not persuade the leading black athletes to boycott the Olympic Games in Mexico City that year, he did urge the participants to protest racism in their own way. Sprinters Tommie Smith* and John Carlos* bowed their heads and raised their gloved fists in a black power salute during the playing of the American national anthem as they were receiving their medals. The U.S. Olympic Committee suspended them from the team and gave them only forty-eight hours to leave Mexico, but Smith and Carlos had focused the attention of the world on the status of the black athlete in America.

Black women also distinguished themselves in a sport that many white Americans viewed as too masculine for proper females. Although Mildred "Babe" Didrikson (of Norwegian ancestry) and Polish immigrant Stella Walsh* had earned international fame, their "mannish" public images discouraged many other white women from testing themselves on the track. As white females rejected the sport, African American women asserted themselves, especially after World War II. Tuskegee Institute led the way, forming the first highly competitive women's track team in 1929. Its team dominated women's track during the 1930s and 1940s, winning eleven of twelve AAU outdoor championships between 1937 and 1948. Tennessee State University then challenged Tuskegee for supremacy in female track, producing many Olympians. During the 1950s African American women constituted more than two-thirds of American women chosen to compete at the major international meets and the Olympics. Alice Coachman* was the first black woman to win a gold medal at the Olympics when she placed first in the high jump in 1948 in London. Mildrid McDaniel also starred in the high jump, setting a world record while winning the gold medal in 1956 in Melbourne. Wilma Rudolph* was a sensation in 1960 in Rome, capturing three gold medals.

Track and field began as an ethnic sport; the original clubs were the foundation of modern athletics, including the Olympic Games. Ethnic clubs that supported track-and-field athletes are also significant as the precursors of the many small clubs that are more social than athletic in their purpose. These clubs are the basis of the long-distance running boom of the late twentieth century. With the increasing prestige of the Olympic Games and the rise of major college track-and-field programs, African Americans of both sexes earned international renown. By the end of the twentieth century track and field had lost most of its original ethnic and immigrant character, but the success of black athletes had demonstrated the fruits of increasing opportunities for African Americans.

SELECTED BIBLIOGRAPHY: Arthur R. Ashe, Jr., *A Hard Road to Glory: A History of the African-American Athlete, 1919–1945*, vol. 2 (1988); Bob Considine and Fred G. Jarvis, *The First Hundred Years: A Portrait of the NYAC (New York Athletic Club)* (1969); John Cumming, *Runners and Walkers: A Nineteenth Century Sports Chronicle* (1981); Gerald Redmond, *The Caledonian Games in Nineteenth-Century America* (1971); Steven Riess, *City Games: The Evolution of American Urban Society and the Rise of Sports* (1989); Len Wallach, *The Human Race* (1978).

Pamela Cooper

TREVINO, LEE (1 December 1939, Dallas, TX–   ). A Mexican American golfer, he is the son of Juanita (Barrett) Trevino, a domestic worker. He was raised by his mother and her father, Joe Trevino, a grave digger, who was born in Mexico and as a child moved to Texas in search of farmwork. Trevino was raised on the outskirts of North Dallas, and when he was seven, he moved with his family to a primitive house near the Glen Lakes Country Club and began his golf career as a caddie. He excelled in sports in school, but because of financial needs of his family, he had to drop out of school at age fourteen to find a job. He began working at a Dallas driving range, which gave him ample time for practice and opportunities to learn about the game and business. At seventeen he joined the U.S. Marine Corps and spent much of the next four years playing golf for marine teams. He then returned to his driving range job in Dallas and entered many local competitions. In 1965 he became assistant pro at an El Paso, Texas, country club and in 1967 was accepted for the Professional Golfers' Association (PGA) Tour. Trevino's first major victory came the next year when he won the U.S. Open. After that he won many tournaments, including the U.S. Open again in 1971, the British Open in 1971 and 1972, the Canadian Open in 1971, 1977 and 1979, and the PGA Championship in 1974 and 1984. Trevino was a Ryder Cup team member seven times and was team captain in 1985. He was elected to the PGA Hall of Fame and the World Golf Hall of Fame in 1981. He entered full-scale PGA Seniors play in 1990 and has earned several senior titles. Trevino is proud of his Mexican heritage and his nickname of "Super Mex."

SELECTED BIBLIOGRAPHY: Myron Cope, "A Firm Hand on a Carefree Cat," *Sports Illustrated* 28 (17 June 1968): 49–52; Thomas W. Gilbert, *Lee Trevino* (1992); Barry

McDermott, "The Unseen Side of Lee Trevino," *Sports Illustrated* 54 (15 June 1981): 74–79, 85, 87–88.

Richard V. McGehee

TUNNEY, JAMES JOSEPH ("Gene") (25 May 1898, New York City–7 November 1978, New York City). A prizefighter, he was born in the Greenwich Village section of Manhattan to Irish Catholic parents John Joseph Tunney (a longshoreman) and Mary Lydon Tunney. He graduated from the Christian Brothers high school, La Salle Academy, in 1915, then worked as a clerk in the Ocean Steamship Company of New York. With America's entry into World War I he joined the Marine Corps and was sent to France with the American Expeditionary Force. Following the trench warfare of World War I his boxing abilities came to the fore, and in Paris in 1919 he won the light-heavyweight championship of the American armed forces in Europe (AEF). Still boxing as a light-heavyweight back in the United States after the war, Tunney knocked out the popular French fighter Georges Carpentier in 1924 and then decided to fight regularly in the heavyweight class. Losing only one of sixty fights up to this time, Tunney entered the ring in Philadelphia in 1926 to face the immensely popular Manassa Mauler, heavyweight champion Jack Dempsey.* In a bout fought in the rain, a run-down Dempsey was perhaps distracted by legal problems with his former manager, Jack Kearns. He was finished by the tenth round, and Tunney became the new champion. In September 1927 Tunney and Dempsey were to meet again for the championship in what has often been described as the most controversial fight of the century. Tunney, boxing well in the return bout, was knocked down by Dempsey in the seventh round. Dempsey, enjoying give-and-take with ringsiders, failed to go to a neutral corner as required. The referee's attempts to get him to do so resulted in the famous "long count." A now clear-headed Tunney went on to outbox Dempsey and win the fight. He fought only one more time, winning a technical knockout over Tom Heeney in 1928, after which he retired as the undefeated heavyweight champion. Tunney, a devout Roman Catholic, stated that religion was his highest ideal in his 1932 book, *A Man Must Fight*. He went on to hold directorships and executive positions with various banks and corporations and directed the U.S. Navy physical fitness program during World War II. He remains, arguably, the most atypical boxing champion of the twentieth century.

SELECTED BIBLIOGRAPHY: Paul W. Gallico, "By Horatio Alger Jr.," in *Farewell to Sport* (1938), 81–91; C.H.L. Johnson, "James Joseph ('Gene') Tunney: Champion Heavyweight Boxer in the World," in *Famous American Athletes of Today* (1928), 1st ser. 67–95; W. O. Inglis, "Gene Tunney, Captain of Fistic Industry," in *Champions Off Guard* (1932), 284–311.

Lawrence Huggins

TURNERS (TURNVEREIN). Through the turnverein movement, German immigrants contributed greatly to the development of physical education, exercise, and gymnastics programs in the United States. The first turnverein club had been founded in 1811 by a Prussian patriot turned German nationalist named Friedrich Ludwig Jahn (1778–1852). He was an instructor at an academic high school who sought to enroll the youth of Berlin in the resistance against the Napoleonic domination of their homeland. He named his program after what he believed was an extinct Teutonic word, "turnen," and erected the first gymnastic field, or "Turnplatz," on a field outside Berlin called the Hasenheide. Here the new club placed a running track, a jumping ditch, and standardized measures for high jumping and pole vaulting and also erected apparatus, such as the horse, the balance beam, the horizontal bar, and ladders, some of which had evolved from older models, some relatively recently invented for use in experimental German schools, and some, like the parallel bars, created by Jahn and his associates for use in the club. When the club was only a few months old, it held its first "turnfest," a gymnastics festival open to the public, which was a great popular success and symbol of German revival following Prussia's humiliation at the hands of the French.

The turners welcomed the war that overthrew French domination, even though it cost them many of their younger followers. But they found their desire for political participation suddenly suspect in the repressive atmosphere of post-Napoleonic Europe. The turners then undertook an increasingly desperate struggle to promote their vision of a new and unified German state. Their efforts were crushed in 1819, when the various governments united in the German Confederation, led by the conservative Austrian prime minister Clemens von Metternich, moved to suppress all expressions of liberal nationalism. As a part of this crackdown, the turnverein was banned, its practice areas closed, and its apparatus dismantled. Jahn himself was imprisoned, but even after his release in 1825, he was barred from teaching or gymnastic work.

German immigrants introduced gymnastics into the United States in two stages. During the 1820s a trio of refugees from the repressive Prussian policies arrived in New York and Boston. Charles Beck, Charles Follen, and Francis Lieber contributed significantly to the adoption of physical education programs at several schools and colleges. Beck, a disciple of Jahn, taught Latin and gymnastics at the Round Hill School at Northampton, Massachusetts. In 1825 that school became the first literary or industrial institution in the United States to require physical training in its curriculum. Follen became a German instructor at Harvard, and in 1826 he persuaded the college authorities to allow him to construct some apparatus on a ground called the Delta, a facility that became the first college gymnasium in America. Lieber arrived in Boston in 1827 and took over the supervision of a gymnasium that Follen had founded in Boston. But this flurry of excitement over the German system soon faded, for the Round Hill School closed its doors in 1834, and during the 1830s attendance dropped precipitously at both the Harvard and Boston gymnasiums.

A much larger wave of German immigrants popularized the sport of gymnastics in North America after 1848. The ban on turnverein clubs that had been imposed in the German Confederation was gradually lifted in the more liberal atmosphere of the 1840s, when the drive for a liberal and unified Germany culminated in the revolution of 1848. Turners played a major role in the revolutions, and when they were suppressed, they constituted a significant component of the emigration to America. These "Forty-Eighters" soon founded turnverein clubs in various American cities, mostly in the Midwest and mid-Atlantic regions. The first turnverein in the United States is generally considered to be the one founded in Cincinnati in 1848, inspired in large part by Frederick Hecker, who fled to America following the final defeat of the rebellion in South Baden earlier that year. Over the next three years, newly arrived Germans organized at least twenty-one additional turnverein clubs in Louisville, Philadelphia, Baltimore, Brooklyn, New York City, Boston, Utica, New York, Newark, New Jersey, and other towns. By 1860 their number had reached 157 and counted 10,000 members from among the slightly more than 1 million German immigrants who arrived in the United States between 1848 and 1860.

These clubs joined together in larger unions, called turnerbunds, that sponsored national gymnastic festivals in Philadelphia (1851), Baltimore and Cincinnati (1852), and Louisville and New York (1853). These events were held annually until the Civil War caused a five-year interruption. The gatherings featured a variety of athletic competitions for three categories of participants, grouped by age: juniors, actives, and seniors. There were military events (target shooting, fencing with sabre and foil, and bayonet thrusting) and "free-turning" (wrestling, weight lifting, sprint running, hurdles racing, high jumping, javelin throwing, stone putting, swimming, and stilt walking). However, the featured attractions were always the apparatus exercises: rope climbing and work on the horizontal and parallel bars, swinging rings, and vaulting horse.

The turnverein clubs played an important role for the German community as the newcomers promoted democratic social and political reforms, resisted nativist attacks and temperance campaigns, and debated the hotly contested issue of slavery. Northern and midwestern turners tended to be antislavery, and during the Civil War the German turner organizations contributed substantial numbers to the ranks of the Union army, with large numbers of recruits (and sometimes entire companies) enrolling in New York City, Newark, Philadelphia, Cincinnati, St. Louis, Chicago, Milwaukee, and Indianapolis. However, most turners who resided in the Confederacy fought for the South.

After peace returned, the turnerbunds launched new campaigns for gymnastics and also various political, social, and educational reforms. In November 1866 the National Turnerbund Normal School opened in New York City as a training academy for German gymnastics. By 1867 the North American Turnerbund included eighteen districts, 148 clubs, and a total membership of 10,200. Its platform proclaimed that its special task was to give its members "a proper understanding of the efforts at radical reform in social, political, and religious arenas, to assist in their realization, as well as in the protection of the rights with which men were born." It also announced that gymnasts will "fight every effort to limit freedom of conscience, along with all efforts to abridge human rights," and also "support all efforts to expand adult education, and to promote as much as possible a free and ethical education for young people through founding and supporting good schools."

For the remainder of the nineteenth century the turners worked on a number of fronts to promote the cause of physical education and fitness in the United States. First, they labored to expand programs for the training of instructors in German gymnastics. They also launched a crusade to pass state laws mandating the inclusion of German gymnastics in public school curricula. In addition, they revitalized their gymnastics festivals, and since 1885 the national turnfests have been held every four years, with the exception of the eras of the two world wars. Finally, they expanded opportunities for girls and women to participate in physical education and gymnastics programs.

The German turnverein movement reached its peak in numbers and influence during the late nineteenth and early twentieth centuries. In 1895 the national bund reported 314 clubs, totaling 40,000 members, but by 1920 the numbers had decreased to less than 200, with enrollment under 33,000. By the 1990s there were only about sixty turnverein clubs in the United States, with about 14,000 members in the national society. The effects of the two world wars, the increasing assimilation of Germans into mainstream American society, and the proliferation of non-German gymnastics clubs and programs have all contributed to this decline. Nonetheless, no other immigrant group has matched the record of the German turners in promoting physical education and gymnastics in the United States.

SELECTED BIBLIOGRAPHY: Robert K. Barney, "German Turners in America: Their Role in Nineteenth Century Exercise Expression and Physical Education Legislation," in Earle F. Zeigler, ed., *A History of Physical Education and Sport in the United States and Canada* (1975); Robert K. Barney, "The German-American Turnverein Movement: Its Historiography in North America," in Roland Naul, ed., *Turnen and Sport* (1991); Robert K. Barney, "Forty-Eighters and the Rise of the Turnverein Movement in America," in George Eisen and David K. Wiggins, eds., *Ethnicity and Sport in North American History and Culture* (1994); Erich Geldbach, "The Beginnings of German Gymnastics in the United States," *Journal of Sport History* 3 (1976): 236–272. Henry Metzner, *History of the American Turners*, 4th rev. ed. (1989).

Forrest F. Steinlage, George B. Kirsch, and Claire E. Nolte

TYSON, MICHAEL GERALD (30 June 1966, Brooklyn, NY–   ). An African American boxing champion, he was the youngest of three children of Lorna Tyson and John Kilpatrick. He grew up in the Bedford Stuyvesant area of Brooklyn—a locale known for its violence and street gang culture. As a boy he was bullied, and eventually, boxing allowed him a measure of esteem and self-respect. At the age of thirteen Tyson was sent to a reform institution called the Tyron School for Boys in upstate New York. He eventually came under the tutelage of the legendary boxing trainer Cus D'Amato. Despite winning the 1984

National Golden Gloves heavyweight championship, Tyson was never an American Olympian. On 22 November 1986 Tyson won the World Boxing Council heavyweight championship, becoming the youngest ever boxer to hold a "partial" world championship. He eventually won both World Boxing Association and International Boxing Federation versions of the heavyweight title. His June 1988 knockout of Michael Spinks made him the undisputed heavyweight champion of the world. Despite considerable fistic success, a much publicized divorce from actress Robin Givens after incidents of wife abuse, and his reaction to the deaths of mentors and confidantes D'Amato and comanager Jim Jacobs gained him a reputation as a controversial and confrontational celebrity. On 10 February 1990 James "Buster" Douglas, lined up as an "easy target," created a sensation by knocking out Tyson in the tenth round. Tyson's comeback march was derailed when, in 1992, an Indianapolis jury found him guilty of raping an African American beauty queen contestant. He was released from prison in March 1995 and allowed Don King* to continue as his manager, guru, spokesman, and promoter. A tandem deal with the MGM Grand in Las Vegas and Showtime Event Television guaranteed vast riches for Tyson, and the general expectation was that Tyson, despite his age and an erosion of his striking ferocity, had too much power for the existing crop of fighters. However, in November 1996 Evander Holyfield slugged it out with Tyson and eventually overpowered him. Their rematch on 5 July 1997 in front of 16,331 at the MGM Grand Garden Arena and a huge pay-per-view audience had pundits wondering if this might be one of the classic encounters of modern boxing. What eventuated was the absolute nadir of sport, much less boxing. Tyson was disqualified by referee Mills Lane in round three for biting Holyfield on both ears. The Nevada State Athletic Commission fined Tyson and suspended him for a year. Comeback odysseys are synonymous with professional boxing, but in Tyson's case the specter is of a disturbed athlete tormented by too many demons. Sadly, the Holyfield debacle left Tyson defined as a crazed pugilist. At his prime, however, in his early twenties, he was a fearsome antagonist.

SELECTED BIBLIOGRAPHY: Robin Givens, "So How Do You Like Me Now," *Playboy* 41 (September 1996): 120–130; Richard Hoffer, "Feeding Frenzy," *Sports Illustrated* 87 (7 July 1997): 32–38; David Miller, *Our Sporting Times* (1996); Joyce Carol Oates, "Interview," *Playboy* 40 (November 1993): 63–76; John Robertson, "Mike Tyson," in David L. Porter, ed., *African-American Sports Greats: A Biographical Dictionary* (1995); John M. Sloop, "Mike Tyson and the Perils of Discursive Constraints: Boxing, Race and the Assumption of Guilt," in Aaron Baker and Todd Boyd, eds., *Out of Bounds: Sports Media and the Politics of Identity* (1997), 102–122.

Scott A.G.M. Crawford

TYUS-TILLMAN, WYOMIA (29 August 1945, Griffin, GA–   ). An African American track champion, she is the daughter of Willie Tyus, a dairy farmer, and Maria Tyus, a laundress. As a child her father encouraged her to participate in sports, but her mother was less supportive because she believed athletics to be unfeminine. In high school Wyomia excelled in both basketball and track, winning the girls' national Amateur Athletic Union title at 100 yards in 1962 and setting an American age group record of eleven seconds. When she enrolled at Tennessee State University in 1963, she joined the legendary Tigerbelles track team, earning her bachelor's degree in 1968. She gained international fame by winning the gold medal in the 100-meter final in the 1964 Olympic Games in Tokyo, Japan, adding a silver medal in the 400-meter relay. Four years later she became the first Olympian to successfully defend a sprint title when she repeated as 100-meter champion at Mexico City. There she also won a third gold medal by anchoring the world record-setting 400-meter relay team. In Mexico City she also lowered her world record time for 100 meters to eleven seconds. After marrying Duane Tillman and having her first child, she left the amateur ranks and joined the Professional International Track Association. She competed as a professional for three years, remaining undefeated in the sixty-yard dash. After her retirement she worked in public relations in Los Angeles and conducted sports clinics for youngsters. She was elected to the National Track and Field Hall of Fame in 1980.

SELECTED BIBLIOGRAPHY: Cheryl Bentsen, "Tigerbelle Tradition," *WomenSport* 5 (February 1978): 52–53; Lewis H. Carlson and John J. Fogarty, *Tales of Gold* (1987); Michael D. Davis, *Black American Women in Olympic Track and Field: A Complete Illustrated Reference* (1992); Michael Levy, "All-Time Greats," *WomenSport* 6 (June 1984): 37–41; Scott Ostler, "Wyomia Tightened Up to Loosen Up for Gold," *Los Angeles Times*, 25 July 1984, 12.

George B. Kirsch

U

UKRAINIANS. Large-scale Ukrainian immigration to the United States can be divided into five periods: 1870–1900 (240,000); 1900–14 (42,000); 1914–39 (20,000); 1945–52 (100,000); 1952–present (20,000). The most heavily settled states of the United States for Ukrainian newcomers were Pennsylvania, New York, Maryland, Michigan, and Illinois. Early Ukrainian settlers were employed mostly in coal mining in Pennsylvania and in agriculture in the other states. Ukrainian participation in U.S. sports began early in the twentieth century. In 1912 Frank Gotch became the first Ukrainian to win a world championship in wrestling. In 1915 an organization named "Sichovi striltsi" was founded by Peter Zadoretzky. Members competed in baseball, basketball, bowling, softball, and track and field. In 1928 Steve Halaiko, a boxer, and John Kojak, a swimmer, represented the United States at the Olympic Games in Amsterdam. In 1933 the Ukrainian Youth League of North America was founded. Their members were involved in basketball, baseball, softball, bowling, volleyball, and golf. In 1932 and 1936 Peter Fik was a member of the U.S. Olympic swimming team. In 1936 a Ukrainian track-and-field meet took place under the auspices of the Ukrainian Catholic Youth League near Philadelphia. Also in 1936 the first Ukrainian Olympiad, held in Philadelphia, attracted over 150 youths from fourteen Ukrainian clubs in the United States. It included competition in swimming, track and field, and baseball.

Ukrainian organized sport in the United States consists of eight sports clubs and two youth organizations, which are involved in various athletic activities. They are Ukrainian American Sports Association "Lions" (Chicago); Ukrainian Sports Club "Kryla" (Chicago); Ukrainian Sports Club "Chernyk" (Detroit); Ukrainian American Sports Club "Lviv" (Cleveland); Ukrainian American Sports Club "Tryzub" (Philadelphia); Ukrainian Sports Association "Sitch" (Newark, New Jersey); Ukrainian Sports Club of New York (New York City);

Sports Club "Krylati" (Yonkers, New York); Ukrainian Youth Organization "Plast," U.S.A.; Ukrainian American Youth Association, U.S.A.

Most Ukrainian clubs are involved in such sports activities as soccer, volleyball, swimming, track and field, tennis, softball, skiing, baseball, bowling, basketball, and hockey. The Ukrainian clubs have an umbrella organization called Association of Ukrainian Sports Clubs of North America (USCAK), a governing body of Ukrainian sports clubs network on the North American continent. In 1988, under the auspices of the USCAK, a Ukrainian American Millennium Olympiad was held in Philadelphia. Eight hundred athletes competed in eight sports: soccer, volleyball, track and field, tennis, swimming, golf, table tennis, and chess.

Ukrainian athletes have distinguished themselves in soccer. The "Tryzub" club of Philadelphia, playing under the name of the Ukrainian Nationals, was U.S. soccer champion four times in the 1960s (1960, 1961, 1963, 1966), and the "Sitch" club of Newark also captured the U.S. soccer title once. The soccer boom of the 1960s produced outstanding soccer players who have represented the United States in Olympic and World Cup competitions. Among these are Zenon Snylyk,* two-time All-American for the University of Rochester, who holds the national record of having been selected three consecutive times to the U.S. Olympic soccer teams (1956, 1960, 1964); goalie George Kulishenko; winger Jimmy Stachrewsky; fullback Myron Krasij; fullback Myron Worobec; center-halfback Nick Krat; goalie Orest Banach; fullback George Chapla; and forward Walter Chyzowych,* who later served as the U.S. national soccer coach. Other Ukrainian soccer coaches include Dr. Leonard Lucenko of Montclair State College and Ostap Stromecky at the University of Alabama.

Ukrainians have also become prominent in a variety of other sports. Taras Liskewych was a coach in volleyball. In football there have been many All-Star performers, including Chuck Bednarik,* Bronco Nagurski,* Mike Ditka,* George Andrie, John Machuzak, Don Chuy, Bill Malinchak, Andy Stynchula, Bill Keman, Ted Stahura, Jim Ninowski, Frank Kuchta, John Guzik, and Bohdan Newsiacheny. Prominent tennis players include Alex Olynec, George Glowa, Mike Kopach, Roman Kupchinsky, Andrew Chaikowsky, Leo Worobkewych, George Sawchak, Mike Shyjan, Roman Rakotchyj, Jr., and his sister Areta Rakotchyj, the late Dr. Volodymyr Huk, John Durbak, Zenowij Jackiw, George Felinsky, Dr. Zenon Matkiwsky, Victor Herlinsky, Zenon Snylyk,* Constantine Bon, and Theodore Stopnycky. The professional ice hockey teams never lacked for aggressive Ukrainian players, such as Danny Lewicky of the New York Rangers, Terry Sawchuk, originally of the Detroit Red Wings, and Bill Mosienko of the Chicago Blackhawks. National competition of the best in Ukrainian tennis and swimming talent continues to grow in the USCAK-sponsored meets. At the present time, the Ukrainian organized sports scene is being dominated by soccer, volleyball, tennis, track and field, bowling, and golf.

SELECTED BIBLIOGRAPHY: Metodij Boretsky, *Ukrainian Sports Club "Tryzub"* (1991); Walter Dushnyk, *The Ukrainian Heritage in America* (1991); Alexander Lushnycky, *Ukrainian Olympiad* (1988); George Tatomyr, *Beyond the Uke Line* (1992).

Metodij Boretsky

UNITAS, JOHN C. ("Johnny") (7 May 1933, Pittsburgh–   ). A football player, he was born John Jonaitis, the son of Lithuanian immigrants. His father, Leonard, owned a small coal delivery business, which his mother, Helen, continued after her husband's death in 1938. She later worked at menial jobs and as a bookkeeper. Unitas began playing football at St. Justin's High School in Pittsburgh. A star quarterback who weighed 140 pounds, he did not receive an athletic scholarship from Notre Dame, but he did accept an offer from the University of Louisville, Kentucky. His body weight filled out to 190 pounds by the time he graduated in 1955. Unitas was picked in the ninth round of the 1955 draft by the Pittsburgh Steelers. After being dropped by the Steelers, Unitas worked at construction jobs and played for the semiprofessional Bloomfield Rams team. In 1956 the Baltimore Colts approached Unitas with a contract valued at $7,000. This began his extraordinary career with the Colts. Unitas led the Baltimore Colts to five National Football League (NFL) championships in 1958, 1959, 1964, 1968, and 1970 and the Super Bowl Crown in 1971. In 1973 he was traded to the San Diego Chargers before he retired from professional football in 1974. Unitas established an impressive list of football records. These included the most pass attempts (5,186); most completions (2,830); most total yards (40,239); most touchdowns (290); and the most 300-yard games (twenty-six). His greatest record of the most consecutive games throwing touchdown passes (forty-seven) has been considered to be the NFL equivalent of the great Joe DiMaggio's* fifty-six-game hitting streak in baseball. Voted the Most Valuable Player in the NFL in 1959, 1964, and 1967, he was named the "Greatest Player" of the first fifty years of professional football. In 1979 he was inducted into the Pro Football Hall of Fame.

SELECTED BIBLIOGRAPHY: *Baltimore News American*, 25 July 1974; Hal Butler, *Sports Heroes Who Wouldn't Quit* (1973); Lud Duroska, ed., *Great Pro Quarterbacks* (1972); Edward E. Fitzgerald, *Heroes of Sport* (1960); *New York Times*, 17 January 1971.

Sigitas Krasauskas

UNITED GOLFERS ASSOCIATION. The United Golfers Association (UGA) was formed in 1928 to provide African American golfers the opportunity to compete in regional and national tournaments, since they were excluded from participation in most golf competitions sponsored by whites-only private and public clubs. A forerunner to the UGA, the Colored Golfers Association, established in Washington, D.C., in 1925, changed its name to the United Golfers Association during its annual tournament at the Mapledale Country Club in Stow, Massachusetts, in 1928. The UGA consisted of regional organizations of black golfers, such as the Eastern Golfers Association, which would periodically stage competitions for individual members and interclub matches. The UGA coordinated the scheduling of these events and sponsored an annual national championship held at various black clubs throughout the country. What was to become the first UGA championship was played in 1925 at the Shady Rest Country Club* in New Jersey. The winner of the inaugural event was Harry Jackson of Washington, D.C., and the runner-up was John Shippen.*

Throughout the years, when black professionals were unable to compete on the Professional Golfers' Association Tour, the UGA served as the only opportunity for these golfers to showcase their abilities and, for some time, to earn at least a modest living playing golf. It also represented a social network for middle-class blacks who were otherwise excluded from the social institutions associated with the game.

The principal people involved in the history of the UGA were Mrs. Anna Mae Robinson, the first president and founder of the Black Golfers Hall of Fame, Mrs. Paris Brown, former tour director of the UGA, and Mrs. Ethel Williams, founding member of the Wake-Robbins Golf Club, the first black women's golf club.

As restrictions on African American golfers diminished throughout the 1950s and 1960s, the role of the UGA also diminished. Rose Elder attempted to revitalize the activities of the UGA in 1992. The UGA continues to generate interest in establishing a permanent home for the Black Golfers Hall of Fame at Wilberforce University in Ohio.

SELECTED BIBLIOGRAPHY: Guilford Jones, "Past Greats," *Black Sports* (July 1973): 65–66; Richard Porter Preiss, "Black Country Clubs along the East Coast, 1920–1929," paper presented at the American Culture Association Convention, Atlanta, GA (2–6 April 1986).

Larry Londino

V

VALVANO, JAMES T. (10 March 1946, Queens, NY–28 April 1993, Durham, NC). An Italian American basketball coach, his father, Rocco, was a high school basketball coach. A graduate of Seaford High School on Long Island, Valvano went on to earn his B.A. in English from Rutgers University. He worked on his master's of philosophy of education degree at Rutgers from 1968 to 1969 before becoming head basketball coach at Johns Hopkins University. He was an assistant coach at the University of Connecticut before becoming head coach at Bucknell and Iona. His success at Iona gained him national fame and the top post at North Carolina State University in 1980, where he coached until 1990. Valvano, known simply as "Jimmy V.," achieved a unique brand of fame in his lifetime as a sports celebrity, rising into the national spotlight on three distinct occasions. First, he gained notoriety as a coach when he led an underrated, underappreciated North Carolina State Wolfpack team to the national collegiate basketball title in 1983 with a dramatic, last-second win over the University of Houston. Valvano won a number of Coach of the Year awards for the 1983 season; however, the later years of Valvano's coaching tenure would be marred by many allegations of ethical violations, fixing grades, hiding drug-test results, and giving money and cars to his players. A National Collegiate Athletic Association (NCAA) investigation cleared Valvano of those charges but did find that his players were selling complimentary tickets and sneakers and put NC State on two years of probation. Allegations arose again in 1990 that Valvano's team was shaving points from its victories, and the coach (who had also served as the school's athletic director for three years) was forced to resign amid the controversy. He then became a noted television commentator for ABC and ESPN, receiving an ACE Cable award for excellence in cable television sports analysis. Finally, Valvano appeared in the national consciousness on a sadder note, as his fight against cancer inspired countless Americans. When he was diagnosed with metastatic adenocarcinoma, a form of cancer, he became a symbol of hope. Appearing on ESPN's *American Sports Awards* show to receive the Arthur Ashe* Award for courage, he moved the audience and America when he took the podium to announce the forming of a Jimmy V. Foundation to fight cancer. He ended the speech by imploring the audience, "Don't give up, don't ever give up."

SELECTED BIBLIOGRAPHY: "Jimmy Vee Hung in There," *Sports Illustrated* 78 (10 May 1993): 72; *New York Times*, 29 April 1993, B16; *Newsweek* 121 (10 May 1993): 49; *Time* 141 (10 May 1993): 27; *U.S. News and World Report* 114 (10 May 1993): 18; Jim Valvano and Curry Fitzpatrick, *Valvano* (1991); Dick Vitale, "Unforgettable Jim Valvano," *Reader's Digest* 144 (April 1994): 78.

Zachary Davis

VAN BROCKLIN, NORMAN (15 March 1926, Eagle Butte, SD–2 May 1983, Social Circle, GA). A collegiate and professional football player of Dutch heritage, he was the son of Mac, a farmer and watchmaker, and Ethel Van Brocklin. He graduated in 1943 from Acalanes High School in Walnut Creek, California. After completing a tour of duty with the U.S. Navy, he matriculated at the University of Oregon and received a B.S. degree in physical education. His passing led the University of Oregon to the Cotton Bowl in 1948. Known as "the Dutchman," he was renowned as a great passer-punter and is numbered among football's greatest quarterbacks. He was All-American in 1948. He played in eight Pro Bowls. He spent nine seasons with the Los Angeles Rams of the National Football League (NFL) and, in 1951, led them to their only league title. At age thirty-two he was traded to the Philadelphia Eagles before the 1958 season—one of the most important trades the Eagles ever made. He was named league Most Valuable Player (MVP) in 1960 after he led the Eagles to an NFL championship. Surgery put an end to his twelve-year professional on-field football career. When he was not chosen to succeed retiring Eagles coach Lawrence "Buck" Shaw in 1961, he became coach of the Minnesota Vikings, a position he held until 1967, when he joined the Atlanta Falcons (NFL), coaching them in middling fashion until midway in their 1974 campaign. In 1948 he was elected to the College Football Hall of Fame and in 1979 to the Pro Football Hall of Fame.

SELECTED BIBLIOGRAPHY: Tom Bennett, ed., *The NFL's Official Encyclopedic History of Professional Football* (1977); William A. Gudelunas, "Van Brocklin, Norman," in David L. Porter, ed., *Biographical Dictionary of American Sports: Football* (1987); Ronald L. Mendell and Timothy B. Phares, *Who's Who in Football* (1974); Beau Riffenburgh, ed., *The Official NFL Encyclopedia of Football* (1986).

Thomas E. Bird

VANDERBILT, HAROLD S. (6 July 1884, Oakdale, NY–4 July 1970, Newport, RI). A yachtsman and the inventor of contract bridge, he was the son of William Kissan Vanderbilt and Alvia E. (Smith). Of Dutch heritage and a member of one of the nation's wealthiest and most prominent families, he graduated from Harvard University in 1907 and from Harvard Law School in 1910. A French card game, *plafond*, involved declaring the players' intention to take a specific number of tricks. Vanderbilt and a group of his friends tried out variations of the game, combining the *plafond* principle with the rules of auction bridge, and called it "contract bridge." It provided that only tricks bid and made count toward game, with extra tricks counted as bonuses. Having perfected it, Vanderbilt published his rules of this new game (*Contract Bridge*, 1929; *New Contract Bridge*, 1930), and they became internationally accepted as official, as his version of the game became preeminent. In 1928 Vanderbilt donated "the Vanderbilt Trophy," an annual award perpetuated by a $100,000 trust fund under the terms of his will. It was contested each year until 1958 as a separate championship. In that year it became part of the Spring North American Championships. Winners constitute a "Who's Who in Bridge" or a Bridge Hall of Fame. A legendary yachtsman, Vanderbilt also revised yachting rules, which were also widely adopted following World War II. He won major trophies in American yachting—the Astor Cup and the King's Cup—a total of fourteen times. He was one of two men to skipper three America's Cup defenders: the *Enterprise* (1930), the *Rainbow* (1934, beating Chandler Hovey's *Yankee* for the honor of defending the Cup by just one second), and the *Ranger* (1937).

SELECTED BIBLIOGRAPHY: Wayne Andrew, *The Vanderbilt Legend: The Story of the Vanderbilt Family 1794–1940* (1941); Louis Auchincloss, *The Vanderbilt Era: Profiles of a Gilded Age* (1989); Edwin Hoyt, *The Vanderbilts and Their Fortunes* (1962).

Thomas E. Bird

VELASQUEZ, JORGE (28 December 1946, Chepo, Panama–   ). One of sixteen children, he was raised by his great-aunt. A top rider in Panama, he was brought to the United States in the 1960s by Fred Hooper. A quick success in this country, Velasquez was the leading rider in 1967 with 438 wins. In 1985 he rode winners of fifty-seven stakes, a single-season record. He rode Pleasant Colony to win the 1981 Kentucky Derby and Preakness and top fillies Chris Evert (1974) and Davona Dale (1979) to sweep New York's Acorn, Mother Goose, and Coaching Club American Oaks series. He was also the rider of Chris Evert in her match race victory over Miss Musket at Hollywood Park in 1974. In 1978 Velasquez guided Alydar in that colt's thrilling second-place finish to Affirmed in the Kentucky Derby, Preakness, and Belmont Stakes. Among other notable achievements, Velasquez piloted Proud Truth to victory in the 1985 running of the $3 million Breeders' Cup Classic. In grass races, the veteran jockey also excelled; he won the 1979 Washington, D.C., International with Bowl Game. Between 1963 and his induction into the National Thoroughbred Racing Hall of Fame in 1990 he earned more than $108 million in purses, winning 6,117 races out of a total of 35,288 mounts (17.3%). He was one of a select few ever to win more than 6,000 races and more than $100 million in purses.

SELECTED BIBLIOGRAPHY: *Annual Racing Review* (1974); Ron Smith, *The Sporting News Chronicle of Twentieth Century Sport* (1992); Michael Watchmaker, "Horse Racing," in *Athletics* (1985).

Courtesy of the National Thoroughbred Racing Hall of Fame

W

WAGNER, JOHANNES (JOHN) PETER ("Honus" or "Hans," "the Flying Dutchman") (24 February 1874, Chartiers, PA–6 December 1955, Carnegie, PA). A baseball player and the son of German immigrants, his father (Peter) was a coal miner, and his mother (Katheryn or Katharina) was a homemaker. After grammar school, he went to work in the mines. Wagner left the mines in 1895 to sign a minor league baseball contract. He reached the National League with the Louisville Colonels in 1897, transferred to the Pittsburgh Pirates in 1900, and played through 1917. Generally regarded as the greatest shortstop ever and by some the greatest player ever, he won eight batting titles, the National League record, and hit over .300 seventeen consecutive years, the major league mark. Sturdily built with a massive chest, long arms, and big hands, he was an exceptional fielder in an era of tiny gloves. Wagner led the Pirates to four National League pennants and played in two World Series, including a celebrated matchup against Ty Cobb and the Detroit Tigers in 1909. He also served as a model for clean living, once forcing a tobacco company to withdraw from the market a trading card with his image on it. Wagner coached college baseball and basketball and coached for the Pirates. He owned a sporting goods store in downtown Pittsburgh and was elected a charter member of the Baseball Hall of Fame in 1936.

SELECTED BIBLIOGRAPHY: Dennis DeValeria and Jeanne Burke DeValeria, *Honus Wagner: A Biography* (1996); William Hageman, *Honus: The Life and Times of a Baseball Hero* (1996); Arthur D. Hittner, *Honus Wagner: The Life and Times of Baseball's "Flying Dutchman"* (1996); "Honus Wagner," in Martin Appel and Burt Goldblatt, *Baseball's Best: The Hall of Fame Gallery* (1977).

Steven P. Gietschier

WALKER, HERSCHEL (3 March 1962, Wrightville, GA–). An African American football star, his parents were Willis Walker, Sr., who worked in a clay factory, and Christine (Taylor) Walker, who was employed in a pants factory. As a stellar college athlete at the University of Georgia Walker became only the seventh junior in National Collegiate Athletic Association (NCAA) history to win the Heisman Trophy award. He was a three-time consensus All-America selection after rushing for 5,259 yards (third in NCAA history) in three seasons at Georgia. Walker was a singular athlete in that he had power, strength, and great acceleration. He was an extraordinary "workhorse" who surprised everyone, but not himself, by carrying the ball forty-seven times in a 1981 game against the University of Florida. The 6'1", 225-pound running back rushed for an average of 159 yards per game. His academic major was criminal justice. In February 1983 Walker joined the New Jersey Generals in the fledgling U.S. Football League (USFL). He was a dominant figure in the league's short three-season life span. He led the league in rushing in 1983 and 1985, the year in which he ground out 2,411 rushing yards, thereby setting the professional football single-season record. Signed by the Dallas Cowboys in August 1986, following the demise of the USFL, Walker achieved a degree of success. However, his glorious record as a collegian and a USFL participant was never to be repeated in the National Football League. Nevertheless, his hallmark of consistency and reliability was maintained with Dallas, the Minnesota Vikings, and the New York Giants. At the 1992 Albertville Winter Olympics Walker was a member of the two-man U.S. bobsled team, a reminder of his college track sprinting ability.

SELECTED BIBLIOGRAPHY: Robert T. Bowen, Jr., "Herschel Walker," in David L. Porter, ed., *African-American Sports Greats: A Biographical Dictionary* (1995); Saleem Choudhry, Pro Football Hall of Fame Library-Research Center, Canton, OH; Press Relations Office, Dallas Cowboys, TX.

Scott A.G.M. Crawford

WALKER, MOSES FLEETWOOD, JR. (7 October 1857, Mt. Pleasant, OH–11 May 1924, Steubenville, OH). An African American baseball player, he was the son of Moses W. Walker, a physician, and Catherine O'Hara. Walker spent his first few years in a small Quaker community that served as a way station on the Underground Railroad. Walker attended integrated schools as a child and in 1878 enrolled at Oberlin College. While at Oberlin and later at the University of Michigan, his fascination with the increasingly popular sport of baseball exceeded his interest in academic subjects. After twice lettering in baseball at Michigan, in 1883 he left college and joined the Toledo Blue Stockings, a minor league team that captured the Northwestern League title in his first year. When Toledo entered the American Association the following year, Walker became the first African American baseball player to compete in the major leagues, over sixty years before Jackie Robinson* joined the Brooklyn Dodgers. His brother, Weldy, who joined the team later that year, became the second. A catcher, Walker suffered an injury that ended his first, and what became his only, year in the majors. After the conclusion of the season, the Toledo club released Walker, but he continued to play for five more years in the minor leagues for the Cleveland; Waterbury, Connecticut; Newark; and Syracuse teams in four different leagues. In the minors, he was one of only a handful of black players, as the trend moved toward the formal exclusion of blacks from the minor and major leagues. Walker and other African American ballplayers of his time paid a heavy personal and professional price for playing organized baseball. Walker himself had been refused hotel accommodations, threatened with violence, and benched by his manager. By the late 1880s African American players experienced a more open and intense hostility to their participation in organized baseball. In 1887 the International League officially established a color line, and with the failure of the League of Colored Base Ball Clubs, it became apparent that blacks would soon be excluded from the sport. After Walker left organized baseball in 1889, he became a successful businessman, inventor, and author. In 1908 he published a booklet, *Our Home Colony*, in which he advocated the emigration of blacks from the United States.

SELECTED BIBLIOGRAPHY: Larry Bowman, "Moses Fleetwood Walker: The First Black Major League Baseball Player," in Peter Levine, ed., *Baseball History: An Annual of Original Baseball Research* (1989); Jerry Malloy, comp., *Sol White's History of Colored Base Ball, with Other Documents on the Early Black Game 1886–1936* (1995); Robert Peterson, *Only the Ball Was White* (1970); Dean A. Sullivan, comp. and ed., *Early Innings: A Documentary History of Baseball, 1825–1908* (1995).

Larry K. Menna

WALSH, EDWARD AUGUSTINE ("Big Ed") (14 May 1881, Plains, PA– 26 May 1959, Pompano Beach, FL). A baseball player, his father (Michael) was an Irish immigrant and a miner. He attended parochial schools for five years and then worked in the mines. Walsh joined the Chicago White Sox in 1904 after playing minor league baseball for two years. Strictly a fastball pitcher, he learned to throw the spitball from teammate Elmer Stricklett during spring training with the White Sox in 1904. He won seventeen games to help the "Hitless Wonders" of 1906 defeat the New York Highlanders for their first American League pennant. He then won two World Series games as the White Sox defeated the Chicago Cubs. Walsh had his most memorable season in 1908. He appeared in 66 of his team's 156 games, setting a modern major league record of 464 innings pitched. With a 40–15 record, he fell one victory short of Jack Chesbro all-time record. He ended his career with the Boston Braves in 1917. His lifetime record was 195–126 and an earned run average of 1.82, the lowest in major league history. Walsh managed in the minor leagues in 1920, umpired in the American League in 1922, coached the White Sox from 1923 to 1925 and 1928 to 1930, and coached at Notre Dame University in 1926. He was elected to the Baseball Hall of Fame in 1946.

SELECTED BIBLIOGRAPHY: "Ed Walsh," in Martin Appel and Burt Goldblatt, *Baseball's Best: The Hall of Fame Gallery* (1977); Richard Lindberg, *Who's on Third: The*

Chicago White Sox Story (1983); David S. Neft, Roland T. Johnson, Richard M. Cohen, and Jordan A. Deutsch, *The Sports Encyclopedia: Baseball* (1976); Hy Turkin and S. C. Thompson, *The Official Encyclopedia of Baseball* (1977).

William Francis

WALSH, STELLA (3 April 1911, Wierzchowina, Poland–4 December 1980, Cleveland, OH). A track-and-field athlete, she was born Stanislawa Walasiewicz. She immigrated to the United States with her parents in 1912. She had an exceptionally long career, setting twenty world records and capturing forty-one Amateur Athletic Union titles in sprints, long jump, and discus throw. In 1930 Walsh became the first woman to break the eleven-second mark for 100 yards. She was considered a virtual certainty to medal for the United States at the 1932 Olympics, but her job as a clerk for the New York Central Railroad was eliminated due to financial constraints. Her only job offer came from the Cleveland Recreation Department, but accepting that position would have ended her amateur status. Still a Polish citizen, Walsh also received a job offer from the Polish Consulate, which would have allowed her to enter the Olympics, though as a Pole. The day before she was to finalize her U.S. citizenship, Walsh decided to withdraw her naturalization papers and accept the job with the consulate. She competed for Poland in the Olympics and won the gold medal in the 100-meter event in a time of 11.9 seconds. Walsh encountered a great deal of resentment in the United States, not just because she ran for Poland but also because of American society's hostility to women's athletics at that time, especially track. After the Los Angeles Olympics "the Polish Flyer" competed throughout Europe and the United States. In 1936 she ran in the Berlin Olympics, again representing Poland. She improved her time in the 100 meters to 11.7 seconds but finished second to American Helen Stephens. Walsh competed in Europe until the outbreak of World War II, when she returned to the United States. She became a United States citizen in 1947 and continued to compete until 1954. That year she won her final AAU title at age forty-three, twenty-four years after her first championship. Walsh played and coached women's basketball and softball and wrote for sports newspapers. She was very active in Polish American organizations, particularly the Polish Falcons* of America, and competed in the Falcons' meets. While shopping for decorations for the Polish national women's basketball team, she walked into a robbery attempt and was shot to death. An autopsy revealed that she had a rare condition known as mosaicism, which involves ambiguous sexual organs. Although press reports charged that Walsh was a man, the coroner concluded that she "lived and died a female."

SELECTED BIBLIOGRAPHY: Reid M. Hanley, *Who's Who in Track and Field* (1973); *New York Times*, 6 December 1980, 20; "Slain Star Stella Walsh Active in Sports 'Till End," *Cleveland Plain Dealer*, 6 December 1980, 1, 6; "Stella Walsh (1911–1980)," *Track and Field News* 33 (December 1980): 40; "Walsh Questions Unresolved," *Track and Field News* 34 (February 1981): 51.

Thomas M. Tarapacki

WASHINGTON, EVELYN ASHFORD (15 April 1957, Shreveport, LA–   ). An African American track-and-field star, she is the daughter of Samuel Ashford, a U.S. Air Force sergeant, and Vietta Ashford. A military child, Evelyn moved frequently as a youth, attending Clements High School in Athens, Georgia, in 1972–73 and Roseville High School in Roseville, California, from 1973 to 1975. The recipient of one of the first athletic scholarships awarded by the University of California at Los Angeles to a woman, she first gained notice in the international track world for her fifth-place finish in the 100-meter final in 1976 at Montreal, Canada. Over the next sixteen years she was a dominant sprinter at the national and international levels. Her chief rivals were East Germans, especially Marlies Oelsner Göhr. Denied an opportunity to compete for a gold medal in 1980 because of the U.S. boycott of the Moscow Games, she finally achieved her goal in 1984 at the Los Angeles Olympics, when she won the 100-meter race and anchored the victorious American team in the 400-meter relay. Later that year Ashford defeated Göhr (who did not run in Los Angeles because of the communist nations' boycott of the Olympics) at a meet in Zurich, Switzerland. There she broke her own 100-meter world record with a time of 10.76 seconds. After marrying Ray Washington and dropping out of competition to have a baby, she returned to the world track scene in 1988 to capture a silver medal in the 100-meter race (behind Florence Griffith Joyner*) and a gold medal in the 400-meter relay. Her remarkable career ended in 1993, one year after she earned her fourth Olympic gold medal running the first leg in the 400-meter relay at Barcelona. During the 1980s she achieved celebrity status in American society, as the media portrayed her as not only powerful and athletic but also feminine, graceful, and glamorous.

SELECTED BIBLIOGRAPHY: Michael D. Davis, *Black American Women in Olympic Track and Field: A Complete Illustrated Reference* (1992); Jon Hendershott, *Track's Greatest Women* (1987); Michael Kort, "Evelyn Ashford, Olympic Sprinter," *Ms.* 12 (May 1984): 40, 42–43; C. Neff, "She's Back, Running like the Wind," *Sports Illustrated* 60 (7 May 1984): 24–25; James A. Page, *Black Olympian Medalists* (1991).

George B. Kirsch

WASHINGTON, KENNETH S. ("Kenny") (31 August 1918, Los Angeles– 24 June 1971, Los Angeles). A football player, he was one of the first blacks to star in sports on the West Coast. When a national magazine polled 1,600 collegiate football players in choosing its All-American team for 1939, only one player in the entire country was selected by every opponent he faced. That player was Washington, a big, fleet halfback from the University of California at Los Angeles (UCLA). Washington had been All-Pacific Coast Conference choice the season before, as the Bruins beat Stanford for the first time in four seasons and the University of Washington for the first time in seven. In 1939 Washington, known by some as the "almost-perfect player," gained 863 yards in 141 carries and completed thirty-two of seventy-six passes for 497 yards from his tailback position. He led UCLA to what was at the time the greatest season in its history. Segregation and World War II delayed Washington's professional career. By the end of the war, the Los Angeles Rams had signed Washington, and he played for three years before his retirement in 1948.

SELECTED BIBLIOGRAPHY: Donald Bogle, *Toms, Coons, Mulattoes, Mammies, and Bucks* (1994); Edwin Henderson, *The Black Athlete: Emergence and Arrival* (1970); *New York Times*, 26 June 1971, 32; R. S. Rinnert, *African American Answer Book: Sports* (1995).

C. Keith Harrison

WASHINGTON, ORA MAE (16 January 1899, Philadelphia–? May 1971, Philadelphia). Known as the black Helen Wills Moody, she was a national champion in amateur tennis and basketball. Washington won eight American Tennis Association* (ATA) singles championships between 1929 and 1937. She also claimed eight consecutive New York state singles titles between 1926 and 1933 and several ATA Southeastern Section, Pennsylvania state, and Cockburn Trophy titles. In addition, Washington won numerous doubles and mixed doubles championships at the state, regional, and national levels in the 1920s and 1930s. The first true star of the ATA, she was an unprecedented phenomenon who completely dominated the black game. Washington played tennis using a unique style, gripping the racquet at midhandle and rarely following through on her swing. During the winter, Washington played the center and guard positions in six-on-six basketball for the Otto Brigg's Philadelphia Tribune Girls club team, a team organized in 1931 and sponsored by the *Philadelphia Tribune*, a black newspaper. As team captain, she displayed quick footwork and speed on the court. For most of the 1930s, black newspapers declared the Tribune Girls team to be the national champions. In February and March 1938, the team barnstormed in the South, playing black college and club teams and giving clinics. Black America's first premier female sports team, the Tribune Girls disbanded in 1940. Washington went on to play for the Germantown Hornets basketball team.

SELECTED BIBLIOGRAPHY: Arthur R. Ashe, Jr., *A Hard Road to Glory: A History of the African-American Athlete, 1919–1945*, vol. 2 (1988); *Pittsburgh Courier*, 5 February 1938, 17, and 26 August 1933, 2d sec., 4; Ora Mae Washington file, International Tennis Hall of Fame, Newport, RI.

Susan Rayl

WEISSMULLER, PETER JOHN ("Johnny") (2 June 1904, Windber, PA– 20 January 1984, Acapulco, Mexico). A swimmer and water polo player, he won five Olympic gold medals and was single-handedly responsible for pushing swimming into the world's spotlight during the 1920s. His father, Peter, was an

Austrian immigrant who moved his family to Chicago when Johnny was a child. A failed saloon keeper, before dying of tuberculosis, he was a heavy drinker who regularly beat his wife and children. A fragile youth, Weissmuller was advised by a doctor to take up swimming. In 1920 he joined the Illinois Athletic Club and began training under the U.S. Olympic coach Bill Bachrach. Under the tutelage of Bachrach Weissmuller developed the remarkable ability to push a bow wave ahead of him, then to arch his back and ride that wave like a hydroplane. In 1922 he became the first man to swim 100 meters in less than a minute. By the 1924 Paris Olympics Weissmuller had grown to 6'3" and 195 pounds and was fast enough to challenge the world's best. In the much awaited 400-meter freestyle Weissmuller captured the gold medal in world record time (5:04.2), defeating Arne Borg of Sweden and Andrew Charlton of Australia. Weissmuller also took gold in the 100-meter freestyle and the 4 × 200-meter freestyle relay, as well as a bronze as a member of the U.S. water polo team. At the 1928 Olympics in Amsterdam, Weissmuller won gold medals in the 100-meter freestyle and in the 4 × 200-meter freestyle relay. Following the games he turned professional, swimming in exhibitions throughout Europe and Japan to the cheers of adoring crowds. Hollywood noticed his star quality, as MGM Studios picked him in 1932 to star in a series of Tarzan movies. He made twelve over the next sixteen years, then made sixteen more films as the star of the Jungle Jim series. Weissmuller dominated swimming for a decade, setting twenty-four world records, winning fifty-one Amateur Athletic Union titles, and holding every freestyle world record from 100 yards to the half mile when he retired. He was voted in 1950 as the greatest swimmer of the first half century by 250 sportswriters and was made a charter member of the International Swimming Hall of Fame in 1965 and the U.S. Olympic Hall of Fame in 1983.

SELECTED BIBLIOGRAPHY: Zander Hollander, *Great American Athletes of the Twentieth Century* (1966); *Lincoln Library of Sports Champions*, vol. 13 (1974); Bill Mallon and Ian Buchanan, *Quest for Gold: The Encyclopedia of American Olympians* (1984); James R. Parish, *The Great Movie Series* (1971); Ellen Phillips, *The Olympic Century*, vol. 8: *VII Olympiad Paris 1924, St. Moritz, 1928* (1996); Bert R. Sugar, *The 100 Greatest Athletes of All-Time* (1995); David Wallechinsky, *Sports Illustrated's Complete Book of the Summer Olympics* (1996); Johnny Weissmuller, *Water, World, and Weissmuller* (1967); Alexander M. Weyand, *The Olympic Pageant* (1952).

Dennis Ryan

WELCH, MICHAEL ("Smiling Mickey")

WELCH, MICHAEL ("Smiling Mickey") (4 July 1859, Brooklyn, NY–30 July 1941, Concord, NH). A baseball player, he was the son of Irish immigrants John and Bridget Quinan Welch. He played from 1880 to 1892, pitching complete games in his first 105 starts in the major leagues. He was known as a right-handed control pitcher, with a good curveball, change-up, screwball, and fastball. He began his career in 1880 with the Troy Trojans of the National League. On 14 July 1881, he won both ends of a doubleheader, a feat he would duplicate on his birthday in 1885. In 1883 he moved to the New York Giants, where he played the outfield on days when he wasn't pitching. On 28 August 1884, he struck out nine batters in a row against Cleveland. The following year he won seventeen consecutive games while going 44–11. His .800 winning percentage led the league. During his early years in New York, he was assigned to report to the games an hour early in order to watch the turnstiles. Though he was instrumental in the founding of "the Brotherhood," the players' union that sparked the Players League rebellion of 1890, he did not jump to a Players League club, as many star players did. On 10 September 1889, he became the first pinch hitter in major league history, though he struck out. After retiring, he lived in Holyoke, Massachusetts, and, later, Brooklyn, running a tavern and working at the Polo Grounds and Yankee Stadium in various positions. He was the third pitcher in history to top 300 career victories, with a final mark of 307–210. He was named to the Baseball Hall of Fame in 1973.

SELECTED BIBLIOGRAPHY: George Bulkley, "Why Did Mickey Smile?," *The Baseball Research Journal* 11 (1982): 127–129; Lowell Reidenbaugh, "Mickey Welch," *Baseball's Hall of Fame: Cooperstown: Where the Legends Live Forever* (1993).

Timothy J. Wiles

WILKENS, LEONARD R. ("Lenny") (28 October 1937, Brooklyn, NY–   ). An African American basketball player and coach, he is the son of Leonard R. and Henrietta (Cross) Wilkens. As a youngster he was a standout in Catholic Youth Organization* competition, and later he excelled in academics and athletics at Providence College. Wilkens was one of the early African American athletes to star at the point-guard position. Typically, this position had been reserved for the white players, because it was thought to require thinking, cognitive abilities, and court presence. Wilkens would make the most of this opportunity from this highly responsible position in basketball. After starring for the St. Louis Hawks, Seattle Supersonics, Cleveland Cavaliers, and Portland Trailblazers in the National Basketball Association (NBA), Wilkens began a long and illustrious coaching career. He led the Seattle Supersonics to two World Championship final round appearances, winning one of the two in 1979 against the Washington Bullets. Wilkens picked up the appropriate nickname "the Solitary Bird" during his playing and coaching career, in which he quietly turned around the Cleveland Cavaliers and the Atlanta Hawks. For his efforts, Wilkens passed the legendary Red Auerbach* for total wins by a National Basketball Association head coach in 1995. Wilkens would add one more achievement to his trophy case. In the summer of 1996 Wilkens led the Olympic basketball team to a gold medal, a first for an African American coach in this sport.

SELECTED BIBLIOGRAPHY: Raymond Hill, *Unsung Heroes of Pro Basketball* (1973); Zander Hollander, ed., *The Pro Basketball Encyclopedia* (1977).

C. Keith Harrison

WILLIAMS, BILLY (15 June 1938, Whistler, AL–   ). An African American baseball player, he is the son of Frank Williams, a laborer who played semiprofessional ball, and Jesse Mary Williams. Williams graduated from Whistler High School and competed for a local team, the Mobile Black Bears. As a youth his experience with manual laboring jobs motivated him to pursue a better opportunity as an athlete. In 1956 he signed a contract with the Chicago Cubs and spent the next few leagues in the minor leagues in the South. The pressures of competition and racial discrimination and a stomach ulcer led him to consider quitting, but he persevered and made it to the major leagues for a few games in 1959 and 1960. His breakthrough year came in 1961, when he became a regular and was voted the National League's Rookie of the Year. For the remainder of the 1960s and the early 1970s he starred in the outfield for the Cubs before ending his career with two seasons with the Oakland Athletics. Among Cub fans in his prime he ranked second to Ernie Banks* in popularity. He led the National League in batting in 1972 (.333). Upon his retirement in 1976 he held the National League record for consecutive games played (1,177); he batted .290 over eighteen seasons with 2,711 hits and 1,475 runs batted in (RBIs). After his playing days ended, he coached for both Chicago and Oakland. He was elected to the National Baseball Hall of Fame in 1987.

SELECTED BIBLIOGRAPHY: Eddie Gold and Art Ahrens, *The New Era Cubs 1941–1985* (1985); Billy Williams and Irv Haag, *Billy, the Classic Hitter* (1974); "Williams Enters Hall of Fame," *Cubs Vineland* 2 (February 1987): 6–7.

George B. Kirsch

WILLIAMSON, ANSEL (? 1806, VA–18 June 1881, Lexington, KY). He was an African American thoroughbred trainer. Ansel probably took his name from the white Williamson family whose members were prominent in American racing from colonial times in New York to the 1850s in California. Ansel first made the headlines in 1855 as the still-enslaved trainer of the fabulous distance horse Brown Dick. Shortly before the Civil War, Lexington thoroughbred owner A. Keene Richards bought Ansel and brought him to Kentucky. After Richards lost his fortune, Robert A. Alexander, a Scottish citizen and the wealthiest horseman in the Bluegrass, bought Ansel, freed him, and put the cream of his Woodburn Farm thoroughbreds in Ansel's hands. After Alexander's death in 1867 Ansel worked for H. Price McGrath, for whom he developed the 1874 champion runner Tom Bowling. Ansel was a leading trainer at Churchill Downs at its 1875 inaugural meet, winning both the Kentucky Derby and New York's Belmont Stakes that year.

SELECTED BIBLIOGRAPHY: Alexander Mackey-Smith, *The Race Horses of America 1832–1872: Portraits and Other Paintings by Edward Troye* (1981); Lynn S. Renau, *Racing around Kentucky* (1995).

Lynn S. Renau

WINN, MARTIN J. ("Col. Matt") (30 June 1860, Louisville, KY–6 October 1949, Louisville, KY). An executive in thoroughbred horse racing, he was the son of Irish immigrants. His father, Patrick Winn, was a grocer; his mother was Julia Flaherty Hession. A graduate of Bryant & Stratton Business School, Louisville, he first worked in the wholesale grocery business, then owned his own successful tailoring business. He became vice president and general manager of New Louisville Jockey Club (Churchill Downs) in 1904, when the track was on the verge of bankruptcy. In 1905 Winn created the American Turf Association and served as the organization's president. By 1907 he was general manager of six tracks, including Empire City in Yonkers, New York. He successfully rebuffed reformers' efforts to close Churchill Downs in 1908 by reintroducing pari-mutuel wagering, a strategy for which he received a colonelcy in Kentucky's honorary militia. When antigambling forces closed tracks throughout the East, Winn kept the southern circuit open by operating a racetrack in Juarez, Mexico, from 1909 to 1917, when his fund-raising efforts for the Red Cross made him and tracks he managed positively patriotic. Having gained considerable national clout, he shepherded an alliance of Kentucky racetracks first through another antigambling challenge in the 1920s, then the depression and World War II. In 1938 he was appointed president as well as executive manager of Churchill Downs, Inc., the only major track not closed by the Office of Defense Transportation from 1942 to 1945. Winn died the fall after the seventy-fifth Kentucky Derby was run.

SELECTED BIBLIOGRAPHY: Frank G. Menke, *Down the Stretch: The Story of Colonel Matt J. Winn* (1945); Lynn S. Renau, *Racing around Kentucky* (1995).

Lynn S. Renau

WOJCIECHOWICZ, ALEX (12 August 1915, South River, NJ–13 July 1992, South River, NJ). A collegiate and professional football player, he was the son of Andrew and Anna (Chartowicz) Wojciechowicz, both Polish immigrants. In 1934 he graduated from South River High School and then attended Fordham University, where he earned All-America honors in 1936 and 1937 as the center of the famed "Seven Blocks of Granite" line. He led the team to national prominence, losing just two games in his three seasons. "Alex the Great" was Detroit's number one draft pick in 1938. A true "iron man," he played linebacker on defense and center on offense. As a linebacker, the 6', 230-pounder was known as an outstanding pass defender with sixteen career interceptions. As a center he anchored the offensive line and controlled the middle of the field. He played center using an unusually wide stance. At that time pro football was not a lucrative sport, and Wojciechowicz relied on various business interests to support his family. Early in the 1946 season the Lions honored his request to play in the East so that he could be close to those interests. Wojciechowicz joined the Philadelphia Eagles and played primarily on defense as linebacker. He and Joe Muha were the linebackers in coach Greasy Neale's innovative 5–2–4 alignment. "Wojie" was an integral part of the defense that helped the Eagles win three straight divisional titles (1947–49) and two National Football

League (NFL) titles (1948 and 1949). The four-time All-Pro retired after the 1950 season and worked in real estate. He also helped found the NFL Alumni Association, which was established to help former pro football players in need. He was inducted into the College Football Hall of Fame in 1955 and the Pro Football Hall of Fame in 1968.

SELECTED BIBLIOGRAPHY: Ben Chestochowski, *Gridiron Greats: A Century of Polish Americans in College Football* (1997); Ray Didinger, "The Best Team of the Best Years," *Pro!* 3 (January 1983): 69–75; George Sullivan, *Pro Football's All-Time Greats: The Immortals in the Pro Football Hall of Fame* (1968).

Thomas M. Tarapacki

WOODARD, LYNETTE (12 August 1959, Wichita, KS–). An African American basketball player, she is the daughter of Lugene and Dorothy (Jenkins) Woodard. Her father was a fireman. A pioneer and trailblazer in women's basketball, her skills first gained national attention in 1977, when she was a senior at Wichita North High School in Wichita, Kansas, leading her team to a women's state high school basketball championship. That fall she became a Lady Jayhawk for Kansas University. During all four of her college years, 1978–81, she was named Kodak All-American, and for two years she was Academic All-American. She graduated with a bachelor's degree in speech communications and human relations. Upon graduation her record of 3,649 points made her college basketball's all-time leading scorer. At Kansas University's Allen Field House her retired jersey hangs near those of Wilt Chamberlain* and Danny Manning. In 1981 Woodard was named Outstanding Female of the Year in the Big Eight Conference, Woman of the Year by the National Association for the Advancement of Colored People (NAACP) chapter of Wichita, Kansas, and winner of the Wade Trophy for being the outstanding women's college basketball player of the year. In 1984 Woodard captained the U.S. Olympic women's basketball team, which won the gold medal. The following year she was inducted into the Women's Sport Foundation's Hall of Fame. Woodard made history in 1985, when she became the first woman to play for the world-famous Harlem Globetrotters.* Her career with the Globetrotters lasted for two years. Between 1989 and 1993, she played professional basketball in Italy and Japan. Returning home after playing basketball overseas, she became director of athletics for the Kansas Missouri School District, 1993–94. Later she became vice president of marketing for MAGNA Securities Corporation, the first brokerage firm to be both African American- and woman-owned. In 1997 she signed to play for the Cleveland Rockers, a team in the newly formed Women's National Basketball League (WNBA).

SELECTED BIBLIOGRAPHY: Steve Beitler, "Basketball," *Women's Sports* 5 (November 1983): 38; University of Kansas Basketball Media Guide, 1983–84.

Gai I. Berlage

WOODS, ELDRICK ("Tiger") (30 December 1975, Long Beach, CA–). An African American golfer, he is the son of a retired Green Beret lieutenant colonel in the U.S. Army (Earl) and a former secretary in the U.S. Army office in Bangkok (Kultida). Woods entered professional golf in 1996 at age twenty as the most decorated amateur in the game's history. Woods started by perfectly imitating his father's golf swing with a sawed-off club while only eleven months old. By age four he was able to beat players ten to twenty years his elder. He won an unprecedented six consecutive U.S. Amateur titles, the 1991, 1992, and 1993 U.S. Junior Amateur and the 1994, 1995, and 1996 U.S. Amateur. He also won the 1996 National Collegiate Athletic Association's individual golf title while a sophomore at Stanford University. After only two years at Stanford and immediately following his 1996 U.S. Amateur title, he turned professional. In only his fifth start as a professional golfer, Woods won the 1996 Las Vegas Invitational, beating Davis Love III in a play-off. Two weeks later he won again at the Walt Disney World/Oldsmobile Classic in Orlando. Besides winning twice in his first seven professional tournaments, he had five top-five finishes, earned nearly $800,000 in prize money, and qualified for the season-ending Tour Championship in Tulsa, a tournament reserved for the Professional Golfers' Association's top thirty money earners. He captured his first major title by winning the 1997 Masters tournament. As a rookie professional he had an immense impact on the sport of golf. His diverse personal background, which includes African American, Native American, Thai, Chinese, and European ancestry, has focused attention on the ethnic and racial significance of golf in the United States for golfers, fans, sportswriters, and scholars. Woods adds color to a sport traditionally played and watched by wealthy whites. In addition, his multiracial heritage has caused many to question American society's apparent need for racial classification. The Nike and Titleist corporations have invested in the appeal of Woods' youth and transcendence of traditional racial and ethnic divisions by signing him to multimillion-dollar endorsement deals. His early popularity has introduced the game of golf to a wider and more diverse audience, especially minority youngsters.

SELECTED BIBLIOGRAPHY: Jaime Diaz, "Roaring Ahead," *Sports Illustrated* (2 September 1996): 22–26; Rick Reilly, "Top Cat," *Sports Illustrated* (28 October 1996): 46–50; Gary Smith, "The Chosen One," *Sports Illustrated* (23 December 1996): 29–52; Gary Van Sickle, "Jackpot!" *Sports Illustrated* (14 October 1996): 36–38.

Troy D. Paino

WORLD BOCCE LEAGUE. The World Bocce League is the professional circuit for bocce in the United States. The league was organized in August 1993 by Philip Ferrari, one the nation's top players and administrators. The league sponsors a series of tournaments throughout the country each year, with prize money comparable to that of the other major sports leagues. The centerpiece tournament is the annual "Super Ball Classic" in Chicago. Although few players earn their sole living from bocce, league tournaments do average over 400 competitors. As physical size is not a prerequisite to success, competitors range in all ages and all backgrounds. A tournament weekend also includes a women's and mixed-pairs competition, so that normally the number of female players is quite high. Bocce's popularity has even spread across the border, with the Canadians now fielding a strong contingent. As in other sports, the top players do earn some money from product endorsements, instructional books and videos, and private tutoring. The World Bocce League is an ardent supporter of the Special Olympics. On behalf of the league, Philip Ferrari serves as a senior adviser to the national bocce team and most recently worked with the squad at the 1996 Games in Connecticut. In addition, a portion of the proceeds from league tournaments is donated toward the Special Olympics. The World Bocce League works in tandem with the World Bocce Association, the sport's national governing body. For more information about the league, contact the World Bocce Association at 1098 West Irving Park Road, Bensenville, IL 60106 or via telephone no. 800\OK-BOCCE (800\652–6223).

SELECTED BIBLIOGRAPHY: Marilyn and Philip Ferrari, eds., *Rolling Generation: The Magazine of the World Bocce Association* (1995–   ).

Philip Ferrari and Ciro C. Poppiti

WORLD JAI ALAI. The leading organization in the sport of jai alai in the United States, World Jai Alai has three frontons. The Miami fronton, the first in the United States, opened on 24 February 1926 and is often called "the Yankee Stadium" of jai alai. Besides the fronton in Miami, there are World Jai Alai frontons in Tampa and Ocala, which opened in 1954 and 1973, respectively. In addition, World Jai Alai previously owned frontons in Fort Pierce, Florida, and Hartford, Connecticut. World Jai Alai has been an innovator in the gaming industry. In the mid-1940s it was the first to introduce quiniela and perfecta wagering and brought the two forms of betting to prominence in other pari-mutuel facilities. Quiniela wagering requires the bettor to select the two players or teams to finish first and second, in any order. Perfecta wagering requires that the two players or teams must finish in the exact order chosen. Furthermore, in 1979 World Jai Alai introduced the bet-cash system. Miami Jai Alai was the first to have a system that permitted the patron to both buy and cash mutuel tickets at any betting window in the fronton. This computerized system is now used in almost every pari-mutuel facility in the United States. In November 1978 a merger took place between World Jai Alai, Inc., a public company, and WJA Delaware, Inc., a Delaware corporation wholly owned by WJA Realty, a Massachusetts limited partnership whose principals are the members of the Wheeler family of Tulsa, Oklahoma.

World Jai Alai has French, Spanish, and American champions playing professionally at each fronton. Recently there has been an upsurge of interest by American children in playing jai alai. World Jai Alai's training school, North Miami Amateur Jai Alai, is largely responsible for the rise of American-born players. Once dominated by Basque players, fronton rosters are now full of American jai alai stars.

SELECTED BIBLIOGRAPHY: J. Garcia Lourdes, "*Jai Alai* Flourished in Florida," in *International Prosperity, Florida in Shape for the Future* (1984); Miami Jai Alai Press Kit, Miami, Florida; the ABC's of World Jai Alai, Miami, Florida.

James R. Varella

WRIGHT, GEORGE (28 January 1847, Yonkers, NY–21 August 1937, Boston). A baseball player, he was the son of English immigrants Samuel and Ann (Tone) Wright. He was a sportsman who had a distinguished athletic career as a cricketer, baseball player, sporting goods merchant, and pioneer of American golf. His father was a professional for the St. George Cricket Club* of New York, and his older brother Harry* was a noted cricketer and baseball player. Following in the footsteps of his brother, as a boy and young man during the 1860s he starred in cricket for the Dragon Slayers of St. George and for a number of amateur baseball nines in the New York vicinity. In 1869–70 he gained national fame as the hard-hitting shortstop of the Cincinnati Red Stockings, organized and managed by his brother Harry as the first all-professional baseball club in the United States. From 1871 to 1875 George played for the Boston Red Stockings in the first professional league, the National Association of Professional Base Ball Players. Managed by his brother, that club won four pennants. Soon after his arrival in Boston in 1871 he opened a sporting goods store. After taking on a partner, Henry Ditson, his company expanded into the Wright and Ditson Company, a leading merchandiser in the growing business of athletic equipment and clothing. In 1876 he again signed up with his brother to play for the Boston franchise in the new National League of Professional Baseball Clubs, but he switched to Providence in 1879 as player-manager, and his team won that season's championship. He closed out his baseball career with two more years in Boston and one in Providence. After his retirement from baseball he competed for the Longwood Cricket Club in Brookline, Massachusetts. He was also one of the first to introduce the Scottish game of golf in the Boston area, laying out a nine-hole course in 1890 in Franklin Field, a public park. Boston's George Wright Municipal Golf Course was dedicated in his honor just a few weeks before his death. He was inducted into the Baseball Hall of Fame in 1937.

SELECTED BIBLIOGRAPHY: James D'Wolf Lovett, *Old Boston Boys and the Games They Played* (1906); H. B. Martin, *Fifty Years of American Golf* (1936); *New York Times*, 22 August 1937, Sec. 2, 6; Harold Seymour, *Baseball: The Early Years* (1960). A. G. Spalding, *America's National Game* (1911); George V. Tuohey, *A History of the Boston Base Ball Club* (1897).

George B. Kirsch

WRIGHT, HENRY ("Harry") (10 January 1835, Sheffield, England–3 October 1895, Atlantic City, NJ). One of the pioneers of American amateur and professional baseball, he was the son of Samuel and Ann (Tone) Wright and the older brother of noted sportsman George Wright.* As a young boy he traveled with his parents to New York City in 1836, and a few years later his father became the professional for the St. George Cricket Club* of Manhattan. Young Harry attended grade school in New York and then was employed by a jewelry manufacturer. But his true love was athletics; as a young man during the 1850s he excelled as a professional bowler for the Dragon Slayers of St. George. At that time he also took up the game of baseball, playing with the New York Knickerbocker nine, which had introduced new rules for the sport in 1845. After the Civil War in 1866 Wright accepted a position as a professional cricket player and instructor with the Union Cricket Club of Cincinnati, but before long he switched his allegiance to baseball. Captain, pitcher, and then center fielder for the new Cincinnati Red Stockings Base Ball Club, in 1869 he managed and starred for the nation's first fully professional baseball team. For two seasons the Red Stockings traveled across the nation, winning eighty-four consecutive games. In 1871 Wright played a major role in the formation of the first professional league, the National Association of Professional Base Ball Players. In that circuit he guided the Boston Red Stockings to four pennants in five seasons. He continued his career as a manager in Boston after the creation of the National League of Professional Baseball Clubs in 1876, winning two more championships. During the 1880s he also managed clubs in Providence and Philadelphia before becoming chief of umpires of the National League. He was elected to the Baseball Hall of Fame in 1953.

SELECTED BIBLIOGRAPHY: Harry Ellard, *Base Ball in Cincinnati* (1907); George Morland, *Balldom* (1926); Harold Seymour, *Baseball: The Early Years* (1960); A. G. Spalding, *America's National Game* (1911).

George B. Kirsch

Y

YAMAGUCHI, KRISTI (12 July 1971, Hayward, CA–   ). A figure skater and an American of Japanese descent, her parents are Jim Yamaguchi, a dentist, and Carole Yamaguchi, a medical secretary. Her mother was born in an internment camp during World War II, and her father spent part of his early childhood in an internment camp. Kristi began skating at age six. In 1988 she won the World Singles Junior Championships and the World Pairs Junior Championships with partner Rudi Galindo. The following year she and Galindo won the gold medal in pairs at the U.S. National Championships, and she also won the silver medal in the women's singles event. In 1990 Yamaguchi decided to concentrate on her singles career. In 1991 she won the World Championships and in 1992 took first place at the U.S. National Championships. In 1992 she won the gold medal at the Albertville Winter Olympics. Yamaguchi capped off her amateur career in 1992 by winning the World Championships. She turned professional in 1992 and won the World Professional Skating Championships. Yamaguchi decided against returning to the Olympics in 1994, when professional skaters were permitted to be reinstated as amateurs and return to Olympic competition. During the late 1990s she continued to skate as a professional in the Discover Card "Skate on Ice" tour.

SELECTED BIBLIOGRAPHY: Stuart Kim, "Kristi Yamaguchi: A Biography," www. polaris-net/-shnhew/bio.html; E. M. Swift, "Silver Lining," *Sports Illustrated* 76 (24 February 1992): 14–17; "Yamaguchi, Kristi," *Current Biography Yearbook* (1992), 616–618.
Alison M. Wrynn

YANCEY, JOSEPH J., JR. (12 October 1910, New York City–22 February 1991, Teaneck, NJ). Born in the Hell's Kitchen section of New York City, he attended Saratoga High School, Virginia State College, and New York University. After university, he entered his father's undertaking business and competed in track and field for the Mercury Athletic Club of Harlem. Yancey was also a reserve captain in Harlem's 369th Regiment. Later he became a revenue officer with the Internal Revenue Service. In 1936 Yancey was one of the founders of the New York Pioneer Club* of Harlem. The club's goals included encouraging education and interracial understanding as well as track and field. The membership was originally African American but was officially integrated within a few years. The many athletic successes of the club members under Yancey's coaching brought international recognition. The U.S. State Department sent Yancey abroad as a goodwill ambassador to give advice and coaching expertise. Between 1948 and 1968 Yancey coached Olympic track-and-field teams for Jamaica, Trinidad and Tobago, the Bahamas, British Guiana, and the Virgin Islands. In 1952 the Jamaican relay team that Yancey coached won the Olympic gold medal in the 1,600-meter relay.

SELECTED BIBLIOGRAPHY: Jesse P. Abramson, "Democratic Ideal: The Pioneer Club," *Amateur Athlete* (September 1945): 11, 15; Theodore Corbitt, "Testimonial to a Pioneer: Joseph J. Yancey," *Road Runners Club New York Association Newsletter* 65 (1975): 10; *New York Times*, 25 February 1991, B10.

Pamela Cooper

YASTRZEMSKI, CARL ("Yaz") (22 August 1939, Southampton, NY–   ). A baseball player of Polish descent, he is the son of Carl and Hattie (Skonieczny) Yastrzemski. His father was a farmer, semiprofessional baseball player, and coach of youth sports teams. At Bridgehampton High School Yastrzemski was class president and excelled in basketball and baseball. After his graduation in 1957 he attended Notre Dame University for one year on a baseball scholarship. After a tryout with the New York Yankees he signed with the Boston Red Sox. After spending two years in the minor leagues, he began his major league career with the Boston Red Sox in 1961. Expectations for Yastrzemski were high since he was replacing the recently retired Ted Williams as the Red Sox's left fielder. Although he had only a mediocre rookie season, he improved dramatically over the next five years, winning the batting title with a .321 average in 1963. The year 1967 proved to be magical for both himself and his club, as Yastrzemski won the Triple Crown with a .326 batting average, forty-four home runs (tied with Harmon Killebrew), and 121 runs batted in. He starred in the Red Sox's pennant drive and in his team's loss to the St. Louis Cardinals in seven games in the World Series. His heroics at bat and in the outfield that season earned him honors as the American League's Most Valuable Player, *Sports Illustrated's* Sportsman of the Year, and Associated Press Male Athlete of the Year. Although over the remainder of his twenty-three-year career he never again attained the heights of his performance in 1967, he did win one more batting crown in 1968. He also led the Red Sox to another American League pennant in 1975, only to suffer another seven-game defeat in the World

Series, this time to the Cincinnati Reds. Throughout his career he was also a superlative fielder, winning a Gold Glove Award seven times. Over his career he played in 3,308 games and recorded 3,419 hits and 452 home runs. He was inducted into the Baseball Hall of Fame in 1989.

SELECTED BIBLIOGRAPHY: Robert B. Jackson, *Let's Go, Yaz* (1968); Shepard Long, *Carl Yastrzemski* (1993); *Sports Illustrated* 14 (3 April 1961): 27, 38 and (21 August 1967): 12; Carl Yastrzemski and Gerald Eskenazi, *Yaz: Baseball, the Wall, and Me* (1990).

George B. Kirsch

YCAZA, MANUEL (1 February 1938, Panama City, Panama–   ). He began competing in his native country of Panama at age fourteen and rode for a time in Mexico before settling permanently in the United States in 1956, where he quickly developed a reputation for brilliant, skillful, and aggressive riding—to the delight of racing fans and the consternation of race stewards. For ten of the sixteen years that he rode in this country, Ycaza was under contract to Capt. Harry Guggenheim's Cain Hoy Stable, for which he rode the two standout horses of his career—champions Never Bend, which he later said was the best horse he ever rode, and Bald Eagle, which he said was his favorite. Other good horses he rode for Cain Hoy included Make Sail, Heavenly Body, Hidden Talent, One-Eyed King, Iron Peg, Battle Joined, and Ack Ack. For other owners, Ycaza rode such standouts as Dr. Fager, Fort Marcy, Damascus, Sword Dancer, Dark Mirage, Ridan, Gamely, Lamb Chop, Intentionally, Top Knight, Cyane, and Silky Sullivan. He won the 1964 Belmont on Quadrangle and also three Washington, D.C., Internationals, four Kentucky Oaks, Two Travers, two Florida Derbys, and one Queen's Plate. Injury forced his retirement in 1971, but he returned in 1983 to win eight races. Over his career he won 2,367 times out of 10,561 mounts (22.4%) and was inducted into the National Thoroughbred Racing Hall of Fame in 1977.

SELECTED BIBLIOGRAPHY: *Thoroughbred Record* (15 July 1967).

Courtesy of the National Thoroughbred Racing Hall of Fame

YONAMINE, WALLY (24 June 1925, Lahainaluna, HI–   ). A superb all-around athlete, Wally Yonamine crossed racial and ethnic frontiers in both professional football and baseball. Yonamine's father was born in Okinawa and migrated to Hawaii to work in the sugar fields. There he met Yonamine's Japanese-born mother. Yonamine first caught the sporting world's attention in the mid-1940s as a Honolulu high school football "phenom" and then as an exciting open field runner for an eleven called the Hawaiian All-Stars after World War II. Yonamine was then signed by the San Francisco 49ers, who at that time competed in the now defunct All-American Football Conference. Also at that time, considerable prejudice existed in California against people of Japanese ancestry. Nevertheless, Yonamine made the 49ers in 1947 and, in the process, became the first and only Japanese American to play major league

American professional football. The 1947 season, however, was Yonamine's first and last for the 49ers. While pursuing a career in football Yonamine emerged as one of the best baseball players on the Hawaiian islands, which were filled with multiethnic, multiracial nines. In 1950 the San Francisco Seals of the formidable Pacific Coast League gave him a tryout. He did not make the Seals but impressed enough mainlanders in organized baseball to win a roster spot on the Pioneer League's Salt Lake City team. Yonamine batted .335 for Salt Lake City in 1950 but rather than move up the U.S. minor league ladder Yonamine became a Japanese major leaguer in 1951. While Yonamine possessed Japanese ancestry, he was still viewed in Japan as an outsider in a significantly ethnocentric society. Yonamine, moreover, brought to Japan a tough competitiveness that Japanese baseball supporters identified, in a frequently critical way, with American baseball. Yonamine, nevertheless, became one of the best hitters in the history of Japanese major league baseball and the first non-Japanese citizen to become a coach and manager. He was selected for the Japanese Baseball Hall of Fame.

SELECTED BIBLIOGRAPHY: Center for Labor Education and Research of the College of Continuing Education, *The New Rice and Roses Presents Hawaii's Plantation Heroes*, Video (1992); Sadaharu Oh and David Faulkner, *Sadaharu Oh: A Zen Way of Baseball* (1984); Robert Whiting, *You Gotta Have Wa* (1989).

Joel S. Franks

YOUNG, ANDREW SPURGEON ("Doc") (29 October 1919, Danbrooke, VA–6 September 1996, Los Angeles). A 1941 graduate of Hampton Institute, Young was a sportswriter who began his journalistic career as sports editor with the *Cleveland Call and Post*. In 1949 he became sports editor of the *Los Angeles Sentinel*, the largest black newspaper west of the Mississippi River. In addition to his duties with the *Sentinel*, Young assumed the position as West Coast editor of the *Chicago Defender*, the famous black weekly owned and operated by John H. Johnson. He eventually moved to Chicago and served six years as an associate editor for the *Defender*. Young was a prolific writer. He published literally hundreds of magazine articles and syndicated columns in well-known black and white newspapers. He also wrote several notable books, including *Negro Firsts in Sports* (1963), *Great Negro Baseball Stars* (1953), and *Sonny Liston: The Champ Nobody Wanted* (1963). Besides his many publications, Young was closely involved with a number of black Hollywood movies. He was also involved in Republican politics, participating in the gubernatorial campaign for Nelson Rockefeller in 1964 and the presidential campaigns for Richard Nixon in 1968 and Gerald Ford in 1976. Young was instrumental, moreover, in major league baseball's decision to open a black wing to its Hall of Fame in Cooperstown, New York. Young was a member of the National Association for the Advancement of Colored People (NAACP), Baseball Writers Association of America, Cleveland Press Club, Los Angeles Urban League, Sigma Delta Chi Fraternity, and other civic groups and organizations.

SELECTED BIBLIOGRAPHY: Arthur R. Ashe, Jr., *A Hard Road to Glory: A History of the African-American Athlete* v. 3 (1988); *Chicago Defender*, 15 September 1996; Shirelle Phelps, ed., *Who's Who among African Americans, 1998–99* (1997).

David K. Wiggins

YOUNG MEN'S HEBREW ASSOCIATION. Modeled on the Young Men's Christian Association, the Young Men's Hebrew Association (YMHA) was founded in 1854 in Baltimore to promote moral recreation, sociability, literature, physical fitness, and spiritual values among young German Jewish men. These pioneers of "muscular Judaism" admired the "muscular Christianity" movement among Protestants, which stressed the positive role of physical training in religion. By the mid-1870s there were several dozen YMHAs, as affluent second-generation German Jews established their own facilities when they were excluded from the leading metropolitan men's clubs because of anti-Semitism. The institution organized in Manhattan in 1874 evolved into the 92d Street YMHA, which sponsored numerous cultural and sports programs and premier teams and athletes in the twentieth century. By 1900 about 100 Ys enrolled 20,000 members, including both German and Eastern European (especially Russian) immigrants and their children. In 1921 the National Jewish Welfare Board (JWB) became the national governing body for YMHAs and YWHAs,* as it merged with the National Council of Young Men's Hebrew and Kindred Associations. Later in the twentieth century the JWB encouraged the merger of YMHAs and YWHAs into Jewish Community Centers (JCC).

During these formative years the directors and managers of the YMHAs had several goals. First, they aimed to use sports to help Jewish newcomers preserve their religious identity while they assimilated into the mainstream of American culture. Their mission was to encourage wholesome recreation and competition in popular games, thereby strengthening both Jewish values and also American citizenship and patriotism. Second, they hoped to use Jewish participation in athletics to counter the prevailing cultural stereotype of the Jew as a weakling who neglected physical activity in favor of intensive religious and intellectual study.

During the early 1900s the YMHAs sponsored a wide variety of recreational and competitive athletic programs, including gymnastics, basketball, volleyball, boxing, track, handball, swimming, soccer, baseball, bowling, bicycling, rifle shooting, billiards, and other sports. Many of the Jewish American athletes who excelled in national and international competitions prior to World War II either honed their skills at Ys or played for Y teams. Boys and young men at YMHAs played against settlement house teams, other YMHAs, YMCAs, and in sanctioned Amateur Athletic Union events at various age levels and in local, regional, and even national events. New York City's 92d Street Y was a national powerhouse in several sports, especially basketball. Nat Holman* headed its professional physical education staff, earning a $5,000 salary from the Y while he also coached the City College of New York's varsity basketball team. During the 1930s its senior basketball team consistently drew large crowds to its home games, especially when it played strong clubs such as the all-black New York Harlem Renaissance* five. In boxing, numerous Jewish fighters learned their craft at YMHAs, including "Slapsie" Maxie Rosenbloom* at the 92d Street Y.

After World War II, as second- and third-generation Jews successfully assimilated into society, YMHAs and JCCs shifted their primary focus from helping newcomers adjust to American culture to fostering stronger ethnic ties within the Jewish communities of cities and suburbs. As Jewish neighborhoods deteriorated or disappeared in center cities, and as many Jews were losing their sense of identity, leaders of the YMHAs and JCCs resolved to rebuild and revitalize their institutions to renew Jewish community ties. Realizing the popularity of athletics in mainstream culture, they used recreational and competitive sports programs to attract new members to Jewish institutions, whose space and facilities substituted for the lost ethnic worlds of earlier generations. At the end of the twentieth century the YMHAs and JCCs provided many educational, cultural, and recreational services for their members, but they rarely, if ever, produced the star athletes or teams that competed for the YMHAs during the golden years of the early to mid-1900s.

SELECTED BIBLIOGRAPHY: *Building Character for 75 Years: 75th Anniversary of the Young Men's and Young Women's Hebrew Association, New York City* (1949); Peter Levine, *Ellis Island to Ebbets Field: Sport and the American Jewish Experience* (1992); Benjamin Rabinowitz, "The YMHAs (1854–1913)," in *Publications of the American Jewish Historical Society* 37 (1947): 221–326; Steven A. Riess, *City Games* (1989); Steven A. Riess, ed., *Sports and the American Jew* (1998).

George B. Kirsch

YOUNG WOMEN'S HEBREW ASSOCIATION. In 1902, Mrs. Bella Unterberg founded the first Young Women's Hebrew Association (YWHA) located in New York City, and served as the first president of this organization. As a separate association from the Young Men's Hebrew Association,* this YWHA is the oldest existing organization for Jewish girls and women that developed activities in "religious work, gymnasium, social work and educational work" to promote the social and physical welfare of Jewish females. The forerunner to the YWHA in 1888 was the Ladies Auxiliary of the New York YMHA, organized by Jewish philanthropist Julia Richman. In fact, most YWHAs in the early twentieth century existed as Ladies Auxiliaries to YMHAs to assist immigrant and working-class girls and women; Americanization efforts emphasized domestic skills as well as physical education to aid Jewish females in adjusting to American life. As Mrs. Bella Unterberg reminded her fellow YWHA workers, "it is the finest thing a Young Women's Society can start with, with the gymnasium and the basket-ball teams for your recreational work." To help organize new groups and advance their activities, some YWHAs joined together to form regional Associated YWHAs in the early twentieth century.

In most of the YWHAs affiliated with Young Men's Hebrew Associations,* women secured limited access to the use of the gymnasiums and swimming pools with inadequate buildings and lack of female physical training instructors. The Louisville YMHA, founded in 1890, provided an extensive physical education program, but until 1912, women's activities in the association were rather limited, although there was a gym class for women. This gym class led to other gym activities for Jewish females at the Louisville YMHA like the formation of a basketball team: the Y was among the first organizations of the country to pioneer in physical education and health classes for women.

In 1921 the National Jewish Welfare Board (JWB) became the national governing body for YMHAs and YWHAs, and the National Council of YMH and Kindred Associations combined with the JWB. The JWB actively promoted the merger of YMHAs and YWHAs to develop them into Jewish Community Centers (JCCs). The JWB mission integrated Jewish life, education, and sports for both sexes in JCCs. To foster girls' and women's physical activities, JWB field-workers often noted the need to have athletic facilities accessible to females and to secure appropriate personnel for women's programs.

As YWHAs procured space for members' use, they offered physical training classes and athletics like gymnastics, swimming, tennis, basketball, volleyball, badminton, track and field, bicycling, and bowling. Basketball for women, endorsed by Jewish American physical educator Senda Berenson (Abbott)* of Smith College, gained popularity at YWHAs. Basketball teams from YWHAs and YM-YWHAs played not only other Jewish Ys but Young Women's Christian Association (YWCA) and women's industrial teams as well. The Hartford, Connecticut, YWHA, founded in 1915, encouraged members to play basketball; in 1920 the Hartford YWHA boasted of their "two basketball teams and the girls have picked out the five best players and challenge any team in the State." Hartford's YWHA basketball team won the state championship in 1930 and 1931.

For women's sports, the New York City YWHA served as a model with its independent executive officers and an outstanding new building in 1914 equipped with athletic facilities. The YWHA developed an extensive program of swimming contests, tournaments, and athletics at their 31 West 110th Street building. The YWHA's new swimming pool opened in 1916, and this modern pool hosted health classes as well as national competitive swimming championships. The YWHA held swimming meets featuring prominent national and Olympic champions like Aileen Riggin and Gertrude Ederle in the 1920s. Aileen Riggin, 1920 Olympic gold medal diving champion and 1924 Olympic medalist, recalled how as a member of the Women's Swimming Association of New York, founded by Charlotte Epstein,* she swam at this YWHA pool for a national championship.

In the 1940s Jewish Community Centers expanded, housing enlarged sports facilities and sponsoring more athletic contests, but the JWB still emphasized that JCCs needed to provide adequate sports activities for women and girls. Increasingly in the last decades of the twentieth century, JCCs furnish numerous athletics and sports competitions for females of all ages, extending the programs initiated by forerunners at YWHAs.

SELECTED BIBLIOGRAPHY: Linda J. Borish, "Jewish American Women, Jewish Organizations and Sports, 1880–1940," in Steven A. Riess, ed., *Sports and the American Jew* (1998); Louis Kraft, "Center, Jewish," in Isaac Landman, ed., *The Universal Jewish Encyclopedia* (1941); Benjamin Rabinowitz, *The Young Men's Hebrew Association, 1854–1913* (1948); "Second Triennial Convention. Conference: Girls,' and Women's Work," *Publications of the Council of Y.M.H. and Kindred Associations* (November 1916); Hartford, Connecticut, Young Women's Hebrew Association Archives, Jewish Historical Society of Greater Hartford, Hartford, CT; National Jewish Welfare Board Archives, Records of the Young Men's Young Women's Hebrew Association, American Jewish Historical Society, Waltham, MA; Young Women's Hebrew Association Records, 92d Street Young Men's-Young Women's Hebrew Archives, New York.

Linda J. Borish

Z

ZAHARIAS, MILDRED DIDRIKSON (26 June 1914, Port Arthur, TX–27 September 1956, Galveston, TX). A track athlete and golfer, she was born Mildred Ella Didriksen to Norwegian immigrants Ole and Hannah Didriksen. She changed the spelling of her last name in 1932. Didrikson is regarded as one of the best all-around female athletes ever. She grew up in Beaumont, Texas, and was nicknamed "Babe" for Babe Ruth after she hit thirteen home runs in a neighborhood softball game. Prior to her senior year in high school, she accepted a secretarial job at the Employers Casualty Company of Dallas and competed on the company basketball team, the Golden Cyclones. In 1932, entered as a one-woman team, Babe won the eighty-meter hurdles, high and broad jumps, shot put, javelin, and baseball throw at the Amateur Athletic Union track championship meet. That year she won gold medals at the Olympic Games in Los Angeles in the eighty-meter hurdles and javelin events. She would have won a third gold medal in the high jump, but she was disqualified for her technique. After her Olympic track career, she was tremendously successful in golf. In 1946 and 1947, she won seventeen consecutive golf tournaments, including the U.S. and British Amateur Championships. Some of her accolades include Associated Press Greatest Female Athlete of the First Half of the 20th Century (1950); Ladies Professional Golf Association (LPGA) Hall of Fame (1951); Professional Golfers' Association (PGA)/World Golf Hall of Fame (1974); National Track and Field Hall of Fame (1974); International Women's Sports Hall of Fame (1980); U.S. Olympic Hall of Fame (1983). As a young track star she was a controversial figure because of her outspoken personality and her masculine image. But after she became a golfer (and especially after her marriage), the media and the public praised her more traditional, feminine appearance and behavior. When cancer caused her untimely passing, the press honored her for her courage and her athletic achievements.

SELECTED BIBLIOGRAPHY: Susan E. Cayleff, *Babe: The Life and Legend of Babe Didrikson Zaharias* (1995); Betty Hicks, "Foremothers: Babe Didrikson Zaharias," *Women's Sports* 2 (November–December 1975): 18–28; William Johnson, *Whatta-gal!* (1977); Babe Didrikson Zaharias, *This Life I've Led* (1955).

Shawn Ladda

ZALE, TONY (29 May 1913, Gary, IN–20 March 1997, Portage, IN). A prize-fighter, he was born Anthony Florian Zaleski, the son of Polish immigrant parents. His father, Joseph Zaleski, died when he was one year old, and his mother raised the family. Tony followed his older brothers into the boxing ring and shortened his name so that his mother would not see it on the local boxing cards. His muscular physique and blue-collar roots earned him the nickname of "the Man of Steel." After an outstanding amateur career Zale turned professional in 1934. He struggled early and quit the ring to return to the steel mills of Gary in 1935. In 1937 he returned to boxing and began a steady ascent up the middleweight rankings. In 1940 he defeated Al Hostak to win the National Boxing Association (NBA) middleweight crown; in 1941 he was recognized as world middleweight champion when he defeated Georgie Abrams. Zale's title was "frozen" during World War II. When he came out of the navy, a sensational young puncher named Rocky Graziano* was ready to challenge him. The body-punching Zale and the free-swinging Graziano were contrasts in personalities as well as fighting styles. Zale was a soft-spoken navy veteran known for his "clean living," while Graziano was a colorful product of New York's "Hell's Kitchen" who served jail time for deserting the army and punching an officer. Boxing observers still regard their three fights between 1946 and 1948 as one of the most exciting and hard-hitting series in the annals of boxing. (Zale won the first and third bouts.) Just over three months after the final Graziano bout the thirty-five-year-old Zale fought Frenchman Marcel Cerdan and lost his title when he could not come out for the twelfth round. He then decided to retire and devoted much of his time to teaching boxing in Chicago with such groups as the Catholic Youth Organization.*

SELECTED BIBLIOGRAPHY: Dan Daniel, "Hostak Toughest Foe Says Zale," *The Ring* 45 (December 1966); *New York Times*, 21 March 1997, B-9; Gilbert Odd, *Encyclopedia of Boxing* (1983); Bert R. Sugar, *The 100 Greatest Boxers of All Time* (1984); Stanley Weston, "Tony Zale, Boxing's Man of Steel," *Boxing and Wrestling* 6 (June 1956).

Thomas M. Tarapacki

ZASLOFSKY, MAX (7 December 1925, Brooklyn, NY–15 October 1985, New Hyde Park, NY). After graduating from Thomas Jefferson High School, Max "Slats" Zaslofsky attended college at St. Johns in New York in 1945–46. He left after his freshman year and became one of professional basketball's first premier Jewish players. Zaslofsky starred for Chicago from 1946 to 1950. He was chosen to the All-League team in each of those four seasons, the first three of which were spent in the Basketball Association of America (BAA), and the last of which was in the National Basketball Association (NBA) after the BAA merged with the National Basketball League (NBL). The best year of his career was 1947–48, when he led the league with 1,007 points scored in forty-eight games, a 21.0 average. Zaslofsky would break the twenty-point barrier again the next season with a 20.6 average, which was high in the days before the twenty-four-second clock. He regularly finished among the top five scorers in the league. In 1950, when the Chicago franchise folded, Zaslofsky was the subject of a controversy when the remaining teams in the league tried to divvy up the players from Chicago. After most of the players had been handed over to a new team, the only players left were Zaslofsky, Andy Phillip, and Bob Cousy. There were three teams left to receive a player: Boston, New York, and Fort Wayne. All three wanted Zaslofsky, and New York won the lottery to receive him. He spent three years there, with his 1952–53 season cut short with a broken arm. He led the team in scoring in the 1951 playoffs with a 17.9 scoring average. Zaslofsky finished his career with Fort Wayne, compiling a lifetime scoring average of 14.8 points per game, and then went on to coach the New York Nets of the American Basketball Association (ABA) for two seasons from 1967 to 1969.

SELECTED BIBLIOGRAPHY: Zander Hollander, ed., *Modern Encyclopedia of Basketball* (1979); *New York Times*, 17 October 1985, D27; *The Sporting News*, 11 November 1985.

Zachary Davis

Selected Bibliography

Arbena, Joseph L., ed. *An Annotated Bibliography of Latin American Sport*. Westport, CT: Greenwood Press, 1989.

Ashe, Arthur R., Jr. *A Hard Road to Glory: A History of the African-American Athlete*. Vol. 1, *1619–1918*; Vol. 2, *1919–1945*; Vol. 3, *Since 1946*. New York: Warner Books, 1988.

Blady, Ken. *The Jewish Boxers Hall of Fame*. New York: Sapolsky, 1988.

Cavallo, Dominick, *Muscles and Morals: Organized Playgrounds and Urban Reform, 1880–1920*. Philadelphia: University of Pennsylvania Press, 1981.

Chalk, Ocania. *Pioneers of Black Sport*. New York; Dodd, Mead, 1975.

Coursey, Leon. "Pioneer Black Physical Educators." *Journal of Physical Education and Recreation* 51 (May 1980): 54–56.

Culin, Stewart. "Games of the North American Indians." In *Twenty-Fourth Annual Report of the Bureau of American Ethnology, 1902–1903*. Washington, D.C.: Government Printing Office, 1907.

Davis, Michael D. *Black American Women in Olympic Track and Field*. Jefferson, NC: McFarland and Company, 1992.

Dixon, Phil, and Hannigan, Patrick J. *The Negro Baseball Leagues: A Photographic History*. Mattituck, NY: Amereon House, 1992.

Early, Gerald. "House of Ruth, House of Robinson: Some Observations on Baseball, Biography, and the American Myth." In Robert Atwan and Valeri Vinokurov, eds., *Openings: Original Essays by Contemporary Soviet and American Writers*. Seattle: University of Washington Press, 1990, 221–249.

———. "Baseball and African American Life." In Geoffrey C. Ward and Ken Burns, *Baseball: An Illustrated History*. New York: A. A. Knopf, 1994, 412–417.

Edwards, Harry. *The Revolt of the Black Athlete*. New York: Free Press, 1969.

———. "The Sources of the Black Athlete's Superiority." *Black Scholar* 3 (November 1971): 32–41.

———. " 'Sport within the Veil': The Triumphs, Tragedies, and Challenges of Afro-American Involvement." *Annals of the American Academy of Political and Social Sciences* 445 (1979): 116–127.

Eisen, George, and Wiggins, David K. *Ethnicity and Sport in North American History and Culture*. Westport, CT: Praeger, 1994.

Fleischer, Nathaniel. *Black Dynamite: The Story of the Negro in the Prize Ring from 1782 to 1938*. 5 vols. New York: *Ring Magazine*, 1947.

Frank, Stanley. *The Jew in Sport*. New York: Miles, 1936.

George, Nelson. *Elevating the Game: Black Men and Basketball*. New York: Harper-Collins, 1992.

Gissendanner, Cindy. "African-American Women and Competitive Sport, 1920–1960." In Susan Birrell and Cheryl Cole, eds., *Women, Sport and Culture*. Champaign, IL: Human Kinetics, 1993, 81–92.

Goodman, Cary. *Choosing Sides: Playground and Street Life on the Lower East Side*. New York: Schocken Books, 1979.

Gorn, Elliott J. *The Manly Art: Bare-Knuckle Prize Fighting in America*. Ithaca, NY: Cornell University Press, 1986.

Govan, Michael. "The Emergence of the Black Athlete in America." *Black Scholar* 3 (November 1971): 16–28.

Green, Tina Sloan, Oglesby, Carole, Alexander, Alpha, and Franke, Niki, eds. *Black Women in Sport*. Reston, VA: American Alliance for Health, Physical Education, Recreation, and Dance Publications, 1981.

Harris, Othello. "Race, Sport, and Social Support." *Sociology of Sport Journal* 11 (1994): 40–50.

Harrison, Walter L. "Six-Pointed Diamond: Baseball and American Jews." *Journal of Popular Culture* 15, No. 3 (Winter 1981): 112–118.

Hauser, Thomas. *The Black Lights: Inside the World of Professional Boxing*. New York: McGraw-Hill, 1986.

Henderson, Edwin Bancroft. *The Negro in Sports*. Washington, D.C.: Associated Publishers, Inc., 1939; rev. ed. 1949.

———. *The Black Athlete: Emergence and Arrival*. Cornwell Heights, PA: Pennsylvania Publishers Company, 1968.

———. "Physical Education and Athletics among Negroes." In Bruce L. Bennett, ed., *Proceedings of the Big Ten Symposium on the History of Physical Education and Sport*. Chicago: Athletic Institute, 1972.

Holway, John B. *Voices from the Great Black Baseball Leagues*. New York: Dodd, Mead, 1975.

———. *Blackball Stars: Negro League Pioneers*. Westport, CT: Meckler, 1988.

———. *Black Diamonds: Life in the Negro Leagues from the Men Who Lived It*. Westport, CT: Meckler, 1989.

Hoose, Phillip M. *Necessities: Racial Barriers in American Sports*. New York: Random House, 1989.

Kahn, Lawrence M. "Discrimination in Professional Sports: A Survey of the Literature." *Industrial and Labor Relations Review* 44 (April 1991): 395–418.

Kirsch, George B. *The Creation of American Team Sports: Baseball and Cricket, 1838–72*. Urbana, IL: University of Illinois Press, 1989.

Lee, George L. *Interesting Athletes: Black American Sports Heroes*. New York: Ballantine, 1993.

Levine, Peter. *Ellis Island to Ebbets Field: Sport and the American Jewish Experience*. New York: Oxford University Press, 1992.

Lynn, Erwin. *The Jewish Baseball Hall of Fame*. New York: Shapolsky, 1987.

MacDonald, William W. "The Black Athlete in American Sports." In William J. Baker and John M. Carroll, eds., *Sports in Modern America*. St. Louis, MO: River City Publishers, 1981, 88–98.

Manley, Effa, and Hardwick, Leon H. *Negro Baseball before Integration*. Chicago: Adams Press, 1976.

Melville, Tom. *The Tented Field: A History of Cricket in America*. Bowling Green, OH: Bowling Green State University Popular Press, 1998.

Metzner, Henry. *A Brief History of the American Turnerbund*. Pittsburgh, PA: National Executive Committee of the American Turnerbund, 1924.

Nasaw, David. *Children of the City: At Work and at Play*. Garden City, NY: Doubleday, 1985.

Olsen, Jack. *The Black Athlete: A Shameful Story*. New York: Time Life Books, 1968.

Orr, Jack. *The Black Athlete: His Story in American History*. New York: Lion Books, 1969.

Oxendine, Joseph. *American Indian Sports Heritage*. Lincoln: University of Nebraska Press, 1995. Reprint.

Paraschak, Victoria. "Native Sport History: Pitfalls and Promises." *Canadian Journal of History of Sport* 20 (May 1989): 57–68.

Parry, Jose, and Noel Parry. "Sport and the Black Experience." In Grant Jarvie, ed., *Sport, Racism, and Ethnicity*. New York: Falmer Press, 1991, 150–174.

Peterson, Robert W. *Only the Ball was White*. Englewood Cliffs, NJ: Prentice Hall, 1970.

———. *Cages to Jump Shots: Pro Basketball's Early Years*. New York: Oxford University Press, 1990.

Postal, Bernard, Silver, Jesse, and Silver, Roy. *Encyclopedia of Jews in Sports*. New York: Bloch, 1965.

Redmond, Gerald. *The Caledonian Games in Nineteenth-Century America*. Rutherford, NJ: Farleigh Dickinson University Press, 1971.

Regalado, Samuel. *Viva Baseball!: Latin Major Leaguers and Their Special Hunger*. Urbana: University of Illinois Press, 1998.

Ribalow, Harold. *The Jew in American Sports*. New York: Bloch, 1948.

Ribalow, Harold, with Ribalow, Meir. *Jewish Baseball Stars*. New York: Hippocrene Books, 1984.

Riess, Steven A. "A Fighting Chance: The Jewish American Boxing Experience, 1890–1940." *American Jewish History* 74 (March 1985): 223–254.

———. *City Games: The Evolution of American Urban Society and the Rise of Sports*. Urbana: University of Illinois Press, 1989.

———. *Sport in Industrial America, 1850–1920*. Wheeling, IL: Harlan Davidson, 1995, ch. 3.

———, ed. *Sports and the American Jew*. Syracuse, NY: Syracuse University Press, 1998.

Rogosin, Donn. *Invisible Men: Life in Baseball's Negro Leagues*. New York: Atheneum, 1983.

Rust, Edna, and Rust, Art, Jr. *Art Rust's Illustrated History of the Black Athlete*. Garden City, NY: Doubleday, 1985.

Sammons, Jeffrey. *Beyond the Ring: The Role of Boxing in American Society*. Urbana: University of Illinois Press, 1988.

———. " 'Race' and Sport: A Critical, Historical Examination." *Journal of Sport History* 21 (Fall 1994): 203–278.

Sinnette, Calvin H. *Forbidden Fairways: African Americans and the Game of Golf.* Chelsea, MI: Sleeping Bear Press, 1998.

Slater, Robert, ed. *Great Jews in Sport.* Rev. ed. Middle Village, NY: Jonathan David Publishers, 1992.

Sports in North America: A Documentary History. Thomas L. Altherr, ed., vol. 1, *Part 1, Sports in the Colonial Era, 1618–1783; Part 2, Sports in the New Republic, 1784–1820,* 1998; Larry K. Menna, ed., vol. 2, *The Origins of Modern Sports, 1820–1840,* 1995; George B. Kirsch, ed., vol. 3, *The Rise of Modern Sports, 1840–1860,* 1992; George B. Kirsch, ed., vol. 4, *Sports in War, Revival, and Expansion, 1860–1880,* 1995; Gerald R. Gems, ed., vol. 5, *Sports Organized, 1880–1900,* 1996; Steven A. Riess, ed., *Sports in the Progressive Era, 1900–1920,* 1998. Gulf Breeze, FL: Academic International Press, 1992–1998.

Tarapacki, Thomas M. *Chasing the American Dream: Polish Americans in Sports.* New York: Hippocrene Books, 1995.

Thompson, Stephen I. "The American Indian in the Major Leagues." *Baseball Research Journal* (1983): 1–7.

White, Solomon. *Sol White's Official Baseball Guide.* Philadelphia: Camden House, 1984. Reprint.

Wiggins, David K. "Clio and the Black Athlete in America: Myths, Heroes, and Realities." *Quest* 32, No. 2 (1980): 217–225.

———. "From Plantation to Playing Field: Historical Writings on the Black Athlete in American Sport." *Research Quarterly for Exercise and Sport* 57 (June 1986): 101–116.

———. " 'Great Speed but Little Stamina': The Historical Debate over Black Athletic Superiority." *Journal of Sport History* 16 (Summer 1989): 158–185.

Young, Andrew S. *Great Negro Baseball Stars.* New York: Barnes and Company, 1953.

———. *Negro Firsts in Sports.* Chicago: Johnson Publishing Co., 1963.

Index

Page numbers in **bold** refer to main entries.

About the Editors and Contributors

GEORGE B. KIRSCH is Professor of History and Chair of the History Department at Manhattan College, Riverdale, New York. He is a specialist on nineteenth-century American baseball and has written and edited several books on U.S. sport history.

OTHELLO HARRIS is Associate Professor of Physical Education and Chair of the Department of Physical Education, Health, and Sport Studies at Miami University, Oxford, Ohio. His research interests include race relations, social stratification, and race and sport involvement. His work has been published in numerous journals and books.

CLAIRE E. NOLTE is Associate Professor of History and Director of the International Studies Program at Manhattan College, Riverdale, New York. Her major field of research and publications are in the area of Central European history, with a specialty in the Czech sokol movement.

ROGER ALLAWAY is a copy editor at the *Philadelphia Inquirer* and is a former president of the Society for American Soccer History.

E. JOHN B. ALLEN is Emeritus Professor of History at Plymouth State College in Plymouth, New Hampshire. He is a specialist in the history of skiing and the historian for the New England Ski Museum in Franconia, New Hampshire.

DAVID ANDREWS is Assistant Professor and Coordinator of Graduate Studies and Research in the Department of Human Movement Sciences and Education at the University of Memphis in Memphis, Tennessee.

VERNON ANDREWS is a member of the American Studies Department at the University of Canterbury in Christchurch, New Zealand.

WILLIAM J. BAKER is Professor of History and formerly Chair of the History Department at the University of Maine in Orono, Maine.

C. ROBERT BARNETT is Professor and Chair of the Division of Health, Physical Education, and Recreation at Marshall University in Huntington, West Virginia.

DAN BENNETT is a senior technical service associate at the National Baseball Hall of Fame and Museum in Cooperstown, New York.

GAI I. BERLAGE is Professor of Sociology at Iona College in New Rochelle, New York.

THOMAS E. BIRD is a member of the Slavic Studies faculty at Queens College at the City University of New York and also Assistant Historian of the St. Nicholas Society of the City of New York.

METODIJ BORETSKY is press coordinator for the Regional Ukrainian Olympic Committee of Philadelphia. He has published extensively on the Ukrainian American community and Ukrainian sports.

LINDA J. BORISH is Associate Professor of History at Western Michigan University in Kalamazoo, Michigan. She is a specialist on the history of Jewish women in sports in the United States.

DOUGLAS A. BROWN is an Assistant Professor in the Department of Kinesiology at the University of Lethbridge in Lethbridge, Alberta, Canada. His research focuses on the cultural and aesthetic nature of modern sport.

FRANK J. CAVAIOLI is Professor Emeritus at the State University of New York at Farmingdale and also a coeditor of *Italian American History and Culture: An Encyclopedia*.

THOMAS CESA, a graduate of Manhattan College with a B.A. in history, earned his M.A. in Public Communication and Media Studies from Fordham University.

SHANKAR CHAUDHURI is a doctoral candidate in Modern History and Literature at Drew University in Madison, New Jersey.

JAMES R. COATES, JR., is a member of the Department of Education at the University of Wisconsin—Green Bay.

PAMELA COOPER is an editor at *Runner's World* and a specialist on the history of the marathon.

SCOTT A.G.M. CRAWFORD is Professor of Physical Education at Eastern Illinois University in Charleston, Illinois, and book review editor of *The International Journal of the History of Sport*.

DIANE D'ANGELO earned her M.A. from the University of Maine at Orono, where she specialized in twentieth-century American and sports history. She also holds an M.S. in Library Studies from Florida State University.

ZACHARY DAVIS is former Assistant Sports Editor of the Duke University *Chronicle* and is now a law student at the University of Michigan.

PAUL J. DELOCA is a writer and a specialist on speed skating, residing in Greensboro, North Carolina.

RICHARD N. DEMIRJIAN is a retired first lieutenant from the U.S. Army Reserves, a businessman, and an active member of various Armenian American sports organizations. He has published books on Armenian American athletes and heroes of World War II.

PETER P. DUSEK, JR., is Professor of Physical Education (retired), Cuyahoga Community College in Cleveland, Ohio, and Director of Men, American Sokol Organization, Northeastern District.

ANTHONY O. EDMONDS is Professor of History at Ball State University in Muncie, Indiana.

PHILIP FERRARI is President of the World Bocce Association and League in Bensenville, Illinois.

RICHARD FITZPATRICK is Professor of Management at Manhattan College in Riverdale, New York.

WILLIAM FRANCIS is a journalist who formerly wrote for the *Cooperstown Independent* in Cooperstown, New York.

JOEL S. FRANKS teaches Asian American Studies and Ethnic Studies at San Jose State University in San Jose, California. He is the author of two forthcoming books on sports and ethnicity.

DAVID J. GARBER is executive director of the U.S. Curling Association in Stevens Point, Wisconsin.

JAMES L. GATES, JR., is Librarian at the National Baseball Hall of Fame and Museum in Cooperstown, New York.

GERALD R. GEMS is the Health and Physical Education Department Chair at North Central College in Naperville, Illinois. He has published three books and numerous articles on sport history.

STEVEN P. GIETSCHIER is Director of Historical Records at *The Sporting News* in St. Louis, Missouri.

JULIANA F. GILHEANY is Adjunct Assistant Professor of History at Manhattan College in Riverdale, New York. She also teaches at Fordham University and New York University.

JOSEPH M. GIOVANNETTI is a member of the Ethnic Studies Department at Humboldt State University in Arcata, California.

EDWARD GOBETZ is Professor Emeritus of Sociology at Kent State University in Kent, Ohio, and Executive Director of the Slovenian Research Center of America, Inc., in Willoughby Hills, Ohio. He is the author of numerous books and articles and is a specialist on Slovenian immigrants in the United States.

ROGER A. GODIN, former Director and Curator of the U.S. Hockey Hall of Fame, 1971–1987, is the author of numerous essays on American hockey players.

ELLIOTT J. GORN is Associate Professor of History at Purdue University in West Lafayette, Indiana.

PAT HARMON is a historian affiliated with the National Football Foundation and College Hall of Fame.

GREGORY S. HARRIS is Director of the film, video, and recorded sound collection at the National Baseball Hall of Fame and Museum in Cooperstown, New York.

C. KEITH HARRISON is Assistant Professor in the Department of Sports Management and Communication and Director of the Paul Robeson Research Center for Academic and Athletic Prowess at the University of Michigan in Ann Arbor, Michigan.

LESLIE HEAPHY is Professor of History at the Stark Campus of Kent State University in Canton, Ohio.

DEBRA A. HENDERSON is Assistant Professor in the Department of Sociology and Anthropology at Ohio University in Athens, Ohio.

MARGARET MARY HENNESSEY is a public relations officer in the College Relations office of Manhattan College in Riverdale, New York.

LAWRENCE HUGGINS is Professor of Management at Manhattan College in Riverdale, New York.

LESLEY L. HUMPHREYS was formerly a Senior Library Associate at the National Baseball Hall of Fame and Museum in Cooperstown, New York.

MILTON JAMAIL is a lecturer in the Department of Government at the University of Texas at Austin.

KATHERINE M. JAMIESON is Assistant Professor in the Department of Exercise and Sport Science at the University of North Carolina-Greensboro. She has published several articles on Latinas in U.S. sport.

COLIN JOSE is the historian at the National Soccer Hall of Fame in Oneonta, New York, and the author of five books on soccer history.

ALAN S. KATCHEN has taught at the University of California at Santa Barbara and Howard University. He was formerly regional director of the Anti-Defamation League in Columbus, Ohio and is a consultant on racial and ethnic issues.

RANDY B. KLIPSTEIN is a member of the Society for American Baseball Research (SABR) and his work has been published in SABR periodicals. He is employed by IBM as a financial analyst and lives in Tarrytown, New York.

MICHAEL J. KOPANIC, JR., is a member of the faculty at the Altoona campus of Pennsylvania State University. He has written extensively on the history of Slovak Americans.

SIGITAS KRASAUSKAS is Senior Advisor and former President of the Lithuanian Athletic Union of North America. He is a specialist on Lithuanian sports.

ORLIN KRUMOV is a member of the Society of Professional Journalists of the United States.

TIMOTHY L. KUZMA is First Vice President for Membership Services for the Polish Falcons of America, in Pittsburgh, Pennsylvania.

SHAWN LADDA is Assistant Professor of Physical Education and Human Performance at Manhattan College, Riverdale, New York.

LARRY LONDINO is Chair of the Department of Broadcasting at Montclair State University in Upper Montclair, New Jersey.

MARGHERITA MARCHIONE is Professor Emerita of Italian Language and Literature at Fairleigh Dickinson University in Madison, New Jersey. A Fulbright Scholar and member of the Religious Teachers Filippini in Villa Walsh, Morristown, New Jersey, she is the author of thirty-four books on political and religious topics.

BRUCE MARKUSEN is a Senior Researcher at the National Baseball Hall of Fame and Museum in Cooperstown, New York.

RAÚL MAYO-SANTANA is Professor of Psychology at the Department of Physical Medicine, Rehabilitation, and Sports Medicine at the School of Medicine, University of Puerto Rico in San Juan, Puerto Rico.

MARY G. MCDONALD is Assistant Professor in the Department of Physical Education, Health, and Sport Studies at Miami University in Oxford, Ohio.

RICHARD V. MCGEHEE is Adjunct Professor of Geology and Physical Education at Concordia University, Austin, Texas. He is a specialist in the history of modern sports in Mexico and Central America, the International Multisport Festivals of the Americas, and the participation of Hispanics in sport in the United States.

DAVID R. MCMAHON is a doctoral student at the University of Iowa in Iowa City who specializes in immigration/ethnic history and twentieth-century U.S. history.

LARRY K. MENNA is an Assistant Professor of History at the State University of New York at Farmingdale, New York. He is a specialist in U.S. political and popular culture.

SCOT E. MONDORE is a Senior Researcher at the National Baseball Hall of Fame and Museum in Cooperstown, New York.

PHILIP M. MONTESANO teaches U.S. history at the City College of San Francisco, Evening Division.

RICHARD J. MOSS is Professor of History at Colby College in Waterville, Maine.

RAY MULLEY is a journalist and life-long hockey historian dedicated to preserving the names of past National Hockey League players prior to the league's major expansion in 1967. He resides in Niagara Falls, Ontario.

LES E. NIEMI was formerly the Director of Planned Giving at Suomi College in Hancock, Michigan.

NICHOLAS NOTARIDIS is publisher of the newspapers *Omogeneia* and *Athlitismos* in New York City. He is a specialist on Greek American ethnic sports.

KURT OELER is night editor of CNET News.com and was previously associate editor of *Historical Abstracts* and the *Journal of Democracy*. He has published numerous rugby articles in the United States and abroad.

LEONARD P. OLIVER is the founder of Oliver Associates, a public policy consulting firm in Washington, D.C. He was inducted into the National Soccer Hall of Fame in 1996 and is a specialist on the ethnic aspects of soccer in the United States.

TROY D. PAINO is an Assistant Professor of Twentieth Century Cultural History at Winona State University in Winona, Minnesota. He is currently working on a manuscript about the cultural history of Indiana high school basketball.

VICTORIA PARASCHAK is Associate Professor in the School of Human Kinetics at the University of Windsor in Windsor, Ontario, Canada.

CLYDE PARTIN is Professor in the Department of Health, Physical Education, and Dance at Emory University in Atlanta, Georgia.

FRANK PIPAL is editor of *The Boules Broadsheet*, the newsletter of the Federation of Pétanque U.S.A., published in Kenwood, California.

CIRO C. POPPITI of Wilmington, Delaware, is a partner in w.h.a.t.t., an entertainment company specializing in filmed and audio entertainment. He is an active leader with the National Italian American Foundation, the Order Sons of Italy in America, Italo-Americans United of Wilmington, and the World Bocce Association.

JULIANNA PUSKAS is affiliated with the Hungarian Academy of Sciences in Budapest, Hungary. She is a specialist on overseas migration from Hungary and the Hungarian American community.

SUSAN RAYL is Assistant Professor in the Department of Movement Arts, Health Promotion, and Leisure Studies at Bridgewater State College in Bridgewater, Massachusetts.

MILOSLAV RECHCIGL, JR., is one of the founders and current president of the Czechoslovak Society of Arts and Sciences in Washington, D.C. He is a specialist on the history of immigration from the former Czechoslovakia.

LYNN S. RENAU is a specialist on the history of horse racing in Kentucky. She is an antiques consultant in Louisville, Kentucky.

RICHARD RENOFF is Professor of Sociology at Nassau Community College (State University of New York) in Garden City, New York. He has published on religion and ethnicity among Carpatho-Rusyns.

ROLAND RENSON is Professor at the Institute of Physical Education and Physiotherapy at the Katholieke Universiteit Leuven, in Louvain (Heverlee), Belgium.

JILL E. RENWICK was formerly a Library Associate at the National Baseball Hall of Fame and Museum in Cooperstown, New York.

STEVEN A. RIESS is Professor of History at Northeastern Illinois University in Chicago, Illinois. A former editor of *The Journal of Sport History*, he is the author of several books and numerous articles on sports in the United States.

LA VERN J. RIPPLEY is Professor of German and Chairman of the German Department at St. Olaf College in Northfield, Minnesota. He is the author of some fifteen books and 200 articles on German-related topics, most concerning the German American experience.

GEORGE RUGG is Curator of the Joyce Sports Research Collection at the Hesburgh Library at the University of Notre Dame, in Notre Dame, Indiana.

DENNIS RYAN is a graduate of McGill University in Montreal, Quebec, and is a candidate for his M.A. in sport history at the University of Western Ontario in London, Ontario.

GARY A. SAILES is Associate Professor in the School of Health, Physical Education, and Recreation at Indiana University in Bloomington, Indiana.

COREY SEEMAN was formerly Director of Technical Services of the National Baseball Hall of Fame and Museum in Cooperstown, New York.

WILLIAM M. SIMONS is Professor of History at the State University of New York at Oneonta, New York. He is a specialist on the participation of Jews in sports in the United States.

MARC SINGER is a graduate student in American Studies at New York University in New York City.

VLADISLAV SLAVIK is a Vice-President of the World Sokol Federation and member of the Board of Governors, American Sokol Organization. He is active in sports and is the author of many articles in Czech and American magazines.

EARL SMITH is Chair of the Department of Sociology at Wake Forest University in Winston-Salem, North Carolina.

THOMAS M. TARAPACKI is Sports Editor of the *Polish American Journal*, the largest independent monthly Polish American newspaper in the English language. He is a specialist on Polish American sports.

JAMES R. VARELLA is a publicist for Miami jai alai in Miami, Florida.

THOMAS VENNUM, JR., is Senior Ethnomusicologist at the Smithsonian Institution's Center for Folklife Programs and Cultural Studies in Washington, D.C.

DAVID K. WIGGINS is Professor in the Department of Health Fitness and Recreation Resources at George Mason University and also editor of *The Journal of Sport History*.

RALPH C. WILCOX is Professor and Chair in the Department of Human Movement Sciences and Education at the University of Memphis in Memphis, Tennessee. He has published extensively in the fields of sport history and the sociocultural dimensions of sport.

TIMOTHY J. WILES is Director of Research at the National Baseball Hall of Fame and Museum in Cooperstown, New York.

LAUREN F. WINNER has studied at Cambridge University in England and is Richard Hofstadter Fellow in the Department of History at Columbia University.

ALISON M. WRYNN is Assistant Professor in the Department of Physical Education and also Interim Coordinator of the Women's Studies Program at the State University of New York at Cortland, New York.

JOEL WURL is Curator and Assistant Director of the Immigration History Research Center at the University of Minnesota in St. Paul, Minnesota.

ISBN 0-313-29911-0

9 780313 299117

HARDCOVER BAR CODE